God Beyond Boundaries

Perry Schmidt-Leukel

God Beyond Boundaries

A Christian and Pluralist Theology of Religions

Waxmann 2017
Münster • New York

Original title: Gott ohne Grenzen. Eine christliche und pluralistische Theologie der Religionen. By Perry Schmidt-Leukel

Translated into English by Ulrike Guthrie, Carolina Weening, Charlie Cahill, and Perry Schmidt-Leukel.

Bibliographic information published by the Deutsche Nationalbibliothek
The Deutsche Nationalbibliothek lists this publication in the Deutsche Nationalbibliografie; detailed bibliographic data are available in the Internet at http://dnb.d-nb.de

Print-ISBN 978-3-8309-3739-5
E-Book-ISBN 978-3-8309-8739-0

www.waxmann.com
info@waxmann.com

Cover design: Inna Panomareva, Düsseldorf
Typesetting: Stoddart Satz- und Layoutservice, Münster
Print: CPI Books GmbH, Leck

Printed on age-resistant paper, acid-free as per ISO 9706

MIX
Papier aus verantwortungsvollen Quellen
FSC www.fsc.org
FSC® C083411

For John H. Hick

Contents

Part III:
Testing a Christian and Pluralist Theology of Religions in Interreligious Encounter

Preface to the English Edition

I am glad, grateful and relieved that my study *God Beyond Boundaries* ("Gott ohne Grenzen") is now available to an English speaking readership. Apart from offering my reflections and argumentations on Christianity's self-understanding among and in relation to other religions, the book also provides an opportunity for getting some glimpses of the discourse in Germany, even if the bulk of the literature discussed in this work stems from the English speaking world.

My relief is due to the fact that the translation process has taken unusually long. Getting as close as possible to the German original involved far more difficulties than originally foreseen. Several drafts and three translators were involved, while I myself gave the manuscript a final check. My gratitude goes to Ulrike Guthrie, Dr. Carolina Weening and Dr. Charles Cahill for all the time and effort they invested in producing the English text of this book. I'm also grateful to Dr. Natalie Watson (formerly at SCM Press) who strongly supported the project during the first years of the translation process and to Dr. Ursula Heckel from Waxmann Publisher who supervised the final production of the book after the project had been transferred from SCM Press to Waxmann. The staff at Waxmann have been wonderfully supportive and highly professional in getting this book published. I feel sad that Carolina, a fine scholar in her own right, who in 2012 died from a rapidly growing cancer, has not been able to see the final result.

The translation of *God Beyond Boundaries* not only took much time and effort, it also required significant financial support. Grants have been given by *The Weisfeld Foundation*, the *Cluster of Excellence "Religion and Politics"* at the University of Muenster and the *Stiftung Apfelbaum*. I am very grateful to all three funding institutions and their representatives who decided to support the project.

I have been asked whether my more recent book *Religious Pluralism and Interreligious Theology* (Orbis Books 2017) would make *God Beyond Boundaries* redundant. Anybody who takes a look at the present work will soon realize that this is not the case. *Religious Pluralism and Interreligious Theology* starts where *God Beyond Boundaries* ends, with the need for an interreligious theology. And while the more recent book only provides a summarized sketch of pluralist approaches in Christianity, *God Beyond Boundaries* deals in much detail with the various theological questions raised by these approaches. Moreover, *God Beyond Boundaries* shows with regard to both Christian doctrinal issues in general and Christian dialogue with Judaism, Islam, Hinduism and Buddhism in particular what the numerous and significant advantages of a pluralist approach over against its rival option of Christian exclusivism and Christian inclusivism are. The arguments presented here are still as topical and pertinent as they were more than ten years ago. There is only one point where the theological discussion has moved forward considerably. While the last chapter of *God Beyond Boundaries* emphasizes the need for more theological reflection on the question of multi-religious identity (cf. chapter 16, note 51), this issue has now indeed caught more theological attention and found some excellent scholarly treatment, though here too still more work needs to be done.

Muenster, May 2017 Perry Schmidt-Leukel

Preface

Even in the era of internet and computerized word processing, books continue to be "born." While this obviously applies to the drafting of texts, on a deeper and more fundamental level it is even more true of the thoughts themselves that make up the books. Thoughts need time to develop, time to allow their implications to unfold and gradually take on the form in which they will then see the light of literary day. Certainly books too are "children of their times," clearly marked by the atmosphere and circumstances in which they came into being; it follows that they may be outdated before long, and superseded by new ones. Yet until then they continue to work and, as it were, reproduce themselves: in the thoughts of others as well as sometimes in the creation of new books.

Usually the birth of a book is preceded by a longer pre-history. In the case of the volume at hand, its concept and structure derive from a particular course of lectures I held, first at the University of Salzburg in the summer semester of 1999 and not long thereafter at the University of Munich in the 1999-2000 winter semester. Although I had been officially banned from teaching by authorities of the Roman Catholic Church, colleagues and good friends of mine—for whom academic freedom is of great importance—actively lent their support to make these courses possible. In the turmoil of this situation, that both threatened my livelihood as well as jeopardized my family's well-being, many of my ideas had to remain in embryonic form. Still, I never abandoned the hope that the driving ideas behind this lecture series would one day emerge as a book.

In spring 2000 I was appointed to the newly established Chair of World Religions for Peace at the University of Glasgow. Now in Scotland one rarely encounters that cynicism regarding the European Enlightenment and its values so widespread on the Continent. On the contrary: the Scots are thoroughly proud of the not insignificant contribution made by their country to the Enlightenment, and it comes then as no great surprise that they continue to foster the Enlightenment tradition of freedom of thought in speech and in writing. In contrast to the situation on the Continent, control and censorship at secular universities, whether by the churches or by other ideological entities, is quite unthinkable in Scotland and legally prevented. Indeed some churches have accommodated themselves to this very well. The teaching staff of Glasgow's Department of Theology and Religious Studies, to which I belong, represents a number of different denominations and religions, and the current (2004) chairperson is a Muslim lady—a fact that by no means prevents the largest ecclesiastical denomination in Scotland, the Reformed Church of Scotland, from continuing to educate its ministerial candidates in this department. Even outside the University it is not uncommon to encounter signs of an exemplary social openness. The German and French prohibitions against the wearing of a *hijab*, or headscarf, by Muslim women in certain official positions, together with the often pseudo-intellectual discussion surrounding these measures, is in Scotland more likely to be greeted with a puzzled shake of the head. The traditional police uniform in Glasgow has been supplemented with a turban decorated with the police emblem and the famous checkerboard hatband so as to enable access to police service even to those who belong to the religious community of Sikhs and as such are duty-bound to wear a turban.

In this liberal (in the best sense of the word) climate of Scotland I was able not only to continue my academic work but also finally to realize my plans for this book. Some of what I have published in recent years is included here in revised format and now appears in what I hope is a unified and coherent form. I have made an effort to refer frequently to contemporary discussions on the theology of religions, though it has not been my intention to do so in a comprehensive way. My coverage has been largely selective, because my primary concern has been to present my own position on the theology of religions, relating this to other positions only when necessary. Anyone interested in a more comprehensive presentation of the state of the discussion will find this in some of my earlier publications (particularly in Schmidt-Leukel, 1997) as well as in the numerous references to the broader literature mentioned throughout this book.

The fundamental issues in the theology of religions are far too important to be left only to theological specialists. I have therefore tried to write this book in such a way that it can, on the one hand, be read with understanding by non-theologians, while still appealing to specialists on the other. Hence I must ask the latter to forgive what may appear to be unnecessary explanations, and the former for forbearance if there is presumably still too much theological shoptalk.

There remains the debt of thanks which I owe to many people who contributed to the coming-into-being of this book—a duty I am only too glad to fulfill. First are to those who made my German-Austrian farewell lecture possible: Heinrich Schmidinger from the University of Salzburg and Heinrich Döring from the University of Munich. The extent to which the ongoing discussions and thematically cutting-edge seminars at the Institute headed up by Heinrich Döring informed my thinking and broadened my horizon can hardly be assessed. Without this foundation, the present book would never have been written. Yet it also could not have been written without the granting of an entire sabbatical year for research. For this I am indebted to the Department of Theology and Religious Studies of the University of Glasgow for relieving me of teaching duties during the 2003-2004 winter semester, and to the British Arts and Humanities Research Board for magnanimously supporting this project through a generous financial grant, thus making it possible for me to prolong my research-leave in the summer semester of 2004. In particular, I thank my former Glasgow colleague John Barclay, without whose energetic encouragement I probably would not have taken up this project so quickly. I owe special thanks as well to Shulamit Spain-Gayer and Philip Spain, who read the chapter on Christianity and Judaism and gave me valuable suggestions from their Jewish-influenced perspective. (In the end, of course the final responsibility for the handling of this topic in the book lies with me.)

It was not only the university that had to release me for this work but my family as well. Too often, they had to endure the fact that my thoughts were not with them but with this book; too often their attempts to discover whether I might be approachable at a given moment were met on my part with annoyance. I particularly thank Doris for investing so many hours of her time, yet again, in proofreading. Thanks also to Diedrich Steen of the Gütersloher Publishing Company for the enthusiasm with which he accompanied the book and thus spurred on its author. One glance at the German-language publications on the theology of religions demonstrates the enormity of this publishing house's contribution to the ongoing vitality and topicality of this discussion over the years.

To mention here the names of all those who have informed my thinking would exceed the bounds of a foreword. Yet there is one author and fatherly friend whom I must name: John Hick. After my lengthy study of the Buddhist-Christian dialogue I began to extend the scope of my theological work by taking up the fundamental systematical questions of a comprehensively conceived theology of religions. In this process, no other theologian inspired me as much as did John Hick. And I am not the only one who has benefitted in this way. For almost four decades John Hick has pushed forward the international discussion on a Theology of Religions—far beyond the circles of Christian theology. It is to him therefore that this work is dedicated as a token of my particular gratitude.

Glasgow, September 2004 Perry Schmidt-Leukel

1. Introduction

October 27, 1986 – September 11, 2001

The twentieth century will likely go down in history as the period in which the major world religions began to engage with one another on a large scale and in an unprecedented spirit of openness and dialogue. This spirit became symbolized and also concretized in the interreligious prayer meeting at Assisi on October 27, 1986, convened by Pope John Paul II and broadcast by many TV networks around the globe. Roughly 150 representatives of numerous religious communities had gathered in Assisi. Both individually and collectively, these representatives gave expression in their own particular ways to their desire for peace and to their conviction that an unshakeable commitment to peace was inherent in their understanding of religion.[1]

Since then however a second event of great symbolic power has overshadowed the event of Assisi. Similarly it generated images that were transmitted throughout the world and have left an indelible impression in the consciousness and sub-consciousness of countless people. While not a religious event, it nonetheless contained an undeniable religious dimension: the horrific attacks of September 11, 2001, conceived and carried out in the name of God. The perpetrators put the ultimate seal upon their conviction that this mass murder would serve the cause of God by deliberately sacrificing their own lives, for which they are today honored as martyrs in the circles of those similarly minded. 9/11 drove home two resounding points: first, that religion is a most powerful factor, and not to be ignored in our future life together on the planet; and second, that this factor continues to have a dangerous, violent dimension.

The symbolic intensity of the events of September 11 and October 27 illustrates the ambiguous mix of expectations and potentialities inherent in global religious encounters.[2] On the one hand, given the inevitably increasing interconnectedness of the world's countries and cultures in the wake of globalization processes, diverse religions contain the potential to exacerbate the conflicts and problems among com-

1 In light of the conflict that had flared up in theological circles before this event had even taken place, Rome went to considerable lengths to "clarify" the Church's position: Participants would not be gathering in order to pray *together*, "but rather they were coming together in order to pray" (J. Mejia, cited in Waldenfels 1989, 26). Fortunately, such casuistry is too difficult to reach the public at large and thus the symbolic power of the event did not suffer any diminution. The Assisi texts can be found in Waldenfels 1987.

2 For that reason on January 24, 2002, an interreligious assembly met once again for prayer in Assisi. Rather than succumbing to the psychological atmosphere set off by the events of September 11, 2001, this gathering explicitly invoked the spirit of Assisi in 1986.

munities. On the other hand, however, the same religions could play a decisive role in the resolution of these problems as well, and offer active assistance in overcoming conflicts in ways that are both just and peaceful. They could move us to tackle the challenges of the contemporary world and of our common future with imagination, creativity, and above all with confidence. Since the early beginnings of the human race religions have been able to awaken, sustain and renew within their respective cultural realms an abiding awareness of the presence of a supreme transcendent reality. Religions have imparted meaning and purposefulness, and despite all their dark aspects have contributed to the best and highest achievements of human life. Might not the various religions prove able to make comparably beneficial contributions to our future life together within a worldwide community? – I am referring here to that cultural coexistence which will come to define not only globalized society in general but also, and increasingly, life *within* each individual society on the planet. This in turn will be wholly dependent upon the nature of religions' relationships to one another. In any event, what the Chief Rabbi of Great Britain, Jonathan Sacks, wrote in his noteworthy and widely acknowledged response to the events of September 11 holds true: "If religion is not part of a solution, it will certainly be part of the problem."[3]

Interreligious Encounter and the Emergence of Pluralism

Just which of those two roles religions are to play in the future will be closely bound up with the way in which they apprehend and take stock of one another, the way in which they approach the teachings and practices of the others as well as how they deal with the fact that there *is* religious diversity at all: Is this diversity considered a regrettable evil ultimately to be overcome, or seen as an opportunity for reciprocal enrichment and common spiritual growth? Ultimately decisive however will be the question of how each religion will come to view its own place within the context of such diversity. And all this in turn will be shaped by how well and how deeply the religions (more precisely: their respective adherents) know and understand one another. It is here that we can recognize the significance of those interreligious encounters which became so widespread in the twentieth century.

An example of such recognition can already be seen at the first Parliament of the World's Religions, convened in Chicago in 1893, in conjunction with the World Exposition.[4] One of the most impressive speeches was given by the renowned Neo-Hindu Vivekananda. Friedrich Heiler, the German scholar of religions, reported the following reaction: "…as Vivekananda left the lecture hall a listener said

3 Cp. Sacks 2003, 9.
4 Cp. Seager 1993.

spontaneously: 'This man a heathen?! And we're sending missionaries to his people. It would be better if they were to send missionaries to us!'"[5]

Apparently, for the first time in his life, this Christian had encountered an authentic Hindu and been confronted with Hindu spirituality. His spontaneous remark gives expression to the insight that Christians must change their ways of thinking and acting if there are people of the caliber of Vivekananda among the supposed "heathens" that are to be evangelized. Vivekananda himself perceived that an encounter among the world religions should elicit such reactions on *all* sides. When he once again took the podium at the final session of the World Parliament, he closed with the words:

> If the Parliament of Religions has shown anything to the world it is this: It has proved to the world that holiness, purity and charity are not the exclusive possession of any church in the world, and that every system has produced men and women of the most exalted character. In the face of this evidence, if anybody dreams of the exclusive survival of his own religion and the destruction of the others, I pity him from the bottom of my heart, and point out to him that upon the banner of every religion will soon be written, in spite of resistance: "Help and not Fight," "Assimilation and not Destruction," "Harmony and Peace and not Dissension."[6]

Nowadays interreligious conferences of global scope are no longer a rarity. One hundred years later a second Parliament of the World's Religions met in Chicago and formulated the "Declaration Toward a Global Ethic."[7] In this important document the signatory representatives of the various religions reconfirmed the conviction that there is significant agreement among the different religious traditions as to fundamental ethical values, norms, and attitudes. Not only did they commit themselves to working together to implement this global ethic, they also pledged to strive for "better mutual understanding." This procedure was further strengthened in the follow-up meetings held in Capetown in 1999 and Barcelona in 2004. There, all religious institutions and their representatives were called upon to promote an attitude of "respect and mutual welcome" with respect to each other and "to strengthen the search for those shared ethical and spiritual values and principles that can enable religious and spiritual communities to engage creatively with each other and with the world."[8]

Here one could list a goodly number of further international and interreligious organizations that have dedicated themselves to the peaceful coexistence of all peoples as well as to an improved understanding among the religions—for example, the World Conference of Religions for Peace, the World Congress of Faiths, the Temple of Understanding, Religions United, *et al.*[9] Perhaps even more significantly, com-

5 Heiler 1967, 36.
6 Vivekananda 1994, vol. I, 24.
7 For the text of this Declaration and for the story of its origins, see Küng, Kuschel 1996.
8 Council for a Parliament of the World's Religions 1999, 18.
9 For an overview of interreligious organizations, see Böhle 2001.

munal inter-faith councils have since sprung up in any number of cities and larger towns—and their numbers continue to rise.

The English industrial city of Birmingham presents a particularly evolved example of this within Europe, having been shaped by enormous cultural and religious diversity for many years. An "Inter-Faith Council for Birmingham" has been in operation since 1975.[10] John Hick, a British professor of the philosophy of religion and by then an ordained minister in the Presbyterian Church of England, was decisively involved in setting up the Council, and played a crucial role in a number of other interreligious activities as well.[11] In 1967, after holding teaching positions in England and the U.S. (Cambridge, Cornell and Princeton), Hick was appointed to the H.G. Wood Chair in the Theology Department of the University of Birmingham, a position he held until 1982 when he became Danforth Professor at the University of Claremont, California. Since his retirement in 1992, Hick once again lives in Birmingham. At the beginning of his career Hick's views on theology and philosophy had been quite evangelical and conservative but his early encounter with the religious diversity of Birmingham led him to a radical rethinking, which he himself describes in the following words:

> ... I was drawn into the work which is variously called 'race relations' and 'community relations'[12], and soon had friends and colleagues in all these non-Christian religious communities as well as in the large black community from the Caribbean. And occasionally attending worship in mosque and synagogue, temple and *gurdwara*, it was evident that essentially the same kind of thing is taking place in them as in a Christian church—namely, human beings opening their minds to a higher divine Reality, known as personal and good and as demanding righteousness and love between man and man. I could see that the Sikh faith, for instance, is to the devout Sikh what the Christian faith is to the sincere Christian; but that each faith is, naturally enough, perceived by its adherents as being unique and absolute. Visits to India and Sri Lanka, amounting together to nearly a year, mainly to study Hinduism and Buddhism, further revealed something of the immense spiritual depth and power of these two oriental religions. Without ever being tempted to become either a Hindu or a Buddhist I could see that within these ancient traditions men and women are savingly related to the Eternal Reality from which we all live.[13]

10 On the interreligious situation in Birmingham, cp. Ustorf 2005 and Conway 1996.

11 In his autobiography, Hick reports more extensively on his involvement in Birmingham, particularly with AFFOR ("All Faiths for One Race"), Hick 2002, 159-192.

12 Here, Hick alludes particularly to his participation in multi-religious campaigns against racism and fascism. His political writings, which were an integral part of this participation, are unfortunately hardly known. Yet just how seriously his opponents took his involvement can be seen in the death threat he received (cp. Hick 2002, 190) as a result of his pamphlet against the racism of the British National Front (Hick 1977b), and his pamphlet against the racism of the then South African government (Hick 1980b) promptly led to his blacklisting (cp. Hick 2002, 246).

13 Hick 1982, 5.

Soon Hick began to reflect on the latent consequences of his new experiences for a theology of religions and to develop the results in a series of publications.[14] In so doing he also drew upon the experiences and reflections of others who had reached similar conclusions. Wilfred Cantwell Smith, a scholar of Middle Eastern and Oriental Studies and the History of Religions, and a Reformed theologian, had a particularly strong influence on Hick. Smith and Hick in turn attracted other theologians, for example the U.S. Catholic academics Paul Knitter and Leonard Swidler. 1986 marked a watershed: A group of theologians met together with a number of critics at a conference in Claremont in order to formulate and propagate a new *theology of religions*, which had been known for several years as "religious pluralism" or "pluralist theology of religions."[15] In retrospect, proponents as well as critics of religious pluralism came to refer to this conference as the "Rubicon Conference," for it was the "Rubicon" of *Christian absolutism* that was here being crossed. In its place, these scholars suggested a fundamental equality of the major religious traditions as spaces of uniquely distinct but no less genuine forms of *revelation/experience* of the divine reality and as equally valid paths of salvation.

One year later, Hick and Knitter published the pro-pluralism papers of the Rubicon Conference in a collection entitled *The Myth of Christian Uniqueness: Toward a Pluralistic Theology of Religions*.[16] At the same time (1986-87) John Hick received a special honor in the field of the philosophy of religion: the invitation to hold the Gifford Lectures at the University of Edinburgh. Hick used this opportunity to set forth his approach to a pluralist theology of religions in a philosophically secured form. These lectures were later turned into the book, *An Interpretation of Religion*, honored in 1991 with the renowned Grawemeyer Award and since then translated into a number of languages.[17]

At this point the critics of Hick's position became quite vocal. In 1990, a group which included several of the critics who participated in the Rubicon Conference published a response under the title: *Christian Uniqueness Reconsidered. The Myth of a Pluralistic Theology of Religions*,[18] edited by Hick's former student, Gavin D'Costa. Since then, the dispute between the advocates and opponents of a pluralist theology of religions has by no means abated. In the German-speaking context, religious pluralism was the object of intense controversy at the 1994 annual conference of Roman-Catholic systematic theologians.[19] In a widely publicized speech in 1996, Josef

14 Particularly noteworthy among Hick's publications on the Theology of Religions from the first Birmingham period are: Hick 1973, Hick 1980a, as well as two volumes he edited: Hick 1977a and Hick 1974. For a summary review of Hick's works, see Schmidt-Leukel 2001b.

15 Cp. Race 1983, Hick 1983b.

16 Hick, Knitter 1987.

17 Cp. Hick 1989.

18 D'Costa 1990.

19 Published in Schwager 1996. Beyond this, in the German-speaking context it is principally the following monographs and discussion volumes that should be noted: Bernhardt 1990, Bernhardt 1991, von Brück, Werbick 1993, Peter 1996, Schmidt-Leukel 1997, Schwandt 1998, Breid 1999, *Die Theologie der Religionen in der Diskussion* 2000, Müller, Serretti 2001, Hüt-

Cardinal Ratzinger identified the pluralist theology of religions as one of the greatest theological challenges of the present day.[20] That same year the *International Theological Commission*—the advisory committee of the Vatican's Congregation for the Doctrine of the Faith—published an extensive document on the theology of religions, a document consisting for the most part of a critical confrontation with the pluralist position.[21] The Roman Catholic Church's most adamant rejection of religious pluralism (at least for the present) was set out in the declaration *Dominus Iesus*, issued by the Congregation for the Doctrine of Faith in 2000. [22] "(T)o consider the Church as *one way* of salvation alongside those constituted by the other religions, seen as complementary to the Church or substantially equivalent to her" (No. 21)—clearly the pluralist position—is sharply denounced in this document.

Reactions to *Dominus Iesus* were extremely mixed. In the German-speaking context, the most vociferous protest to *Dominus Iesus* arose in response to a few anti-ecumenical remarks,[23] whereas its statements concerning theology of religions often met with agreement—among Protestants as well as Catholics.[24] At the global level, alongside some predictable agreement on the one hand and some radical dissension (Leonardo Boff, for example, and Aloysius Pieris) on the other, the responses were on the whole reserved or, at the most, cautiously critical.[25] The publication of *Dominus Iesus* was accompanied both before and after by a battery of sanctions and censorial measures directed against Roman-Catholic advocates of a pluralist approach.[26] Such measures significantly narrowed the possibilities for a free and unhindered discussion even within academic contexts—to the extent that university theological departments are subject to control by the Roman Catholic Church (as is the case primarily but by no means exclusively in the German-speaking countries). Thus it is difficult to gain a clear picture of the degree to which Roman Catholic theologians accept a pluralist theology of religions at the present time.

tenhoff 2001. Particularly noteworthy German works specifically on John Hick's philosophy of religion and Theology of Religions include: Gerth 1997, Joswowitz-Schwellenbach 2000, Heller 2001, Koziel 2001. Gerhard Gäde's work unfortunately suffers from numerous misunderstandings and erroneous renderings of Hick's thoughts (see my extensive discussion of this book in Schmidt-Leukel 1998b). For further bibliographic references to a pluralist theology of religions see chapter 6.

20 Ratzinger 1996; on this, see also Hick's response in Hick 1998.

21 International Theological Commission 1996.

22 The German and Latin texts of *Dominus Iesus*, along with some supportive statements as well as the Congregation for the Doctrine of Faith's statement as to the measures taken against the Jesuit theologian Jacques Dupuis can be found in Müller 2003.

23 Cp. Rainer 2001.

24 In some ways the document issued by the theological commission of the Protestant churches in Germany ("Kammer für Theologie der Evangelischen Kirche in Deutschland") *Christlicher Glaube und nichtchristliche Religionen* (EKD Texte 77) presents a kind of German-Protestant counterpart to *Dominus Iesus*.

25 With regard to Asian responses see Chia 2003, 55-107.

26 Cp. the reports by John Allen in the *National Catholic Reporter* ("Doubts about Dialogue," 27.8.1999, and "Perils of Pluralism." 15.9.2000).

The reactions among other churches or ecclesial organizations to the idea of religious pluralism were generally milder but also considerably less specific. However, the closing declaration of the 1990 Baar consultation convened by the World Council of Churches (hereafter: WCC) constitutes something of an exception.[27] This document displays a cautious but unmistakable opening for a pluralist understanding of religions. So, for example, we read there:

> We see the plurality of religious traditions as both the result of the manifold ways in which God has related to peoples and nations as well as a manifestation of the richness and diversity of humankind."[28]

Accordingly, the document views the plurality of religions not as "an obstacle to be overcome, but rather as an opportunity for deepening our encounter with God and with our neighbours..."[29] Yet afterwards, even within the WCC, the Baar declaration did not yield any noteworthy consequences, and the WCC's *Ecumenical Considerations for Dialogue and Relations with People of Other Religions* (2003) returns to the nebulous position which Hans Küng had characterized as "ambiguous" more than twenty years previously, rightly attributing such indecisiveness to the conflict of positions among the WCC's member churches.[30]

Nevertheless, advocates of a pluralist position took a significant step forwards in Birmingham, September 2003, as they gathered for an interreligious conference to discuss the possibility of arriving at a pluralist understanding of religions *from within* the various religious traditions themselves. For if the pluralist conviction is correct in its claim that humanity's major religious traditions refer to an ultimate transcendent reality in ways which are indeed different and yet in principle equally valid, then it must be possible for each particular religious tradition to express this claim in its own specific way and on the basis of its own presuppositions. This then means that there should be a pluralist theology of religions expressible *as* a Jewish, or Christian, or Islamic, or Hindu, or Buddhist[31] theology.[32]

27 "Religious Plurality. Theological Perspectives and Affirmations," in *Current Dialogue* 19 (1991) 47-51.
28 Ibid, 48.
29 Ibid. 49.
30 Küng, Ess, Stietencron, Bechert 1984, 53.
31 With regard to Buddhism the term "theology" is, of course, to be understood in a broader sense, much in the way the term is used by the Buddhist authors in *Buddhist Theology: Critical Reflections by Contemporary Buddhist Scholars*, (Jackson, Makransky 2000), that is in the sense of a critical and academic type of referring to one's own religious tradition, in order to relate it freshly and authentically to today's world, (cp. ibid., p. IX).
32 A sampling of the contributions to this symposium appears in P. Knitter (ed.), *The Myth of Religious Superiority*, Maryknoll 2005.

An Outline of the Argument

With this in mind, the present book aims at a delineation of the fundamental characteristics and advantages of a theology of religions which would be both pluralist and at the same time Christian. My argument unfolds in three major parts. In *Part One*, I explain why I believe a Christian and pluralist theology of religions is necessary—in other words, I set forth the problems a theology of religions needs to address, and lay out the approaches which are available for resolving these problems. All this will be examined in detail later, but for now let us simply sketch out these approaches. First to be considered is the *exclusivist* position, which insists that it is Christianity alone among all the religions that witnesses to and mediates a salvific knowledge of God; secondly, there is the *inclusivist* position, which maintains that although fragmentary and embryonic forms of salvation and revelation can indeed be discerned in other religions, alone in Christianity are salvation and revelation to be encountered in a form that is uniquely superior to all others; and lastly we come to the third approach: the *pluralist* position, according to which salvation and knowledge of the reality designated by Christianity with the word "God" is witnessed to and mediated by various religions in diverse but equally valid ways, such that no religion is uniquely superior to all the others.

Now there are to be sure a number of variations upon these three basic positions (as will be seen in later chapters) but there are no other *basic options* left from which to develop a Christian theology of religions. Thus a theology of religions must reflect upon, carefully evaluate and choose from among these three options, taking into consideration as well their respective theological consequences, so as to arrive at a choice grounded in sound and cogent argumentation.

During the course of Part One all three options will be considered, and I shall present arguments which, I believe, demonstrate that the exclusivist and inclusivist positions are both deficient—although the inclusivist option does indeed represent an advancement over the exclusivist option that should not be underestimated. It will be vital to realize that a pluralist theology of religions does not at all negate or abandon the progress represented by the inclusivist position; on the contrary, this progress is developed yet further. This is to say that inclusivism will be freed, as it were, from its exclusivist remnants—specifically: freed from Christianity's claim of the exclusive or sole superiority of revelation in Jesus Christ.

Of course serious objections have also been advanced against the pluralist position. Is this position *philosophically* consistent, i.e., is it logically coherent or does it suffer from insurmountable inner contradictions? And we must ask too whether religious pluralism can honestly be considered as a *Christian* theological position, as the present book claims. We must take up the question as to whether such pluralism is not grounded in conditions that are ultimately incompatible with central Christian beliefs. In other words, is a pluralist theology of religions *theologically* consistent?

Now whether or not religious pluralism can be seriously considered as a possible theological option at all depends on how convincing the answers to these questions are found to be. These concerns are pursued in *Part Two*, where I demonstrate that a pluralist theology of religions can indeed hold up to scrutiny, albeit only under quite specific philosophical and theological presuppositions, which are developed in the course of *Part Two*. The first and most fundamental presupposition concerns the understanding of God as a transcendent reality necessarily exceeding all human comprehension and speech. What then follows takes up the problem of why and in what sense we both can and must speak of this transcendent reality, despite its inconceivability and ineffability. Key to the understanding of religious discourse as here expounded is the link between revelation and experience. At its core lies a conception of revelation understood not as a divine communication of propositional truths but rather as the self-disclosure of divine reality within the many and diverse forms of human experience. Such an understanding of revelation, coupled with an unequivocal acknowledgement of God's transcendence, clears the way for a theological hermeneutic open to a coherent and consistent pluralist reading of the incongruent and even seemingly contradictory varieties of religious speech. The next task will then be to clarify the connection between such an understanding of revelation and religious experience on the one hand, and the salvific function of the religions on the other. In what sense, and under what conditions can religions be considered as paths of salvation—indeed, as possibly equally valid paths of salvation? The answers to these questions lead directly into the field of Christology, which is to say, into the question of how Jesus Christ can be spoken of as revealer, as mediator of salvation, and as incarnation of the Divine. My proposal will, I believe, preserve a justifiable and sustainable understanding of these claims while being at the same time compatible with a pluralist theology of religions.

Those who find themselves in fundamental agreement with the presuppositions of a Christian and pluralist theology of religions as set out in *Part Two,* and also find themselves agreeing with the critique of the alternative options as presented in *Part One,* will come to consider a pluralist theology of religions as both possible and indeed advisable. Yet can such a theology of religions also find its confirmation in real-world encounters with other religions? What can we learn from both past and present relations between Christianity on the one hand, and Judaism, Islam, Hinduism, and Buddhism on the other? In *Part Three* I hope to show that here too—in the delicate area of interfaith relations—a pluralist approach seems to bear much promise. Now to be sure, the encounter and dialogue with these religions constitutes a vast and to date still largely unexplored terrain; thus my statements on these issues will necessarily remain provisional and fragmentary. Yet through select examples I will demonstrate that despite a history heavily burdened and stamped by exclusivism, inclusivist approaches have indeed managed to open up new perspectives and precisely these perspectives are now further developed via pluralist approaches.

By way of conclusion I will suggest a few possible steps into the future—suggestions which, however, are intended neither as a contribution to some sort of theological futurology nor as an exercise in prognostic speculation. Their aim instead will be to highlight those areas where a theology of religions which will be both Christian and pluralist can be recognized as unquestionably relevant for the future. In this regard we will above all need to inquire into the consequences of such a theology for Christianity's practical relations with non-Christian religious communities. And more: We will need to carefully consider the kind of contribution this theology might make to a gradually emerging "world theology" which draws upon several religious traditions and what significance it will have for the further development of an interreligious spirituality as it is increasingly taking shape among us.

Part I:

The Need for a Christian and Pluralist Theology of Religions

2. Theology of Religions: What's It About?

The Dual Question Addressed by the Theology of Religions

To the great achievements of the Christian Middle Ages belongs the notion that theology should be understood as a science and therefore practiced according to scientific, rationally controlled methods. Particularly famous and influential was Thomas Aquinas' (1225-74) understanding of theology as a derivative science. As optics depends on geometric principles and as harmonics on aesthetics, so the work of theology is grounded in divine revelation. This lends theology a unifying perspective in so far as it considers God in God's relationship to the world and the world in its relationship to God.[1] Its main interest, according to Aquinas, is speculative and focuses primarily on establishing the truth as well as defending against error.[2]

The core features of the conception of theology as a science can still be valid and fruitful today. Then as now its maxims should be the rationally controlled search for truth and elimination of errors. Yet today, far more clearly than in the times of the scholastic pioneers, the human and in particular the historical and socio-cultural conditioning of our receptivity to revelation must be taken into account. And the sensibility that we have in the meantime attained in the philosophy of science demands that we distance ourselves from apodictic claims of infallibility and irrefutable proofs, and understand our assertive judgments as preliminary, hypothetical, and at best probable.[3] But all this can and must occur in the spirit of the maxims here mentioned and not in a spirit of turning away from them.

In light of this, theology today stands in danger of no longer understanding itself as a science, but rather primarily or indeed only in a pragmatic or ideological sense. Christian faith is often implicitly, and sometimes even explicitly, considered as an element of social, cultural, and particularly political life, and theology as its explication for the purpose of societal articulation and implementation of practical concerns and interests along with the attendant values.[4] What then determines

1 Cp. Summa Theologiae I 1, 2-3, 7.
2 Cp. Summa Theologiae I 1, 4 & 8.
3 Cp. Pannenberg 1987a, esp. chapter 5.3, as well as Loichinger 1999, esp. chapter 16.
4 This is true, for example, of many classical proponents of Liberation Theology as well as of defendants of a non-cognitive interpretation of faith, who disavow any actual truth content in faith and honor faith as only an expression of certain basic existential notions. On this, cp. Schmidt-Leukel 1999a, 54ff. There is even a strong tendency among proponents of so-called "Radical Orthodoxy" to replace the question of the truth of faith with the question of its socio-political relevance or to reinterpret the question of truth in terms of its practical relevance. This corresponds to the fact that "Radical Orthodoxy" employs ideas of postmodern

how beliefs and their traditional formulation are interpreted is above all their practical utility within societal discourse. Consequently the discussion of theological ideas is frequently dominated by the question of their social or political appropriateness. The unveiling of allegedly every theology's practical or non-cognitive interests is regarded as the most important analytical tool ("hermeneutics of suspicion," "deconstruction") and theological creativity happens primarily through reinterpretation or reformulation.

One can observe this process in both coarse and more subtle forms, and it is by no means limited to particular theological standpoints or groupings. It can be found equally in progressive or liberal as well as in conservative theological circles. Although these differentiate themselves strongly from each other in determining *what* they deem opportune, they agree *that* it is that kind of opportunity that is the first criterion within theological debates. Abandoned in the process is theology's scientific (and traditional!) interest, that is, the rationally controlled question about the possible truth or falsehood of beliefs. Although on the path of functionalization and ideologization, of reconstruction and deconstruction, of interpretation and reinterpretation, traditional beliefs can be protected from otherwise perhaps unavoidable correction, the price that is paid for such an "orthodoxy" is a rapidly increasing loss of intelligibility and credibility.

To make oneself aware of the process I have only briefly sketched here is particularly important in those areas of theology that are of considerable and far-reaching practical or socio-political relevance, as is unmistakably the case with the theology of religions. It is not uncommon to find among its critics the opinion that a pluralist theology of religions exemplifies a theology that understands itself as principally pragmatic or ideological. On the one hand this may be because some critics themselves understand all theology this way. But on the other hand it may also be because some proponents of pluralist theology express themselves in such a way that lends itself to this interpretation. Yet all in all, this understanding of a pluralist theology of religions is inaccurate. I plead for not only a pluralist theology of religions but theology of religions in general to be understood and carried out in the traditional sense of scientific theology. That is, as every form of scientific theology, theology of religions has to do with God and God's relationship to the world and with the world and its relationship to God, and its concern is not primarily practical but speculative. Certainly its practical implications should be clarified and considered, but these must not take precedence over the question of truth.

The general theological reflection on the relationship between God and the world is concretized in the theology of religions by focusing on religions as part of the world. Wilfred Cantwell Smith expressed this fittingly in the following aphorism:

relativism in order to immunize the Christian faith against rational critique. On this, see also below pp. 41-50.

> We explain the fact that the Milky Way is there by the doctrine of creation, but how do we explain the fact that the Bhagavad Gita is there?[5]

On the one hand, taking the Christian understanding of revelation as a point of departure, theology of religions focuses on developing as plausible an explanation as possible for what we encounter in the world of religions. Yet this is only one side of the coin. To stay with Smith's example: The *Bhagavadgītā* is one of the most significant writings of Hinduism. Mahātma Gandhi praised it as the "infallible guide of conduct" for his life, and, like countless other Hindus, experienced it as the source of spiritual insight and wisdom, and as a testimony to divine revelation. [6] To interpret the world of religions in the light of Christian revelation thus inevitably requires dealing with whatever claims of revelation and knowledge of transcendent reality are witnessed to in and by these religions. So, on the other hand, a theology of religions also has to consider how to view and interpret the Christian understanding of God—as it has been formed on the basis of the revelation witnessed to by Christianity and the experiences underlying that revelation—in the light of non-Christian religions.

Both avenues of inquiry are closely and indivisibly related. If, for example, there are good reasons to consider as authentic the immense wealth of spiritual insight of other religions, how then from a Christian perspective can we explain that such a spiritual treasure exists outside of Christianity? If, as Smith says in his aphorism, the majesty of creation is attributed to God through the doctrine of creation, must we then analogously attribute the authentic spiritual insight of other religions to God through the doctrine of revelation? This would mean extending the doctrine of revelation to include other religions and admitting that revelation is not only testified to by Christianity. Yet this stirs up far-reaching questions about the self-understanding of Christianity and of its own fundamentals of faith, because these then need to be freshly understood and thought through in light of this broader understanding of the revelation event.

A Christian theology of religions is therefore concerned with both questions: *How does Christianity understand and assess other religions?* And: *How does Christianity understand and assess itself in light of other religions?*[7] Like two sides of a coin, these questions are inseparable. Christianity's assessment of other religions has direct consequences for how Christianity understands itself. And by the same token Christianity's self-understanding has consequences for its assessment of other religions. Both questions together can be viewed as one dual question. The importance of realizing the interconnectedness of the two questions is illustrated by the well-known anecdote which the Ceylonese theologian D. T. Niles recounted about Karl Barth: In § 17 of his *Church Dogmatics,* Karl Barth labels religion in general

5 Smith 1976, 16.
6 Cp. Gandhi 1957, 265.
7 See also document of the International Theological Commission "Christianity and the World Religions" (September 30th, 1996), No. 7.

and non-Christian religions in particular as "unbelief." In connection with this, Niles once asked Barth if he had ever met a Hindu. Barth said he had not. Niles responded by asking how Barth could then know that Hinduism was unbelief. And Barth's response was, "A priori."[8] In other words: What follows implicitly from Barth's understanding of the gospel and of Christianity is that all non-Christian religions have to be unbelief—regardless of what one finds in them. But it is precisely this that constitutes the problem: preconceived notions are not examined against the concrete realities of other religions; the second part of the dual question is given short shrift. But if the theology of religions suit is to fit, then it is the "customer" who needs to be measured.[9] And if the suit doesn't hang right, then it isn't the client that needs to be altered, but the suit.

So if Christian claims are not to be raised totally independent of or even in opposition to those facts to which they refer explicitly or implicitly, then any conclusions about other religions that are derived from Christian self-understanding need to be appraised within the concrete encounters with those religions and, if necessary, to be modified or revised in light of these experiences. In other words, a Christian judgment about non-Christian religions that allows itself to be informed by the concrete appearance of those religions can under certain circumstances lead to a change in Christian self-understanding, but in so doing can also become more connected to reality and therefore gain in credibility. Precisely this is the subject of a pluralist theology of religions.

The dual question of the theology of religions issue can be concretized by looking at five different themes that every Christian theology of religions needs to consider. In the remainder of this chapter I give an overview of these themes. As my argument develops, these themes provide the basis for assessing the different options in the theology of religions.

The Dogmatic Problem

Do non-Christian religions have salvific relevance? That is, do Christian doctrinal presuppositions *and* our improved knowledge of non-Christian religions—which, in principle, is now available and can be further deepened through concrete dialogical encounter—allow us or even demand us to attribute a positive salvific meaning to non-Christian religions?

The starting point for this question is the widely held belief within Christianity that God desires the salvation of all human beings and does not exclude any unwitting person from the possibility of such salvation. Granted, this understanding is not shared by all Christians.[10] However, to seriously deny the universal salvific will of

8 Cp. Niles 1969.
9 With regards to this image, cp. Knitter 1985, 206
10 On this, cp. chapter 4.

God leads to grave difficulties with regard to the concept of God itself. A God who arbitrarily excludes persons from salvation without any fault of their own, who creates persons only to damn them, can hardly be considered as the most perfect being, or, as Anselm of Canterbury wrote, as "that greater than which nothing can be conceived," but rather takes on the characteristics of a cosmic tyrant.

According to Christian understanding, broadly speaking, the salvation of persons consists in a healing or healed relationship with God that is only made possible through God's self-revelation to humanity. If one affirms belief in God's universal salvific will, then this presupposes a general revelation that is fundamentally accessible to all human beings. But this then raises many questions that are pivotal for our problem: How can such a general, salvific revelation be conceived so as to truly include all persons? Do the various religions play a role in mediating this revelation, and if so, what is it?[11] So even if it does reach far into the realm of soteriology, the dogmatic problem has to do mainly with the theology of revelation: *From a Christian perspective, is the salvific knowledge/revelation of a transcendent reality mediated only through Christianity or also through other religions?*

There are two main arguments that can be made in favor of a constructive role of religions in this regard. The first is that all human life is bound by a culturally determined web of relations, and thus any possible divine revelation or human knowledge of God must be seen as socio-culturally articulated and mediated; it cannot be conceived of in an isolated and individualistic way. The second argument is that the religions represent that particular cultural phenomenon which explicitly thematizes the divine-human relationship.[12] This then raises the question of the relationship between the various conceptions of non-Christian religions and the Christian understanding of revelation and salvation.

It is a fact of the history of religions that not only Christianity but also all the other religions each in their own way claim to be paths of salvation or claim to witness to and mediate a salvific knowledge or revelation of transcendent reality. Judaism assumes that the covenant that God made with the Jewish people is unchanged and continues to be valid, and that the way of salvation consists of trusting in God's promise and following God's commandment. Islam proclaims that God sent Muhammad as the seal of the prophets and that the Qur'an contains the ultimate guidance for all those who, as the first Sūrah says, "walk on the straight path, the way of those on whom Allah has bestowed grace." Buddhism teaches that on the night of his enlightenment the Buddha discovered the path of liberation, the Noble Eight-

11 See Seckler 1986 for his critical calling into question particularly Karl Rahner's view of such a role for religions. Among other things, Seckler justifiably raises the question of how there can be a way of salvation for *all* people if religions, which after all don't reach every person, are assumed to play a constructive role in mediating this revelation. Chapter 10 delves deeper into this problem.

12 Thus both of Karl Rahner's decisive arguments in Rahner 1964, esp. 151ff. Wolfhart Pannenberg reaches similar conclusions. See Pannenberg 1987b, Pannenberg 1988, 127-132, and Pannenberg 1989.

fold Path, which if followed leads a person to ultimate release from suffering and transience, as well as from the roots of all evil, greed, hatred, and delusion. Daoism teaches the Dao as the "eternal path" and promises that whoever follows this path "will see the mystery of mysteries." (*Daodejing,* 1). Based on Vedic revelation, Hinduism teaches that it is the three paths of right conduct (*karma mārga*), of meditative knowledge (*jñāna mārga*), and of love of God (*bhakti mārga*) which will lead a person "from the unreal to the real, from darkness to light, from death to immortality"[13]

The dogmatic problem can therefore be pointedly expressed like this: *Can Christians endorse the claim of non-Christian religions to be paths of salvation, or do they have to dispute this claim?* Revelation was and is often understood by Christianity as excluding the possibility of affirming the salvation and revelation claims of other religions. Yet if one accepts that there is a fundamental connection between God's universal salvific will, a universal possibility of salvation, a universal salvific revelation, and the socio-cultural role of religions as mediators, then exactly the opposite seems likely. That is, it is rather the Christian understanding of revelation itself that suggests ascribing a basic truthfulness to other religions' claims of salvation and revelation. Of course we then still need to clarify more precisely how the concrete explications of salvation and revelation or knowledge of the transcendent in non-Christian religions relate to what is considered to be salvation and revelation in Christianity. For if the claims of salvation and revelation of those other religions are found to be in deep and irreconcilable opposition to the Christian understanding of salvation and revelation, it will be difficult from the Christian perspective to ascribe a constructive role to the other religions' mediation of salvific knowledge of the transcendent. Thus the dogmatic problem leads directly to the question of how the diversity of religious claims of salvation and truth might be interpreted. Is it a case of a radically incompatible diversity without any points of connection? Or are there significant commonalities, similarities, functional equivalents, etc., that allow this diversity to be understood as in principle compatible and even in the end perhaps as complementary? As we shall see, these questions also stand in the background of the other problem areas that a theology of religions has to address.

The Practical Problem

Broadly speaking, the practical problem consists of the following question: *As Christians, how should we encounter the individuals and institutions of other religions?* Any discussion of practical interreligious relations has to begin with the clear recognition that, to a large extent, the history of interreligious encounters was and partly continues to be one of mutual animosity, hostility, and even of outbursts of crass vio-

13 Bṛhadāranyaka Upaniṣad 1:3, 28.

lence: Christianity used violence against Judaism, against the Greek and Roman religions, against the Celtic and Germanic religions, against Islam, and in the course of missionary activity in modern times, against Shintoism, Buddhism, and Hinduism as well as against the traditional religions of Africa, Asia, and America. In addition, as is well known, the history of Christianity is full of often bitter fights between the different Christian churches. Already in the New Testament, so-called "heretics"—in other words, Christians with different theological convictions—are likened to "irrational animals, mere creatures of instinct, born to be caught and killed" (2 Pet 2:12 NRSV). Islam in turn violently fought the polytheistic religions of the Arabian Peninsula, followed later by Hinduism, Buddhism, and the traditional religions of Africa. Despite its relatively tolerant stance toward Judaism and Christianity, parts of Islam were and are embroiled in massive violent confrontations with these religions too. Like Christianity, Islam also has a long history of bloody conflicts between the different Islamic traditions, including the unspeakable pogroms that were carried out in the last decades against the Bahai religion, itself an Islamic descendant. Even if Asia's history of religions has, by comparison, been generally less violent, there are nonetheless several examples of violent interreligious conflicts: following the reign of Emperor Ashoka, Hindu Brahmins fought Buddhism that they perceived as a threat. Still today, Ceylonese Buddhists fight what they consider to be threatening Hindu Tamils. Likewise there have been bloody persecutions of Buddhists in Tibet and China, prompted by adherents of the Bon religion, Daoism, and Confucianism. And Buddhists and Shintos in seventeenth-century Japan carried out one of the bloodiest persecutions of Christians to date. Up to the present day Hindus, Muslims, and later also Sikhs in India remain enmeshed in sometimes extremely violent conflicts.[14]

Quite often interreligious conflicts are explained as resulting merely from a misuse of religion. According to such an interpretation, these conflicts are not truly religious in nature, but result from other motivations. Thus one runs across comments like the following from the former German president, Roman Herzog: "Religions do not divide. Religious wars only ever come about because of political misuse of religion."[15] No matter how well intentioned, such depictions seem to me dangerously trivializing and naïve. The examples I have named show that numerous cases of interreligious conflict are predominantly and at times even exclusively motivated by religious reasons. The thesis of the political misuse of religion can be rebutted not only by historical example. In itself, it is also completely implausible. Let us assume, as the thesis does, that religions in themselves are not a divisive but rather a fundamentally peace-promoting factor. Then why is it possible that they can be so easily misused for allegedly non-religiously motivated conflicts? I am not disputing that there are and have been many cases in which those responsible for the outbreak of

14 For a brief overview of religiously motivated and potentially highly violent conflicts and tensions of the present, see Jenkins 2002, 163-188.

15 "Gegen die Maler von Feindbildern" (Against the creators of bogeymen), in *Die Woche*, 13.11.1998, p. 27.

violence have been motivated by something other than religion and have indeed instrumentalized religions for these purposes. Yet such a misuse of religion is only possible because there is a high potential for conflict within religions, and that this potential allows itself to be misused. If a person wants to see a house burn, he or she will pour gasoline and not water onto the flames. The thesis about the political misuse of religion implies in itself that there are not only peace-promoting factors in religions, but also a dangerous potential for conflict that one can apparently all too easily exploit.[16]

If there is such a thing as a genuinely religious potential for conflict, then it must be connected to the salvation and truth claims of the religions. Wolfhart Pannenberg has repeatedly drawn our attention to the fact that at the root of interreligious conflict lies a conflict in their claims to truth and validity.[17] Yet we need to differentiate between three important components here. First, there is the *tight connection between truth and salvation claims* characteristic of religions. This means that religions assume that the truth or revelation to which they witness is of decisive importance for the salvation of persons, salvation being the highest of all possible goods. Engagement on behalf of a truth perceived as decisive for salvation is therefore, in the context of religion, often a passionate and extreme engagement. Such an engagement is of course ambivalent. Committing oneself passionately on behalf of saving truth will always be understood religiously as a selfless sacrifice for the sake of one's fellow humans. Yet depending on how the situation is assessed, precisely this motive can assume very different forms and in so doing be both non-violent and also prepared for violence. As ethical discussion on tyrannicide, rebellion, defensive war, etc., shows, use of force cannot always be judged negatively. Who would want to dispute that the Christians involved in the July 20th attack on Hitler were truly and seriously motivated by their religion and that a success of this assault would most likely have prevented untold further suffering? It is important to recognize that the use of force in the context of interreligious conflicts feeds on similar motives. According to Thomas Aquinas, it is precisely the commandment to love one's neighbor that obliges us to stop a heretic, with force if necessary, since the heretic's unhindered action endangers the eternal salvation of countless fellow humans. And so the love for one's fellow human beings commands one to preserve them from this harm.[18] Similar reflections presumably play a significant role in many religious conflicts: the true faith must be protected for the salvation of beings, if necessary by the use of violence.

Yet the link between the question of salvation and truth only partially explains the religious roots of interreligious conflicts. Passion for salvation can after all be manifested peacefully and without force; it is not inevitably accompanied by conflict or the use of violence. That this however was and still is often the case is connected with two further factors related to the content and validity of religious claims about

16 In this connection, see also Herrmann 1996; Schmidt-Leukel 2004.
17 See Pannenberg 1989, 104ff; Pannenberg 1979, esp. 270ff.
18 Summa Theologiae II/II, 11, 3, & 4. On this, see also Schmidt-Leukel 2000.

truth: the assumption that religions contradict each other in relation to the truths they consider as decisive for salvation, and the corresponding intention of either establishing one religion's truth claims offensively or at least protecting them defensively against the truth claims of others. For example, according to Karl Rahner, Christianity claims to be "the absolute religion destined for all persons…*the* path of salvation that God has made for all and has made, in principle, obligatory for all."[19] Even if other religions mostly do not go so far in expressing their claims as to insist that the paths of salvation to which they witness are "obligatory for all," they do nonetheless assume their truth claims to be universally valid and typically offer their path of salvation as objectively superior to any others.[20] When it comes to missionary religions, we see an effort to translate such claims into action. But by doing so, these religions unavoidably slip into a tense, conflictive relationship due to the reciprocal claims of truth and validity that they raise against one another,

But how unavoidable are the rudiments of this conflict potential? Must the truth claims of the various religions considered decisive for salvation inevitably be understood as irreconcilable? Or is there an acceptable and credible interpretation that can understand the uncontested differences of truth and salvation claims as an, at least partially, reconcilable, compatible, or even complementary diversity? In such a case religions would no longer be forced to insist on their own exclusive validity or reciprocal superiority, and religious conflict potential would thus be nipped in the bud.

A pluralist theology of religions maintains that it can offer such an interpretation of religious diversity and grounds its particular practical relevance on this fact. Yet two important aspects must be highlighted here. First we need to emphasize that from the standpoint of academic theology the insight into the close connection between the different theology of religions' options and practical interreligious relations must not be allowed to give precedence to pragmatic considerations over theological arguments. Second, even a pluralist theology of religions does not entail that *all* differences in questions deemed crucial to salvation can be interpreted in terms of a basically compatible diversity. Also, one cannot rely on all religious persons wanting to adopt a pluralist standpoint. Therefore, in light of the religious potential for conflict, the need to contain and control it through secular authorities and through the acceptance of modernity's command of tolerance—in the sense of a toleration of what one does not appreciate—remains indispensable.[21]

For several decades the question of how Christians are to encounter persons of other religions has been intensely and passionately discussed under the rubric "Mission or Dialogue?".[22] There is no lack of attempts to declare this presentation of the

19 Rahner 1967, 355f (translated from the German original)

20 Compare the apt comment by John May (2003, 149) that behind religions' claims to uniqueness and superiority there lurks the danger of deriving from this a justification for violence.

21 Compare Schmidt-Leukel 2000, Schmidt-Leukel 2002, as well as chapter 6 below, pp. 162-164.

22 On this, compare Helfenstein 1998, Zehner 1992, Rosenstein 1991, Samartha 1981.

issue as redundant claiming that it would be based on an incorrect way of framing the question. The solution, it is said, would be to talk about "Dialogue *and* Mission." Together, both of these should and could determine the practical relationship of Christianity to the non-Christian religions. Yet such a rash solution conceals the fact that behind this alternative lies the problem I have just outlined about opposing truth and validity claims. According to its traditional understanding, mission ideally aims at the Christianization of the world and consequently the overcoming of all other religions. Andreas Laun correctly summarizes this understanding when he says: "the fact that that there are other religions—meaning people who have not recognized Christ—is an evil that mission desires to overcome."[23] Yet such a stance inevitably results in a strained relationship to other religions. As Laun himself emphasizes, this tension can be countered when simultaneously both a fundamental tolerance and the principle of religious freedom are affirmed. The basis of the tension itself, however, and the *potential* for conflict remain. In the face of this, the call to dialogue is often understood as a clear alternative, as a call to a stance that does not yearn for the conversion of the other, but rather only for rapprochement and understanding, with the goal of learning from and with one another. So the decisive difference and contrast between mission and dialogue lies precisely in the fact that the traditional concept of mission sees other religions fundamentally as an evil to be overcome, whereas such a notion is alien to the program of dialogue.

This is a weighty distinction, for on it depends whether practical interreligious relationships are fundamentally relaxed or strained. What we see with most of the attempts to declare mission and dialogue as compatible is that this opposition can only be resolved by either so modifying the concept of dialogue that it can coalesce with the basic concerns of mission, or even becomes subservient to it, or, by contrast, so modifying the concept of mission that it effortlessly adapts to the goals of the dialogue-program. In the first case, for example, it is said that dialogue is the form most suitable for effectively conveying the gospel to adherents of non-Christian religions. In the second case, one argues that the willingness of the dialogue partners to understand and learn invites mutual witness. But such alignment of the idea of dialogue with mission, or the other way around, does not erase the fundamental opposition between them, but rather at best glosses over it. At the root of this opposition is the differing assessment of non-Christian religions according to the different options in the theology of religions, and this inevitably affects the corresponding practical relationships. So, as argued above, the reciprocal assessment of religions which determines the kinds of practical relationships between them now rests on the one hand on internal theological assumptions, but on the other hand should follow a knowledge of other religions that is as precise as possible and that is

23 Laun 1992,269. Karl Rahner also says "One can and must say that these non-Christian religions in themselves have been, in principle, done away with and superseded by the coming of Christ (…), so that the historic expansion of Christianity, which even today is not over, is identical to a progressive abolition of the legitimacy of these religions." Rahner 1967, 371f. (Both quotations translated from German originals.)

led by a genuine attempt at understanding. Yet in order to move from understanding to appraisal, interreligious assessment has to rely on the application of suitable criteria, which brings us to the next set of problems.

The Criteriological Problem

The in many ways notable document of the Roman Catholic Church "Dialogue and Proclamation" (1991) points to the ambivalence of religions. On the one hand, the religions reflect humanity's sinfulness and limitations. On the other hand, religions also contain "elements of grace capable of sustaining the positive response of their members to God's invitation." In order to discern and identify these elements the document affirms that suitable criteria have to be established (No. 30).[24] This is exactly what constitutes the criteriological problem: *According to which criteria can we assess other religions?*

What criteria may appear to be suitable depends in the first instance on the categories of the critical assessment. In the context of forming an interreligious judgment, the categories are *truth*, *goodness*, and *holiness*. The related criteria consequently have to be of a rational, ethical, and religious or soteriological nature. This means that assessing truth claims demands *rational* criteria, assessing claims about values and norms of behavior needs to be determined by *ethical* criteria, and in order to assess claims and practices that in a more narrow sense have to do with the religious orientation or salvation of persons one needs *soteriological* criteria. Of course, the fact these three strands are typically tightly intertwined with each other in religions means that while they can be differentiated from one another they cannot really be separated.

The first problem we encounter in more closely working out an interreligious criteriology is the challenge of *relativism*, which has emerged powerfully out of postmodernist philosophical trends. There are two reasons to examine relativism somewhat more closely here. On the one hand, it deserves attention because in the West relativism has by now grown into a broad current of intellectual and cultural sensitivity that has taken hold—particularly in its more superficial and popular forms—in broad spheres of the media world and general societal discourse. On the other hand, relativism needs to be addressed, because pluralist theology of religions is often, whether intentionally or not, confused or identified with relativism.[25]

The challenge of relativism has repercussions for all three strands named here and their corresponding criteria. This means that the validity of the rational, ethical,

24 Dialogue and Proclamation, 812.

25 A particular prominent example of this is Cardinal Josef Ratzinger, who branded pluralist theology of religions as relativism in his 1996 speech "Relativism: The Central Problem of Faith Today," which was widely publicized and translated into several languages. For a critical response to this text by John Hick see Hick 2001b. 157-160.

and soteriological criteria is challenged by a cognitive relativism, an ethical relativism, and an ideological or religious relativism. It is not always easy to exactly specify relativist standpoints since they are often presented rather diffusely. But what is contested from the perspective of relativism is usually the universal validity of normative views and their corresponding criteria. Typically this contestation is based on the two following assumptions.

First, according to a relativist understanding perspectives, norms, and criteria—whether of rational, ethical, or of a more narrowly religious nature—do not have universal but only "local" validity. In other words, for the relativist, the validity of such norms and criteria is dependent on, limited by, and therefore relative to their particular historical, cultural, social, and religious context. Combined with this relativist point of departure is the *second* assumption: that these contexts are radically or irreducibly different, and that this radical difference in contexts results in an irreducible difference of the respective normative views and their spheres of validity. Most often, this difference is described as "incommensurability," although it is not always clear what precisely this should mean. In a weaker sense it simply expresses that the respective contexts and norms are incompatible. In a stronger and likely more commonly intended sense, it means incomparability, untranslatability, or even mutual incomprehensibility.[26]

From this thesis of the contextually bounded nature of all norms and criteria, it follows that there can be no neutral or independent perspective beyond or above the various individual contexts. No matter what is said about various contexts and thus about cultures and religions, it is itself traceable back to a particular context from which it receives its validity. From the incommensurability thesis follows that any judgment about other contexts as well as the criteria supporting that judgment are *only* valid in this particular context. This in turn means that every context, every system, every culture, every religion, etc., can only be judged according to its own criteria *and* that incommensurability excludes the possibility of any overarching general validity of norms and criteria. The formation of interreligious judgments is thus ultimately impossible, or at least not possible in the sense of something that will be equally acceptable to all sides. Wherever such a judgment arises, it merely reflects the claims and views of those making the judgment, without any justified claim to general validity. The superiority of one's own system is unavoidable in this type of judgment-formation and in a sense presupposed by the immanent logic of the system: one's own system is the only one able to finally fulfill one's own specific criteria. Yet precisely for this reason, such superiority claims cannot claim any general validity. When this is nonetheless done it constitutes a form of ideological "imperialism."

Relativist positions can lead to two distinct but related reactions. On the one hand, they can evoke a feeling of indifference and irrelevance that bears a resemblance to skepticism and nihilism insofar as they all share a sense that a specific

26 On this, compare the differentiated presentation and discussion on the thesis of incommensurability in N. Hintersteiner 2001, 155-206.

decision can only be justified within its particular system and cannot be rationally justified in any intrinsic or general way. The other reaction can be characterized as decisionistic or fideistic. If all thought and action is unavoidably bound to a particular standpoint, and there is no possibility of objectively privileging one standpoint over another, then one can all the more unhesitatingly and decisively adopt and represent any standpoint one chooses (for any reason whatsoever). Relativist arguments can thus even be used to immunize one's own ideological or religious position. For according to a relativist understanding, one's own standpoint or in this case one's own religion cannot justifiably be criticized or called into question from another standpoint. And yet from one's own standpoint one can make something like a judgment about all others so long as one renounces any claim to objective or universal validity and instead consciously characterizes the formation of this judgment as a kind of discourse and understanding within one's own system.

Numerous Christian theologians and philosophers, embracing what is sometimes described as "Radical Orthodoxy," also pursue similar views and strategies in various forms and to varying degrees of radicality.[27] As Peter Donovan has rightly remarked, such a "defense" of orthodoxy is considerably more distant from the original concerns of orthodoxy than the liberal and modern positions indebted to the Enlightenment against which such postliberal and postmodern defenses of orthodoxy are directed.[28] For in contrast to relativist postmodernism, traditional orthodoxy shares with the Enlightenment a fundamentally realist epistemology and an interest in universally binding truth claims, value judgments, and concepts of salvation.

So how might we respond to the challenge of relativism? For starters, a thorough relativism is self-refuting, and this holds for both of its two basic assumptions. *First* there is the question of whether or not the relativist claims universal validity for his or her own contestation of universal claims of validity. If the former, then the self-contradiction is apparent, and if the latter, the relativist thesis becomes irrelevant. For if the relativist tries to remain consistent by accepting the limited validity of his or her own thesis from the start, then it is no longer possible to conclude from that thesis what is intended—that is, the limited validity of *all* judgments.[29] Relativism then becomes nothing more than a mere claim and as such possesses no argumentative strength in the face of rival positions.[30] Yet when relativists argue on behalf of their position, they do in fact assume something like the universal validity of arguments, evidence, logical rules, and so forth.[31]

27 For example, cp. Phillips 1988, Lindbeck 1984, MacIntyre 1985, Milbank 1990, Milbank 1997, Milbank, Pickstock, Ward 1999, Hemming 2000, D'Costa 2000. For an overview of postmodern relativistic types of argumentation among critics of pluralist theology of religions, see Knitter 1995, 38-53.

28 Cp. Donovan 1993, 224f.

29 Cp. Kreiner 1992, 46f.

30 Cp. O'Grady 2002, 148f.

31 Ibid., 146f.

The *second* assumption of relativism, the thesis of incommensurability, is likewise self-refuting, at least if incommensurability is understood in the sense of untranslatability or unintelligibility. For in order to be able to claim with some justification that diverse contexts are fundamentally unintelligible to one another, the relativist would have had to understand both contexts. He or she would thereby implicitly postulate a sort of metacontext within which such subcontexts would be intelligible, which are claimed to be mutually unintelligible. The denial that there are such encompassing and connecting metacontexts, however, is precisely one of the central concerns of relativism. Thus to be consistent, the relativist could only say about himself that he or she is unable to understand any other context apart from his or her own one—a position with no bearing on the fundamental intelligibility or unintelligibility of those contexts. If one embraces a weaker form of the incommensurability thesis by allowing for a certain degree of intelligibility and translatability, one presupposes the existence of commonalities that overlap different contexts—which are necessary for any amount of understanding and translation—commonalities such as common points of reference, background assumptions, structural or functional similarities, and so on.[32] Yet such a diminished incommensurability thesis contradicts the basic relativist assumption that the respective contexts are in every regard incomparably and irreducibly different. The existence of some specific or limited incommensurabilities that are at the same time accompanied by significant commonalities and comparable features or that can be related to some common background does not offer relativism any support.[33] Indeed, as Paul O'Grady has commented, one is quite justified in asking whether this type of difference can even appropriately be described as "incommensurability" at all.[34]

The critique of the incommensurability thesis has weighty repercussions on the relativist assumption that all judgments, norms, and criteria are context-dependent. For if one cannot demonstrate something like a pervasive incommensurability, if the differences between contexts are always also accompanied by significant commonalities, then what should the purported context-dependence actually mean? Presumably the strongest possible meaning would be one of logical dependence. Yet this neither necessarily limits the general validity nor does it imply that the assumed logical dependence is necessarily of an exclusive nature. When, where, and under what conditions a particular view arises does not say anything about the validity of that view. Even statements that have a high degree of logical dependence on certain particular conditions—as for example propositions with a time and place indicator (e.g., at

32 Following H. Sankey, Hintersteiner has argued against D. Davidson not to equate untranslatability with incomprehensibility. That is, it is possible for two languages not to be able to be translated into one another, but still be understandable to one and the same subject. Yet in such cases, the untranslatable languages ought to be defined as "sub-languages in the context of a common background language" (Hintersteiner 2001, 176), so that the claim of incommensurability is reduced to a local and limited incommensurability. In the end, Hintersteiner too declines the thesis of a fundamental incommensurability (see ibid., 205).

33 Cp. O'Grady 2002, 161.

34 Ibid., 163, 169f.

t-time, person x was at place p)—despite their close context-dependence, are, if true, absolutely true.[35] Moreover, judgments, norms, and criteria, even when they logically derive from particular context-bound conditions, can under certain circumstances and in other contexts also be derived from other context-bound conditions. For example, agreement on a particular value judgment is entirely possible on the basis of different ideological or religious background assumptions.

There can of course be weaker forms of contextual dependence besides logical dependence. The context can for example merely constitute a setting for discovering certain judgments, norms, or criteria, which could be discovered equally well in other contexts, meaning their validity is not dependent on the particular discovery context. Context dependence can also result from a particular form of expression or a special embodiment of a truth, a norm, or a criterion, in such a way that that the relevant truth, norm, or criterion could also be expressed or embodied in a different way in another context. All of this is possible without thereby in any way supporting the thesis of incommensurability and the relativist contestation of commonly applicable judgments and norms.

It is not only the above mentioned logical objections that speak against the claims of incommensurability. In addition, one can also produce empirical objections. By this is meant the empirical demonstration that "human cultures … show far more specific invariables"[36] than had been assumed under the influence of earlier anthropological or ethnological studies, studies which often inspired the relativist assumptions discussed above. According to Elmar Holenstein, modern linguistics and behavioral studies have yielded numerous proofs of this.[37] The empirically demonstrated intercultural dispersal of logical rules and types of argumentation contests a cognitive or rational relativism that assumes the existence of incommensurable rationalities.[38] Against ethical relativism, the existence of numerous examples of intercultural and interreligious commonalities in basic ethical assumptions has been demonstrated and newly confirmed in the course of the "Global Ethic Project," a project largely co-initiated by Hans Küng.[39] The debate about relativism is of course more difficult and contentious in regard to religious or soteriological assumptions. Are there also empirical proofs for interreligious commonalities regarding soteriology? Is there significant interreligious common ground concerning what is perceived as being salvific? Are there criteria for this whose validity and factual acceptance is not limited to just one particular religious tradition?

According to John Hick, the various religions' conceptions of salvation/liberation can be understood as variations on a central and common theme, which he describes as the "transformation of human existence from self-centeredness to Real-

35 Cp. O'Grady 2002, 149.
36 Holenstein 1985, 125.
37 Ibid., 125ff.
38 On this, compare for example Paul 1994.
39 Cp. Küng 1995; Küng, Kuschel 1996.

ity-centeredness,"[40] in which the term "Reality" or "the Real" always refers to the ultimate, transcendent, or divine reality. This central and basic soteriological motif, according to Hick, is also at work within the religious critique of religion, in other words, in that critique which exemplary religious figures have practiced towards certain religious manifestations of their day. For this critique was primarily shaped by a fundamental soteriological concern. It is this concern that, according to Hick, should dominate over the religious assessment of religions. In other words,

> Religious traditions and their various components—beliefs, modes of experience, scriptures, rituals, disciplines, ethics and lifestyles, social rules and organisations—have greater or less value according as they promote or hinder the salvific transformation.[41]

Certainly, there need to be additional criteria that can function as indicators of whether the salvific transformation really occurs. According to Hick, the criteria for this should be taken from the religions themselves, and yet not from their particular peculiarities but from what is common to them, because it is only in this way that an interreligious recognition of these criteria is ensured. Hick proposes we look for these commonly held criteria in what the various religions consider to be the spiritual and moral fruit of salvific transformation. We can begin by looking at the various religions' ideals of saintliness, as the "saints" present the ideal embodiments of salvific transformation, so that the criteria for salvific transformation can be derived from the criteria for saintliness. It is true that there are specific and characteristic differences between the ideals of saintliness. But there are also commonalities in certain fundamental spiritual characteristics such as transparency to the transcendent reality, love of neighbor, friendliness, self-control, patience, inner peace and calm, freedom, joy, etc. According to Hick, the most significant criteriological commonality is found in the ethical sphere as an integral part and aspect of the salvific process.[42] For salvific transformation "shows itself, within the conditions of this world, in compassion (*karuṇā*) or love (*agapé*)."[43]

Incidentally, a quite similar notion was previously advocated by Cardinal Josef Ratzinger. As he says:

> ...it is not the system and the practice of a system that saves a person; rather, what saves a person is something that is more than any system and that represents the opening up of all systems: namely love and faith, which are the true cessations of egoism and of self-destructive hubris. The religions are effective for salvation in so far as they lead persons into this attitude; they hinder salvation in so far as they hinder persons taking on such attitude.[44]

40 Cp. Hick 1989, 36-53.
41 Hick 1989, 300.
42 Cp. Hick 1989, 299-342.
43 Hick 1989, 164.
44 Ratzinger 1969, 356 (translated from the German original)

John Hick has called attention to the fact that to a certain extent this ethical criterion emerges from our human nature, and that it is not only at work in the religions' self-understanding and in the formation of interreligious assessment but that the ethical criterion is already operating in the acceptance of a religion by its followers. Would the first Christians have accepted Jesus as the "Son of God" if he had preached hatred instead of love? Would Gautama have been seen as the enlightened one by the first Buddhists if he had proclaimed egoism instead of selflessness? And would the first Muslims have followed Mohammed as the prophet of God if he had not lived up to the ethical demands that he preached?[45] However, it is not only ethical criteria but also criteria such as the opening of a new and fulfilling understanding of ultimate reality in face of the experience of evil and suffering, as well as the experience of a transforming power that lies at the root of a religion's acceptance by its members. These criteria are thus certainly bound to the particular standpoint of the respective religion, and yet do not depend on it in an exclusive sense; otherwise they could not be effective as criteria of the acceptance of this particular religion.[46]

Such observations point to another important direction for research in the search for an adequate interreligious criteriology—the search for a transcendental grounding of such criteria in the structure of the human mind. This direction of research must also begin with certain empirically tangible religious phenomena, before returning to the general mental or intellectual conditions that make their existence possible. In this regard Rudolf Otto proposed his epochal attempt to demonstrate relationships between the concrete phenomena of the history of religions and a human religious *a priori*—amongst other things also with the goal of establishing criteria for judging religion.[47] There have been other attempts in this same vein,[48] for example Karl Rahner's reflections on a "transcendental" and more precisely a "searching Christology."[49] Rahner is concerned with the conditions for the possibility of recognizing and accepting Jesus as the "absolute savior." According to Rahner, for this to happen certain criteriologically effective expectations have to be present, whether consciously or unconsciously. The person must have somehow already more or less known what he or she was expecting or searching for, when he or she comes to believe that it is found in Jesus. Rahner tried to concretize these criteria. By way of the absolute savior, God affirms as meaningful and possible that which would seem meaningless and impossible without such affirmation: to venture oneself in total love to one's fellow humans, to willingly accept one's own death, and to live hopefully into a future of total reconciliation.[50] Because Rahner views the searching Christology as anchored transcendentally in the characteristically human conditions of existence he assumes that signs of this "search" are to be found within the totality of

45 Hick 1989, 325f.
46 Cp. Hick, *On Grading Religions*, in Hick 1988, 67-87.
47 Cp. Otto 1923.
48 See for example Ward 1991, 178-92.
49 Cp. Rahner 1976, 206-211, 287-295, 303-312.
50 Cp. Rahner 1975.

religious history, especially in the mythic or historic savior figures of particular religions. However, Rahner assumes that the ultimate fulfillment of this "search" is to be found exclusively in Jesus, and therefore describes the savior figures of other religions as "anticipations," that is as forms of a prescience of what was only in fact realized in Jesus. Yet the criteria of a searching Christology in themselves do not seem to justify this opinion. For why should the testimony to such saviors in non-Christian religions not also be understood as evidence that the transcendental search for the absolute savior has been fulfilled authentically and validly at several places in the history of religion?

If despite the different religious conceptions of salvation something like a formal, perhaps also rudimentary substantial agreement or at least a compatible criteriology of salvation can be identified—whether that be in a primarily empirical or transcendentally analytical way—then such a criteriology will also permit the idea that there can be a salvific relation to transcendence in different but equally valid forms.

Let us take another look back. The relativist challenge confronts the search for a suitable criteriology in interreligious assessment with the following dilemma: In order to be unbiased and universally valid, such a criteriology would have to take as its point of departure a sort of "Archimedes point outside of all religious traditions."[51] Since, however, there is no such point, every criteriology is always bound to the perspective and standpoint of its own religion, and will therefore be neither unbiased nor universally valid, but due to its own boundedness will inevitably assume the superiority of its own religious tradition. Anyone who claims to be able to avoid this would in reality likewise insist on the superiority of his or her own religious or philosophical standpoint and thus be playing the same game. As unavoidable as these superiority claims might be, there exists no possibility for them to be tested or confirmed in any universally valid and unbiased way.

As the critique of relativism sketched above makes clear, this supposed dilemma is contingent upon a whole series of untenable and unjustified assumptions. There may in fact be nothing like an Archimedian stance *external* to all religions and ideologies. After all, what would such a positionless position be? However, such a stance is by no means necessary. For in order to be unbiased, universally valid, and therefore in principle also acceptable above and beyond the stance of one's own religion, the only thing required is that the criteria for assessing religions are not tied exclusively and incommensurably to the standpoint of one particular religion. Such a criteriology need not be derived from an illusory point outside of all religions and ideologies. Rather, it can be developed by starting with those criteria which are already operative within the religions and upon which the acceptance of one's own religion as well as one's assessment of other religions depends. That in each case such criteria are tied to the context of the respective individual religion does not mean that they are *a priori* unsuitable for a generally applicable interreligious criteriology. In order to be in principle acceptable for several religions it is sufficient that these

51 G. D'Costa 1993a, 90.

criteria do not possess an exclusive logical dependence on their context. Inter-religious dialogue will therefore also have the task of negotiating the criteria for reciprocal evaluation. On the one hand, this means asking what relevant norms and criteria religions possibly have in common. On the other hand, one has to investigate whether in the case of divergent criteria the differences are irreconcilable or whether these can be seen as compatible or even complementary. There is no good reason for the insistence often raised from a postmodern perspective that the only person who really takes the diversity and multiplicity of religions seriously is the one who regards them as radically and irreducibly incompatible. Diversity can be incompatible as well as compatible. The claim that diversity is only taken seriously if one characterizes it as incompatible arises from the relativist incommensurability thesis, and is as false as the latter.

So the *first* step is to ask (along the lines of John Hick and Karl Rahner) on which criteria one's acceptance of one's own religion depends. A *second* step is then to assess the salvation and truth claims of other religions according to the same criteria. In so doing, of course, one needs to observe the oft-stated ground rule of all comparative evaluation: that one must not compare the ideal of one's own religion with a less ideal reality of the other, but rather that ideal can only be compared with ideal, and reality only with reality. In addition to this, with religions that have existed for a long time one has to take into account a diachronic perspective that informs us about which positive and which negative fruits have so far resulted from these religions. There is no reason, however, to abstain from any judgment, nor would such abstention be always possible. Many will agree that from a Christian perspective there are good reasons and appropriate criteria to dismiss completely the quasi-religious claim of salvation associated with Adolf Hitler ("Heil Hitler"). But if this is the case, why shouldn't the same reasons and criteria allow us to come to a positive assessment of other claims of salvation and other saviors? Those who demand that we completely withhold any kind of judgment rob themselves of the possibility to practice critique where it is called for. Yet if one assumes that in certain situations such a critique is not only unavoidable but even necessary, one will hardly be able to produce persuasive arguments that Christian judgments on other religions and ideologies are only permissible when they are negative. Whatever does not correspond to the demands of reason, of morality, or of a Christian understanding of salvation cannot be endorsed from a Christian perspective. But the reverse is also true: that Christians should likewise not deny the due endorsement of everything they encounter in other religions that is actually true, good, and holy.

As the *third* step, we need finally to inquire about the convergence and divergence of criteria operative in Christianity and other religions. As we have already seen, Christian norms can be compatible with those of other religions, even when they differ from one another in particular ways. This inquiry is a protracted and arduous process, for it assumes one will learn to see oneself through others' eyes. Yet this labor is worthwhile. For it carries the promise that one will learn to understand far better and perceive more realistically one's interreligious partner and oneself. In the meantime there are a series of signs that interreligious dialogue is gradually penetrating into this sphere, and this is a sign of its increasing maturity.[52] The mutual opinions about each other and the criteria that determine them will then become more transparent and more easily comprehensible for all sides. This could in the future lead to much improved and more appropriate opinions and to the development of a more precise and differentiated criteriology that is not limited solely to one's own religious tradition.[53]

The search for a suitable criteriology serves the goal of forming adequate interreligious judgments. But a judgment can only be adequate if what is to be judged is properly understood. For that reason, the criteriological problem is closely connected with the question of the possibility of interreligious understanding, to which we now turn.

The Hermeneutical Problem

Understanding a Buddhist means being able to see the world through his eyes: this is how Wilfred Cantwell Smith described the maxim of interreligious hermeneutics.[54] It expresses the intuitive insight that properly understanding the religious stranger means understanding him or her as he or she understands him- or herself and his or her life in the world. Every hetero-interpretation, that is every interpretation by another, must in the first instance make every effort to arrive at a good understanding of the auto-interpretation, the self-understanding.[55] But is such an understanding actually possible, if it is attempted from the perspective of another religion? *Can other religions be properly understood from the perspective of one particular religion?* This question seems more than justified when one considers that in the course of interreligious controversy the depiction of other religions has only too often been—and continues to be—crudely distorted and that such distortion unmistakably grew out of polemical and apologetic roots. Max Müller, one of the great pioneers of the science of religion, commented on this in the nineteenth century:

> No judge, if he had before him the worst of criminals, would treat him as most historians and theologians have treated the religions of the world. Every act

52 Examples include: Griffith 1990, Grünschloss 1999, Gross, Muck 2000, Schmidt-Leukel 2001a, Ridgeon 2001.

53 The matter of interreligious criteriology has until recently been a largely unresearched field. For first steps compare Schlette 1998, Kellenberger 1993. The contributions to a symposium on this subject held in Basel in 2004 are to be published as Bernhardt, Schmidt-Leukel 2005.

54 Cp. Smith 1989, 47, 82; 1997, 132f.

55 As far as I know, the helpful terminological distinction between auto-interpretation and hetero-interpretation was first introduced by Piet Schoonenberg in connection with the discussion about Karl Rahner's term "anonymous Christians" (cp. Schoonenberg 1975, esp. 171ff.). In the meantime the distinction has gained wider dissemination, even beyond the German-speaking sphere (cp. D'Costa 2000, 100f.) but people do not always seem to be aware of its origin.

> in the lives of their founders, which shows that they were but men, is eagerly seized and judged without mercy; every doctrine that is not carefully guarded is interpreted in the worst sense that it will bear; every act of worship that differs from our own way of serving God is held up to ridicule and contempt. And this is not done by accident, but with a set purpose, nay, with something of that artificial sense of duty which stimulates the counsel for the defense to see nothing but an angel in one client, and anything but an angel in the plaintiff on the other side. The result has been—as it could not be otherwise—a complete miscarriage of justice, and utter misapprehension of the real character and purpose of the ancient religions of mankind (...).[56]

Müller's chosen comparison with defendants and accusers underlines his analysis: The widespread distortion and false depiction of religions results from their standpoint-bound perspective. Yet this is by no means a harmless perspective; it is deeply shaped by tension and conflict. Hence the image of a court case. From his perspective the accuser *has* to depict the accused as negatively as possible, just as the defense attorney is bound to doing the opposite. The consequence that pioneers of the science of religion derived from this analysis of the theological approach was that a correct understanding of religions is only possible when one practices *epoché*, in other words when one's own religious or philosophical preferences are bracketed or excluded. But this implies that theology *as* theology is denied the possibility of understanding other religions correctly. For, as Joseph Kitagawa has put it, "a theological science of religions [is] bound by being based in an apologetic interest, and this apologetic interest is inherently inclined to distort the perspective and structure of religions that are different from one's own."[57] The adequate undistorted understanding of religions—so the thesis goes—thus depends on the practice of *epoché* and is consequently a monopoly of the science of religions. However, if one ties the possibility of a correct understanding of religions to the condition of bracketing or abstaining from any standpoint, then this implies also the impossibility of *inter*religious understanding (and presumably also the impossibility of a proper religious auto-interpretation, since this is after all anything but lacking in a particular standpoint). As late as the year 1988 Hans-Jürgen Greschat could write that only the science of religion scholar was "free to research foreign faiths without bias." For theologians, by contrast, it would hold that "their faith... as the true one confronts every other faith as a false one."[58]

But is this postulated and demanded bracketing or exclusion of one's own convictions altogether possible? Not infrequently, as Slater and Lewis have noted, "historians of religion might be observed as doing the very thing which they forbade the theologians and philosophers to do, entering the field with presuppositions of their own or presuppositions accepted from others."[59] Is this pure carelessness, or does

56 F.M. Müller, *Lectures on the Science of Religion*. New York 1872, 102-3.
57 Kitagawa 1963, 37-66, here p. 65.
58 Greschat 1988, 130.
59 Slater, Lewis 1966, 5.

it indicate that the demand of the *epoché* is unrealistic and fundamentally unfeasible? Over the last few decades numerous discussions have taken place about this in religious studies. It seems to me that three particularly strong arguments emerged against the possibility of an *epoché:* First, that *epoché* is "psychologically impracticable" since, as Panikkar says, "I cannot simply abstract my deepest convictions or concoct the fiction that I have forgotten or laid aside what I hold to be true."[60] Second, a pure description as it is envisaged by the ideal of *epoché* would be *hermeneutically impossible,* since every description that is more than simply a quotation includes elements of explanation or interpretation, which in turn is never fully free from implications pertinent to a particular worldview.[61] Finally and thirdly, *epoché* would be *inadequate* to the object of research, since it cannot do justice to the existential challenges that issue from religious messages.[62]

The possibility of a genuine interreligious understanding is, however, not only called into question by those who demand *epoché.* Raimon Panikkar has repeatedly advocated the position that understanding is the same as being convinced: "I can only understand the ideas of another if I am convinced that these ideas are right. I can only understand a religious belief if I hold it to be true."[63]

Panikkar, who can be counted among the decided critics of *epoché*, demands here that in order for an understanding to be successful, it must identify without reservation with the standpoint of the other, that is, with the other's auto-interpretation. If this is not possible, Panikkar concludes that no understanding has been achieved:

> It is contradictory to imagine I understand another's view when at the same time I call it false (...) When I say I understand a proposition and consider it untrue, in the first place I do not understand it, because by definition truth alone is intelligible (...); in the second place I certainly do not understand it in the way of someone who holds it to be true. Accordingly, to understand is to be converted to the truth one understands.[64]

The consequences of Panikkar's thesis are truly wild, since it means that the rejection of a statement is always based on lack of understanding and is therefore in the final analysis unjustified. For how can something justly be rejected that has not been understood? It is obvious that Panikkar, by this thesis, is trying to take into account the hermeneutical maxim that the other is to be understood as he or she understands him- or herself—for the other will assume the truth of his or her own convictions. But sufficient justice has already been done to this hermeneutical maxim if one understands the reasons why the other is convinced of the truth of his or her convictions and further, if one understands why these reasons are compelling to the

60 Panikkar 1978, 45.
61 Cp. Heelas 1978, 1-14.
62 Cp. Cahill 1982, esp. 106ff., 148ff.
63 Panikkar 1975, 137 (translated from the German original).
64 Panikkar 1978, 9.

other.[65] Yet this does not imply that one has to share these reasons and the convictions that result from them.[66]

Both the proponents of the demand for *epoché* and Panikkar's thesis equating understanding and conviction perceive the difference between one's own standpoint and that of the religion under examination as the decisive hermeneutical obstacle. This is the reason behind both, the problematic (and presumably impossible) demand of bracketing one's own standpoint and the even more problematic demand of complete self-alignment with the standpoint of the other. But is it really true that one's own standpoint necessarily renders impossible interreligious understanding? Of course interreligious understanding cannot be reached quickly, easily, or effortlessly. And one cannot exclude the danger that one's personal religious and philosophical assumptions lead to a distorted perception of the other. Perhaps one can best appreciate the difficulty by approaching the problem from the opposite direction. For example, can a non-Christian properly understand Christianity? Can a non-Christian learn to see the world through the eyes of a Christian without having to convert to Christianity to do so? That this will not be achieved easily is obvious. But to declare it to be completely impossible would be tantamount to agreeing to the relativistic thesis of incommensurability. Yet, as we saw above, that is not a very plausible option. So how can one deal with one's own religious perspective in such a way that it does not stand in the way of interreligious understanding but is rather in a certain sense even made helpful to it?

Of course I am not talking here about mimicking certain postmodern trends that plead for a carefree bias. It is rather a case of becoming conscious of the assumptions of one's own religious or ideological background and disclosing rather than hiding them from the research community. Explicitly identifying one's own pre-understandings allows their influence on the process of understanding to be better comprehended and controlled than if this influence remained obscured by claims of objectivity and neutrality. At times in more recent religious studies the demand for *epoché* has been corrected and redefined in this sense.[67] In order to avoid allowing the specific pre-understanding to lead to misunderstandings and distortions, this control must be exercised not only through the critical discourse of the research community. Rather, wherever it seems possible such control also constitutes a central task of interreligious dialogue. For dialogical scrutiny, as Wilfred Cantwell Smith rightly emphasized, provides the scholar of religion with a type of "experimental control"[68] for his attempt to understand the faith of other persons:

65 Similarly Smith 1997 133f.

66 For a detailed discussion of Panikkar's thesis concerning understanding as being convinced, see Schmidt-Leukel 1992, 381-397.

67 Cp. Smart 1984, esp. 260. Similarly also Streng 1985, 12f.

68 Smith 1959, 43.

> … about the meaning that the system has for those of faith, an outsider cannot in the nature of the case go beyond the believer; for their piety *is* the faith, and if they cannot recognize his portrayal, then it is not their faith that he is portraying.[69]

But if in attempting to understand people of other religions in this way, one's own religious background and its effect on the process of understanding is consciously made explicit and thematized in the interreligious dialogue itself, then the unavoidable consequence is that the inter-religious dialogue passes into an intra-religious dialogue.[70] To the extent that we learn to understand what faith means to people of other religions, and to the extent that we bring our own faith into play with this dialogically, the faith of the other person becomes an entirely personal challenge that we must not avoid. If in this process one recognizes in the other's faith something good, true, or holy, then one must search for ways in which to "creatively integrate" these into one's own faith—a process in which one will not remain unchanged.[71] The process of interreligious understanding does not necessarily have to lead to conviction, as held by Panikkar, yet this possibility should not be closed off from the start either. Creative integration is thus the alternative to the change of religion. The acid test of Christian faith—as for the faith of other religions as well—is therefore whether it is capable of such a transformation if the dialogical process should lead to it.

Perhaps the pivotal reason why many pioneers of the science of religion concluded that a religious approach to the study of other religions would necessarily result in their distortion and misrepresentation lay in their assumption that every religion was more or less intent on establishing all other religions as false or at least deficient. The early advocates of *epoché* were convinced—as Max Müller's image of the disputing parties in court makes clear—that being bound by a particular religious standpoint in itself already implies being at variance with all other religions. On this conviction, something along the lines of a hermeneutical credit of trust,[72] a positive initial suspicion that even the religious stranger has something true, good, and holy to offer, appears to be impossible from the start, and instead the distortion and misrepresentation of the religious other seem to be predetermined.[73] Among other things, a pluralist theology of religions focuses on disputing this conviction, at least as a generalizing assumption. A pluralist theology of religions proves that being bound to a religious standpoint does not inevitably imply the falsehood or the inferiority of the religious other, and that there are even good systematic theological reasons that justify something like a hermeneutical credit of trust. Here we see

69 Ibid., 42.
70 Cp. Panikkar 1990, 100ff.
71 On the concept of "creative integration" in this context cp. von Brück 1987, 357ff.
72 For the significance of this principle for inter-human understanding in general and interreligious understanding in particular, see Grünschloss 1999, 299ff.
73 Since the demand for *epoché* works counter to such an advance of trust, more sensitive pioneers in the science of religion have tried to balance out *epoché* with the demand for *methexis*, i.e. religious empathy.

the connection between the hermeneutical problem and the dual question of the theology of religions. How we, as Christians, understand other religions will always be connected to our Christian self-understanding. And for that reason it is possible that an improved and more profound understanding of the other, as achieved in dialogue, can by all means result in transformations of the Christian self-understanding. That this proves advantageous in the search for a rationally justifiable faith is made clear by the final problem area.

The Apologetic Problem

The apologetic problem emerges from the question raised by the critique of religion as to *whether the claims of the various religions do not in fact refute one another by their differences and contradictions.* As with the dogmatic problem, this problem also primarily affects the theology of revelation. Enlightenment critics of religion formulated the problem like this: Every religion bases its claims in one way or another on an appeal to revelation. But, as Paul Thiry d'Holbach (1723-1789) writes, the purported revelations "have never in any two countries held literally the same language: that although they are said to have spoken in many places, that they have always spoken variously."[74] This, however, naturally undermines the credibility of each religion's claims. For if revelation is genuine and there is one unique source of revelation, then one would expect a higher degree of conformity among the putative revelations.

This argument gains further weight if the various religions themselves characterize the revelatory claims of all other religions as being lies, deceit, error, projection, etc. For then, as David Hume (1711-1776) describes it, the situation resembles a court case in which all the witnesses name the other witnesses as liars.[75] Such a situation suggests to the judge—meaning here critical reason—that he should not trust any of the witnesses, that is to say, any of the religions. For there is no reason to consider one witness more trustworthy than all the rest, since the structure or quality of their testimony, the very appeal to revelation—or as Hume said with regard to the miracle-based apologetics of his time—the appeal to miracles as that which was meant to substantiate revelation, is the same in every case. More recently, Antony Flew has extended this reasoning to the entire field of religious experience.[76] In other words, the decisive source of religious truth claims is untrustworthy because it leads to such divergent and contradictory claims.[77]

I think one ought not to underestimate the force of this objection. To many contemporaries the diversity of religions, which nowadays is much more evident than

74 D'Holbach 2005, vol II, chapter 3.
75 "An Enquiry Concerning Human Understanding", cp. Hume 2000, 121.
76 Cp. Flew 1966, 126f.
77 Cp. to this Davis 1989, 166-192; Loichinger 1999, 801-807.

ever before, is precisely in the sense of this objection a reason to doubt the credibility of all religions. On the other hand, this objection also exhibits to what extent its argumentative power rests in the fact that religions until now have mostly judged each other quite negatively. If this situation were to change, that is, if religions were able to understand their diversity in such a way that it no longer speaks against the credibility of religion in general, then this objection would lose its force, as had been conceded by John Leslie Mackie, one of the leading twentieth-century critics of religion.[78] Yet in recent times there have also been voices from the atheist side that have newly underscored the striking force of this objection, among other things by arguing that attempts at a harmonizing interpretation of religious difference have proven to be unconvincing.[79]

John Hick has explicitly placed the development of a pluralist theology of religions in the context of this issue. That is, a pluralist theology of religions attempts to show that the diversity of religions does not necessarily weaken the reliability of religious experience as a source of credible truth claims.[80] It is precisely for this reason that it is necessary to refute the assumption of the critics of religion, that—as Hume expresses it—"in matters of religion, whatever is different is contrary; and that it is impossible the religions of ancient Rome, of Turkey, of Siam, and of China should, all of them, be established on any sound foundation."[81] A theology concerned with the question of the truth of the Christian faith cannot ignore or dismiss as irrelevant such objections simply because they are supposedly part of another language game. If faith is to be reasonable, that is, if it is to have a rationally recognizable chance to be true, then addressing such objections lies in faith's own best interests and therefore forms a significant part of the theology of religions. For that reason it would be desirable that even those who take positions in the theology of religions other than the pluralist one remain conscious of this problem, and that they test their own position for what it contributes to the questions of the credibility of religious experience in light of this objection.[82]

After this overview of the particular tasks of a theology of religions, in the next chapter I turn to a basic classification of the possible options in the theology of religions. In so doing, let us hold fast to the insight attained in addressing the dual question of a theology of religions by means of an exploration of five problem areas: namely, that what stands at the center of the theology of religions is the question of the right interpretation of religious diversity in light of Christianity and of the right interpretation of Christianity in light of religious diversity. From a Christian perspective, must we characterize as wrong or at least deficient everything that differs from Christianity with regard to the question of salvific revelation or knowledge of

78 Even if with a clearly ironic tone. Cp. Mackie 1982, 14
79 Cp. Firth 1996, 212-216; Paul 2000.
80 Cp. Hick 1989, 227-229; Hick 1990, 77-80, 109-119.
81 Hume 2000, 121.
82 As a critic of a pluralist understanding, William Alston has conceded the importance of this problem. Cp. Alston 1991, 255-285.

transcendence? Or is there the possibility of understanding at least a part of this religious diversity as different but basically equally valid forms of a genuine and salvific relation to transcendence?

3. Classifying the Options

The Tripartite Classification

Since the beginning of the 1980s, a schema has become widely used to classify the different positions in the theology of religions.[1] This typology assigns these positions to three different groups:

- Exclusivism,
- Inclusivism,
- Pluralism.

Although this schema continues to be widely used, since the 1990s it has also become the object of at times severe criticism.[2] Some of the sharpest attacks have come from Gavin D'Costa, who earlier had based his own work on this schema[3] and defended it against initial attacks.[4] In the meantime D'Costa has come to see the schema as "untenable" or as a "faulty typology."[5] Not infrequently does one find the opinion voiced by Wesley Ariarajah, the longtime leader of the dialogue program of the World Council of Churches: namely, that the classification had "increasingly become one of the stumbling blocks to progress in the discussions on how Christians should understand and relate to religious plurality."[6] Paul Knitter, who likewise up till now has used the tripartite schema, albeit in his own versions, has in the meantime broadened it with a fourth position, which he characterizes as the "acceptance model."[7] Yet more recently both advocates (like Alan Race) and critics of the plu-

1 Before the composition of the tripartite classification, each of its three terms has already been used for a longer time in connection (though not exclusively) with questions about a theology of religions. As far as I can tell, the predicates, "exclusive," "inclusive," and "pluralistic", as referring to three different options in the theology of religions first appeared in Whittaker 1981, 147ff albeit only in loosely connected fashion. Approximations of this same terminology appear in Hicks' publications from the years 1981 and 1982. In terms of a systematic classification this terminology was introduced in 1983 by John Hick (cp. Hick 1983b) and his student Alan Race (cp. Race 1983).

2 For example, relatively early criticisms can be found in DiNoia 1990 and 1992, 47-55, and in Markham 1993, 33-41.

3 Cp. D'Costa 1986.

4 Cp. D'Costa 1993b.

5 Cp. D'Costa 1996, D'Costa 2000, 19-52.

6 Ariarjah 1997, 30. Tilley (1999, 326) makes a similar judgment.

7 Cp. Knitter 2002, 192-237. The "acceptance model" includes, according to Knitter, the position of Mark Heim as well as those of some representatives of comparative theology (such as Fredericks and Clooney).

ralist position (such as Paul Eddy) have defended the schema.[8] In the last few years there have also been both critical[9] and supportive voices[10] in the German-speaking arena, among them two notably comprehensive and constructive discussions,[11] which primarily address the logical reinterpretation of the schema[12] that I proposed.

Since I continue to be convinced of the inner consistency, the theological aptness and the productiveness of this classification for the discussion on the theology of religions, I will once again explain the basic idea of my logical interpretation of this tripartite schema, as well as clarify the associated terminological precision. After that, I will discuss the most important critical objections. Finally, I will deal with the thesis that some authors have recently proposed as an alternative to the form of a theology of religions set down in the tripartite classification, namely that of a "comparative theology."

The fact that the tripartite classification is so widely used in no way means that this schema is always understood in the same sense or defined in the same way. Quite to the contrary: the various ways the terms "exclusivism," "inclusivism," and "pluralism" are used is unfortunately a source of constant misunderstanding, which unnecessarily burdens and makes difficult constructive debate in the theology of religions. For it is obvious that discussions about "exclusivism," "inclusivism," and "pluralism" cannot lead to fruitful outcomes when the parties involved associate different meanings with each of the terms. One reason for these difficulties may be that each of these three terms is also used independent of this particular classification. But the "external" uses of these terms are often not the same as the sense ascribed to them in the context of the tripartite schema of the theology of religion. It is there-

8 Cp. Race 2001, 21-42; Eddy 2002, 3-13. Yet neither of them pushes through to a logical interpretation, but rather stays on the level of descriptive understanding, which weakens their defense. Eddy argues for restricting the schema in turn to its epistemological and soteriological aspects. Race and Eddy's objections are partially addressed by the critiques presented in this chapter. In addition to these, Eddy raises one further objection, which is addressed to any and every *a priori* classification.

9 According to G. Gäde (2002, 169), "neither the Christian message nor other religions, in so far as they proclaim an unsurpassable truth that encompasses all of reality ...allow themselves to be categorized in such preconceived and supposedly 'logical' models." Similarly Müller 1998, esp. 162-170.

10 Cp. for example C. Heller: "In the face of this clear division of options regarding the theology of religions, so far it has not been possible, in my opinion, to show that there are other possible ways of relating religions to one another. Of course every model allows for a wealth of possible variations, yet their fundamental components can always be ascribed to the three...conceptions mentioned." Heller 2003, 67, n. 1. Albeit with a fundamental reservation toward construing models of the theology of religions, von Stosch reaches a similar judgment (Stosch 2002, 295ff., n. 3; Stosch 2001, 324ff.).

11 Cp. Grünschloss 1999, 15-43; Hüttenhoff 2001, 29-77. Whereas Grünschloss ascribes a "heuristic" value to the classification, in the final analysis the schema is insufficient, in his opinion (Grünschloss 1999, 27-30). In contrast, Hüttenhoff argues for using the schema, with a few modifications and qualifications (Hüttenhoff 2001, 75-77).

12 Cp. Schmidt-Leukel 1993a; 1996; 1997, 65-97. Reinhold Bernhardt was the one who proposed the initial starting point for a logical interpretation of the classification. Cp. Bernhardt 1990, 26-40.

fore absolutely necessary in any theology of religion discussion regarding one of the three classified options to clarify as precisely as possible what is to be understood by it. In what follows, I will therefore suggest exact definitions, which will then form the basis of the further argumentation in this book.

A Logically Comprehensive Classification

The problem of the terms exlusivism, inclusivism, and pluralism being used in such different ways is closely connected to the fact that some authors use the tripartite schema as a purely descriptive typology whereas others intend it as a logical classification.[13] And the differences between the two ways of classification are serious. Whereas a logical classification strives for logical completeness and clear-cut distinctions, a descriptive classification attempts to list factually existing positions, and name these according to their most prominent characteristics.[14] The latter process therefore strives neither for logical completeness nor necessarily for systematic uniformity with regard to the defining characteristics. A typology that is descriptive in nature always allows for the possibility of seeking or developing positions that up until that point have not been charted. This is not possible with a logical, comprehensive classification, if it is free of errors. For such a classification covers all logical possibilities, and does so independent of whether they are really advanced or not. For this reason, the division of options has to be narrowly oriented to a systematically unified question and carry a strictly disjunctive character. Some may consider this a disadvantage, because such a unified systematic division does not reflect the multifaceted or even heterogeneous character of various individual theological approaches. On the other hand, the advantage of a logically strict classification lies precisely in the fact that on the basis of it one has no need to look for other positions, because there can be no other positions. Given a sound logical classification, the discussion can therefore concentrate solely on deciding between them on the basis of the advantages or disadvantages of the classified positions. Whether this advantage outweighs the specified disadvantage is not a matter of subjective preference but rather can be measured according to whether the unified central idea and the determination of the individual disjunctions of the logical classification are appropriate for the fundamental problem of a theology of religions. If someone prefers another way of posing the problem, one would need to clarify whether or not such an

13 Bernd Elmar Koziel also points to the difference between the various definitions of exclusivism, inclusivism, and pluralism and to the connection of this with the respective classification process (cp. Koziel 2001, 449-469).

14 For example, cp. Thomas 1969, who lists the following approaches: rationalism, romanticism, relativism, exclusivism, dialectic, reconception, tolerance, dialogue, catholicism, and presence. Less expansive but following the same principles, Rössler 1990 enumerates the following positions: intolerant exclusivism, relativism, syncretism, enhancement, and universalism.

alternative approach is still dealing with the "theology of religions" or whether it is about something else. That is why it was important to state first as precisely as possible the task of a theology of religions before now moving on to the classification of the possible options.

According to the explanations of the previous chapter the general way of stating the dual question of a theology of religions is this: *How does Christianity understand and assess other religions?* And: *How does Christianity understand and assess itself in light of other religions?* As was shown earlier, what is preeminently at stake here is how the Christian claim of witnessing to or of mediating a salvific knowledge/revelation of transcendent reality relates to comparable claims of other religions. By "transcendent reality" I mean a reality that in a qualitatively *in*finite and *un*limited way "goes beyond" (the literal meaning of "transcends") finite, limited reality.[15] I speak of a "salvific" knowledge/revelation of this reality in as much transcendent reality is the highest good and human salvation consequently depends on whether a person is in the right relationship to this reality (before and after death).[16] "Knowledge" and "revelation" are paired up here for two reasons.[17] First, because revelation only occurs when it actually reaches a being in the form of some sort of knowledge/realization (to the one who knows or understands nothing, nothing is "revealed"). Second, because in common parlance "revelation" is often linked to a personal or theistic conception of transcendent reality, while in connection with non-theistic conceptions of transcendence it may be more appropriate to speak of "manifestation" or simply of "understanding/realization." That the revelation or manifestation of a transcendent reality actually reaches or has reached human understanding is something that religions testify to and thus, if this testimony is true, this understanding or knowledge is also mediated by this testimony.

Let us designate this "mediation of/witness to salvific knowledge/revelation of a transcendent reality" as *P*. The question at the heart of the dual question of the theology of religion is then: Is there such a thing as *P* among the religions, including Christianity? I am not asking whether any of the religions claim to have *P* (because this is undisputedly so), but rather whether—and if so, to what extent—this claim is valid, that is, whether it is true. Hence the question which forms the point of departure for our classification is:

Is *P* found among the religions?

To this there are the following four possible answers:

1) *P* is not present in any religion.
2) *P* is present in only one religion.
3) *P* is present in more than one religion, but is found only in one single religion in a form that surpasses all the rest.

15 Cp. chapter 7.
16 Cp. chapter 10.
17 Cp. chapter 8.

4) *P* is present in more than one religion, without one religion surpassing all the others.

Through these four answers we now have a division that is logically comprehensive because it is unified and strictly disjunctive: namely, either *P* is present (among the religions) or not. If there is *P*, then it is present only in one religion or in more than one. If *P* is present in more than one religion, then either there is one uniquely superior form, or there is not.

Is *P* present among the religions?

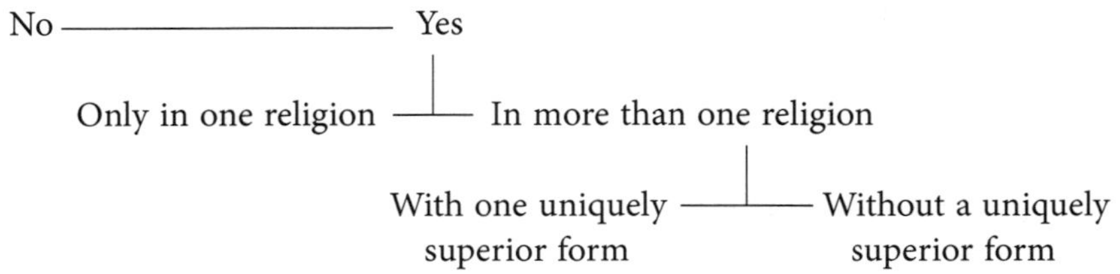

Any other conceivable claim about the presence of *P* among the religions is included in this classification. It is logically complete. There can be no claim about the presence of *P* that is not effectively covered by this classification, although there are several possible claims that represent sub-forms of the basic positions defined here. For example, it remains an open question whether the respectively superior forms of *P* are conceived of in terms of an absolute maximum that cannot develop more highly, or only in terms of relative, i.e. currently superior forms. Both options are included in the definitions of position 3 and 4. Moreover, positions 3 and 4 cover various options with regard to the question of whether the deficient manifestations of *P* include further gradations and whether some religions are completely devoid of *P*. The definition of position 4 includes those positions that assume an equally high incidence of *P* in all religions as well as those that claim this of only a few (but at minimum two) religions. Further, the classification does not say anything about the modality of the claims regarding the presence of *P*, e.g. as a mere possibility, as a well-supported hypothesis, or as an apodictic assertion. The classification is only about the content of each claim not about its logical modality. And in this regard it is complete.

If we now relinquish the formalization, we arrive at the following four definitions:

1) *Atheism/Naturalism:* Salvific knowledge/revelation of a transcendent reality is mediated by none of the religions.
2) *Exclusivism:* Salvific knowledge/revelation of a transcendent reality is mediated by only one religion.

3) *Inclusivism:* Salvific knowledge/revelation of a transcendent reality is mediated by more than one religion, but only one of these mediates it in a uniquely superior form.
4) *Pluralism:* Salvific knowledge/revelation of a transcendent reality is mediated by more than one religion, without any one religion surpassing the others in this regard.

The first option is based on the conviction that something like a transcendent reality does not actually exist. In other words, all that exists is finite, limited reality, and therefore all claims by religions to a salvific knowledge of a transcendent reality are false. The dual characterization of this position as *Atheism/Naturalism* clarifies that this does not refer to atheism in the sense of non-theism, that is to a non-theistic conception of transcendence, but rather to the naturalistic denial of any transcendent reality. Within the interpretation of religious diversity this atheist/naturalistic option represents a clear logical possibility as well as a rational philosophical alternative to religious interpretations. Yet it is not a possible *theological* position, that is, a position which presupposes the existence a transcendent reality.[18] Therefore as options within the theology of religions in the strict sense only *exclusivism, inclusivism,* and *pluralism* are left.

Understood through the interpretation of the tripartite schema as it is introduced here, every religion can, in principle, determine its relationship to other religions in the sense of one of the three named options. So, in principle, there could be a Buddhist, Hindu, Jewish, Islamic, etc. exclusivism, inclusivism, or pluralism. Whether or not this is factually the case depends, as it does with Christianity, on the one hand on the doctrinal presuppositions of each religion and on the other on that religion's concrete evaluation of the other religions. Moreover, when this classification is applied to the positions of a specific religion then one's own religion will be naturally regarded as the one to which exclusive validity or inclusive superiority is predicated, or as the one in relation to which the pluralist equality of other religions is stated. But in this case, would it not also be conceivable that from the perspective of a Christian theology of religions the superiority of another religion with regard to the salvific knowledge of God is acknowledged, in other words, that for example a Christian would hold the position of an Islamic inclusivism? As I noted in other places, in this case one would have to assume that someone holding such a view has converted, at least as an act of inner conviction, to Islam, which means that we

18 Hüttenhoff's suggestion of allowing this position as a variant of a theology of religions, somewhat like the criticism of religion expressed by Karl Barth and other dialectic theologians (cp. Hüttenhoff 2001, 31 plus fn. 4), is something I cannot comprehend. Neither Barth nor any other of the theologians Hüttenhoff mentions leaves any doubt that salvific knowledge of God is testified to and thus mediated within Christianity alone. Otherwise Barth's statements on mission would be incomprehensible according to which Christianity alone is commissioned and authorized by God "to confront the world of religions as the one true religion, with absolute self-confidence to invite and challenge it to abandon its ways and to start on the Christian way" (Kirchliche Dogmatik I/II, 392; translation: Barth 1956, 357).

would not be talking about a position tied to a Christian perspective.[19] One would need to respond the same way to the question of whether a Christian theology of religions could hold an Islamic, Buddhist, etc., exclusivism, or a form of pluralism that would not count Christianity among the group of equally superior religions. Thus as positions of a *Christian* theology of religions only three positions are left, which can now be characterized as follows:

Christian Exclusivism maintains that it is only within Christianity that salvific revelation/knowledge of transcendence can be found, and not in any other religion. This definition of exclusivism (and herein lies an important difference from other usages/definitions of the term) does not depend on the issue of the individual non-Christian's chance of salvation. Radical exclusivists would tend to exclude any chance of salvation for a non-Christian. Moderate exclusivists can conceive of a chance of salvation for individual non-Christians (for example by encountering Jesus after their death, or as a result of an isolated individualistic choice of conscience), but they do not ascribe any kind of positive role to non-Christian religions regarding this chance of salvation. Undecided exclusivists leave open the question of whether a non-Christian can be saved, but, like all other stripes of exclusivists, deny any kind of positive salvific role of the non-Christian religions.[20]

Christian Inclusivism maintains that a deficient form of salvific revelation/knowledge of transcendence can also be found in non-Christian religions, but that Christianity has it in a way that is superior to all others. This definition includes numerous variants of such an inclusivism, both as regards a more precise understanding of the

19 Cp. on this point Schmit-Leukel 1997, 79, n. 42, and 82f. Andreas Grünschloss (1999, 21-24) expanded this issue into an objection to my claim of logical completeness of the classification, but in so doing does not sufficiently take into account the fact that the position of "inferiority" or "exoticism" which he adds to the classification is nothing but what I define as "inclusivism"—only expressed from the perspective of the inferior point of view. In his nuanced and balanced discussion of this question, Michael Hüttenhoff (2001, 68-71) likewise points to the fact that inferiority does not constitute any additional position if the classification is stated in an independent way, that is, not from the perspective of one particular religion. And yet, along with Grünschloss he assumes that in an exposition of the classification from the perspective of a particular religion the inferiority option would need to be added as a further position (cp. ibid., 75). Yet this means that the issue is really a matter of applicability, not of logical completeness or incompleteness! Hüttenhoff cites my response, that in the case of inferiorism one would need to assume at least an inner conversion and that for this reason precisely *as a perspective-bound judgment* inferiorism is not an option. In his response to this rebuttal he does seem to suggest that it is possible that for particular reasons an exterior change in one's religion cannot occur. And yet this changes nothing about the fact that even in this case an "inner" conversion has already taken place. Yet how it is supposed to be possible from the perspective of a Christian theology of religions to embrace an Islamic (etc.) inclusivism or even exclusivism, neither Grünschloss nor Hüttenhoff explains. Grünschloss and Hüttenhoff do rightly emphasize that a certain superiority can be attested to another religion in relation to particular elements or aspects. I have myself earlier drawn attention to this, but also pointed out that if this is done, the question necessarily follows of what consequences result from such a judgment for the underlying question of a theology of religions regarding the salvific knowledge of transcendence (cp. Schmidt-Leukel 1997, 86f.) See also n. 40 below.

20 For further information on Christian Exclusivism, see chapter 4.

supposed deficit of other religions (whether for example this is understood in terms of them having only implicitly what is explicit in Christianity, or in terms of vagueness in contrast to clarity, as fragmental in contrast to fullness, as fundamentally surpassable or unsurpassable, as continuous or discontinuous, as partial or comprehensive, etc.) as well as the more precise fashion in which salvific revelation is ascribed dogmatically to Jesus of Nazareth.[21]

Finally, *Christian Pluralism* maintains that salvific revelation/knowledge of transcendence is found in non-Christian religions and in Christianity, without one of the different forms in which it is witnessed and mediated surpassing all the rest. This means that from a Christian perspective, other forms of knowledge of transcendence or revelation, despite their differences to the revelation in Christianity, are recognized as being of equal value. This definition too leaves room for a range of sub-types and variants. So theoretically one could imagine a comprehensive pluralism that insists on the equal validity of *all* religions. However, I don't know anyone who would seriously support this position, and yet it is the position that is often referred to as *the* pluralist position in anti-pluralist polemic. Christian pluralists typically assume that while not all religions testify equally well to salvific revelation or knowledge of transcendence, several of them do, whereby Pluralists may significantly differ in the more precise determination of the radius of this assessment. At times only *one* further religion is considered as equivalent, namely Judaism.[22] One could also extend pluralist equivalence only to the theistic religions.[23] However, most pluralists include prominent non-theistic religions, such as certain forms of Buddhism, Hinduism, Daoism, or Jainism. Many pluralists leave open to debate the assessment of smaller and younger religions. The definition of pluralism chosen here makes it possible to have an exclusivist or an inclusivist stance toward some manifestations of religion or quasi-religious worldviews—something that indeed is found in the deliberations of various pluralists. John Hick, for example, has criticized as being decidedly non-salvific[24] destructive cults such as the Jim Jones movement, the Waco community, Satanism, or a "secular religion" such as National Socialism, but has taken an inclusivist stance toward certain forms of atheist humanism.[25] This would be inconsistent only if pluralism would be defined as the position that everything in religion was of equal value, which, however, as I have said, is not the case except for in polemical insinuations.

Compared to both the other options, the pluralist position therefore holds sway over the greatest evaluative latitude. As regards the central question of salvific

21 For further information on Christian Inclusivism, see chapter 5.

22 See for example theologians Paul van Buren, A. Roy Eckardt, J. Coos Schoneveld, and J.T. Pawlikowski (cp. the overview in Pawlikowski 1988). On this subject, see also chapter 12 below.

23 Among those who tend in this direction are Vroom 1990, esp. 89f. In the final analysis, however, Vroom does assume—in an inclusivist manner—the superiority of the gospel (cp. Vroom 1996, 157, 163).

24 Cp. Hick 1989, 326; Hick 1995, 44.

25 Cp. Hick 1983a, 88; Hick 1999, 326; Hick 1991, 83; Hick 1995, 80f.

knowledge of transcendent reality, the exclusivist can only judge other religions negatively. At most the exclusivist may differentiate between a total absence of knowledge of God and a non-salvific knowledge of God (in the sense of a revelation "as judgment on themselves.") For an exclusivist, there is no other option. The inclusivist on the other hand, can identify both a complete absence of the knowledge of God in some religions as well as numerous gradations of such knowledge in others. Exemplified in the well-known "onion layers model" of the Second Vatican Council, this approach differentiates religions (and Christian denominations) according to the degree to which they correspond with the Roman Catholic Church.[26] And yet *as* an inclusivist, the inclusivist can never assess any other religion as equally valid, no matter how much he or she identifies of truth, goodness, and holiness in it. In contrast, all three options are open to a pluralist. Depending on what concrete appearance and theological evaluation suggest, the pluralist can, in exclusivist fashion, evaluate certain manifestations of religion as purely negative, deem others, in inclusivist fashion, as deficient forms of salvific knowledge of transcendence, and rank still others as being equal to Christianity.

The following graphics illustrates the different evaluative possibilities of the various positions, as well as their defining characteristics. Here, the outer rings symbolize different religions, whereas the inner black areas indicate the presence of *P*, in other words the mediation of salvific knowledge/revelation of transcendence. The defining characteristics and the logically comprehensive character of the classification (never—once—singular superiority—equality) are indicated by the rectangle.

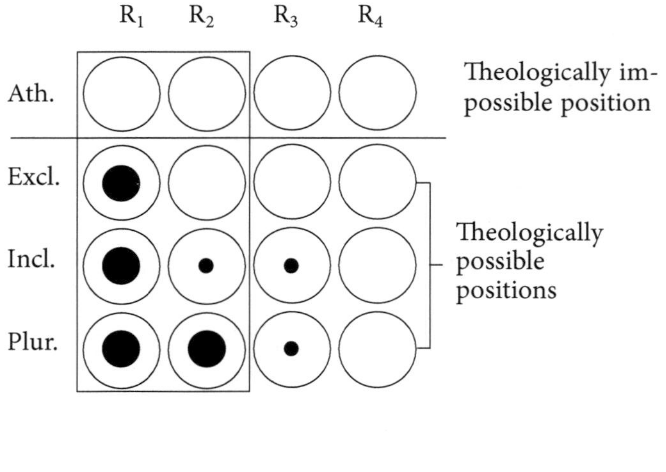

26 Cp. Bernhardt 1990, 116ff.; Zehner 1992, 37-47; Grünschloss 1999, 272ff.

Clarification of Terms

As already mentioned, the international discussion on theology of religions in part deploys the individual terms of the tripartite schema in very different ways, which often causes unnecessary misunderstandings and confusion. The logical interpretation of the classification suggested here leads to clear and unambiguous definitions, which in order to reduce misunderstandings shall once again be explicitly differentiated from some current alternatives in use.

(1) My interpretation of the tripartite classification refers to *judgments about religions or religious traditions.* In this, it differs from interpretations that apply the schema to different positions on the question of the possible salvation of individual non-Christians. From this, several significant differences result in determining the three central terms:

If one interprets the schema in relation to the possibility of individual salvation then "exclusivism" is typically taken to mean the denial that non-Christians can be saved. "Inclusivism" then refers to those positions that in various ways nonetheless allow non-Christians a chance of salvation, whether it is through a posthumous encounter with Christ, through the doctrine of the "baptism of desire", through invisible church membership, through an anonymous relationship to Christ, etc. Finally, "pluralism" then refers to either a way of salvation for the non-Christian that occurs independent of Christian ties, or to universal salvation of some kind, in other words the doctrine of *apokatastasis,* which says that in the end all people attain eternal salvation.

According to the interpretation I have suggested, (Christian) "exclusivism" refers only to the position that denies a positive salvific role of the non-Christian religions, independent of the question of an individual's possible salvation. Accordingly, I use the term "inclusivism" only for those viewpoints that ascribe a positive salvific significance to non-Christian religions, yet still consider Christianity or a particular form of it to be superior in this respect. And according to my definition, "pluralism" has nothing to do with the question of universal salvation, but rather refers only to the recognition of a fundamental equality with regard to the religions' mediation of salvific knowledge of transcendence. In this sense, "pluralists" can take both, the view of a universal salvation as well as a more restricted position, while those who believe in universal salvation can in relation to the theology of religions just as well be exclusivists or inclusivists.

(2) The terms "exclusivism," "inclusivism," and "pluralism" are often also used in an *epistemological* or *hermeneutical* sense, which at times enters the theology of religions debates and then occasions no small confusion.

In the epistemological sense, "exclusivism" can refer quite generally to the "exclusive" nature of truth claims. This is not a matter of specifically religious truth claims, but of the general fact that every truth claim for logical reasons "excludes" the truth of an opposite, contradictory claim. In this sense, "exclusivism" truly is unavoidable.

To deny this kind of "exclusivism" would amount to intellectual suicide, since a position that excludes nothing also no longer claims anything. Of course, in this sense of "exclusivism" all three theology of religions positions that I have classified are "exclusivist" since each one of them excludes the truth not only of both other positions but also of numerous other possible counter positions (for example a Christian exclusivism precludes an Islamic exclusivism, and so forth, as long as in each instance the claims refer strictly to the same content under the same aspect). But this also shows that qualifying all three positions as "exclusivist" in the epistemological sense of the word assumes no prejudgment as to whether a position is exclusivist, inclusivist or pluralist, in the sense of my definitions, that is, from a theology of religions perspective.

The term "inclusivism" too is used as an epistemological denotation and may indicate, for example, that on the one hand all human understanding in principle reaches for the whole, but on the other hand in so doing "includes" everything it encounters concretely in its own specific horizon, a horizon which though it can change, nonetheless always represents one's own perspective. As Michael Bongardt has aptly remarked, in this epistemological or hermeneutic sense: "Understanding is inclusive, or it is nothing at all."[27] Of course in this sense of "inclusivism" each of the three theology of religions positions is "inclusivist," in that each position, tied as it is to its own perspective's formulation, gains its understanding of other religions by starting from one's religious background, although this background may change in the course of this understanding. In the same way as in the case of epistemological exclusivism, so too it is true that by identifying "inclusivism" in an epistemological or hermeneutical sense no prejudgment is made about which of the three possible theology of religions positions is taken within the horizon of epistemological inclusivism. For it can equally well be either an exclusivist, an inclusivist or a pluralist one.

"Pluralism" too is at times used in the epistemological sense, where to a greater or lesser extent it typically signifies some form of relativism. How strong relativism is in one or the other case depends on how radically the idea of incommensurability is conceived. In an extreme case, epistemological pluralism can even lead to the postulate of collective solipsism, according to which radically incommensurable contexts of understanding create equally radically incommensurable worlds. More mild forms of epistemological pluralism are compatible with all three theology of religions models, for these forms merely notice something like a plurality of epistemological inclusivisms.[28] But if one pushes epistemological pluralism to the point that it means abandoning the idea of a comprehensive reality, then this sense of "pluralism" cannot be reconciled with any of the three theology of religions options presented here, since they all presume the existence of an ultimate transcendent reality, a reality that is by no means only thought of as a context-dependent construct.

27 Cp. Bongardt 2000a, passim.
28 In this regard, cp. also the overview in Bernhardt 1996.

In this sense of "pluralism," neither exclusivism, inclusivism, or pluralism would be "pluralist."

(3) Finally, two particular terminological delineations of "pluralism" as a term in the theology of religions should be pointed out. In the theology of religions the pluralist option is also referred to as "religious pluralism," particularly in the English-speaking world. This can lead to misunderstandings if by "religious pluralism" one understands the purely descriptive statement of *religious plurality* or *diversity*—in other words, the fact that there is a multiplicity of religions. In the theology of religions "pluralism" is not meant to be descriptive but rather encompasses a normative judgment about the theological interpretation of religious plurality. "Pluralism" as a position in the theology of religions is also sometimes confused with the political demand for *societal pluralism*, in other words with the sociopolitical maxim to enable people of very different world views and religious convictions to live together in a way that is fair and to a large extent free of repression. But in my opinion, in order for this to work we need only the imperative of tolerance and a legal guarantee of freedom of conscience, opinion, and religion. We do not need a pluralist theology of religions for this, because the demand for tolerance and religious freedom can be supported by exclusivists, inclusivists, and pluralists alike without any inner contradiction. The call for sociopolitical pluralism therefore does not result in an argument either for or against "pluralism" as an option in the theology of religions.[29]

A Discussion of Some Objections

As will now become evident, these terminological clarifications are also important when addressing the critical objections to the tripartite classification. These are based partly on terminological misunderstandings, partly on interpretations of the tripartite classification as a descriptive schema. Yet in some cases they are also related to the interpretation of the schema as a logical classification.

(1) *The tripartite schema has an inconsistent structure, "because the positions are not of the same genre and do not address the same questions."*[30] So goes one objection that T.W. Tilley and I. Markham have raised. Their objection may or may not apply to one or other descriptively oriented versions of the schema. But it does not hold for the logical interpretation presented here. All four positions as defined here have a single reference point (the religions) and address the same question (the mediation of salvific knowledge of transcendence).

29 In this regard, cp. the explanations on the question of tolerance in chapter 6, pp. 162-164. Yet things are different when the religious community is identified with the political community, as partly happens among Muslim thinkers. For then the debate in favor of sociopolitical pluralism tends to coalesce with the debate in favor of a theology of religions pluralism.

30 Tilley 1999, 324, similarly Markham 1993, 34.

(2) *The tripartite schema is misleading, because it obscures or misses the real issues of a theology of religions.* We find this objection raised, for example, by J.A. DiNoia, T.W. Tilley, and G. D'Costa. But they differ in what they consider the actual subject of a theology of religions to be. According to DiNoia, it is the question of how the universality of Christianity can be reconciled with its particularity,[31] according to Tilley it is about recognizing the "religious other *as other*, not as a mere outsider to, reflection of, extension of, or unwitting member of one's own tradition,"[32] and according to D'Costa it is a matter of justification, clarification, and the reciprocal relationship between different truth claims, but not about "how many are saved."[33] Now of course everyone is free to construct a theology of religions as he or she considers appropriate. Yet if one takes seriously the Christian claim to testify to and mediate salvific knowledge of God and the analogue claims of other religions, then the tripartite schema is not only not "misleading" but directly touches the core of a theology of religions. If in addition one pays attention to the connection explored in the previous chapter between the dual question of a theology of religions and the aforementioned five problem areas, then what is also clear is that the topics which DiNoia, Tilley, and D'Costa mention are themselves in one way or another closely related to the question of the mediation of salvific knowledge of transcendence.

(3) *The schema is too narrow, for there are more than three options.* This objection is likewise presented in quite diverse ways. To name just a few examples: S. Ogden proposes there is a fourth option, not included in the schema, which according to him differentiates itself from pluralism by holding "not that there *are* many true religions, but only that there *can be*."[34] According to A. Grünschloss, as a logical classification the schema needs to be amplified with the further option of exoticism or inferiorism, which claims the superiority of another religious tradition over one's own.[35] As already mentioned, P. Knitter also expanded the schema with a fourth position, calling it the "acceptance model."[36] R. Plantinga considers "universalism", the belief in the salvation of all, to be a fourth possibility,[37] while G. Gäde suggests "interiorism" as a fourth position. Here, Christ is neither being set exclusivistically *against* religions, nor inclusivistically *above* them, nor pluralistically *alongside* them, but rather is "recognized *within* the religions."[38]

The examples I have given should suffice to clarify how we can resolve this objection. To the extent that the tripartite schema is understood as a descriptive classification, it can always be expanded in whatever ways. Things are different when one reconstructs it as a logical classification. For if this reconstruction is correct, then

31 DiNoia 1992, 180.
32 Tilley 1999, 323.
33 D'Costa 1996, 225 and 232.
34 Ogden 1992, 83.
35 Grünschloss 1999, 21-30. See also above n. 19.
36 See above, n. 7
37 Cp. R. Plantinga 1999, 6. However, he restricts this objection by explaining that universalism could also be seen as a type of pluralism.
38 Cp. Gäde 2002, 184ff.

apart from the option of atheism/naturalism there is no other choice left. In other words, every other alternative option turns out to be either a sub-form of one of the options suggested by the schema, or a position that does not address the question whose answers are subject to this classification. S. Ogden's "potential pluralism" is therefore not another possible option, but rather presents the pluralist option in another modality.[39] Likewise, Grünschloss' postulated "inferiorism" or "exoticism" does not really offer a new logical possibility, but rather reiterates inclusivism, only this time from the perspective of the inferior position.[40] We can tell from M. Heim's, F. Clooney's, and J. Fredericks' approaches, which P. Knitter terms the "acceptance model," that these either—as is the case with Heim and Clooney—represent inclusivism as I have defined it here, or that, as in the case of Fredericks, they do not address the question underlying the classification.[41] Plantinga's universalism likewise says nothing about whether religious traditions mediate salvific knowledge of transcendence and for that reason also does not fit into the classification suggested here. Yet as soon as one clarifies in what relationship universalism stands to the role of religions, it becomes clear whether or not "universalism" refers to an exclusivist, inclusivist, or pluralist position. Gäde's "interiorism" can also be seen as a form of inclusivism. For according to Gäde, the Christ *within* the religions, the one who gives them their truth, can only be recognized by Christians. Thus, according to Gäde, the Christian message does not proclaim a "greater" truth than the other religions. But it is only in the Christian message that what remains "veiled" in the non-Christian religions becomes "universally understandable and proclaimable." In an unambiguously inclusivist way, a higher form of clarity is here claimed for the Christian witness to revelation. What remains is of course to ask Gäde whether in his opinion a higher salvific relevance is connected in any way with this increased clarity, or whether the alleged greater clarity is in the final analysis irrelevant to salvation.[42] Gäde's interiorism would have to be classified differently if—as Panikkar's work suggests[43]—we allowed that Christ is the "hermeneutical key" to understanding other religions only for Christians, while to non-Christians their own truth is disclosed in equally good

39 See likewise Hüttenhoff 2001, 54.

40 It is noteworthy that at its heart the alternative classification model Grünschloss proposes is not really different from the tripartite classification. His model is based on three basic relationships: "distant," "hierarchical," and "harmonious." Whereas Grünschloss associates the distancing relationship with exclusivism and the harmonizing one with pluralism, he subdivides the hierarchical relational model into a "superior" and an "inferior variation." The superior one is then linked with inclusivism, and the inferior one with "exoticism"—which however is now, at the systemic level, distanced from its perspective-bound formulation and is linked with "conversion"(!) (see the schematic representation in Grünschloss 1999, 82, "Systemebene": " Relationierung"). Obviously this corresponds exactly to my criticism of Grünschloss' insistence on having demonstrated the necessity of enlarging the schema (on this, cp. above n. 19).

41 On Heim, see below chapter 5, p. 139-45; on Clooney and Fredericks compare the explanations in the last section of this chapter.

42 But why then should the Christian message be understood as a "service" to the religions, as Gäde claims?

43 Cp. on this chapter 14, pp. 366-371, below.

though different ways by "hermeneutical keys" of their own religions. Yet there is no hint of such a perspective in Gäde.

(4) *The schema is too broad, for there is actually only one single option.* According to Gavin D'Costa, exclusivism is the only tenable option, because "both pluralism and inclusivism are subtypes of exclusivism." Each of the positions of a theology of religions follows "the logic of exclusivism," he says, since in every instance particular truth claims are proposed whose opposite is explicitly or implicitly rejected as false.[44] A. Plantinga likewise defends exclusivism as being the only possible option.[45] Yet D'Costa also remarks that one could see exclusivism and pluralism as being "only sub-types of inclusivism."[46] This points in the direction of those who, like R. Bernhardt,[47] M. von Brück,[48] M. Bongardt,[49] H. Kessler,[50] and A. Grünschloss,[51] consider an epistemological or hermeneutical inclusivism to be insurmountable and therefore argue for describing interreligious relationships in the sense of a "mutual" or "reciprocal inclusivism," while at least some among these authors understand "mutual inclusivism" as a hermeneutical reconstruction of pluralism or as something like a rapprochement between pluralism and inclusivism.

This objection is fundamentally based on a confusion of what the terms "exclusivism" and "inclusivism" could mean in an epistemological sense compared to their sense in the theology of religions that I have suggested here. As explained above, epistemologically the terms refer to certain *formal* features that apply to any kind of truth claim (namely that such claims logically and unavoidably *exclude* the truth of an opposite claim) or to *structural* features of cognition (namely that new insights are always *included* in one's own horizon of understanding), without necessarily prejudicing the *content* of the respective truth claims or cognition processes.[52] This content, however, is the topic of the three theology of religions positions distinguished here, each of which makes a different statement about the mediation of salvific knowledge of transcendence through religions. The affirmation that in an epistemological sense all assertions in the theology of religions follow an exclusive logic says nothing about whether the content of these assertions reflects an exclusivist, inclusivist, or pluralist position in the theology of religions sense.[53] The feature of exclusivity as it applies in an epistemological sense to any of the three positions as propositions has no impact whatsoever on the difference in content between

44 D'Costa 1996, 225.
45 Cp. A. Plantinga 2000, esp. 174.
46 D'Costa 1996, 225.
47 Cp. Bernhardt 1996; 1997; 1999.
48 Cp. von Brück 1993, esp. 88ff.
49 Cp. Bongardt 2000a, 2000b, 2000c.
50 Kessler 2001, esp. 218ff.
51 Grünschloss 1999, 313ff.
52 Yet Grünschloss seems to fall victim to this error in writing: "In the final analysis, the so-called theology of religions 'inclusivism' therefore remains *hermeneutically* insuperable." (Grünschloss 1999, 297, emphasis mine.)
53 A similar dismissal of this objection with reference to A. Plantinga is found in Basinger 2002, 4ff, and with reference to G. D'Costa in Eddy 2002, 10ff.

these three positions. In this respect, D'Costa's comment that pluralism and inclusivism are "sub-types" of exclusivism is quite revealing. For this shows that at the level of "sub-types" the tripartite schema continues to thrive undisturbed. The same thing is true, *mutatis mutandis*, of an epistemological or hermeneutical inclusivism. This too allows that the inclusive nature of cognition may lead either to the exclusivist position of the falsehood of another religion, or to it being ranked as deficient, or to it being viewed as equal.[54] Yet if "reciprocal inclusivism" is not meant in the epistemological sense, but rather in the theology of religions sense of reciprocal superiority claims, then this cannot count as a valid position but merely as the description of the actual problem in the theology of religions, which manifests in the various religions reciprocally emphasizing their superiority over each other. To the extent they do this in strictly the same respect, such a reciprocal inclusivism is from a logical perspective just as impossible as two siblings each being one year older than the other.

(5) *The schema exerts an "act of subtle force" in that it does not represent "the self-understanding of the so-called exclusivists and inclusivists," but instead serves a pluralist agenda.* This objection, as brought by Gerd Neuhaus, commits as much an "act of subtle force" as it claims to find in the proponents of the schema.[55] First of all we simply need to note that the tripartite schema was and is by no means only used by theology of religions pluralists, but rather also by inclusivists and exclusivists, as a way of characterizing theology of religions positions.[56] The terminology does not serve some kind of sinister pluralist intentions and it can be changed according to one's preferences. [57] A good reason for such a change would be the circumstance that, as shown above, the use of the same terminology beyond the realm of a theology of religions discussion becomes a frequent cause for misunderstanding. Yet I cannot see that the terminology in itself is in any way misrepresentative or offensive. Terms such as "exclusive" are in particular circumstances associated with very positive values (often equivalent to "exquisit" or "special") and even the predicate "inclusive" in certain contexts denotes a positively connoted openness. Whatever the case, some exclusivists prefer to call their viewpoint something else, for example, "par-

54 Regarding this differentiation, compare also Hüttenhoff 2001, 271: "Even if they are pluralist on the basis of their content, judgments about other religious systems of orientation are *structurally inclusive*, because they are motivated by the assumed convictions of their own position" (italics mine).

55 Cp. Neuhaus 1999, 86. The allegation that the logical interpretation of the schema serves only pluralistic interests can also be found in Grünschloss 1999, 28.

56 To name only a few examples: On the inclusivist side, the schema is for example used by C. Pinnock (1997, 14f.) and by G. D'Costa when he himself still adhered more clearly to an inclusivist position (cp. D'Costa 1986). On the exclusivist side, we find it used by Hempelmann 2000, incidentally with unmistakable pride about the predicate "excluisivist," and we find it in Netland 1991, esp. 8-35, and in Eddy 2002.

57 According to Neuhaus, pluralists want to use the schema and its terminology to "create an appropriately dark background contrast and it is only against this background that the theology of religions model they favor can assume the desired contours." Neuhaus 1999, 86.

ticularism."[58] Hüttenhoff[59] (in many ways like Bernhardt[60]) has made the thoroughly sensible suggestion of calling inclusivism "superiorism" because it is solely the claim to singular superiority that is actually the determinative characteristic, and superiority would not necessarily presume a relationship of inclusion. I agree that the term "superiority" is indeed equally well suited and perhaps even better suited to naming the second option, and yet I stick to the existing terminology because it has become so common, and because all terminology, even new terminology, can be misunderstood and because in any case what matters is not so much the names but the ideas and positions signified by them. That the positions characterized here as exlusivism and inclusivism are not the result of some hidden pluralist agenda can already be seen by the fact that in terms of substance and concept both of them existed long before a pluralist theology of religions was developed.[61]

What might be behind Neuhaus' suspicion of a hidden pluralist agenda linked to the schema is the fact that a logical interpretation of the tripartite classification deliberately emphasizes the necessity of deciding between the different logically possible options. Yet this fact can be used equally well by each of the three positions. If for example the exclusivist is able to provide hard-hitting arguments against inclusivism and pluralism, then logically speaking it is clear that the only theology of religions option to remain is exclusivism.[62] The intention of staking out all possible options in the field through logical analysis and of highlighting the necessity of making a decision between them serves the goal of constructively channeling the theological discussion. In other words, we should not waste time and energy searching for other options—which for logical reasons don't exist—, but rather invest it in discussing and weighing against each other the different options which are possible. Within this framework, defenders of all three (and if we include atheism, four) positions can clarify the arguments that advocate for their positions and against others.[63]

58 Cp. the contributions of A. McGrath, D. Geivett, and G. Phillips in: Okholm, Phillips 1995.

59 Hüttenhoff 2001, 45ff. But each and every claim to superiority naturally assumes a common point of comparison. I consider it to be less decisive whether one speaks of this in terms of a "inclusive relationship" or not. For that reason I also do not agree with Hüttenhoff's notion that the transition from inclusive to non-inclusive forms of a claim to superiority is somehow more decisive as the transition from inclusivism (or superiorism) to pluralism. Cp. also ibid. 73ff.

60 Cp. Bernhardt 1990, 36ff.

61 For example, already in 1963 Heinrich Ostermann wrote that: "Theoretically there are three ways of evaluating the big religions: 1. Either one says: *All religions are equally valid.* 2. Or one says: *Christianity alone is the true religion. …* 3. Or one says: *Christianity is the only true religion, but also the other religions have partial truths.*" Ostermann 1963, 76ff.

62 Cp. for example Netland 1991, p. X. "After carefully reflecting upon the various alternatives advanced in the current debate, I am persuaded that the proposed alternatives suffer from even greater difficulties than those associated with exclusivism."

63 Two exemplåry examples of this are: The volume *More Than One Way?* edited by D. Okholm and T. Phillips (Okholm, Phillips 1995) which presents a debate between a pluralist, an inclusivist, a moderate exclusivist, and two radical exclusivists. And volume 4:2 (2000) of the *Salzburger Theologische Zeitschrift* which offers a discussion between an atheist, an exclusivist, an inclusivist, and a pluralist.

In this way, one particular position is not served in a covert manner (this objection is typical of a "hermeneutics of suspicion"!); rather, such open discussion serves the scientific goal of a rationally controlled search for truth. The pressure to decide between them is not artificially *introduced* through the schema, as Grünschloss maintains, but rather it is *highlighted* by the schema.[64] For the pressure originates not so much in the schema itself as in the logical facts illuminated by it. If one has to decide between various alternatives and if logical analysis shows that these alternatives are irreconcilable and unavoidable, then it doesn't seem particularly reasonable to attribute the blame for this situation to logic.

The following objections also pertain to the clarification of the necessity to make a decision as it emerges from the logical interpretation of the tripartite classification.

(6) *The schema divides things more sharply than reality warrants.* Hüttenhoff raised this objection, and particularly applied it to the following problem: Determining the pluralist position by rejecting the inclusivist claim to a singular superiority implies that there is an equality between at least two religions in relation to the guiding aspect of the classification.[65] Hüttenhoff postulates that in this context "equality" has "a quantitative, and not a qualitative sense."[66] Yet in a strictly quantitative sense, the equality between religions, for example as regards their salvific efficacy, cannot be tested, and for that reason we cannot exclude that one religion can indeed be superior to another—superior in the quantitative sense—even if only minimally and therefore barely noticeably. In order for it to be useful, the definition of pluralism therefore would have to be applied less stringently, in other words in the sense of an "approximate" equality. But in so doing one could no longer clearly differentiate such a definition of pluralism from that kind of superiorism which leaves undetermined whether a particular religion, and if so which, is in fact superior. This leads to the dilemma that either the categorization of religions remains logically precise, but is then artificial, or that it is re-presented in a more realistic way, but thereby sacrifices some of its logical precision. Yet even in a less precise version, Hüttenhoff admits, a pluralist position could still be distinguished sufficiently from some forms of superiorism or inclusivism in so far as pluralism would be determined by calling into question a particular religion's claim to sole or superior validity.[67]

Through this critique, Hüttenhoff undoubtedly highlights a certain weakness of the logical reconstruction of the tripartite schema. But at the same time he also makes clear that this does not affect its practical relevance and that its distinctions still remain clear enough to differentiate the various positions from one another. Nonetheless I do not agree with all points of his argument, particularly with his premise that deeming religions equal is meant only in a quantitative and not in a qualitative sense. The problem of how we can speak here of equal ranking or equal

64 Cp. Grünschloss 1999, 28-30.
65 Cp. Hüttenhoff 2001, 71-75.
66 Ibid. 72.
67 Ibid. 74ff.

validity by no means has to do only with how we define the pluralist position, but is also an issue in defining inclusivism. For pluralism uses "equality" in the same sense in which inclusivism insists on "superiority." Only then is the systematic uniformity of the classification truly retained. Thus if it is seen as possible, in principle, to insist on one religion's superiority over the others in some particular sense, then it is, in principle, also possible to assume equality of some religions in the very same sense. The real question is therefore whether a gradation is permissible at all.[68] If so, then this will also include the possibility of assessing religions as equal.

Yet is it necessary to view this equality (and therefore implicitly any gradation between religions) as being solely quantitative, and not qualitative, as Hüttenhoff assumes? I see no reason for that to be so. Elsewhere, I showed with reference to Bernhardt's analyses and to some factual examples that a gradual ranking (and hence also equivalence) can fundamentally be understood as both quantitative and also qualitative.[69] Qualitative gradations appear to be conceivable in all three of the aforementioned criteriological fields, that is, with reference to the good, the true, and the holy. Even the "soteriological effectiveness" of a religion, to which Hüttenhoff relates (by drawing on Hick), by no means has to be understood only in a quantitative sense, but can also be conceived and evaluated qualitatively, in the sense of a fundamental salvifically effective potential, quite independent of how much (a quantitative assessment) of this potential is manifested at different times and at different places.

We must agree with Hüttenhoff that comparatively assessing religions is anything but easy and that our possibilities of acquiring any knowledge in that area are quite limited. This, however, is true not only regarding statements of equality, but also in relation to claims of superiority or exclusivity. We will always have to remain conscious of this limitation. And yet there are such things as signs or indicators that confirm or falsify. Exclusivist, inclusivist, and pluralist positions can be unpacked in such a way that one can derive particular prognoses or—more cautiously—expectations from them, which are not immune to falsifying or confirming evidence. Moreover, the three positions can always be tested for internal consistency, and can be evaluated comparatively on the basis of the price that they may have to pay for retaining this consistency. Yet as far as I can tell, Hüttenhoff does not intend to question this. This insight, however, has important consequences for how we respond to the two following and tightly interconnected objections.

(7) *The schema is misleading in that it does not do justice to the complexity of religions.* This objection is raised in two different forms. According to the first, represented primarily by Grünschloss and Schenk (but to which, in modified form, Hüttenhoff and others also subscribe), the complexity of religions pushes us to different conclusions with regard to different individual aspects. This could consequently lead to mixed results in such a way that, for example, the assessment of a particular reli-

68 I have already pointed to this in all my earlier work on the tripartite schema. Cp. Schmidt-Leukel 1993a, 177f.; 1996, 239f; 1997, 80f.

69 Cp. the references in the previous note.

gion could be exclusivist regarding the question of salvation, pluralist regarding its veneration of a merciful god, inclusivist regarding the more precise way this god is characterized, and even "inferioristic" regarding its spiritual praxis (in other words, recognizing the superiority of another religion in this regard). Yet, so the objection goes, this kind of differentiated and combined judgment at the level of different elements of a given religion makes a firm classification of it on the systemic level problematic if not impossible.[70] As Reinhold Bernhardt had already stated before:

> A Christian will find elements in all religions which he can discard without compromise, elements that he would rank positively but object to as being outmoded; still others that he could see as a good move in the right direction, capable of fulfillment, and finally still others that could stand as equally valid alongside his own faith position and even enrich it.[71]

For that reason, says Bernhardt, the different theology of religions positions "do not lend themselves to judging entire religions, but rather to assessing particular phenomena and convictions within them."[72]

In his discussion of this objection, Hüttenhoff rightly emphasizes that difficulties in applying the classification only result if there is no single reference point undergirding the classification. [73] However, if such a unified reference point is present, then each of the undoubtedly necessary individual judgments at the elemental level (as Grünschloss calls it) can be questioned and assessed as to what significance it holds regarding an exclusivist, inclusivist, or pluralist claim in relation to the main undergirding reference point. So if—as I have suggested—the main reference point of the classification is the mediation of salvific knowledge of transcendence, then we can ask whether the judgments about individual elements or aspects of other religions confirm or negate the claim of one's own religion to being the sole mediator of salvific knowledge of transcendence, or the claim to singular superiority, or to essential equality.[74] Differentiating between elemental and systemic levels does not then make the application of the classification at the systemic level problematic or even impossible, as Grünschloss holds.[75] Instead, it shows the way in which, in light

70 My presentation of the objection follows primarily Grünschloss 1999, 24ff. A similar version of the objection is also found in Schenk 1999, and Thomas 1990, 58.

71 Bernhardt 1990, 235.

72 Ibid. 234.

73 Cp. Hüttenhoff 2001, 35.

74 It is this connection between the judgments at the elemental and systemic levels to which Grünschloss does not give sufficient credence, and also not with respect to his second larger point of critique—his request to extend the schema to include inferiorism. For on the elemental level, at least to a limited extend, another religion can be deemed superior (therefore in so doing claiming one's own religion to be inferior), but only in so far and as long as this does not touch upon the main reference point of the classification on the systemic level. If however the latter is in fact the case, then such declarations of inferiority will either not be found or conversion results. On this, see again above n. 19.

75 Cp. his perhaps a bit too big claim that in relation to "the choice between exclusivism, inclusivism, and pluralism" "science of religion has had the rug pulled out from under it." Grünschloss 1999, 27.

of and despite the complexity of the various religions, we can nevertheless strive toward making clear judgments at the systemic level. A glance at existing versions of a theology of religions confirms that, when using the main classifying categories suggested here, we can in most cases without great difficulty categorize them as either exclusivist, inclusivist, or pluralist.[76]

In another variation of this objection, found particularly in J.A. DiNoia and M. Heim, it is held that a unified reference point of the classification founders on the complexity and multifacetedness of religions. DiNoia and Heim, for example, emphasize that religions have very different conceptions of salvation which resist being put together into one single understanding of salvation in the context of the tripartite schema.[77]

In response to this objection, it needs to be asserted that the main reference point of the classification, particularly in its logical reconstruction, indeed has to be unified. But this does not presuppose (as the objection insinuates) that one would have to assume that the religions have an identical concept of salvation in a descriptive sense. Those who hold an exclusivist position usually claim, as one of their arguments, that other religions' concepts of salvation—and consequently the life of a non-Christian oriented by such a concept—are incompatible with the Christian concept of salvation and that precisely because of that incompatible difference, other religions cannot be granted any kind of positive salvific meaning. Inclusivists, for their part, often refer to a partial conformity between the Christian concept of salvation and non-Christian religions' concepts of salvation and/or a corresponding praxis. The extent to which a positive salvific role is granted to other religions depends on the degree and/or kind of conformity between them. The pluralist is in a different situation. Though he or she is not obliged to claim a complete identity of the religions' concepts of salvation, he or she must nevertheless assume at least an indirect compatibility and perhaps also complementarity in relation to those religions which are categorized as being equally valid. In other words, from a pluralist perspective it has to be possible to interpret the diversity of the respective concepts of salvation and the corresponding paths of salvation as a diversity of equally valid or soteriologically equally effective paths and concepts. For that reason, the objection by DiNoia and Heim is not to the schema as such, but to the pluralist position, and in DiNoia's case, also presumably to the inclusivist position, although his pronouncements on inclusivism are not always unambiguous. Assessing the salvific nature of non-Christian religions is in other words precisely what—on the basis of the classification—re-

76 Cp. Schmidt-Leukel 1997, 87, n. 54. Hüttenhoff interpreted this "in most cases" in the sense of an admission that the classification in fact is not complete (cp. Hüttenhoff 2001, 35). Surely this must be a misunderstanding. For the fact that one cannot always undertake an unambiguous categorization has to do not with the incompleteness of the classification system, but with the sometimes insufficient clarity of certain conceptions of the theology of religions, for example, when no clear consequences can be drawn at the systemic level on the basis of some given particular judgments.

77 Cp. Heim 1995b, esp. 4; DiNoia 1990 and 1992, esp. 47-55.

mains contentious between exclusivists, inclusivists, and pluralists. The classification schema does not presuppose that the various religions have substantially an identical concept of salvation, but merely, as Hüttenhoff also notes, that their salvation concepts are comparable and open to mutual evaluation.[78] The objection would be more targeted to the classification as such if it were based on a radically conceived notion of incommensurability.[79] Yet even protecting the objection with the relativistic armor of incommensurability would not prevent that from a logical perspective the objection then itself assumes an exclusivist position, albeit an exclusivism that would have to admit that it is contingent on not understanding other religions because they are incommensurable.

So we turn now to the last of the objections to be addressed here.

(8) *The schema is too unrefined. It does not do justice to the complex and nuanced form of existing versions of a theology of religions.* This objection is partly the result of the assumptions of the foregoing objection:[80] Consider a situation in which a theologian combines various judgements regarding different aspects at the elemental level. In other words, if in one respect he judges exclusivistically, in another inclusivistically, and in still another pluralistically, but then in the final analysis is categorized within the tripartite schema only according to the relevance of each of these individual aspects with respect to the main reference point of the classification, the schema, so the objection goes, necessarily leads to an abbreviation and simplification of what is essentially a far more subtle, complex, and nuanced theology.

Although this objection identifies an obvious danger of the logically reinterpreted tripartite classification, the use of this schema does not entail succumbing to this danger. In the first place we need to establish that among other things a logically oriented classification explicitly and deliberately differentiates itself from a descriptive typology in that the descriptive typology orients itself by the typical characteristics of factually present theological approaches, whereas a logical classification abstracts from them. This latter type of classification asks, quite independent of existing theological approaches, what answers to a specific question are in principle logically possible and then surveys extant theological approaches to discern which of the logically possible responses are proposed by them. In doing so, the logical classification thus creates a focus on what is most pertinent, if the initial question and reference point of the classification is indeed targeted to what is essential within the theology of religions. On the one hand, this focusing on what is most essential creates an unmistakable clarification, which is why even critics of this schema do not dispute its having a heuristic value. On the other hand, the corresponding danger of an

78 Cp. Hüttenhoff 2001, 67.

79 This remark is anything but groundless, for J. DiNoia, like G. Lindbeck and to some extent also M. Heim, do indeed refer back to relativistic postmodern strategies but, if I am seeing things correctly, keep their distance from a really strictly conceived notion of incommensurability. On this, see the more detailed discussion in Schmidt-Leukel 1997, 146-164.

80 On this, cp. Grünschloss 1999, 26f. (where he clarifies this objection using Tillich); Hüttenhoff 2001, 35f.; Schenk 1999.

inadmissible abbreviation and simplification can be countered by researching more carefully why and how an individual theological approach leads to its particular response regarding the central question of the classification. In other words, we should pay attention to why, in the final analysis, a particular theological approach amounts to an exclusivist, inclusivist, or pluralist position. In this sense, the schema may also help to uncover possible inconsistencies and ambiguities in the factually extant approaches of a theology of religions, for example, when we see that various particular assessments by the same theologian lead to incompatible results or a nebulous overall judgment. Moreover, the schema can also help us to discern fundamental difficulties within each of the three options in the theology of religions so that, in a sort of inverted research direction, particular approaches in the theology of religions can be investigated as to whether and how these fundamental difficulties are handled or even solved by them. To this extent, as Hüttenhoff also notes, "the schema proves itself to be a valuable means by which to analyze theology of religions approaches."[81] But if one should discover a particular individual approach in the theology of religions that cannot in any way be classified as being part of the schema, the logical completeness of the schema makes it clear that categorizing this approach is impossible because the respective author simply does not make any statement at all regarding the substantial problem underlying the categorization. However, where there is no position taken, of course nothing can be classified.

Comparative Theology as an Alternative?

As far as I can tell, the fact that the formal logical reinterpretation of the tripartite schema indeed leads to a logically complete way of categorizing the possible options in the theology of religions has not been rebutted by a single argument. And any successful rebuttal could of course only be achieved by arguments of a similarly formal logic.[82] What is being contested is rather the appropriateness and usefulness of such a formal logical reinterpretation for the tasks of a theology of religions. I hope to have shown by discussing the various objections that the schema is capable of ensuring both. If so, the schema continues to show with undiminished clarity that a Christian theology of religions is in the end about the choice between one of the three classified options, and that, inasmuch as one pursues a theology of religions, the necessity of such a choice is unavoidable. Yet according to Klaus von Stosch, this creates for a consciously *Christian* theology of religions the following "fundamental dilemma":

81 Hüttenhoff 2001, 76.

82 Admittedly Grünschloss (1999) has seriously attempted to do this, only—in my opinion—without success. On this cp. again above p. 64, n. 19 and p. 71, n. 40.

> On the one hand, it is concerned as a confessional theology to be faithful to its own claims of truth and unconditioned validity, which for Christians is above all exemplified in the confession of Jesus of Nazareth as *the* Christ, savior, and Son of God. On the other hand, it at the very least aims not to evaluate negatively those who believe differently simply because they are different. [...]
>
> The fundamental dilemma of every theology of religions consists [...] in the fact that the wish to hold on to what is one's own (a wish inherent to the inner logic of the Christian faith), while simultaneously being able to approve the value of the Other, cannot be fulfilled in any of the conceivable models of the theology of religions.[83]

According to von Stosch, exclusivism and inclusivism retain the confession of Jesus Christ in an undiminished way. Yet exclusivism, says von Stosch, is due to its theoretical presuppositions unable to positively evaluate other religions, and inclusivism can only assess them as "a deficient form of one's own," rather than being able to appreciate them in their genuine otherness.[84] In comparison to this, pluralism takes great pains to establish a "genuine appreciation of religious diversity,"[85] yet because of the "necessary de-potentization of Christology", as it is implied by its presuppositions, pluralism is unable "adequately to hold on to the Christian truth claim."[86] However, as von Stosch admits, for logical reasons there is no other option left.[87] According to von Stosch, there is therefore only one way out of this dilemma:

> ... the efforts to create theology of religions models (would have to be) ... replaced by a comparative theology, which would compare concrete religions or world views with regard to narrowly determined problems.
>
> Comparative theology ... addresses particular concrete instances and thus rather specific areas of debate. Comparative theology is not concerned with making generalized pronouncements as to the truth of one or several religions, but rather with the back and forth discussion between concrete religious traditions as regards particular issues, in order to discover anew what connects and what divides religions.[88]

Von Stosch thus sets out on a path that is pursued especially by James Fredericks[89] and Francis Clooney[90] (although, as we shall see in a moment, Clooney is less consistently abstinent regarding the adoption of theology of religions models).[91] According to Fredericks, the theology of religions discussion about exlusivism, inclusivism, and pluralism has reached an impasse. Pluralists have successfully pointed

83 Stosch 2002, 294ff. Similarly, see Stosch 2001, 345-352.
84 Cp. Stosch 2002, 294ff.
85 Ibid. 297. Yet von Stosch does express some doubts as to whether pluralism actually could succeed in doing so.
86 Ibid., 297f.
87 Cp. ibid., 295f.
88 Ibid. 307.
89 See esp. J. Fredericks 1995 and 1999.
90 Cp. Clooney 1990; 1993; 1995; 1996; 2001.
91 Norbert Hintersteiner also signals a more muted agreement. Cp. Hintersteiner 2001, 318-20.

out the shortcomings of exclusivism and inclusivism, says Fredericks, yet the criticism of pluralism has shown that pluralism is also inadequate. In this situation, he says, comparative theology can be an alternative to all three models and thus point a way beyond the impasse.[92] And yet this alternative does not consist of an alternative model or position in the theology of religions:

> Comparative theology is not another theology of religions. All theologies of religion, be they of the exclusivist, inclusivist, or pluralist variety, are theoretical approaches to religious diversity. They think of religious diversity as a theoretical problem to be solved. Comparative theology, in contrast, is a process or a praxis, not a theory.[93]

This praxis consists of comparative attention to particular areas of interreligious discussion. Yet what is expressly not intended is a return to interreligious comparison as practiced in the phenomenology of religion. "Comparative theology" does not understand itself to be "comparative religion," but rather, as Clooney puts it, as "the doing of constructive theology from and after comparison."[94] "As theology," according to Clooney, "comparative theology consists most basically in faith seeking understanding; its ultimate horizon can be nothing less than knowledge of the divine, the transcendent." Within this horizon, it is characterized by "its commitment to the detailed consideration of religious traditions other than one's own"[95] Fredericks expresses it similarly: "Doing Christian theology comparatively means that Christians look upon the truths of non-Christian traditions as resources for understanding their own faith."[96] In doing theology this way, Fredericks and Clooney declare unanimously, one's own faith can get changed. According to Clooney, through attentive observation of other religions theology is "deeply changed."[97] According to Fredericks, in other religions theology encounters "demanding and transforming truths" that have the power "to inspire new insights within us."[98] Yet both Clooney and Fredericks equally emphasize that comparative theology "remains rooted"[99] in its own tradition and does not betray its commitment to Christianity.[100] According to Fredericks, the "tension between commitment to Christianity and openness to other religious truths" has to be maintained and endured, while each of the three theology of religions options would resolve this tension in its own way.[101] The stipulation of a faithfulness to a confessional standpoint that excludes any possible revisions, signals a clear difference to other theologians also working comparatively,

92 Cp. Fredericks 1999, 8f.
93 Ibid. 9.
94 Clooney 1995, 522.
95 Ibid. 521.
96 Fredericks 1999, 140.
97 Clooney 1995, 522.
98 Fredericks 1999, 170.
99 Clooney 1995, 522; Fredericks 1999, 170.
100 Cp. Clooney 1990, 522; Fredericks 1999, 170.
101 Fredericks 1999, 170f.

such as, for example, Keith Ward.[102] Ward too holds that comparative theology is not pursued from a "tradition-neutral" position, but rather "from a particular perspective."[103] Nevertheless comparative theology ought to be "prepared to revise beliefs if and when it comes to seem necessary."[104] This difference is illuminating for the understanding of the entire project.

There is no doubt that it makes a methodological difference whether one is dealing with the basic systematic questions and problems of a theology of religion or if one is comparing specific texts, thinkers, ideas, rituals, etc., of Christianity with those of another religious tradition, as Clooney does in an exemplary way in his works on Christianity and Hinduism.[105] We can agree with Fredericks and others when they speak in this sense of comparative theology as being another path.[106] Drawing on Grünschloss' terminology, we may say that this kind of theological work operates primarily at the elemental level, whereas a systematic theology of religions has to do primarily with the systemic level. Moreover, at the elemental level comparative theology usually focusses on only very few aspects, and typically confines its comparative work to a very narrow range from one's own and another religious tradition. But is this all tantamount to saying that comparative theology offers an alternative to the controversial questions discussed in the theology of religions, to questions that according to von Stosch and Fredericks are to be avoided because they necessarily lead to a "fundamental dilemma" or an "impasse"?

Whoever practices comparative theology may initially—as Fredericks requires[107]—keep a suitable distance from the problems of a systematic theology of religions and turn, from a Christian perspective, to the comparative treatment of a specific phenomenon of another religion. This turn to comparison does not have to be necessarily linked explicitly and in advance to one of the three positions in the theology of religions. Yet given that the comparative work is meant to be done from one's own Christian point of view, it cannot be excluded that, implicitly and perhaps unconsciously, such a position is in fact taken. At least, one's Christian perspective will include those systematic elements which are in some way or another relevant to the construction of a position in the theology of religions. According to theoreticians of comparative theology, the praxis of comparative work should be of a theological and not only phenomenological nature; in other words, "ultimately" such work should focus on the search for truth. If this is indeed so, then sooner or later comparative work will reach a point at which the question of the logical compatibil-

102 Ward contributed outstanding pioneering works to the futuristic project of pursuing Christian systematic theology in light of the world religions. Here, cp. Ward 1987; 1994; 1996; 1998; 2000.
103 Ward 1994, 47 and 49.
104 Ibid., 48.
105 Compare once again Clooney's works named above in n. 90. Somewhat paradoxically, Fredericks presents himself predominantly with work on the more general problem of a systematic theology of religions.
106 Cp. Fredericks 1999, 167f. Cp. again with the quotation by von Stosch above, n. 87.
107 Cp. Fredericks 1999, 167f.

ity of certain Christian beliefs with the corresponding non-Christian objects of comparison arises. At this point, four logical possibilities for moving forward will present themselves: (1) Either the Christian and the corresponding non-Christian belief are both wrong. (2) Or one of the two is true and the other false. (3) Or one of the two expresses the truth more completely and adequately than the other. (4) Or both can be seen as equally true. As is not hard to recognize, what we have here is the same four options that underlie the logical reconstruction of the theology of religions classification that I suggested earlier. So what will the comparative theologian do now? She or he may stay true to the maxim that comparative theology is meant to be "theology" and is thus compelled to the search for truth. Hence he or she will try, via appropriate argumentation, to arrive at a decision on one of the four possible options. Yet in so doing, questions about the systematic coherence of each of the possible options with further beliefs arise, whether on the part of the Christian or non-Christian system. The comparative theologian thus crosses over into the field of theology of religions. Now she or he will remember that theoreticians like von Stosch and Fredericks have warned precisely about this happening, because this path would allegedly lead to an "impasse" or a "fundamental dilemma," against which comparative theology after all is meant to guard. So the comparative theologian backs off from the courageous stance she or he had just taken and decides instead not to pursue questions of truth any further, but to let them be. But then she or he remembers that renouncing questions of truth characterizes precisely that form of comparison that the phenomenology of religion recommends and that therefore unavoidably falls short of the theological aspiration of comparative theology. Where to look for advice now? It will come from Fredericks. For, as one reads in his works, it is crucial to endure the tension and not strive for its dissolution by adopting one of the theology of religions options. But what does this mean methodologically? Presumably nothing other than settling down in the no man's land between comparative religion and comparative theology, unable to advance in either the one or the other direction, and remaining stuck at an "impasse" and with a "fundamental dilemma." But had he or she not been promised that comparative theology is precisely the path leading beyond the "impasse" and the "fundamental dilemma"?

Based on the experience of his own comparative work, Clooney has allowed that there is a point at which, for example, the comparison between particular Christian and Vedāntic texts leads inescapably to a confrontation between the Vedāntic claim that all salvation is rooted in the knowledge of Brahman, and the Christian claim that Christ is the source of all salvation.[108] Or, to take another example of Clooney's, the comparison of Shaivite and Vaishnava texts with Christian ones will sooner or later arrive at a point where the question of whether God is the God of Jesus Christ or Nārāyana (Vishnu) or Shiva becomes unavoidable. As does the question whether

108 Cp. Clooney 1993, 189ff.

God became human only in Jesus Christ, and not in Rāma and Krishna.[109] So how then should the comparative theologian judge?

In his writings, Clooney offers several responses. On the one hand, he never tires of emphasizing that any response to this question does not come easy and takes time.[110] For at least a certain length of time the search for a systematic response should be set aside, simply confessing a kind of helplessness.[111] But from whence shall help then come? Even Clooney seems to recognize that such advice either does not take us any further or that in the final analysis the recommended waiting needs to serve that careful weighing of arguments that eventually encourages a decision for one of the positions in the theology of religions. Yet, "the sequence" writes Clooney, "is important." *First* comes the concrete and comparative work, *after that* the step to the level of theology of religions may follow.[112] In order to be taken seriously in the context of comparative theology, each of the three theology of religions models would need to attend to concrete examples and details far more than it has done to this point.[113] But in the final analysis, according to Clooney, the inclusivist position turns out to be the superior one, in that it is faithful to the universal claims of one's own religious tradition as well as recognizing the truth that lies beyond confessional borders.[114] Clooney clarifies what this means to him concretely with reference to the two aforementioned examples. Regarding Vedānta the comparative theologian would stay with the notion that salvation comes from Christ, yet—after the comparison—no longer combine this with the claim that knowledge of Brahman is not salvific.[115] And in relation to Shaivism and Vaishnavism one could hold fast to the truths of the Christian faith "without compromise," without however at the same time having to assert that Shiva is not God and that Vishnu did not become incarnate for the sake of human beings.[116]

Yet how are we to understand Clooney's admissions regarding the theology of religions in light of the insistence that comparative theology is to be seen as an alternative to a theology of religions? Has Clooney become weak and given in? Or is he not a satisfactory representative of the program? As Clooney's examples show, sooner or later comparative theology ends up at that point where the dilemma identified above presents itself: either to give up the theological aspiration and retreat to interreligious comparison at a purely phenomenological level, or to remain true to the theological aspiration and thus enter into the arena of the theology of religions and decide for one of the available options. But if this decision is declined, then it is clear that it is not theology of religions but comparative theology that leads to an

109 Cp. Clooney 2001, 180.
110 Cp. Clooney 1993, 189ff; Clooney 1996, 298ff.
111 Cp. Clooney 1996, 310.
112 Clooney 1990, 66.
113 Cp. Clooney 1993, 194.
114 Cp. Clooney 1993, 194f. Similarly, Clooney 1990, 66, 72-79.
115 Cp. Clooney 1993, 194f. Similarly Clooney 1990, 66, 72-79.
116 Cp. Clooney 2001, 180f. This last statement however will presumably burst the boundaries of inclusivism and lead to something like a "potential" pluralism.

impasse. This, however, can be avoided if comparative theology remains open and sensitive to the problems discussed in the theology of religions, if it learns from the systematic discussion in that field and for its part tries to produce specific arguments won by the direct comparison with non-Christian religions that would support one or the other of the options in the theology of religions. But in so doing it does nothing but what is the task of a serious interreligious dialogue.[117] What is still problematic about this is Clooney's and Fredericks' insistence that comparative work must not—as Keith Ward proposes—result in the possibility of having to revise one's own beliefs. Thanks to this stipulation, it repudiates not only its own affirmation of the transformative power of comparative work, but also—as Clooney makes particularly clear—prejudices the decision for an inclusivist position. For in Clooney's work this is founded less on the concrete results of any comparison (and therefore stands in opposition to his own agenda) as it is on the necessity of holding onto Christianity's unchanged claims of validity.

Von Stosch too cannot escape all of this. He tries, via his reference to Wittgenstein's philosophy, to offer comparative theology methodological help in more adequately implementing its comparisons, namely by taking into account not only the cognitive content of religious doctrines but also their grammatical function. As von Stosch notes, this at times may allow for compatibilities at the level of rules even if there is simultaneously an incompatibility of content. But of what use are these no doubt fruitful suggestions, if they do not in the final analysis contribute to a decision about the different positions in the theology of religions, where it is an inevitable question of whether such compatibilities at the level of rules are to be interpreted either in the sense of inclusivism or in the sense of pluralism or whether a possible incompatibility would not actually support exclusivism. One notices that von Stosch himself admits—albeit only in the "small print"—that one ought to "be careful about giving up completely the achievements of the traditional model construction of a theology of religions in favor of the micrology of comparative theology." For it is not "a priori wrong…if we, as Christians, conjure up a picture of the others as effecting their salvation through an anonymous relationship to Jesus Christ."[118]

The discussion of the theses of comparative theology once again clarifies some important considerations of this chapter. In the theology of religions the decisions made at the elemental and systemic levels remain connected to one another and are at least partially interdependent. In other words, even narrowly defined questions—as raised in a comparative theological assessment of individual aspects of Christianity and a non-Christian religion—may nevertheless have serious repercussions for the principal decision for or against one of the available positions in the theology of religions. Comparative theology or interreligious dialogue can for that reason of-

117 In the meantime, Clooney has establish the dialogical character of comparative theology more strongly than before. Cp. Clooney 2001, 7ff.

118 Stosch 2002, 308, n. 40.

fer important help in making one's choice in the theology of religions.[119] Yet here we must also note the reverse dependence— namely that the explicit or implicit preliminary decisions or relevant background assumptions regarding one's own position in the theology of religions will also have an effect on the range of judgments deemed possible in carrying out concrete comparative or dialogical work. If we want to prevent these preliminary decisions from prejudicing the results of comparative work, then we should, with Ward, demand that one should be open to the possibility that the results of dialogue and theological comparison might also under certain circumstances lead to a revision of previously held beliefs.[120]

The range of the options, as ultimately available in the theology of religions, is determined in a comprehensive sense by the logically interpreted classification. From a Christian perspective—and apart from the atheist/naturalist position—this can be only variations of exclusivism, inclusivism, and pluralism.[121] Yet the decision for one of these options does not depend solely on those perspectives that result from the concrete comparative or dialogical interaction with other religions. Rather, those perspectives are complemented by other aspects which also play a role in arriving at a decision and which are connected to the systematic implications of the respective options in the theology of religions. The first line of inquiry is taken up in the third part of this book, while the remaining chapters of this first part as well as the entire second part are dedicated to the systematic implication of the different theology of religions options. Since the chief concern of this study is to explain the pluralist option as a possible Christian position, in the following two chapters I will only address exclusivism and inclusivism in an abbreviated way, focusing primarily on why I do not find either of these positions to be convincing.[122]

119 My own theology of religions development incidentally was like this. It was the prolonged, detailed, sometimes painful, but deeply rewarding interaction with Buddhism that finally convinced me of the superiority of the pluralist option, and which further strengthens that conviction. Cp. Schmidt-Leukel 1984; 1992; 1993b; 1995; 199b; 2001a; 2003a.

120 Compare here also the following comment by Paul Knitter with reference to the representatives of comparative theology: "While we have to be aware that we bring our theological baggage to the journey of dialogue, that doesn't mean that during the journey we may not have to rearrange, or even dispose of, some of that baggage." Knitter 2002, 236.

121 The "journey of dialogue" as Knitter calls it can however very well also lead to conversion. Yet even then, from the perspective of the new religion of the convert, it is only the three aforementioned positions which are available.

122 For a more extensive presentation and discussion of both these models, cp. Schmidt-Leukel 1997, 99-235.

4. A Critique of Christian Exclusivism

One of the biggest festivals in Hinduism, one celebrated by nearly all Hindus, is Diwali, the Festival of Lights (actually Dīpāvalī=chain of lights). It takes place in autumn (October/November) and lasts five days, during which India is bathed in a sea of lights. It celebrates the triumph of Vishnu over Bali and the triumph of Krishna over Naraka, in short, the triumph of the divine over the world's darkness.[1] The Southern Baptist Convention—an amalgamation of Baptist churches, which with its 41,000 member congregations and 15.8 million members represents the largest protestant denomination in the USA—published a prayer guide on the occasion of Diwali in October 1999. The guide urged members to consider the 900 million people who are "lost to the hopeless darkness of Hinduism," and to pray for their conversion to "the one true path" of Christianity. "Satan"—so reads part of the publication—"has retained his hold on Calcutta through Kali and other gods and goddesses of Hinduism. It's time for Christ's salvation to come to Calcutta." In response to critical comments, William T. Neal, an official representative of the Southern Baptists, asked what was so novel about this prayer guide. After all, he said, Southern Baptists have been praying for almost two hundred years for the conversion of other religions.[2]

Indeed, there is a long tradition of exclusivism in Christianity, one that reaches back considerably further than the two hundred years of the Southern Baptist Convention. Even in the present, this exclusivism has by no means been overcome, but rather enjoys an impressive amount of support, both theoretically and practically. Before I give a short historical theological overview of Christian exclusivism and mention several contemporary developments, I must first distinguish between three different forms of exclusivism.

Forms of Exclusivism

In the last twenty years of theology of religions discussion, one often encounters a definition of exclusivism that determines Christian exclusivists as assuming that access to salvation is exclusively linked to certain conditions tied to Christianity, such as for example membership in the Christian church through baptism and/or personal faith in Jesus Christ and a life lived accordingly. In other words, there is no

1 Cp. Lipner 1999, 295f.
2 Cp. *ENI Bulletin,* No. 20, 10. November 1999, 8f., items 99-0406 and 99-0407.

chance of being saved outside of Christianity, and all non-Christians are eternally lost. Such a definition of exclusivism is, however, not the same as the one I suggested in the previous chapter. Whereas the definition of exclusivism just mentioned is primarily concerned with making a judgment about the possible salvation of the individual non-Christian, my suggested definition focuses on the religions. In other words, I define Christian exclusivism as the notion that it is only in Christianity (and for some exclusivists only in one particular form of Christianity) that a salvific knowledge of God is mediated whereas the possibility that other religions can mediate salvific knowledge of God is denied. Yet such a definition does not automatically preclude the eventual possibility of a non-Christian being saved. Rather, at least as I define exclusivism, it involves three different positions:[3]

(1) *Radical Exclusivism.* This refers to the understanding I just quoted, namely that there is no possibility of salvation for non-Christians at all. Anyone who does not believe in Jesus Christ or who does not join a Christian church through baptism, cannot attain salvation, even if she or he has never heard the gospel or come into contact with the church and therefore has never had the opportunity to be baptized or to believe in Jesus.

(2) *Moderate Exclusivism.* Moderate exclusivists assume that individual non-Christians can attain salvation, but that non-Christian religions—in contrast to Christianity—have no positive significance, and in fact are hindrances. If a non-Christian does attain salvation, then it is not thanks to the help of his or her non-Christian religion but rather despite their participation in it. Within the context of moderate exclusivism there are basically two ways of thinking about such individual possibilities for salvation of a non-Christian: Either one assumes that the conditions for salvation for the individual non-Christian are accessible in this life, or the possibility of salvation presents itself only at or after death.[4]

The first option is typically associated with traditional Catholic authors who embraced (and to some extent still embrace) the notion that a non-Christian, despite his or her belonging to a non-Christian religion, can attain a salvific relationship to God through an ultimately upright act of conscience. Yet this salvific act of conscience is nonetheless conceived of in such a way that any shaping or influence of the conscience by non-Christian religions is considered either irrelevant or, more likely, dangerous. Another theory, disseminated especially but by no means only in Protestant circles, consists of the hypothetical assumption of additional or special revelations for individual non-Christians, revelations that provide them the possibility of a salvific faith in Christ.

The second form of holding that despite the exclusivist position there nonetheless exists a possibility of salvation for non-Christians, speculates on them having an encounter with Christ either in death or—as most authors assume—after death

3 On this division, cp. Schmidt-Leukel 1997, 99ff. Hüttenhoff (2001, 211-213) makes a similar division, but uses different terminology.

4 Cp. on this Hüttenhoff 2001, 213f, giving numerous examples and references.

which then gives the non-Christian the chance of making a positive and salvific response. This scenario essentially also takes up the notion of a special revelation, yet not as happening through dreams, apparitions, and auditions during one's lifetime, but rather after death.

(3) *Undecided Exclusivism.* This type of exclusivism also claims that the mediation of salvific knowledge of God is confined to Christianity. And yet it views the question of whether, and if so, how, salvation can be attained by individual non-Christians as open, and ultimately unanswerable. Christians, so it says, ought not to make a judgment about this, but rather leave it to God. The Christian theologian ought to base his or her judgment entirely on what revelation says on this matter; in other words he or she should proclaim that salvation is to be found only through faith in Jesus Christ and baptism in his name.

However, it is not always clear in theological and especially in official ecclesial statements whether the position of undecided exclusivism is assumed or whether they are simply abstaining from a theology of religions judgement. This difficulty stems not only from the lack of clarity of many texts. Occasionally, such abstention can be inconsistent, so that, for example, a position such as radical exclusivism is given clear disapproval but then nothing else is said about it, neither with regard to a moderate or an undecided exclusivism, nor with regard to one or the other variants of inclusivism or pluralism. Yet in principle it is possible to clearly distinguish between undecided exclusivism and theological abstinence. For undecided exclusivism is undecided only regarding the question of the possible salvation of individual non-Christians, while decisively denying any positive salvific value in non-Christian religions. In contrast to this, a theology of religions abstinence amounts to opting neither for an exclusivist nor for an inclusivist nor for a pluralist position regarding the question of a possible salvific role of the non-Christian religions (and also typically regarding the question of the salvation of individual non-Christians).

So what all three variations of Christian exclusivism have in common is the exclusive limitation of salvific knowledge of God to Christianity, and therefore the denial that such salvific knowledge is also witnessed to and mediated by non-Christian religions. An important practical implication results from this commonality: for if no positive significance regarding human salvation can be ascribed to non-Christian religions, if this is something unique to Christianity, then it is theologically desirable that all non-Christian religions be replaced by Christianity. From time to time, even exclusivists are sober enough to recognize that this is possibly an unrealizable ideal, and they can develop theories about why non-Christian religions are to be tolerated. Yet the ideal remains Christianizing the world, and this they try as best as possible to realize through missionary efforts.

Before I discuss the various forms of exclusivism, I want next to give a brief overview of the place of Christian exclusivism within the history of theology.

Exclusivism in the History of Theology: An Overview[5]

Clearly the New Testament does not yet contain anything along the lines of an elaborate theology of religions, particularly not one that is based on a good knowledge of other world religions. The New Testament authors had no knowledge of Hinduism, Buddhism, Confucianism, or Daoism, and Islam did not yet exist. So if there are any inklings in the New Testament of a theology of religions these have to be considered either in the context of internal Jewish conflicts—for early Christianity after all understood itself initially as an inner-Jewish movement. Or they are molded in reference to various Greek and Roman forms of religion. And yet the New Testament contains a couple of sayings to which exclusivists continually refer and which *prima facie* do seem well suited to buttress exclusivist claims. Let me briefly mention a few examples. In Mark 16:16 we find: "The one who believes and is baptized will be saved; but the one who does not believe will be condemned." Or in John 14:6, Jesus says the words: "I am the way, and the truth, and the life. No one comes to the Father except through me." Exclusivists also often like to quote Peter's words in Acts 4:12: "There is salvation in no one else, for there is no other name under heaven given among mortals by which we must be saved."

My intention here is not to pursue the question of to what extent, from exegetical perspectives, such sayings are appropriately commandeered by exclusivists to support their position, because this would take us into the wide field of detailed historical-critical analyses. Yet it seems to be that none of the aforementioned sayings was formulated with the intention of making a judgement in the context of a theology of religions. So, for example, Peter's word about there being "no other name given among mortals" is not intended as a claim about other possible names, such as for example Krishna, Buddha, or Muhammad. Rather, this saying is about confessing Jesus in a situation in which shortly before he was accused and convicted by the religious authorities of blaspheming against God. It is to this situation that the heightened words refer, and in this situation they are certainly understandable. For that reason we can at least say that it is not entirely unproblematic to derive an exclusivist position in the theology of religions directly from such sayings. At the very least one would need a more extensive justification for doing so. But what I am solely concerned about here is to draw our attention to the fact that there are sayings in the New Testament which *prima facie* seem to support exclusivist claims and to that end have been and are continually drawn upon by exclusivists. This makes it more understandable that in times in which there were neither the methods nor the awareness of the need for a historical critical interpretation of biblical texts, it appeared more obvious to consider a theology of religions exclusivism as biblically grounded. And this also explains why this same understanding continues to be espe-

5 On the following matter, compare also the overviews in Kern 1980, Bernhardt 1990, 63-70, and Sullivan 1992.

cially widespread in those places where one does not particularly value the historical-critical efforts to understand the biblical writings appropriately.

Christianity's contention with Judaism and Greek and Roman forms of religion increased considerably during Patristic times. It was also during this time that inner-Christian controversies became more acute. As a result of this, the question arose not only as to how one ought to judge Judaism and non-Jewish religions, but also the question of how one ought to evaluate other Christian groups. Under exclusivist premises Christians fought each other as "false teachers" or "heretics." Much like the term "idolater," the term "heretic" of course never represented anyone's self-understanding—who after all has ever admitted that he worshipped idols or proclaimed heresies?—but served as a polemical demarcation. So eventually the triad of "Jews, pagans, and heretics" became established as a well-known rhetorical term, and marked the three-fold boundary by means of which an exclusivist self-understanding became established.[6]

In the third century, the North African Bishop Cyprian (†258) formulated the renowned exclusivist axiom, *salus extra ecclesiam non est*—"There is no salvation outside of the church,"[7] or as Cyprian expressed it in another formula: "Whoever does not have the Church as mother, cannot have God as father."[8] As an allegorical image of the church's exclusivist claim to salvation numerous church fathers repeatedly drew upon the biblical story of the flood. Just as once Noah's ark alone offered sanctuary from divine judgment, so too now do all people stand under God's judgment, and cannot escape it—except for those who find shelter in the ark, meaning the church. In its explicit form, Cyprian's words were aimed "only" at heretics and schismatics. That their implications however applied equally to Jews and members of non-Christian religions, i.e. "pagans," soon became explicit in different ways. In the year 380, Emperor Theodosius I (379-95) through his edict *De fide catholica*, prescribed the Nicene Creed as binding on all his subjects, and, backed by a threat of serious punishment, subsequently forbade not only the Arian form of Christian worship, but also that of all non-Christian cults. Countless non-Christian temples were closed and either destroyed or transformed into Christian churches. Pogroms against Jews, adherents of other religions, and Christians with other beliefs were no longer a rarity. The Cyprian principle of "No salvation outside of the Church" was now understood also explicitly as an articulation of radical exclusivism and applied to the entire triad of "Jews, pagans, and heretics."[9] Fulgentius of Ruspe (468-533), an avowed follower of Augustine's theology, offers an especially clear formulation of this view:

> Most firmly hold and by no means doubt, that not only all pagans, but also all Jews, and all heretics and schismatics who die outside the Catholic Church,

6 The overview D'Costa proposes (1990b) is lacking in that it overlooks this threefold demarcation.

7 Cyprian, Ep. (73) ad Judaicum 21 (PL3, 1169).

8 Cyprian, De unitate Ecclesia 6 (PL 4:502).

9 On this, see also Sullivan 1992, 24ff.

> will go to the eternal fire that was prepared for the devil and his angels (Mt 25:41).[10]

Yet Fulgentius goes one step further than this. Augustine had already taught double predestination, in other words, that God has predestined some people to salvation and others to damnation.[11] For Fulgentius, the fact that numerous people never hear the gospel is a clear sign that God does not want them to be saved, and that they therefore belong with those who from the outset are excluded from redemption, or predestined to be damned.

> If it were true that God universally willed that all should be saved and come to the knowledge of the truth, how is it that Truth itself has hidden from some people the mystery of his knowledge? Surely, to those whom he denied such knowledge, he also denies salvation. ... Therefore, he willed to save those to whom he gave knowledge of the mystery of salvation, and he did not wish to save those to whom he denied the knowledge of the saving mystery. If he had intended the salvation of both, he would have given the knowledge of the truth to both.[12]

In the sixth century, exclusivism was now also turned into strict religio-political practice. Emperor Justinian I (527-65) ordered all remaining non-Christians to be baptized on pain of complete dispossession and deprivation of their rights.

In this way, exclusivism became the reigning theological position and determined the treatment of "Jews, pagans, and heretics." Numerous magisterial pronouncements of the Middle Ages emphasized the axiom "No salvation outside of the church" (*extra ecclesiam nulla salus*). In this regard, alongside the relevant pronouncements of the Fourth Lateral Council (1215) and the Papal Bull *Unam Sanctam* of Pope Boniface VIII (1302), the Council of Ferrara-Florence (1442) is particularly noteworthy for the following pronouncement, which directly draws on statements of Fulgentius:

> [The Holy Roman Church] ... firmly believes, professes and preaches that 'no one remaining outside of the Catholic Church, not only pagans,' but also Jews, heretics and schismatics, can become partakers of eternal life; but they will go to the 'eternal fire prepared for the devil and his angels' [Mt 25:41], unless before the end of their life they are joined (*aggregati*) to it. (...) 'And no one can be saved, no matter how much alms one has given, even if shedding one's blood for the name of Christ, unless one remains in the bosom of the Catholic Church.'[13]

10 Fulgentius, De fide, ad Petrum, 38,79 (PL 65:704), cited according to Dupuis 1997, 92. D'Costa is clearly wrong in claiming that Fulgentius applies the axiom "Extra ecclesiam nulla salus" not to followers of other religions but only to schismatics (Cp. D'Costa 1990b, 138).

11 On this, cp. Flasch 1990.

12 De veritate praedestinationis, 3, 16-18 (PL 65:660-61), cited according to Dupuis 1997, 92.

13 Cp. Denzinger-Schönmetzer, 1351, cited according to Dupuis 1997, 95f.

Almost a hundred years later (1529/30) Martin Luther in his *Large Catechism* expressed this no less unambiguously:

> … for where Christ is not preached, there is no Holy Ghost who creates, calls, and gathers the Christian Church, without which no one can come to Christ the Lord. (…) For all outside of Christianity, whether heathen, Turks, Jews, or false Christians and hypocrites, although they believe in, and worship, only one true God, yet know not what His mind towards them is, and cannot expect any love or blessing from Him; therefore they abide in eternal wrath and damnation. For they have not the Lord Christ, and, besides, are not illumined and favored by any gifts of the Holy Ghost. [14]

Luther thus also unmistakably embraces the axiom "No salvation outside of the church," even though with a Christological focus. And just as much as the Council of Florence, Luther also applies it to the familiar triad of "Jews, pagans, and heretics," albeit the "Turks"—meaning Muslims—now stand alongside the pagans, and the identification of the "heretics" or "false Christians" is inverted by now aiming at the Roman Catholics.

The Christological concentration of exclusivism is even more clearly seen in the sixteenth century Anglican Articles of Faith. Yet the conclusion is not much different. Thus, Article 18 says:

> They also are to be had accursed that presume to say, That every man shall be saved by the Law or Sect which he professeth, so that he be diligent to frame his life according to that Law, and the light of Nature. For Holy Scripture doth set out unto us only the Name of Jesus Christ, whereby men must be saved.

Calvin repeats the perspective that Fulgentius already articulated. For him, the circumstance that people have never heard of Christ or have not accepted the gospel is a sign that they do not belong to the elect, but rather to the reprobate, i.e. to those that God has from the beginning predestined to eternal damnation.[15]

Despite this exclusivist unanimity which ruled theology from the end of the early Church to modernity, it was nonetheless disputed whether one was really to understand the axiom *extra ecclesiam nulla salus* in the sense of a *radical* exclusivism. Here, the following questions played a significant role: What about all those who died as infants before being baptized? Would it not be repulsively unjust if these children were condemned to eternal damnation because of their unintended early deaths? And what about those people who have never heard of Jesus? What about the righteous of the Old Covenant, such as Abraham, Isaac, and Jacob? Are we to assume that these persons, whom Scripture views as the patriarchs of the faith, are

14 *Of the Creed: Article III* of the *Larger Catechism* by Martin Luther, quoted from: http://bookofconcord.org/lc-1-intro.php.

15 Cp. Institutio III, 21: 7 and 24:12. Cp. also Sullivan 1992, 76-78. Correspondingly, the exclusivist position also found acceptance in the Presbyterian Westminster Confession (X.4) of 1648. For the Anglican Articles see: http://anglicansonline.org/basics/thirty-nine_articles.html.

eternally damned simply because they were not explicitly Christians and had not been baptized? Or again, what are we to think of the wise among the "pagans," such as Plato or Aristotle? After all, many church fathers and theologians not only assumed that their thoughts were, in some respects, thoroughly in line with the Christian faith, but even significantly relied on their work in their own theological systems. Were such persons simply to be viewed as lost, even though they never had the opportunity of becoming Christians? Or should one even believe that they were predestined to such a hopeless fate by God?

On the basis of such questions, three doctrines arose that watered down the radical exclusivist interpretation of *extra ecclesian nulla salus* and offered a more moderate exclusivist meaning: (1) The doctrine of "Christ's descent into Hell," (2) the doctrine of the "limbo" (or the "edge of hell"), and (3) the doctrine of the *votum*, i.e. the "will," which stands in place of the deed. Since these teachings continue to exist in the various forms of a moderate exclusivism to the present time, even if in somewhat altered ways, and because they also have an undeniable significance for the development of inclusivism, it is worth examining each somewhat more closely.

With the support of New Testament texts such as 1 Peter 3:18ff and 4:6 (and numerous texts from the Old Testament interpreted along these same lines), the notion developed in the Early Church that between his death and his resurrection Jesus had descended into hell, in order to bring the righteous of the Old Covenant the news of the redemption achieved on the cross so that he could now free them from hell. This teaching about Christ's descent into hell became part of the Apostolic Creed and from that time on was bindingly proclaimed in the Western Church. But since this teaching is not found in the Nicene Creed, it did not achieve this same definitive status in the Eastern Church, although it has been equally widely disseminated there.

Connected to the teaching about Christ's descent into hell is also the teaching about the "limbo." The assumption that only the righteous of the Old Covenant were freed as a result of Christ's descent into hell, and not the "damned" in general, suggests a differentiation within hell. And thus over time a distinction between various forms of hell developed, enabling a further watering down of radical exclusivism. Soon a two-layered "edge of hell" ("limbo" literally means "edge" or "hem") could be distinguished from the hell of the damned. First there was the *limbus patrum* or "limbo of the fathers," which originally identified the dwelling place of the righteous of the Old Covenant during the time before Christ descended into hell. Yet subsequently this expanded to include the righteous beyond the Jewish people, and thus offered a "solution" for the eschatological fate of the good and the wise among the non-Christians. Along with the *limbus patrum* there also developed the idea of a *limbus puerorum* or "limbo of the children," a "place" for those children who had died unbaptized at an early age. In contrast to what Christ did in the *limbus patrum* one assumed that he had not been able to free the infants from limbo upon his descent because they could not have had even an implicit faith (cp. Thomas Aquinas, *Summa Theologiae* II 52,7). Although the limbo was originally conceived of as a place of punishment, even if of a milder nature, the image of the "edge of hell" eventually transformed into a kind of "edge of heaven." Although being in limbo excluded the beatific vision of God (*visio beatifica*), it did allow a certain natural beatitude. Still disputed was the more precise allocation of the good and wise pagans, particularly (but not only) of those who had lived before the time of Christ. Whereas some theologians believed that they were freed from the limbo by Christ along with the righteous of the Old Covenant and were taken to the beatific vision of God, Dante saw their fate as being eternally linked with that of the unbaptized infants. Representatives of radically exclusivist positions of course rejected such theories as an unacceptable watering down of the church's exclusive claim to salvation. For example, the influential medieval theological school of Laon judged the children who had died before being baptized as follows: "They are nothing but excrement and corrupt flesh (...). And nothing is owed them in terms of justice."[16]

The doctrine of the *votum implicitum* (or of the "implicit will") or "baptism of desire" represented an even greater watering down of radical exclusivism. It is again closely related to the teaching on limbo, as we can see from the different judgments about the eschatological fate of the righteous of the Old Covenant and of the unbaptized infants. For the reason why the lot of the Old Testament righteous was regarded more optimistically was the assumption that though having no explicit Christian faith, they nonetheless had a faith that was implicitly directed to Christ. Some church fathers thought that because of this implicit faith the Old Testament righteous already were part of the church in some sense, which is why one spoke of an "Ecclesia ab Abel," that is of a "Church since Abel," the son of Adam and the first righteous one. If this implicit faith establishes some kind of church membership, then in a way it replaces baptism. The argument goes that if the righteous of the Old Covenant had heard the gospel, they would have desired to become part of the church, that is, they would have desired baptism. In this sense their faith was counted as an implicit will (*votum implicitum*) to be part of the church. This alleged implicit desire for baptism ("baptism of desire") could be regarded as a substitute for the actual water baptism. As a result, the term "church" encompassed more than just the visible institution of church. In this way the original formula of "no salvation outside of the church" could be retained, but at the same time it could be interpreted to imply that all those non-Christians who do receive salvation belong to the church in this wider sense.

The teaching on the *votum* and "baptism of desire" was then further buttressed by concrete experiences of early Christendom. In the early church, it was customary that those desiring to be baptized first had to be instructed about the Christian faith as catechumens for a protracted period before they were allowed access to baptism. Now if such catechumens or baptismal candidates died before their baptism, perhaps even became victims of a persecution and suffered martyrdom, did they have a chance of being saved? On this point most if not all theologians decided in

16 Gross 1965, 39.

their favor. In other words, in this case the longing for baptism, the baptismal desire, takes the place of baptism itself and thus replaces it; the baptismal desire becomes the "baptism of desire". Or, as was also argued, martyrdom, which unambiguously proved this desire, could replace water baptism as a kind of "baptism of blood."

Now in the case of Christian catechumens the desire for baptism is both explicit and unambiguous. But what would happen if such a baptismal candidate did not die shortly before his or her baptism but at a point when he or she had not yet even heard the gospel? Can we in that case assume that—analogous to the case of the righteous of the Old Covenant—there had been something like an implicit or latent desire for baptism, which only becomes explicit and manifest after the actual encounter with the gospel? A positive response to this question would mean that through the doctrine of the "implicit will" (*votum implicitum*) or "baptism of desire" the possibility of salvation in principle is extended to all human beings, because one could assume for everyone, even if they have never heard or listened to the gospel, the existence of this implicit will. More than this, if one assumes that there are people who, although they have heard of the Christian message have never really understood it in such a way as to recognize God's call in it, then these people basically find themselves in a similar position to those who never had the opportunity of hearing the gospel. So one could impute even to them an implicit *votum* by assuming that if they had fully understood the gospel they would have affirmed it and accepted it in faith.

On the basis of these far-reaching consequences it is no surprise that the theological recognition of the *votum implicitum* remained disputed for such a long time. Yet in the modern era official statements from the Roman Catholic Church moved ever more clearly in the direction of a positive response. Thus in the year 1713 the notion was condemned that outside of the church there was no working of grace (D 2429). Several magisterial statements followed up on this, each of which expressed an undecided exclusivism (for example, Pope Pius IX's pronouncement, *Singulari quadam*, of 1854). Finally the magisterium moved with increasing clarity towards an affirmation of the doctrine of the *votum implicitum*. As a result of the conflict with the American Jesuit Leonhard Feeney, who defended a radical exclusivism, the Vatican's magisterium explicitly affirmed the doctrine of the salvific potential of the "implicit will:"

> To gain eternal salvation it is not always required that a person be incorporated in reality (*reapse*) as a member of the Church, but it is required that he belong to it at least in desire and longing (*voto et desiderio*). It is not always necessary that this desire be explicit, as it is with catechumens. When a man is invincibly ignorant, God also accepts an implicit desire, so called because it is contained in the good dispositions of the soul by which a man wants his will to be conformed to God's will.[17]

17 From the Letter of the Holy Office to Archbishop Cushing (1949), quoted after Sullivan 1992, 137.

Through this declaration, the magisterium of the Roman Catholic Church officially adopted a moderate exclusivism. However, as the further development of the magisterial pronouncements shows, this position could easily develop into inclusivism. This became apparent in the Second Vatican Council (1962-65), but became even more evident in magisterial documents such as the encyclical *Redemptoris missio* of 1990 and the declaration *Dialogue and Proclamation* of 1991. We will return to this in the next chapter on Christian inclusivism. But now we shall turn to some other current counter-developments that either continue to or newly support exclusivist positions within the various Christian churches, including the Roman Catholic Church.

Recent Developments

In 1996, the *International Theological Commission* of the Roman Catholic Church declared in its document *Christianity and the World Religions:*[18] "The object of discussion today is not the possibility of salvation outside the Church of those who live according to their conscience. This salvation (…) is based on the universal presence of the Spirit" (No. 81). In addition, the document states, the more recent magisterial development suggests the possibility that the non-Christian religions take on a positive role regarding the non-Christians' chance of salvation (Nos. 84-87), "insofar as they impel man to seek God, to act in accord with his conscience, to live a good life" (No. 86) and above all "to true love" (No. 87). Yet some Roman Catholic theologians have made an effort to downplay such a positive salvific role of the non-Christian religions.[19] The resulting tension is reflected especially in *Dominus Iesus,* a declaration published in 2000 by the Roman-Catholic *Congregation for the Doctrine of the Faith*, which is primarily directed against the pluralist theology of religions, but also against a more broadly conceived inclusivism.[20] *Dominus Iesus* contains a series of immediately contradictory statements that are well-suited to arouse new doubts regarding the affirmation of a significant salvific role of the non-Christian religions.

In Nos. 20-22, *Dominus Iesus* stresses that salvation is accessible also to "those who are not formally and visibly members of the Church" (No. 20). In No. 7, *Dominus Iesus* distinguishes between what it calls "*theological faith*" and "*belief* in the other religions". According to this distinction, "theological faith" is "a gift of grace"

18 International Theological Commission, 1997. (The document carries the year 1997 but was actually released on 30. September 1996. See also the analysis in Tilley 1999.

19 Cp. Dörmann 1988, as well as the contributions of R.M. Schmitz, L. Scheffczyk, R. Knittel, and E. Keller in Breid 1999.

20 For the text of *Dominus Iesus* see Congregation of the Doctrine of Faith 2000. That *Dominus Iesus* is also directed against a broadly conceived inclusivism was also underlined by the fact that shortly after *Dominus Iesus* Jacques Dupuis was censored, who may be considered as a notable representative of an inclusivist position. For the text regarding Dupuis and for the official commentary see: Congregation for the Doctrine of the Faith 2001a and 2001b. On Dupuis, see also below, chapter 5, pp. 131-136.

through which humans concur in a salvific way with God and the truth revealed by God. In contrast, "belief, in the other religions, is that sum of experience and thought that constitutes the human treasury of wisdom and religious aspiration, which man in his search for truth has conceived and acted upon in his relationship to God and the Absolute." Therefore, theological faith which responds to God's revelation must not be confused "with belief in other religions, which is religious experience still in search of the absolute truth and still lacking assent to God who reveals himself." Yet how can one justify the possibility of salvation for non-Christians, if the "belief" of non-Christians is not at least implicitly rooted in the "theological faith" that is, in a faith responding to divine revelation? There is no indication that *Dominus Iesus* intends to divert from the doctrine of the *votum implicitum* and would instead assume that a possibility of salvation is only offered after a person has died. Yet how then should one interpret such contradictory statements?

In No. 8 *Dominus Iesus* reaffirms that God "does not fail to make himself present in many ways, not only to individuals, but also to entire peoples through their spiritual riches, of which their religions are the main and essential expression (...)." For that reason, the sacred scriptures of other religions contain "elements (...) by which countless people throughout the centuries have been and still are able today to nourish and maintain their life-relationship with God." The "elements of goodness and grace" which are found in these scriptures stem "from the mystery of Christi." Nonetheless, *Dominus Iesus* declines to designate these writings as "inspired." For, so it says, the designation "inspired texts" refers exclusively "to the canonical books of the Old and New Testaments, since these are inspired by the Holy Spirit." Yet how do the writings of non-Christian religions "receive from the mystery of Christ the elements of goodness and grace" if not through the inspiration of the Holy Spirit?

In No. 21, *Dominus Iesus* states: "Certainly, the various religious traditions contain and offer religious elements which come from God, and which are part of what 'the Spirit brings about in human hearts and in the history of peoples, in cultures, and religions'. Indeed, some prayers and rituals of the other religions may assume a role of preparation for the Gospel, in that they are occasions or pedagogical helps in which the human heart is prompted to be open to the action of God. One cannot attribute to these, however, a divine origin or an *ex opere operato* salvific efficacy, which is proper to the Christian sacraments." So after having first emphasized that some elements, like prayers and rituals, of non-Christian religions "come from God" and are effected by the divine Spirit, the very next sentence teaches that one "cannot attribute" these prayers and rites to "a divine origin."

The cited contradictions unmistakably manifest the conflict between a moderate exlusivist and an inclusivist position. The best explanation for why these contradictions are found unresolved in *Dominus Iesus* seems to me that *Dominus Iesus* reflects a tension that remains similarly unresolved among the various bearers of the magisterium in the Roman Catholic Church. The theological persuasiveness of this document is, of course, significantly reduced by its inner contradictions.

While the Roman Catholic Church thus wrestles with how to consistently follow the path set out since the Second Vatican Council, Protestant churches have not yet managed (as far as I can tell) to break through to an inclusivist position. Official declarations announce either a moderate or an undecided exclusivism, or, like most of the statements of the World Council of Churches,[21] they maintain abstinence from a theology of religions.[22] Two documents need to be mentioned with respect to the situation in Germany: the 1991 study entitled *Religions, Religiosity, and Christian Faith* (*"Religionen, Religiosität und christlicher Glaube"*) published by the United Protestant Lutheran Church of Germany (or VELKD=*Vereinigte Evangelische Lutherische Kirche Deutschlands)* along with the Churches of the Arnholdshain Conference, and the EKD's (*Evanglische Kirche in Deutschland*) 2003 guidelines entitled *Christian Faith and non-Christian Religions* (*"Christlicher Glaube und nichtchristliche Religionen"*).

In *Religions, Religiosity, and Christian Faith*,[23] Karl Rahner's inclusivism and Paul Knitter's pluralism are pretty clearly rejected. By contrast, what remains unclear is the study's own evaluation of non-Christian religions. These religions, it says, are not "simply an expression of demonic power" nor are they simply "human contrivance." Rather, through them, "God acts in the lives of people."[24] Yet this divine involvement is explained as God's "mundane action" or God's "creative action" and the references to Acts 17:27 and Rom 1:23 suggest that what is meant is a limited witness of God, and not the mediation of salvific knowledge of God: "God acts in the world both in religions and behind them with the goal that humanity might find him…yet people pervert God's action according to their wishes."[25] One also does not read anything in this study about the chance of salvation of the individual non-Christian. Theo Sundermeier, one of the study's co-authors, comments on this in the following words: "The protestant churches are being pressed from many sides finally to come clean about their relationship to other religious and to say bindingly whether and in fact that there is salvation in other religions outside of the church." This

21 While it is true that within the World Council of Churches there are consistent attempts to emphasize the significance of the problems in the theology of religions, for understandable reasons it cannot however offer any binding or representative answers for all member churches. And so the relevant publications concentrate mainly on questions of how to practically enact interreligious relations. Typical examples of this are the *Guidelines on Dialogue with People of Living Faiths and Ideologies* (1979) and the *Ecumenical Considerations for Dialogue and Relations with People of Other Religions* (2003).

22 This is true also of Anglicanism and of the Orthodox Churches. For the first consultation of the Anglican Network for Inter Faith Concerns (NIFCON) in Bangalore in 2003, see the report online: www.anglicannifcon.org/BangaloreRpt1.htm. See also the joint Lutheran-Anglican Declaration *Guidelines for Inter Faith Encounter in the Churches of the Porvoo Communion* (2003): https://www.churchofengland.org/media/36605/porvooguidelines.doc. Nonetheless, radical exclusivism is dealt a clear blow in No. A where it says "… it is not for us to proclaim limits to God's saving mercy." For Orthodox perspectives, cp. Phidas 1997 and Papandreou 1998.

23 On this, see the detailed analysis in Schmidt-Leukel 1992b.

24 *Religionen, Religiosität und der christlicher Glaube* 1991, 127.

25 Ibid. 128.

judgment, according to Sundermeier, cannot be conceded, "because part of such a judgment would be establishing boundaries and conditions under which salvation would be possible and when it would not be possible. Yet in such a situation one is no longer open to finding the truth; rather one would assume the judgment seat of Christ which is not our due."[26] Given this comment, the statements of the study are presumably to be understood in the sense of an undecided exclusivism.

Christian Faith and non-Christian Religions (Christlicher Glaube und nichtchristliche Religionen) does not present the situation much differently. The text primarily emphasizes the contrasts and differences between the religions, which—the book suggests—are so extensive that even the commonalities between the religions are affected by them. "The notion of an 'ecumenism of religions' similar to that of Christian ecumenism" is dismissed as a "false path."[27] The text characterizes the most important difference between Christianity and non-Christian religions as follows: As Creator, God is equally close to all people, Christians and non-Christians, yet:

> This proximity of the Creator to all people is disclosed in all its abundance and irrevocably in Jesus Christ. In him, God encountered humanity historically and concretely, and in the gospel of Jesus Christ God turns *graciously* toward all persons. ...The *difference* between Christians and people of another religion is ... based on the experience of God's salvific attention to humanity in the story of Jesus Christ, an experience that only a person who believes in Jesus Christ can have. Christianity differentiates itself from all other religions through *faith in Jesus Christ.* (...) This differentiation does not put into question God's gracious devotion to all people, but rather makes it clear that other religions do not convey the experience of God coming close to all humanity through Jesus Christ. Hence what connects the Christian faith with persons of all religions (namely, that God is gracious to all persons) is simultaneously also what separates them.[28]

Unfortunately, this statement is in a decisive sense ambiguous. Did God *graciously turn* to humanity *only* through Jesus Christ, which would mean that receiving this grace presupposes faith in the gospel? Or is it the case that *only* through Jesus it becomes *clear* that the grace of God indeed is for all people? Let us assume for a moment that the document intends to emphasize the second alternative (although in fact the document provides no unambiguous clarity on this point). In this case, the difference between Christianity and other religions would consist primarily in a kind of advanced recognition: Through the revelation of God in Jesus Christ Christians know and witness to the fact that God is gracious to all persons. Although this grace reaches also people of other religions, it is not witnessed to in their religions. But is the gracious devotion of God really the same toward all people if it has produced a conscious recognition of its presence only through Jesus Christ and only in Christianity? If it really reaches all people, why has the grace of God not also made

26 Sundermeier 1991, 187.
27 *Christlicher Glaube und nichtchristliche Religionen,* 2003, 19.
28 Ibid. 8.

itself known in other religions? Why should the various testimonies to divine grace, which are factually present in other religions, not be taken as being what they claim to be, that is, as genuine evidence of experiences of grace? Or does the document perhaps want to say that the grace of God that embraces all people has become evident to Christians through Jesus Christ, but that it is possible that this grace was witnessed to and mediated similarly, albeit in a different way, through other historical figures? At one place, the document says that Christians "(encounter) other religions in the expectation that one may find in them likewise somehow experiences with this truth."[29] Yet it seems to me that "this truth" here refers only in a general way to the "truth of God," and not to a salvific experience of grace. Why else should the document, as cited earlier, reinforce the notion that the testimony to a grace for all people is precisely what differentiates Christianity from all other religions? So in the final analysis *Christian Faith and non-Christian Religions* follows an exclusivist trajectory. And as was suggested in *Religions, Religiosity, and Christian Faith,* here too a possibility of salvation outside of Christianity is not *unambiguously* affirmed, even if some statements might perhaps be interpreted in this way.

Nowadays, radical exclusivism is found particularly in evangelical and pentecostal circles, although there too it is no longer uncontested. In the last few years, there have been noteworthy forays into an inclusivist theology of religions among evangelical[30] and pentecostal[31] theologians, most notably and influentially by Clark Pinnock.[32] A radical exclusivist attitude, more typical of an evangelical position, is displayed in the following quote from Eddy Lanz, a theology teacher at the evangelical Bible School of Wiedenest:

> Without Christ there is no redemption, and we can add that without Christ being proclaimed to and accepted by people, there is no redemption.... God's love in Christ desires to save, to save for all eternity, precisely because the only alternative to Christ is being lost for all eternity. What is born of the flesh, is flesh and therefore lost. Only those who claim their personal salvation in the Crucified One can live forever.[33]

Similar ideas lie behind evangelical statements such as in the Southern Baptists' prayer guide mentioned at the beginning of this chapter, or also the following statement of the 1960 evangelical Congress on World Mission held in Chicago:

29 Ibid. 16.
30 Cp. the summary review in Heim 1995, as well as the extensive overview complete with numerous bibliographic references in Strange 2002, 16-35 and 294-331.
31 Cp. Yong 2000 and 2003.
32 See especially Pinnock 1995 and 1997, as well as Strange 2002, on the evangelical discussion of Pinnock.
33 Lanz 1996, here p. 64f. Further examples of radical exclusivism in the realm of evangelical theology can be found with bibliographic references in Netland 2001, 320.

> In the years since the war, more than one billion souls have passed into eternity, and more than half of these went to the torment of hellfire without even hearing of Jesus Christ....[34]

Sometimes one encounters the opinion that exclusivism is a matter of the past, overcome by theology, and therefore is not to be taken seriously any more by a contemporary theology of religions. Yet this is a grave misjudgment of the true theological situation. In all three of its forms, exclusivism is still a very widespread position. Considering the vast numerical strength of evangelical and pentecostal forms of Christianity with their strong inclination to radical exclusivist positions, radical exclusivism might even be, just as before, the most common form of exclusivism.

Also within the academic theological discourse one can still find numerous apologists for exclusivist positions. Here I will mention only a few important and widespread trends. Still influential is the exclusivism of dialectical theology, as laid out systematically above all by Karl Barth[35] and supported with arguments from the history of religions by Hendrik Kraemer.[36] However, as was the case with Barth and Kraemer, what we find here is typically a moderate exclusivism. This is true also of the American Lutheran, George Lindbeck, who tries to link the discontinuity thesis of dialectical theology with the incommensurability thesis borrowed from postmodern relativist thinkers.[37] On the evangelical side, Alister McGrath can be named as a particularly prominent representative of a moderate exclusivism.[38] The position of undecided exclusivism can be found not only among numerous evangelical theologians; it was also represented by the British theologian and committed ecumenist, Lesslie Newbigin (1909-1998),[39] who continues even today to exert great influence both within the WCC and beyond.[40] It is a particularly noteworthy development that in the last few years analytical philosophers of religion have represented exclusivist positions, among them several philosophers from the school of reformed epistemology such as Alvin Plantinga,[41] Peter van Inwagen,[42] David Basinger,[43] as well as other philosophers such as Stephen Davis,[44] Richard Swinburne,[45] and William Lane Craig.[46] Craig is a former student of John Hick and Wolfhart Pannenberg who has

34 Quoted from Hick 1982, 30.
35 Cp. especially Barth, *Church Dogmatics* I/II, §17.
36 Cp. Kramer 1959, and 1962.
37 Cp. Lindbeck 1984, and Lindbeck 1997. On Lindbeck, see the analysis in Kreiner 1992b and the pertinent remarks in Stosch, 2001, 325ff.
38 Cp. McGrath 1995. For further evangelically oriented defenses of exclusivism, see also Netland 1991, Stetson 1994, and Strange 2002.
39 Cp. Newbigin 1989 and 1995.
40 On Newbigin, see also Foust et al. 2002.
41 Cp. A. Plantinga 1997 and 2000.
42 Cp. Inwagen 1995.
43 Cp. Basinger 2002.
44 Cp. Davis 1990.
45 Cp. Swinburne 1989.
46 Craig 1989, 1993, 1994, 1995, and 2003.

proposed the presumably most imposing and influential attempt to date at defending radical exclusivism.

In the next section I want to show that exclusivism suffers from two serious problems, both of which can be remedied but whose remedy in my opinion makes exclusivism not so much stronger as rather less plausible. These two problems have to do, first, with the question of salvation, and second, with the question of interreligious parallels.

Critical Discussion

The Question of Salvation

Most exclusivists take it for granted that God, as it says in 1 Tim 2:4 "desires everyone to be saved and to come to the knowledge of the truth." This "universal salvific will of God," meaning God's love of every single person, is for many exclusivists the most important reason for mission: Because God loves all human beings, the saving news should be brought to everyone. But how then is one to reconcile this with the position of radical exclusivism? The notion that all non-Christians, whether they lived before or after Jesus, whether they were able to hear the gospel or not, are lost forever, thus excluding the vast majority of humanity from salvation, undoubtedly stands in tension with the claim that God desires the salvation of all.

From a logical perspective, the most "simple" solution to this problem of exclusivism consists in disputing God's universal salvific will. As I have mentioned before, Fulgentius of Ruspe pointed to the large number of people who never could have heard of Christ as proof that there is no universal salvific will of God.[47] According to Augustine as well, the just-cited text from the First Letter of Timothy does not mean that God desires the salvation of all persons, but rather that no one attains salvation unless God wishes so.[48] In modern time, similar disputes regarding the universal salvific will of God can be found particularly among those theologians who are heavily influenced by Augustine, like for example Luther[49] and Calvin.[50] It is especially due to the influence of Calvin's theology that we frequently encounter this motif in the present. For if one accepts, in line with tradition, that salvific faith comes from hearing the gospel, as Daniel Strange explains,

47 Again, cp. above p. 93.
48 *Enchiridion*, 27, 103.
49 *De servo artibrio* (St A 3:170-356—254: 10-13).
50 *Institutio* III, 24:16.

> ...then those who never hear must lie outside God's salvific will and Christ's atoning provisions. (...) God does not wish to save them and so there is no need to construct a theology that includes them.[51]

This is undoubtedly logically consistent. Yet what are the implications of denying a universal salvific will of God for the image of God? Is it not repulsively unjust if only a small portion of humanity is predestined for redemption, and all the rest for damnation? Defenders of this position counter this accusation of injustice with two different strategies. On the one hand, following the Augustinian tradition, they argue that humans cannot determine whether God is just: "God does not stand under justice as a norm but is himself the norm."[52] On the other hand, they argue that from the vantage point of justice, what all people *deserve* is not redemption but judgment. What is just is only the punishment, and this is universal since sin is universal. Grace, by contrast, is something that God gives of his own free will to a chosen a few, without their deserving it.[53] If two criminals who have been proven guilty are led to the scaffold and the ruler at the last moment for no particular reason shows mercy to one of them, then this, according to William Lane Craig, is not a case of injustice.[54] Therefore, according to Craig, denying the universal salvific will of God does not raise questions about God's justice but rather about God's love. For if God elects only some people to receive grace, then God, though still being just, is not equally gracious to all persons.[55] For this reason Craig has suggested a different way of defending radical exclusivism.

According to Craig[56] God most certainly desires the salvation of all human beings, yet because of several stringent logical reasons, it is impossible, even for God, that everybody can achieve salvation: First of all, the possibility of grace or forgiveness depends on Jesus' death on the cross, which Craig understands as an atonement for our sins and hence as constitutive of our salvation. Second, human freedom implies the possibility of being able to decline God's offer of grace. Normally this offer of grace is tied to the proclamation of the gospel, and whoever rejects the gospel, according to Craig, excludes himself from grace. If one assumes that God respects human freedom, then in this case it is even for God impossible to save such persons. Third, Craig assumes that God not only knows all our free choices in advance, but also knows the truth or falsity of all counterfactual propositions (in other words, God possesses what Molina called the *scientia media*). God therefore knows what

51 Cp. Strange 2002, 284f. Strange names contemporary examples for this position (ibid., 280-285 and 307-310) and identifies them as a theological option with which he is obviously closely aligned.

52 Carl Henry: "Is it Fair" in Crockett and Sigountos (eds.): *Through No Fault of Their Own?* Grand Rapids, 1992, 255, cited in Strange 2002, 282.

53 Cp. Strange 2002, 281ff, 309ff.

54 Other evangelical philosophers, such as Stephen Davis, continue to consider it deeply "unfair" if for no particular reason some are denied the offer of grace (Davis 1990, 181).

55 Cp. Craig 1995, 123ff.

56 See especially Craig 1989.

free decisions each person would have made even under such circumstances that never became or will become reality. Thus God knows who would accept the gospel and who would not, even if in fact those persons never got to hear it. Craig assumes that all those who, even if they had heard the gospel, would have rejected it were created in such places and such times that they never did in fact get to hear the gospel. Put another way: "If there were anyone who would have responded to the gospel if he had heard it, then God in His love would have brought the gospel to such a person. (…) Hence, no one is lost because of lack of information due to historical or geographical accident."[57]

But why then did God at all create those persons whom he knew would reject his offer of salvation under all conceivable circumstances? Could God not have created a world in which only such people existed as God knew from the outset would not reject his grace? Craig does not dispute this possibility. Yet he suggests that this might possibly be a world with only a handful of people in it. For it is logically conceivable that, due to particular circumstances, creating persons who accept grace freely makes the creation of other people whom God knows will reject grace simply unavoidable. In order to increase the numbers of the redeemed a loving God will accept the need to also create such persons whose redemption is impossible. However, according to Craig, a loving God will ensure the optimal balance between the redeemed and the lost, in other words, God will bring about the largest possible number of redeemed persons and the least possible number of lost ones. It is conceivable that this situation corresponds exactly to our actual world. Those who would under no circumstances accept the gospel were created in those times and in those places in which they never actually heard the gospel, and they were created solely because this was an unavoidable condition for making as large as possible the number of those who would accept the gospel. The position of radical exclusivism therefore does not contradict the assumption of a maximally good God, a God who wants all to be saved and who brings about the salvation of the largest number of people possible.

Yet Craig's attempt to reconcile radical exclusivism with the broader salvific intention of God fails even if one shares all of Craig's presuppositions. According to Craig, the creation of the reprobate is necessary in order to increase the number of the redeemed. For Craig does concede that God could have created a world in which all people are redeemed, but that this probably would have been a very small world. But then God could have increased the number of those redeemed by creating a large number of such sparsely populated worlds (either in chronological order or as spatial or multidimensional parallel worlds). This however makes Craig's main argument untenable, according to which God was forced to create the reprobate due to his love for the redeemed. Moreover, even if it were tenable, Craig's argument would presumably have a side effect highly unwelcome for evangelical Christians. For in this case they would have to accept that essentially, the vast majority of the

57 Craig 1989, 185.

redeemed do not owe their redemption to the atoning death of Jesus but rather to the torment of the damned—since their creation was the price God had to pay for it.[58] Or to put it more precisely, through their suffering the damned pay the price for the salvation of the redeemed!

Beyond these internal problems, Craig's attempt rests on a range of problematic presuppositions. Philosophically, it is controversial whether free decisions can be known by God in advance and still be considered to be free. More problematic still are Craig's theological presuppositions. As opposed to other radical exclusivists, Craig is not willing to connect the acceptance of the divine offer of grace to an explicitly Christian faith. For if he were to do so, then it would necessarily follow that even the righteous of the Old Covenant were not redeemed. Yet this contradicts a number of biblical statements, so that, as Harold Netland admits, the biblical witness concerning the righteous of the Old Testament presents a serious problem for any kind of Christian exclusivism.[59] For this reason, Craig concedes that God's offer of grace does not necessarily have to come to people in the form of the Christian gospel. This means that in principle there could be "anonymous Christians" but, says Craig, they "are relatively rare."[60] Yet what is the basis of this limitation? Certainly not the acceptance of God's universal salvific will, which Craig allegedly wishes to defend, but rather—as he himself writes—the scriptural witness according to which "the mass of humanity do not (…) respond" [to the offer of grace. P.S.-L.].[61] But is the scriptural testimony really as unambiguous in this regard as Craig supposes? Other evangelical theologians who are more optimistic about salvation than Craig have applied the notion of the *scientia media* in a quite contrary way. God knows of all persons whether they would have accepted the gospel under certain particularly favorable circumstances. If they would have, then for God this is as good as an actual acceptance, even if they never actually did so.[62] In the final analysis, this position is similar to the doctrine of the *votum implicitum*, which could thus equally well be justified on the basis of Craig's epistemological position.

Furthermore, Craig makes the highly problematic assumption that everyone who declines the gospel thereby rejects God's offer of grace; that is, he assumes that such rejections are always and in every case guilty rejections. Yet it is very well conceivable, as David Myers has objected to Craig, that non-Christians might reject the gospel out of epistemological reasons (such as insufficient evidence of the gospel, or a subjectively stronger plausibility of another religious or philosophical tradition).[63] Craig has responded to this by arguing that the evidence of the gospel is supported by the testimony of the Holy Spirit; in opposing the gospel, then, the non-Christian

58 "…the terrible price of filling heaven is also filling hell…" Craig 1989, 183.
59 Cp. Netland 1991, 266f.
60 Craig 1989, 186.
61 Ibid., 176.
62 Thus Donald Lake, cited in Strange 2002, 327.
63 Cp. Myers 2003a.

becomes guilty of opposing the Holy Spirit.[64] Yet as Myers says, this assumption is completely lacking in plausibility and moreover assumes every educated non-Christian to be lacking in moral and religious integrity.[65]

As the final problematic theological presupposition one needs to point out that Craig's whole argument—like that of almost all Christian exclusivists—is based on the assumption that Jesus' death on the cross is constitutive of salvation. Yet this assumption is intertwined with a whole host of theological difficulties to which I will return later.[66]

Independent of the problematic nature of these theological presuppositions, we can conclude that radical exclusivism so far has not yet proven its compatibility with the doctrine of God's universal salvific will. Yet denying God's universal salvific will has fatal consequences for the image of God. Undoubtedly such an image of God would not correspond to the New Testament witness that God is love (1 Jn. 4:8). And the "justice" of such a God would also be seriously in question: If one responds by saying that God ought not to be measured according to our norms of justice, then what is being openly admitted by this response is that according to "our" norms, God is not just. This God then, according to our norms, is more akin to a partisan and extremely brutal cosmic tyrant. This is why we must also raise questions about the moral, spiritual, and psychological consequences, side effects, and origins of venerating such a being.

Yet is it at all possible to raise such an objection against radical exclusivism from the perspective of a pluralist theology of religions? As we will see in more detail later,[67] a pluralist theology of religions assumes that God is far removed from everything that we can conceive or name, and that therefore statements like "God is love" are not in a position to describe the nature of God such as it is in itself. But does not pluralism thereby deprive the critique of radical exclusivism of its basis?[68] In light of this objection, we should first point to the fact that the aforementioned critique of radical exclusivism depends on internal presuppositions of this position. For an exclusivist either assumes there to be a universal salvific will of God, as for example Craig does, but then fails in consistently explaining why the damnation of all non-Christians should be inevitable. Or the exclusivist denies God's universal salvific will and then is in tension with the New Testament concept of God as love, in contrast to his or her claim on the scriptural adequacy of the exclusivist position. This particular objection advanced against pluralism furthermore overlooks that the ineffability and inconceivability of God is not claimed in the sense of an unqualified negation of all human conceptualizations and expressions, but rather is the consequence of the idea of the infiniteness of God that transcends all finite concepts; so it

64 Cp. Craig 2003.
65 Cp. Myers 2003b.
66 On this, cp. below chapter 11, p. 243-251.
67 See below chapters 7 and 8.
68 On this objection, cp. D'Costa 1986, 30ff.; D'Costa 1987, 93-117; Pinnock 1997, 45f; Hüttenhoff 1999, 222ff.

is possible to assign the positive statements about God a legitimate place as part and parcel of this process of ultimately transcending all concepts and of the existential experience of transcendence. In addition, it is sometimes overlooked that in talking about a universal salvific *will* of God or of God's *love* for all people we are using a language that expresses in personal forms a "cosmic optimism"[69] which however can also be expressed in terms of impersonal symbolizations of transcendent reality.[70] The thesis of the transcendent nature of ultimate reality does not, as Hüttenhoff seems to suggest,[71] imply the invalidity of both types of religious expression, but rather establishes that and in what sense both are equally possible. From the pluralist perspective, radical exclusivism therefore not only presents an inappropriate limitation and morally questionable representation of transcendent reality, but also a lamentable backslide from the cosmic optimism which, in principle, has been achieved in both Christianity and the other major religious traditions.

It is this apparently insurmountable tension with the universal salvific will of God that makes radical exclusivism appear unacceptable even in the eyes of other exclusivists. They therefore profess either a moderate or an undecided exclusivism. Yet both positions are theologically unstable. Undecided exclusivism is theologically inconsequential and half-hearted. Moderate exclusivism carries the inevitable tendency of turning into a kind of inclusivism. And this is true of all its forms.

Let us assume one holds that after death non-Christians experience a revelation of Christ, which opens to them the possibility of a salvific faith. Then the question arises of whether the life that he or she led *before* his or her death has any bearing whatsoever on the decision reached after death. In this respect can we not assume that the postmortem decision for or against God's offer of grace is prepared by that personality development which the non-Christian underwent before, that is in his or her earthly life? Anyone who wants to dispute this would have to declare the earthly life of a non-Christian to be completely irrelevant. But if one admits that a certain type of character development occurs during life here and now that is decisive for the postmortem decision, then one can no longer deny the importance of all those factors which shape this life. But then the question immediately poses itself of whether non-Christian religions could not also have a positive function for such character development. In other words, one would have to ascribe to non-Christian religions at least the function of a *praeparatio evangelii*, or "preparation for the gospel," even if the proclamation of the gospel should happen only after death. Yet this function assumes a certain continuity between the other religions and the gospel. How else would the other religions be able to positively prepare people for the gospel if not through the working of the Holy Spirit in them? But this would mean that one has arrived at a cautiously inclusivist position.

69 For the term "cosmic optimism" see Hick 1989, 56-69.
70 On this, cp. Hick 1990b, 190. Cp. also Gerth 1997, 112f.
71 Cp. Hüttenhoff 1999, 224ff.

The same argument applies if one assumes that a chance of salvation is offered to the non-Christian through certain special or private revelations in this life. Here too we must ask whether the previous molding of the person via a non-Christian religion could be completely without relevance for the experience of and reaction to a supposed private revelation. Moreover, the witness of such special Christian revelations among non-Christians is an extremely rare phenomenon, making this path of argument unsuitable for accounting for a universal chance of salvation as it would correspond to the universal salvific will of God—unless one assumes that these "special revelations" are nothing but the salvific revelatory quality of non-Christian religions themselves, which would mean that one has adopted an inclusivist position.

The same is true, but in an even stronger sense, when one pursues a moderate exclusivism in the sense of the doctrine on the *votum implicitum*. One can only realistically conceive of such a *votum* if one accepts the formative importance of the entire setting of a person's life. But this is precisely how religions attain their salvific function. If for example this *votum* is primarily identified with an individual good decision of conscience, then one cannot dispute that religions play an important role in forming the individual conscience. Thus, it is no wonder that from the moment that the magisterium of the Catholic Church unambiguously pronounced itself in favor of the doctrine of the *votum implicitum*, developments within Catholic theology very quickly led to inclusivism.

On account of this inner inclination of moderate exclusivism toward inclusivism, many exclusivists draw back from moderate exclusivism just as they do from its radical variant. But what then remains is a retreat into undecided exclusivism.[72] This claims that the judgment as to whether an individual non-Christian can be saved or not is not up to theology but should be left entirely up to God. Undoubtedly, we should not place ourselves, as we read in the quote from Sundermeier above, on the "judgment seat of Christ."[73] But this is not what is intended here. For the moderate exclusivist does not assume judgments about particular individual people, but rather exposes the theological consequences of confessing God's universal salvific will. If a person is not prepared to draw these consequences, then this unavoidably calls into question the seriousness of the affirmation of a universal offer of grace. In this sense, refraining from making a judgment would not be humble modesty, but rather a sign of a lack of theological consistency.[74]

In addition, undecided exclusivism necessarily awakens the impression of half-heartedness. For if undecided exclusivists feel capable of firmly rejecting particular non-Christian claims to salvation—if theologians, for example, say unambiguously that it was the duty of each and every Christian to deny the National Socialists' claim to "salvation" as expressed in their "Heil Hitler"—then why should Christians not also be in a position to endorse positive claims to salvation from

72 Similarly Netland's position, 2001, 323.
73 Cp. above, p. 101 at n. 26.
74 See likewise Hüttenhoff 2001, 214.

outside of Christianity? Either Christians are not permitted to make any judgment whatsoever—including negative ones. Or they are entitled to form responsible judgments, of course with all provisos due to the recognition their human proclivity to err. But then it is hard to see why these judgments should only be of a negative type.

To summarize: Radical exclusivism stands in stark contrast to faith in the universal salvific will of God. There are only three options available to radical exclusivism to dispel this contradiction: Either it refutes the existence of a universal salvific will of God at the cost of having a diminished, and morally highly questionable image of God. Or it gives up its position of restricting salvation to the few and instead adopts the viewpoint of moderate exclusivism. Given that exclusivism can always make that move, Hüttenhoff holds that the question of salvation is only of "limited" value in the critical discussion of Christian exclusivism.[75] However, as Hüttenhoff himself notes, moderate exclusivism tends to evolve into some kind of inclusivism,[76] and this is literally "fatal" for exclusivism. So the exclusivist is more or less left with only the third alternative, i.e. undecided exclusivism, which pays for its stance with the price of theological half-heartedness and inconsequence. Thus, none of the three alternatives manages to convince, and for that reason in my opinion the question of salvation by itself is completely sufficient to exclude Christian exclusivism from the circle of theologically credible positions.

Yet there is a second weighty objection to Christian exclusivism, one that affects all forms of exclusivism forms equally. This was already hinted at in what was just said about undecided exclusivism, and concerns the existence of interreligious parallels.

The Question of Interreligious Parallels

Obviously one can find numerous parallels in non-Christian religions to what counts as an expression of salvific knowledge of God in Christianity. In other words, we also find many aspects of faith in God in non-Christian religions that correspond with its Christian forms. In addition, one often finds in the lives of non-Christians those very characteristics that in Christianity are considered as the fruit of the Holy Spirit and as signs of true faith: "love, joy, peace, patience, kindness, benevolence, faithfulness, gentleness, and self-control" (Gal 5:22)—and these signs do not appear in spite of the non-Christians' belonging to a non-Christian religion, but precisely because of their authentic non-Christian spirituality. Is exclusivism capable of explaining the existence of such parallels in the faith and lives of Christians and non-Christians? Do such parallels not contradict the exclusivist assumption that only Christianity mediates salvific knowledge of God? For exclusivist claims to ring

75 Cp. Hüttenhoff 2001, 221, 215.
76 Cp. ibid., 215.

true, wouldn't the existential fruits of salvific knowledge of God be found only in Christianity?

Two possible responses remain for exclusivists in light of this objection. *First*, the exclusivist can claim that all similarity between the faith and life of Christians and non-Christians is superficial or deceptive. In truth, the non-Christian neither knows the true God, nor are his or her works of love genuine. Rather, these are simply a cover for pious hypocrisy and self-righteousness, or it is even a case of demonic imitation (*imitatio diabolica)* of the sacred. The thesis of *imitatio diabolica* was the standard argument of exclusivist minded missionaries whenever they stumbled upon doctrinal and existential parallels to Christian faith in other religions. This thesis is hard to disprove with logical arguments. For how can one conclusively refute that hiding behind what seems to be signs of a genuine salvific relationship to God is in truth only hypocrisy, self-righteousness, or the deceitful work of demons? Nevertheless, this defense of exclusivism is weak. For such skepticism towards appearance must finally also undermine any trust in the genuineness of Christian faith and life. For example, it perplexed many Christians that Mahātma Gandhi's life, which in many respects was more Christ-like than that of most Christians, drew from the spiritual wells of Hinduism and Jainism. In light of "the whole problem of, for instance, Gandhi"—and from an exclusivist perspective Gandhi is doubtless a "problem"—Hendrik Kraemer reminds us that the "most sincere representative of the most impressive forms of piety or of quality of life may happen to be the farthest from the Kingdom of God." The life of such a person could, according to Kaemer, very well represent a repetition of the "Fall", the desire-to-be-like-God.[77] But if Gandhi's life were only made up of works-righteousness and pious self-affirmation, in short if it were simply extreme human pride and a repetition of the fall, with what right could one then regard the life of a Francis of Assisi or a Jesus of Nazareth in a different way? Or let us take an example from the area of beliefs: When Tiru Mular, a scholar and saint of Hindu Shaivism writes that "God is Love,"[78] why in this instance should that be an expression of vain idolatry, whereas it is regarded as an expression of salvific revelation in the First Letter of John?

In light of the objection based on the interreligious parallels, the exclusivist can, *second*, adopt the position that while such parallels in faith and life may be genuine, they are nevertheless irrelevant to the question of the saving nature of faith. Karl Barth was, for example, prepared to allow for "a sea of more or less adequate, but at any rate fundamentally unmistakable, parallels and analogies."[79] By no means did Barth represent the view that only Christianity claims to rely on revelation and grace. Rather, he saw numerous and significant parallels especially to this claim in other religions. Christianity, according to Barth, differs from other religions not so

77 Kraemer 1956, 365. On p. 84 Kraemer states that behind the "sublimity of religious experience" may well be "Satan disguised as the Angel of Light".

78 Tirumantiram 257. Cp. Dhavamony 1971, 128.

79 Barth 1932-70, (CD I/2 §17) 282.

much because of its form as a religion of revelation and grace, but rather because it is only in Christianity that the claim of revelation and grace is true. For according to Barth the reality of revelation is not tied to the form of a religion of revelation[80] and the reality of grace is not tied to the form of a religion of grace.[81] So according to Barth how can we establish which religion rightly claims revelation and grace and which does not, in other words, where are revelation and grace witnessed to in truth and where not? According to Barth, the interreligious parallels make clear that,

> only one thing is decisive for the distinction between truth and falsehood in religions. That one thing is *the name Jesus Christ.*[82]

In fact, Barth expressly emphasizes that the difference

> is actually enclosed in all the formal simplicity of this name …[83]

Thus according to Barth the truth of Christianity consists neither of the content of any beliefs connected to this name, nor of any particular characteristics of a lived life:

> It is not enclosed, therefore, in its more or less explicit structure as the religion of grace, nor in the Reformation doctrines of original sin, representative satisfaction, justification by faith alone, the gift of the Holy Ghost and thankfulness. All this (…) the heathen, too, can in their own way teach and even live and represent as a church. Yet that does not mean that they are any the less heathen, poor, and utterly lost.[84]

Several times Barth repeats that anything that cannot be proven to be "incontestably original,"[85] in other words, anything that "has its more or less exact parallel outside the Bible"[86] cannot, precisely for that reason, "be the very essence of the matter"[87] and therefore cannot be considered as the decisive criterion to establish the unique truth of Christianity. It is only the name "Jesus Christ" that is without parallel. And it is only "the formal simplicity of this name" because everything that is connected to this name above and beyond its "formal simplicity" is not actually unique. The name alone is decisive. And so Barth even declares:

80 Barth, 1932-70, (CD I/2) 329. This is emphasized in the German original while the emphasis has been dropped in the English translation.
81 Barth, 1932-70, (CD I/2) 339.
82 Barth, 1932-70 (CD I/2), German original, p. 376. Translation on the basis of the German original ("daß über Wahrheit und Lüge zwischen den Religionen nur Eines entscheidet. Dieses Eine ist *der Name Jesus Christus*") which is somewhat softened in the English version (p. 342).
83 Barth, 1932-70 (CD I/2), p. 342. The German original (p. 376) reads: "Wirklich in der ganzen formalen Simplizität dieses Namens…".
84 Barth, 1932-70 (CD I/2), p. 342.
85 Barth, 1932-70 (CD I/2) 342.
86 Barth, 1932-70 (CD I/2) 11.
87 Ibid.

> Neither the ethics of the Sermon on the Mount (…), nor the healing of the blind, lame and possessed, (…) nor love to God nor love to neighbour, nor the passion and death of Christ, nor the miraculous raising from the dead—nothing of all that has any value, inner importance or abstract significance of its own in the New Testament, apart from Jesus Christ being the Subject of it all. His is the name in which it is all true and real….[88]

But in focusing on the "name" is Barth referring to the person designated by this name? The answer to this is not entirely clear. For Barth is conscious of the fact that we only have access to the historical person of Jesus via that testimony of faith which confesses him as the "Christ," meaning that the revelation can only come to us by way of this testimony, that is, by way of the "name." In a discussion with Paul Tillich, Barth even says that the matter of Jesus' historicity is not in the final analysis "of any fundamental significance."[89] This indicates that even the historical person of Jesus fades in importance compared to the formal name, or rather compared to the confession expressed by it. Be that as it may, in light of the existence of far-reaching parallels in faith and life between Christians and non-Christians, Barth tries to attach the exclusivist claim of sole validity to something that is in fact without parallel, and ends up with a formalism that declares the formal simplicity of a name as the decisive criterion that—from the perspective of interreligious comparison—renders as meaningless everything that is connected to this name in a cognitive, ethical, or spiritual sense. So the price of insisting on Christian singularity in the face of the existence of interreligious parallels therefore consists in a dramatic emptying of Christian content. According to Barth, anything in Christianity that is true, good, and holy is so only on account of its relation to the name of Jesus, not because it is intrinsically true, good, or holy. In an interreligious sense Barth therefore ends up in a pure tautology: despite numerous parallels in the faith and life of other religions, Christianity nonetheless is uniquely true, because only here do we find an explicit reference to the name of Jesus. Put even more briefly: Only Christianity is true because there is truth only in Christianity. Yet even such claims are not without non-Christian parallels. For, as Wilfred Cantwell Smith has soberly remarked: "A claim to uniqueness is not unique."[90]

In a modern variation on Barth's position, the American Lutheran George Lindbeck has proposed that nothing in the faith and life of a non-Christian could possibly be *Christian* faith or *Christian* life, because in the case of the non-Christian it is not shaped by the reference to the name of Jesus or by a Christian language game.

88 Ibid. 10f.

89 "No 'empirical fact' *is* in itself what revelation is. No 'recognition' of such fact *is* in itself what faith is. The entire historical 'life of Jesus', for example, is, separate from the witness of those who encountered majesty in his humiliation, in itself nothing but the possibility, highest probability of *the annoyance*, and the hypothetical 'non-existence of this fact,' without being of any fundamental significance ("ohne von besonderem prinzipiellem Belang zu sein"), may carry this to extremes." Translated from the German original as in Barth 1987 (1923), 106.

90 Smith 1987, 64.

For example, no matter what loving deeds a non-Christian does, it could never be a case of Christian *agape*.[91] Beyond what has already been said, I do not wish to discuss any further this type of defense of exclusivism,[92] but only point to one implication of this strategy. If Barth and Lindbeck are right, then apparently Jesus made a huge mistake in presenting the merciful Samaritan as a model of life lived under the kingdom or rule of God. For no matter what this Samaritan did, it did not occur with any formal reference to the name of Jesus, nor was it *agape* as shaped by the Christian language game. And to his disciples' question of how one can distinguish a true prophet from a false one, Jesus likewise did fail to instruct them: Pay attention to whether the name of Jesus Christ, in all its formal simplicity, can be found in their proclamations. Rather, Jesus pointed to the criterion of the fruit of the alleged prophets' work, quite independent of any context marked by a particular religious label (Mt 7:15ff and 24:11f.). I can therefore not avoid the impression that such attempts at rescuing exclusivism not only lack any persuasive power, but that in reality they are also much less orthodox than they pretend to be.

When we theologically recognize as genuine the parallels in other religions to what in Christianity counts as an expression and fruit of salvific knowledge of God—in other words, when the authenticity of that which we encounter in other religions as being good, true, and holy, is not drawn into question simply because it doesn't arise from Christianity—then we have discarded exclusivism and crossed the boundary into inclusivism.

91 Cp. Lindbeck, 1984, esp. 39ff, and 46ff, as well as Lindbeck 1997.
92 On this, cp. Schmidt-Leukel, 1997, 122-164.

5. A Critique of Christian Inclusivism

On June 23rd, 1990, Pope John Paul II described in a letter to the Bishops of Asia the tasks and perspectives for the new millennium. Among other things, the letter says:

> On the eve of the third Christian millennium, an ever greater commitment to evangelization is imperative for all the local churches in Asia (…). Their special challenge is to proclaim the Good News where different religions and cultures meet, at the crossroads of social, political, and economic forces in today's world. (…) Although the Church gladly acknowledges whatever is true and holy in the religious traditions of Buddhism, Hinduism and Islam as a reflection of that truth which enlightened all men, this does not lessen her duty and resolve to proclaim without fail Jesus Christ who is "the way, and the truth, and life" (John 14:6) (…) The fact that the followers of other religions can receive God's grace and be saved by Christ apart from the ordinary means which he has established does not thereby cancel the call to faith and baptism which God wills for all people. It is a contradiction of the gospel and of the Church's very nature to assert, as some do, that the Church is only one way of salvation among many, and that her mission toward the followers of other religions should be nothing more than to help them being better followers of those religions.[1]

Compared to the remarks of the Southern Baptists' prayer guide that I mentioned at the beginning of the preceding chapter, these words show the advantage of Christian inclusivism over exclusivism. Compellingly and without dancing on theological eggshells, inclusivism emphasizes that God's grace does indeed reach all persons and that it forms the basis of a genuine possibility of salvation for all non-Christians. With this in mind, it is possible to "gladly acknowledge" everything good, true, and holy in non-Christian religions as a sign of the universality of grace. In contrast to the exclusivist perspective of the Southern Baptists, here Hinduism is not seen as a pervasively dark power controlled by Satan, but rather as a reality in which the light of Christ is reflected. Inclusivism's advantage over exclusivism becomes clear precisely with relation to the latter's two basic weaknesses: Inclusivism recognizes a universal possibility of salvation and it allows a theological appreciation of the parallels between Christianity and non-Christian religions as an expression of the universality of revelation and grace. Yet at the same time the words of the Pope show that the inclusivist esteem for non-Christian religions is not connected with a recognition of theological equality. According to inclusivism, non-Christian religions are not equal-

1 Quoted from in Sherwin, Kasimow 1999. 50ff.

-y valid paths of salvation. All salvation that comes from God, including the salvation of non-Christians, is mediated through Jesus Christ. But given that this truth is attested to only by the Christian church, it remains her duty to call all people to the Christian faith and to entrance into the church through baptism. On this point, Christian inclusivism does not differ from exclusivism: Like exclusivism, inclusivism too is concerned with the Christianization of the world and thus also, in the final analysis, with overcoming all other religions. This remains the ideal that needs to be pursued even if one acknowledges that under realistic conditions this ideal may not be attainable.

It is significant that in a central part of his letter the Pope refers to *Nostra aetate*, that is, the Second Vatican Council's "Declaration on the Relation of the Church to the Non-Christian Religions." For the Roman Catholic Church, this council marked the transition from moderate exclusivism to inclusivism. But similar to exclusivism, Christian inclusivism also has very old roots.

Inclusivism in the History of Theology: An Overview

As already mentioned in the preceding chapter, the New Testament does not yet contain anything like an elaborate theology of religions, but rather at best a few partial notions or individual elements that can be drawn upon to develop a theology of religions. In this spirit, I mentioned some verses to which representatives of exclusivist positions consistently refer. Alongside these, we also find other verses that express what one might rather call an inclusivist tendency. One may think here of Mt 8:10f where Jesus comments on his encounter with the Gentile centurion from Capernaum: "Truly I tell you, in no one in Israel have I found such faith. I tell you, many will come from east and west and will eat with Abraham and Isaac and Jacob …". Apparently this affirms the possibility of a salvific faith for those who do not belong to the Jewish people, which enables them to participate in the eschatological meal, a metaphorical image of the eternal fulfillment of the kingdom of God. A similar saying is found in the "Judgement of the Nations" in the Gospel of Matthew where Jesus makes a promise to those who never knew him but who did good in their lives: "Just as you did it to one of the least of these who are members of my family, you did it to me" (Mt 25:40). There seems to be a particular inclusivist emphasis in the Apostle Paul's so-called Areopagus sermon. Referring to an altar that is dedicated "To an unknown god," Paul announces to the Athenians that he has come to make known to them the God whom earlier they had worshipped as unknown. At the end, Paul says about people who do not know Christ that they should "search for God and perhaps grope for him and find him—though indeed he is not far from each one of us. For 'In him we live and move and have our being;' as even some of your own poets have said, 'For we too are his offspring'" (Acts 17:27-28). So Paul here even cites non-Christian authors in order to buttress a theological insight. Further texts in the book of Acts have similar leanings, and thus modify the verse from Acts so often deployed by exclusivists, according to which no other name but the Name of Jesus is given us for our salvation. So for example Acts 14:17 says that God "has not left himself without a witness" among the nations, and in Acts 10:35 that "in every nation anyone who fears him and does what is right is acceptable to him."

We meet much more defined inclusivist conceptions among a range of early church fathers. On the one hand, they developed these positions in order to determine the relationship of Christianity to pre-Christian Judaism, and then carried this over, on the other hand, in response to particular manifestations of the Greek-Roman religion, especially with respect to the religiously inflected Greek philosophy. The basic pattern they employed was the notion that the Logos (that is, the revelatory "word" of God—later identified as the second person of the Trinity) had become incarnate in all its fullness in Jesus Christ, while traces, fragments, or "seeds of the Logos" (*logoi spermatikoi)* can also be discerned outside of Christianity. Reflections along those lines are, for example, found in the church fathers Irenaeus (†c. 200), Clement of Alexandria († before 215), Origen (†250), Eusebius (†339), Ambrose (†397), and Augustine (354-450). Yet Justin Martyr (†165) was the first who expressed this idea. He writes (II. Apol 10:1-3):

> Our doctrine surpasses all human teaching, because we have the Word in his entirety in Christ, who has been manifested for us (...). All the right principles that philosophers and lawgivers have discovered and expressed they owe to whatever of the Word they have found and contemplated in part (...). The reason why they have contradicted each other is that they have not known the entire Word, which is Christ.[2]

The characterization of fullness and fragment is typical here: The fullness of the Logos, that is, of divine revelation, is found in Christ, while in others we find at best only "parts" or fragments of it. Yet Justin by no means considers these fragments of the Logos as being paltry. As he writes elsewhere (I Apol 46):

> Those who have lived in accordance with the Logos (*meta logou*) are Christians, even though they were called godless, such as, among the Greeks, Socrates and Heraclitus, and others like them; among the barbarians, Abraham, Ananias, Azarias, Misael, and Elijah, and many others ...[3]

Almost three centuries later, Augustine came to similar conclusions. In his late work *Retractationes* (I, 13,3), he writes:

> The very thing which is now called the Christian religion existed already among the ancients, nor was it absent at the beginning of the human race, until the coming of Christ in the flesh when the true religion which already existed began to be called Christian.[4]

2 Justin Marty, after J. Daniélou as quoted in Dupuis 1997, 58.
3 Ibid. 58.
4 Augustine, Retractationes I, 13:3. Ibid. 81.

Thus, in the first centuries of Christianity, there were not only exclusivist but also inclusivist views and the latter even seemed to dominate. As explained in the previous chapter, this changed in the fifth and sixth centuries, so that from that point on exclusivist understandings won the upper hand. However, inclusivism did not simply disappear without a trace, even if it clearly receded into the background for nearly fifteen hundred years. Individual theologians, such as Peter Abelard from the High Middle Ages (1079-1142) or Nicholas of Cusa (1401-1464) in the transition to modernity, represented inclusivist understandings. In Nicholas it is almost possible even to speak of an inclination toward pluralism.

Inclusivism regained its earlier dominance only in the theology of the twentieth century. Let us begin with a short glance into the Protestant camp. In the first two World Missionary Conferences, Edinburgh (1910) and Jerusalem (1928), which together more or less mark the beginning of the ecumenical movement among the Protestant churches, an inclusivist perspective became quite concrete—even if it did not ultimately prevail—in the appraisal of other religions. Participants in Edinburgh explicitly latched on to the inclusivist approaches of the early church fathers and judged "that in fact all these religions without exception disclose elemental needs of the human soul that Christianity alone can satisfy, and that in their higher forms they plainly manifest the working of the Spirit of God."[5] Even more unambiguous were statements from the Jerusalem World Missionary Conference. The Declaration of the International Missionary Council from the 8th of April 1928 contains statements that sound like a blueprint for *Nostra aetate*, "The Declaration on the Relation of the Church to the Non-Christian Religions," passed almost forty years later by the Second Vatican Council. In the Jerusalem Declaration it says:

> We know that, even apart from conscious knowledge of Him [i.e. "the living Jesus Christ"], when men are true to the best light they have, they are able to effect some real deliverance from many of the evils that afflict the world; And this should prompt us the more to help them to find the fulness of light and power in Christ (...) We rejoice to think that just because in Jesus Christ the light lightens every men shone forth in its full splendour, we find rays of that same light where he is unknown or even is rejected. We welcome every noble quality in non-Christian persons or systems as further proof that the Father, who sent His Son into the world, has nowhere left himself without witness. Thus, merely to give illustration (...) we recognize as part of the one Truth that sense of the Majesty of God and the consequent reverence in worship, which are conspicuous in Islam; the deep sympathy for the world's sorrow and unselfish search for the way of escape, which are at the heart of Buddhism; the desire for contact with ultimate reality conceived as spiritual, which is prominent in Hinduism; the belief in a moral order of the universe and the consequent insistence on moral conduct, which are inculcated by Confucianism (...)[6]

5 World Missionary Conference 1910, 267.
6 The Christian Life and Message 1928, 487 and 490f. Insertion in square brackets is mine.

And yet the inclusivist tendencies of the Edinburgh and Jerusalem Conferences did not prevail within the International Missionary Council nor the World Council of Churches, into which the Missionary Council was later integrated. Already at the Third International Missionary Conference, in Tambaram/Madras (1938), the exclusivist counter position rose up powerfully. Hendrik Kraemer, whose theology was strongly influenced by the exclusivist theology of Karl Barth, offered an impressive defense of exclusivism at this conference. On the whole it can be said that the influence of Barth and the so-called "Dialectical Theology", which depended strongly on him, as well as the influence of evangelical circles are responsible for the fact that many Protestant churches today still tend towards exclusivist stances. One consequence of this is that within the World Council of Churches (WCC) no type of the theology of religions prevailed and that therefore the declarations of the WCC mostly abstained from any clear decisions in the theology of religions, although within the WCC one certainly gave considerable weight to the praxis of interreligious dialogue and the resulting theological questions.

The situation developed differently within Roman Catholic theology. In the nineteenth and first half of the twentieth century, as already mentioned in the previous chapter, a trend toward a moderate exclusivism became clearly discernible within the official pronouncements of Rome. Numerous significant Catholic theologians transformed this trend into an inclusivist position in their work. In this connection the Catholic missiologists Otto Karrer and Thomas Ohm deserve special mention, as well as influential systematic theologians such as Yves Congar and Henry de Lubac. Yet it was Karl Rahner who initiated by far the most effective changes. With his theory of "anonymous Christians" and "anonymous Christianity" Rahner created a consistent inclusivist theology of religions, which is also deeply rooted in his transcendental theology. I will briefly sketch Rahner's reflections here because of their far-reaching effects.

According to Rahner, since the beginning of humanity every person has lived under the influence of grace. Because this is a feature of every human being's existence, Rahner refers to this as the human being's "supernatural existential." In this context, "grace" means nothing less than that God himself is present to each human being. In fact, a human being is *the* kind of being that is open to the presence of God. In contrast to animals, only a human being is in a position consciously to discern the finite as being finite. Yet in recognizing the finite nature of the finite, the notion of the infinite is presupposed. Everything finite is recognized as being finite in an essentially endless, infinite horizon. Despite its constant and, in a sense, "quiet" presence this infinite horizon can itself never be comprehended. Every act of recognition and comprehension has the structure of definition, that is, something is comprehended by placing it into a larger and more comprehensive whole. But this entails that the ultimate, infinite horizon of all comprehension cannot itself be comprehended or understood. For the person of faith, this mysterious and inconceivable ultimate horizon is nothing else than the reality of God. For this reason Rahner holds that some awareness of God is given to each human being on the basis of the structure of human cognition as such. In other words, God is present to everybody in a "transcendental" sense, that is, as the condition of the possibility of human cognition or understanding. If a person takes the courage of entrusting oneself to this mysterious infinity, this "holy mystery," and if, as Rahner puts it, he "abandons himself to the absolute mystery whom we call God,"[7] then this person accepts the grace of divine presence or divine "self-communication". This abandoning of oneself occurs in quite concrete acts of life: in performing acts of unselfish love, in accepting death, in hoping for an absolute and ultimate future. In humanity's religious traditions this awareness of the infinite mystery is made explicit as referring to the divine reality and thereby they make this fundamental attitude of faith possible. Non-Christian religions thus shape the concrete environment in which the non-Christian can and must put salvific faith into practice.

According to Rahner, Jesus Christ is a person who completely and perfectly accomplished this abandonment of oneself to the mystery of God and whose life—including his death and resurrection—has therefore become the perfect expression of this promise or assertion of the grace that is available to every person. Consequently for Rahner, Jesus is "the unique and *highest* instance of the actualization of the essence of human reality"[8] and as such is the perfected word of God to us all.[9] For that reason, Christianity is superior to all other religions in as much as it mediates this final word of God, which is Jesus himself. According to Rahner, non-Christian religions do indeed have genuine salvific significance for their adherents, but only as long as they have not heard the message of Jesus Christ, or as long as they have not yet heard this message in such a way that they were able to grasp in it the ultimate promise of the grace of God. Thus for Rahner Christianity is "the absolute religion, intended for all men, which cannot recognize any other religion beside itself as equally valid."[10] Rahner expresses the consequence of this in the following way:

> One can and must say that these extra-Christian religions are 'in themselves' and in principle abolished and superseded by the advent of Christ (...), so that the historic expansion of Christendom, which even today is not yet simply completed, is identical with a progressive abolition of the legitimacy of these religions.[11]

The legitimacy of non-Christian religions is therefore only of a temporary nature and consists of forming vague anticipations of that message that has attained its full and unambiguous shape in Jesus Christ. This hidden relation to Christ makes

7 Rahner 1978, 218 (German original: Rahner 1976, 216); see also Rahner 1978, 126-133.

8 Rahner 1978, 218.

9 Cp. ibid. 202, 214f. [Rahner interprets Jesus as the assertion or affirmation of divine grace for all of us. But note that the word "offer" which William v. Dych used to translate Rahner's "Zusage" ("assertion" or "affirmation") is clearly less optimistic than Rahner's own term.]

10 Thus the first thesis from Rahner's groundbreaking essay, "Christianity and the Non-Christian Religions." Rahner 1964. Here quoted from the translation in Hick, Hebblethwaite 2001, 22.

11 Rahner 1967, 371f. Translation from the German original.

it meaningful to speak of them as an "anonymous Christianity" and of their adherents as "anonymous Christians." Yet as soon as the message of Christ enters the consciousness of non-Christians with complete clarity, they can no longer remain "anonymous Christians" but are called to become explicit or confessing Christians. In this way Christianity is on the one hand the fulfillment of non-Christian religions, but on the other, as Rahner says, "*de iure*" also their abolition, in other words, it is that what actually and in the long run makes their existence superfluous.

Given the immense influence that Karl Rahner's theology exerted on Roman Catholic theology of the second half of the twentieth century, the inclusivism it represented became almost a standard model for Roman Catholicism. Yet in more recent years opposing influences have become stronger. To some Roman Catholic theologians, Rahner's position in the theology of religions goes too far. They want to stop at a moderate exclusivism and reject the notion of other religions as possible ways of salvation, even if this role, as Rahner suggests, is only of a temporary nature.[12] Other theologians try to develop further Rahner's inclusivism. This is particularly true of Jacques Dupuis, to whose reflections I will return below. For a time it was also true of Gavin D'Costa, who, though still representing an inclusivist position, has nonetheless to some extent moved back to a position before Rahner.[13] Still other Catholic theologians of religion, who initially also followed Rahner, soon saw the need to depart from Rahner's standpoint and embrace a pluralist orientation, no doubt partly in the sense of further developing Rahner's own ideas. Examples of such theologians include Raimon Panikkar[14] and Paul Knitter.[15] Yet for many Roman Catholic theologians, Rahner's position still continues to provide a kind of guideline in the theology of religions. Among other things, this could have to do with the fact that numerous official doctrinal pronouncements of the Second Vatican Council are close to Rahner's position and testify to his influence. The Council's pronouncements on a theology of religions can be summed up into the following three pertinent points:

First, the Council unambiguously underscored that even for those who do not belong to the Roman Catholic Church there exists a possibility for salvation. Thus, in *Lumen gentium* 16 it says: "Those also can attain to salvation who through no fault of their own do not know the Gospel of Christ or His Church, yet sincerely seek God and moved by grace strive by their deeds to do His will as it is known to them through the dictates of conscience." The Council extends this possibility of salvation even "to those who, without blame on their part, have not yet arrived at an explicit knowledge of God" in other words to atheists whose atheism results from subjectively honest motives.

12 Cp. for example Schmitz 1999, Scheffczyk 1999.
13 Cp. D'Costa 1986 and D'Costa 2000.
14 On this, cp. chapter 14, pp. 366-371.
15 On this, cp. chapter 6, pp. 152, 161f. and chapter 10, p. 235-238.

Second, the Council recognizes that authentic experiences of divine reality do occur in non-Christian religions, and indeed in this context it even employs the word "perception" (*perceptio*) of divine power. Hinduism and Buddhism, Islam and Judaism are explicitly acknowledged. Whatever truth and holiness is found in the religions, is according to the Council's declaration *Nostra aetate* 2, "a ray of that Truth which enlightens all men" and has found its fullness in Christ. In the decree on mission *Ad gentes,* the Council explicitly draws on the patristic notion of the *logoi spermatikoi* and speaks of the "seeds of the Word" which are to be found in non-Christian religions (*Ad gentes* 11).

Third, the traditional axiom *extra ecclesiam nulla salus* ("There is no salvation outside of the church") is now interpreted as meaning that only those who know about the necessity of the church for salvation and yet do not become part of it or do not stay in it fail to attain salvation (*Lumen gentium* 14). Beyond this—and this is significant for a theology of religions—the Council developed the notion of a graded membership of the church (*Lumen gentium* 14-16). In this connection, some speak of an "onion layers model," because membership in the church is imagined as being like a series of concentric circles layered like onion skins around the center. In a narrow and strict sense, it is only members of the Roman Catholic Church that belong to the church, to the extent that they possess the full Catholic faith informed by love. However, through the band of baptism and numerous commonalities in faith all other Christians are linked with them. As further layers or circles of a graded church membership, the Council at first mentions the Jewish people, then all those who recognize a creator, as especially the Muslims, furthermore "those who in shadows and images seek the unknown God" and finally all people of good will.[16]

With its first point, that is, with its confirmation of a possibility of salvation for non-Christians, the Council is still fully in line with the moderate exclusivism that the magisterial development had begun to follow prior to the Council. The renewed affirmation of the "seeds of the Word" and the "rays of the light" of Christ in non-Christian religions as well as their graded association with the church indicate the view that non-Christian religions can have a positive function for the salvation of non-Christians—even though the Council has not actually expressed this point unambiguously. The Council essentially introduced the transition from moderate exclusivism to inclusivism, a transition which at first was consistently advanced by the post-conciliar magisterial development, until the declaration *Dominus Iesus* (2000) brought matters to its present standstill at a highly ambivalent position.[17]

16 This model is repeated in the so-called "World Catechism" (Catechism of the Catholic Church, Nos. 836-848).

17 On this, cp. above chapter 4, pp. 98f.

Recent Developments

Post-Conciliar Doctrinal Developments in the Roman Catholic Church

Already in his inaugural encyclical, *Redemptor hominis* (1979), Pope John Paul II expressed his understanding "that the firm belief of the followers of the non-Christian religions (...) is also an effect of the Spirit of truth" (No. 6). In *Redemptoris missio* (1990) he repeated the notion of the presence and effectiveness of the Holy Spirit in non-Christian religions and explicitly connected this working of the Spirit with the possibility of salvation for non-Christians (Nos. 28-29, 55-56). At the same time he clarified "that the Church is the ordinary means of salvation and that she alone possesses the fullness of the means of salvation" (No. 55).

One year after *Redemptoris missio*, in 1991, the Congregation for the Evangelization of Peoples and the Pontifical Council for Interreligious Dialogue jointly published the document *Dialogue and Proclamation*. The document states: "Concretely, it will be in the sincere practice of what is good in their own religious traditions and by following the dictates of their conscience that the members of other religions respond positively to God's invitation and receive salvation in Jesus Christ, even while they do not recognize or acknowledge him as their savior (...)." (No. 29). The document continues to explain that religions contain "elements of grace capable of sustaining the positive response of their members to God's invitation" (No. 30). Everything salvific that is found in other religions is owed to the redemption in Christ. For this reason Christianity holds a unique position: for "Christians know this through their faith, while others remain unaware that Jesus Christ is the source of their salvation" (No. 29). Therefore the proclamation "aims at guiding people to explicit knowledge of what God has done for all men and women in Jesus Christ, and at inviting them to become disciples of Jesus through becoming members of the church" (No. 81). On the one hand, *Dialogue and Proclamation* therefore retains the claim of a singular superiority for Christianity among the religions, because it is only in Christianity that the true source of salvation is known and it is only in Christianity that it is proclaimed. On the other hand, this document just as clearly underscores the potential salvific function of other religions, that is, it declares that it has a positive salvific value if non-Christians put into practice whatever is true and good in their religions and which has its origin in the work of divine grace.

The position of *Dialogue and Proclamation* found further confirmation in the 1996 document *Christianity and the World Religions* officially published in 1997 by the Vatican's *International Theological Commission*. The document first makes a connection to *Redemptoris Missio* and then explains (No. 84): "Given this explicit recognition of the presence of the Spirit of Christ in the religions, one cannot exclude the possibility that they exercise as such a certain salvific function; that is, despite their ambiguity, they help men achieve their ultimate end." The document gives relatively concrete examples of how one should understand the salvific function of other religions (Nos. 86-87):

> Salvation is obtained through the gift of God in Christ, but not without human response and acceptance. The religions can also help the human response, insofar as they impel man to seek God, to act in accord with his conscience, to live a good life (...).The religions can be carriers of saving truth only insofar as they raise men to true love.

Finally, the superiority of the church is once again highlighted (Nos. 85-86):

> In the religions the same Spirit who guides the Church is at work. But the universal presence of the Spirit cannot be compared to his special presence in the Church of Christ.(...) Only the Church is the body of Christ, and only in it is given in its full intensity the presence of the Spirit. Therefore, to no one can belonging to the Church of Christ and participation in the fullness of the saving gifts which alone are found in it be a matter of indifference (...). The religions can exercise the function of a *praeparatio evangelica*; they can prepare different peoples and cultures for welcoming the saving event, which has already taken place. (...)The religions can therefore be, in the terms indicated, means helping the salvation of their followers, but they cannot be compared to the function that the Church realizes for the salvation of Christians and those who are not.

Dialogue and Proclamation and *Christianity and the World Religions* thus completed the process begun at the Second Vatican Council in which the Roman Catholic Church moved from a position of moderate exclusivism to one of inclusivism. It affirmed that non-Christian religions mediate a saving knowledge of God, but that within Christianity—and particularly within the Roman Catholic Church—this knowledge exists in a manner surpassing all others. The fundamental matrix however remains one of fragment and fullness: Other religions do contain the working of the Spirit, but the fullness of the Spirit-given means of salvation is found only in the church.

Pluralizing Inclusivism: Mark Heim and Jacques Dupuis

The developments within Roman Catholic theology did not fail to influence the Protestant arena. Most notable in this respect is the aforementioned departure of some evangelical theologians to an inclusivist position, Clark Pinnock above all. Pinnock's proximity to the inclusivism of Roman Catholic theology is unmistakable.[18] By his own admission, he gives preference to the thought on this matter found in the documents of the Second Vatican Council, rather than to most of the evangel-

18 Cp. for example Pinnock 1995.

ical positions.[19] Pinnock's main concern is to take into account the universal salvific will of God and to acknowledge theologically that sanctity is also found "in persons and religions other than Christian."[20] At the same time, Pinnock warns against a wholesale recognition of other religions as paths of salvation. Religions neither all teach the same things, nor do they have the same goals, nor do they all correspond equally to the will of God. Nonetheless, God can use non-Christian religions—or elements of them—as means of grace. In this sense, Christ is and remains the norm and measure of their Christian assessment.[21]

Apart from the fact that Pinnock does not give his inclusivism an ecclesiological focus, his position hardly differs from the more cautious versions of Roman Catholic inclusivism. In recent years, however, two other theologians have proposed new forms of inclusivism: Mark Heim, like Pinnock originally of an evangelical background, and Jacques Dupuis, a Roman Catholic. Both attempt in their own way to introduce certain pluralizing elements into inclusivism, and both identify their position as "pluralistic inclusivism."[22]

Mark Heim developed and increasingly nuanced his approach in three books published between 1985 and 2001.[23] Basic to his ideas is his critique that in the theology of religions the typical debate on the salvific role of non-Christian religions operates with a uniform concept of salvation assuming a single goal of salvation that is identical for all people. This, he holds, does not do justice to the fact that the conceptions of salvation differ significantly, at times even radically, among the various religions. Every religion essentially teaches its own path of salvation, a path oriented to that particular goal of salvation which is peculiar to this specific religion. Thus the Buddhist path of salvation, in Heim's view, does not lead to the Christian goal of salvation, just as the Christian way of life does not lead to the Buddhist Nirvāṇa.[24] Heim then proposes the hypothesis that the various religions' different goals or ends of salvation correspond to different but nevertheless real eschatological states. The salvific paths of the various religions are therefore true and effective paths of salvation, but each one of them leads to a different "salvation." Exclusivists thus correctly emphasize, according to Heim, that Christ alone is the way to salvation *as it is understood by Christians*. But they fail to recognize that the soteriological ends pursued by other religions do have some value and can be attained by following the corresponding path of salvation. *Pluralists,* says Heim, either operate with a diffuse and vague notion of salvation, or they assume in a more or less hidden fashion the superiority of one particular notion of salvation, favored by the pluralist, thereby falling back into an inclusivist position. An *inclusivism,* such as for example the one represented by Rahner, harms the integrity of other religions and ignores that these do

19 Cp. Heim 1995, 73.
20 Pinnock 1995, 102.
21 Cp. Pinnock 1995, 99f., 113f., 116f. and Pinnock 1997, 106-110.
22 Heim 1994, 355; Dupuis 2002, 95, 255. Dupuis also proposes the term "inclusive pluralism."
23 Cp. Heim 1985, 1995b, 2001.
24 To this extent Heim agrees with DiNoia's understanding. Cp. DiNoia 1992.

not in fact lead to the salvation of Christ in some unclear or anonymous way, but rather are clearly and appropriately oriented toward the salvation they themselves proclaim. Thus, according to Heim, the fundamental problem of all three positions in the theology of religions consists of the assumption of one single eschatological goal of salvation for all. The "pluralistic inclusivism" Heim represents seeks to avoid this "mistake."

What if God, asks Heim, allowed all persons to reach that eschatological goal that they themselves desire or for which they strive? What if Nihilists attained an irreversible annihilation, Buddhists Nirvāṇa, advaitic Hindus unity with Brahman, Muslims the Qur'anic paradise, and Christians communion with the triune God? At first such a thought might seem strange. And yet Heim reminds us that the Christian tradition did not always only operate with the binary alternative of either eternal damnation or eternal bliss, but rather reckoned with the possibility of a certain diversity of eschatological states, as, for example, various types of hell punishments, several forms of limbo (*limbus puerorum, limbus patrum*), purgatory (*purgatorium)* and "heaven."[25] Yet how might we conceive of theologically a possible diversity of eschatological states in relation to the different salvific ends of various religions and philosophies?

In answering this question, Heim went through a certain development. In his 1985 book *Is Christ the Only Way?* Heim judged that the Buddhist Nirvāṇa, the Hindu unity with Brahman, and even humanistic, purely this-worldly notions of the future are "not noticeably different from hell. In all of these there is separation from the personal God known in Jesus, the extinction of personal and bodily existence, the end of all relationship. "[26] Yet at the same time, Heim assumed that for all those who, despite their affiliation with a non-theistic religion or atheistic system, had nevertheless certain inclinations toward a personal relationship with God, there might be the possibility of a further personal development after death and a postmortem encounter with Christ.[27] Thus Heim initially supported a version of moderate exclusivism.

In *Salvations* (1995) Heim expresses himself in a considerably more nuanced way. As before, he advises Christians to consider alternative religious ends "as something to be avoided, even in cases carrying some measure of the meaning of 'damnation.'" [28] But these ends should not be seen "as positive evils (though such evils may also be live possibilities), but they are aims different than the best that Christians know and hope for."[29] Heim thus differentiates between three basic eschatolog-

25 In all three works Heim particularly refers to Dante cp. Heim 1985, 146ff.; 1995b, 164; 2001, 99ff., 275ff.
26 Heim 1985, 146.
27 Cp. ibid. 148f.
28 Heim 1995b, 163.
29 Ibid.

ical possibilities: *first,* "lostness," which he conceives of as ultimate annihilation[30]; *second,* "penultimate religious fulfillments," in other words, the various salvific ends of non-Christian religions; and *third*, the final fulfillment in "communion with the triune God."[31] At the same time, Heim already indicates here that the Trinity provides the matrix for the ontological connection among the "penultimate" salvific ends as well as their connection with the ultimate salvific goal of Christianity.[32] The penultimate salvific goals of non-Christian religions are possible on the basis of certain aspects of the Trinity and the Trinity's relationship to the world. From that perspective, it appears that non-Christian religions envision their goals in a somewhat isolated way, because they are unaware of the fullness of the divine Trinity.[33] Heim claims that the Christian salvific end of "communion with the triune God...encompasses dimensions of other fulfillments" and is therefore "better because more consistent with the nature of the ultimate, and so more inclusive."[34]

In *The Depth of the Riches* (2001) Heim further develops and concretizes this notion. In contrast to his *Salvations* of 1995, Heim now no longer uses the term "salvation" in the plural, but rather reserves it for the Christian salvific end, the communion with the triune God and with God's creatures in and through Christ. Only *this* end is "salvation" in its full and genuine sense. Only here does one attain full communion with God, whereas the salvific goals of other religions get stuck in a limited relationship to God or, better, to certain aspects of the Trinity.[35] Heim clarifies this using the examples of Buddhism, advaitic Hinduism, and Islam.[36] According to Heim, intra-trinitarian relationships are characterized on the one hand by a kind of apophatic emptiness, in so far as each of the divine persons points completely away from itself to the others; an emptiness or selflessness in which—as Heim says—each divine person "makes space for the others." A similar observation holds for the Trinity's relationship to the world, in that God retreats or "contracts" in order to "make space" for the creation and grant creatures their autonomy. It is this emptiness and selflessness that Buddhism grasps correctly and around which Buddhist conceptions of salvation are oriented. On the other hand, intra-trinitarian relationships are characterized by a complete reciprocal interpenetration of divine persons, a total coinherence or immanence. And this holds similarly for God's relationship to creation, to the extent that God is immanent to every creature. Advaitic Hinduism correctly understands this aspect of the Trinity, namely, the unity which underlies all differentiation. This unity is reflected in the Advaitic end of a non-dualistic unity between Brahman and Ātman. A genuine and specific relationship to God therefore under-

30 Later, Heim differentiated again between the idolization of an isolated good creation that leads to a kind of hellish or pre-hellish existence, and the total rejection of creation which ends in annihilation. Cp. Heim 2001, 272f.

31 Cp. ibid. 165.

32 Cp. Heim 1995b, 65ff; Heim 2001, 198.

33 Cp. Heim 1995b, 165f.

34 Ibid. 165.

35 Cp. Heim 2001, 19, 179, 289, and elsewhere.

36 Cp. Heim 2001, 209-239; Heim 2001b.

girds both Buddhism and Advaita, yet in both cases the relationship is not characterized by personal communion and therefore lacks the full reality of the Trinity and of the God-world relationship.

Given the unity of the three divine persons, creation encounters God as a single unified reality. The unified impression God leaves with creation can be understood impersonally as a kind of eternal law or personally as the divine commandment or divine will. Heim suggests Islam as an excellent example of the latter. The salvific end as conceived by Islam is not characterized by an impersonal relationship to God; rather, the relationship here takes on unquestionably personal characteristics, indeed characteristics of a personal communion with God. However, since Islam shares neither the belief in a Trinitarian God, nor in the incarnation, it neither grasps the depths of divine existence *as* communion nor humanity's participation in the inner-divine communion as it is made possible through the incarnation. The ultimate intensity of communion with God thus also falls outside the scope of the Islamic salvific end.

Thus while the Christian goal of salvation includes all dimensions of communion with God, the salvific goals of other religions represent gradual approaches to God and remain limited to specific dimensions or aspects of God. Nevertheless, according to Heim, we are talking about real eschatological states. Hence there exists a plurality of ultimate salvific ends and within this plurality there is a hierarchy according to which the highest salvific end encompasses all other dimensions.[37] And yet the "penultimate" salvific ends have, compared to the Christian salvation, their own specific individuality in as much as they, in a sense, represent an isolated aspect of the divine nature, in which they thus participate in an intensity not available in the same way within the Christian salvific end.[38]

Taking into account the belief in God's universal salvific will, Heim assumes that no person without any fault of their own is denied the attainment of the highest, in other words, the Christian goal of salvation. Thus he reckons with the possibility that the salvific ends of non-Christian religions may either constitute final eschatological states or interim stages on the way to the Christian salvation.[39] Therefore a person born and socialized into a non-Christian religion nonetheless may still have the chance, after reaching the salvific end of his or her own religion, to finally attain the full communion with the triune God. There is even a certain pull in this direction. Not only because God desires the full salvation of all persons, but also because the other salvific ends are rooted in different dimensions of the divine Trinity. Since the dimensions of the Trinity are tightly interconnected, each aspect of the Trinity is inherently related to the full Trinitarian community.[40] To this extent, all religions that mediate a genuine salvific end are rooted in an authentic revelation of the Trin-

37 Cp. Heim 2001, 255.
38 Cp. Heim 2001, 238, 283; Heim 1995, 166.
39 Cp. Heim 2001, 268, 279.
40 Cp. Heim 2001, 268f.

itarian God, though not in the complete revelation of God *as* the triune One.[41] All salvation, even that in the form of fragmented, "penultimate" salvific ends, is made possible by Christ, but is not—except in the case of Christian salvation—mediated through an explicit faith in Christ.[42]

Although there is a kind of pull from God in the direction of full salvation, it can be resisted through sin, whether through completely closing oneself off to God, or through a partial closing off that stops at one single dimension of divine life and resists the full personal communion with the triune God.[43] From a Christian perspective the salvific ends of other religions are to be evaluated positively only to the extent that they are rooted in a genuine relationship to the Trinitarian God and serve as eschatological interim stages on the way to genuine salvation. Yet these salvific ends are to be evaluated negatively and as a form of lostness when people fail to move past them, so that to them these "penultimate" ends become the final, ultimate stage.[44]

The inclusivist nature of Heim's conception is obvious. Ultimately, Heim too understands the function of non-Christian religions as a "preparation for the gospel" (*praeparatio evangelii*), yet shifts this preparation into the realm of postmortem speculation. In so doing, he falls prey to his own critique of Rahnerian inclusivism. In *Is Christ the Only Way?* Heim sharply dismisses the thesis of "anonymous Christianity" as being "imperialistic," and criticizes it by emphasizing the differences and diversity of the many religious ends and paths of salvation.[45] This objection is still present in *The Depth of the Riches,* where Heim says that the designation of "anonymous Christianity" is not an "accurate" description of another religion, and that "its ordinary function there is to its own religious end, not the Christian one."[46] Yet at the very same place Heim confirms his own understanding that the salvific ends of other religions have the "capacity to serve as a step toward salvation," that is, toward the Christian salvation, because and to the extent that these ends are rooted in a genuine relation to a particular dimension of the triune God. According to Christian belief, the respective religious end "can only with difficulty remain isolated from the entire triune life of which it is one dimension."[47] Thus Heim postulates that the salvific ends of non-Christian religions have a hidden or anonymous inclination to the higher Christian end of salvation. Hence it is not surprising to find the image of concentric circles, so characteristic of inclusivism, also in Heim's scenario—albeit not in the form of the Roman Catholic onion layers model, which grades all other religions according to their proximity to or distance from the Roman Catholic Church, but in the form of Dante's conception of several circles of heaven and hell,

41 Cp. ibid. 275.
42 Cp. ibid. 286.
43 Cp. ibid. 272ff., 288f.
44 Cp. ibid. 289.
45 Cp. Heim 1985, 137f.
46 Heim 2001, 269.
47 Ibid.

to which Heim refers repeatedly.[48] For Heim, the measure is not ecclesiological but doctrinal. His concentric grading of the salvific ends of other religions relates their proximity to or distance from a full understanding of the Trinity (that is, the Trinity as it is understood by Heim). Regarding his oft-repeated concession that other religions could develop similar scenarios in which they place their particular salvific end at the center, and then rank those of other religions as being preliminary, fragmentary, or lacking, Heim remarks that:

> … the notion of the "best" religious end goes hand in hand with the understanding of the nature of God or the ultimate reality. One will not view salvation [i.e. the Christian salvation] as the true religious end unless one believes in the triune God and desires communion with that God.[49]

This reveals that Heim's inclusivism is based on the simple idea of Christianity as having the truest description of God, so that the truth and potential salvific efficacy of other religions is graded according to how much or how little their conceptions of transcendent reality have in common with this most accurate description. Yet his claim that in this way he does better justice to the diversity, integrity, and differences of religions than is done from a pluralist perspective or from the perspective of a Rahnerian inclusivism escapes my comprehension. Moreover, Heim's "pluralistic inclusivism" stays as it were at the lower end of the inclusivist spectrum.[50] For whereas Christian inclusivists typically acknowledge that non-Christian religions can contribute to the full salvation of non-Christians, Heim views them as leading only to deficient salvific ends, even if in the end they can be seen as potential transition stages to full Christian salvation.

The Belgian Jesuit Jacques Dupuis (1923-2004) taught from 1948-84 at the Theological Jesuit Institute of Vidyajoti in New Delhi, and from 1984-98 at the Pontifical Gregorian University in Rome. In Rome he also worked as a consultant for the Pontifical Council for Inter-religious Dialogue. His first book on the theology of religions appeared in 1989 in French and in 1991 in English translation with the title *Jesus Christ at the Encounter of World Religions.*[51] In *Toward a Christian Theology of Religious Pluralism* (1997)—which appeared in both English[52] and French and to great international acclaim[53]—Dupuis presented his own version of inclusivism, which had been indicated in the earlier work, a systematic exposition. In 1998, the Roman Congregation for the Doctrine of the Faith launched an investigation into

48 Heim 1995, 164; Heim 2001, 101 and frequently.
49 Heim 2001, 284. Insertion in square brackets is mine.
50 On this, cp. also the similar critique leveled by Hick 2001c.
51 Cp. Dupuis 1993.
52 Cp. Dupuis 1997.
53 In 1999 a Portuguese translation appeared and in 2000 a Spanish translation. In Dupuis, 1999, Dupuis refers to 47 English and French reviews. According to O'Collins 2003, 389, more than 100 reviews have meanwhile appeared worldwide. For a thorough German-language discussion of this book, see Waldenfels 1999.

this work. This led to a "Notification"[54] published in January 2001 that was closely connected, chronologically and content-wise, with the publication of *Dominus Iesus.*[55] The "Notification" presents itself "as a refutation of erroneous or harmful opinions, which, prescinding from the author's intentions, could be derived from reading the ambiguous statements and insufficient explanations found in certain sections of the text."[56] Dupuis signed this "notification" and in so doing "committed himself to assent to the stated theses and, in his future theological activity and publications, to hold the doctrinal contents indicated in the Notification," as well as adding the text of the notification to all future editions and translations of the book.[57] During his clash with the Congregation of Faith, Dupuis was working on a shorter edition of his 1997 work, which appeared in the Italian language in autumn 2001 and in English,[58] French, and Spanish translation in 2002. In this work Dupuis clarifies his position in light of the charges leveled against him.

As Christian Heller aptly noted, Dupuis' theology can be described "as elliptical. His position circles around two main points: the qualitatively unattainable role of Jesus Christ on the one hand and the appreciation of the plurality of religions on the other."[59] On the one hand Dupuis advocates a number of classical Christian-inclusivist positions:[60] Jesus is personally identical with the eternal Son of God, the second person of the Trinity, and as such is unique.[61] In his person and especially through his death and resurrection, Jesus is "constitutive" of the salvation for all humanity.[62] In addition, Jesus is the unsurpassed and unequalled revealer: "No revelation, (...), either before or after Christ can either surpass or equal the one vouchsafed in Jesus Christ, the divine Son incarnate."[63] The description of God as Trinity, as rooted in

54 The official English text of the "Notification" and the official commentary are both found on the Vatican's website. On the legal procedure, see also Chia 2003, 49ff. and Waldenfels 2001.

55 On *Dominus Iesus* cp. above chapter 4, pp. 98f.

56 See: http://www.vatican.va/roman_curia/congregations/cfaith/documents/rc_con_cfaith_doc_20010124_dupuis_en.html

57 Cp. ibid. According to Chia 2003, 51, this interpretation of the signature was added to the text of the "Notificatio", without Dupuis' knowledge, after he had signed the notification. Allegedly Dupuis had however decided not to challenge this procedure in order to avoid a further extension of the process and the "shock and trauma" associated with it. In an official Foreword to the publication of *Dominus Iesus* and the "Notificatio" in Müller 2003, the Congregation on the Doctrine of Faith explains: "Certainly the declaration *Dominus Iesus* and the notification should not hinder healthy theological discussion ('die gesunde theologische Erörterung')..." (Müller 2003, 12). Given this context, this word choice is deeply shocking. Apparently here a "healthy" theological discussion is being distinguished from what is implied as an unhealthy or sick theological discussion and the criterion that distinguishes between health and sickness in theology is not an academic or scholarly one but one of conformity to Rome. How often in human history have rigorous reprisals been defended by saying that they are directed only at "unhealthy" phenomena?

58 Cp. Dupuis 2002 and O'Collins 2003.

59 Heller 2003, 177.

60 On this cp. also the careful analyses in Heller 2001, 421-446, and Heller 2003.

61 Dupuis 1997, 191, 294ff.

62 Dupuis 1997, 387; similarly ibid. 295, 297, 304f, 350.

63 Dupuis 1997, 250, see similarly also ibid. 204, 283, 286, 318f., 388.

God's revelation in Jesus Christ, is not only one image of God among many, but "objectively, though imperfectly and only analogically, corresponds to the reality of the Absolute."[64] Compared to this, the insights of other religions into the divine mystery are incomplete and in need of fulfillment in Christ.[65] The Christ-event is the culmination of salvation history.[66] Therefore, the mystery of salvation in Christ has its overt and explicit presence only in the Church and is completely mediated only by her. "In other religious traditions, it is present in an implicit, concealed manner, in virtue of an incomplete mode of mediation constituted by these traditions."[67]

On the other hand, Dupuis is clearly at pains to go beyond certain impasses of Christian inclusivism. According to Dupuis, the basic question of all current theology of religions is whether the plurality of religions is but to be accepted or tolerated as a historical fact (pluralism *de facto)* or whether this plurality can be welcomed theologically and evaluated as a positive factor in the divine plan of salvation (pluralism *de iure*).[68] He clearly opts for the latter.[69] Truth and grace in other religions ought not to be reduced to mere "seeds" or "stepping-stones" that can be used and superseded by Christian revelation. Rather, each of them possess their own autonomous value.[70] The relationship of Christianity to other religions is no longer to be characterized in terms of "realization here and stepping-stones there" or even in terms of "absoluteness (...) and only potentialities," but rather as "relational interdependence"[71] or as "complementarity"[72]—and this not in the sense of the "fulfillment theory" according to which only Christianity unilaterally brings to fulfillment the fragmentary truths of other religions, but rather in the sense of "mutual complementarity" or "mutual enrichment and transformation."[73] For not every truth and grace that is found in other religions is contained in Christianity in the same way.[74]

No doubt, Dupuis' appreciation of religious plurality is remarkable. But can it be consistently reconciled with his basic inclusivist position? Heller appropriately asks "whether one can, as Dupuis advocates, coherently embrace in one position both centers of his ellipsis (the uniqueness and constitutiveness of Christ—the appreciation of religious diversity)..."[75] According to Paul Knitter, Dupuis' Christology, which sees Christ as constitutive of salvation, prevents him from being able to surmount the traditional fulfillment theory.[76] Conversely, Cardinal Josef Ratzinger em-

64 Dupuis 1997, 263.
65 Cp. ibid, 279.
66 Cp. ibid. 303.
67 Ibid. 319.
68 Cp. Dupuis 1997, 11, 211; Dupuis 2002, 255.
69 Cp. Dupuis 1997, 386ff; Dupuis 2002, 255.
70 Cp. Dupuis 1997, 388.
71 Ibid. 204.
72 Ibid. 326.
73 Ibid. 326 and 389.
74 Cp. ibid. 388.
75 Heller 2003, 177.
76 Cp. Knitter 1999, 229 and 342.

phasizes that "the average reader" of Dupuis' 1997 book "despite all his [i.e. Dupuis'] loyalty to the uniqueness of Jesus Christ nonetheless must take from it an inclination to the pluralist position."[77]

Dupuis attempts to combine both poles of his thought by the following reflections on the nature of *revelation*, the role of the *Spirit*, and the *Kingdom of God*.[78] According to Dupuis, the diversity of religions mirrors the diversity of God's revelation to humanity.[79] If it is taught that Jesus Christ embodies the fullness of revelation, this "fullness" needs to be understood in a "qualitative," not a "quantitative" sense. In the qualitative sense Jesus is the fullness of revelation because of his unique identity with the eternal Word of God, the second person of the Trinity. In the quantitative sense, however, Jesus does not represent this "fullness," since his human consciousness unavoidably shares in the limitations of the human spirit.[80] "No human consciousness, even the human consciousness of the Son of God, can exhaust the Divine Mystery."[81] "The historical particularity of Jesus imposes upon the Christ-event irredeemable limitations." His revelation therefore remains "incomplete". The incarnation of the Logos in Jesus does not exhaust the work of the Logos, which is and remains effective also in other religions and other savior-figures before and after the Incarnation.[82] Something similar is also true of the divine Spirit.[83] Divine salvific activity occurs through the universal working of the Spirit, which attained its zenith in Jesus Christ, but is not restricted to a particular time.[84] Since the working of the Logos and of the Spirit transcends the particularity of the Christ-event and of Christianity, the kingdom of God is, according to Dupuis greater and wider than the church.[85] It is not only individual non-Christians, standing in grace, who belong to the Kingdom of God, but the non-Christian religions too can contribute to the expansion of the Kingdom of God through the true and salvific elements found within them. Wherever Christians and non-Christians are engaged in the integral liberation of persons and promote religious or spiritual values, they are working together on building up the Reign of God and are together heading towards its eschatological

77 Ratzinger 2003, 44. Insertion in square brackets is mine.

78 It is in fact at precisely these points that the Roman "Notificatio" sees the danger that Dupuis' book could occasion "erroneous and harmful opinions." According to the notification it is "contrary to the Catholic faith" to hold, "that revelation in Jesus Christ (or the revelation of Jesus Christ) is limited, incomplete or imperfect" (No. 3), or "that the salvific action of the Holy Spirit extends beyond the one universal salvific economy of the Incarnate Word " (No. 5), or "to consider the different religions of the world as ways of salvation complementary to the Church" (No. 6).

79 Dupuis 1997, 387.

80 Cp. ibid. 249.

81 Ibid. 249.

82 Ibid. 298f., similarly ibid. 320, 388.

83 Cp. ibid. 300.

84 Cp. ibid. 197, similarly ibid. 207, 298-300, 321.

85 Cp. ibid. 341, 344f.

fulfillment. It is this already extant and deeply spiritual communion that can become explicit in and through interreligious dialogue.[86]

The mutual complementarity of Christianity and non-Christian religions can turn into convergence through dialogue and the common work on the Kingdom of God. The convergence Dupuis has in mind is oriented toward the eschatological fullness of the Kingdom of God, when, according to Dupuis, all religions will be subordinate to Christ as the one Lord, or better, when Christ will finally become apparent as the source of eternal salvation.[87] Thus, Dupuis' appreciation of religious diversity does not change the view that all religions, to the extent that they contain what is good, true, and holy, are ultimately related to Christ as their true source and subordinate to him as their eternal Lord. What will become apparent in the eschaton holds true already in the here and now: Christianity and non-Christian religions represent "various, though not equal, paths" of salvation.[88] The complementarity between Christianity and non-Christian religions, as Dupuis has meanwhile clarified terminologically, is "mutual but asymmetrical."[89] In other words,

> whereas other religious traditions can find, and are destined to find, in the Christ event their fullness of meaning—but without being absorbed or dispossessed—the reverse is not true: God's self-manifestation and self-giving in Jesus Christ are not in need of a true completion by other traditions (…).[90]

Yet if the revelation of God in Jesus, as testified to by Christianity, is superior to the revelation of all other religions from beginning to end; if—to put it another way—Dupuis maintains his inclusivist position undiminished, what then becomes of his intention not only to acknowledge the plurality of religions as a matter of fact but also to legitimize and appreciate it theologically as a "pluralism *de iure*"? If other religions are not equal to Christianity, and if eschatologically the Lordship of Christ over other religions will eventually and ultimately become obvious, in what sense are we then to understand Dupuis' talk of a "lasting role"[91] of the religious traditions? According to Dupuis this should be viewed in analogy to the notion of the "unbroken covenant" of God with the Jews. The covenant that God made through Noah with the peoples of the world continues unaltered and is just as little obliterated by the climax of God's salvific action in Christ as is God's covenant with Israel.[92] Given Dupuis' consistent emphasis on the inequality of the various "covenants" or paths of salvation, this must be a matter of an enduring provisional situation that will only be ended eschatologically—and then only in one direction! Yet has this idea really achieved a theological appreciation of religious diversity? If "pluralism *de iure*" means—as Dupuis says it does—that religious diversity is not "only per-

86 Cp. ibid. 346.
87 Cp. ibid. 389.
88 Ibid. 328.
89 Dupuis 2002b, 65, similarly Dupuis 2002, 257.
90 Dupuis 2002, 257.
91 Dupuis, 1997, 211.
92 Cp. ibid. 232f.

mitted by God" but "positively willed by him",[93] then Dupuis' suggestion would ultimately amount to the conclusion that God wants this temporariness and inequality to continue until its eschatological resolution. This would mean that God wants some people to have access to the highest revelation, while others have to be satisfied—permanently—with "less deep," "preliminary," "incomplete," "not definitive," "qualitatively surpassable"[94] forms of revelation. This would be a more or less inclusivist version of double predestination: though non-Christians are not predestined to damnation, they are nevertheless predestined to permanently (!) follow deficient paths of salvation. Presumably Dupuis did not intend this consequence. And yet this is the unavoidable result of his inclusivist premises. If one shares the inclusivist conviction of the unique superiority of God's revelation in Jesus Christ and the deficient character of non-Christian religions in comparison to Christianity, then any talk of a "*de iure* pluralism" makes no sense, or rather only in a counter-productive way. An honest inclusivist conviction should ideally aim at sharing with all people, as far as possible, the one revelation that is superior to all others, in other words to Christianize the world and thus ideally overcome religious diversity. If people nonetheless oppose the call to conversion to Jesus Christ, then, from an inclusivist (and exclusivist) perspective, the diversity of religions is to be tolerated as a "*de facto* pluralism." Yet to speak of a "*de iure* pluralism" on the premises of an inclusivist theology, would not do justice to the universal salvific will of God, but rather imply that God wants the majority of humanity to participate lastingly in inferior paths of salvation In the theology of religions, talk about a "*de iure* pluralism" only makes sense if plurality is linked to equality. But this is precisely what would burst the limits of inclusivism.

Critical Discussion

In the theology of religions inclusivism is naturally criticized from two sides: For exclusivists, inclusivism goes decidedly too far; indeed, in their eyes inclusivism seems like a half-hearted pluralism. For pluralists, inclusivism does not go far enough. It takes a step in the right direction, but then stops in mid-course by re-coining the original claim of exclusivism as a claim of the singular superiority of Christianity. I do not wish to go further here into the critique that exclusivists direct at inclusivism. Mostly they accuse inclusivism of presenting a reduced form of Christian belief, of deviating from the biblical witness, and of undermining the motivation for mission—a critique that depends totally on the highly problematic exclusivist way of reading the "biblical witness." From my perspective, inclusivism offers a significantly stronger theological position than does exclusivism. For inclusivism precisely avoids

93 Dupuis 1997, 386.

94 See the list of Dupuis' various characterizations of revelation in non-Christian religions in Heller 2001, 445.

the two most basic weaknesses of exclusivism: on the one hand, inclusivism is far better able than exclusivism at allowing for the universal salvific will of God, and it assumes that salvific faith, also in the case of non-Christians, manifests itself and has its impact already in this life (and not only after death). On the other hand, it is no problem for inclusivism that there are many significant parallels to Christian faith in the faith and life of non-Christian religions and their adherents. In these parallels, inclusivism is wont to see the "seeds of the Word of God" and in this sees its own position confirmed. So in what follows I concentrate on those objections that are predominantly leveled against inclusivism from a pluralist perspective.[95]

Evaluating Religious Diversity

Perhaps the most widespread critique of inclusivism is that it illegitimately usurps other religions and thus assumes an attitude that is counterproductive to dialogue. Hans Küng, for example, early on raised this objection to Rahner's theory of "anonymous Christianity" and has repeated it many times since. According to Hans Küng, this "factually reduces other religions to having a lower or partial knowledge of the truth, whereas it elevates one's own religion to the status of a supersystem from the get go. What looks like tolerance, in practice turns out to be a kind of conquest through embrace, a kind of integration through relativization and loss of identity."[96] According to Küng, "it would be impossible to find anywhere in the world a sincere Jew, Muslim or atheist who would not regard the assertion that he is an 'anonymous Christian' as presumptuous. To bring the partner to the discussion into our own circle in this way closes the dialogue before it has even begun."[97] Hans Küng himself is not a pluralist; he has repeatedly distanced himself from not only exclusivism but also inclusivism and pluralism without clarifying his own position in the theology of religions. Yet pluralists have frequently repeated his objection that inclusivism makes an illegitimate usurpation,[98] while some exclusivists have also adopted it as an argument against inclusivism.[99]

To my mind, the charge of an illegitimate usurpation of other religions is a particularly weak argument against inclusivism. Every religion that forms a judgment about other religions and world views does so on the basis of its own religious understandings. In so doing we can by no means exclude the possibility that the representatives of the religion or world view in question will not agree with the way how it is interpreted or judged. However, I do not see what is illegitimate here. For

95 See the more extensive treatment in Schmidt-Leukel 1997, 171-235.

96 Küng 1986, 76.

97 Küng 1978, 98. German original: Küng 1980, 108.

98 Cp. for example Race 1983, 63; Race 1986, 179f.; Samartha 1981, 103; Knitter 1986, 64ff; Knitter 1989, 512f; Hick 2001a, 31, 41f, 75.

99 For example, Lindbeck 1984, 61; Sundermeier 1991, 181ff, 189, as well as Heim during his exclusivist phase (Heim 1985, 139f).

if one wanted to propose the maxim that from a Christian perspective one could only say about people of another religion or world view what they themselves would confirm, then this could under certain circumstances lead to absurd results. If, for example, from a Christian perspective one were not allowed to term an atheist an "anonymous Christian" because the atheist does not understand himself that way, then can one from a Christian perspective call an atheist a human being created by God? There is no question that an atheist does not understand him- or herself as someone created by God. So according to this maxim one could no longer say that an atheist — even though he or she is unaware of it— is nevertheless a human being created by God. As not to make demands on someone contrary to his or her self-understanding one would therefore have to say that God only created those persons who consider themselves explicitly to be creatures of God—which would obviously be an absurdity. Yet if it is and must be possible to understand an atheist as someone created by God, although he himself is not aware of his creatureliness, why would it then not be equally legitimate, for example, to understand a Buddhist as someone who lives in a salvific relationship to God made possible or represented by Christ, although the Buddhist is not consciously aware of it?

In the context of the discussion on inclusivism, the Dutch theologian Piet Schoonenberg has—as previously mentioned—developed a terminological distinction that is most useful in this regard.[100] He differentiates between the auto-interpretation of a religion, meaning the way it interprets and judges itself, and the hetero-interpretation, meaning the way one religion is interpreted and judged by another. What is necessary in interreligious dialogue and reciprocal evaluation is that both sides make an effort to grasp and understand the other's auto-interpretation as well as possible, because the hetero-interpretation must relate to the auto-interpretation. But one cannot demand that the hetero-interpretation merely repeats the auto-interpretation. So for example if a Christian wants to form a judgment about Buddhism, he or she ought first to get to know and understand Buddhism as well as possible. And that includes understanding Buddhists as they understand themselves. This understanding of someone's auto-interpretation, something that needs to be constantly checked and possibly modified, ought to be the reference-point of the Christian hetero-interpretation. But the hetero-interpretation does not need to agree with the auto-interpretation in all regards. Otherwise one would end up with the untenable thesis that understanding is identical to being convinced.[101]

Therefore, I think that the allegation of an illegitimate usurpation is not a valid objection against inclusivism. Yet I believe that this allegation does contain one significant aspect that leads to a truly weighty objection against inclusivism. What is presumably behind the allegation of a presumptuous usurpation is the inclusivist assumption that non-Christian belief finds a clearer and more perfect expression, that is its fulfillment, in Christianity. As I have shown, one way or another inclusivism

100 Schoonenberg 1974. See above chapter 2, p. 50, n. 55.
101 Cp. to this chapter 2 above, pp. 52f.

always moves within the matrix of fragment and fullness, of a beam of light and full illumination, of seed and ripe fruit, and so forth. Likewise the notions of "implicit and explicit," "hidden and clearly visible," "unconscious and conscious," which underlie the talk of an "anonymous Christianity," also correspond to this inclusivist schema. According to the inclusivist understanding, whatever is true about the faith of non-Christians refers in a hidden and unconscious way to Christ and is elevated to a full consciousness of itself in Christianity. In other words, if a Buddhist, for example, lives in a salvific way then he or she is in truth someone implicitly connected to Christ, so that Christianity would make a better expression of his or her salvific life than does Buddhism. For in the inclusivist understanding Buddhism can only be truly relevant to salvation if it—though in a hidden way—leads to Christ.

This, however, expresses the conviction that there can basically only be one single correct expression of the salvific relationship to God, namely Christianity. Within the framework of an inclusivist approach, the value of non-Christian religions is in the end measured solely by the degree to which they conform to Christianity (or a particular denominational version of it). This is graphically portrayed by the image of concentric circles that appears in different forms in inclusivism. The more another religion conforms to Christianity, which is placed at the center,—or to the revelation of God in Jesus Christ, seen by Christianity as central—the more it is viewed as true, good, and holy. Yet to whatever extent another religion is different from Christianity it is regarded as being deficient, unclear, pervaded with errors, and so forth. That is why from an inclusivist perspective a positive evaluation of religious diversity and multiformity is either impossible or only possible within very tight limits.

This is also evident in the foundational inclusivist conviction that Christianity testifies to or mediates a revelation that is superior to all others. If there is a revelation that is superior to all others or even just a testimony of revelation that is superior to all others, then these other revelations or testimonies can at most be ascribed a temporary value. Yet this means that "in themselves" and "in principle," as Rahner says, the "extra-Christian religions...are abolished and superseded by the advent of Christ."[102] The preliminary value of religious diversity consists in leading to that unique religion which is superior to all others—even if only eschatologically (as becomes evident with particular clarity in Heim's model or in Dupuis' notion of the eschatological reign of Christ over all religions). Thus even if, realistically speaking, the conversion of all people to the one superior religion cannot be achieved under pre-eschatological conditions, according to inclusivist thinking it would clearly be ideal if religious diversity were rescinded to the benefit of the one most true religion. As Rahner unequivocally concedes, this ideal remains the actual goal of mission.[103] To the extent that the Christian inclusivist is honestly convinced that Christianity is superior to all other religions, he or she will explicitly or implicitly wish that

102 Rahner 1967, 371. See above p. 121 at n. 11.
103 Ibid. 371f.

all people should be members of this best religion. And this implies the wish that all other religions disappear in favor of Christianity.

Suppose this vision could indeed be realized. Suppose one day all other religions really might be replaced by Christianity or even by one particular version of Christianity so that the world might consist only of Roman Catholics or of Lutheran Christians. Would this, from a religious perspective, actually be a desirable situation, or perhaps rather a lamentable impoverishment? I do not doubt that there are numerous Christian who would honestly welcome such a situation. But I assume that there are also numerous Christians (and certainly non-Christians) who do not consider such a situation a desirable goal. They intuitively consider the diversity of religions to be a value. It is this intuition to which inclusivism is unable to do justice.

However, in my opinion, diversity is not a value in itself. Rather, diversity increases both positive and negative values. If ill and evil exists in a diversity of forms, the negative value of the evil is increased. For example, torture does not become less horrific, but rather more so by the fact that humanity has invented many different kinds of it. Yet the same also seems to be true of the opposite: if beauty, goodness, and truth exist not just in one single form but in a rich diversity of forms, their value is not thereby reduced but increased. Is this not also true of the holy? Doesn't what is good, true, and holy in religion become even more valuable through there being a diversity of forms of it? It seems to me that this is precisely the case and that this has to do deeply with the diversity of human existence itself. If religion, at its heart, is about the relationship between human beings and transcendent reality, then it seems to be the case that this relationship must exist in as many different forms as human beings themselves exist in a huge diversity and variety. To the question "How many ways to God are there?" Cardinal Ratzinger once gave the surprising answer in an interview: "As many as there are human beings."[104] I believe that, in the final analysis, inclusivism is unable to take this insight into account. At least it is not in a position to appreciate religious diversity in a genuinely theological sense. Yet I admit that this objection is an intuitive argument. It may appeal to many people, but it might not have the strength of a substantial defeater. I find a stronger objection, however, in the following reflection.

Insufficient Empirical Evidence

As a rule, inclusivists assume that divine revelation does not occur without purpose, but usually serves salvation. Revelation is the precondition for a salvific faith, as well as for a salvific life. The more overt and clear the revelation, the better is the chance that a corresponding faith-life will be realized. Now if the revelation in Jesus Christ is supposed to far surpass all other forms of divine revelation, then Chris-

104 Ratzinger 1996b, 35.

tianity must presumably offer the best precondition for a salvific life. In this, Karl Rahner saw a decisive argument for the legitimation of the missionary task from an inclusivist perspective. Though there is a possibility of salvation outside of Christianity, since Christianity offers the clearest articulation of a salvific knowledge of God, it therefore also offers the "better" or "greater chance at salvation."[105] Or, as the document from the International Theological Commission on "Christianity and the World Religions" says about the (Roman Catholic) Church: "only in it is given in its full intensity the presence of the Spirit", and in it alone is found the "fullness of the saving gifts" (No. 85).[106] According to Clark Pinnock, Christianity mediates "a fuller experience of salvation"[107] and regarding those non-Christians who have already responded positively to the grace of God, the message of the gospel calls them to a "higher" and "deeper" relationship with God, in other words "to know God better and love God more."[108]

Throughout its different writings, the New Testament maintains the belief that a salvific life expresses itself in corresponding works and fruits. As the fruit of the Holy Spirit, Paul names "love, joy, peace, patience, kindness, generosity, faithfulness, gentleness, and self-control" (Gal 5:22f.). Jesus himself says that one can tell the true prophet from the false prophet by the fruits of their work (Mt 7:15-20). And the First Letter of John states, "everyone who loves is born of God and knows God" (1 Jn 4:7). Today we know that other major religions rank the spiritual value of these fruits similarly. They too praise love, selflessness, and inner peace as characteristics that proceed from a life which is rightly oriented to the highest reality. The teachings and the histories of humanity's major religious traditions show that these characteristics have and continue to contribute to the development of salvific lives and the corresponding fruits. Of course all religions also have lamentable ills. As the International Theological Commission fittingly says, in each of them one also sees "the presence of the spirit of evil, the inheritance of sin, the imperfection of human response to God s action (…)."[109] But is this any different in Christianity? If religions are compared without prejudice regarding their good fruits, one cannot recognize any evident superiority of Christianity. This, however, speaks against inclusivism. For according to the inclusivist presupposition that the "fullness of the saving gifts", or the "greater chance of salvation" or the "deeper" relationship to God is mediated only by Christianity, this would have to be apparent by a corresponding superiority at the level of the fruits and signs of a salvific relationship to God.

John Hick repeatedly drew on this argument as a central objection to inclusivism.[110] Neither at the individual nor the social or collective level can one say after

105 Cp. Rahner 1964, 156; 1964b, 365; 1970, 514.
106 http://www.vatican.va/roman_curia/congregations/cfaith/cti_documents/rc_cti_1997_cristianesimo-religioni_en.html.
107 Pinnock 1997, 178.
108 Pinnock 1995, 120.
109 International Theological Commission: "Christianity and the World Religions" (No. 85).
110 Cp. for example, Hick 1988, 38, 106f.; Hick 1988b, Hick 1987.

unbiased examination that Christianity, measured by its fruits, has produced recognizably more saintliness and more humaneness than any other religion.[111] At times, the nature of this objection has been understood, or rather misunderstood, as if Hick were trying to prove the truth of religion by means of practical criteria.[112] This would indeed be a hopeless undertaking.[113] What he is actually doing is offering a critique of inclusivism on the basis of one of inclusivism's own two premises: The *first* premise entails that the mediation of salvific revelation evokes a salvific life with the corresponding fruits. And the *second* premise is that Christianity is singularly superior in mediating salvific revelation. Hick shares the first premise and on the basis of it he refutes the second, since otherwise the claimed superiority of Christianity would have to be apparent in a clear superiority on the level of these "fruits." The argument then proceeds, still on the basis of the shared first premise, to the conclusion that the equality at the level of fruits speaks for an equality at the level of revelation or mediation of revelation.

The history of theology shows that earlier inclusivist positions indeed assumed that the superiority of Christianity at the level of its existential fruits could be proved easily. But inclusivists who know the history of religions better and particularly those who have gained a deeper insight into the inner life of other religions—who as it were can sense some of what it is like to live in the dwelling of another faith—no longer see themselves in a position to make such judgments. They typically then defend their position with the argument that although Christianity has the superior revelation, this does not necessarily mean that Christians factually live better or that they should live better than adherents of other religions. In the individual case this view might certainly be true. But I don't think that it works as a defense of inclusivism. A comparison might be illuminating here: Let us imagine two different civilizations. From a medical perspective, civilization 1 is at a minimally developed level and has at its disposal not more than a rudimentary herbal medicine, which moreover is also connected to numerous ineffective practices. Civilization 2 has at its disposal a highly developed medicine and an exceptionally well-developed health care system. Now it can certainly happen that an individual member of civilization 1 is healthier and lives longer than a particular member of civilization 2. But in general one would expect that the average level of health and the life expectancy

111 Especially in Hick 1987.

112 Cp. for example Vroom 1993. One cause of this misunderstanding is apparently that Hick, in the context of his discussion of an interreligious criteriology, suggests the "fruits" as a criterion to differentiate between authentic and inauthentic religion. Yet he does so on the basis of the premise, shared by inclusivism, that salvific knowledge of transcendence becomes apparent in these "fruits." Only on this premise can "fruits" function as a distinguishing criterion. That is, they cannot prove the truth of religion without this premise.

113 Hick makes it quite clear that in his opinion there is no argument whatsoever that would prove the truth of any religion nor make its truth more probable than that of an atheistic or naturalistic position. The arguments for and against a transcendent reality hold the scales in balance. That is why a religions stance (as also a non-religious one) in the final analysis remains a matter of belief or a matter of rational trust. Cp. Hick 1970; Hick 1989, 73-230.

in civilization 2 is significantly higher than in civilization 1. If this were not the case, then civilization 2's claim of medical superiority would not be credible. In this case one would have to question whether the medicine practiced and health care provided in civilization 1 are really as underdeveloped as initially assumed. Similarly, if revelation is to be considered as a somehow effective means of salvation, bringing about the appropriate existential fruits, then inclusivism's claim of superiority must correspond to a different situation than seems factually to be the case. Otherwise the question arises of whether the knowledge of transcendence mediated by other religions is really less salvific than that of Christianity.

At this point it is worth looking once more at the connection between this argument and the critique of exclusivism. Radical exclusivism collapses—as I have shown—in light of its irreconcilability with belief in the universal salvific will of God. The critique of radical exclusivism and the intellectual insufficiency of undecided exclusivism therefore necessitate a transition to a moderate exclusivism. Yet moderate exclusivism, in all its forms, has a clear leaning toward inclusivism. For no matter how one actually imagines the possibility of salvation for non-Christians—whether through an encounter with Christ after death, or through special revelations or as a result of a subjectively good life in accordance with one's conscience—in all cases one must admit that non-Christian religions are not totally irrelevant to the respective disposition of the individual non-Christian. Anyone, however, who assumes that non-Christian religions can have a negative influence on the individual's disposition, can in principle not exclude the possibility of a positive influence either. The existence of parallels in the history of religions comes into play here, for the existence of these parallels at both the level of belief and of life suggests a positive role of non-Christian religions in mediating salvation. Thus if one fundamentally allows the possibility that non-Christian religions have a positive role to play in promoting salvation, the question of whether they actually do so will probably be answered on the basis of doctrinal and existential parallels between non-Christian religions and Christianity, that is by the extent of doctrinal commonalities and the ability of other religions to promote the development of those very qualities that Christianity identifies as the fruit of the Holy Spirit and thus as signs of a salvific relationship to God. But then the transition from a moderate exclusivist to an inclusivist position is complete. Yet the result of this transition is an inclination toward a pluralist position. For at this point one needs to consider the theological implication of the fact that at the level of the fruit of the Spirit no superiority of Christianity over the other religions can be discerned. The next step is taken if one agrees that non-Christian religions should not be assessed solely according to the degree of their similarity to Christianity, but that it is necessary to reckon with a legitimate diversity and variety of what is true, good, and holy in the religions. However, this combination of the recognition of salvific equality with a theological appreciation of diversity is no longer possible in the context of inclusivism, but rather denotes the further transition to pluralism. So radical exclusivists are not entirely wrong in their suspicion that any movement toward inclusivism will in the short or long term eventually lead to pluralism. Yet to my mind this is already the case if one abandons radical exclusivism in favor of its moderate version. This step, however, seems to me to be unavoidable. Whether all further steps then likewise follow is perhaps primarily a question of consequence and consistency.

For numerous inclusivist authors, what stands in the way of the transition from inclusivism to pluralism are primarily dogmatic considerations. These particularly concern Christology, soteriology, and the doctrine of God. But how strong is the supposed dogmatic evidence in favor of inclusivism really?

Dogmatic Evidence?

According to Karl Rahner, Christianity:

> … cannot recognize any other religion beside itself as of equal right (…) because it rests on the Incarnation, death and resurrection of the one Word of God become flesh" and "is God's own interpretation in his Word of this relationship of God to man founded in Christ by God himself.[114]

For Jacques Dupuis:

> the uniqueness and universality of Jesus Christ are neither 'relative' nor 'absolute'. They are 'constitutive,' that is, they belong to the essence of salvation insofar as Jesus Christ has saving significance for all human beings, and insofar as the Christ event—in particular the paschal mystery of his death and resurrection—is the true 'cause' of salvation for all human beings. The Christ event (…) constitutes the privileged channel through which God has chosen to share the divine life with human beings.[115]

Further, according to Rahner, Christianity sees itself:

> as the only true religion to the extent that it alone properly and fully expresses the divine self-communication in the depths of the graced person and the history of this self-communication of God to humanity, which attained its zenith and highest tangible historical form in Jesus Christ (…).[116]

And according to Dupuis:

> For Christian faith, (…), the Triune God cannot be viewed as a manifestation or an appearance, among others, of an Ultimate Reality (…). It is not a penultimate sign of the Real an sich, it is the Ultimate Reality itself.[117]

114 Rahner 1964, 139. Translation from Hick, Hebblethwaite 2001, 22.
115 Dupuis 2002, 166; similarly see Dupuis 1997, 283.
116 Rahner in Szczesny 1971, 128f.
117 Dupuis 1997, 263.

These quotations outline the *three* dogmatic cornerstones of Christian inclusivism:

- the uniqueness of God's incarnation in Jesus Christ,
- Jesus' constitutive role in the salvation of all human beings,
- the doctrine of the Trinity as the most adequate description of transcendent reality.

I think we frankly need to admit that these three points taken together (and also each in their own right) make Christianity's claim to a singular pre-eminence among the religions inevitable. But how strong is the dogmatic evidence for each of these three points both in terms of the history of doctrine and with reference to the insights available to us today into the exegetical, historical, and philosophical aspects and problems of these three topics?

Rahner himself proposed an understanding of the incarnation according to which even the union of the divine and human nature in Jesus:

> is distinguished from our grace not by what has been offered in it, which in both instances, including that of Jesus, is grace. It is distinguished rather by the fact that Jesus is the offer for us, and we ourselves are not once again the offer, but the recipients of God's offer to us.[118]

Such an understanding of the incarnation necessarily raises the question of whether the divine offer or promise of salvation was made to humanity through Jesus alone, or whether this in fact happened in many different ways and through many different mediators.

According to Dupuis—and with reference to Rahner—it is not Jesus but God the Father who alone is the "original," "ultimate," and "primary" cause of salvation.[119] Jesus is the constitutive cause of salvation only,

> secondarily, insofar as the Christ event is the efficacious expression of the divine saving will and action.[120]

Here the affirmation of Christ as the savior is not that much understood in the sense that he is the "constitutive cause" of salvation but more along the lines of seeing him as "representative" of salvation. For Jesus' "causation" is understood as an efficient expression of God's salvific will, which is the ultimate cause.[121] Yet this raises the question of whether the one divine source of all salvation has not also been expressed in equally effective ways by other mediators.

To his claim that the doctrine of the Trintity describes the divine reality as it truly is, Dupuis add the following modification:

118 Rahner 1978, 202. German original: Rahner 1976, 202. Again, note that the term "offer" in the English translation is much weaker than the German word "Zusage" ("assertion" or "affirmation") which Rahner uses here.
119 Dupuis 2002, 167.
120 Ibid.
121 The difference between a "constitutive" and a "representative" understanding of Christ as savior is developed more fully in chapter eleven. See below pp. 243-251.

> This is not to say that the Divine Reality is in itself within the purview of a direct human apprehension by mode of a positive representation; for the intrinsic mystery of God remains irremediably beyond our full grasp: *de Deo quid sit nescimus!*[122]

Here too the question arises as to whether this modification does not demand an interpretation of the doctrine of the Trinity that no longer upholds it as necessarily the best or most adequate description of God. One cannot claim on the one hand that divine reality as it is in itself is beyond all positive description, and at the same time insist that the doctrine of the Trinity is the best description of it. Like hardly any other twentieth-century theologian, Karl Rahner emphasized, in deep agreement with the tradition of negative or apophatic theology, the nature of God as an essential and irrevocable mystery. But then his claim that only Christianity expresses the divine self-communication "properly and fully" appears highly questionable. As André Gerth rightly clarifies, there is, precisely in the light of Rahner's insistence on the mystery of God,

> clearly the possibility (...) of understanding the different beliefs of the religions as expressions of the experience of the divine self-communication, which are in no way inferior to the Christian conception of the divine self-communication, and therefore can be considered as equally valid.[123]

The response to the question of whether Christian inclusivism is unavoidable despite its weaknesses or whether one can move beyond it and accept a pluralist position therefore depends to a great extent on the interpretation of the three aforementioned dogmatic points; that is, it depends on the *understanding of religious language in the light of the mystery of God*, the *understanding of incarnation*, and the *understanding of Jesus as the cause and mediator of salvation*. The second part of this study will pursue these questions in more detail. For now, let us keep hold of the notion that the doctrinal evidence in favor of an inclusivist Christian position is by no means as unambiguous as the representatives of inclusivism at times pretend.

122 "We do not know of God what God is" Dupuis 1997, 263.
123 Gerth 1977, 80.

6. Religious Pluralism

> ... the Christian churches have always known that religions were plural, that there were other religions than our own. This consciousness of plurality raised few theological problems, because the church was convinced on a number of grounds that Christianity was the only truly valid religion, the only effective "way". That we now speak of theological implications of plurality, and clearly intend *serious* implications, thus bespeaks a new sense or understanding of plurality, a new evaluation of its meaning. This new understanding of plurality, therefore, includes and adds the concept of "parity" or "rough parity," to that of plurality: we recognize, often against our will, that in some sense the sole efficacy or even superiority of Christianity are claims we can no longer make, or can make only with great discomfort.[1]

With these words from the previously mentioned pluralist polemic *The Myth of Christian Uniqueness,*[2] the American theologian Langdon Gilkey describes the motivation for, as well as the core of, a pluralist theology of religions: both exclusivist claims about the unique validity of Christianity and inclusivist claims as to its singular superiority have become increasingly implausible. The theological alternative is to understand the place of Christianity among other religions in terms of an equivalent plurality. As Gilkey correctly says, as a whole this understanding is relatively "new." Yet we can nonetheless identify a few "precursors." So next I will present a short overview of such precursors, paying particular attention to those diverse theological roots that in the recent past have led to the development of this new position in the theology of religions.

Pluralism in the History of Theology: An Overview

As mentioned in the two previous chapters, there are several verses that exclusivists and inclusivists repeatedly offer as biblical support of their views. Can the same be said of the theology of religions pluralism? Are there any biblical texts that point in a pluralist direction? We do well to remind ourselves again that there is no elaborate theology of religions in the books of the Hebrew Bible and the New Testament. But there are sayings that can be understood in a pluralist way: For example, Amos 9:7 where God speaks through the prophet: "Are you not like the Cushites to me, O

1 Gilkey 1987, 37.
2 Hick, Knitter 1987. See above p. 23.

people of Israel? … Did I not bring up Israel from the land of Egypt, and the Philistines from Caphtor and the Syrians from Kir?" And in the New Testament one can find support in the saying of 1 Jn 4:7: "everyone who loves is born of God and knows God," or in Jesus' word about the great eschatological banquet with "many… from east and west" (Mt 8:11). Of course such passages can also be interpreted inclusivistically. Yet to my mind they are not necessarily tied to an inclusivist interpretation, but are in principle open also to a pluralist interpretation.

If we inquire into the appearance of pluralist positions within theological and church history the results will be rather meager. As shown above, both exclusivist and inclusivist approaches can be found in the first few centuries of Christianity. Between the fifth and seventh centuries, exclusivist positions gained the upper hand, until inclusivist approaches once again took center stage in the twentieth century. Only occasionally does one find alongside these positions traces—and even then only by insinuation—of a pluralist theology of religions. In pre-modern times, such traces are found especially among smaller Christian groups that did not live in the Christian West, but rather in cultures shaped by the presence of other world religions. An intimate familiarity with other religions is the logical and factual prerequisite for being able to evaluate them as theologically equal with Christianity, in other words the prerequisite for the development of a pluralist position. One possible example of this are the Nestorian Christians. After their expulsion from the Latin West, they went to China, where they survived for a long time. The renowned stele of Sianfu, which the Nestorians erected in 781, carries an inscription that says, among other things:

> The teaching (Tao) has no particular name and the Wise One is not embodied in any particular person. Religions have been created in different regions of the world so that redemption is within the grasp of all living beings…[3]

In mission studies, so far, such statements were more or less always classified as "not being meant seriously" or interpreted as simply a strategic adaptation to the non-Christian context. Yet why should we not reckon with the possibility that this quotation was indeed—and with theological justification—intended precisely as it sounds?

The Saint Thomas Christians in South India, a group also shaped by Nestorian theology, are another example of this. According to an old tradition, the Apostle Thomas brought Christianity to India in the first century. It is to his ministry that the pre-colonial Christian churches of India trace their existence. There are various indications that the Saint Thomas Christians of the pre-colonial era fostered good and in some cases quite close relations with their Hindu neighbors. One especially convincing piece of evidence is that in the year 1599 the Synod of Diamper, under pressure of Roman Catholic Portuguese, condemned various forms of close con-

3 Cp. P. Y. Saeki, *The Nestorian Documents and Relics in China,* Tokyo, 1937. Although this is an excerpt from an Imperial decree, it is apparently quoted affirmatively.

tact that the Saint Thomas Christians had up to that point maintained with Hindus. Moreover, the Synod condemned a range of "errors" allegedly found in the teachings of the Thomas-Christians. Among these one also finds the following rejection:

> Each one can be saved in his own law; all laws are right: This is fully erroneous and a most shameful heresy: There is no law in which we may be saved except the law of Christ our Saviour.[4]

The fact that the synod condemned this understanding along with other beliefs and practices of the Saint Thomas Christians suggests that such notions were apparently widespread among them.

As far as I can tell, hints of pluralist positions in the Christian West can be found only in modern times, that is, since the beginning of the discovery of non-European cultures and their religions. Of particular importance in this regard are several leading theologians of the so-called Deist movement. Herbert of Cherbury (1582/83-1648) and Matthew Tindal (1657-1733) argued that everything necessary for salvation was available in every religion to the same extent. Yet the Deists were less concerned with a theological appraisal of religious diversity. They were far more concerned to prove that those articles of faith, the knowledge of which was considered as necessary for salvation, can be found in all religions.[5] Besides the Deists, one can also regard Nicholas of Cusa ("Cusanus") (1401-1464) as a type of precursor of pluralist positions; he presented the thesis of "one religion in a variety of rites." Yet Nicholas ultimately follows mostly an inclusivist approach.

Inklings of a pluralist position are found during the height of the Enlightenment. Thus Immanuel Kant, for example, put forth the notion that there could be one true religion clothed in a variety of different types of belief.[6] And Friedrich Schleiermacher in the fifth of his "Speeches on Religion" judged that: "as nothing is more irreligious than to demand general uniformity in mankind, so nothing is more unchristian than to seek uniformity in religion."[7]

Pluralistic tendencies appear more often at the beginning of the twentieth century. Yet only since the second half of the twentieth century do we see carefully thought through and fully developed attempts at pluralist positions. While there are certainly significant differences in their details, the following theologians can all be said to embrace pluralist positions in the sense suggested in the third chapter. In other words, they all suggest that regarding the mediation of salvific knowledge of transcendence Christianity is not superior to all other religions, but rather that de-

4 Actio III, Decretum IV, art. 37, 39. Quoted following Kuttianimattathil 1995, 15. Cp also Aleaz 1995, 219ff.

5 Cp. Bryne 1989.

6 Cp. I. Kant, Die Religion innerhalb der Grenzen der bloßen Vernunft (*Religion within the Limits of Bare Reason)*, 2nd edition (1794), pp. 154ff.

7 F. Schleiermacher, Über *die Religion. Reden an die Gebildeten unter ihren Verächtern.* First ed., (1799), p. 310. Translation following John Oman (Schleiermacher 1958, 252).

spite their many differences they do share a real equality. The emergence of a pluralist position can be ascribed to seven different currents.[8]

(1) *Pluralism as the result of interreligious dialogue.* Many theologians who have engaged in dialogue with other religions initially did so by starting with an inclusivist outlook, and then developed a pluralist position as a result of their dialogical experiences. Particularly well known examples of this from the *Christian-Hindu* dialogue are the Catholic theologians Raimon Panikkar[9] and Francis D'Sa,[10] as well as the Benedictines Henri Le Saux[11] and Bede Griffith,[12] who developed their theological reflections from a lived spiritual praxis of a Hindu-Christian symbiosis. Also worth mentioning in this context is Stanley Samartha,[13] a member of the Church of South India who for a long time led the dialogue unit of the WCC. Regarding dialogue with *Buddhism*, the two Sri Lankan theologians Lynn de Silva[14] and Aloysius Pieris,[15] the Japanese exegete Seichi Yagi,[16] and the American Process theologian Paul Ingram[17] should also be mentioned. Michael von Brück[18] developed his variant of a pluralist position in dialogue with both Hinduism and Buddhism. For the reformed theologian and historian of religion Wilfred Cantwell Smith,[19] it was the encounter with *Islam* that played a central role in the development of his pluralist position; with Rosemary Radford Ruether[20] and Leonard Swidler,[21] it was their encounter with *Judaism*. The third part of this study will go into greater detail regarding the significance of concrete interreligious dialogues for the development of a pluralist theology of religions as well as the significance of a pluralist theology of religions for the further progress of interreligious dialogue.

(2) *Pluralism as a working hypothesis in religious studies.* The ideas of Christian scholars in religious studies were also of great significance for the development of a pluralist position. Some pluralist tendencies emerge in the later work of Friedrich Heiler[22] and Gustav Mensching.[23] They are still more pronounced in the work of

8 For a discussion on the broader societal motives which foster the development of pluralist positions, see Bernhardt 1998.
9 Cp. Panikkar 1990, 50-81; 1990b; 1991, 133-187; 1999. On Panikkar, see also below chapter 14, pp. 366-371.
10 Cp. D'Sa 1987; 1998.
11 For Le Saux see Hackbarth-Johnson 2003.
12 Cp. Griffith, B. 1983; 1990.
13 Cp. Samartha 1981; 1991.
14 Cp. De Silva 1998.
15 Cp. Pieris 1986; 1989; 1994.
16 Cp. Yagi 1987; 1988. On Yagi, see also Fritsch-Oppermann 2000.
17 Cp. Ingram 1988; 1997.
18 Cp. von Brück, Michael 1987; 1991; 1993; von Brück, Lai 1997.
19 Cp. especially Smith 1967; 1981. On this, see also below chapter 13, pp. 334-338.
20 Cp. Ruether 1978, 1987.
21 Cp. Swidler 1990, 73-121; 1991; 1994.
22 Cp. Heiler 1963.
23 Cp. Mensching 1995; 1964.

Helmuth von Glasenapp[24] and Willard Oxtoby.[25] More recently, Stephen Kaplan[26] has argued for a polycentric pluralism[27] as a hypothesis for religious studies. Yet the most influential contribution from a religious studies perspective comes from Wilfred Cantwell Smith.[28] As a specialist in Islamic studies and a historian of religion, Smith published important works on the methodology of religious studies in which he criticizes the un-dialogical and typically reductionist attempts found in contemporary religious studies. As an alternative, Smith developed a methodological approach that takes seriously the faith of religious persons, and attempts to integrate it, on a pluralist basis, by developing a "world theology." Smith undoubtedly stands as one of the fathers and most eminent representatives of a pluralist position.

(3) *Pluralism as a hypothesis of systematic theology and philosophy of religion.* The first moves in theological-philosophical thinking toward a pluralist perspective are already found in the later work of Ernst Troeltsch[29] and Paul Tillich.[30] Beginning around 1970, the British philosopher of religion and Reformed theologian John Hick[31] systematically developed a pluralist position. Although each in their own way, it can be said that Protestant theologians Gordon Kaufman,[32] Langdon Gilkey,[33] Tom Driver,[34] Alan Race,[35] and Glyn Richards[36] hold pluralist positions. Among those who have come close to a pluralist position—in particular with regard to their Christological implications—is also the Anglican systematic theologian and former chairman of the Church of England's Doctrine Commission, Maurice Wiles,[37] as well as the influential theologian John Macquarrie.[38] The Anglican Keith Ward,[39] who like Wiles was previously a professor of divinity at the University of Oxford, embraces a "convergent pluralism" according to which true religion is to be

24 Cp. Glasenapp 1972, esp. 385-398.
25 Cp. Oxtoby 1986.
26 Cp. Kaplan 2002.
27 On this terminology, cp. Hüttenhoff 2001, 45. On Kaplan and for a critique of polycentric pluralism see below pp. 158-161.
28 Cp. esp. Smith 1976; 1977; 1978; 1979; 1987; 1987b; 1989; 1993; 1997. For more on Smith see also Grünschloss 1994 and Hughes 1986.
29 Cp. Troeltsch 1994.
30 Tillich 1994. On the development of Tillich's theology of religions reflections, see also Siedler 1999.
31 *An Interpretation of Religion* (Hick 1989) must count as John Hick's principal work on the theology of religion, along with the Christological "Postscript: The Metaphor of God Incarnate" (Hick 1993). Among his numerous works, of narrower importance to the theology of religions are especially: Hick 1973; 1980; 1982; 1988; 1993b; 1995; 1999; 2001b. See also above chapter 1, pp. 22-24.
32 Cp. Kaufman 1987; 1991; 1993.
33 Cp. Gilkey 1987; 1993.
34 Cp. Driver 1987.
35 Cp. Race 1983; 1986; 1991; 2001.
36 Cp. Richards 1989.
37 Cp. Wiles 1992, 1993.
38 Cp. Macquarrie 1993, 1995, 1997.
39 For Keith Ward's attempt at a "convergent pluralism" see Ward 1991.

found in the convergence of the diversity of concrete religions. Reinhold Bernhardt[40] conceived of his own variant of a pluralist position in the sense of a reciprocal but hermeneutically understood inclusivism. Paul Schwarzenau[41] and Reinhard Kirste[42] accentuate their versions of pluralism with a psychology of religion and pedagogy of religion edge. Deserving particular mention among Catholic systematic theologians are, alongside the aforementioned Leonard Swidler, Chester Gillis,[43] Paul Knitter,[44] and Roger Haight.[45] Along with Hick and Smith, Knitter stands as one of the pioneers of a pluralist approach. Haight contributed significantly to the formulation of a pluralist Christology. At the purely philosophical level, Peter Bryne[46] has defended the pluralist position in the last few years, after having initially, like Keith Ward and Chester Gillis, opposed it.

(4) *Pluralism as metaphysical axiom in the Traditional School.* A special version among the philosophical models of religious pluralism is found in the so-called school of *religio perennis,* or *Traditional School.* It defines itself on the one hand through a strict metaphysical and decidedly anti-modern perspective; yet on the other hand it clearly embraces religious pluralism. The school has adherents in all the major religions. Its spiritual fathers are René Guenon[47] and Frithjof Schuon.[48] Both have a Christian background, but Guenon later converted to Islam. Schuon has not formally converted, but rather has let himself be accepted into a Sufi order and later himself led a Sufi-oriented brotherhood. To the particularly renowned and competent adherents of this School can be counted the Hindu philosopher and philosopher of religion, Ananda Coormaraswamy,[49] the Buddhist Marco Pallis,[50] the Christian philosopher of religion, Huston Smith,[51] and the Islamic philosopher of religion Seyyed Hossein Nasr,[52] who was the first non-Western thinker granted the honor of giving the Gifford Lectures. The intellectual impact of this school has not yet been sufficiently researched.[53] Currently it is particularly influential among Muslim pluralists, especially those in Iran.

(5) *Pluralism as a guiding vision in ecumenical theology and mission studies.* A series of praxis-oriented theologians from the field of Christian ecumenism and mission studies have switched to pluralistically oriented work. Among the ecumenists, this occurred on the basis of an expansion of the ecumenical conversation beyond

40 Cp. Bernhardt 1990; 1993; 1996; 1997; 1999.
41 Cp. Schwarzenau 1993; 1999; Schwarzenau, Gerlitz 1999.
42 Cp. Kirste 1991; 1999; 2002.
43 Cp. Gillis 1993.
44 Cp. Knitter 1985; 1987; 1991; 1995; 1996; 1997a; 1997b; 2002.
45 Cp. Haight 1992; 1999.
46 Cp. Bryne 1995; 2003a.
47 On Guenon and the Traditional School as a whole cp. Nasr 1990, esp. 93-176.
48 Cp. Shuon 1981; 1984; 1986; 1993.
49 Cp. Coomaraswamy 1977.
50 Cp. Pallis 1989.
51 Cp. H.Smith 1991; Smith, Griffin 1989.
52 Cp. Nasr 1989; 1993.
53 On Schuon see also Schmidt-Leukel 1997, 251-270. A dissertation by André Gerth on Schuon is close to being finished.

the boundaries of Christianity. A particularly good example of this is the American Catholic theologian, Leonard Swidler,[54] who edits the *Journal of Ecumenical Studies*, one of the major international journals in ecumenics. Usually, theologians in mission studies came to a new, pluralist-oriented understanding of their discipline as a result of both the impulses from systematic theology and an improved knowledge of other religions. Dialogue and a willingness to learn from the religious other came to replace reciprocal conversion strategies. "Mission" in the sense of a divine commission in the world is understood as a calling and task that encompasses all religions. As examples of this we can name Eugene Hillman,[55] who moved to a pluralist position in his old age, and especially Kenneth Cracknell,[56] Diana Eck,[57] Wesley Ariarajah,[58] and Hans Ucko. Ariarajah followed Samartha in leading the dialogue unit of the WCC, and Ucko is Ariarajah's successor.

(6) *Pluralism as the basis for interreligious liberation theology.* As is well known, the primary concern of liberation theology is the preferential option for the poor, which is meant to encourage theology to do its part in liberating the poor from the misery inflicted upon them. Yet how does one pursue a liberation theology in those countries in which the poor are mainly adherents of non-Christian religions? Do these persons first have to be evangelized and converted to Christianity, or do the liberating impulses of the Gospel have their equivalents in non-Christian religions? Some liberation theologians affirm the latter and see in pluralist attempts a theologically adequate basis for a plausible interreligious liberation theology. Among these theologians are the aforementioned Aloysius Pieris,[59] Felix Wilfred,[60] who teaches in India, and the Sri Lankan theologian Tissa Balasuriya,[61] who has become known to many in the West as a result of his temporary excommunication. In addition, here we need once again to mention Paul Knitter,[62] who likewise works toward a close connection between a pluralist theology of religions and liberation theology.

(7) *Pluralism as the basis for an interreligious feminism.* The basic concern of feminism, to overcome all socio-culturally assigned gender roles that show preference to the male gender, and in so doing to pay close attention to how women describe their experiences, has by its own admission an intercultural and therefore also interreligious dimension. To the extent that feminist theologians study religions not only as social phenomena but are also interested in their religious truth, here too the question of the basic evaluation of non-Christian religions arises, though in con-

54 Cp. Swidler 1987; 1990; 1990b; 1991; 1992.
55 Cp. Hillman 1989.
56 Cp. Cracknell 1990.
57 Cp. Eck 1993.
58 Cp. Ariarajah 1985l 1997; 1999.
59 See above n. 15. On the discussion within the Ecumenical Association of Third World Theologians (EATWOT) compare the contributions in Balasuriya 1988b as well as the declaration of the EATWOT Consultation on "Religion and Liberation" in New Delhi, 1987, in Balasuriya 1988a, 152-171.
60 Wilfred 1988, 1993a, 1993b.
61 Cp. Balasuriya 19881a, 152-171. On his excommunication see Evers 1997.
62 See for example Knitter 1991.

nection with the specifically feminist concern.[63] As examples of feminist theologians who use pluralism as their point of departure, we can refer next to Rosemary Radford Ruether,[64] especially to Ursula King,[65] Marjorie Hewitt Suchocki,[66] and in the German-speaking arena, to Manuela Kalsky.[67]

Within Christianity, although pluralist positions still represent a minority position, in recent years it has gained influence and significance, which one can also recognize in the strong counter reaction, particularly from the magisterium of the Roman Catholic Church. As already hinted at in the discussion of the "Traditional School" or *religio perennis*, the development of pluralist conceptions of interreligious relations is not limited to Christianity. For this reason I want to cast at least a quick glance at the pluralist efforts in other religions.

Pluralist Approaches in Other Religions

The traditional stance within Islam is inclusivist towards monotheists and those considered "people of the book" (in other words, particularly toward Jews and Christians), and exclusivist towards religions considered polytheistic. Yet there are also Qur'anic roots[68] that approach a pluralist attitude. Points of reference often quoted in pluralist positions are Sūrah 16,36 and 5,48 (translation following Paret 1988):

> In every community we have let a messenger rise up (with the challenge): 'Serve God and avoid the idols.'
>
> For each of you (who are members of various confessions) we have determined an (individual) tradition (?) and an (individual) path. And if God had so wanted, he would have made you all part of one community. But he (divided you into a variety of communities) and (so) wanted you (i.e. each group of you) to put you to the test in whatever he had given you (from revelation). So compete with each other for whatever is good!

Particularly among Islamic mystics there exists a whole slew of hints that point in a pluralist direction. In the ninth century, Al-Junaid wrote with reference to the differences between religions: "The colour of the water is the same as that of its container."[69] In the tenth century, Al-Hallaj answered the question "What are religions?" with the curt response "a ground-root with many branches."[70] The following saying

63 On the connection between theology of religions and feminist theology cp. Gössmann 1996. See also Fletcher 2003.
64 Cp. Ruether 1987; 1991; Ruether, Gross 2001.
65 Cp. King 1998.
66 Cp. Suchocki 1987.
67 Cp. Kalsky, 2000.
68 For a nuanced analysis of the perception of religious others in the Qur'an cp. Grünschloss 1999, 86-134.
69 Quoted following Hick 1989, 241.
70 Quoted following Schimmel 1995, 69.

by Rūmī, the great thirteenth-century Islamic mystic, aims in this same direction: "The lamps are different, but the light is the same."[71] Perhaps the strongest statement comes from Ibn ʿArabi, who was likewise active in Spain in the thirteenth century:

> I will no longer say to one whose religion is different from mine: My religion is better than yours. For my heart is ready to assume any form, to be a meadow for gazelles, a monastery for monks, a temple for idols, the Ka'ba for whom who has made a vow, the tablets of the Torah, the scroll of the Qur'an. For me, the only thing there is, is the religion of love: Wherever her ascent leads me, there will be my confession and my faith.[72]

In contemporary Islam one finds pluralist positions with the already mentioned Seyyed Hossein Nasr,[73] as well as Hasan Askari,[74] Mohammed Arkoun,[75] Mahmut Aydin,[76] Mahmoud Ayoub,[77] Ashgar Ali Engineer,[78] Farid Esack,[79] Abdulaziz Sachedina,[80] and Abdulkarim Soroush.[81] Adnan Aslan[82] and a series of other Islamic theologians hold a position close to pluralism. Similar to the case with Christianity, it seems that from all of this a stronger theological direction could emerge.

Traditionally, inclusivist positions dominate in *Judaism* as well. They principally depend on the notion that before and alongside the particular covenant with Israel, God made a covenant with all peoples, which is represented by the covenant with Noah and his sons. The religions of non-Jews witness to divine revelation, even if in dim and distorted ways, and non-Jews can attain salvation if they follow the Noahide Laws. However, nowadays there are Jewish theologians who, as Dan Cohn-Sherbok puts it, approve a pluralist position "in which the Divine, rather than the Jewish tradition, is at the centre" so that Judaism is equal to other religions in their orientation toward this divine center.[83] Among the Jewish pluralists are, next to Cohn-Sherbok himself, David Hartman,[84] Norman Solomon,[85] and, to some extent, Jonathan Sacks,[86] the Chief Rabbi of Great Britain.

71 Quoted following Hick 1989, 233.
72 Quoted following Zirker 1996, 198.
73 On Nasr, see above n. 52. An interview with Nasr and Hick is found in Aslan 1996b (reprinted in Aslan 1998, 257ff.).
74 Cp. Askari 1985; 1991b; 1992; 2002.
75 Cp. Arkoun 1993; 1998.
76 Cp. Aydin 2000; 2001; 2002a and 2002b.
77 Cp. Ayoub 1997 and 2004.
78 Cp. Engineer 2001.
79 Cp. Esack 1997.
80 Cp. Sachedina 2001.
81 Cp. Soroush 2000.
82 Cp. Aslan 1996a; 1998.
83 Cohn-Sherbok 1994, 23f. (similarly ibid. 157ff.).
84 Cp. Hartman 1990 and 1999.
85 Cp. Solomon 1996.
86 Cp. Sacks 2003. The first edition of *The Dignity of Difference* appeared in 2002. In the revised 2003 edition, due to considerable pressure from conservative circles, Sacks had to tone down in particular those deliberations that had a pluralist bent.

It is also true of *Hinduism* that an inclusivist position traditionally prevails. There are already clearly inclusivisitic tendencies in the Bhagavadgītā,[87] that sound like a Hindu variation on the theory of "anonymous Christianity" or of the church fathers' teaching about the Logos. Thus Krishna speaks the following verses in the Bhagavadgītā (7:21f):

> Whatever form, [whatever god,] a devotee
> With faith desires to honour,
> That very faith do I confirm in him,
> Making it unswerving and secure.
>
> Firm stablished (*yukta*) in that faith,
> He seeks to reverence that [god],
> And thence he gains all his desires,
> Though it is I who am the true dispenser.
> (translation from Goodall [1996], 242)

However, time and again we find passages in the sacred Hindu Scriptures that could also be considered indicative of a pluralist view. Perhaps the best known of these is the following verse from the Ṛgveda (I, 164, 46):

> They call it Indra, Mitra, Varuna, Agni (...). To what is One, sages give many a title (...).

In more recent times, pluralist tendencies are to be found particularly among the thinkers of so-called Neo-Hinduism. Even though they exhibit, on the one hand, a particular closeness to the basic Hindu inclusivist paradigm, on the other hand some of them develop such a strong appreciation of religious diversity that it bursts the framework of inclusivism. Particularly noteworthy in this regard are Vivekananda,[88] Tagore,[89] Gandhi,[90] and Radhakrishnan.[91] Finally, among contemporary philosophers of religion who take Hinduism as their primary starting point, Ram Adhar Mall[92] and Arvind Sharma[93] have advocated pluralist ideas.

In ancient *Buddhism*, one finds numerous sayings that indicate either an exclusivist or cautiously inclusivist stance.[94] Among them is the well-known but often misunderstood parable of the blind men and the elephant, which can be found in the Udāna (6:4), one of the writings of the Pāli Canon. Asked about why there are so many different religious teachings whose representatives often fight with one another, the Buddha tells the following parable: A king chooses several men who were born blind and come from a rural area where there are no elephants, and he has

87 On this point, see also Grünschloss 1999, 153-178.
88 Cp. on this the overview in Heiler 1967.
89 Cp. on this Sinha 1993.
90 Cp. on this Hall 1989.
91 Cp Radhakrishnan 1961a; 1961b, and Sinha 1993.
92 Cp. Mall 2003 and the bibliography mentioned there on p. 362, n. 5.
93 Cp. Sharma 1990, 152-165,
94 Cp. Grünschloss 1999, 189-225.

them led to an elephant. Each blind man has to touch the elephant at a different part of its body and then describe what an elephant looks like. The one who touches the elephant's ear describes the elephant as being like a winnowing basket. The one who touches a tusk describes the elephant as being like a ploughshare. The one who touches the elephant's leg describes it as being like a tree trunk, and the one who touches the elephant's tail describes the elephant as being like a broom. The blind men consequently start badly fighting with one another, much to the amusement of the king. This story explicitly addresses the bickering of those "who (only) see one part of the whole." On the other hand, the seeing king quite likely represents the Buddha and his comprehensive knowledge. Even if this identification is not made explicitly, the structure and context of the parable leave hardly any doubt about this. As Grünschloss has demonstrated with reference to the final verse of Udāna 6:5, the seemingly inclusivist parable could actually even have an exclusivist point since the text says that the partial knowledge of the other teachers is insufficient to show the way to salvation.[95]

A saying from the Mahāparinibbāna-Sutta (Dīgha-Nikāya 16), another text in the Pāli Canon, is similarly ambivalent. To the question of whether there are saints and liberated persons in other religious schools, the Buddha responds that there are saints and liberated persons of all degrees in any teaching that contains the Noble Eightfold Path. But, continues the Buddha, this is only the case in his own teaching, not in the teaching of any of his contemporaries (16:5, 27).

The tendency toward inclusivism increases in Mahāyāna Buddhism. This is particularly promoted by the basic hermeneutical positions of Buddhism surrounding the doctrines of "skillful means" (*upāyakauśalya*) and "two truths" *(dvāyasatya)*. According to these, ultimate reality supersedes all human conceptualizations and verbalizations. Religious teachings, including those of Buddhism, are, in the final analysis, to be transcended and relativized, or to be viewed as pedagogical "means", in favor of the trans-conceptual insight into the highest truth. To the extent that these "means" are considered in hierarchical fashion—as is the case in many traditional Mahāyāna schools—we are dealing here with an inclusivist model. But, in principle, it is possible to accept a set of equally effective but different "means" or religions, and thus this concept is also fundamentally open to a pluralist interpretation. In the present, individual Buddhist teachers and thinkers have favored such an interpretation. Particularly to be noted in this regard within Theravāda Buddhism is the Thai reformer Bhikkhu Buddhadāsa,[96] who was influenced by Mahāyāna Buddhism. The Vietnamese master Thich Nhat Hanh[97] can be cited as an example among Mahāyāna Buddhists, as well as the American Shin Buddhist Alfred Bloom.[98] Some Buddhist philosophers of the Kyoto school, such as Keiji Nishitani[99] and Shizuteru

95 Cp. Grünschloss 1999, 202ff.
96 Cp. Buddhadāsa 1967; 1989, 146-155.
97 Cp. Thich Nhat Hanh 1995.
98 Cp. Bloom 1992.
99 Cp. Nishitani 1982, 310-319. Cp. also the quotation in Waldenfels 1976, 84.

Ueda,[100] come close to a pluralist stance, as does Masao Abe,[101] whose writing in his later years approached a pluralist position.

In each of the four named religious traditions we therefore find significant exclusivist traits that are not to be overlooked. Yet as a whole, inclusivist stances dominate. This is also true of Christianity as far as the first four hundred years of its existence and the last few decades are concerned. This means that in actual interreligious encounters either mutual claims to exclusive validity or inclusive superiority are raised and clash with one another. Yet reciprocal claims of exclusivity and superiority lead to a stalemate that in the context of exclusivist and inclusivist approaches cannot be resolved, since it is produced precisely by these approaches. A resolution to the stalemate would however be possible on the basis of pluralist conceptions, and usually the representatives of pluralist approaches within the various religious traditions are quite aware of this. Only the interreligious understanding mediated by pluralist positions can overcome the scenario in which each religion perceives the claims of all others as lies or blindness, or at best as containing only a deficient part of the highest truth. Pluralism can transform this to a situation in which the insights of religions are understood as different but nevertheless equally valid perceptions of a reality that equally transcends all religions and their human limitations. The prerequisites for such a perspective seem to be present in all the major religious traditions—which in itself could be taken as an indication of the possible truth of the pluralist thesis.

Before further explaining the presuppositions of a pluralist position within Christianity in the second part of this study, I will first add a few more clarifications and distinctions, and will specify the most important problems that a pluralist theology of religions poses if taken as a Christian option.

Clarifications and Distinctions

Polycentric Pluralism?

In 1991 Reinhold Bernhardt published a collection of essays from various authors entitled *Horizontüberschreitung* [*Crossing Horizons*], which made a decisive contribution to making religious pluralism known in the German-speaking world. In the Introduction to the book, Bernhardt differentiates between two forms of pluralism: A "unitive" or "monistic" pluralism which has as its point of departure one "common ground" or "transcendent ground" of the religions, and a "strict" pluralism which "[lets] the pluriform religious traditions stand alongside one another uncon-

100 Cp. Ueda 2001.
101 Cp. Abe 1995, 17-51.

nectedly without subsuming them under an overarching transcendent horizon."[102] Hüttenhoff picked up on this distinction and suggested instead the terms "monocentric pluralism" and "polycentric pluralism." In monocentric pluralism, the equal validity of different religious claims rests on the fact that ultimately they all have "the same" or a "common" referent, whereas in polycentric pluralism the equal validity of different religious claims relies on the fact that these all are related to "different" referents.[103]

If one accepts a concept along the lines of a "polycentric pluralism," then the question inevitably arises as to whether one should view the different realities to which the different religious claims supposedly refer as being equal. For if the Christian claim to the mediation of salvific transcendent knowledge refers to the absolute reality called "God," then accepting other reference points of religious claims as valid implies that the realities to which these refer are different from "God." So are these other realities then also ultimate realities? Can there actually be such a thing as an ultimate reality in the plural? If not, the so-called "polycentric pluralism" implies that the truth claims of other religions do not refer to a similarly ultimate reality. The supposed "polycentric pluralism" would then turn out to be a kind of "polycentric superiorism"[104] or inclusivism, perhaps even a kind of exclusivism. Thus Hüttenhoff is right to explain that within the "context of a Christian theology … the claims of different religious orientations (can) only then be judged as potentially equally valid if they can be understood as relating to that one ultimate reality which Christians call 'God.'"[105] "Polycentric pluralism" is therefore also in my opinion ruled out as a truly pluralist position in the theology of religions.

If one takes a closer look at those authors who are occasionally classified as "strict" or "polycentric pluralists," typically one can confirm that their position approaches either a "polycentric" inclusivism, as with John Cobb for example,[106] and explicitly Mark Heim,[107] or that a unifying transcendent ground is only supposedly disputed, so that the diversity of religious reference points turns out to be a diversity of different aspects of that one transcendent reality, as, in my opinion, is quite clearly the case with Raimon Panikkar.[108]

To date, Stephen Kaplan has proposed the most elaborate attempt at a polycentric pluralism.[109] According to Kaplan, one should not understand religions—as commonly suggested—as different paths to the same summit, but as different paths to different summits. Soteriologically, they are all equally effective, yet they are all

102 Bernhardt 1991, 22.
103 Cp. Hüttenhoff 2001, 41-45.
104 Cp. Hüttenhoff 2001, 264, 272.
105 Cp. Hüttenhoff 2001, 271
106 Cp. Cobb 1999.
107 Cp. Heim 1995b; 2001b. On this see also above chapter 5, pp. 126-131. Heim's assignation of the various salvific goals to different aspects of the Trinity moreover makes it particularly questionable as to whether one can even speak of "polycentrism" in this case.
108 On this topic, see also the relevant comments in Hüttenhoff 2001, 44, n. 67.
109 Cp. Kaplan 2002.

aiming at different salvific goals based on a plurality of "ultimate realities." Does Kaplan succeed in consistently applying this understanding?

One could easily view the attempt to attribute the plurality of religions to the assumption of a multitude of real but different ultimate realities as a quasi "polytheistic" concept of pluralism. In *An Interpretation of Religion,* John Hick presents what are in my opinion two compelling arguments against such a concept.[110] First of all, the deities of the different religions are not compatible with one another. Second, accepting the existence of a plurality of ultimate realities would necessarily disrupt their ultimate status. According to Hick, "polytheism reduces each of the gods from ultimacy to penultimacy."[111] Now Kaplan notes right at the beginning of his study that the image of "different summits" that he himself uses is inadequate in that a notion of spatially different goals could foster a polytheistic understanding, which is not his intention.[112] Instead, Kaplan prefers the metaphor of a holographic presentation, because of its ability to unite complex actualities in one and the same space. On the one hand, one can differentiate the hologram from the holographic image—Kaplan speaks of the "implicate" and the "explicate domain"—although both appear so to speak at the same place: Yet although the holographic image looks three-dimensional, the hologram itself is captured on a two-dimensional surface. Thus one can perceive, at one and the same place, both a three-dimensional and a two-dimensional reality. On the other hand, the holographic image can be observed from various sides and changes its appearance accordingly. Whereas the three dimensional structure of the holographic image is made up of numerous particularities that are different from one another, the hologram itself is not an image but a pattern of waves confined to a surface whose individual parts create the same effect as the hologram in its entirety.

Kaplan finds in these characteristics of holographic presentation a parallel with the coexistence of various ultimate realities. Christianity's Trinitarian image of God corresponds to the holographic image, or the "explicate domain." Non-dual "emptiness" (*śūnyatā)* of Mahāyāna (and especially Yogācāra) Buddhism and the non-dual divine self of Advaita-Vedānta correspond to the hologram, or the "implicate domain." On the one hand this is "empty" or "not-self" in as much as it is not actually the holographic image; on the other hand it is thoroughly the *one* "self" to the extent that each of its parts has the same wave structure and therefore is in fact the entire hologram. Among those of the "implicate domain," however, Kaplan also counts the Christian understanding of God—yet not with respect to its Trinitarian structure but rather to the substantial unity of God's divinity.[113] What Kaplan identifies as different "absolute realities" thus actually represents different but simultaneous structures or aspects of one unified metaphysical reality.[114] These correlate with

110 Cp. Hick 1989, 269-271.
111 Ibid. 269.
112 Kaplan 2002, 6 and 26, n. 11.
113 Cp. ibid. 148f.
114 Cp. ibid. 41f, 140f, 150f.

correspondingly diverse soteriological orientations. One can speak of multiple "ultimate realities" only to the extent that the diverse structures or aspects of a single metaphysical reality enables or represents different "ultimate" soteriological goals.[115] Kaplan admits that an "ultimate reality" in the sense of the highest reality must in the final analysis be "singular."[116]

Given such modifications the question arises whether Kaplan's attempt is really so different from the basic notion of a "monocentric pluralism." Kaplan rightly emphasizes two theoretical requirements of a pluralist conception: First, the various religions bear witness to characteristically different practices leading to different results.[117] A pluralist theology of religions must not blur this. Second, in contrast to exclusivism and inclusivism, a pluralist attempt has to hold fast to the idea of soteriological equality.[118] Yet in order to do justice to both these demands, it is neither necessary nor—I would suggest—possible to count on a multiplicity of different "ultimate realities." It makes far more sense—and Kaplan's own attempt makes this clear—to assume a plurality of different aspects or perceptions of ultimate reality, which are interlinked with different experiences of this reality and which are manifest in different but nevertheless equally salvific existential orientations.

Pluralism and the Ability to Dialogue

Opponents of a pluralist theology of religions often allege that it is defended primarily on the argument that only on the basis of a pluralist theology of religions can one establish and accomplish interreligious dialogue. In other words, pluralists allegedly insist that one can only enter into genuine dialogue with a person of another faith if from the beginning one considers that person's faith as equally valid to one's own. A dialogue in which one assumes unique ownership of the truth or at least to know the truth better than the other person would not deserve the name "dialogue." The document of the International Theological Commission "Christianity and World Religions" considers this to be the central motive of a pluralist theology of religions.[119]

Indeed there are some proponents of a pluralist theology of religions who have expressed this argument several times, like for example Paul Knitter,[120] though he later corrected himself on this point.[121] Critics often admit the importance of interreligious dialogue, but reject the view that a precondition for dialogue should be

115 Cp. ibid. 42.
116 Ibid. 42.
117 Cp. ibid. 161.
118 Cp. ibid. 18, 31.
119 Cp. International Theological Commission 1997, Nos. 93ff.
120 Cp. Knitter 1988, 158-163 and 1997a, 171f (this text dates from 1987).
121 Cp. Knitter 1995, 184, n. 10: He says that his insistence that genuine dialogue assumes a common ground in the pluralist sense was rash. Dialogue, Knitter now holds, does not assume that what the conversation partners say is equally true or valuable, but rather that they have equal rights and should both be treated equally (See also Knitter 1995, 29; 1996, 23.)

to accept in advance that the opinions of one's dialogue partner are true. To my mind, this objection is completely justified. It goes against the spirit of dialogue if dialogue is only allowed to consist of the dialogue partners affirming each other in their opinions. Instead, dialogue can and must be open to the discussion of controversial notions. Otherwise there could, for example, be no dialogue between Christians and Atheists. For the two parties bring to such a dialogue completely opposite views regarding the existence or non-existence of God. The only things in my view that are required as a precondition of dialogue are willingness to dialogue and fair, meaning primarily repression-free, dialogue conditions. In addition, a culture of dialogue requires virtues such as a commitment to rational argumentation, a willingness to self-critically examine one's own standpoint, and the desire and ability to understand the other person as well as possible. But in my opinion what is not part of such a culture is to admit to one's dialogue partner from the outset the truth of his or her convictions. A pluralist theology of religions can therefore not be established by the argument to be the only theological basis for a meaningful interreligious dialogue. Rather, one can enter into interreligious dialogue from a pluralist stance as well as from an inclusivist or exlusivist stance.

And yet the presuppositions of the respective options in the theology of religions do make a difference with regard to the theological expectations linked to the dialogue. The exclusivist will solely expect to understand better how most effectively to proclaim the Gospel to his or her non-Christian dialogue partner. The inclusivist will expect to discover seeds of that Word or glimpses of that light which, as he or she believes, has found its sole and unparalleled fullness in Jesus Christ. By contrast, the pluralist will expect to learn something truly new as a result of the dialogue: to see in what other salvific way the non-Christian dialogue partner is oriented towards the one divine reality through his own religious tradition, a reality that we as Christians know through its revelation in Jesus Christ.

Pluralism and Religious Tolerance

The issue of religious tolerance bears some similarities to the previous objection. Critics ascribe to pluralists the claim that it is only on the basis of a pluralist theology of religions that something like religious tolerance is even possible. Religious tolerance is the need of the moment because it is only through tolerance that people from different religions can live together both on a global scale and in multi-religious societies. Therefore, pluralists allegedly claim, it is mandatory to accept as quickly and as broadly as possible a pluralist theology of religions. In contrast to this, critics of religious pluralism emphasize that the demand for tolerance implies that people with different religions and world views coexist in reasonable peace, precisely if they are not particularly well disposed toward each other and clearly assume that the beliefs of the other are wrong or at least insufficient. So what one therefore needs is not so much a theology that affirms the equal truth of the other, but rather a theology or theory that enables religious groups to interact peacefully with one another despite their rival stances.[122]

I also agree completely with this critique. To my mind it makes no sense to substantiate a pluralist theology of religions by claiming that it represents the only truly tolerant point of view. Such a stance I consider to be both counterproductive and even dangerous. Today, the notion of tolerance is often used in a rather watered down fashion. At times, any critique of other religions or world views is branded as "intolerant." This practice implies a completely unacceptable confusion of the command for tolerance with the abstention from a critical attitude.[123] Furthermore, there is a tendency to equate tolerance with appreciation.[124] To my mind, tolerance has nothing to do with an uncritical attitude and it should also be strictly differentiated from appreciation. There is good reason to follow the tradition of modernity and understand "tolerance" as the "endurance" or "toleration" of a religious or philosophical conviction that one neither appreciates nor shares.[125] At its core, the call for tolerance is about religious communities allowing other communities, whose views they neither appreciate nor share, the right and the possibility to live nonetheless according to their own convictions. Said another way, it is about religious communities appropriating the demand for freedom of opinion and religion. Religious intolerance thus consists of denying theoretically and practically the right of those whose convictions one neither likes nor shares to practice their beliefs and stand for their convictions.

Without doubt the history of Christendom is in this sense to a shockingly great extent and for a long period a history of intolerance. Equally uncontested is that exclusivist positions stand in the background of this history. They more or less indicated which convictions were not valued and why not. To this extent, Christian exclusivism was actually indeed a condition of Christian intolerance. Yet even inclusivism can lead to intolerance, for example when it is tied to maxims such as "no right to error."[126] But exclusivism or inclusivism, as positions in the theology of religions, do not have to be intolerant *necessarily*. A person who in an exclusivist or inclusivist sense does not appreciate another religion at all or only in a limited way can nonetheless advocate for tolerance of that which he or she does not like. By contrast a

122 Cp. for example Härle 1992, Feldkeller 1998, and Neuner 2003.

123 Netland rightly opposes this, 2001, 142-146.

124 Gustav Mensching in particular has encouraged this equation with his differentiation between "formal" and "substantive tolerance." He defines "formal tolerance" in the sense of toleration, whereas "substantive tolerance" means the "positive recognition of foreign religion as a genuine and justified religious possibility for encountering the holy" (cp. Mensching 1995, 16.) To my mind what is problematic about this is not the position that Mensching describes as "substantive tolerance" but its being subsumed under the ideal of tolerance and therefore under the reasons for tolerance.

125 I have dealt extensively with the question of religious tolerance in Schmidt-Leukel 2000 and 2002.

126 This is a maxim that was frequently used in establishing the public prohibition of non-Catholic religious communities in traditionally Roman Catholic countries.

pluralist theology of religions has nothing to do with tolerance, but rather with appreciating a particular religion. For when one no longer despises another religion or regards it as deficient, the demand for tolerance becomes superfluous. It is obvious that one would not challenge a person's right and freedom to exist whose beliefs are considered as being as valid and valuable as one's own. But given that a religious pluralist will never appreciate or share everything in the arena of religion, there will always be situations in which the pluralist is also called to be tolerant. So if tolerance is understood in its original sense of enduring ("tolerating") what one does not appreciate, then the call for religious tolerance has lasting importance and retains its good sense in general, independent of the stance one takes in the theology of religions. But then it is equally true that there will also be limits to tolerance. In other words, that which is not appreciated can occasionally be so negative and threatening, even in the realm of religion, that tolerance is no longer a responsible choice. Yet we are talking here of extreme situations, and the identification of such an extreme situation must be based on hard and legally demonstrable evidence, not on religious beliefs or theological speculation. A belief that, for example, another religion is putting the eternal salvation of its members in jeopardy must therefore never legitimate the praxis of religious intolerance.

Problems of a Pluralist Theology of Religions

Quite soon after Wilfred Cantwell Smith, John Hick, and Paul Knitter had presented the first comprehensive outlines of their pluralist approaches, the pluralist theology of religions became the object of fierce theological debates. These debates heated up after Hick and Knitter published the pro-pluralist collection *The Myth of Christian Uniqueness* in 1987. There were numerous attacks in the context of these discussions that had the character of extreme polemics, and partially also of slanderous insults, rather than of sober objections. A single example will have to suffice here. According to Thomas Ruster, the pluralist theology of religions is not only "not pluralistic;" "it is not at all interested in the actual lived realities of religions in their historical and cultural particularity;" is it "not theology, at least not Christian theology;" it "leads to apathy toward God;" the "ethical impulse that comes from such an understanding is weak;" it makes a person "incapable of critiquing religions;" and "above all" it makes a person incapable of critiquing "capitalism".[127] Ruster makes no effort at providing arguments that would substantiate this condemnation. Likewise Ruster offers no supporting evidence from the works of religious pluralists, nor does he, for that matter, offer some more differentiated judgments. It is not worthwhile, in my opinion, to engage with this kind of unfounded criticism—not even when said criticism is found in a work that, in the German-speaking theological world, became a theol-

127 Ruster 2000, 196f.

ogy of religions bestseller! Instead, in what follows I want to describe three ways of looking at the problem that are of central importance in any sound academic discussion of a pluralist theology of religions. These have to do with the theoretical status of a pluralist theology of religions, and its philosophical and theological consistency.

On the Theoretical Status of a Pluralist Theology of Religions

Particularly among critics of a pluralist theology of religions, one repeatedly finds the objection that it assumes a theoretical position above all religions, that is, a kind of "bird's eye view" or "God's eye view."[128] This objection combines three different critiques: *First,* that such a "bird's eye view" abandons the insider perspective of Christian faith in favor of an seemingly neutral meta-perspective, which puts Christianity on a plane with all other religions. *Second,* that such a meta-perspective is pure fiction. In reality no one could ever assume such a meta-perspective, for no one has the kind of comprehensive knowledge that would allow them to assess the equal validity of the major religions. *Third,* that a pluralist theology of religions thereby gets entangled in a kind of performative self-contradiction. Thanks to its alleged "bird's eye view," a pluralist theology of religions claims to have a more complete and better understanding of religious reality than it accords to any individual religious tradition. In so doing, it actually elevates itself to a position superior to all religions and is therefore in truth a concealed form of inclusivism. Stated with the parable of the elephant and the blind men, the objection holds that the pluralists claim for themselves the role of the seeing king, whereas they ascribe the role of the blind men to the religions.[129]

Let us turn first to the *second* point of criticism. If a pluralist proposes the thesis that the other major world religions mediate salvific knowledge of transcendent reality in equally valid though different forms, we are dealing here with a hypothesis. I agree that no one can rightly claim that he or she knows with infallible certainty that the pluralist thesis describes things as they actually are. As humans we are not privy to a "God's eye view." After all, we cannot even prove beyond doubt that the reality we call "God", and hence something such as salvific knowledge of God, actually exists. These are instead basic matters of faith. Yet even if it is not strictly provable, faith in the existence of God or a transcendent reality, can still be justified rationally if it can be shown that such faith might at least be possibly true (among other things by satisfactorily refuting counterarguments). Epistemologically, such an assumption of faith can be characterized as a possible hypothesis. If therefore belief in the existence of God and in God's revelation through Jesus Christ can be regarded as rationally justified, then why should it not, in principle, likewise be legitimate

128 This critique is also found among those who—like R. Bernhardt, for instance—try to reconstruct pluralism as a reciprocal (hermeneutical) inclusivism.

129 Cp. Feldkeller 2000, 283f.

to expand this faith perspective to other possible bearers of revelation? Moreover, the pluralist position in no way distinguishes itself in this respect from inclusivism or exclusivism. The inclusivist too undertakes such an expansion; the only difference is that the inclusivist does not recognize other mediations of revelation as equally valid. And the exlusivist assumption that all other religions' claims of salvation and revelation are merely based on lies and deception is likewise not, of course, founded on conclusive proofs, but also presents a claim based on faith. None of the three positions, neither exclusivism, nor inclusivism, nor pluralism can claim a God's eye view for itself, if by that is meant an infallible certainty in the epistemological sense. On the other hand, however, all three positions are making claims about the place of Christianity among the religions and in so doing unavoidably assume a certain meta-perspective or bird's eye view. I see nothing wrong with this as long as it is clear that we are talking here of hypotheses or faith claims, which must then be examined in detail regarding their respective plausibility.

This also provides the answer to the *first* point of critique: The hypothetical acceptance of such a meta-perspective does not in itself constitute a relinquishing of the Christian insider perspective or of the Christian standpoint. Otherwise one would have to conclude that every decision that Christian theology tries to make about the place of Christianity among the religions constitutes an abandonment of the Christian perspective. That would, however, be completely nonsensical. So behind the first point of critique lies presumably, at least for some critics, the premise that the Christian perspective does allow only for an exclusivist or inclusivist position. Yet this would amount to reaching a dogmatic decision on an issue that is actually up for discussion. If one defines *a priori* that the only those positions can be called "Christian" which confirm the absolute primacy of Christianity over all other religions, then of course the pluralist position would have to count as an abandonment of the Christian perspective. But such restriction of Christianity to either an exclusivist or inclusivist position needs to be based on sound arguments and be open to critical review.

We can thus say the following about the methodological status of a pluralist theology of religions: As with exclusivism and inclusivism, so pluralism too needs to be seen as a theological hypothesis about the relationship of religions to one another. As already explained in the third chapter, every religious community can in principle adopt exclusivist, inclusivist, and pluralist positions regarding its relationship to other religions. As Christian positions the three options in the theology of religions refer to Christianity's place among the religions. Although each position entails necessarily making a meta-statement (about Christianity's status among the religions), the pluralist hypothesis—just like the inclusivist and exclusivist hypotheses—remains tied to a perspective that is fundamentally Christian in orientation. In so doing, one assumes that it is not essentially contrary to the Christian standpoint to hold a pluralist position, meaning to recognize a genuine equality between Christianity and other religious traditions regarding the mediation of salvific knowledge of transcendendence. The validity of this assumption of course requires theological discussion.

But doesn't the tying of each position in the theology of religions to the perspective of its own religion itself already indicate that a pluralist position is impossible? Is it thus not a contradiction in itself to insist on the existence of a position which is simultaneously Christian *and* pluralist? According to Reinhold Bernhardt, there is no such thing as a "privileged meta-perspective, but rather only the outward looking inside perspective, which can then integrate such outside perspectives. Inclusivism is thus hermeneutically unavoidable. Understanding always involves integrating what is to be understood into the frame of reference of one's preconception as it has been shaped by one's own tradition."[130] But does such a hermeneutical inclusivism also prejudice the content of a theology of religions in favor of an inclusivist position? Does hermeneutical inclusivism necessarily presuppose the superiority of the salvific and revelatory claims of one's own religion above all others?[131] By no means. For even if the way in which a decision in the theology of religions is made continues to be bound structurally or hermeneutically to a Christian preconception, that *alone* does not necessarily determine what the content of this decision will be, that is, whether from a Christian perspective the relationship to other religions is understood exclusivistically, inclusivistically, or pluralistically.[132] Unless of course one assumes that the content of the Christian preconception is already confined to just one of these three options. Yet this is precisely one of the substantive points being up to a discussion which cannot be decided in advance by drawing upon structural or hermeneutic principles.

From this emerges also an answer to the *third* aspect of the question regarding the theoretical status of a pluralist theology of religions. On its own, the fact that a pluralist theology of religions—just like an exclusivist and an inclusivist theology of religions—implies a judgment about all of religious reality is not tantamount to the inclusivist claim of the superiority of one's own religion over all others. The endorsement of a pluralist position certainly does entail that it is the superior hypothesis compared to an exclusivist or inclusivist position. But this does not necessarily constitute a performative self-contradiction. This might perhaps be the case if one

130 Bernhardt 1999, 41.

131 In my opinion, on this question Hüttenhoff is not entirely consistent. On the one hand he admits that "judgments about other religious systems of orientation" can be "pluralist in terms of their content" although they are hermeneutically or, as he says, "structurally" inclusivistic. On the other hand he seems to see a tension between substantive pluralism and structural inclusivism when he explains that argumentation for a pluralist position becomes "more difficult because it goes against the grain of the inclusivistic structure in (the religion's) way of thinking" (Hüttenhoff 2001, 271). Yet here Hüttenhoff confuses the different levels of content and hermeneutical structure. If a hermeneutical inclusivism were at the same time to prejudice the content of the theology of religion toward inclusivism, then exclusivism would also be in tension with it. Yet one would hardly want to insist that Christian exclusivism is fundamentally in tension with a Christian preconception or frame of reference. So why should this be the case with pluralism?

132 Here, cp. again chapter 3 above, pp. 67, 72f.

wanted to assert that *only* one's own religion is able to develop a consistent pluralist position. One could perhaps accuse such a "*primus inter pares*-pluralism"[133] of a certain self-contradiction. But even in that case one would still have to keep in mind that—as Kaplan rightly points out—the formulation of a pluralist position does not claim for itself anything akin to a religious or soteriological dignity, but only the status of a particular model regarding the possible validity of the salvation and truth claims of religions.[134] But it is more or less part of the "logic" of the pluralist thesis that each of the religions that are considered equally valid could develop a pluralist interpretation of their relationship to one another and that this is not thus the privilege of a single religion.

From this discussion we can now derive several important requirements for a pluralist theology of religion: (1) As a hypothesis that wants to be truth-apt, a pluralist position must allow itself to be formulated in a philosophically consistent manner. (2) As a hypothesis that claims not to give up the Christian perspective, it must demonstrate its Christian ties in a theologically consistent manner. (3) In line with its own logic, a Christian version of pluralism must intend to align with the pluralist approaches of other religions, thereby further developing the pluralist thesis within the context of interreligious dialogue or a world theology.[135]

A large part of the more serious criticism of a pluralist theology of religions focuses on the first two of these three requirements. In other words, this criticism contests the philosophical as well as the theological consistency of a Christian and pluralist theology of religions.

Philosophical Consistency?

According to Armin Kreiner, "one of the most pertinent objections" against a pluralist theology of religions is connected with "the issue of truth."

> This objection is based on the observation that the truth claims raised in the various religious traditions diverge from, compete with, or even directly contradict one another. From this one would have to conclude that the pluralist insistence on equal validity must apparently be erroneous.[136]

Within the context of a pluralist theology of religions, the problem of divergent truth claims lies in how equality can be predicated of different forms of knowledge of transcendence when these differences manifest in propositions that appear to contradict one another. For if such differences are indeed incompatible contradictions, then for logical reasons it is impossible, from the outset, to consider them

133 At times some neo-Hindu thinkers, such as Vivekananda, can be read as coming close to such a position.
134 Cp. Kaplan 2002, 43-54.
135 On this, see below chapter 16, pp. 429-431.
136 Kreiner 1996a, 253. See also Kreiner 1996b.

equally true. One could consider them equally untrue, yet that would no longer amount to a pluralist position but an atheist or naturalist one.

Generally speaking, the pluralist solution to this problem consists of contesting the contradictory character of those divergent claims that are considered to be expressions of equivalent knowledge of transcendence. In other words, it is admitted that such claims at first sight give the impression of being strict opposites, but that they do not necessarily have to be understood this way. But it is not the goal of a pluralist theology of religions to contest the contradictory character of *all* truth claims posed by different religions. Given that the claimed equivalence refers fundamentally to the mediation of salvific knowledge of transcendence, the contestation of an irreconcilable contradictoriness refers primarily to those claims that have to do with transcendent reality itself. In some religions this is depicted as an impersonal reality, for example as the *Dao*, meaning the eternal way or eternal harmony, or as *Brahman,* the divine, as the *Dharmakāya,* the highest reality of a law that rules over all, or as *Nivāṇa,* meaning the "unconditioned" and "deathless" reality in which suffering, greed, hatred, and delusion are forever extinguished .Other religions depict transcendent reality as a personal reality or, more precisely, in *monotheistic* form as a single person or in its *polytheistic* form as a multiplicity of persons, or in terms of *Trinitarian* theism as three persons of a single divine nature. Is it not true that such diverse depictions of divine or absolute reality seem like utter contradictions, so that at best only one of them can apply or else all are equally false? How is it possible to understand these claims in such a way that they can be considered as different ways of expressing an equally valid knowledge of transcendence?

Pluralist theology of religion has to offer a consistent solution to this problem. Otherwise it would be impossible to consider it as a possibly true hypothesis. Although the solutions suggested within the different pluralist approaches vary to some extent and have their own specifics, nearly all of them depend on viewing the divergent depictions of transcendent reality as not—or not entirely—offering exact descriptions of transcendent reality. Instead, such depictions are traced back to different aspects or to different experiences of transcendent reality. Hence, the most incisive critical objections to a pluralist theology of religions focus on the claim that this "solution", in all its variants offered from the pluralist angle, can be shown to be inconsistent, so that, as Keith Yandell suggests, the pluralist position is a "tissue of inconsistencies."[137]

137 Yandell 20041, 201.

Theological Consistency?

If there is only one single divine incarnation—namely in Jesus of Nazareth—Christianity is unavoidably superior to all other religions, because then it is only in Christianity that this sole incarnation of God has been properly recognized and because then Christianity is the sole religion truly founded by God in person. As already noted in the previous chapter, it is for precisely this reason that several theologians hold firm to an inclusivist position.[138] For Rahner, for example, what belongs "to the Christian and Catholic faith [is]... the belief that Christianity, at least for now, is the only religion founded by God himself through Christ, the absolute religion, intended for all persons, *the* path of salvation that God's salvific will has created and principally made mandatory for everyone."[139] On such premises, a pluralist theology of religions seems to be incompatible with the Christian doctrine of incarnation. Indeed, most of the theological objections to pluralism stem from the insistence that it is incompatible with Christology. In order to demonstrate that it is a possible Christian position, a pluralist theology of religions must therefore above all clarify and justify its implication for Christology.

Now the belief in the incarnation of God in Jesus Christ is indeed one of the bedrocks of the Christian faith. Much less clear, however, is what, exactly, is meant by the term "incarnation." In order to arrive at an adequate understanding of "incarnation" a number of relevant issues have to be taken into account: questions of a logical and philosophical nature, but also questions that arise from the insights of historical-critical exegesis and from research into the history of doctrine. It is only once we have more precisely established what should and can be meant by "incarnation" that we can ask the question anew—and eventually also answer it anew—about whether Jesus of Nazareth is necessarily the only person in whom one can say that God was incarnate. Nowadays many pluralists argue for an understanding of incarnation which—to use Hick's words—"open(s) up the possibility of seeing God's activity in Jesus as being of the same kind as God's activity in other great human mediators of the divine."[140] But to what extent is such an understanding compatible with the key elements of Christian belief in incarnation?

Pluralism — a Christian Option

The goal of the first part of this study consisted in pointing out the necessity of a Christian and pluralist position. In brief, this depends on the following four points: *First,* there are no further theological alternatives beyond an exclusivist, inclusivist,

138 Cp. above chapter 5, pp. 144f.
139 Rahner 1967, 355f.
140 Hick 1988, 36.

or pluralist position. *Second,* both exclusivism and inclusivism suffer from substantial and presumably unresolvable problems. *Third,* pluralism is able to do precisely that which neither exclusivism nor inclusivism can do, namely to appreciate other religions both in what they have in common with Christianity as well as in their own distinctiveness from Christianity. So only pluralism is therefore in a position to offer a genuine appreciation of religious diversity. *Fourth,* only pluralism takes into account that according to the criterion of the "fruit of the Spirit" one cannot discern a superiority of the Christian mediation of salvific knowledge of transcendence, but rather that in this respect at least the major religious traditions seem to be equal. At the end of the first part of this study we have, however, arrived at the question of whether a pluralist position is actually a *Christian* possibility. After all, it could be the case that the pluralist understanding of religious diversity, though a logically possible option, is, like atheism, excluded as a Christian-theological option. John Hick has suggested the following short formula for a Christian form of a pluralist theology of religions:

> ...the belief that there is an ultimate transcendent Reality which is the source and ground of everything; that this Reality is benign in relation to human life; that the universal presence of this Reality is reflected ("incarnated") in human terms in the lives of the world's great spiritual leaders; and that amongst these we have found Jesus to be our principal revelation of the Real and our principal guide for living.[141]

Is this a possible Christian position? The answer to this depends basically on the solution to both of the just-mentioned problems, in other words on whether a pluralist theology of religions proves to be philosophically and theologically consistent: *First,* is Christian faith compatible with a theological hermeneutic that views the various claims of the religions about transcendent reality in such a way that they no longer appear to be contradictory opposites? And *second,* is Christian faith compatible with an understanding of incarnation in which incarnation is not exclusively confined to the person of Jesus?

I believe that both questions can be answered in the affirmative, although only under specific philosophical and theological presuppositions. In particular, these are:

1) The *metaphysical* presupposition, according to which transcendent reality is a reality that surpasses all human comprehension;
2) The *epistemological* presupposition, according to which this reality is known by humans in the form of religious experience;
3) The *hermeneutical* presupposition, according to which the interpretation of religious language about transcendence should focus on the respective forms of its specific relation to experience;

141 Hick 1993a, 163.

4) The *soteriological* presupposition, according to which salvation consists of a transformation from self-centeredness to an orientation toward transcendent reality and the loving attention to one's fellow humans;
5) The *Christological* presupposition, according to which Jesus is neither the only nor the superior mediator of salvific knowledge of transcendence.

A pluralist position becomes possible under these presuppositions. And in so far as these presuppositions can be considered as compatible with a Christian self-understanding, they make a pluralist theology of religions a possible Christian option. In the five chapters of the second part of this study, I will explicate these presuppositions in more detail in order thereby to prove the possibility of a theology of religions that is Christian *and*, at the same time, pluralist.

Part II:

Presuppositions of a Christian and Pluralist Theology of Religions

7. Belief in a Transcendent Reality

Nicholas of Cusa begins his fifteenth-century writing *Dialogus de Deo Abscondito* (Dialogue about the Hidden God) with the following scene.[1] A "pagan" sees a "Christian" having "most devoutly prostrated" himself and "shedding tears of love-not hypocritical tears but heart-felt":

> *Pagan*: What are you worshipping?
> *Christian*: God.
> *Pagan*: Who is [this] God whom you worship?
> Christian: I don't know.
> *Pagan*: How is it that you worship so seriously that of which you have no knowledge?
> *Christian*: Because I am without knowledge [of Him], I worship [Him].
> *Pagan*: I marvel that a man is devoted to that of which he has no knowledge.
> *Christian*: It is more amazing that a man is devoted to that of which he thinks he has knowledge. (...)
> *Pagan*: I ask you, Brother, to lead me to the point of being able to understand you regarding your God. Tell me: what do you know about the God you worship?
> *Christian*: I know that whatever-I-know is not God and that whatever-I-conceive is not like God but that God excels [all this].[2]

Only a reality that "exceeds" everything, that "transcends" everything, and that is therefore inconceivable and ineffable deserves to be called "God." Only to such a reality can we direct our adoration. This, according to Nicholas, constitutes the heart of the Christian understanding of transcendent reality. In this view, Nicholas follows a long tradition, one which exists not only within Christianity but also within all other major religions.

The Concept of Transcendent Reality

I want to approach the concept of transcendent reality in a way that might initially seem like a detour, namely by way of the concept of religion. For a long time belief in God has been considered as constitutive of the concept of religion. Thus the

1 The exact date of its creation is unknown but it is generally dated to before 1445. I am indebted to Dr Karl Baier of the University of Vienna for alerting me to this scene.
2 *De Deo Abscondito* 1f, 8. Translation by Hopkins 1994, 300, 302.

Brockhaus encyclopedia of 1960 follows a very old tradition in still defining "religion" as "the faithful veneration of a god." Yet more recent scholarship on religion is increasingly of the conviction that it is neither possible nor meaningful to regard the concept of god as *the* constitutive element of religion as such. There are primarily two reasons for this change: On the one hand, it was recognized that "the faithful veneration of a god" is not constitutive for many of the phenomena we describe as "religion," for example, for religions in which not *one* but many gods are honored, or those in which faith in one personal god or many does not occur or does not play a central role, as in Buddhism, some forms of Hinduism, Jainism, Daoism, and in parts of Confucianism. Moreover, it has often become standard usage in religious studies to describe the major secular ideologies of the twentieth century—such as fascism or communism—as "political" or as "secular religions." On the other hand, one became increasingly conscious of the fact that much more and many other things occur in religions than simply the faithful veneration of a god. In our daily usage we apply the words '"religion," "religions," and "religious" to extremely diverse and complex phenomena. Among the many things we denote as "religious" are: people, ideas, feelings, motives, behaviors, dietary regulations, vows, buildings, institutions, societies, conflicts, festivals, music, books, and numerous other phenomena.

For this reason, many scholars of religion have concluded that one cannot define the intrinsic nature of religions in a way that is acceptable to everyone.[3] The heterogeneous multiplicity of actual language usage precludes a definition of "religion" that would accommodate the entire breadth of the term. And yet in the arena of phenomena deemed "religious," one characteristic plays an undeniably important role: In religions, convictions are nurtured, whether consciously or unconsciously. The philosopher of religion, William A. Christian, divided these convictions into three classes. These include:

1) Assertions about the nature of reality,
2) value judgments, and
3) directions on how to act.[4]

Christian does not suggest that religions do no more than cultivate convictions. Rather, this is just one aspect of religion among numerous others. Yet according to Christian, in the realm of religious convictions one can determine something like a *basic religious conviction*, in other words a conviction that makes it possible to speak of *religious* convictions at all. This is the conviction, explains Christian, according to which there is "something more important than anything else in the universe."[5] The three aforementioned types of conviction flow together in this basic religious conviction. That is, in religions we find

3 On this, see the overviews in Kerber 1993; Arnal 2000; Kunin 2003.
4 On this cp. Christian 1987, 41ff, 161ff.
5 "...a religious interest is an interest in something more important than anything else in the universe. [...] So, if M is religious, then for M there is something *m* such that, for any *n*, *m* is more important than *n*." Christian 1964, 60. Cp. also ibid 84ff, 243ff.

1) the conviction that there *is* indeed such a reality that exceeds all others in importance;
2) that this reality constitutes the highest *value* or the highest good;
3) that *right behavior* has to orient itself according to the existence and unsurpassed value of this reality.

To my mind, Christian's reflections offer three advantages:

First, Christian does not limit religions to one particular aspect, in this case to the cognitive aspect of doctrinal convictions. Instead he remains quite conscious of the fact that this is just one aspect, albeit a rather significant one, of the multi-layered complex of religious phenomena.

Second, Christian's proposal offers us the possibility of also including so-called secular religions in the discussion. To secular religions, this *something* that is more important than anything else is a political ideal, as is for example the ideal of a classless society in Communism, or the ideal of a particular people or race as in National Socialism and Fascism. In other words, in each case it is a mundane reality that in the secular religions is held above all other worldly realities as the highest and most significant reality. In the major religions and in numerous smaller religious communities, however, this *something* is regarded as a reality that is not part of this world but rather surpasses all finite and limited mundane realities.

Third, on the basis of Christian's proposal we can now clarify how some reality that is generally regarded the highest and most significant religious reality can be designated in a narrower sense as a *transcendent* reality: namely when the highest and most significant reality is not only a partial reality of the finite and limited world, but when it is a reality that surpasses the entire finite and limited reality and thus in this sense is a *un*-limited or *in*-finite reality. To express it in Anselm of Canterbury's (1033-1109) genial words, in its limitlessness it is something "than which nothing greater can be conceived" (*Proslogion* 2).

For a large proportion of religions we can therefore express the basic religious conviction thusly: the reality which is more important than everything else in the world is not part of this world, but rather, as Karl Rahner puts it, something that forms the "infinite horizon" of all finite realities. Apart from that, this basic religious conviction adopts the same structural place as described in Christian's general analysis. In other words, religions *first* sustain the conviction that such a reality that transcends everything finite really exists. *Second,* they regard this reality as the highest value or highest good; and *third,* they assess right action or living according to whether it is oriented to the existence and highest value of this transcendent reality.

Christian's abstract analysis thus shows itself to be fundamentally compatible with normative concepts of religion, as these are held in the various religions. Christian is not interested in an understanding divorced from the particular religions but rather in analyzing the convictions as they are held in the particular religions. In the context of theistic religions the basic religious conviction with its three connotations of a factual assertion, a value judgement and a practical direction can be summarized in the simple phrase that what is most important in religion is serving God, or, expressed in Christian terms: "Seek first the Kingdom of God" (cf Mt 6:33). If giving a soteriological emphasis to the basic religious conviction, one may say in summary: The salvation of persons consists in living with the right attitude toward the highest or transcendent reality. In this sense, Max Seckler, for example, drawing on Thomas Aquinas, defines the "theological concept of religion" as "a salvific relationship to God."[6]

In an analogous way, this is also true for religions that envision transcendent reality not as a personal god, not as a *theos*, but rather as an impersonal reality. For these religions, such as parts of Hinduism, Buddhism, Daoism, or parts of Confucianism, salvation or liberation also consists of the human being's right orientation to transcendent reality, even if this is not perceived as a personal god, but rather, as in Advaita-Vedānta, as the triad of *sat-cit-ānanda,* i.e. as being, spirit, and bliss, or, as in Buddhism, as the "deathless" (*amṛta*) or as Nirvāṇa, meaning the ultimate "fading away" of suffering, greed, hatred, and delusion, or, as the Dao, as the eternal word or the eternal way.

In all the major and ancient world religions, regardless of whether they are theistic or non-theistic in form, in other words, regardless of whether they refer to the highest reality in personal or impersonal ways, the reality that is more important than any other and which constitutes the basis of human salvation/liberation is regarded as a *transcendent* reality, as a reality that surpasses all finite reality and that forms its infinite horizon. I will mention only a few examples of this: Yahweh, of whom one cannot, according to Ex 20:4 make any image, is described by Deutero-Isaiah as the one who is to be compared with nothing (Isa 40:18). And in 1 Kings 8:27 Yahweh's transcendence is described with the beautiful phrase that the heaven of heavens cannot contain him. We read a quite similar passage in the second Sūrah of the *Qur'ān (2,256)* where it says that Allah's throne encompasses heaven and earth. *Sūrah 112* describes Allah's transcendence with the succinct statement that: "God is One. He is eternal…No one is like Him." In the revelatory scriptures of Hinduism known as the Vedas, divine reality is presented as the One, beyond being and non-being *(Ṛg-Veda 10:129),* or, as it says in the Upanishads, the "One without a Second" *(Chāndogya-Upaniṣad 6:2:1),* in other words, as that which is beyond all numerical, countable, and therefore finite multiplicity. It is "neti, neti" meaning "not this, not that" *(Bṛhadāranyaka-Upaniṣad 4:5:15).* The *Śatapabrāhmaṇa (10:3:5:10-11)* states: "This Brahman is the highest, for nothing exists that is higher than this Brahman…This Brahman neither has something before itself nor after itself." Or as it says in the *Chāndogya-Upaniṣad (3:14:2):* it is "greater than the earth, greater than the atmosphere, greater than the heavens, greater than all these worlds." In Buddhism, Nirvāṇa is the "unconditioned" (*asaṃskṛta*), that which is distinct from all other conditioned, and therefore also transitory, reality. In contrast to that which underlies conditioned origination and destruction, that which is born and dies, Nirvāṇa is "the peace, inaccessible to reason, imperishable, that is the not-

6 Cp. Seckler 1985.

born, not-made, devoid of sorrow and passion; the cessation of all forms of suffering, the blissful appeasement of all conditioned processes" *(Itivuttaka 43)*. Or, as it says in another place: "It is…neither earth nor water, neither fire nor air, neither… this world nor another world…neither coming nor going, nor staying, nor destruction, nor origination. It is not fixed, without beginning, without a foundation…" *(Udāna 8:1)*. About the Dao we read in the *Chuang-tzu (6:1)* that it is "higher than heaven." And in the *Daodejing*, the Dao is described as "vast and deep," as the "ancestor of all things" and as the "mother of the ten thousand beings" (*4:12* and *1:2*).

The Inconceivability of Transcendent Reality

There is an important consequence tightly connected with the notion that the highest and most important reality is one that transcends all finite reality, namely the insight in the necessary inconceivability of transcendent reality. This consequence has been made particularly clear by Karl Rahner. As already mentioned in the fifth chapter, Rahner characterizes transcendent reality as the infinite horizon of all finite reality. However, all conceptual understanding has the structure of a defining categorization. I comprehend a particular thing by differentiating it from other things and then by sorting all into a larger framework of concepts, that is, into a comprehensive system of categorization. But if I want to grasp the concept of ultimate reality, a reality which is transcendent in the sense that it is the final, infinite, or unconfined horizon of all other reality, then such a reality has to be determined, on this presupposition, as that which cannot be determined, as something that cannot be comprehended because it forms the final horizon which comprehends all reality and which therefore cannot be conceived by subsuming it into a still wider horizon. Rahner writes:

> …the horizon itself cannot be present within the horizon …The ultimate measure cannot itself be measured. The limit by which everything is "defined" cannot itself be defined by a still more ultimate limit. The infinite expanse which can and does encompass everything cannot itself be encompassed. But then this nameless and indefinable term of transcendence … becomes that which is absolutely beyond our disposal. It is beyond the control of the finite subject not only physically, but also logically. (…) And for this reason the term of transcendence is mystery.[7]

Holmes Rolston has endorsed the same view on the basis of his research in comparative religion. He sums up the primary reason for the incomprehensibility of transcendent reality in the following way:

7 Rahner 1976, 72f. Translation (W. v. Dych) from Rahner 1978, 64f.

> That comprehensive ultimate is, almost analytically, incomprehensible. Comprehended by it, we cannot comprehend it.[8]

Indeed there is something like a formal-logical confirmation of this. As Volker Beeh has shown, Cantor's notion of dissimilarity, Gödel's theorems of incompleteness, and Russell's antinomy all point to a fundamental tension between completeness and consistency. In other words, they point to the impossibility of creating a logically consistent concept of the whole or of the "set of all sets." In this, according to Beeh, they have a connection with the inconceivability of God, in as much as God cannot be conceived of as a part of a more comprehensive, larger whole, but rather represents the ultimate, all-encompassing reality.[9]

Structurally all these examples are about the problem that although our conceptual thinking tends to go beyond all possible boundaries, whether these are defined in terms of particular sets, or systems, or categories, it thereby inevitably ends up with certain paradoxes that explode conceptual thinking. So while logical thought certainly points stringently toward the concept of the whole or the all-encompassing, the attempt to construct such a concept in a self-consistent manner leads to insurmountable problems. Though the notion of the all-encompassing is logically attainable, it cannot be described without contradiction. With help from Russell's antinomy, this can be exemplified as follows: We can divide the set of all sets (the totality of all classifications) into two sub-sets. *Type 1:* Sets that do not contain themselves; *Type 2:* Sets that contain themselves. For example, the set (or classification) "philosopher" is part of *Type 1*. While it does contain people like Socrates, Plato, Śankara, or Nāgārjuna, it does not contain itself, since the term "philosopher" in itself is not a "philosopher". The set of all things which are not "philosopher", does contain itself and hence belongs to *Type 2*. The set of all sets that do not contain themselves (that is, the set of all sets of *Type 1*) can, however, not be described without contradiction. For if one asks the question concerning what type of set this is, then the following paradox results: If it does not contain itself, then it has exactly the same character as its parts and hence contains itself. But if it contains itself, then it is no longer the set of all sets that do not contain themselves.[10] Put another way, it contains itself precisely when it does not contain itself, and it does not contain itself precisely when it contains itself. But if the set of all sets that do not contain themselves is not describable without contradiction, then this is true also for the set of *all* sets, because the set of all sets also contains the set of all *Type 1* sets.

Whenever the human intellect attempts to conceive the concept of the whole or of the all-encompassing, it tries to "de-fine", that is to set a defining limit to it, and yet still wants to go beyond this limit toward that which is still greater. That what is "greatest" in this sense cannot be conceived if it is thought of as something finite or limited. And it cannot be conceived either if it is thought of as something infinite or

8 Rolston 1985, 136.
9 On this, cp. Beeh 1994; 1995.
10 Cp. Sainsbury 1993, 156.

unlimited. In this way human thought touches a boundary, where it goes beyond itself and enters the realm of what can no longer be conceived of or, put another way, into the territory of that which can only be thought of as the unthinkable. Ludwig Wittgenstein hinted at this in the final sentences of his *Tractatus logico-philosophicus*. The famous concluding phrase of the *Tractatus* reads as follows:

> Whereof one cannot speak, thereof one must be silent. *(7)*

This is preceded by Wittgenstein's statement:

> There is indeed the inexpressible. This *shows* itself; it is the mystical. (*6.522*)

And *how* does the inexpressible show itself? To this, Wittgenstein responds:

> The contemplation of the world *sub specie aeterni* is its contemplation as a limited whole. The feeling of the world as a limited whole is the mystical. (*6,45*) (Translations follow C. K. Ogden, with a modification in 6,45b.)

In recognizing the world as finite, or as Wittgenstein says, as a "limited whole," we are already presupposing the larger notion of the infinite or unlimited. In other words, I consider the world *"sub specie aeterni"*, that is, from the angle of eternity or the infinite. It is precisely this infinite as the ultimate, unlimited horizon of everything else, as the horizon of the world as a limited whole, that can no longer be consistently described and conceived, but rather is only properly understood when its necessary inconceivability is grasped.[11] This, one might say, is the logic of the mystical. Here language becomes self-contradictory and unspeakable, and transitions into silence.

The idea that divine reality, if conceived of as a truly transcendent reality, necessarily has to be thought of as an inconceivable and ineffable reality, is a notion seen as self-evident by all church fathers of rank.[12] We can name at least a few examples of this: Augustine captures it succinctly: "If you understand it, then it is not God."[13]

In Gregory of Nyssa we read: "The godhead is precisely that which essentially exceeds all possible knowledge and that which always eludes the grasp of the mind."[14] Thomas of Aquinas reduces it to this formula: "The ultimate human knowledge of

11 In this regard, Magnus Striet is fully right in stating that "the inconceivability of God is a *conceived inconceivability* … (italics P S-L). Therefore an apophatic doctrine of God is right from the start essentially different from … the tired and resigned agnosticism, such as it is widely found in today's cultural situation." Striet 2003, 25.

12 With Avicenna, Maimonides, and Thomas Aquinas in mind, David Burrell has made clear that even "simpleness" in the sense of that metaphysical determination that for God denies a difference between essence and nature, is not to be understood itself as an attribute of God. Rather, simpleness defines the manner in which all attributes are applicable to God, namely in strict differentiation from their applicability to creatures. The emphasis on the simpleness of God is therefore another form of emphasizing God's transcendence. It does not stand in opposition to the inconceivability and ineffability of God but rather actually is the foundation of these (cp. Burrell 1986, 46-51).

13 "Si enim comprehendis, non est Deus." (*Sermo* 117).

14 *Life of Moses*, Migne, P.G. 44, 377c.

God is knowing that we do not know God."[15] It is in Anselm of Canterbury's writings that one finds perhaps the most logically concise definition of the inconceivability of God. As already mentioned, in the second chapter of his tract *Proslogion* Anselm defines God as that "than which nothing greater can be conceived." Yet in the fifteenth chapter of the same writing Anselm adds a crucial supplement to this: God is only that "than which nothing greater can be conceived" if God is "greater than anything that can be conceived" (*Proslogion* 15). The logic of this statement is clear and compelling. If God is so perfect that something even more perfect ("greater") cannot be conceived, and if one may assume that beyond every conceivable perfection there is an even greater, inconceivable perfection, then God must be thought of in the sense of such an inconceivable perfection.[16]

The insight that God is correctly determined precisely when one recognizes that the infinite reality of God exceeds all comprehension and description has serious consequences for the interpretation of human talk about God. A first consequence is a kind of confirmation of Wittgenstein's tenet that one has to be silent about the unspeakable. In other words, the insight into the necessary inconceivability of God is the crucial substantive reason for the justification of "negative theology," in other words for that theological notion which suggests we only speak appropriately about God if we negate every statement about God.

Thus for example Pseudo-Dionysius the Aeropagite, the crown witness of "negative theology", writes:

> But no Unity or Trinity or Number or Oneness or Fecundity or any other thing that either is a creature or can be known to any creature, is able to utter the mystery, beyond all mind and reason, of that Transcendent Godhead which super-essentially surpasses all things. It hath no name, nor can It be grasped by the reason; It dwells in a region beyond us, where our feet cannot tread. Even the title of "Goodness" we do not ascribe to It because we think such a name suitable; but desiring to frame some conception and language about this Its ineffable Nature, we consecrate as primarily belonging to It the Name we most revere. ... nevertheless the actual truth must still be far beyond us.[17]

Yet even among such sober church fathers as Irenaeus of Lyons we find quite unambiguous statements on this matter. Thus Irenaeus writes about the denotation of God as "simple," "Spirit," "Light," or "Source of all Goodness":

> He is, however, above [all] these properties, and therefore indescribable. For He may well and properly be called an Understanding which comprehends all things, but He is not [on that account] like the understanding of men; and He may most properly be termed Light, but He is nothing like that light with which we are acquainted. And so, in all other particulars, the Father of all is in no degree similar to human weakness. He is spoken of in these terms accord-

15 "illud est ultimum cognitionis humanae de Deo quod sciat se Deum nescire...". *De potentia*, q.7., a.5.

16 On this, cp. also Kenny 2004, 15 and 29.

17 *De divinis nominibus* XIII, 3. Quoted from the translation in C.E. Rolt (no year).

ing to the love [we bear Him]; but in point of greatness, our thoughts regarding Him transcend these expressions.[18]

Thomas Aquinas has very precisely articulated the connection between the necessary inconceivability of God and divine ineffability. According to Thomas Aquinas, every human concept corresponds to a finite notion. But if God is a reality that exceeds everything finite, then God's infinite reality must necessarily exceed all human understanding and every representation by means of human concepts:

> for no created species, whether it be that by which an external sense is informed, or by which the imagination is informed, or by which the intellect is informed, is representative of the divine essence as it is. ... Therefore, the vision of the divine essence is not attained through any species. ... for nothing finite can represent the infinite as it is; but every created species is finite ... Now a created intellectual substance is finite; hence it knows in a finite way. And since God is infinite in power and being, and as a consequence is infinitely knowable, he cannot be known by any created intellect to the degree that he is knowable. And thus he remains incomprehensible to every created intellect.[19]

Nicholas of Cusa also clearly articulated the substantive basis of "negative theology" and did not shy away from applying its principles to the doctrinally central Christian understanding of God, that is to the doctrine of the Trinity. In his *De docta ignorantia*, Nicholas writes:

> ... according to the simple consideration of itself infinity is neither the Father nor the Son nor the Holy Spirit. (...) For according to the consideration of infinity God is neither one nor many. (...) From these [observations] it is clear (...) that in theological matters negations are true and affirmations are inadequate.[20]

As shown, the notion that the reality which is most important in the religious sense is at the same time a transcendent reality in the more specific sense of the term is by no means found only in Christianity, but rather in all the major religious traditions. Accordingly, in other religions too, the conclusion was drawn that this reality exceeds all human conceivability and therefore in the final analysis is ineffable. I will offer a few brief examples here:[21]

18 *Adversus Haereses* 2, 13, 4. Translation from http://www.earlychristianwritings.com/text/irenaeus-book2.html.

19 *Super Evangelium S. Joannis Lectura,* ch 1, Lectio XI, 1, Nos. 211 and 213. From the translation by James A. Weisheipl, O.P. Online: http://dhspriory.org/thomas/John1.htm.

20 *De docta ignorantia* I, 26, 88f. Translation from Hopkins 1985, 46.

21 Particularly noteworthy among more recent comparative studies on the inconceivability and ineffability of transcendental reality in different religions are: Rolston 1985 (relying on Augustin, Al-Ghazālī, Śankara, and Nāgārjuna); Burrell 1986 (comparing Avicenna, Maimonides, and Thomas Aquinas); Williams, J.P. 2000 (comparing Dionysius Areopagite, Maximus Confessor, and Dōgen), as well as Sturm 1996 (a most impressive comparative study of the use of the four-fold negation in eastern and western religious and philosophical traditions).

"There is nothing whatever like unto Him," says in the Qur'an (*Sūrah 42,11*). According to al-Asch'arī God is "not a form, ... not a person, neither substance nor attribute, ... in no way does he come close to being like his creatures.... He is different from anything that reason can think of or fantasy can imagine...".[22] According to Al-Ghazālī, "no one [knows] the essence of God except God himself."[23] Similar to Augustine, Aquinas, and Cusanus, Al-Ghazālī judges: "The end result of the knowledge of the knowers (...) is their inability to know him, and their knowledge is, in truth, that they do not know him."[24] Or as Rūmī puts it: "Everything you can think of is fleeting; that which cannot be grasped by any thought is God!"[25]

In the *Kena-Upaniṣad* (*1:3*) the divine Brahman is identified as being that "to which no eye can go, nor speech, nor thought," and "it is only known by those who (say they) do not know it; it is not known by those who (say they) know it" (*2:11*). Śankara, the most important representative of Advaita-Vedānta, says: "Brahman cannot be grasped, since it is transcendent. It cannot be comprehended since it comprehends everything. (...) Brahman cannot be defined. It is beyond the capacity of thought and speech ..."[26]

The Pāli Canon refers to the Buddhist Nirvāṇa not only as "the not-born, the not-brought-to-being, the not-made, the not-conditioned" (*Udāna 8:3*), but also as something "for which there is nothing similar anywhere" (*Sutta Nipāta 1149*) and as the "limit of that which can be explained" (*Majjhima-Nikāya 44*). Regarding ultimate reality, Nāgārjuna writes that it "is not knowledge or knowable, not existent nor non-existent, not one nor many, not both nor neither, ... inconceivable, incomparable, ... not within the range of words [or] knowledge ..."[27]

The *Daodejing* begins with the famous verse: "The name that can be given is not the eternal name. The nameless is the origin of heaven and earth" (*Daodejing 1:1b-1:2a*). Therefore it holds true that: "He who knows does not talk about it; he who talks about it does not know" (*56:129*).

From all of this we can now derive a first and most *fundamental* consequence for a pluralist theology of religions, or, more accurately for a solution to the problem of divergent truth claims within the context of a pluralist theology of religions: It is quite evident that all major religious traditions emphasize, each in their own way, that there is an ultimate, transcendent reality whose transcendence surpasses all human conception and all human attempts to describe it. This implies that the claims of these religions about transcendent reality do not contradict each other in this central point, but rather that they converge in here. This in turn has a crucial impact on the proper understanding of the divergent statements that the various religions make about transcendent reality. Thus when this reality is referred to by both

22 Quoted following Becker 1987, 321f.
23 Miskāt a-anwār. Al-Ghazālī 1987, 23.
24 Al-Maqsad al Asnā. Quoted following Rolston 1985, 136.
25 Quoted following Schimmel 1996, 45.
26 Vivika-cudāmanī. Quoted following Shankara 1990, 121.
27 Acintyastava 37-39. Quoted following Lindtner 1982, 153.

impersonal and personal conceptions, we have to keep in mind the premise, found in every major religion, that in its infiniteness transcendent reality cannot be adequately grasped and described by any notions, regardless of whether these are personal or impersonal. Therefore we have to distinguish strictly between *transcendent reality as an inherently infinite and therefore inconceivable and ineffable reality and such conceptions and descriptions which are used in the various religions as pointing to this transcendent reality.* This differentiation is made in every religion which is conscious of the fact that a truly transcendent reality can necessarily only be determined as an inconceivable reality.

As John Hick has expounded in all his writings on theology of religions, this differentiation—made in one way or another by the religions themselves—between transcendent reality in its inconceivable and ineffable infiniteness and our mental approximations to this reality in the form of finite concepts and images constitutes the essential basis of a pluralist theology of religions. For it is this differentiation that offers a solution to the problem of divergent truth claims. Under the presupposition of this differentiation, what the major religions say about transcendent reality cannot be taken as opposing and mutually exclusive *descriptions*, but has to be understood as different verbal *approximations* to a reality which according to these religions exceeds all description. For this reason we do not need to ask whether a transcendent reality is better described and grasped by way of an impersonal, a personal, or even a three-personal conception. According to the fundamental hermeneutic principles of all the major religions, none of these conceptions should be understood as offering an adequate description or an adequate comprehension of transcendent reality. Rather, all of these conceptions are only apt in so far as they point beyond themselves to the inconceivability and ineffability of transcendent reality.

Of course one can also find contrary tendencies in the major religions—tendencies toward a dogmatism which is in danger of abandoning the transcendence of ultimate reality and considering it to be a fundamentally comprehensible and describable reality, and thereby as a highest but in the end inner-worldly reality. The only alternative to "negative theology," according to Maimonides, is "idolatry," the worshipping of a finite creaturely image instead of the true God.[28] Nicholas of Cusa concurs and holds that:

> ... the theology of negation is so necessary for the theology of affirmation that without it God would not be worshiped as the Infinite God but, rather, as a creature. And such worship is idolatry; it ascribes to the image that which befits only the reality itself.[29]

Since traditional insight into the inconceivability of transcendent reality forms the first and fundamental presupposition of a pluralist theology of religions, the critique of a pluralist theology of religions can begin with a refutation of the inconceivabili-

28 *Guide of the Perplexed* 1, 160. Cp. Burrell 1986, 63.
29 *De docta ignorantia* I, 26, 86. Translation from Hopkins 1985, 45.

ty and ineffability of God.[30] If human reason is capable of, at least in principle, correctly grasping the highest religious reality and if this reality can be adequately described in human words, then the various claims of the different religions have to be understood as competing descriptions. Then it would be reasonable to suppose that only one of them describes the highest reality in the most accurate manner and that therefore only this description is true or at least is comparatively more appropriate than other, different descriptions. Armin Kreiner is thus completely right in his judgement that in the discussion on a pluralist theology of religions, "the question of the mysteriousness of transcendent reality" takes on a key position:

> The more radical and consistent the ineffability or inconceivability of the transcendent is thought to be, the more plausible seems the pluralist hypothesis as developed by Hick. Conversely, it becomes less and less convincing the more optimistic the possibilities of the human intellect are judged with reference to the divine reality.[31]

Thus it is only consistent that when, in *Dominus Iesus,* the Congregation for the Doctrine of the Faith of the Roman Catholic Church in its attempt to fend off a pluralist theology of religions claims:

> The truth about God is not abolished or reduced because it is spoken in human language; rather, it is unique, full, and complete...[32]

Yet it is deeply surprising how readily the Congregation for the Doctrine of the Faith thus significantly diverges from the traditional teaching of the limitation of all human language in the face of the mystery of God and in so doing sets itself up in flagrant opposition to the majority of the Christian theological tradition.[33] If one

30 Keith Yandell in particular pursues this strategy. Cp. Yandell 1993; 1994, 61-115; 1999, 65-80; 2004a, 2004b.

31 Kreiner 1996b, 131.

32 *Dominus Iesus* No. 6. And linked to this is of course the insistence "that the Holy Spirit ... will teach this entire truth (...) to the whole Church." Ibid. See also Müller 2003.

33 The most thorough criticism of negative theology to date, as far as I know, has been presented by Magnus Striet (cp. Striet 2003). Striet quite frankly admits that the denial of apophatic or negative theology constitutes a radical break with broad sections of the Christian theological tradition. Striet, however, construes a much simplified opposition between, on the one hand, the idea of the absolute oneness and simplicity of God as shaped by Neo-Platonism, and, on the other hand, the biblical notion of a God who is free and governs over history. I am not denying the enormous influence of neo-platonic thought on Christian theology, nor that in various biblical writings God is often depicted as acting freely in history. The problematic simplification is rather to be found in the fact that the biblical writings do not offer an elaborate and carefully thought through doctrine of God and therefore also do not seriously address or respond to the question of the literal or metaphorical understanding of the biblical statements. Striet's concept of the biblical understanding of God is undoubtedly a post-biblical, or more precisely, a modern construct. In addition, Striet reflects too little on the motives why Christian theologians were so receptive to neo-platonic considerations. Talking of neo-platonic "influence" by itself does not explain the substantive reasons that made such influence possible. Likewise Striet does not reflect on the parallel reception of neo-platonic thought in post-biblical Judaism or on the different forms of the apophatic tradition in non-Christian religions that are beyond a neo-platonic influence. In general, Striet

abandons the notion of the inconceivability and ineffability of transcendent reality, according to Keith Yandell, "nothing is lost."[34] In any case, says Yandell, the inconceivability and ineffability of transcendent reality are advocated by only a minority within the different religions, primarily in the writings of a few mystics, and are mostly in tension with their respective religious tradition.[35] According to Peter Byrne, Yandell in this way only exhibits his ignorance of these traditions. Byrne holds that the emphasis on the inconceivability and ineffability of transcendence is of central importance in many religions. To me, Byrne is correct, and this not only from a historical perspective. If it holds true—as I have tried to argue with reference to various representatives of these traditions—that the insistence on the inconceivability and ineffability of transcendent reality directly results from the affirmation of its transcendent status, then it is not only false that "nothing is lost" by its abandonment. Rather, in so doing, what would be lost is the truly transcendent nature of the highest reality itself. In the words of Maimonides and Cusanus, it would amount to confusing the truly transcendent with the finite images that we make of it.

The Relevance of Transcendent Reality

Yandell's view that nothing is lost by abandoning divine inconceivability and ineffability corresponds with his perspective that the existence of a reality characterized in that way has no religious relevance whatsoever. Again and again, opponents of a pluralist theology of religions have attacked its supporters, especially John Hick, with the accusation that the pluralist way of resolving the problem of divergent truth claims, namely by drawing on the connection, affirmed in all religions, between the transcendence and the inconceivability of ultimate reality, will lead to religious irrelevance. In this way, the critics hold, transcendent reality becomes an "ineffable X" about which one cannot say more than that it exists and that it is ineffable. Yet such an "ineffable X" lacks any kind of religious significance. It is thus a pointless concept, void of meaning and of no interest to any religion. Whether or not such an inconceivable X exists or not is completely irrelevant. Basically, such an X is redundant, and this would show that behind a pluralist theology in general, and behind

seems to have made an unacknowledged prejudgment that appropriate knowledge of God is found exclusively in the "biblical" image of God that he favors, but not in any non-biblical traditions. Although Striet mentions the importance of the question of negative theology for the discussion on the pluralist theology of religions (Striet 2003, 31-37), the deficits I just pointed out show that the issues of a theology of religions remain irrelevant for the primary questions of his study. Therefore his study remains stuck in the framework of the somewhat outdated debate about the Hellenization of Christianity. However, precisely the contrapositions of this debate could be significantly opened up by the advances within the theology of religions. Nevertheless, in spite of these deficits, Striet's work undoubtedly makes an important contribution to the broader debate about negative theology.

34 Cp. Yandell 1994, 115.

35 Cp. Yandell 2004a, 199f.

John Hick's theology in particular, lies just a concealed atheism.[36] This objection has its classical precursors: In the fourth part of his *Dialogues Concerning Natural Religion*, David Hume asks in what way the mystical insistence on the absolute inconceivability and ineffability of God is actually different from the atheistic insistence on the non-existence of God. And in *The Essence of Christianity* Ludwig Feuerbach characterizes the insistence on the unknowability and indefinability of God as practically a form of atheism.

The response to this critique, as Hick himself has repeatedly clarified,[37] must begin with the relevance of transcendent reality for the world. But first we need to keep in mind that the claim that transcendent reality is inconceivable and ineffable does not refer to some random and arbitrary X. Rather, as we have seen, it is about the inconceivability of a reality that infinitely surpasses every finite reality and forms the ultimate horizon of all reality. Hick describes it as a "reality which transcends everything other than itself but is not transcended by anything other than itself."[38] Should such a reality actually exist, then our finite universe would have a different character than if there were no such infinite reality that transcended everything else. For if the finite universe itself is meant to be the ultimate reality, then the meaning and the potential of the universe are confined entirely by its own finite limits. But if there is indeed a reality that infinitely exceeds the finitude of the universe, then this bursts open the limitation of the universe's own finitude. In other words, then there is a hope that exceeds the hope as it is possible within the boundaries of the universe's finitude. Therefore, the relevance of transcendent reality consists of the fact that its existence provides the entire existence of finite reality with a different meaning.

As Hick has shown convincingly in the first part of *An Interpretation of Religion*, his *opus magnum* in the theology of religions, the existence of a transcendent reality is, in all the major religions, at the root of their "cosmic optimism" and correspondingly of their salvific hope for the individual. If there is a reality that goes beyond all limitations, then the transience of the universe and the mortality of each individual, the countless sufferings, injustices, and supposed absurdities of existence need not have the last word. That the existence of such a reality gives us reason to hope is what the religions express in different ways, in that each of them depicts transcendent reality in its relationship to the world and to us as a *good* reality:[39] theistic religions do this by speaking of ultimate reality as of a loving, gracious, and merciful person, and non-theistic religions do so by depicting this ultimate reality through impersonal images, such as "the deathless," "being-spirit-bliss," the "eternal path," the ultimate "law," and so on. Thus in their depictions of transcendent reality, religions

36 Besides Yandell's work (cp. above fn. 34 and 35) this objection can for example be found in Barnes, 1990; Loughlin 1987, 505; 1990, 43; D'Costa 1991, 9; and especially in Eddy 2002, 168-182.

37 Cp. for example Hick 1993b, 3-16; 1995 71-76; 2001b, 95-112.

38 Hick 1993b, 164. Cp. also Hick 1995, 65-67.

39 Cp. Hick 1995, 63.

do not describe this indescribable reality but rather they express in different ways their hope for salvation, which is tied to the belief in a reality that transcends all limitations and finitude.

Yet the existence of a transcendent reality is not only the warrant of a cosmic optimism and individual hope for salvation. Above and beyond this, it ensures, as Hick has responded to Yandell,[40] the authenticity of religious experience and therefore forms the realistic basis of religious life—without necessitating the exclusivist limitation of this realism to only one religious tradition. As we have seen, the notion that transcendent reality is necessarily inconceivable and ineffable is by no means an invention of a pluralist theology of religions, but rather belongs to the traditional inventory of the religions of humankind. The achievement of a pluralist theology of religions consists rather in its pointing to an important consequence of this notion that until now had only rarely been recognized in religious traditions: namely that on the basis of the inconceivability and ineffability of transcendent reality it is possible to grant authenticity not only to the religious experience of a small part of humanity, but rather to the a large variety of religious experiences as expressed in the world's major religions.

In the following two chapters I will delve more deeply into this connection between transcendent reality on the one hand and the variety of religious experience and religious language on the other.

40 Cp. ibid. 59f.

8. Revelation and Experience

Revelation as Divine Self-Disclosure

How is it possible for people to recognize the presence of a transcendent reality and to enter into a saving relationship with it? Within Christianity, this question is answered by the doctrine of revelation. That is, it is God who reveals himself or allows himself to be recognized, and thus enables the Divine-human relationship.

In the history of theology one can see significant shifts in the conception of "revelation."[1] These changes also carry extraordinary significance with respect to the presuppositions of religious pluralism. In the early days of Christian theology the notion of "revelation" was not yet used as a systematic category, but was applied in a rather unspecific way to diverse manifestations and forms of God's appearance. Only later an understanding of revelation developed according to which "revelation" means divine instruction, that is, the term refers to particular propositional truths or texts communicated by God (the so-called *instruction-model* of revelation). Primarily under the influence of the modern critique of revelation—but also in light of a better understanding of the historic genesis and development of biblical texts and Christian doctrines—the instruction-model was broadly recognized as misleadingly narrow and untenable, and was replaced by a communication-model of revelation, according to which God does not reveal propositions or propositional content but rather himself, or better: God-self, and in so doing enables people to live in relation to God. However, this transition is by no means complete. Despite all of the criticisms against it, remnants of the instruction-model and its corresponding ways of thinking can still be found throughout the theological world and continue to thrive particularly in evangelical or conservative circles.

Several influential theologians of the twentieth century, among them Karl Barth, Wolfhart Pannenberg, and Karl Rahner, have helped propel forward the development of a communication-model of revelation. The reasons for this change in the concept of revelation have been repeatedly analyzed. The respective work of Max Seckler offers one example of such analysis. In particular, Seckler clearly shows that the Enlightenment critiques of revelation play a key role in the conceptual change regarding "revelation".[2] The Enlightenment critique of revelation was multifaceted, and targeted a variety of things. But three motifs stand out quite strongly:

1 On this, see the overviews in Eicher 1977, Dulles 1983; Waldenfels 1996.
2 Cp. Seckler 1981; 1985b; Seckler, Kessler 1985.

First, there is the critique of the assertion that knowledge derived from revelation obtains over a *higher degree of certainty* than knowledge derived from human experience and rational conclusions. This was refuted by Enlightenment critics with the argument that whatever is regarded as revelation can never have a higher epistemological certainty than the arguments on which the claim that something has in fact been revealed is based. But if one admits that the existence of revelation cannot be demonstrated with infallible certainty, and that not even the existence of God can be proved beyond doubt, then that what is supposed to be a revelation cannot offer any greater certainty. Instead, it remains a matter of faith as to whether there is such a thing as revelation at all, as well as whether in a particular instance one is actually dealing with revelation.

Second, the Enlightenment critique of revelation takes issue with the insistence on the *supernatural character* of the content of revelation. This critique, of course, was entirely directed at an instruction-model of revelation. Against those who considered the books of the Holy Scripture as revealed in the sense that these were verbally inspired to the biblical authors by God, the Enlightenment critics pointed out that the biblical scriptures contain errors and mistakes as well as numerous time-bound and culturally conditioned notions. Therefore, critics argued, these writings are human documents through and through. To the extent that theology had assumed that the central doctrines of the Christian faith—namely the Christological and Trinitarian doctrines—represented the true content of revelation, the critics sought to prove that these doctrines were products of protracted theological discussions, and not an information that God had shared with humanity through Jesus. Additionally, they criticized the notion, often connected to the instruction-model, that the doctrines revealed by God were mysteries of the faith in the strict sense, in other words, propositions which even after their revelation remain completely incomprehensible to people. If revelation is thought of in this way, then in the end—so the thrust of this critique—nothing becomes evident to persons and hence nothing is revealed.

The *third* motif of Enlightenment critique of revelation touches directly on the problems of a theology of religions. It concerns the soteriological meaning as well as the *salvific necessity* of revelation. If divine revelation consists of the communication of particular texts or propositional mysteries of faith, and if one also assumes that knowing these revealed mysteries of faith is a necessary condition of salvation, then it inevitably follows that God has denied the majority of humanity what is necessary for their salvation. Thus, for example, the critique from the French Enlightenment scholar Paul Thiry D'Holbach:

> Indeed, every [belief in] revelation presupposes that for a long time the Godhead has been able to conceal to mankind the knowledge of the truths most important to their wellbeing. If revelation is given only to a small number of chosen people, then above all this witnesses to a partiality and unjust predi-

lections in that being which can hardly be reconciled with the goodness of the common father of the human race.[3]

These Enlightenment critiques of revelation were thus, as mentioned before, directed against the concept of revelation as a divine communication of particular texts or beliefs. Yet if one understands revelation in the sense of divine self-disclosure, according to which God does not reveal certain propositions, texts, or propositional contents, but rather makes *him/her/it-self* accessible to people, then the aforementioned objections lose their punch. Indeed, they can even be positively appropriated on behalf of a further development and clarification of a theology of revelation.

Two aspects are particularly decisive for such an altered understanding of revelation: On the one hand, that knowledge of God as enabled by revelation really is about knowing this divine reality itself. On the other hand, and as a result of this, that the statements in the so-called documents or records of revelation and in texts relevant to revelation, such as the biblical writings, creeds, doctrinal definitions, etc. attain a different status. No longer can they be considered revealed texts, but rather are to be understood as various expressions of the human response to revelation in the sense of divine self-disclosure. That is, they now move entirely into the domain of humanity. In view of the criticism of revelation, these two aspects have the following repercussions:

Regarding the question of the *certainty* of revelation, it must be admitted that the existence of revelation is not, and cannot be, more certain than the existence of God. For if revelation is to be understood as God's self-disclosure, then both belong inescapably together. Stated positively: we may indeed trust and believe that God reveals him/her/itself, but we must admit that God's revelation is not of such a coercive evidence that any rational doubt is no longer possible. Rather, as Blaise Pascal once put it, God reveals himself in a way that offers enough light to those who want to see, and leaves enough darkness for those who wish otherwise (*Pensees* 430).

The issue of the *supernatural content* of revelation can also be easily resolved on the basis of a communication-model of revelation. First, we can fully agree with the critique of revelation that the formulations of faith are not supernatural. Rather, these are thoroughly human articulations that bear the imprint of true humanity: that is, they contain errors and are unmistakably shaped by their particular historical and socio-cultural context. The only supernatural content of revelation is *God him/her/itself.* Our articulations of faith essentially present human responses to divine self-disclosure.

Regarding the question of the *salvific necessity* of revelation, we can hold fast to the idea that human salvation is found in one's proper orientation to God, and that this orientation is only possible because God allows him/her/itself to be recognized by human beings. Since divine self-disclosure is not tied to the communication of particular propositions and texts, it is also no longer automatically implied that, as

3 Following the German translation in D'Holbach, 1978, 359.

D'Holbach put it, "the Godhead has been able to conceal to mankind the knowledge of the truths most important to their wellbeing." Rather, it now seems fundamentally conceivable that God reveals or has revealed him/her/itself to all people. The diversity of testimonies to revelation in the various religions need not count against the credibility of revelation. Rather, within the framework of a communication-model of revelation, this diversity points to a multitude and multiplicity of different human responses to the divine self-disclosure; responses that are just as numerous and diverse as the people whose testimonies record their responses to the divine self-disclosure.

In this way, we take an important further step toward a pluralist solution of the problem of divergent religious truth claims. The various statements about transcendent reality found in the major religious traditions of this world can be interpreted as *different expressions of the human response to divine self-disclosure.* In this sense, the understanding of revelation as divine self-disclosure is another presupposition of a pluralist theology of religions. Yet let me emphasize once more that this presupposition is now theologically widely accepted, regardless of the position that one takes within the theology of religions. This concept of revelation is thus just as little a product of the pluralist theology of religion as is faith in the inconceivability and ineffability of transcendent reality. In fact the inverse is more true: the possibility of a pluralist theology of religions is due in part to this change in our concept of revelation. At the same time this implies that for all those who continue to hold to an instruction-model of revelation a pluralist position in the theology of religions is ruled out. For them, there are particular propositions or texts that, because they come directly from God, contain the only or at least the highest form of knowledge of God, so that other propositions or texts, to the extent that they diverge from these, cannot be accepted as an expression of equivalent knowledge of God or as equally valid revelatory documents.

To this point we have thus established two basic presuppositions of a pluralist theology of religions: *First,* the recognition that if transcendent reality is thought of as inconceivable and ineffable, then the concrete personal and impersonal notions of this reality that we find in the various religions cannot have the status of directly applicable descriptions, and that therefore we need not understand their diversity as constituting incompatible descriptions. If it were indeed a case of mutually exclusive descriptions, then it would be impossible to regard these notions as equally valid expressions of human knowledge of transcendence. Yet if it is a case of various approximations that all point beyond themselves and in their own ways to an inconceivable transcendent reality, then it is, in principle, possible that despite their differences such approximations are nevertheless equally valid. The *second* theological presupposition consists in interpreting revelation in the sense of divine self-disclosure. It is none other than the infinite transcendent reality itself that reveals itself to humans. Thus it is no longer the faithful acceptance of supposedly revealed propositions or texts but rather the recognition of transcendent reality itself that is at the center of the revelatory event. The diverse testimonies and documents of revelation in the religions can then be interpreted as expressions of human responses to the transcendent reality's universal self-disclosure.

What remains for this chapter is to explain how one can imagine in a feasible way such a self-disclosure of infinite transcendent reality to the finite human spirit, and what further consequences this has for our understanding of the diverse statements about this reality.

Receiving Revelation via Religious Experience

Revelation is a relational concept. That is, "revelation" indicates a particular relationship between the one who reveals and the one who receives the revelation. One can only speak of revelation if indeed the revelation is imparted to someone. A revelation that reaches no one would not be a revelation. As Wilfred Cantwell Smith has said, "Revelation is always a revelation to somebody."[4] That is, "…it does not mean anything to say that God has revealed Himself unless He has revealed Himself to some person."[5] Both the reception and the receptor of revelation are therefore integral aspects of the event we call "revelation."

Now if revelation means God's self-disclosure then the human dimension of revelation, the receiving of revelation, is nothing other than the recognition by which a person becomes aware of the existence and presence of the infinite transcendent reality. According to the countless testimonies in the history of religion, this does not occur primarily by means of speculative reflection, but rather by means of religious experience. The patriarchs and prophets of the Old Testament did not believe in the existence of God because they had developed the one or the other argument for the existence of God. Rather, for them the existence of God was a matter of vivid religious experience. The same also holds true for Jesus and his disciples, and for the prophet Muhammad. The situation is no different in the great Asian religions. The Vedic seers and the compilers of the Upanishads became aware of the presence of an ultimate transcendent reality through mystic, meditative, and partially trance-like experiences. According to the Buddhist scriptures, the Buddha awakened to the presence of an unconditioned and deathless reality in the enlightenment he experienced while meditating. Something similar applies to the mystics of Daoism. Also with respect to other ancient religious traditions, such as for example Africa's autochthonous religions, there can be no doubt that in the first instance people became aware of the existence and presence of transcendent reality through religious experience and not through intellectual reflection and theoretical speculation. Religious experience is the wellspring and lifeblood of the religions.

4 Smith 1989, 173.
5 Ibid.

Revelation and religious experience are not opposed to one another as two alternative paths of knowing God. Revelation, if it consists of a person becoming aware of the existence and presence of God, reaches people via religious experience. This does not suggest that every religious experience must be an expression of a genuine revelation. But it does suggest that every genuine revelation is always imparted to people by way of religious experience. Johannes Hessen expressed this clearly:

> The core of religion is religious experience or the experience of religious value. (…) In religious experience we become aware of the true value-object—the holy or the divine. (…) This means that somehow the Holy discloses itself to us. (…) What from a human perspective seems like religious experience, is, from God's perspective, divine revelation.[6]

This triggers the following questions: What is the nature of the experience that has to be considered the subjective side of the revelation event, that is, the human reception of revelation? And is revelation, in this sense, at all possible, if it means the self-disclosure of the infinite God to the consciousness of finite persons? Does not the old Calvinist principle *finitum non capax infiniti*—"the finite cannot grasp the infinite"—imply that a self-disclosure of the infinite God to the finite and limited consciousness of humans is fundamentally impossible?

Let us begin with the last question. For the answer to this will simultaneously lead us to an answer for the first question. Indeed, the consequence of the ontological difference between the infinite reality of God and the finite reality of humans is that God's infiniteness cannot be conceived. God always has to be denoted as that reality which surpasses all conceptual limitations and all, inevitably, finite concepts. Therefore there can be no religious experience in which a human could comprehend God in God's infinite nature. According to Thomas Aquinas, it even holds true for the *visio beatifica*, that "blissful vision of God" which is promised after death, that a human being will not be able to grasp God in his infiniteness.[7] Rather, a human being can only ever recognize as much of God—whether now or in the eschatological vision of God—"as is possible by his power of cognition." Yet the human power of cognition is always finite or limited, so that a human can only grasp the infinite God, even eschatologically, in a sort of finite reflection.[8] This view is in line with Thomas Aquinas' epistemological premise that the known is in the knower according to the mode of the knower. So if "the known"—in this case God—is infinite and "the knower" finite, then a human being can only know the infinite God in a finite way.

Yet this in no way means that knowledge or experience of God would be completely impossible. Rather, a genuine experience of God—and thus genuine revelation—must be interpreted as a *finite experiential impression of an infinite reality*. That is, when revelation occurs, the person stands in an experientially genuine relation-

6 Hessen 1963, 28.
7 Cp. *Super Evangelium S. Joannis Lectura* Cp. I. lect X1, 1. Thomas Aquinas 1986, 155-157.
8 Cp. on this Schmidt-Leukel 1998a.

ship to the infinite God and he or she does become aware of God's presence. But the awareness of God's presence is mediated by such limited contents of consciousness as correspond to human finitude. In this the person realizes that God is a reality that is always greater than everything we experience or know about it. The following analogy might be helpful here: The night view of a clear, starry sky brings us into genuine experiential contact with the universe. What we see is truly the immeasurably wide universe itself. But we do not see the universe in its immeasurable width. Rather, we see only that limited section of it that we can recognize. But at the same time we can also grasp that the universe by far exceeds our capacity of perception and our current experience of it.[9]

Thus, because of its conceptual structure, the human mind is geared toward understanding the finite. And yet it is simultaneously open to the infinite. This observation presents an influential motif of modernity's philosophy of religion. Descartes introduces this idea in the third of his Meditations. On the one hand, Descartes keeps hold of the idea that God is the infinite and that it is part of the nature of the infinite not to be able to be grasped by finite humans.[10] And yet—according to Descartes—humans are open to the idea of the infinite because the idea of the infinite forms the necessary conceptual correlate to what humans can grasp, namely the finite. Indeed, says Descartes, the concept of the infinite in some ways precedes that of the finite.[11] In other words, only under the presupposition of the idea of the infinite can the finite be recognized *as finite*, namely as a restriction of the infinite.

Friedrich Schleiermacher further develops this motif. For Schleiermacher, religion is "sense and taste for the infinite,"[12] or, more precisely, the contemplation of the infinite in and through the finite. If we become conscious of the finite *as* finite, that is, if we consciously experience finite reality under the aspect of its finitude, then this experience implies the idea of the infinite. For—according to Schleiermacher—"Everything finite exists only through determining its limits, which, so to speak, need to be excised from the infinite."[13] Thus, as in Descartes, we also find in Schleiermacher the idea that the notion of the finite is logically formed in the sense of a restriction of the infinite, such that a person can only become conscious of the finitude of the finite because and to the extent that he or she is simultaneously conscious of the infinite. Thus, according to Schleiermacher, religion can awaken the feeling for the infinite by teaching humans to regard "everything that is finite as a representation of the infinite."[14]

In the previous chapter, I already pointed out that this motif can also be found in Wittgenstein's *Tractatus logico philosophicus*, in which Wittgenstein talks about the "contemplation of the world … as limited whole" as that in which the mystical

9 Cp. the similar response by Descartes to Caterus in: Descartes 1994, 102f.
10 Meditations III, 50.
11 Meditations III, 49.
12 *On Religion: Second Speech* [1st edn. p. 53]. Schleiermacher 1985, 36.
13 Translation follows the German original of the first edition. Ibid. 37.
14 Ibid. [56] 39.

or the "inexpressible ... shows itself." But it was Karl Rahner who, more than anyone else in the twentieth century, made this thought the basis of his theology. According to Rahner, in every finite understanding we reach beyond the finite and into the inconceivable and unobtainable realm of the infinite. For this reason, all humans are by the very structure of their mind open to the notion of an incomprehensible, infinite horizon of all finite reality. The person of faith interprets this as openness to God. That is why Rahner speaks of this as a "transcendental revelation." That is, through the openness of our mind to an incomprehensible, infinite horizon humans are already in some sense familiar with God, are given a knowledge of God as the "holy mystery" surrounding all of our understanding which is always directed toward the finite.

Yet it is by no means obligatory to interpret this openness to the idea of the infinite as an openness to God. It cannot be conclusively demonstrated that the *idea of the infinite* actually corresponds to the *existence* of an infinite, divine reality. Therefore, the atheist will simply interpret the notion of the infinite embedded in our mental structure as a fiction, rather than the awareness of an actually existing infinite ultimate reality. Two things become clear through this: On the one hand, God's self-revelation does not occur in such a way that thereby the existence of God is made indubitably certain. Rather, God reveals him/her/itself in such a way—to cite Pascal once more—that leaves enough light for faith and enough darkness for doubt. On the other hand, what also becomes clear is that every experience of God, that is, every reception of revelation, is mediated by an interpretive act that occurs within the experience itself. That is, if I experience the infinite horizon of the world *as* the infinite God, and if this experience, this "sense for the infinite" as Schleiermacher calls it, becomes real to me through the insight into the finitude of the world, then this experience in itself already contains an interpretive element, namely the interpretation of the infinite *as the infinite reality of God.* Because the experience of God contains interpretation, the experience is a conceptually mediated experience. Regarding the question about the kind of experience which can be interpreted as the subjective reception of revelation in the sense of divine self-communication, we can therefore respond: It is a conceptually mediated experience, in which the finite is experienced as a representation of the infinite, namely in such a way that the infinite appears as the infiniteness of the divine reality. With the help of the following reflections by John Hick, I now want to clarify further how we might understand the conceptual mediation of this experience.

Experience and Interpretation

The question about the nature, the possibility, and the structure of religious experience constitutes one of the central themes of John Hick's thought. Long before Hick became one of the leading representatives of a pluralist theology of religions, he was concerned with the epistemological problems of religious experience. Thus already in his early work, *Faith and Knowledge* (1957) he developed a model of religious experience which, in essence, he still maintains to this day and which has contributed—as can be seen from the development his work—to the formation of his pluralist position.[15]

According to Hick, not only religious experience but all experience has an interpretive element to it. For experience only becomes possible by our consciousness processing, and in so doing interpreting, certain data that are usually received by our sense organs. This process of interpretation happens spontaneously and mostly unconsciously along with the act of perception. And yet involved in this is an active interpretive effort by our mind, an interpretive effort that is not necessarily determined. This can be demonstrated by so-called flip-flop images. Our visual perception presents us with particular lines and dots, while our mind forms a picture from this. If the lines are such that they allow several interpretations, then our mind wavers. Take, for example, the well-known "rabbit-duck illusion":

Sometimes we interpret this image as a duck—and then we *see* a duck (looking left); sometimes we interpret it as a rabbit—and then we *see* a rabbit (looking right). That is, we have here a real act of the interpretation of particular sensory data. The interpretation is not predetermined. Nor does it come only after the experience, but rather in the very act of the experience itself.

According to Hick, every experience has this kind of structure. To experience something always means experiencing something *as* this or *as* that. Experiencing is "experiencing-as;" that is, experience is interpreted perception. Interpretation is an inner constituent of the process of experience itself and not only the product of later reflection. Despite its spontaneous character, this interpretive element is an active process in the sense of a free, not completely predetermined activity.

In this sense, Hick identifies religious faith as the interpretive element within religious experience. In other words, it is faith that makes us experience particular finite impressions as representations of a divine reality. Faith in this sense is not an intellectual, theoretical construct. It is rather an attitude that directly informs the way in which we experience the world. The interpretive activity that happens in this faith is not necessarily predetermined. An Old Testament prophet, for example, experienced certain historical events *as* deeds of God. We are talking here not about

15 For a short bibliographical overview see Schmidt-Leukel 2001b. More extensive explorations can be found in Heller 2001 and Koziel 2001.

a subsequent interpretation but about an interpretation that occurs in the act of the experience itself. Yet these events by no means *had* to be interpreted or experienced in *this* way. Another person at the same time could just as well experience the same historical events as being purely political events.

Experiencing historical events as deeds of God and thus as a form of indirect divine self-revelation is, according to Hick, only a small sample of a big palette of religious experiences.[16] Yet all of them have the epistemological structure of "experiencing-as." For example, someone can experience an icon *as* a sacramental image of the glory of God, or the Eucharist *as* an event of divine presence. Some people experience a particular place *as* a holy place that fills them with awe. A dream can be experienced *as* a divine message, a person *as* a divine prophet and messenger, or a book *as* the word of God. In fact, the entire reality that surrounds us can in moments of strong religious experience become the medium of an intensively experienced presence of God. And the mystic might experience a vision or even a supraconscious state of absorption *as* becoming one with God.

The range of the available sets of interpretation—that is, the terms and categories one has at hand—plays a crucial role for the particular kind of interpretation that undergirds the respective act of experience. For the interpretation that happens in and through the experience works through the application of particular concepts. This is as true of experiencing simple objects as it is of experiencing complex situations. For example, I see or experience this "something" before my eyes *as* a "computer," the place where I am at the moment *as* the "university," and the situation in which I find myself *as* a "research leave." Therefore in the process of experiencing, I structure my perceptions by applying certain concepts like "computer," "university," or "research leave" to them. Yet these concepts are complex, extremely artificial, and to a high degree time- and culture-bound. A Neanderthal who suddenly found himself in my office thanks to a time machine would have absolutely no chance of having the same experiences as I do. Although he and I have access to the same sensory perceptions, he would not be able to see the object in front of my eyes as a computer, recognize the place where I am as a university, nor understand the situation in which I find myself as a research leave—simply because he lacks the concepts and the understanding connected with these concepts.

Now the same is also true of religious experience. Here too, in the act of experience, perceptions of anything from simple objects to complex situations, become connected to particular concepts that are not simply universal givens but rather are tied to particular historical and cultural situations. If one accepts the hypothesis that it is within particular religious experiences that a person becomes aware of the existence or presence of God, and that such experiences are mediated and structured by terms and categories tied to a particular time and culture, then what follows is that humans' experience of God is necessarily shaped by the interpretational tools

16 Cp. on this Hick 1995b.

of their particular time and culture. We can therefore understand the diversity of religious experiences and their verbal articulation as reflections of different perceptual conditions that are primarily connected to the differences in human culture. Or, to put it theologically: if revelation refers to the process in which God discloses him/her/itself to humans, then one must not imagine the human as an abstract being divorced from its time and culture, but rather in each case as a concrete person, shaped by his or her own personality, culture, society, and historical situation. God's self-revelation will therefore only ever be able to reach humans in a diversity of different forms, which correspond to the diversity of its recipients. Thus Hick's thesis that:

> It is in relation to different ways of being human, developed within the civilisations and cultures of the earth, that the Real, apprehended through the concept of God, is experienced specifically as the God of Israel, or the Holy Trinity, or as Shiva, or as Allah, or as Vishnu, … And it is in relation to yet other forms of life that the Real, apprehended through the concept of the Absolute, is experienced as Brahman, or as Nirvana, or as Being, or as Sunyata …[17]

According to this thesis, the various cultures work rather like different lenses through which people experience the same transcendent reality in different ways. In turn, this means that religious experience is always qualified by a specific and particular perspective.

The Perspectivity of Religious Experience

To my mind the epistemological approach that best corresponds to a pluralist theology of religions is that of critical realism, or more precisely (borrowing the term from Andreas Grünschloss) that of a *"perspective-dependent realism."*[18] According to this, the major religious traditions embody different perceptions of the same transcendent reality. Yet because of the finite and limited nature of human cognitive abilities on the one hand, and the infinite or limitless nature of transcendent reality on the other hand, no one can grasp transcendent reality in its infinite plenitude. Nevertheless within the various religions and cultures of this world there are equally authentic experiences of this reality that can be interpreted as finite experiential impressions of an in itself infinite reality. We can therefore interpret the differences in these experiences in terms of different perspectives. Different perspectives arise through different perceptual conditions on the part of the perceiving subject. One mountain can be seen or experienced quite differently by different subjects, depending on the optical perspective one has of the mountain, on one's mental situation

17 Hick 1989, 245.

18 Grünschloss speaks of W.C. Smith having a "perspective-dependent proviso." Cp. Grünschloss 1994, 193, 205, 286, etc.

or mood, on the symbolic meaning mountains have for the one perceiving it, on whether mountains are a familiar phenomenon or something completely new, and so on. In religious experience as well, so goes the central thesis, we are dealing with the perception of one and the same transcendent reality. Yet one's perception of it is mediated by the different ways, in which the finite can appear as a representation of the infinite.[19] This occurs concretely by way of different religious interpretations that have arisen and developed in different cultures of the world. Analogous to the diversity in perspectives, we are also dealing here with different perceptual conditions, each dependent primarily on the differences present within the respective interpretive material available to the perceiving subject.

Such an epistemology is significantly different from both an epistemological absolutism (or naïve realism) and from postmodern relativism. Absolutism assumes that the religious experience of one's own tradition and its respective concepts and ideas contain the only truth. This standpoint thus negates the perspectival limitedness of human experience. But if one assumes such a perspectivity, then absolutism is simply a matter of confusing one's own limited perspective with an all-encompassing perspective. A perspective-relative realism, however, is also clearly different from a relativism according to which each religion constructs its own reality, which is unconnected to the realities of other religions, but rather stands in an incommensurable relationship to them. Such a relativistic position is basically not different from collective solipsism. That is, each culture and religion lives in its own self-created world. According to this position, there is no such thing as one underlying objective reality common to all. Consequently it would make no sense from such a relativist standpoint to talk about a perspectivity of perception, or of various perspectives of perception. For different perspectives are constituted by a common reference, in other words, a common point toward which these perspectives are oriented despite and in their differences. The epistemology of a perspective-dependent realism recommended here thus preserves the basic intuition that despite all our religious, cultural, and individual differences we do ultimately participate in a common reality, rather than each person living in his or her own separate universe. At the same time, it allows for the real differences and constraints of our individual and collective forms of experiencing the world and God. It is precisely in this way that this position offers an epistemological framework within which it seems meaningful and possible both to make an effort to understand the other's perception of reality, as well as to allow the possible insights of other perspectives to challenge and enrich one's own.

After this clarification of the epistemological presuppositions of a pluralist theology of religions we can now more closely determine how to understand religious

19 This is true even of an immediate vision of God. For here too, as has been said above in connection with Aquinas, we would still have the situation of the finite cognition of an actually infinite reality—independent of how one might conceive a finite cognition in this particular case.

language. In so doing, we are concerned primarily with two questions: *First*, is it at all possible—and if so, in which sense—to speak about transcendent reality if this is claimed to be inconceivable and ineffable? *Second*, what consequences does a more refined understanding of religious language have for a pluralist theology of religions as a theological theory? Both questions will be addressed in the next chapter.

9. Religious Language and Experience

How and Why We Must Speak about God

In his *Tales of the Hasidim,* Martin Buber relates the following anecdote about Rabbi Schneur Salman, the Rabbi of Reussen:

> The Rabbi addressed a student, who had just come to see him, as follows:
> "Mosche, what is that 'God'?"
> The student kept silent.
> The Rabbi asked a second and third time.
> "Why are you silent?"
> "Because I don't know."
> "Well, do I know?" said the Rabbi.
> "But I *must* speak; for that's how it is, that I have to speak it:
> He is clearly there, and apart from him nothing is there clearly, and *that* is God."[1]

Although the only adequate knowledge about God consists of the insight that God cannot be conceived or "known," and that therefore strictly speaking one cannot talk about God, there are nonetheless reasons why one must speak about God. One, and perhaps the most important of these reasons, is named in this story: the experience of God's presence.

Despite the widespread insight among human religious traditions regarding the necessary ineffability of transcendent reality, these traditions speak and have spoken about such a reality, steadily and in a multitude of ways. At first sight, this seems like a contradiction or paradox. Yet these religious traditions also developed hermeneutical theories whose express function consists of mediating between the effability and ineffability of transcendence, or of explaining more precisely how, given the ineffability of transcendence, we are properly to understand religious talk about and of transcendence. As some of the most prominent examples of this I may mention the medieval teaching of analogy in Christianity, Kabbalistic symbolism in Judaism,[2] or the teachings on "the two truths"[3] and "skillful means"[4] in Hinduism and Buddhism. In this chapter I first want to explore three important reasons that make speaking about transcendent reality unavoidable, without abandoning the insistence

1 Translation following the German text in Buber 1949, 417.
2 Cp. on this Fine 1984.
3 Cp. on this: Sprung 1973; Eckel 1987.
4 Cp. Pye 1978. For John Hick's interpretation of the theory of the "skillful means" in the context of a pluralistic theology of religions, cp. Hick 1993b, 119-136.

on its ineffability: a *logical*, a *semantic*, and a *spiritual* reason. As I will show, these three reasons correspond to particular *forms* of speech about transcendence, which can be identified easily as the three classical ways of talking about God: the *via negativa*, the *via eminentiae,* and the *via affirmativa.*

A Logical Reason and the *via negativa*

The *first* reason why, despite its ineffability we must still talk about transcendence is a *logical* reason. For whoever says that strictly speaking ultimate reality is ineffable has of course already said something about it. The human way of talking about God that corresponds to this insight is the so-called *via negativa*, that is, a limitation to expressions that negate. In this vein, only negative statements about God are considered to be true. In truth we can only speak about God by saying what God is not, rather than saying positively what God is. What can be said and what has to be said is exclusively the ineffability of God. The paradox of Wittgenstein's maxim, "Whereof one cannot speak, thereof one must be silent" (*Tractatus logico-philosophicus 7)* is thus underlying the negative or apophatic way of speaking. For here too it is true that through its very formulation—in short by the fact that it does not keep silent—this maxim contradicts itself. As Karl Rahner aptly explains, this paradox represents the basic structure of theological hermeneutics:

> … the word 'God' … is our opening to the incomprehensible mystery. … It is always open to Wittgenstein's protest, which bids us to be silent about things which we cannot speak about clearly. Notice, however, that he violates this rule in formulating it. The word itself agrees with this maxim if correctly understood. For it is itself the final word before wordless and worshipful silence in the face of the ineffable mystery.[5]

There have been attempts in the history of religion to escape this paradox—for example, through not only negating every affirmation but at the same time also negating every negation. An example of this is Dionysius' deliberations in his writing *On Mystical Theology*, where he says that God is

> not … equality, or inequality, … nor does It belong to the category of non-existence or to that of existence; … nor is It darkness, nor is It light, or error, or truth; nor can any affirmation or negation apply to It; for while applying affirmations or negations to those orders of being that come next to It, we apply not unto It either affirmation or negation, inasmuch as It transcends all affirmation by being the perfect and unique Cause of all things, and transcends

5 Cp. Rahner 1978, 51.

> all negation by the pre-eminence of Its simple and absolute nature—free from every limitation and beyond them all.[6]

It is evident that Dionysius is here emphasizing God's "transcategorial" nature.[7] That is, any affirmation *and* negation is related to categories that are not applicable to God, because they are part of a sphere of reality that, as Dionysius says, is "next to" or underneath God. Even this, however, does not finally override the paradox, but only shifts it to another level. For the negation of the applicability to God of all linguistic and conceptual categories again implicitly introduces a new kind of category, that is, the category of the "transcategorial". Thus the paradox remains.

This is true also of those attempts to avoid the paradox through recourse to total silence, as for example in the renowned ninth chapter of the Buddhist *Vimalakīrti Nirdeśa Sūtra*. Here, a gathering of high-ranking enlightened Bodhisattvas are asked to explain the entry into "the Dharma-door of nonduality," that is, the mystical surpassing of the world of conceptual distinctions. After each of the thirty-one Bodhisattvas had given an, in terms of the Buddhist tradition, exquisite response, it is Mañjuśrī's turn, the wisest Bodhisattva of them all. And he says:

> "Good sirs, you have all spoken well. Nevertheless, all your explanations are themselves dualistic. To know no one teaching, to express nothing, to say nothing, to explain nothing, to announce nothing, to indicate nothing, and to designate nothing—that is the entrance into nonduality."

After this statement, Mañjuśrī turns to Vimalakīrti, the main character of the text:

> "We have all given our own teachings, noble sir. Now, may you elucidate the teaching of the entrance into nonduality!"
>
> Thereupon, the Licchavi Vimalakīrti kept his silence, saying nothing at all.
>
> The crown prince Mañjuśrī applauded the Licchavi Vimalakīrti:
>
> "Excellent! Excellent, noble sir! This is indeed the entrance into the nonduality of the bodhisattvas. Here there is no use for syllables, sounds, and ideas."[8]

But even the *Vimalakīrti Nirdeśa* cannot escape the logical paradox. For the recording of this artful episode itself violates its own verdict.

Radical critics like Keith Yandell discard the notion of the inconceivability and ineffability of transcendent reality as "a logically contradictory doctrine, sharing with all contradictions the inelegance of being false."[9] Yet it is not at all the intention of those whom Yandell criticizes in this way to claim that transcendence can be described in a consistent, non-contradictory way. The inconceivability and inexpressibility of transcendence would be denied if one wanted to insist—as Yandell's objection presupposes—that they could be expressed without any contradiction. Put

6 Cp. Dionysius the Areopagite, *On Mystical Theology*, 5. English translation from Rolt (no year).
7 Thus fittingly John Hick (Hick 2001b, 76-89).
8 Thurman 1976, 77.
9 Yandell 1994, 115. For a similar critique see Rowe 1999.

another way, it would be inconsistent if one wanted to postulate a non-contradictory describability of what is indescribable. It is far more adequate to present divine ineffability and inconceivability by means of a paradox. The actual point of contention thus resides in the question of whether one considers it to be possible in principle that there is a reality that surpasses the human ability to grasp it, and can therefore only be expressed in a paradoxical way. Therefore the discussion about the conceivability or inconceivability of transcendence is also simultaneously a discussion about the limited or unlimited capacity of the human intellect.

A Semantic Reason and the *via eminentiae*

Is the negative and paradoxical (in its climax as a double negation) way of speaking the only possible form of speaking about God, given the fundamental inexpressibility of transcendence? In my opinion, this is not the case for the following reason: One has to say *which* reality is claimed to be absolutely ineffable and transcategorial. Let us once again turn to the example of Vimalakīrti. The totality of the Bodhisattvas' statements that preceded his silence serves, in the end, to qualify his silence. That is, they show whereof and why in the end only silence remains. Without this qualification Vimalakīrti's silence would not be a telling silence. For, as the Buddhist philosopher Dharmakīrti once concluded: Silence alone does not make one a wise man![10] Despite his radical notion that God is beyond every affirmation and negation, Dionysius too cannot escape clarifying to what kind of reality this transcategoriality applies; and he does so by describing it as "the perfect and unique Cause of all things."

Thus it is necessary to first achieve an at least preliminary verbal clarification of what kind of reality it is that finally needs to be qualified as inexpressible.[11] This *semantic* reason is usually closely connected with a specific argumentative aspect: For it is not just some "ineffable X,"[12] any random something, that than just happens to be claimed as inconceivable and ineffable, but rather that ultimate, all-embracing, and thus all-transcending reality, which is claimed to be ineffable precise-

10 Cp. Vetter 1964, 33.

11 In this sense I agree with Keith Ward that the insistence on the inexpressibility of God has to begin by first stating concrete attributes such as God's power, wisdom, etc., but will then remove their limitations and thereby contest their adequacy for God (cp. Ward 1993, 211). Yet this 'ascent' can be performed not only by beginning with a personal theistic image of God, but rather can take off from every type of concretely conceived conception of transcendental reality.

12 For this reason Yandell is wrong in insinuating that a pluralist theology of religions simply assumes the existence of some X, about which no more can be said than that it exists and that one can refer to it (Yandell 2004a, 197). In the end, Yandell's critique is based on the objection that a pluralist theology of religions, for the sake of its own consistency, could not assume more than such an "ineffable X," which would be completely irrelevant in any religious sense.

ly because of its transcendent character.[13] As Peter Byrne appropriately puts it, "we know enough to know that we cannot comprehend the transcendent."[14] Moreover, it is only by means of this determination of the ineffable reality that we can clarify that and how negative or apophatic theology differs from that kind of negation which in a materialistic, naturalistic, or nihilistic sense contests the existence of a transcendent reality, and considers only what is finite to be real.[15]

Yet negative theology by itself is insufficient to adequately determine the undeterminable without thereby abandoning its essential ineffability. This can only be achieved by identifying certain relationships that allow, by means of surpassing, to arrive at the borderline notion of inconceivable transcendence—relationships as for example the apparent to the real, the imperfect to the perfect, the many to the one, the composite to the simple, the founded to the foundation, the penultimate to the ultimate, etc. The decisive step into ineffability is taken by that act of surpassing which in the context of the respective relation denies with respect to the transcendent any limitation and finitude and hence any conceivability and speakability. Hence it is that form of speech traditionally known as the *via eminentiae* that corresponds to the *semantic* necessity of talking about the ineffable. The *via eminentiae* thus builds the indispensable basis for the *via negativa*.

Thomas Aquinas' doctrine of analogy offers a good example of this. First, Aquinas emphasizes that everything we say about God is borrowed from our experience of the created and, as such, finite and diverse reality. In contrast to this, God's being is of infinite perfection and pure oneness and simpleness beyond all diversity and complexity while also being the creative source of all things. Therefore according to Aquinas it is "impossible for something to be predicated about God and the creatures in strictly the same sense (univocally)" (*Summa theologiae I 13,5)*. Yet Aquinas also refutes the notion that one can only speak of God negatively (*Summa theologiae I 13, 2)* or totally equivocally, that is with a complete difference in meaning (*Summa theologiae I 13,5*). As an alternative, Aquinas suggests that we understand our words about God in sense of an analogy: "In this way, whatever is spoken about both God and the creatures is spoken in the sense that creatures are related to God as their origin and their cause, in which all things are found before they come to exist, and do so in the most superior way" (*Summa theologiae I 13, 5*). Hence, according to Aquinas, in speaking about God in terms borrowed from the creatures "there is neither a completely identical meaning (…) nor a completely different one" (ibid.) but rather a similar one or, better, one in the sense of an analogy.

Aquinas explains this similarity in the following way: To the extent that "God being absolutely and in every respect perfect contains within Himself, and previous to the creatures, all of their perfections, (…) every creature represents Him and is sim-

13 "One can put this by stressing that this idea of the ineffable is not just of some ineffable thing or other; it is the idea of an ineffable *God*…" Ward 1993, 211.

14 Byrne 1995, 141.

15 Cp. on this above, chapter 7, pp. 187-189.

ilar to Him in the sense that it has some perfection…" (*Summa theologiae I 13,2*). This is why God can be positively designated by means of the perfections found in the creatures, though only in an incomplete way. So if for example one calls God "good" then this means that that which "we identify as being 'good' in creatures (...) preexists in God, and this in in a higher form (*Summa theologiae I 13,2*).

However, Aquinas suggests that this "in a higher form" implies something higher "than we are capable of conceiving or expressing" (*Summa theologiae I 13,2 ad 2*). This implies that, "we cannot know God's being in this life as it is in itself" (*Summa theologiae I 13,2 ad 3*). Therefore "with reference to God (…) that what is signified remains uncomprehended and exceeds the meaning of the [signifying] name" (*Summa theologiae I 13,5*). Thus, according to Aquinas, all statements about God in the sense of analogy are always, and inevitably so, constructed from just one end of the two ends of the analogy. We know the meaning of the names that we apply to God only regarding the perfections of creatures, yet we do not and cannot know what these predicates mean with respect to God. Though according to Aquinas we can justifiably say that God is "good" or "wise," but in the final analysis we only understand what this means with respect to human beings, not to God. Revelation does not change this fact. According to Aquinas, thanks to revelation we can say things about God that—like for example his Trinitarian nature—we cannot deduce from creation. But since we do not really understand any of these, it is also true that we even "by revelation .... do not know the essence of God and thus are united to God as to one unknown" (*Summa Theologiae I 12,13, ad 1*).

One may easily think that a doctrine of analogy conceived in this way is at the end of the day useless and remains fundamentally unable to move beyond purely negative statements. For what have we gained if, according to Aquinas, one can justifiably call God "good" but have no idea what this attribute means with respect to God?[16] This critique is sound to the extent that Aquinas indeed achieved no more than what "negative theology" affirms. But presumably Aquinas does not want to achieve any more than this, in case this "more" entails abandoning God's inconceivability. Yet Aquinas' doctrine of analogy is, as a variant of the *via eminentiae*, an advance on a mere *via negativa* in that it provides a semantic foundation for the *via negativa*. It clarifies by way of analogy which reality we need to identify as ineffable and why. Indeed, Aquinas does not get beyond the *via negativa*. His achievement consists rather in giving this a profound semantic substructure. Through the negative statements of the *via negativa* and the relational statements of the *via eminentiae* it gets sufficiently clear that it is only transcendent reality that has to be designated as being necessarily inconceivable and ineffable.[17]

16 Cp. to this critique often leveled at Aquinas the summary in Vardy 1990, 42: "We can say that language about God can truly be applied to God, but we do not know what this language means when it is so applied." Similarly Byrne 1995, 151.

17 Similarly also Byrne 1995, 140.

A Spiritual Reason and the *via affirmativa*

Now if the *via negativa* and the *via eminentiae* (as a condition of the *via negativa)* can be well justified as possible ways of speaking about the unspeakable, then what about the so-called *via affirmativa*, that is, that form of language that to some extent may be considered as the primary level of religious discourse? It cannot be applied to transcendent reality in any immediate and univocal sense because then the ineffability of the transcendent would simply be contested. So is the only function left for the *via affirmativa* that of speaking in analogies before being finally surpassed and thus pointing beyond itself to the inconceivability and ineffability of God?

The American philosopher Walter Stace suggested a different possibility.[18] The affirmative statements are to be understood neither as analogous nor as symbolic statements *about* God but rather as symbolizations of human experiences of God.[19] With this suggestion Stace touches on the third reason we can give for the need to talk about transcendence although it is actually ineffable. I would like to call this the "spiritual reason," i.e. the fact that knowledge of transcendence is deeply rooted in religious experience. According to Stace, religious talk can be understood as symbolic talk when "that which is symbolized is not a proposition about God but the direct apprehension of His presence in religious or mystic intuition."[20] What Stace here identifies as "religious or mystic intuition" is thus the subjective manifestation of divine presence in human religious experience.[21]

The hermeneutic of religious language that Stace suggests thus corresponds to an understanding of revelation in which the object of revelation is none other than God him/her/itself, and this revelation reaches the human person in the form of religious experience, provided that religious experience is conceived as finite experiential impressions of an infinite reality. For then it still holds that we cannot state anything about God in God's infinite being-in-itself—just as negative theology has always insisted—but have nevertheless due to God's self-disclosure finite experiential impressions of this infinite God, to which the concrete ideas and concept of religious language refer in such a way that this language becomes intelligible. In contrast to the adaptation of the *via eminentiae* in Aquinas' doctrine of analogy, this constitutes a significant expansion in the understanding of the function of religious language. Given the conditions of the traditional teaching on analogy, we are justified in saying, for example, that God is a good father. But we do not know what "a good father" means with reference to God. Yet if the statement, "God is a good father" is to be understood in the sense that God has been experienced and can be ex-

18 Cp. Stace 1952, 50-68.
19 Effectively this comes close to Aquinas' epistemological axiom according to which the thing known is in the knower according to the mode of the knower (e.g. *Summa Theologiae* I 12,4). In light of this axiom it seems appropriate to connect the statements about God not directly to God but rather to humans' experience of God.
20 Stace 1952, 68.
21 Cp. ibid. 65f.

perienced as being like a good father, then we can of course imagine what is meant by this. Such a statement is still either symbolic or analogous, but it is intelligible because its direct reference point lies in human experience. It is only in an indirect manner that anything is said here about God in him/her/itself, insofar as the concrete God, as experienced by us, represents a finite, humanly-formed manifestation of an infinite divine reality far beyond all human conceivability. Compared to the doctrine of analogy, such a hermeneutic not only has the advantage of giving an intelligible meaning to the positive statements about God. It also has the simultaneous advantage of interpreting these statements from their original point of reference, that is, their relatedness to quite concrete experiences of God or transcendence. For the traditional doctrine of analogy does not consider the concrete origin of positive statements about God—that is, its origin in the testimonies to revelation, that is to religious experience—as important for the question of how to properly interpret these statements. In the hermeneutics of the traditional doctrine of analogy, the concrete experiences which led to the positive statements about God remain ultimately irrelevant. At least in the doctrine of analogy this aspect does not become a structural principle of the interpretation of religious language.

On the one hand, Stace's hermeneutical proposal for interpreting religious language therefore remains faithful to the core concerns of the doctrine of analogy—meaning that the ineffability of transcendence is emphasized just as is the necessity of giving negative theology a semantic substructure. On the other hand, our understanding of religious language is significantly expanded and is also brought into alignment with a communication-model of revelation. The proposal of interpreting positive statements about God as not referring immediately to God him/her/itself but rather to human experiences of God is, of course, not just Stace's invention. Rather, it is characteristic of a whole series of new theological and hermeneutical attempts in modern times.

Here once again one has to point in the first place to Friedrich Schleiermacher.[22] Already in his [*Speeches*] *On Religion* he formulates the crucial epistemological foundation of this hermeneutic: the infinite which as such escapes human understanding can nonetheless be perceived or experienced by way of its influence on people. "All perception ["Anschauung"] proceeds from the influence of what is perceived on the perceiver," which, Schleiermacher continues, "is then apprehended, synthesized, and comprehended by the latter according to his nature."[23] Hence it is only through the effect that a perceived object exerts on the subject that the subject can have an experiential knowledge of this object. And this knowledge reflects the particular ef-

22 Relayed by John Oman and Herbert H. Farmer, Schleiermacher's ideas have exercised an indirect yet unmistakable influence on leading pluralists such as Wilfred Cantwell Smith and John Hick. Oman translated Schleiermacher's *Speeches* into English and Farmer was Oman's devoted pupil and successor at Cambridge. Both Smith and Hick studied with Farmer, and both admit to having been strongly influenced by him. Cp. on this Grünschloss 1994, 31f., 199-204, as well as Hick 1998c (Preface to the 1988 reissue); Hick 2002, 83-86, 115.

23 Schleiermacher 1985, 38. Translation follows the first German edition p. 55.

fect of the object on the specific nature of the subject undergoing the experiencing: "Therefore what you look at and perceive is not the nature of things but their effect on you."[24] When we speak of God, we accordingly do not speak of God's own being, since that would be impossible for us to do, but rather of the way in which we experience God. As I mentioned in the preceding chapter, in *On Religion* Schleiermacher still characterizes this experience of God quite generally as contemplating the infinite in the finite or as the sense for the infinite. In *The Christian Faith*, he specifies this in terms of a feeling of absolute dependence. As a result, Schleiermacher suggests that we interpret all the classic attributes of God, such as eternity, omnipresence, holiness, or omnipotence, not as immediate statements about God, but rather as statements about particular forms and aspects which the feeling of absolute dependence can assume in religious experience.[25]

We find the same basic structure, albeit with different variations, in other modern attempts at a theological hermeneutic. Examples of this are Bultmann's concept of "existential interpretation," Karl Rahner's understanding of "mystagogical language," or Paul Tillich's theory of symbolic language. According to Bultmann, for example, any talk of God inadmissibly turns God into an object. Therefore speaking of God is only possible if it is refracted in talking of our own existential affection by God.[26] According to Rahner, in light of God's transcendence and inconceivability, a literal understanding of statements about God is impossible because it would necessarily make God appear to be simply one being alongside other beings. For Rahner, the meaning of positive statements about God lies instead in their ability to refer back to the various ways in which people have existentially experienced themselves as being directed toward the final transcendent horizon.[27] For Tillich it is also true that language about God cannot be understood literally, because in so doing transcendent—or as Tillich prefers to put it—ultimate reality would appear to be like a finite and penultimate reality. When Tillich continues by suggesting we understand all talk of God symbolically, then by symbolic language he means language that is able to arouse a vivid experience of God.[28]

All three theologians that I mentioned were aware that their experience-related interpretation of religious language had serious implications for the Christian understanding of non-Christian religions. And even if this aspect of their work has led Rahner and Tillich to develop their own approaches in the theology of religions, it does not really occupy a central place in their theological work.[29] This is clearly dif-

24 Ibid. 38. Original first edition p. 56.
25 Cp. *The Christian Faith* 1, §§ 50-56.
26 Cp. Bultmann 1958.
27 Cp. Rahner 1964c.
28 Cp. Tillich 1980.
29 As regards Rudolf Bultmann, Yoshinori Takeuchi reported the following instructive anecdote: On a visit in 1961, Bultmann told Takeuchi that the existential message of the Zen Buddhist "ox-herding pictures" (a pictorial and poetic summary presentation of the Zen Buddhist understanding of the path of salvation) conveys the same existential message as

ferent in the case of John Hick. At least since the 1980s at the latest, he recognized that the hermeneutics of religious language play a key role in a theology of religions.

Consequences for a Pluralist Theology of Religions

John Hick's Hermeneutics of Religious Language

Following the tradition of a negative theology, John Hick assumes that God's transcendence necessarily includes its ineffability. Hick repeatedly formulates this view in a manner reminiscent of Dionysius:

> … it [the divine reality; PSL] cannot be said to be one or many, person or thing, conscious or unconscious, purposive or non-purposive, substance or process, good or evil, loving or hating.[30]

But Hick also shares the concern not to leave things at this verdict on all possible God-talk. He too is interested in granting positive language about transcendental reality its due worth. Thus Hick suggests that we interpret the concrete descriptions of transcendent reality as either a personal or an impersonal reality by relating them to the respective experiences with which they are connected. As explained in the previous chapter, Hick assumes that every experience has the structure of "experiencing-as." The concrete notions of transcendence within the major religions reflect such experience-related interpretative categories and therefore also the result of divine revelation or manifestation.[31] That is, transcendent reality can be experienced both as a personal deity and as an impersonal absolute. The positive statements that we find in the religions primarily refer to these *personae* and *impersonae* (as Hick calls them), that is, to the religions' concrete personal deities and impersonal absolutes. Insofar as these *personae* and *impersonae* reflect genuine collective experiential impressions of transcendent reality, which Hick calls "the Real," he suggests the following constellation:

> Our human concepts, drawn as they are from our earthly experience, do not apply to the Real in itself, but only to the Real as humanly thought, experienced and responded to within the different traditions. (…) Such manifestations are formed at the interface between the Real and the various streams of human life. They consist both in the personae of the Real—Adonai, the Holy

Christianity. The only thing lacking in it would be the notion that the truth of this message is realized in history. Takeuchi 1983, 139.

30 Hick 1989, 350. For Hick's own discussion of Dionysius, see Hick 1999, 79-88; 2001b, 78-81.

31 In the mid-1980s, Hick became more critical about the use of the term "revelation," as this is too closely connected with a one-sided personalist understanding of transcendental reality, or is in danger of identifying transcendent reality only with its manifestation as a personal divinity. On this, cp. Hick 1988, 97f, and, for a more recent example, Hick 2001b, 86.

> Trinity, Allah, Vishnu and so on—and its impersonae, Brahman, the Dharmakaya, the Dao and the rest. And our concepts—such as personality, consciousness, goodness, love, justice, power, unity, plurality, substantiality—apply literally, in either the univocal or the analogical mode, to these manifestations. But in speaking literally in these ways about a manifestation of the Real we are at the same time speaking mythologically about the Real in itself.[32]

So here we have assembled the cornerstones of Hick's hermeneutics: He differentiates between transcendent reality as it is in itself ("the Real in itself" or "the Real *an sich*") and the Real as it is in valid but nonetheless typically human ways conceived of and experienced. In itself, the Real cannot be described in human terms due to its transcendence. Instead, all positive statements should be seen as referring to the manifestation of divine reality in human experience. Yet any valid, either literal or analogous, statement about such a manifestation of divine reality in human experience, simultaneously refers in a *mythological sense* to the transcendent reality as it is in itself. In order to better understand what Hick means by "mythological", one has to first look at his general theory of (conceptual) meaning.

According to Hick every experience has the structure of experiencing-as because in the process of experiencing something we assign certain concepts to whatever it is that we perceive. But now what is a concept? What does it mean if we interpret or experience something *as* this or that? Hick adopts a pragmatist approach in this as interesting as complicated field of philosophy known as the theory of meaning. That is, concepts summarize meaning and meaning is primarily to be understood in a practical, dispositional way. If, for example, we designate something as being a bar of soap, then we give it a meaning that is connected to particular expectations, which have a dispositional impact on our actions. For example, we expect to wash our hands with soap, not eat it. So when we consider something to be a bar of soap, then we find ourselves in a particular stance toward this object. The sum of the possible and adequate dispositions toward a thing is, according to Hick, what constitutes its concept. The concept therefore encapsulates the meaning that a thing has *for us*, in such a way that one is "in a distinctive dispositional state in relation to it."[33]

Such a pragmatist theory of meaning is accompanied by a corresponding criterion of truth. According to this theory, an object or situation has been conceptually understood correctly when this concept brings us into the correct or adequate disposition toward this object or situation. If we mistakenly perceive a bar of soap to be an apple, because it has been designed to look like an apple, this is a false apprehension of this object or of the meaning of the respective concept, precisely because we then find ourselves in a wrong disposition toward this object. That is, we would not expect to be able to wash our hands with this object, but if we became hungry we would be disposed to eat the supposed apple. At latest upon realizing this possibili-

32 Hick 1993b, 116f.
33 Hick 1989, 131.

ty we would learn in an unpleasant way that we had not properly grasped what the purported apple really was.

This theory of meaning Hick now applies to religious experience and the conceptual interpretation being at work in it. When he claims that though statements about transcendent reality cannot be true in a literal sense, they nevertheless are true in a "mythological" sense, then he implies an understanding of truth according to which truth consists in the correct apprehension of the meaning that a particular thing has *for us* in a primarily practical-dispositional sense.

Given that religious experience always has the structure of "experiencing-as" and thus always involves an act of interpretation in the sense of the assignment of particular concepts, according to Hick a pragmatic theory of meaning can clarify both the meaning of the respective concepts used and, particularly, the question of their adequacy. That is, although transcendent reality in its infinite being-in-itself surpasses every human concept and representation, humans experience it in a way in which conceptual mediation plays a central role. We experience transcendent reality concretely *as* this or that personal deity or *as* this or that variant of an impersonal absolute. Although none of the concepts by which we form the personal and impersonal notions of a transcendent reality literally apply to transcendent reality in itself, the personal and impersonal notions operative in religious experience and their respective conceptual descriptions can nonetheless be deemed adequate, if they, according to the pragmatic theory of meaning, bring a person into the correct disposition or right attitude toward transcendent reality. That is, the concrete notions and statements made about transcendent reality within the various religions are incorrect if one understands them to be literally true descriptions. Yet nonetheless they can be adequate in the sense that they appropriately grasp the dispositional significance which transcendent reality has for human beings.

Hick chose the term "mythological language" for this interpretation of religious language. According to Hick, even if it assumes abstract and speculative form, religious discourse about transcendent reality is:

> mythological throughout in the sense that it constitutes discourse in human terms about that which transcends the literal scope of human language (…). And the value of myth, whether in the form of a story of theological or philosophical schema, is practical. The truthfulness or untruthfulness of mythological stories, images and conceptions does not consist in their literal adequacy to the nature of the Real *an sich*—(…) the target is totally beyond their range—but in their capacity to evoke appropriate or inappropriate dispositional responses to the Real.[34]

In other words, substantial statements and notions (in contrast to purely formal ones) about transcendent reality count as "mythologically true" if in the sense of the pragmatic theory of meaning they bring a person into the right attitude toward transcendent reality.

34 Hick 1996, 378.

This not only provides an answer to the question of what significance the positive notions of God or transcendence possess when transcendent reality is actually ineffable. In addition, it also offers a criterion by which one can evaluate the different notions of transcendence. They are adequate to the extent that they correctly grasp the dispositional meaning of transcendent reality for us and induce the right existential attitude toward transcendent Reality. According to Hick, this is the case precisely when these notions bring about

> a transformation in human existence from self-centredness to Reality-centredness [i.e. transcendent "Reality"; PS-L]—a transformation which shows itself, within the conditions of this world, in compassion (*karuṇā*) or love (*agapé*).[35]

Thus Hick's criterion explicitly points to the field of soteriology. But how does one establish what the right attitude toward transcendent reality actually is? From where do we draw the criteria to determine what should count as the right or appropriate attitude toward transcendent reality? How should it be possible at all to determine what counts as appropriate in the face of a reality deemed to be an inconceivable and ineffable Reality? Such questions cannot be answered—as Hick also recognizes—without reference to the *central soteriologically normative elements of one's own respective religious tradition.* It is true that the appropriateness of a religious attitude cannot be determined by an immediate recourse to an inconceivable and ineffable reality. The inconceivability and ineffability of transcendence do have a normative significance to the extent that they rebuff dogmatic hubris and are oriented against fantasies of theological omnipotence. Apart from that, however, recourse to normative principles and mediators of revelation within one's own tradition is unavoidable. Accordingly, explains Hick, we measure the appropriateness of the attitude not by the transcendent reality itself but by its genuine manifestations.[36] Put another way, an appropriate attitude toward a genuine manifestation of the Real is simultaneously also an appropriate attitude toward transcendent reality itself.[37] With reference to Christianity, Hick says:

> ...in responding appropriately to God the Father, by imitating divine love in our love of neighbor, we are responding appropriately to the final Reality in which we live and move and have our being.[38]

Thus Hick's basic soteriological position—according to which the appropriate attitude consists of a transformation from self-centeredness to a centeredness on transcendent reality and a fundamental attitude of loving care—unmistakably reflects the dual commandment of love of God and love of neighbor.[39]

35 Hick 1989, 164.
36 Cp. Hick 1989, 248f., 350f.
37 Cp. Hick 1989, 248f.
38 Hick 1991c, 116.
39 Cp. Hick 1989, 321f.

If, however, we measure the appropriateness of a basic religious attitude by the authenticity of a manifestation of transcendent reality, and if, conversely, we assess the authenticity of this manifestation by whether it prompts an appropriate attitude, then, as Hick openly admits, we have arrived at a circular reasoning.[40] But what once again becomes clear at this central point for the construction of a pluralist theology of religions is that, precisely as its critics have cautioned, we cannot create a pluralist theology of religions from the perspective of a "bird's eye view" which would separate itself from the faith perspective of individual religious traditions. Hick himself insists that the pluralist thesis cannot be established through a separation from the perspective of faith, but only through what he calls an expansion the circle of faith.[41] Concretely, this means that we can never prove the genuineness or validity of a manifestation of transcendent reality. Rather it is something assumed by faith within each individual religious tradition. As I said in the previous chapter, revelation cannot be coercively demonstrated; it is already an expression of faith to consider something to be a revelation. However, the confidence that in one's own religious tradition a genuine and saving revelation of God or manifestation of transcendent reality is testified and mediated can be rationally justified even if there is there is no strict proof of it.[42] So if we each use the faith of our own religious tradition as the starting point when encountering witnesses to revelation and religious experience of other religious traditions, and if we consider these to be just as valid and authentic according to the same soteriological criteria, then we are not moving beyond the circle of faith but extending it to embrace various other traditions. Subsequently such an expansion can of course also lead to an expansion of the fundamental soteriological criterion—yet not in the sense of its weakening or dissolution but rather in the sense of enriching its understanding, to the extent that the concrete insight and wisdom of non-Christian paths to salvation can be included in the understanding of salvation and therefore also in a soteriological criteriology.

Yet the condition for such an expansion of the circle of faith is that one accepts the fundamental distinction between the transcendent, inconceivable and ineffable reality on the one hand and its finite manifestations found in human concepts on the other hand. For it is only on the basis of this differentiation that we can assume that the same transcendent reality has elicited different manifestations in other religious contexts, which are equally valid because they induce a similarly appropriate response.[43] Anyone who does not admit this differentiation and completely identifies ultimate reality with one particular manifestation will either, in an exclusivist sense,

40 Hick 1991b, 26; 1995, 77f.

41 Cp. for example Hick 1995, 75.

42 It can be considered as one of the most significant epistemological developments of the twentieth century that—in contrast to the nineteenth century—the criteria for a rationally justified conviction are no longer simply identified with its provability. A conviction can even count as being rationally justified when it is only possibly true, that is if critical objections can be sufficiently resolved. Cp. Kreiner 1992, 542ff; 1993, 11ff.

43 Cp. Hick 1989, 248.

reject as false every manifestation that differs from this or, in an inclusivist sense, will consider it as being deficient.

Hick's epistemology of religious experience and his hermeneutics of religious language is also relevant for another aspect, which is extremely helpful not only for the development of a pluralistic theology of religions but also beyond it: the historicity of religious language.

The personal and impersonal notions that are operative as interpretative categories within human religious experience are concepts and ideas that, according to Hick, have a concrete history. Since people who have religious experiences are historically and culturally conditioned beings, the notions which manifest and summarize people's experiences of God are also undergoing genuine historical developments. The *personae* and *impersonae* of transcendental reality live in and with the history of those peoples and civilizations whose religious experience they reflect and mediate. Thus we can reconstruct, without too much difficulty, the history of Yahweh or, as Hick calls it, of the Yahweh-*persona:* From being a storm and thunder deity with partially quite questionable moral traits, the Yahweh-*persona* evolves into a liberator and protector of the people of Israel, and finally into a monotheistically understood creator-deity of utmost power and highest moral perfection, and then evolves once again, as the Father of Jesus Christ, into the first person of a deity understood as a Trinity. With relatively little effort we can also show comparable developments and changes in the history of religion regarding other gods and impersonal notions of transcendence.

Yet these changes cannot be thought of as changes in God him/her/itself. It would contradict the idea of God if one assumed that God had, as it were, in his youth the character traits of the incalculable Yahweh, then gradually matured to become a monotheistic God of the highest moral perfection, before finally emerging as the Father-God of a three-personal being. And if one wanted to assume that God had always been the one whom he showed himself to be most recently, then why would God have hidden his true form behind such rather dubious roles? But if one explains the early stages of the development of the Christian image of God by human, historical factors, then why not also the later ones? In any way, from a theological point of view the science-of-religions' insight into the historicity of the images of God cannot be countered with a crude realism. The other extreme would of course be the naturalist response, according to which the historicity of religious notions proves that these should be seen entirely as products of human illusion and projection. Hick's hermeneutics of religious language offers to both positions a plausible and therefore theologically attractive alternative. According to this hermeneutics, the historicity of religious notions can be traced back to the historicity of the people producing these notions. To this extent naturalism is certainly right. But at the same time we find in these notions the manifestation of diverse experiences, made by entire peoples and civilizations, of a truly extant yet inconceivable transcendental reality. The different notions of transcendence are therefore on the one hand an entirely human projection, but on the other hand a projection elicited by the genuine presence of a transcendent reality, making humans aware of this presence and of its significance for an appropriate existential conduct. In this sense, the *personae* and *impersonae* are by no means *only* human projections, but rather, theistically speaking, are the results of a genuine revelation in the sense of divine self-disclosure to the human mind. It is here that we find the fundamental truth of a religious realism.

Contradictory Truth Claims? On the Consistency of the Pluralist Solution

In sum, we can repeat that the pluralist solution of the problem of religions' diverse truth claims or the divergent claims about transcendent reality consists in disputing that these claims are of a contradictory nature:

> ...the differing belief systems are beliefs about *different* manifestations of the Real. They're not mutually conflicting beliefs, because they're beliefs about different phenomenal realities.[44]

Here we should note two things. *On the one hand*, we are talking only about such claims and beliefs that refer to transcendent reality. With regard to other questions, for example of an eschatological, cosmological, or historical nature, a pluralist theology of religion does not dispute the existence of genuine contradictions. Here we need to check in each and every case whether and to what extent conflicting doctrines in these areas affect the main issue of a theology of religions, that is, the saving knowledge of transcendence.[45] *On the other hand,* we presuppose that those religions which are regarded by the pluralist thesis as equally valid actually affirm the notion that transcendent reality surpasses all human understanding and description. For it is only under this presupposition that religions are able—and even compelled—to understand their own claims about transcendent reality not as immediate and literally correct descriptions which stand in irreconcilable opposition to other supposed descriptions. And there is indeed a broad consensus among the religions regarding the inconceivability and ineffability of transcendence, a consensus to which a pluralist theology of religions can rightly appeal.[46] And yet in the past, religions have not usually been aware of the implications of this understanding for their relationships to one another, with the result that they have often embraced both the ineffability of transcendence and at the same time the claim of describing transcendent reality better than any other. A pluralist theology of religions exposes and cures this contradiction between the affirmation of transcendence and the claim to superi-

44 Hick 1995, 43.
45 On this cp. Hick 1989, 362-376; 1995, 52-56.
46 Thus also Peter Byrne against Yandell's critique. Cp. Byrne 2004a, 219f; 2004b, 216f.

ority. The fact that there are a few isolated responses that remove this contradiction in the opposite way, that is, by deciding in favor of their own claim to superiority and against the inconceivability and ineffability of transcendence,[47] is regretful but is unlikely to prevail given the strong substantial and historical rootedness of negative theology (and its non-Christian equivalents).

In their responses to a pluralist theology of religions, several critics doubt that the problem of divergent truth claims can be solved in the way just sketched. In Germany, Oliver Wiertz, among others, has advanced this objection.[48] He suggests that in the context of his pluralist thesis, Hick requires more substantial claims about transcendent reality than his insistence on divine ineffability would allow. If one assumes, as Hick does, that transcendent reality manifests itself in religious experience, then this reality must have a "causal relationship" to the subject of religious experience. We would consequently have to consider a statement like "the 'Real in itself' is such that it can be in a causal relationship to persons" as literally true.[49] In addition, due to Hick's description of the individual's saving transformation as well as what he calls "cosmic optimism," Hick's soteriology requires, according to Wiertz, that "transcendent reality be… benevolent and good," or that "the 'Real in itself' is of positive moral quality."[50] Yet these are substantial and descriptive statements. If they are assumed to be literally true, then, says Wiertz, this not only excludes the insistence on divine ineffability, but it also shows regarding the correct description of God that there remain genuine contradictions between religions, with the result that the thesis of equality proves to be untenable.[51]

> Hick's pluralist theology of religions thus is faced with a dilemma: without the ineffability thesis it cannot defend the epistemological equality and compatibility of the world religions since otherwise it has to allow incompatible religious truth claims. But with the ineffability thesis his theology of religions becomes inconsistent.[52]

As an argument against a pluralist theology of religions in general, this objection would be overdone. Even if one gives up or, more precisely, modifies the ineffability thesis so that some substantial descriptions of transcendent reality become possible, a total collapse of the pluralist thesis would not necessarily follow. In this case, we would have to confine the pluralist thesis to those religions whose notions of transcendence, interpreted as being literally true, are compatible with similarly un-

47 On this, cp. again the respective position of *Dominus Iesus* No. 6, above p. 186.

48 Cp. Wiertz 2000 and 2003. The objection in this or a similar form can be found rather frequently, including in Roth 1989; Ward 1990 and 1993; Yandell 1993; Quinn 1995; Insole 2000; Hüttenhoff 2001, 224-233. In other words it is to be found not only among critics of a pluralistic theology of religions but rather also among authors who are sympathetic to a pluralistic attempt, or who even—like Ward—represent this view and yet do so in a way that tries to get away with either a reduced or no thesis about ineffability.

49 Wiertz 2000, 401.

50 Ibid. 413.

51 Cp. ibid. 405f.

52 Wiertz 2003, 334.

derstood Christian talk about God. Or else those descriptions which are to be understood as literally true would need to be limited to a kind of common doctrinal core of several religions.[53] If one takes Christianity as the point of departure for such pluralism, then one would presumably limit the pluralist assertion of equality to the theistic religions. As a result, this position would categorize religions with a non-theistic or impersonal notion of transcendence as being either deficient or totally wrong. Wiertz, however, is correct in saying that such a truncated pluralism no longer corresponds to Hick's pluralist thesis, which explicitly also includes non-theistic religions. Moreover, Wiertz could argue that when one interprets fundamentally substantial descriptions of this kind as literally true statements about transcendence, then one presumably establishes a ranking also among those religions that have these claims in common, so that one among them describes God in a better, more precise, or more adequate way than the others. Thus in the final analysis an inclusivist theology of religions would indeed be the result.

One must not overlook the fact that this critique by Wiertz and others applies not only to a pluralist theology of religions but also hits all significant church fathers, inasmuch as they have accepted negative theology. For they too face the problem of how the affirmation of the necessary inconceivability and ineffability of transcendence consistently fits into their respective theological system. Finding a satisfactory response to the kind of objections raised by Wiertz is therefore by no means only in the interest of a pluralist theology of religions. Now as Wiertz says, we cannot deny that John Hick's pluralist theology of religions (as also do many other theologies) fundamentally assumes that transcendent reality constitutes the ultimate source of religious experience, of cosmic optimism, and of the process of salvific transformation, and that as a truly transcendent reality it is also the ultimate ground and/or horizon of all reality. Yet the decisive question is whether such claims—as Wiertz assumes—are to be understood as substantial and literally true descriptions of transcendent reality, or rather whether they fulfill the semantic function of clarifying *what kind of reality* it is that one claims to be inconceivable and ineffable, that is, whether their function should thus be seen in terms of the *via eminentia* (or its non-Christian equivalents such as "relative truth" or "skillful means"). In this case they would not need to be regarded as literally true descriptions of transcendent reality in itself, but as claims about transcendent reality *in its relation* to us and to all finite reality.[54] Hick too responded to the critical query of whether we could not and should not at the very least describe transcendent reality as good, benign, and gracious by explaining that such predicates would function as a description of transcendent reality in its relation to us.[55] But can we not derive from this also a claim about transcendent reality as it is in itself?[56] Namely: "It is a fundamen-

53 Suggestions pointing in this direction are found in Ward 1991; 162-177, 193-205; Ward 1993; Quinn 1995; Insole 2000, and Hüttenhoff 2001, 255f.

54 Cp on this my extensive discussion in Schmidt-Leukel 1997, 425-455 and 488f.

55 Cp. Hick 1995, 63, 65.

56 Cp. Ward 1990, 10f.

tal characteristic of transcendent reality in itself that in its relation to human beings it is a good reality for them." Such a reformulation is of course possible, but it does not really say more about transcendent reality in itself than was said before. What is said has its concrete meaning in relation *to us*; that is, in the first instance it says something about our nature and our appropriate disposition toward transcendent reality.[57] One can indeed concretely describe and determine the relations between transcendent and finite reality with reference to their finite pole, but we cross into the ineffable when it comes to the infinite divine pole. This is expressed hermeneutically through the reciprocal dependence of the *via eminentiae* and the *via negativa*.

This response may appear unsatisfactory when (but presumably *only* when) one assumes that divine reality must somehow or other be conceivable and describable. Yet this is precisely what negative or apophatic theology contests, because, to use the words of Augustine, that which we can grasp is certainly not God, or put in the slightly different words of Aquinas, because we can comprehend that God is necessarily incomprehensible. The desire to grasp and consistently describe transcendent reality in its infinite being-in-itself is therefore as presumptuous as it is inadequate, and is moreover doomed to failure. Therefore it also cannot be the goal of interreligious encounter to learn more and something new about the Divine as it is in itself. We are more likely to learn more and something new about how humans have experienced transcendent reality. From a pluralist perspective, the richness and diversity of human notions of transcendence show us the riches of an existential experiential treasure: How people open their lives to the presence of the transcendent, how they center their lives to this presence, and how they hope for and experience their salvation therein.

57 Cp. Hick 2001, 86f.

10. Revelation, Salvation, and Religion

As I argued in chapter three, a Cristian and pluralist theology of religions maintains that other religions mediate salvific revelation/knowledge of transcendence in ways different from, but in principle equivalent to Christianity.[1] In the previous three chapters I explained what such a position must presuppose regarding the understanding of transcendent reality, its revelation and knowability, and the expressibility of its knowledge. We turn in this chapter to questions about which understanding of salvation must be presupposed when one acknowledges that other religions mediate *salvific* knowledge of transcendence, and how this *mediation* is to be understood. Both questions are also closely connected with Christology, that is, with the theological understanding of Jesus Christ. For that reason the subsequent chapter discusses and clarifies the Christological presuppositions of a pluralist theology of religions.

What Does "Salvation" Mean?

In his self-proclaimed theological "swan song,"[2] the former Tübingen Old Testament scholar Herbert Haag complains that in theology in general and in dogmatics in particular the term "salvation" ("Heil") is being used with inflationary frequency while thereby remaining a "vague and undefined item" or even having become a mere "word husk."[3]

Haag emphasizes that there is no homogenous terminology in the Biblical Scriptures regarding the understanding of salvation. In the Old Testament we find an array of word choices with differing connotations, among which the following three stick out:

First is the notion of *help* or *rescue* (Hebrew: "js") coming from God, a notion which is particularly associated with the Exodus experience of being saved from slavery. Second is the aspect of *wellbeing, fortune, and peace*, in other words connotations associated with the word "shalom." To the extent that God himself helps the sinner to regain "shalom" despite their sin, this aspect also includes the connotation of *forgiveness* or *reconciliation.* Third, there is the aspect of *righteousness.* This can refer both to that righteousness that comes through the saving and "shalom"-creat-

1 Cp. above p. 65.
2 Haag 1992, 97.
3 Ibid. 81 and 97.

ing activity of God among people, and to the righteousness of God, in the sense of God's utter trustworthiness.

In the New Testament, the term "soteria" ("deliverance, healing") dominates, having already been used in the Septuagint to translate quite different words from the Hebrew Bible. "Soteria" too is used to describe rescue from various forms of hardship and distress and ultimately the rescue from death. But in the center of all this is the thought that help and rescue spring from God's forgiving turning to the sinner. Thus Haag summarizes: "Forgiving sins creates communion between God and humans. This is what every saving and healing intervention of God's aims for."[4] According to Haag, this is also in line with the meaning of the "Kingdom of God" in Jesus' proclamation. This too is about God's loving and forgiving commitment to the human person, which creates communion between God and humans and from which arise both the motivation for and the obligation to love one's neighbor.

Indeed, we must see the pivotal point and central issue of the Christian understanding of salvation in the notion of the God-enabled communion between God and humans, in which the communion with God must always also be realized in a loving communion with one's fellow humans. Jesus' dual commandment to love God and neighbor are the two basic pillars of a life lived under God's rule, that is to say, a life lived in communion with God and in accordance with his will. According to the witness of the New Testament, this communion created by God's loving attention cannot be severed even by death. Therefore, salvation has not only a this-worldly and present dimension, namely that of life lived under the dawn of God's kingdom or reign, but it also has an eschatological and post-mortal dimension: ultimate salvation in the fulfilled reign of God, that is, ultimate communion with God. Standing in the way of salvation is "sin," the ego-centered act of closing oneself off from openness to God and one's fellow human. Following a long theological tradition, Luther fittingly described the human in the condition of sin as "homo incurvatus in se ipsum" or "the human being curved in on oneself." Salvation then consists of God, in a sense, setting upright the person curved in on oneself, and setting him or her free to know and love God.[5] Put differently: "salvation" denotes a person's liberation from sinful self-centeredness and to a loving devotion to God and one's fellow human—a liberation made possible by the preceding forgiving care of God.

In the various branches of Christianity, theologians have repeatedly underlined that this concept of salvation implies a procedural element. That is, liberation from self-centeredness to openness to God and one's fellow human has the character of a process of personal maturation and growth, of a gradual transformation of one's personality. In Western Christianity, one has typically called this process "sanctification," whereas in the East it was often characterized as "theosis" ("deification" or "divinization"). Behind these terms lies the notion—widespread in the ancient

4 Ibid. 96.

5 Cp. WW 3, 183, 4: "...quia erigit curvum hominem in se ipsum ad Deum sursum cognoscendum et amandum in fide."

church—that although God had created humanity in his image, or as "imago dei," the goal of salvation is to mature to "God-likeness" or "similitude dei." The notion of being in the image of God ("imago dei") was primarily related to the mind as the essential feature of the human being, whereas God-likeness ("similitude dei") meant that a person develops those traits and characteristics which are similar to those of God or more precisely to those of God's incarnation in the person of Jesus. In this regard, the New Testament speaks of persons being transformed into the image of Christ (2 Cor 3:18) or of Christ assuming form in his followers (Gal 4:19), while Christ himself is described as the image of the invisible God (Col 1:15; 2 Cor 4:4). The motif of the "new Adam" is also relevant here. When in the context of the New Testament Adam-Christ parallels (cp. Rom 5:12-21 and 1 Cor 15:21-49), Jesus Christ is called the "second Adam" or the "new Adam," it is done so in contrast to the image of the old, sinful Adam. So Jesus Christ is the "new Adam" in the sense that he is a person who represents how God wants humans to be. In following Christ and being transformed into his image one becomes a "new creation" (2 Cor 5:17). As the new Adam, Jesus thus lives out and embodies what it means, according to Christian understanding, to live in a salvific relationship to God. In Jesus it becomes visible what it is to live under God's reign (i.e. under the "Kingdom of God"). This is why the church father Origen could speak of Jesus as the "*autobasileia*", i.e. as being "himself the kingdom (or reign)" of God.[6]

In assessing the salvific claims of other religions, a *Christian* theology of religion will use the cornerstones of a Christian understanding of salvation as its point of departure. In my opinion there is no alternative to this. It would be absurd to demand that a Christian theology of religions must recognize as valid or indeed equally valid even those salvific claims that blatantly contradict the fundamentals of a Christian understanding of salvation, claims which for example might idealize sinful self-centeredness, individual or collective egoism, hate, or merely indifference toward one's fellow humans and which might preach the idolization of worldly goods instead of an orientation toward transcendent reality. The knowledge of transcendence conveyed by other religions can therefore only be recognized as valid in a Christian theological sense if it is fundamentally compatible with a Christian understanding of salvation.

It is in this sense that I argued in the previous chapter, along with Hick, that it is only possible to recognize the authenticity of other manifestations or revelations of transcendent reality by drawing on their soteriological effectiveness, which however can only be evaluated in terms of the revelation witnessed to in one's own religious tradition. This is why one cannot reach a pluralist position by departing from the circle of faith of one's own tradition, but rather only by expanding the circle of faith so that it also applies to other traditions.[7] Representatives of an exclusivist theology of religious, however, contest the possibility of such an expansion. To their

6 Origen, Commentary on Matthew 12:43 and 14:7. Following Osborn 1987, 264.
7 Cp. above p. 216.

mind, the differences between the concepts of salvation—and the respective notions of transcendence—of non-Christian religions and Christianity are too serious to allow such an expansion. In order to strengthen the credibility of this thesis some exclusivists have recently, as has been shown above,[8] drawn upon the postmodern relativist idea of incommensurability. By contrast, inclusivists agree in principle to such an expansion of the circle of faith, yet also sometimes insist that in so doing one has already made a pre-decision in favor of the inclusivist position. Yet this argumentation, as I have likewise shown,[9] is based on a confusion between a hermeneutical or epistemological "inclusivism" and inclusivism as that position in the theology of religions, according to which one single religion—in this case Christianity—is superior to all the other religions regarding its mediation of salvific knowledge of transcendence.

But in order to prove itself, in the face of these exclusivist and inclusivist objections, as a nevertheless possible option, a Christian pluralism needs to assume two things: first that the concepts of salvation in those religions which are included by the pluralist thesis are compatible with the fundamental tenets of a Christian understanding of salvation, and second that despite their differences, they can be assessed as being equally valid. The crucial question is therefore whether one can expand the circle of faith in such a way that it both preserves the normative nature of one's understanding of salvation, without thereby automatically implying its superiority, and retains the recognition of genuine difference. Both conditions can be fulfilled if the particular aspects of one's own religion's concept of salvation are seen as but one *normative example* of a concept of salvation which, in principle, can also be understood in a broader sense. Yet precisely this seems possible if one admits that the approval of the concept of salvation within one's own religious tradition is based on criteria which do not depend in a logically exclusivist manner on this tradition.[10] Under certain conditions, the concepts of salvation in non-Christian religions can then be not only compatible with the Christian understanding of salvation, but also be equally valid and complementary despite and in their difference. The Christian point of departure, according to which the saving knowledge of God as mediated by Jesus is normative, does not exclude the possibility that there are, as Roger Haight has correctly emphasized, "other savior figures of equal status...who may also reveal something of God that is normative."[11] On the contrary, because of its inherently universal dimension, the revelation of God in Jesus even has heuristic value. It motivates us to actively watch out for other mediators and revelatory testimonies of that salvation which is meant for everybody.[12] Thus within a pluralist theology of religions the expansion of the circle of faith leads to a certain expansion of the concept

8 Cp. above p. 43.
9 Cp. above pp. 68, 72f.
10 On this cp. once more my discussion on the criteriological problem in the theology of religions, above pp. 41-50.
11 Haight 1992, 281.
12 Cp. Haight 1999, 409.

of salvation itself. Although remaining bound by its normative limits, such an expansion is nevertheless significant. In this way, the concept of salvation in one's own tradition is seen anew in a larger context, namely as *one* normative example among others that are different from it but nevertheless compatible with it.

In this sense John Hick suggests that we can interpret the various concepts of salvation in religions encompassed by the pluralistic thesis as exemplary concretions of a more general soteriological structure, which he describes as "the transformation from self-centeredness to Reality-centeredness", whereby "Reality" refers to "the Real", the transcendent reality. This does not imply that this "transformation" occurs somewhere in just this, so to speak, bare formality. It occurs only in the diversity of the particular concepts and paths of salvation found in the respective religions.[13] Yet the abstract quality of the formula allows one to understand the path of salvation in another religion, despite or perhaps even because of its difference from one's own religion, as being an equally valid form of this salvific transformation process. Much the same as when one person can recognizes another person as an equally worthy human being, despite their differences in gender, color, language, customs etc. Or to put it more precisely, not *despite* but rather just in their being different, because after all human beings do not exists as the formal and abstract item of "a human being", but only in the concrete diversity of race, gender, culture, etc.[14] Such a recognition of course necessarily brings with it a change in one's self-perception since now one's own way of being human is no longer equated with being the human being as such, as if all others were not or not fully human, but as one concrete example of human existence among others. An analogous change occurs when one views the concept of salvation in one's own religious tradition as a normative example of a basically much broader notion of salvation, as for example in the sense of John Hick's formula. However, just as granting equal value to a person of another race does not exclude that there are other living beings which are not "humans," the proposal of a broader understanding of salvation as "the transformation from self-centeredness to Reality-centeredness" does not exclude that there may be or actually are other concepts of salvation that do not correspond to this formula and should thus be viewed as highly problematic or even as clearly to be rejected. To what extent the followers of the various religious traditions are prepared to recognize other religious traditions' concepts and paths of salvation as being compatible and even equally valid and complementary to one's own understanding of salvation, and how such complementarity may then be articulated in detail, is a matter for dialogical discussion between the respective religions. Therefore it is necessary to come back to this issue in the third part of the book. What we must now pursue further is the question of how

13 Cp. Hick 1989, 36-55. Compare with this interpretation of Hick also Byrne 1995, 95-103.

14 This example is by no means plucked out of thin air. In the history of many great civilizations we can see that in encountering people of another color, race, culture, etc., it was often a contentious matter as to whether these others were in fact humans. Perhaps we still find ourselves in a similar state of uncertainty regarding the recognition of the religions of other peoples.

we can understand the religious mediation of salvation in the context of a Christian and pluralist theology of religions. For this, we first need to return once more to the theology of revelation.

Salvation as the Purpose of Revelation

The Christian concept of salvation is closely connected to the idea of revelation, in that it views revelation as occuring for the sake of our salvation. To put it rather casually, revelation isn't a divine pastime, neither is it simply a luxury good for humanity, not essentially needed for the actual living of people's lives. Rather, the purpose of revelation is no less than the salvation of human beings. In the context of an instruction-model of revelation (an understanding of revelation as the divine communication of texts or propositions) this means that God reveals to human beings that information that they need to know and believe in order to attain salvation. The communication-model of revelation (God reveals him/her/itself rather than texts or propositions) offers an even closer connection between revelation and salvation. At the same time, a communication-model of revelation is far more in line with the biblical foundation of the Christian concept of salvation. For if salvation is mainly about living in loving openness to God and to one's fellow humans, then, as already said, it is precisely God's forgiving self-disclosure that, in the first place, makes it possible to live in such a saving relationship to God. That is, without God's self-disclosure humans can have no relationship to God and therefore also no salvation. In this model, revelation is therefore the condition of salvation in an immediate and consistent sense.

As shown in the discussion on exclusivism and inclusivism from the first part of this book, numerous Christian theologians—though not all—endorse the belief in a universal salvific will of God according to which God wants the salvation of all human beings. This belief is expressed in a terminology that is fully embedded in a personal conception of transcendent reality. To speak of a will, indeed a will of God that is loving and ready to forgive, is only possible if one views divine reality as being a person. In other religions shaped by the notion of a personal God one finds similar beliefs regarding the all-encompassing and unlimited love and mercy of God. But if we bear in mind that the concept of God as being somewhat like a person neither exhausts nor grasps the infinite reality of God, then we have to reinterpret the doctrine of the universal salvific will of God as a particularly strong and personalist expression of that cosmic optimism which results from faith in the existence of a transcendent reality that surpasses all limitations of the world and which thus gives human hope a quite different basis than the world could do on its own. As I have tried to show in the previous chapter, transcendent reality, despite its inconceivable and ineffable nature, has its meaning for understanding our existence and living our life in the right disposition, a meaning that can be adequately expressed by the image or analogy of a merciful and forgiving father who excludes no one from his benevolence, or—as many find equally compelling—through the image of an empathetic, caring mother who excludes none of her children.[15]

If there truly is a genuine possibility of salvation for every person—as expressed in the doctrine of the universal salvific will of God—and if divine self-disclosure is the fundamental condition for any possibility of salvation, then it follows that there must be a universal revelation that reaches every person. Karl Rahner's thesis of a transcendental revelation is still, to me, the most plausible way of how one may conceive a revelation that reaches everybody. That is, the structural openness of the human mind to the infinite, the presence of an incomprehensible horizon which comprehends all our limited knowledge, suggests a fundamental familiarity with the infinite reality of God, even if this is not always reflected as such. Theologically it can therefore be understood as the basic way in which God reveals him/her/itself to the mind of every person.

But if the salvation-yielding revelation essentially reaches all humans, then what role do the religions play in mediating salvific revelation or salvific knowledge of transcendent reality? This is undoubtedly a question of crucial significance to an inclusivist as well as to a pluralist theology of religions. For both positions assume that other religions do mediate saving knowledge of God, even if they appraise the quality of this mediation differently. For this reason, in what follows I will include reflections by pluralist thinkers like Hick, Smith, and Knitter, as well as by Rahner, the still most important representative of an inclusivist approach.

The Salvific Significance of the Religions

Faith, Relationship to God, and Religion

In order to better understand the role that religions play in mediating salvific knowledge of transcendence, it is helpful to begin with the relationship between religious tradition or institutionalized religion and an individual's personal attitude of faith. Broadly speaking, the term "faith" has two dimensions: on the one hand, the cognitive dimension of believing, that is of holding certain statements to be true (as for example in the sense of "I believe that God exists") and on the other hand the non-cognitive or existential dimension of trust or confidence or of an inner orientation towards that in which one trusts (as for example in "I have faith in God", meaning: "I trust in God, I depend on him, I orient my life by him.").

15 In Christianity the notion of God as loving mother is traditionally less developed than in some other religions, even though some biblical texts do occasionally yield motherly references to what God is like. In popular Christian piety, Mary as "the Mother of God" has of course oftentimes functioned as a maternal image of God and has in particular become a personification of God's grace and readiness to forgive.

Wilfred Cantwell Smith, who counts with John Hick as one of the "fathers" of a pluralist theology of religions, devoted a large part of his studies to the concept of faith and to the relationship between faith and religion.[16] According to Smith, the two aforementioned dimensions of faith are to be strictly differentiated, in that only faith in the sense of an existential orientation to God may count as saving faith. However, faith in the sense of believing, that is as merely assenting to the truth of particular statements, is as such not relevant to salvation because such assent can refer to all kinds of things without implying anything about whether a person is living in a salvific attitude toward God and toward his or her fellow humans. Smith differentiates both dimensions by strictly reserving "believing" and "belief" to capture the notion of holding particular statements ("beliefs") to be true, whereas the word "faith" is reserved for a person's existential attitude toward God. Smith defines "faith" as

> an orientation of the personality, to oneself, to one's neighbour, to the universe; a total response; ...a capacity to live at a more than mundane level; to see, to feel, to act in terms of, a transcendent dimension.[17]

In contrast to this, he defines "belief" simply as "the holding of certain ideas."[18] The difference between "faith" and "belief" becomes clear in as much as it is entirely possible to have beliefs without having any faith.[19] Yet there are also points of connection: According to Smith, "faith" can appear in different forms and tinges, and in this the "beliefs" of a person play some role. For the "faith" of a concrete person is shaped, formed, and influenced by his or her era and culture, and by the religious tradition in which he or she lives. The particular historical epoch, culture, and religion also include certain "beliefs," certain general ideas and statements of faith considered to be true. As such, these contribute to the particular tinge of the "faith." Smith thus proposes the thesis "that faith differs in form, but not in kind."[20] He continues:

> just as Christians have been saved by faith of a Christian form, so have Muslims by faith of an Islamic, Andaman Islanders of an Andaman. (...) saved ... by their faith—or, by God through their faith.[21]

In his comprehensive comparative study, *Faith and Belief* (1979), Smith presents and analyzes the different forms and manifestations of faith in Christianity, Islam, Hinduism, and Buddhism in detail. He finds his thesis confirmed that saving faith does

16 Basic to Smith's understanding of the relation between faith and religious tradition is *The Meaning and End of Religion* (Smith 1978), then, on the concepts of faith and belief, the two works *Belief and History* (Smith 1977) and *Faith and Belief* (Smith 1979), and, on the impact on the theology of religions, his *Toward a World Theology* (Smith 1989).

17 Smith 1979, 12.

18 Ibid.

19 Cp. ibid.

20 Smith 1989, 168.

21 Ibid. 168-9.

not always have to take a personalist form, that is, the form of a personal relationship of trust in a God imagined as a personal being. Rather, faith in the sense of an integral existential orientation can also take on forms influenced by religions that are informed by a concept of transcendence as an impersonal reality.

Smith's thesis of one saving faith in various religiously-shaped forms or manifestations corresponds to John Hick's thesis that faith is the interpretative element within religious experience. As shown above, Hick argues that religious experience—like all other kinds of experience—always has the structure of "experiencing-as." So if in religious experience a person experiences a particular event *as* being directed by God, or the starry night sky *as* an expression of the Creator's majesty, or a particular state of contemplation *as* union with the divine Brahman, etc., then it is the interpretive categories from the respective religions that shape each experience. On these grounds, Hick can compare the religions with different lenses through which people in different ways perceive the divine reality.

Similarly, Smith refers to the religious traditions as "channels" of divine self-disclosure and as "instruments" of God's saving work. People receive salvific revelation, in the sense of divine self-disclosure, through "faith," and the respective religious tradition in turn shapes and conveys the concrete form of this faith. Herein lies, according to Smith, the real significance and task of religions: They are to nourish and support people's faith. Of course, the formative power of religions can also have the opposite effect. That is, religions can also weaken and hinder the faith of their adherents instead of fostering it.[22]

Yet according to Smith, the relationship between an individual's faith and the corresponding religious tradition in which the person lives out their faith is by no means only to be understood in the sense of a one-sided influence in which religion shapes "faith." Rather, the effect is reciprocal. It is not only that religions have their impact on the faith of the people living in and by these religion. But rather, and even more so, the living faith of these people forms and sustains the religious traditions to which they belong.[23]

The way how Smith defines the relationship between faith and religious traditions coincides in several respects with Karl Rahner's conception of this relationship. According to Rahner, saving faith is, in its original sense

> …nothing other than the positive and unconditional acceptance of one's own existence as meaningful and open to a final fulfilment, which we call God.[24]

Existentially this acceptance of one's relatedness to transcendence is always lived out in concrete actions and decisions. These show whether people truly trust in and engage with the divine mystery that surrounds their existence, whether they indeed risk abandoning themselves to this mystery, or whether they close themselves off

22 Cp. ibid. 168ff.
23 Smith, 1979,5.
24 Rahner, Weger 1979, 40f. English translation from Rahner, Weger 1981, 25.

to it. In the concrete existential events of life, faith thus—as Rahner says—takes on a "categorical" form, in other words a concrete form in time and place. Yet it is not only a person's faith that in this way assumes a categorical concreteness but rather also the revelation that in the first place enables and sustains this faith. Rahner therefore speaks not only of a transcendental but also of a categorical revelation. For when a person lives in a way that conforms existentially to transcendental revelation, his or her life becomes a historically concrete interpretation of transcendental revelation—and it is this that Rahner characterizes as categorical revelation.

The historically concrete place at which such interpretation occurs, and thus the location of the categorical revelation, is the religions. The categorical expression of faith and revelation in the religions can of course differ in quality. That is, there can be expressions that tend to be pure and felicitous objectifications of what salvific faith is and of what it means for a person to accept their relatedness to transcendence and therewith divine self-disclosure. Yet in the religions one may also find misinterpretations, misconceptions, and culpable depravations of this relatedness to transcendence. Similar to Smith, Rahner too assumes a reciprocal effect between lived faith and its categorical objectification within the religions. Religions are not merely objectifications and manifestations of faith; rather, precisely as such objectifications, religions also influence and shape the faith of those people living in and by the religions.

If the relationship between salvific faith and its religious mediation is defined along the lines of Smith and Rahner, then it is possible that there are genuine theological differences in quality on the level of the religious mediation of salvific knowledge of God. Religions can help or hinder "faith." They can be good, or not as good, channels of divine revelation, better or worse instruments of the divine salvific impact. They can embody both successful and unsuccessful objectifications of human relatedness to the transcendent. This possibility of genuine differences in the quality of the religious mediation of saving faith, as well as of the categorical revelation informing faith, is important both for a pluralist and for an inclusivist position. Inclusivism assumes that, at the level of categorical revelation, there is one single culmination in the mediation of the salvific knowledge of God. Hence it fundamentally presupposes that there are religious differences in quality. Yet pluralists also agree that—as Hick puts it—"not all religious persons, practices and beliefs are of equal value,"[25] or, as Smith says, that by no means "all forms [of religion] are equally valid or effective or acceptable."[26] Like inclusivists, so pluralists too accept that there are differences among the religions regarding the quality of their mediation of salvific knowledge of transcendence. Yet in contrast to inclusivists, pluralists hold that there is not one single religion that stands out as superior to all the rest. Smith himself concisely expressed this difference between his own pluralist position and Rahner's inclusivism in this way:

25 Hick 1989, 299.
26 Smith 1987, 57.

> He [Rahner] has assumed that Christian formulations are the making explicit of the truth of God's relation to humankind, whereas I have observed that they are *an* explicit formulation, but not *the*.[27]

The different positions on this question do not result from a different understanding of the relationship between salvific faith and its religious mediation, but are rather connected to differences in their views of Christology, to which I return in the next chapter. But for now I want to explain in more detail which impact the recognition that there exist genuine differences in quality regarding the mediation of salvific knowledge of transcendence in and by the religions has on a more precise understanding of their relevance for salvation.

The Universal Possibility of Salvation

Let us begin our reflections with the axiom of the universal salvific will of God. If one avoids religious exclusivism, this axiom implies not only the possibility of salvation for all human beings, but also that there exists for every person, already within their present lifetime, the possibility of living within a salvific relationship to God. This is precisely what is presupposed if one assumes that the divine self-disclosure reaches every person, a view which, as has been said, can best be understood in the sense of Rahner's concept of transcendental revelation. That is, already by the transcendental structure of their mind, every person is open to the notion of an infinite reality. Under the condition that such an infinite reality really exists, every person has already been given a certain familiarity with God that makes it fundamentally possible for them to lead their life in orienting toward this divine or transcendent reality. In light of Rahner's, Smith', and Hick's reflections, it can be further concluded that religions embody the concrete spatio-temporal manifestation of such a transcendence-related orientation. To the extent that this orientation is lived-out adequately, the religions convey categorical revelation. It is in this way that they effectively shape the existential relationship to God or orientation toward transcendence of those people living under their influence.

If, however, we assume that in the religions' mediation of categorical revelation there are qualitative differences in clarity or adequacy, would we then have to conclude that this inevitably implies a difference regarding the chance of salvation? As, for example, in the sense in which Rahner concluded that Christianity offers the highest and best chance of salvation because of its, as Rahner supposed, singular superiority? In my discussion on inclusivism, I mentioned that Rahner employs this conclusion to support his view that even within the context of inclusivism there continues to be the need for proselytizing mission.[28] So if one interprets the salvif-

27 Smith 1984, 60.
28 Cp. above pp. 139f.

ic relevance of the religions in the way that I suggested (in following Rahner, Smith, and Hick), must not then the chance of salvation be all the greater for those fortunate enough to belong to a religion in which revelation has attained a clearer and more successful objectification than in another one? And what about those who belong to a depraved religion or none at all? Is their chance of salvation correspondingly smaller, perhaps gone altogether, or only existent in trace quantities proportional to the dim remnants of genuine religious impulses? The consequence of such an unequal distribution of the chance of salvation, as it seems to inevitably result from the conception sketched out here so far, surely can no longer do justice to the axiom of the universal salvific will of God, which is actually the principle underlying this whole conception. As Bert van der Heijden once rightly remarked in his discussion of Karl Rahner's theology, it does not really fit with the idea of the universal salvific will of God to assume that, "from the outset and independent of a person's own stance, God has given some only a miserly chance at being saved."[29]

Thus our deliberations on the salvific relevance of the religions apparently lead to a dilemma: If, on the one hand, one insists that revelation as mediated by religions, i.e. in its categorical dimension, is not completely irrelevant to salvation, then the differences in the clarity and quality of the mediation of revelation seem to require the assumption that there are different degrees in the chance of salvation, which is evidently in conflict with the presupposition of a universal salvific will of God. If, on the other hand, one wants to conclude from the universal salvific will of God the existence of something along the lines of a universal equal opportunity for salvation, then the question of to what religion one belongs or whether one even belongs to a religion at all, becomes both existentially and soteriologically irrelevant. The particular quality or adequacy of categorical revelation, as mediated by the religions, would thus lose any relevance for salvation. Up until now, far too little attention has been paid to this problem in the debate on the theology of religions. But its solution seems to me essential for the construction of a satisfactory theology of religions because it directly concerns a more precise determination of the salvific relevance of the religions. In the following section I briefly propose a possible solution.[30]

The Chance of Salvation and the Salvific Situation

In connection with his discussion on Rahner, Van der Heijden introduced the distinction between the *chance of salvation* ("Heilschance") and the *salvific situation* ("Heilssituation"). According to this distinction, the soteriological relevance of religions does not affect a person's *chance of salvation*, but his or her *salvific situation*. The chance of salvation refers to the basic possibility of being able to lead one's life in a saving relation to God. This chance is indeed equally available to all people, in-

29 Heijden 1973, 292.
30 Cp. on this Schmidt-Leukel 1998c.

dependent of to what religion one belongs or whether one belongs to a religion at all. An atheist too can lead his or her life in such a way that he or she does not let it be determined only by the finite reality of the world, but rather enacts a hope for meaning that surpasses everything that would appear as meaningful from a purely mundane perspective. What nonetheless varies, and what gives religions their respective significance, is not the people's chance of salvation but rather their salvific situation. The salvific situation is marked by differences in the awareness and quality of the respective relationship to transcendence.[31] Thus according to this distinction, and in line with the axiom of the universal salvific will of God, each person is given the *same chance of salvation* relative to his or her present life situation and his or her inner development. But there are marked differences in the actual salvific situation of people. And from this can be concluded that superior or more successful forms of categorical revelation result in correspondingly *higher levels of salvific situations*.

Of course it is always the same God who reveals him/her/itself, but this revelation is also influenced by the quite different cultural, historical, and individual situations of the one receiving revelation. The goal of revelation is the salvific transformation of a person, that is, the transformation from a sinful self-centeredness to a centeredness on the divine reality and to a loving openness toward one's fellow humans. Decisive in terms of the chance of salvation is whether a person lets him- or herself be moved toward this goal, not the point or level at which this movement begins.[32] Each person therefore has the same chance of salvation, because it is, in principle, always possible for a person to follow the transformative impulse. The salvific situation, however, refers to the degree and form of saving transformation that a person has attained or that is attainable to him or her. This can certainly vary depending on the respective clarity of revelation in the context of each particular religion. For with their stories and teachings, with their rituals and institutions, with their commandments, ideals, and conventions, religions can at an individual and communal level either encourage or hinder people's salvific transformation. This is what constitutes the blessing and curse, the promise and fate of religions: Due to their influence on the lives of people, religions can, as signs and instruments of divine grace, in a very real way advance people's salvific situation. They can so aid and abet the salvific transformation of persons that this process can continually reach higher levels. But given their depravation and perversions, religions can also negatively influence the salvific situation. Without removing responsibility from the individual person, religions can nevertheless cultivate a context in which either the fruit of the Spirit flourishes or the undergrowth of greed, hatred, and delusion spreads. We can therefore speak of a "soteriocentrism" of the religions—of their common focus on salvation—in the sense that they can contribute significantly to the improvement of the human salvific situation. Religions can and should indeed be a "sign and instrument" of salvation; that is, they can and should represent and foster mankind's

31 Cp. Heijden 1973, 293ff.
32 Cp. on this the similar reflections in Kraft 1979 216-257, esp. 239ff.

unity with God and with one another, as we may say in expanding the so-called "sacramental ecclesiology" of the Second Vatican Council.[33]

Soteriocentrism

Paul Knitter introduced the term "soteriocentrism" into the discussion on the theology of religions for two reasons. On the one hand, Knitter was responding to critical objections to a "theocentric" understanding of religions, and on the other hand he was aiming at connecting the theology of religions with liberation theology. In contrast to inclusivist approaches, according to which the actual center and fulfillment of the religious life of humanity is found in the Christian church ("ecclesiocentric" approaches) or in Christ ("Christocentric" approaches), John Hick had argued in his earlier writings on the theology of religions—as for example in *God and the Universe of Faiths*[34]—that it is God who stands at the center of all religions. The major world religions are all oriented toward God rather than toward a particular form of divine revelation, as for example God's revelation in Jesus Christ, or toward a particular faith community that testifies to this revelation, as the the Christian church. This position soon became known in the theology of religions debate as the "theocentric" model. The critics, however, argued that a "theocentric" theology of religions would be biased in placing the theistic religions—the religions that conceive of transcendent reality primarily as a personal god—into the center of the history of religions. From a theocentric perspective the major non-theistic religions would, compared to the theistic ones, inevitably appear as deficient. In response to such criticism, Hick specified his approach. The divine or transcendent reality in its fundamental inconceivability equally surpasses both its representation and conceptualization as a personal god and as an impersonal absolute. It is therefore not a personal god who stands at the center of religions, but rather the inconceivable transcendent reality, the "Real", that is manifest in humanity's religious experience both as a personal god and an impersonal absolute.

Paul Knitter responded to this critique of "theocentricism" by suggesting a "soteriocentric" approach in the theology of religion. According to Knitter, the center of all religions lies in their efforts toward liberation, "identifying a dissatisfying or broken state of human affairs which they try to repair…."[35] Given their "shared concern for the suffering that is shaking our earth" religions have a common cause that on the one hand corresponds to the inner concerns of religions and on the other is imposed to each of them "by the reality of the world."[36] This shared foundation fur-

33 On this cp. the Second Vatican Councils's Constitution on the Church, *Lumen gentium 1.*
34 Hick 1973.
35 Knitter 1988b, 26.
36 Knitter 1991, 210. Extensively discussed in Knitter 1995.

nishes both a common basis for interreligious dialogue and also a point of departure for a "Christian liberation theology of religions:"

> A Christian liberation theology of religions, therefore, will propose as the "common" (…) ground or starting point for religious encounter not *Theos*, the ineffable mystery of the divine, but rather *Soteria*, the "ineffable mystery of salvation."[37]

This proposal can easily be misunderstood to mean that Knitter wanted to abandon the idea of a shared transcendent reality as the common ground underlying all religions and revealing itself within them.[38] However, there are many other statements from Knitter that contradict such an interpretation. Also in connection with the statement just cited, Knitter makes clear that soteriocentrism offers the possibility to discover the religions' common relation to transcendence and to spell out concretely its salvific relevance. Knitter writes:

> Within the struggle for liberation and justice with and for the many different groups of oppressed persons, believers from different traditions can experience together, and yet differently, that which grounds their resolves, inspires their hopes, and guides their actions to overcome injustice and to promote unity. (…) In order, therefore, to enter the difficult discussion of whether there is a "common essence" or "ground" within all religions, in order to know whether "God" and "Sunyata" might, after all, have something in common, we must not only pray and meditate together, but we must first act together with and for the oppressed.[39]

Thus Knitter's soteriocentric version of a pluralist theology of religions also operates within the framework of the overarching consideration according to which the authenticity of a supposed manifestation of transcendent reality can be determined only by recourse to its soteriological effectiveness. What Knitter rightly emphasizes is that we must not allow salvation and liberation to be constricted to an individualistic understanding. Or, put another way, if the salvific transformation to loving openness toward one's fellow humans proves itself in how we respond to their suffering, religions as influential institutions are inevitably confronted by the question of whether and how they contribute to the alleviation of suffering on the social and societal levels. Thus we can state both, that Knitter adopted Hick's formula of a "trans-

37 Thus Knitter in his contribution to *The Myth of Christian Uniqueness*, Knitter 1987, 187.

38 Bryne points to this danger (1995, 89f) and Lienemann-Perrin (199, 159) speaks of a Knitter who "after his experiments in religious pluralism" and on the basis of his insight into the "uncircumventable diversity" of the religions, allegedly took his frustrated farewell from pluralism (cp. ibid. 143, 145). Theo Sundermeier went so far as to conclude from this and announce to the assembly of the Working Group of the Christian Churches in German (known as ACK) on March 2, 2000 in Mainz: "…Pioneers of dialogue, such as Paul Knitter, [have] in the last few years become, full of resignation, reticent and quiet, and have turned toward other aspects of the exchange, if they haven't turned away from it completely" (Sundermeier 2000, 326).

39 Knitter 1987, 186f.

formation from self-centeredness to Reality-centeredness"[40] and that Hick pointed out that his formula includes the dimensions of political and economic liberation. In fact, Hick sees in liberation theology one of the most important ongoing developments and enrichments of the religious concept of salvation, precisely because liberation theology pushes this concept beyond its individualistic constriction.[41]

If one compares the histories of the major religious traditions with regard to their salvific effectiveness, that is their potential to advance people's salvific situation, then as far as is humanly possible to tell none of those traditions has fostered the salvific process in a more optimal and obviously more efficient way than any of the others. None of the major religions has proved superior to all others in this regard. They all witness equally well to both the highest ideals of spiritual life as well as to examples of tragic failure. They have all helped excellent fruits of a salvific relationship to transcendence to flourish. Yet they all also have a dark side replete with violence and horror. The good and the bad, the holy and the unholy facets of the major world religions seem to have kept the scales balanced. Hence we cannot conclude, neither with regard to the theoretical teaching of the religions nor to their practical and historical aspects, that only one among them offers the most favorable conditions for the salvific transformation process. The diversity of concrete insights, practical paths, and cultic and ritual symbolizations through which religious traditions are able to advance salvific transformation reflects the individual and cultural diversity of human life in its relationship to transcendence. By discovering this diversity and perpetually learning to understand it better, religions can offer one another quite concrete spiritual assistance, and through this can both enrich and grow with one another—if nothing else even through an increasing recognition and better understanding of the abysses and dangers that lurk in all of them and of the mechanisms which are at work in these.

Certainly we must emphasize that religions cannot force the process of salvific transformation, nor bring it about in a mechanical and monocausal manner, but that they can "merely" promote and foster this process. They can support it by pointing out to people in their cultural and individual differences the ways of opening to God and to their fellow human, by making people sensitive to God's self-disclosure and by encouraging them to respond to it in their own lives, by creating the space in which the salvific presence of God can be experienced. In this respect, John Hick and Josef Ratzinger need to be cited again as their views on this point seem to coincide strikingly. According to Hick:

> Religious traditions and their various components—beliefs, modes of experience, scriptures, rituals, disciplines, ethics and lifestyles, social rules and organisations—have greater or less value according as they promote or hinder the salvific transformation.[42]

40 Cp. Knitter 1991, 215.
41 Cp. Hick 1989, 303-306.
42 Hick 1989, 300.

That is,

> … a transformation which shows itself, within the conditions of this world, in compassion (*karuṇā*) or love (*agape*).[43]

And Josef Ratzinger judges that:

> …it is not the system and the practice of a system that saves a person; rather, what saves a person is something that is more than any system and that represents the opening up of all systems: namely love and faith, which are the true cessations of egoism and of self-destructive hubris. The religions are effective for salvation in so far as they lead persons into this attitude; they hinder salvation in so far as they hinder persons taking on such attitude.[44]

Thus from behind the institutional aspect of religions appears once again the personal element of religion: If salvific openness to transcendent reality is objectivized within religions in a multitude of ways, then it is ultimately through persons who have opened themselves to this reality and who in so doing are and have been liberated to love. Religions can best support the process of salvific transformation if their traditions are the result of exceptional human cases of transparency to God and of loving devotion to one's fellow humans, and if this inheritance stays alive in them. Religions can be "channels," "signs," or "instruments" of God's revealing and salvific work because concrete persons have become such "channels," "signs," and "instruments"—or better: because they became "mediators." Herein lies the significance of those exemplary figures who, as founders and saints of their particular religious traditions, give those traditions their existence and their particular flavor, as well as the significance of those countless people who gain direction and provisions for the journeys of their lives from these religious traditions, and precisely by so doing in turn fill the traditions with life. The following chapter therefore discusses in more detail the founding figure of Christianity and how to understand his mediation of salvation in the sense of a pluralist theology of religions.

43 Ibid. 164. "Karuṇā" is the technical Buddhist term for the religiously motivated loving concern for one's fellow creatures.

44 Ratzinger 1969, 356.

11. Revelation, Incarnation, and the Mediation of Salvation

Some critics, such as Wolfhart Pannenberg,[1] Alister McGrath,[2] and Gavin D'Costa,[3] have described religious pluralism as "not a Christian position" or as an "abandonment" of what is "authentically Christian," and Lesslie Newbigin has even called it "unbelief" and "a form of paganism."[4] The reason for such negative appraisal is typically Christological in nature; in other words, a pluralist theology of religions is rejected because it is supposedly irreconcilable with a Christian interpretation of Jesus.[5] More precisely, the discussion is about three central aspects of Christology: about how to understand firstly, Jesus' mediation of salvation, secondly, the doctrine of the incarnation, and thirdly, the closely related Trinitarian image of God. The key to developing an understanding of all three, the mediation of salvation, the incarnation, and the Trinity, in such a way as is compatible with religious pluralism, lies once again in the theology of revelation. This is what now needs to be shown.

Jesus as Revealer

In chapter eight I explained that revelation can be conceived either according to the instruction-model or the communication-model, in other words either as the sharing of propositional content through which we are instructed about supernatural matters, or as a self-communication of God through which a salvific relationship to transcendent reality is enabled. I further tried to show that a pluralist theology of religions has to presuppose an understanding of revelation along the lines of the communication-model. These basic reflections are now also important for the inquiry about the Christological presuppositions of a pluralist theology of religions. This means, within the framework of a pluralist theology of religions Jesus can only be thought of as revealer if revelation is understood according to the communication-model.

The reasons for this position are by no means primarily produced by the questions of a theology of religions. Quite independent of the theology of religions, it is

1 Cp. Pannenberg 1987b, 188.
2 McGrath 1992, 489.
3 Cp. D'Costa 1996, 226.
4 Cp. Newbigin 1990, 147.
5 As summarized in Eddy 2002, 149f.

recommendable to understand Jesus' function as revealer according to the communication-model. This holds for two reasons: on the one hand simply because of the general advantages of the communication-model over the instruction-model. The communication-model allows for a significantly more plausible distinction between the divine and human part in the event of revelation than does the instruction-model: the "supernatural" content of the revelation is nothing but God alone. Propositions and texts by contrast are not of divine origin but rather expressions of the human reception of revelation.

On the other hand, this general advantage becomes quite concrete with reference to the understanding of Jesus as revealer. Within the context of an instruction-model of revelation Jesus counted as a revealer to the extent that one assumed that Jesus himself revealed or taught all the central beliefs, in particular the Christological and Trinitarian dogmas. Correspondingly, the task of the Church was seen as faithfully defending these revealed "mysteries of faith" against heretical distortions. It was assumed that Jesus understood and proclaimed himself as the eternal Son of God become man, and that he also taught the Trinity of God. Jesus thus counted as a revealer in the sense that he was one of the Trinity, the eternal Son of God, who had become human in Jesus. As the Son of God become man, Jesus instructed us that God was in truth a triune being and that one of the persons of the divine Trinity descended from heaven for our redemption. Nowadays it is indisputably clear that such an understanding of Jesus as revealer is attributable to an unhistorical, anachronistic way of reading the New Testament and to the doctrinal development in the church of the first centuries. This means that what was in fact the result of a long process of theological wrestling about the right interpretation of Jesus—a process that led to the formulation of the Trinitarian and Christological dogmas— was read and projected into the texts of the New Testament. If, however, one reconstructs the gradual development of Christological and Trinitarian thought in a historically correct manner, then it becomes clear that the thesis that Jesus himself revealed these doctrines in the sense of the instruction-model is no longer tenable. The definitions of the early Christian Councils of Nicaea (325) and Chalcedon (451) according to which Jesus is "of one being" with God and according to which he is at one and the same time "truly God and truly man, (…) in two natures without confusion, change, division, or separation," do not quote what Jesus had taught; rather, they interpret Jesus. This interpretation, therefore, needs for its justification a separate and different kind of argumentation. In any case, this interpretation can no longer be justified by claiming that Jesus himself revealed it in this way. How the definitions of Nicaea and Chalcedon may nevertheless be understood in a justifiable way, will be explained in my discussion of belief in the incarnation. But first I want to examine how the role of Jesus as revealer can be understood in terms of the communication-model.

By way of illustration, we can return once again to the previously quoted words of Origen, according to which Jesus is the *"autobasileia"*[6]—in other words, according to which Jesus embodies the *basileia*, the Kingdom of God, or better, life under the kingly reign of God. Today we know that Jesus did not proclaim himself, but rather made the *basileia tou theou,* the "Kingdom" or the "Reign of God" the centerpiece of his proclamation. The basic outline of Jesus' message about the Kingdom of God was shaped by the messianic apocalyptic expectations of his era. In other words, people assumed that those events would soon and forcefully occur, which would usher in the final establishment of the eschatological Reign of God. Within the framework of these common expectations of the coming apocalypse, which Jesus shared, he laid the particular emphasis of his message on describing the nature of the coming Reign of God, and what it meant to submit oneself to this reign. To Jesus, God reigns not like a despotic king, but like a loving, merciful father who is ready to forgive. God's reign dawns wherever people submit themselves to his good will. The two requests of the *Lord's Prayer*—"Your kingdom come" and "Your will be done"—are therefore intimately connected.[7] The Kingdom or Reign of God "comes", that is, becomes manifest, to the extent that people actually submit to God's reign and carry out God's will. Jesus understands the will of God to be summarized in the dual commandment of loving God and loving one's neighbor. The fulfillment of this divine will happens not through an attitude of slavish obedience, but rather by imitating God, having oneself received God's love. "Be merciful as your father in heaven is merciful" (Lk 6:36) proclaims Jesus, and this is precisely what he himself practices. As the Jewish historian Geza Vermes summarizes,

> His [Jesus'] preoccupation was with enacting to perfection, in his own person, the role of son of his Father in heaven, and with teaching his followers to live likewise.[8]

That the love of God, which Jesus proclaims as the principal characteristic of God's reign, is unconditional and forgiving is shown by the fact that no one is excluded from this love. It is a love that equally embraces the righteous and the unrighteous (Mt 5:43-48); indeed, this love desires that it sets the sinner free from the bonds of sinful self-entanglement and enables the person to love God and neighbor (Lk 5:27-32). Hence, the love of God finds its ultimate measure in the love of one's enemies. Jesus stayed true to this message with his own life, up to the moment of his execution. Even the sin that brings him to the crucifixion changes nothing about that love of God that desires the life and conversion of the sinner, but not his or her death (Ezek 18:23; 33:11): "Father, forgive them" (Lk 23:34). The certainty of faith, which came to Jesus' followers after his crucifixion, that he had been raised from the dead

6 Origen's Matthew Commentary 12:43 and 14:7. Following Osborn 1987, 264. Cp. above p. 224.
7 Cp. Vermes 1981, 25.
8 Ibid. 41.

and taken up into heaven, appeared to them as the divine confirmation that God indeed acknowledged both this messenger and this message.[9]

While this reconstruction is the opposite of an instruction-model of revelation, it fits in seamlessly with a communication-model: On the one hand Jesus' interpretation of the Reign of God is profoundly shaped by the Jewish people's history of faith and the experience of God manifest in it. On the other hand, Jesus puts his own personal mark on it. He derives the authority to do so from his own experience of God as the merciful father. What Jesus teaches about the Reign of God and what he lives out himself, is rooted in his personal experience of close proximity to God.[10] What he, out of this experience, teaches and lives now becomes a formative factor in his followers' experiences of God. Joachim Gnilka summarizes this as follows:

> ...Jesus not only proclaimed the coming Reign of God; in him it became manifest, comprising and uniting his words, his deeds, and his person. (...) Since the Kingdom of God denotes God establishing his merciful reign, the presence of the future reign of God in Jesus' ministry means that God is actually at work in him and that in him God's love itself could be experienced.[11]

Or as Hans Kessler put it:

> Jesus lives out the love of God as a human being. That is why one can read it in him; God's love is *occurring* here, and that is why and how it is *revealed*.[12]

And in the words of Thomas Pröpper with reference to the unity of Jesus' life, death, and resurrection:

> Without Jesus' particular way of being human, God would not have been revealed as love; without his readiness to die, the unconditioned seriousness of this love would not have been revealed; and without his resurrection, God would not have become revealed as the true origin of this love.[13]

In this way, Jesus became the formative factor in his followers' faith. The manner in which they themselves experience God can no longer be separated from the embodiment of God's reign in Jesus. In this sense Jesus is the mediator of his followers' own God experience. Along this line of thought, ideas develop in the New Testament which underline the revelatory function of Jesus together with his significance for salvation, and in so doing they provide the substantial basis for the emerging belief in the incarnation.

1) The earliest witness that Jesus' disciples give about him after his death is that "he was a prophet, mighty in deed and word before God and all the people" (Lk

9 On the significance of Jesus' resurrection within the theology of religions debate, see my extensive discussion in Schmidt-Leukel 1997, 542-562.
10 Cp. also Sanders 1996, 349.
11 Gnilka 1990, 258. Translation based on the German original. See also the English edition Gnilka 1997, 254.
12 Kessler 2001, 230.
13 Pröpper 1991, 197.

24:19; cp. also Acts 3:22). According to Mt 21:46, already during his lifetime many considered Jesus to be a prophet. According to James Dunn, we can even "with confidence" assume that this witness corresponds to Jesus' self-understanding.[14] In Mk 6:4 and Lk 13:33, Jesus indirectly describes himself as a prophet. Not a few exegetes tend to consider these words as genuine words of Jesus.[15] In the ongoing development of the New Testament image of Jesus, his understanding as a prophet is extended to his entire existence.

2) Paul calls Jesus Christ the image of God (2 Cor 4:4) and in a paradoxical phrase the Letter to the Colossians speaks of Christ as "the image of the invisible God" (Col 1:15). In other words, God remains invisible and inconceivable; it is forbidden to make oneself an image of God. Yet what can be grasped in a lively and experiential mode about the inconceivable God has become visible and concrete in Jesus.
3) In a structurally similar way, the Gospel of John claims that whoever sees Jesus also sees the Father (Jn 14:9) and the Prologue of John's Gospel sums this up in presenting Jesus as the "Logos" become flesh, the "Word" of God that has appeared in human form. Put a different way: God's attitude toward us, who and what God is for us, is visible and legible in the life, teaching, and person of Jesus.
4) The First Letter of John summarizes it in this way: "God is love" and this was revealed, became apparent, through the sending of the Son (1 Jn 4:7ff). "God's goodness and loving-kindness"—says the Letter to Titus (Tit 3:4)—have appeared in Jesus. Thus, in the New Testament the point of departure for the doctrine of the incarnation of God in the human person of Jesus and for his saving significance consists in Jesus' proclamation of the Reign of God whose *leitmotif* is God's goodness and mercy. Jesus embodies this Reign of God in his own life and puts it into effect up until his death, so that in his life the love of God is reflected, or, as one could say, that in him God's love assumes concrete form.

Jesus as Mediator of Salvation

In the previous chapters I suggested that the decisive precondition of salvation is to be seen in God's revelatory self-disclosure, and that there is a universal chance of salvation, because this self-disclosure of God has always been given to every person. This view is by no means exclusively tied to a pluralist theology of religions position. Rather, it is also firmly represented by a number of inclusivists, like especially Karl Rahner. But is such a universal chance of salvation—as inclusivists insist—perhaps made possible first and only through Jesus Christ? Is it not a widely held belief in Christianity that Jesus Christ is the sole and universal mediator of salvation because he is the exclusive cause of salvation? Religious pluralism would indeed be incom-

14 Cp. Dunn 2003, 137.
15 Cp., for example, Bornkamm 1988, 136; Hahn 1995, 382, n. 2; Vermes 2001, 69.

patible with this belief. So from a pluralist perspective, how is Jesus' role as mediator of salvation to be understood?

First of all we must hold on to the fact that a Christian and simultaneously pluralist theology of religions definitely assumes that Jesus Christ is *a* divine mediator of salvation and revelation. A pluralist theology of religion will frankly confirm that, historically speaking, up to the present day Jesus has been the sole mediator of a salvific relationship to God for untold numbers of Christians[16]—yet not for all people. Furthermore, there is no need for a pluralist theology of religions to deny that what Christians have recognized and experienced of God through Jesus Christ is of universal significance.[17] What a pluralist position excludes is the assumption that Jesus is the *only* mediator of revelation and salvation, and that he is the *singular cause* of the salvation of all people.

From a pluralist perspective one may even accept the idea that *Christ* is the cause of everyone's salvation, *if* by "Christ" one understands the universal *Logos*, as did many church fathers. If Christ is the Logos and if "Logos" (the divine "Word") means the universal self-disclosure of God, then the statement that Christ is the cause of all salvation could be taken as just one specific Christian formulation of the more general statement, that God's self-disclosure is the cause of all salvation. It is in this sense that Raimon Panikkar, for example, speaks of the presence of the "unknown Christ" in Hinduism.[18] As Panikkar clarifies, this is a particularly Christian way of speaking, which "implies no monopoly on the name (…)".[19] As Panikkar explicitly notes, it is in principle also possible to use other names such as "Rama," "Krishna," "Īśvara," or "Purusha" to refer to this this reality.[20] They would then of course represent a Hindu way of approximating the one reality of divine self-disclosure. A similar statement in also found in John Hick:

> All salvation (…) is the work of God. The different religions have their different names for God acting savingly towards mankind. Christianity has several overlapping names for this—the eternal Logos, the cosmic Christ, the Second Person of the Trinity, God the Son, the Spirit. If, selecting from our Christian language, we call God-acting-towards-mankind the Logos, then we must say that *all* salvation, within all religions, is the work of the Logos and that under their various images and symbols men in different cultures and faiths may encounter the Logos and find salvation. But what we cannot say is that all who are saved are saved by Jesus of Nazareth. The life of Jesus was one point at which the Logos—that is, God-in-relation-to-man—has acted; (…) but we

16 Though not for all Christians. As already noted above, in the history of Christian and particularly Catholic popular piety, for numerous people the grace of God or God's forgiving offer of salvation seems factually to have been mediated not through the image of Jesus Christ but through the image of the gracious and merciful Mother of God.

17 On this topic, see the debate between John Hick and Paul Knitter regarding the more precise determination of the universal significance of the revelation that occurred through Jesus, in Swidler, Mojzes 1997, 7-11, 81f, 159ff, 174-179.

18 On this, cp. below pp. 366-371.

19 Panikkar 1981, 164.

20 Cp. ibid., 27.

> are not called upon nor are we entitled to make the negative assertion that the Logos has not acted and is not acting anywhere else in human life. On the contrary, we should gladly acknowledge that Ultimate Reality has affected human consciousness for its liberation or 'salvation' in various ways within the Indian, the semitic, the Chinese, the African … forms of life.[21]

In this sense, pluralists too can affirm that "Christ" or the "Logos-Christ" is the cause of all salvation. As Maurice Wiles fittingly says, it is a Christian way of *identifying* God's work of salvation and revelation in other religions, and of affirming "that there is no ultimate conflict between that revelation and saving presence and those experienced within the Christian Church."[22] And yet, as Wiles also underlines, such a way of talking can all too easily lead to unnecessary confusion, because it implies the danger of identifying the universal saving presence of God simply with his self-disclosure in Jesus, or of considering the latter to be the true and only cause of God's universal work.

The notion that a universal salvific self-disclosure of God was first made possible or caused through the life, death, and resurrection of the person of Jesus would be incompatible with a pluralist theology of religions. For this idea would necessarily imply the superiority of Christianity—a superiority which, as the Roman Catholic document of 1991 "Dialogue and Proclamation" (No. 29) emphasizes, would consist of Christians knowing about the true source of salvation whereas it was hidden from non-Christians.

In order to establish the plausibility of a pluralist position it is therefore important to take into account the objections against the assumption that Jesus is the sole cause of all salvation. These objections depend on how exactly one understands the notion of Jesus being the cause of salvation. One of the most frequent, and in the Christian tradition fairly widespread, forms of such understandings is that only through Jesus' death on the cross a saving relationship to God was made possible. The underlying concept is that God, due to his justness, can only forgive a person of their sin if someone else who is without sin vicariously assumes the just punishment in place of the sinner. This concept, however, is full of serious problems. First, it is certainly right, to quote John Hick, that "forgiveness that has to be bought by full payment of the debt is not forgiveness."[23] Instead, everything would remain at the level of a concept of justice requiring satisfaction. In addition, the idea that God's justice is satisfied by inflicting the "just" punishment not on the guilty person but rather on someone wholly innocent betrays a rather crude understanding of justice.[24] As Schleiermacher rightly notes in his critique of the doctrine of satisfaction, this is a "conception of divine justice which is transferred to God from the

21 Hick 1977c, 181.
22 Wiles 1993, 233.
23 Hick in: Davis 1988, 37 (Cp. also Hick 19931, 127). Pröpper (1991, 63) call it a "a self-contradictory idea" that Jesus has "earned God's grace" on "our behalf."
24 Hick 1993a, 119.

crudest human circumstances."[25] Moreover, this notion contradicts both the image of God found in the Hebrew Bible as well as the image of God in Jesus' own teaching. In the Hebrew Bible, just as in the New Testament, a God is presented who can forgive freely and unconditionally, without insisting on the execution of a punishment. In the parable of the "prodigal son" the father welcomes the returning son unconditionally, and in joyful response slaughters the fattened calf—and not the older "innocent" son in order to be able to receive the lost son once again.[26] Still more, according to Jesus' proclamation, from the very beginning God approaches the sinful person with the attitude of one who is ready to forgive and be merciful, and it is through this that God first effects an honest admission of guilt and a genuine sense of remorse. It is precisely this that Jesus expresses as the heart of his message and of his actual attitude toward "tax collectors and sinners."

Again, the understanding that, in Jesus, it is not just any innocent person who has taken on the just punishment for sin but rather that God himself has done so, that is, God in the form of the second person of the Trinity, leads—as once more Schleiermacher has already shown—to further theological difficulties. For according to the standard orthodox interpretation of the two-natures doctrine it was not the divine nature of Jesus Christ that suffered on the cross, but his human nature. For due to its perfection and immutability, the divine nature was considered as unable to suffer. Hence, on traditional accounts, it would be impossible to say that it was God who suffered, in Jesus Christ, the punishment for human sin.

There is the further problem of how a conception of Jesus Christ, or more precisely of his death on the cross, as the sole cause of salvation is to be reconciled with the inclusivist assumption of universal salvation. For example, how is Christ's crucifixion supposed to have been the cause of Abraham's salvation? Both, the Hebrew Bible and the New Testament take it for granted that Abraham lived in a saving relationship to God. For Paul, Abraham is essentially the crown witness to the fact that before God, persons are not justified through the works of the Law, but rather through their basic trust in God's promise. If one wants to assume that the saving relationship of Abraham to God was based not only in God's care for him and in Abraham's trust in God's promise, but rather that the real cause must be found in the crucifixion of Christ, then one would have to accept something like a chronologically backward causation.[27] This, however, would lead to considerable logical difficulties. For it is heavily debated whether backward causation is even possible. If it were possible then (as one could argue in following Albert Einstein's well-known grandfather paradox) it would have to be possible to cause retrospectively the death of my grandfather before he begot my father, so that I, as the origin of the backward causation would never have existed and therefore the backward causation itself would never have been possible. The notion of backward causation therefore

25 Schleiermacher, Der christliche Glaube [The Christian Faith], § 104,4.
26 Cp. Hick 1993a, 127.
27 Cp. Hick 1988b, 376f.

seems to lead to unsolvable logical problems. Perhaps one can find some particularly sophisticated ways of establishing the possibility of backward causation—but also perhaps not. In any case, the notion that it was only Christ's crucifixion that causally enabled God's saving relationship to Abraham does not seem particularly plausible. A far more consistent solution was the view, held by significant parts of the theological tradition, that Abraham stayed in limbo (more precisely, in the "limbus patrum") till the moment of Jesus' death on the cross and could only attain eternal bliss after the completion of the crucifixion.[28] This notion appears, as I have said, to be more consistent than the notion of backward causation, but not necessarily more plausible.

Also highly problematic is the idea that God might have changed his mind because of the sacrifice on the cross, as if the just wrath of God were assuaged through this deed and transformed into a forgiving love. The idea of a change of mind in God is, as Rahner notes, "metaphysically impossible."[29] In addition, this understanding implicitly rejects Jesus' proclamation about the loving and merciful father, and obscures—again according to Rahner—that the love of God leads to the crucifixion of Christ and not the other way around so that the crucifixion would lead to the love of God:

> The cross and resurrection are there because there is the salvific will of God; but not: God's will for our salvation is there, because there is the cross.[30]

Rahner derives from this the obvious conclusion:

> The event of the crucifixion … must be … the *consequence* and not the cause of God's unconditioned salvific will—at least not the cause in the typical sense of the word.[31]

According to Rahner, Jesus Christ, in the unity of his life, death, and resurrection, is the "sign" of the "saving grace and of its victorious irreversibility in the world."[32] Every non-Christian who lives in a saving relationship to God, in other words every "anonymous Christian," is according to Rahner unconsciously searching for an explicit expression, for an objectivization of the divine self-commitment to us and its salvific significance, which in the final analysis is supposed to be found in Christ alone. In this sense, Jesus would be the "sign" or the "symbolic-reality" ("Realsymbol") of divine saving grace. Although Rahner explicitly points out that the term "cause" does not adequately represent this fact, he nevertheless feels that he can—or perhaps must—hold on to the notion of the "cross' salvific causality"; albeit, as Rah-

28 On this, cp. above pp. 95f.
29 Rahner 1975, 262.
30 Ibid. 261.
31 Ibid.
32 Ibid. 267.

ner himself admits, with a meaning of causality that "otherwise cannot be found and is not to be subsumed under the other familiar understandings of causality."[33]

I personally do not consider it an advisable theological method to reinterpret terms beyond their recognizability or, indeed, up to the opposite of their standard meaning just in order to hold on to established theological formulas even if their original and genuine sense has long since been dismissed. Such theology helps no one but rather contributes to confusion and its own incomprehensibility. If it is at all helpful, then it is to those who want to keep the respective traditional formulas in their original sense. Yet it often seems that theologians, especially those that have to work under the authoritarian restrictions of academic institutions controlled by the Church, see themselves under the pressure of not to formulate their opinions as clearly and intelligibly as possible but rather in as obscured a way as possible. And in so doing, all too often they resort to giving traditional formulations and terms a completely different or even opposite meaning instead of simply leaving them behind. If according to Rahner Jesus is "the cause" of salvation only in a sense of the term "cause" that "is not to be subsumed under the other familiar understandings of causality" then what this means in plain language is that Jesus is not the cause of salvation. The true cause of salvation, in Rahner's understanding, is the universal salvific will of God.

Regarding the role of Jesus Christ as mediator of salvation, the American theologian Schubert Ogden has suggested a terminological clarification which, in contrast to such word acrobatics as found in Rahner, is remarkably lucid and helpful. Ogden differentiates between those theological approaches according to which "the saving event of Jesus Christ (…) *constitutes*" the possibility of salvation and other approaches to which "this event in no way constitutes the possibility of salvation but only *represents* it." "The Christ event cannot be the cause of salvation because its only cause, and the cause of this event itself, is the boundless love of God of which this event is the decisive re-presentation."[34] In the sense of this distinction, a pluralist theology of religion will presuppose that Jesus Christ does not constitute the universal possibility of salvation, but rather that it is constituted by the merciful self-disclosure of God as it is represented by the life, death, and resurrection of Jesus Christ. The salvific significance of Jesus then becomes constitutive only through its fundamentally representative character. That is, Jesus, by metaphorically or symbolically representing that love which is the sole origin of salvation, becomes a mediator of salvation for all those persons who understand this sign and under its influence live their lives according to the love of God. In this sense, and only in this sense, is Jesus also constitutive for salvation. This insight allows the further understanding that the salvific meaning of God's caring attention is represented *neither solely nor with singular clarity* through Jesus Christ, and that therefore Jesus does not have to

33 Ibid. "…obwohl sich die behauptete Ursächlichkeit sonst nicht findet und unter die übrigen bekannten Vorstellungen von Ursächlichkeit nicht zu subsumieren ist."

34 Ogden 1992, 84 and 93. Cp. also Ogden 1991, 97.

be the only mediator of salvation. Undoubtedly Jesus represents God's care and its significance for the salvation of humanity in a unique and distinctive way, but not necessarily in the only unique way. Pluralists emphasize that the salvific presence of God or of transcendent reality has found similarly unique, that is, different but not therefore less effective representations in other religious contexts.

According to Thomas Pröpper the matter of Jesus' significance for salvation

> ... demands clarity from every contemporary theology of salvation: Is the cross the necessary condition for God's forgiveness because of sin (...)? Or is, conversely, the cross the form in which the decisive love of God—a love already encountered in the life of Jesus—corroborates its unconditioned nature? If the latter, Jesus' giving of his life is a condition for forgiveness only in the sense that without this act of God's going to extremes, his attentiveness even to the enemies, would not have become real and hence the groundlessness and excessiveness of his love would not have been revealed, that is, it would have remained without the historically completed expression of its unconditioned nature.[35]

Pröpper himself argues clearly for the second option. The reason for this is that Pröpper too considers Jesus' role as mediator of salvation, "both formally and in terms of content, as a revelatory event."[36] One cannot understand the salvific meaning of Jesus' death isolated from his life and the way it was determined by "his message of the coming reign of the God who is unconditionally good and ready to forgive."[37] In fact, what appears in Jesus' death is, "the victory of the love based in God over the worst that people have done and could do to that love."[38] Consequently Pröpper rejects the notions that through the crucifixion Jesus earned God's grace for us,[39] that the cross propitiated a wrathful God,[40] or that it rendered "satisfaction" to a God "who rages against the one whom he innocently condemned."[41] But does this mean that Pröpper's conception, with the clarity he himself demands, considers the salvific meaning of the life and death of Jesus as being representative instead of constitutive? The answer to this is not that easy, for Pröpper uses a series of formulations in which he seems to take with the one hand what he gave with the other. For according to Pröpper, the unconditional love is not only revealed through the life and death of Jesus, but rather, as Pröpper says against Rahner, "the form of the revelation is so essentially part of its content (...) that this (God's decisive love for humanity) requires that (the historical-symbolic mediation) in order even to become *truth and reality* for us humans."[42] "For love," explains Pröpper, "since it is free, can only be true if it occurs, and God's love can only become truth for humans by enter-

35 Pröpper 1991, 57.
36 Ibid. 64, n. 108.
37 Ibid. 46-48.
38 Ibid. 59.
39 Cp. ibid. 63.
40 Cp. Ibid. 65.
41 Ibid. 66.
42 Ibid. 248. Emphasis mine.

ing into our reality…."[43] It is in this sense that Pröpper speaks of "its", i.e. God's love, "beginning in Jesus,"[44] and that "God's love, being free and always decided for humans, could nevertheless only become the truth for us by becoming humanly *realized* in our history, in that it was mediated by the freedom of Jesus Christ who complied with that love."[45] Hence Pröpper can make the further statement that, "through Jesus Christ … salvation is finally made available to all persons," that it is "underivably established" in him and "related to him as its unsurpassable beginning."[46]

In this way, Pröpper eventually returns to ascribing a constitutive salvific significance to Jesus and his death, and above all one that ascribes this significance, constitutive for the salvation of all, exclusively to Christ. Yet the logical consequence of this is that in so doing Pröpper undermines the actual point of departure of his argument, that is, Jesus' message "of the God who is unconditionally good and ready to forgive." If God's goodness and readiness to forgive become "realized" only and in the first place through their revelation in Jesus' life, death, and resurrection, and if the love of God only becomes true and real by initially entering our lives through Jesus, then up until this beginning this love apparently was not of an unconditioned nature, because its realization was tied to the condition of Jesus' life and death. Furthermore, apparently even after this beginning in Jesus it was not unconditionally valid for all those humans to whom, because of their ignorance regarding Jesus, it had not been revealed, or as Pröpper says, it had not yet become true and real. Then also Jesus' message to his fellow humans to entrust themselves to this love was apparently wrong or at least rash, since this love, according to Pröpper, after all had not yet been completely realized, that is to say it had not yet become constituted through the life, death, and resurrection of Jesus.

Of course we can agree with Pröpper's basic notion that God's love first becomes fully apparent as such *for us* when it is "revealed" to us. As I explained above, we can only speak of "revelation" if this revelation actually reaches people.[47] But this does not mean, as Pröpper apparently insinuates, that the love of God—at least for us—is only realized and constituted through its revelation in Jesus. Rather, something quite different is yielded by the insight that love wants to communicate itself, and that love only exists insofar as it is happens; namely that the love of God, if it really is for all persons, by no means has its beginning in Jesus. If God's love is the actual incitement for its self-communicating revelation, and if that love really does unconditionally encompass all people, then we can assume that it does not first appear in Jesus, but rather pushes for acceptance and realization in the life of every person. But then one should also assume that there have been numerous signs of this before Jesus and independent of Jesus, signs we only have to recognize and interpret. These signs represent this saving love of God in other cultural and contex-

43 Ibid. 122.
44 Ibid.
45 Ibid. 139. Emphasis mine.
46 Ibid. 60.
47 Cp. above, p. 194.

tual situations and—as in the case of Jesus—thereby become co-constitutive for the salvation of those who recognize and respond to these signs. In the words of Roger Haight we can thus say:

> Indeed, if God is as Jesus reveals God to be, i.e. the universal savior, one must expect that there will be other historical mediations of this salvation.[48]

Jesus as Incarnation

As already became clear in connection with the critical discussion on Christian inclusivism, it is not only the question of Jesus' salvific causality which prevents numerous Christian theologians from accepting a pluralist theology of religions position, but also—and perhaps even more so—the belief in Jesus as God become man, or, more precisely, as the single divine incarnation. Once again Karl Rahner may be quoted as an example representing many others:

> Christianity understands itself as the absolute religion, the one intended for all men, which cannot recognize any other religion besides itself as equally valid (…) because it is founded on the incarnation, the death, and the resurrection of the Word of God become flesh,

and because it is

> the interpretation undertaken by God himself in his Word of that relationship between God and men, which in Christ has been inaugurated by God himself for all …[49]

John Hick too holds that the Christian claim to superiority, whether in its exclusivist or inclusivist form, depends primarily on the doctrine of the Incarnation, to which it is "integral"

> that there has been (and will be) no other divine incarnation. This makes Christianity unique in that it, alone among the world religions of the world, was founded by God in person. (…) for must not God want all human beings to enter the way of salvation which he has provided for them?[50]

Thus, in the course of developing his form of a pluralist theology of religions, Hick criticizes the notion of incarnation and accepts it only as a myth and metaphor. Since the so-called two-natures doctrine of the Council of Chalcedon (451) can, with a certain factual and historical right, count as the fundamental formulation of the belief in the incarnation, Hick's critique is directed mainly at Chalcedon.

48 Haight 1992, 281.
49 Rahner 1964, 139; similarly Rahner 1967, 355f. Translation follows the German original.
50 Hick 1988, 34.

How to Interpret Chalcedon?

The notion of incarnation, in other words the notion that God is present in a person, inevitably raises the question of how the divine and the human are related to one another in the incarnation. If God becomes incarnate in a person, is this person then still a true human being? If it is truly God who is present in such a person, is the humanity of this person then only a husk, a mere apparition? Conversely, if the person in whom God becomes incarnate is supposed to still be a true and genuine human being, can one then honestly and seriously claim that it is really God who is somehow present in this person? In the final analysis the intense christological controversies of the first few centuries can be reduced to this basic problem: Either one conceived of the incarnation in such a way as to put into question the true humanity of Jesus (as in the various forms of so-called "docetism"), or one insisted on the true humanity of Jesus so that it remained unclear whether God was really present in him (as in the various forms of "adoptionism"). Against the background of this problem, the Council of Chalcedon defines Jesus Christ as at one and the same time "perfect in Godhead and (…) perfect in manhood; truly God and truly man," in his divine nature being "consubstantial", of one essence, with the Father, while in his human nature being "consubstantial" with us, "like us in all things except sin."

Chalcedon emphasizes that both natures belong to the one person of Jesus. But regarding the question of how one might conceive of the relation between the divine and human nature in one and the same person, Chalcedon makes only negative assertions. That is, according to the formulations of Chalcedon, the two natures can be thought of neither as "confused/changed" nor as "divided/separate." Yet how it is supposed to be possible that in Jesus a truly divine and a truly human nature are so united that they are both "unconfused" and "undivided", Chalcedon does not explain.

This of course raises an enormous logical problem which John Hick puts this way:

> The problem… [lies] in the fact that the Council in effect merely asserted the Jesus was 'truly God and truly man' without attempting to say how such a paradox is possible. The orthodox task is to spell out in an intelligible way the idea of someone having both a fully divine nature, i.e. having all the essential divine attributes, and at the same time a fully human nature, i.e. having all the essential human attributes.[51]

Yet according to Hick this task is impossible to fulfill. It remains completely incomprehensible how it should be possible that one and the same person…

51 Hick, 1993a, 48.

> … is both divinely omniscient and humanly fallible, divinely omnipotent and humanly limited, eternal and yet born in time, omnipresent and yet locally physical.[52]

Since Chalcedon has no response to such questions, according to Hick the Chalcedonian two-natures doctrine is simply unintelligible:

> For to say, without explanation, that the historical Jesus of Nazareth was also God is as devoid of meaning as to say that this circle (…) is also a square.[53]

Hick is right in pointing out that in the Christian tradition one has been quite aware of the incomprehensibility of the Chalcedonian formula. It was considered to be a *mysterium stricte dictum*, a "mystery in the strict sense", i.e. a mystery that is irresolvable as such, under any condition. According to the traditional standpoint, the Chalcedonian statements were nonetheless to be believed as true, because it was held that God himself had revealed them through his Son. And indeed the famous christological formula of Chalcedon ended with the words that the description of Jesus presented here is just "as the prophets of old and Jesus Christ Himself have taught us about Him and the creed of our Fathers has handed down."[54] Thus, the fathers of Chalcedon understood revelation in the sense of the instruction-model, and they viewed the Christological definitions that they had formulated as being essentially in agreement with what Jesus had revealed about himself. Today, however, such a rationale is no longer possible. With an otherwise unusual measure of consensus, New Testament scholarship agrees that in all historical probability Jesus did not understand himself as the incarnation of a divine person, that he did not believe in a Trinitarian God, and that rather his self-understanding and his conception of God are located entirely within the context of Jewish monotheism. Wolfhart Pannenberg fittingly summarizes this finding as follows:

> At the heart of the message of Jesus stood the Father and his coming kingdom, not any dignity that Jesus claimed for his own person that would thus make himself equal to God (John 5:18). Jesus differentiated himself as a mere man from the Father as the one God. He thus subjected himself to the claim of the coming divine rule, just as he required his hearers to do. He could even reject the respectful title "good Master" (Mark 10:18 par.) with a reference to God alone as good.[55]

So how should one interpret the Chalcedonian formula in light of the aforementioned logical problems as well as these historical findings? According to Hick the insoluble logical difficulties of Chalcedon suggest that the entire talk about the incarnation cannot be understood in the sense of a literally true factual claim. For in this sense it would remain unintelligible. He finds it far more advisable to interpret

52 Hick in Hewitt 1991, 208.
53 Hick 1977c, 178.
54 Neuner Roos 1979, 130 (Nr. 178). English translation from Kelly 1977, 339f.
55 Pannenberg 1991, 415. Translation from Pannenberg 1994, 372.

incarnational language as a metaphorical expression in much the same way as one can say of Joan of Arc that she "embodied" or "incarnated" the spirit of the French Resistance. Yet what then, according to Hick, is the literal meaning behind the metaphorical statement that God became incarnate in Jesus? Hick gives a very precise response:

> In the case of the metaphor of divine incarnation, what was lived out, made flesh, incarnated in the life of Jesus can be indicated in at least three ways, each of which is an aspect of the fact that Jesus was a human being exceptionally open and responsive to the divine presence: (1) In so far as Jesus was doing God's will, God was acting through him on earth and was in this respect 'incarnate' in Jesus' life; (2) In so far as Jesus was doing God's will he 'incarnated' the ideal of human life lived in openness and response to God; (3) In so far as Jesus lived a life of self-giving love, or *agape*, he 'incarnated' a love that is a finite reflection of the infinite divine love.[56]

By interpreting the talk about incarnation as metaphorical, Hick sees the Chalcedonian formula as no longer relevant and hence dispensable. Chalcedon wants to say something about how to conceptualize the relation between a divine and human nature in Jesus *if* one understands the talk about incarnation as a literal truth claim. But if one simply interprets incarnation as a metaphor, then the basis that triggers the paradoxical statements of Chalcedon seems to be removed. But is that really so? In my opinion, on this point Hick's critique goes too far. For with his own suggestion of what would have to count as the literal meaning behind the metaphor of divine incarnation, Hick still holds to two fundamental claims: On the one hand he asserts that it really was God whom Jesus experienced, to whom Jesus was open, and to whom he responded in his life. And on the other hand Hick maintains that it was precisely in this way that God "was acting through him on earth" (see the quotation above). Thus Hick can say that "Jesus was so fully God's agent, so completely conscious of living in God's presence and serving God's love, that the divine reality was mediated through him to others."[57] According to Hick it is even true that God "is present to us in and through everything, but most importantly … through other finite persons…."[58] Hick again confirmed this view in his 1993 monograph on Christology, *The Metaphor of God Incarnate.* Here he explicitly clarifies that he does not deny an understanding of incarnation, according to which God is involved in the life of people and thus is present in the midst of the flow of time. Moreover, Hick does not only not deny an understanding of incarnation in which God is just generally present in humanity's life. He neither contests "that in the life of Jesus God was involved in a particular and specially powerful and effective way. In other words, Je-

56 Hick 1993a, 105.
57 Hick 1973, 177.
58 Hick, in Hewitt 1991, 242.

sus was not just an ordinary man, but one whose relationship to God has a universal significance."[59]

First of all, let us be clear that, given the above statements by Hick, several critics, such as Gerhard Gäde,[60] Gerhard Ludwig Müller,[61] Karl-Heinz Menke,[62] and, depending on Menke, Joseph Ratzinger,[63] unjustly accuse Hick of denying in his Christology the immanence of God in the world and in history. More important than this rectification, however, is that even the apparently merely metaphorical understanding of the incarnation, as we find it in Hick, actually still implies, to a considerable extent, a literal understanding of incarnation. But then the question addressed by the council of Chalcedon is anything but irrelevant. What Hick takes as the literal meaning behind the incarnation metaphor is, in my opinion, the biblical and historical core of the incarnation belief, that is, the belief that Jesus truly lived entirely out of his openness to God and thus became for others a mediator of God's presence: a revealer in the sense of the communication-model. But then it still remains a genuine mystery as to how it is possible or conceivable that God can be present in the life of a person and work through this person without that person ceasing to be a true human being.

Not every relation between two different realities that is deeply mysterious should be considered as meaningless. For example, as Thomas Nagel has impressively shown, it remains an absolute mystery how a physical reality, like the sounds of our language or the printed marks in a book, can be bearers of something quite different, the mental or cognitive phenomenon of "meaning".[64] Basically, one could say—following Nagel—that every book and every word has two natures: the physical nature of the sign, and the mental nature of meaning. Yet the nature of the relation between the two and the reason that makes this relation possible remain deeply puzzling.

Or we can take an example to which Hick himself refers in a quite different context. In his exploration of the relationship between mind and brain in *Death and Eternal Life*, Hick admits that "the interaction of body and mind, as entities of basically different kinds, is unique and utterly mysterious."[65] But Hick, who inclines toward the position of dualistic interactionism, is far from discarding this relationship and interaction as meaningless because of its mysteriousness.

One final example leads us back to Christology. In a discussion between Stephen Davis and John Hick, Davis argued against Hick that it is inconsistent if Hick rejects the Chalcedonian formula because of its paradox nature, while at the same time accepting the "paradox of grace" that Donald Baillie makes the basis of his Chris-

59 Hick 1993a, 9.
60 Cp. Gäde 1998, 270 and 279.
61 Cp. Müller 1998, 166.
62 Cp. Menke 1995, 77, 93f.
63 Ratzinger 1996, 361f.
64 Cp. Nagel 1987, 38-46.
65 Cp. Hick 1990c, 120.

tology,[66] a Christology that Hick himself highly appreciates and by which his own understanding of incarnation is significantly influenced. To this objection Hick responded that the paradox of grace is given by experience whereas "the God-manhood of Jesus, with his divine and human natures, is not an observed fact…."[67] But if I am right in that what Hick retains as the literal truth underlying the metaphor of incarnation is still sufficiently "incarnational" to raise the problem of the two natures, then this response to Davis seems to be in tension with Hick's own explanation of his Christology. For according to Hick, Jesus experienced the presence of God in his life, and his followers experienced that the presence of God was mediated to them through Jesus. To me, these experiences seem to be fundamentally in the same category as the experience of the paradox of grace: They are faith experiences, but they are nevertheless genuine experiences.

However if one insists that the only correct understanding of Chalcedon requires the *person* of Jesus to possess, in strictly the same way, all the characteristics of God and all the characteristics of a true human being, then Hick is presumably right that such a statement does not actually lead anywhere. But is it really so unambiguously clear how we need to understand the term "person" in interpreting Chalcedon? After the council of Chalcedon the teaching of monothelitism was condemned. That is, an interpretation of Chalcedon was rejected, which held that Jesus, while having indeed two natures, had nevertheless only one single will. Instead it was affirmed that having two natures also implies having two "wills"—one divine and one human. This may very well indicate that we should not understand the Chalcedonian use of the term "person" or "hypostasis" in the modern sense of "person," in which the word "person" refers to the immediate subject of the will and knowledge. According to Rahner,

> the term "person" brings with it from its *modern usage* the constant danger that the Christological statements will be misunderstood in the sense of monophysitism or monothelitism. For what is understood by this is a *single* center of activity, namely, the divine center. This would overlook the fact that the man Jesus *in* his human reality exists with a created, active and "existentiell" center of activity vis-à-vis God and in an absolute difference from him.[68]

What Rahner is actually saying here is that if one were taking the modern understanding of a person as the basis for interpreting Chalcedon one would have to radically differentiate between the human person of Jesus and the divine "person" of the Logos at work in him. What, in contrast, the fathers of Chalcedon meant by "person" or "hypostasis" which they used as the common reference point for both natures, remains, according to Rahner, "formal and indetermined."[69] If one accepts Rahner's perspective here, then it is no longer possible simply to quote Chalcedon as

66 Cp. on this below p. 258.
67 Hick in Davis 1988, 34.
68 Rahner 1976, 286. Translation from Rahner 1978, 292.
69 Rahner 1976, 285 and 1978, 292

justification for viewing the Antiochene thrust of early church Christology, including that of Paul of Samosata and Nestorius, as heretical. Their concern after all was to preserve the true humanity of the person of Jesus—in the modern sense of "person"—and to understand him, his human person, in terms of his absolute difference from and yet at the same time total relatedness to God. Hence, it is well possible that precisely because of, and not despite, their proximity to the Antiochene school, John Hick and all the other contemporary representatives of a gradualist and functionalist Christology—to which I will return in a moment—are in fact more orthodox than those who so easily and quickly dismiss this form of Christology as unorthodox.

Be that as it may. It seems to me that if one assumes that God worked in and through Jesus, then the problem to which Chalcedon is responding remains as before both topical and unavoidable. Therefore it has to be possible and permissible to ask questions, from a contemporary systematic perspective, about how to interpret Chalcedon, questions that go beyond the purely historical reconstruction of the original intention of the formula. If one accepts that the assertion that God has revealed himself in a salvific way in and through the life of the man Jesus is the genuine substantial basis behind the Chalcedonian two-natures doctrine, then Chalcedon may be interpreted along the following lines: On the one hand, Chalcedon affirms the notion of the true and genuine humanity of Jesus who—as Chalcedon says—"was like us in all things except sin." On the other hand, Chalcedon expresses that this person truly did become the medium of God's self-revelation. The two natures therefore correspond to the medium and to what was mediated: As the mediator of the salvific presence of God, Jesus is truly human, and what he mediates is truly God.

The doctrine of incarnation should thus be understood primarily as a function of the doctrine of revelation. In other words, to the extent that God reveals himself through Jesus and his impact, God is incarnate in this event. In as much as God reveals him/her/itself by means of a finite medium, this medium automatically gains two natures. On the one hand, the infinite God is essentially different from the finite medium of his presence. On the other hand, if the finite is truly a medium of God, then God is really present in and through it. According to Roger Haight, "the doctrine of Chalcedon mirrors this dialectical structure."[70] It is, says Haight, the fundamental structure of every symbolic mediation: Each symbol has as it were two natures, the nature of the symbol itself and the nature of that which is being symbolized. On the one hand, a symbol points beyond itself to that which is symbolized, which is distinct from the symbol itself, and on the other hand, by doing so the symbol makes what is symbolized present in and through the symbol.[71] The clear implication of such an interpretation of the incarnation and the two-natures doc-

70 Haight 1992, 263.

71 It is in this sense that Haight (1999) speaks of Jesus as the "Symbol of God" in the title of his important Christological treatise.

trine is that the incarnation and the symbolic interleaving of divine and human nature is not limited to the person of Jesus, but can be encountered wherever human beings and what belongs to them become the medium of divine self-revelation.

Incarnation as a Singularity or Basic Feature of Divine Immanence?

As revealer, Jesus incarnates God in a double sense: In the *subjective sense*, that Jesus lives completely by, and according to, his openness to God, that is, right until his violent death he lives according to the presence of God as he experiences it in his life. Second, in the *intersubjective sense*, that through this he becomes virtually transparent for the presence of God and in this transparency becomes the mediator of the salvific presence of God in the lives of other persons. These two aspects constitute the basis of two approaches found in numerous current Christologies: a *gradualist* and a *functionalist* understanding of incarnation.

Gradualist approaches in understanding the incarnation assume that Jesus is not essentially different from all other people, but gradually so. Were Jesus essentially different from anybody else then one could no longer say that he was "truly man." Thus the divine in Jesus does not refer to some kind of additional supernatural characteristic but should be understood as referring to a basic feature of genuine human nature. This means that by their existential nature every person is in some sense open to the reality of the Logos, that is, the self-disclosure of God. Yet it is to greatly varying degrees that people positively respond to this divine reality. If a person lives his or her life in such a way that he or she in every regard translates this openness to God into a positive response, then such a person is both a true and perfect human being and at the same time perfectly filled and shaped by the presence of God.

Within Anglo-Saxon theology, Donald Baillie stands as a major representative of this approach, which he develops by drawing on the the paradox of grace: On the one hand, the believer experiences his or her deeds as the result of his or her own freedom and on the other hand ascribes everything good to the grace of God. Now if in this sense human life, at least in part, depends on both human freedom and at the same time on the grace of God, "does not," asks Baillie, "the same or a similar paradox, taken at the perfect and absolute pitch, appear as the mystery of the Incarnation?"[72] According to this understanding of the incarnation, Jesus thus realizes in a perfect way that which is found in less perfect degrees also in the lives of other people, something that, although given by grace, nevertheless presents a fundamental possibility of human life as such. In this sense, the true divinity of Jesus, in other words his perfect dependence on the grace of God, does not stand in opposition to his true humanity. Rather, it is only in this way that true humanity is perfected and fulfilled.

72 Baillie 1997, 118.

A similar approach is found in the work of Geoffrey Lampe. The point of departure for his Christological reflections is the early church conviction that the Spirit of God fills the whole of creation. In this view, the Spirit provides the link between the continuing creative work of God and God's saving revelation: the Spirit works in creation just as it does through the prophets. For Lampe, this is the basic meaning of God's incarnation: "God has always been incarnate in his human creatures, forming their spirits from within and revealing himself in and through them…."[73] According to Lampe, God's incarnation in Jesus needs to be understood in continuity with this comprehensive incarnation: Jesus' life is "a perfected form of inspiration,"[74] Jesus is "'the' prophet who completes and perfects"[75] the revelatory work of all the other prophets.

Karl Rahner also understood the incarnation, or "God becoming man", as the "unique and *highest* instance of the actualization of the essence of human reality…."[76] In Jesus, says Rahner, human nature "has reached the very point towards which it is always moving by virtue of its essence." That is, "the very thing which necessarily takes place in man in an initial way, (…) takes place in an unsurpassable way" in Jesus.[77] In other words, Jesus lived, like all other human beings, under the "supernatural existential" of God's grace, i.e. God's self-communication to the human mind. What differentiates Jesus from other people is not a different type or quality of this divine self-communication, but rather the completely different extent to which Jesus allowed his life to be determined by this existential fact.

Yet alongside this gradualist aspect of incarnation, Rahner also emphasizes the *functionalist* one: not only does Jesus embody in his positive openness to God the apogee of what it means to actualize the essence of human reality, but as such he is also the apogee of what Rahner calls the categorical revelation. Thus Jesus is the form which the absolute "offer/promise" ("Zusage") of God's grace takes in relation to us. In as much as this offer/promise is, on the one hand, truly the offer/promise of God and, on the other hand, the very reality of the person of Jesus, the assertion of the "hypostatic union", i.e. the Chalcedonian definition that in Jesus are united a divine and a human nature, finds here the actual reason for its appropriateness.[78]

The Anglican systematic theologian Keith Ward suggests an especially distinct example of a Christology that understands the notion of incarnation primarily from the perspective of its functional aspect.[79] According to Ward, Jesus is a revealer in so far as his life initiated a process of knowing God and relating to God in new ways. God is present in these effects that Jesus initiated. It is less a matter of exactly how Jesus lived, whether he really was perfectly sinless, etc. What is important is the im-

73 Lampe 1977, 23.
74 Ibid. 12.
75 Ibid. 97.
76 Rahner 1976, 216. Translation from Rahner 1978, 218.
77 Rahner 1976, 216. Rahner 1978, 217-18.
78 Cp. Rahner 1976, 202; 1978, 202.
79 Cp. Ward 1991.

pact that Jesus left behind, as it is attested to in the images of Christ and words of Jesus of the Holy Scripture. These are images or "icons" that disclose new and healing aspects of God, and through which the infinite God makes himself known to finite humans promising them his saving presence.

In contemporary theology, there are numerous attempts beyond the few examples mentioned here to understand the incarnation in gradualist and/or functionalist terms—a fact that is completely independent of the question of a theology of religions. Rather, these christological efforts are concerned with refining the teaching of incarnation in such a way that, on the one hand, nothing is lost from the true humanity of Jesus, while, on the other hand, justice is done to the early biblical records and to what today we can identify as the genuine substantial basis of the notion of incarnation, that is, Jesus' status as revealer. Yet the consequence of these efforts is that they no longer support the notion of the uniqueness of the incarnation. Rather, they are based on an understanding of incarnation according to which incarnation designates an essential feature of divine immanence in as much as it enables people to live a life of openness to God and, in so doing, to mediate God's self-disclosure. When we talk about incarnation in this sense, then we are still speaking of a true intersection between the divine and the human, but—as Hick puts it—

> no longer (…) of an intersection between the divine and the human that occurs, by definition, only in this unique case but of one that occurs in different ways and degrees in all human openness and response to the divine initiative.[80]

But then it holds that the belief in the incarnation of God in Jesus is no longer irreconcilable with a pluralist theology of religion. Rather, this understanding of incarnation opens up—to quote Hick again—

> … the possibility of seeing God's activity in Jesus as being of the same kind as God's activity in other great human mediators of the divine.[81]

Or as Keith Ward puts if from a functionalist perspective:

> …if "incarnation" is the temporal expression of an eternal and infinite reality in a particular human life and social context, there may be other different modes of expression, none of which will exhaust the divine reality and none of which contains the fullness of truth on its own.[82]

Usually, representatives of a Christian and pluralist theology of religions thus advocate a Christology that follows the basic outline sketched here, and presuppose that Jesus is, in neither gradualist nor functionalist terms, the only incarnation of divine reality.[83] Yet the reverse is not true. That is, many representatives of gradualist and/or functionalist approaches to an understanding of incarnation did and do not in-

80 Hick 1993b, 54.
81 Hick 1988, 36.
82 Ward 1991, 117.
83 Cp. on this the further details in Schmidt-Leukel 1997, 528ff.

tend to affirm a plurality of incarnations, at least not in that full sense of "incarnation," which they reserve for Jesus. On the other hand, a clear consequence of these efforts is that they make the notion of the uniqueness of incarnation rather improbable. For example, if Jesus, as Rahner says, represents the unique and highest instance of the actualization of the essence of human reality, then the question inevitably arises why one should suppose that only one single person in human history truly actualized the essence of what it is to be a human being. Also from a functionalist perspective the unavoidable question arises as to whether God has not, in fact, revealed him/her/itself through many persons, especially when one assumes that the anthropological basis for this is universally given. In his discussion of Rahner's Christology and similar approaches by others, Paul Knitter has made this point unmistakably clear:

> ... they hold back from facing what seems to me to be the clear *implication* of what they are saying: that there can be *other incarnations*, other individuals who achieved (or were granted) the same fullness of God-human unity realized in Jesus. ... Also, why must God's full and irrevocable offer of grace be given only once? Granted the huge number of potential recipients, a plurality of offers would seem to make sense. Finally, why should the possibility of other incarnations minimize the historicity and the saving significance of incarnation in Jesus?[84]

Yet there are Christian theologians who, influenced by religious pluralism, have opened themselves to the possibility of plural incarnations as an unavoidable consequence of their understanding of incarnation, such as the Anglican Maurice Wiles,[85] former professor of divinity at Oxford University and chairman of the Church of England's Doctrine Commission, or the influential reformed theologian John Macquarrie who too was a former professor of divinity at Oxford University.[86]

Thomas Aquinas had already discussed the question of whether it was theoretically possible for the Son of God to become incarnate multiple times. And Aquinas answers with an emphatic "Yes." For if one wanted to deny this possibility one would have to accept

> ...that the Personality of the Divine Nature was so comprehended by one human nature as to be unable to assume another to its Personality; and this is impossible, for the Uncreated cannot be comprehended by any creature.[87]

This argument seems to me to be of abiding validity.[88] It also takes us back to that other fundamental presupposition of a pluralist theology of religions, according to

84 Knitter 1985, 191f.
85 Cp. Wiles 1992, 72.
86 Cp. Macquarrie 1993, 1995, 1997.
87 *STh* III, 3, 7, Benziger Bros. edition, 1947. Translated by Fathers of the English Dominican Province. Online at: http://dhspriory.org/thomas/summa/TP/TP003.html#TPQ3A7THEP1
88 Undoubtedly Thomas Aquinas is simply talking about the logical possibility that the Son could have incarnated himself more than once, not that this is actually the case. Yet what Aquinas emphasizes—quite independent of whether one may expect only one or more than

which "God" refers to an infinite transcendent reality, which can be validly experienced by finite beings, but can never be exhausted by them. This has consequences for the connection between revelation and incarnation: Jesus is a mediator of divine revelation, but he is so as a genuine human being with all the limitations of a human. Jesus can thus only mediate the infinite reality of God in such a way as is possible for a finite, limited person, that is, he can only do so as a child of his time with all the cultural and religious influences specific to his time and situation. In light of this, a pluralist theology of religion reckons with the fact that other people have lived their lives in a similarly open and responsive relation to the divine reality, albeit in culturally and religiously distinct contexts. They too have become mediators of divine self-disclosure by means of their life and teachings, even though in quite different forms. These mediators need not stand in irreconcilable competition with one another because, as Aquinas rightly says, no finite creature is able to provide a comprehensive and exhaustive presentation of the infinite God.

The Doctrine of the Trinity in Pluralist Perspective

In the theology of religions—but by no means only there—approaches based on trinitarian thinking are currently experiencing a boom in interest.[89] Whereas a few of these approaches—at the moment probably most prominently that of Mark Heim[90]—follow an inclusivist direction and see the true being of God most appropriately and perfectly represented in the Christian doctrine of the Trinity,[91] some other approaches are closer to a pluralist position.[92] In other words, they see in the "trinitarian doctrine ... an acknowledgement of the plurality and diversity of the divine activity in relation to mankind...."[93]

one incarnation—is that no finite creature can exhaust the infinite God. In his critical response to the pluralist use of this argument Michael Schulz (2001) claims that this changes "Aquinas' intention to its opposite" (ibid. 139). In contrast to Schulz, it seems to me that the danger of such an inversion of Aquinas' intention is more concrete in Schulz' claims in view of Aquinas: "A human being is capable of expressing the infinite deity,... If God could not incarnate as *himself in his immeasurability*, then he could not *incarnate himself as himself*" (ibid. 139). Of course it is no other and no less (since God of course cannot be divided) than the immeasurable God who becomes incarnate. Yet the medium of incarnation remains finite and different from the mediated God. Any other view would not only be in conflict with Aquinas but also with the word of John's Gospel, "The Father is greater than I" (Jn 14:28). However one conceives of incarnation, the view that God either becomes incarnate in God's immeasurability or does not become incarnate at all, seems almost hazardously presumptious. Unless of course it means that even in the incarnation God infinitely exceeds all finitude and thus remains an immeasurable mystery.

89 On this cp. also Bernhardt 2000 and Kärkkäinen 2004.

90 Cp. Heim 2001. On this, see also above pp. 126-131.

91 Besides Heim 2001, for example also Smart, Konstantine 1991; D'Costa 2000; Ipgrave 2003; Kärkkäinen 2004.

92 For example, D'Sa 1987, and the proto-pluralist position in Panikkar 1973.

93 Hick 1991d, 9.

As has been briefly mentioned above, today every form of the Christian doctrine of the Trinity must begin with the historical reality that Jesus himself did not proclaim any kind of trinitarian image of God, but rather that the doctrine of the Trinity developed only gradually and in the course of, at times, most severe theological confrontations. As Karl-Heinz Ohlig recapitulates:

> There is absolutely no evidence that Jesus understood the 'Father,' by whom he felt himself to have been sent and with whom he presumably felt to have a special relationship, in any other way than the monotheistic God of Judaism…. There is no need to further elucidate this consensus of New Testament research.[94]

And from the perspective of the history of doctrine Reinhard Hübner confirms:

> … that the doctrine of the Trinity originally neither explicitly nor implicitly characterized Christian faith, but rather should be regarded as a "theology in the making." Its very first beginnings can be traced to no earlier than 150 AD and resulted in its representatives being accused of ditheism and tritheism, in other words, of the worst kinds of heresy.[95]

An adequate understanding of the Christian doctrine of the Trinity can therefore only be achieved by way of a critical reconstruction of its historical genesis and the motives at work therein.[96] Of course it is not possible here even to roughly sketch this out. Yet it should be noted, that a historical reconstruction of the doctrine of the Trinity will view it as a gradually evolving interpretation of the experience of a salvific divine revelation in and through Jesus. The experience of revelation and salvation as mediated by Jesus forms the point of departure for the development of the doctrine of the Trinity. The doctrine of the Trinity must therefore be understood from the perspective of Christology, and not, vice versa, Christology from the doctrine of the Trinity. Put more succinctly, the experience of God forms the point of departure for the doctrine of the Trinity, the experience made by Jesus himself and by early Christianity through the mediation of Jesus. If we do not want to declare, retrospectively, Jesus' strict monotheism as wrong, then we must reject as inadequate all those tendencies in the numerous formulations of Trinitarian thought that, in their word and content, conceive of the Trinity as tritheism, that is, as a teaching about three gods. Rather, the origin of the doctrine of the Trinity is determined by the question of how the one God of Jesus, who is at the same time the one God of all human beings, can reveal him/her/itself in three distinguishable forms.

An interpretation of the *doctrine of the Trinity that ties it back to Jesus* implies: We speak of God as "Father" in relation to the God to whom Jesus himself referred with the words "my Father and your Father." We speak of Jesus as "Son" to the extent that through addressing God as "Father" Jesus himself becomes identifiable as

94 Ohlig 1999, 29.
95 Hübner 1996, 326.
96 On this claim cp. also Haight 1999, 471.

"the Son." And one can speak of God as "Son" because Jesus in his function as the human, finite revealer is the "image of the invisible God" and the "Word (of God) become flesh." That is, the identification of Jesus as "the Son" is transferable to God to the extent and in the sense that God discloses him/her/itself through this particular person. One can speak of God as "Spirit" to the extent that Jesus became the revealer through being filled with that divine Spirit that inspires all genuine prophets or divine revealers since the beginning of the world, and also because truly hearing and understanding this revelation implies that one begins to share in this "Spirit."

This should make clear that referring the doctrine of the Trinity back to Jesus' experience of God and to the experience of God as mediated by Jesus cannot stop with Jesus, but rather demands a broader *link to the Jewish people's experience of God*. For the God whom Jesus calls "Father" is for Jesus the God who made him/her/itself known in the experience of Israel. And the Spirit that fills Jesus is the Spirit of those prophets who mediated the Jewish experience of God. In the same way, Jesus' self-understanding—in so far as it might be historically established—must be located within the ellipse marked by these two focal points: Jesus' experience of God as completely centered on the "Father" and the hope of his people for the Kingdom of God.

Yet even this is not sufficient. Referring back to the Jewish people's experience of God demands a further *universal and cosmological relinking*. For Israel had long ago identified the God whom Jesus calls "Father" as being far more than a mere tribal deity. God is not only the one who delivered Israel but, according to the word of the prophet Amos, had also delivered other peoples from their own servitude (Amos 9:7). God is the God of all peoples and of all that is: the ultimate origin of all reality and therefore also the only basis for hope in ultimate salvation, ultimate consummation. And the Spirit that led the prophets is also the Spirit that blows through all creation and gives it order, life, and the power for renewal.

When considered from its roots and beyond its later doctrinal (and partially quite problematic[97]) hardening, the doctrine of the Trinity is therefore *first* closely linked to religious experiences. *Second*, the doctrine of the Trinity presents a specific Christian symbolization of this experience, and *third*, it has an inbuilt universal momentum which stretches far beyond the bounds of Christianity: The "Father" of Jesus Christ points to the transcendent horizon of all reality. The "Spirit" of Christ is not limited to Jesus, neither before nor after him. It is being filled with this Spirit—the Spirit of the prophets and the Spirit of liberation (Lk 4:18f)—that makes Jesus the "Son" and, as Paul could still say quite naturally: "for all those who let themselves be led by the Spirit of God are Sons of God" (Rom 8:14).

97 Problematic because it seems that here we are leaving the plane of living religious experience and are cultivating the illusion of being able to reach differentiated conclusions about the inner being of God, moreover with an alleged degree of certainty that in several theologians' eyes justified the execution of those who differ theologically in their views of the Trinity.

So the doctrine of the Trinity has its origin in what theological language describes as "economic Trinity" or "the Trinity of salvation history," that is in three different and yet interconnected forms of God experience symbolically designated with the words "Father," "Son," and "Spirit." Now, if it is true that it is actually the divine reality itself that is disclosed to people in these three basic forms, must it not then follow that God "an sich", God as God is in him/her/itself, is exactly the same as he/she/it appears in his self-disclosure to us? Must not then all assertions about the self-communication of God as Father, Son, and Holy Spirit be understood "in the strict sense," as Karl Rahner says, "as assertions about God *as he is in himself*," since otherwise they would "not be assertions about God's self-communication,"[98] since God has otherwise not disclosed his inner being as such to us?

It is on the basis of this reflection that Rahner formed his well-known thesis about the identity between economic and immanent Trinity, that is, his view that in God's inner divine being, God is exactly as God has revealed him/her/itself to us, namely a unity of three distinct "persons," the Father, the Son, and the Spirit. However, as Roger Haight has argued against Rahner, it is anything but a logically inevitable conclusion that different forms of divine self-disclosure in human experience have to correspond to real differences in God's inner being.[99] In addition, as Haight likewise points out,[100] Rahner's notion that one should understand the assertions about the Trinity strictly as assertions about God's being as such, is at odds with Rahner's other view that God is essentially an absolute mystery and hence remains that mystery also and precisely in God's self-communication, so that God cannot be comprehended by any concepts or any proposition, not even, as Rahner says, by the word "God,"[101] let alone by trinitarian specifications. The insight that trinitarian language is rooted in the economy of salvation, that is, in the experience of salvific divine revelation, does therefore not imply that the distinguishable differentiated forms of this experience represent real internal differences in God. Rather it clarifies that the one holy mystery reveals itself to people in different ways, without thereby ceasing to be that holy mystery.

Christian trinitarian language about God is thus no exception to the hermeneutics of human language about God presented above, which applies statements about transcendent reality not directly to this reality itself but rather to specific forms of human experience of God or transcendence.[102] Moreover, because the trinitarian language presupposes genuine differences in human experience of God, it may very well serve, in a pluralist sense, to strengthening the legitimacy and equal validity of these experiences, as is expressed symbolically through the full and equal divinity of "Father," "Son," and "Spirit." From a pluralist perspective the doctrine of the Trini-

98 Rahner 1976, 142. Translation from Rahner 1978, 137.
99 Cp. Haight 1999, 488.
100 Cp. Haight 1999, 487.
101 Cp. on this above p. 204.
102 Cp. above chapter 9.

ty thus "expresses the richness and versatility of the divine reality in relationship to humanity."[103]

Going further still, some pluralist theologians have suggested to interpret the doctrine of the Trinity not only in its specifically Christian sense, that is as referring to the revelation of God in Jesus Christ, but rather to see it as one special instance of a more general "Trinitarian symbolism"[104] that expands across the entire history of religion. According to this view, what undergirds the Christian doctrine of the Trinity is the differentiation of three elements of a general framework of divine self-disclosure. Roger Haight describes these as follows: *First,* the self-disclosing transcendent reality itself; *second,* its symbolically mediated presence in an external, personal or non-personal medium of revelation; *third,* its presence in an internal principle of appropriation in the understanding of revelation. According to Haight, "this three-fold structure is implicitly at work in all existentially engaging encounters with transcendent reality."[105]

In my mind, one need not dispute that the structure of salvific knowledge of transcendence can be described in this way. But it is controversial to what extent such a description and its connection with the Christian doctrine of the Trinity makes sense from a pluralist perspective. The answer to this is double-edged. On the one hand this may be all to easily, and underhandedly, employed to give preference to a form of Christian inclusivism, according to which in the final analysis the complete truth about God and God's actions in the world only became clear through Jesus and in Christianity. On the other hand, such use of Trinitarian language may only be a form of *hermeneutical* inclusivism according to which one draws on Christian-systematic categories in order to understand and discern, from a background shaped by Christian faith, the working of God in other religions. Such a hermeneutical inclusivism is completely justified in principle and as such does not entail any pre-decision on whether this interpretation results in an inclusivist or pluralist theology of religions. To this extent speaking of a "universal Trinitarian symbolism" functions similarly as speaking about the working of the "Logos" or the "unknown Christ" in other religions. The test of whether such language coheres with a pluralist theology of religions position consists of asking whether, alongside the Christian discernment of a Trinitarian symbolism, non-Christian ways of identifying similar constellations are also approved as being possible and equally valid. Beyond this, the test of whether such language is fruitful for a theology of religions will consist of whether other religions can actually accept it as illuminating.

103 Hick 1989b, 201.

104 Thus Reinhold Bernhardt in his as yet unpublished contribution ("The *Real* and the Trinitarian God") at the "Pluralist Summit" in Birmingham, 2003. Cp. above p. 25, n. 32. [Author's note: A revised version of this paper is published in: P. Knitter (ed.): The Myth of Religious Superiority. Maryknoll: Orbis 2005, 194-207.]

105 Haight 1999, 484.

Potential Pluralism—and Nothing More?

These reflections on an understanding of the Trinity bring to an end the second part of this book. Its task was to clarify the systematic presuppositions of a Christian and simultaneously pluralist theology of religions. If one accepts the *metaphysical* (chapter 7), *epistemological* (chapter 8), *hermeneutical* (chapter 9), *soteriological* (chapter 10), and *christological* (chapter 11) presuppositions as have been expounded here, then a pluralist theology of religions is a possible Christian option. But does this mean that, in the theology of religions, we must stop at the mere affirmation of such a possibility? Undoubtedly, one cannot, in any strict sense, demonstrate the truth of a pluralist theology of religions. The fact that its theological presuppositions cannot be demonstrated in any irrefutable way is more than enough to show that any strict proof of religious pluralism is impossible. But even if one accepts these presuppositions as valid, one cannot compellingly deduce a pluralist position from them. The aforementioned presuppositions simply show that, and how, a pluralist position is possible within Christianity, but they do not make pluralism mandatory.

So can we merely affirm something like a potential pluralism? As a theology of religions option, Schubert Ogden has suggested,

> that there *can be* many true religions without having to claim that there actually *are* such.[106]

With reference to Ogden, Michael Hüttenhoff has also endorsed this position.[107] However, as John Hick makes clear, in a sense, exclusivists and inclusivists can also allow for the mere logical possibility of a pluralist theology of religions.[108] Yet the pluralist thesis itself, *as a thesis*, of course contains more than simply the affirmation of its own possibility. Rather, it wants to assert what it takes to be true.

Yet Ogden too does not simply stop at a potential pluralism. Instead, he claims that potential pluralism contains everything that can be claimed "a priori, in advance of actually encountering specific religions and validating their claims to truth…."[109] Ogden thus applies his potential pluralism only to the systematic presuppositions of a pluralist theology of religions as can be held *a priori*. When Ogden further states that "any and all other religions can also be true in the very same sense" as Christianity, "because or insofar as they give expression to substantially the same religious truth,"[110] then he actually understands this as an invitation to a research program. That is, this position

> … gives one every reason to look for signs of the actuality of the pluralism whose possibility is securely grounded….[111]

106 Ogden 1992, 103.
107 Hüttenhoff 2001, 271.
108 Hick in Swidler, Mojzes 1997, 79f.
109 Ogden 1992, 103.
110 Ibid.
111 Ibid. 103.

According to Ogden, such signs of the actual truth of pluralism—in contrast to its mere possibility—should be sought in the concrete interaction with other religions. In so saying, Ogden calls for what I identified at the beginning of this book as a basic demand of a theology of religion, namely that it must not proceed simply in an *a priori* way, but rather that its conclusions should be attained, tested, and when necessary modified in the interaction with other religions.[112]

If such an interaction with other religions is to be serious, it can only be done dialogically. Faithful members of another religion must be allowed and invited to explain what their faith means to them, and what they believe to recognize in their own life, through the mediation of their own religious tradition, about transcendent reality. Moreover, we also need to pay attention to how followers of other religions perceive Christianity. For this will allow us to differentiate more clearly between internal and external perception, not only in relation to our own religion. Even more, such attentive listening will also allow us to become more sensitive to the fact that we are in exactly the same position with regards to our interpretation of the other's religion as they are in their interpretation of our religion. Hence it is necessary to reckon also with a discrepancy between what the other religion means to its members and what we are able to understand of this.

In view of the christological foundation of his own inclusivist position, Karl Rahner once posed the famous question: "Where else is there someone" who prompts us to "unconditionally to let ourselves get involved with him…other than just the biblical Jesus?"[113] Hans Kessler recently reiterated this question in his own words:

> Who else in all the religions brings this God home to us, in such a pure and authentic way, a God whom one may trust with every fiber of one's being, without fear (such as one must have of other gods and demonic images of gods)? Who else brings to us that goodness that is decidedly for all, not just as a principle or a nice idea, but in such a way that it actually *happens*?[114]

This question is certainly important. Yet it is also open to the just-mentioned danger of neglecting the differences in perception and thus of hermeneutically applying double standards. Was there not also intense fear of the Christian God? Are there not also sayings in the New Testament—including words of Jesus—which significantly fan the flames of such fear? The "purity" of God's revelation in Jesus that we perceive is also due to a (no doubt justified but still unmistakable) selective perception, which we too easily downplay when inquiring into the possible "purity" of other potential divine mediators and mediations, or in the worst case selectively confine to the perception of the less "pure" aspects in the case of others.[115] Jesus' saying about the speck and the log (Mt 7:3) applies just as well—or perhaps especially so—to interreligious dialogue.

112 Cp. above, pp. 32-34.
113 Rahner 1968, 33f.
114 Kessler 2001, 231.
115 Though this last point undoubtedly does not apply to Kessler!

As Alan Race rightly emphasizes in his recent publication, concrete dialogue with other religions and a systematic theology of religions together form the "twin tracks" upon which the train of interfaith encounter can proceed into the future.[116] It is only through interreligious dialogue that we can corroborate whether there are functional equivalents in other religions to what we, as Christians, have experienced through Jesus Christ as salvific knowledge of transcendence. Interreligious dialogue must show how fruitful a pluralist approach might be compared to its exclusivist and inclusivist rivals. Hence it is in interreligious encounter where we need to look for that kind of confirmation that allows us to see in the pluralist position more than just a mere possibility. This will be illustrated in the third part of the book by using the example of some interreligious dialogues. Given the immense breadth, and to some extent also depth, attained by interreligious dialogue in only a few decades, such illustration can only be selective and tentative. So I will not pursue Ogden's suggested research program in the full way that is necessary, but I hope to at least make clear how rewarding it is to embark on such a program.

116 Race 2001.

Part III:

Testing a Christian and Pluralist Theology of Religions in Interreligious Encounter

12. Christianity and Judaism

Christian Anti-Judaism

Historical Overview

As mentioned in the historical sketch on exclusivism, the exclusivist position developed within early Christian theology in terms of a triple demarcation against Jews (to the extent that they did not become Christians), "Heathens" (adherents of non-Christian religions), and "False Christians" or "Heretics" (i.e. Christians with different theological views).[1] The exclusivist distinctions had horrendous consequences in each of these three directions. So-called "heathens" were stripped of their rights and their sacred sites were destroyed. They suffered wars and conquests, were expelled from their lands, and were sometimes forced to be baptized under the threat of brutal violence. The fight against Christians of other persuasions, the so-called "false teachers" and "heretics," is likewise part of the dark and distressing side of Christendom. Already the New Testament says about them: "Yet these people are like irrational animals which are fated by nature to be caught and killed" (2 Pet 2:12).[2] Indeed, for centuries the Christian inquisition acted out this understanding in a sanguinary fashion. Anti-Judaism, however, presents the most shocking chapter in the fight against Jews, heathens, and heretics.[3]

Today there is no more doubt that Jesus understood his own mission as entirely directed to the people of Israel. In the face of what were believed to be the impending apocalyptic events, it was the Jewish people that was the focus of Jesus' call for religious renewal. Christianity too began, and understood itself originally, as a religious group within Judaism. Yet thanks to the mission to the non-Jews and its early successes, Christianity quickly outgrew its close ties to the Jewish people. The proportion of Jewish Christians compared to the number of non-Jewish Christians gradually became smaller and smaller until it was ultimately insignificant. Already in the New Testament one finds documentation of considerable tensions between the followers of Jesus, that is, the developing Christian church, and those Jews who neither could nor wanted to join the Jesus movement. In the period of the early church fathers, these tensions sharpened into a distinct anti-Jewish theology, to

1 Cp. chapter 4, pp. 92f. above.
2 Translated following Ernst Albrecht's literal and unadorned translation.
3 Cp. the overviews in: Grayzel 1968; Flannery 1985; Ruether 1978; Jansen 1990; Cohn-Sherbok 1992.

whose most important elements I will later return. The anti-Jewish theology of the early church turned into anti-Jewish praxis when Emperor Constantine made Christianity a privileged cult and when, in 380 under the Emperor Theodosius, it became the state religion. Already under Constantine, laws were passed that degraded the legal position of Jews vis-à-vis Christians. In the year 315, conversion from Christianity to Judaism became punishable by death. Soon after, Jews were prohibited from owning Christian slaves or from doing any kind of missionary activity. Mixed Jewish-Christian marriages were made illegal. There was an increase in the number of Christian riots against Jews and Jewish facilities such as synagogues, cemeteries, and Jewish quarters of town. Although the Roman state passed a series of laws to prevent such developments, all too often the guilty parties went unpunished. Their deeds were condoned by various church fathers, and at times openly supported. A famous example of this occurred in 388 when a Christian mob, incited by the local bishop, set fire to the synagogue at Callinicum on the Euphrates. The Emperor Theodosius ordered that the responsible bishop pay for the reconstruction from his resources. When Bishop Ambrose heard about this, he became energetically involved in seeing that those responsible escaped without penalty. In a letter to the Emperor, Ambrose identified himself with the arsonists. He wrote:

> I declare that I set the synagogue on fire, at least that I told them to do it in order to get rid of the place where Christ is denied. (...) What does a believer have in common with an unbeliever? Along with the non-believes the testimonials of unbelief have to be rooted out as well.[4]

In the fifth century, Christian pogroms against Jews increased substantially, and we see the beginning of large expulsions. In 414, Bishop Cyril expelled the Jews from Alexandria, a town that for many centuries had been the spiritual center of Judaism in the Diaspora. In 418, the Bishop of Minorca forced all Jews on the island to be baptized. In the fifth and sixth centuries in Antioch, another significant center of Jewish life, we once again see massive anti-Jewish riots. It was here, where already at the end of the fourth century John Chrysostom excelled, in his sermons and writings, as a particular strong instigator against the Jews. Thus speaks the "Golden Mouth"[5] Chrysostom about the synagogue:

> A place where a whore stands on display is a whorehouse. What is more, the synagogue is not only a whorehouse and a theater; it is also a den of thieves and a haunt of wild animals...The Jews have no conception of [spiritual] things at all, but living for the lower nature...Only one thing they understand: to gorge themselves and to get drunk.[6]

4 Quoted following Jansen 1990, 134.
5 "Golden Mouth" is the literal meaning of the honorary name, "Chrysostomos".
6 Chrysostom c. Jud. 1,3,4, cited following Ruether, 1979, 178.

At the beginning of the seventh century after a renewed futile attempt at converting the Jews, all remaining synagogues in Antioch were destroyed once and for all and the Jews killed or driven away.

The Codex Justinianus of 534 significantly reduced the still formally extant laws protecting Jews and further increased the limitations on their civil rights. There were also repeated attempts in the Byzantine Empire to force the conversion of the Jews to Christianity by legal means, for example in the years 632, 721, 870, and 932. Yet all these attempts were unsuccessful.

At the other end of the Christian sphere of influence, in Spain, the situation was hardly better. A whole series of anti-Jewish laws were in place and kings and bishops continually tried to convert the Jews by force. When at last the edict was announced that Jews had to divest themselves of all property and refrain from all business dealings, the Spanish and North African Jews conspired with the goal of delivering Spain to the Muslims, for Jews could hope for more freedom and protection from Muslims than from Christians. The plot was discovered, in response to which Jews were declared to be "slaves in perpetuity." They lost all of their property, and their children were taken away from them in order to be baptized. Yet the Muslim conquest of Spain soon put an end to this misery. Although under Muslim rule Jews by no means enjoyed the same rights as Muslims, they were able to live much better, unhindered lives than in Christian countries. There were neither mass murders, nor mass deportations, nor forced conversions. An almost symbolic example of this can be found in Maimonides (1135-1204), the outstanding representative of medieval Judaism who was born in Cordoba and spent his entire life in countries ruled by Muslims (Spain, Morocco, and Egypt). In Muslim Spain the Jewish community experienced an, by European standards, unusual period of flourishing. The victory of Christianity over the Spanish Muslims changed this situation abruptly and drastically. From the fourteenth century on, and in particular with the completion of the "Reconquista", the Christian "reconquering" of Spain toward the end of the fifteenth century, Jews once again became the victims of sanguinary pogroms, forced baptisms and expulsion, and above all of the newly introduced inquisition. The situation was similar in Portugal. One of the main tasks of the Spanish Inquisition was to sniff out those among the forcibly converted Jews and Muslims who secretly still adhered to their old religion. There was a general obligation to report others, and one was particularly to pay attention to whether former Jews and Muslims showed signs of maintaining the habits of their former religion in their day-to-day behavior (for example, through particular cleanliness or refraining from certain activities on Saturdays) and especially in their eating habits (the form of the food preparation, avoiding pork, etc.).[7] In the long term, the praxis of the Spanish Inquisition led to a general suspicion of all Christians of Jewish descent. The first anti-Semitic race laws originated in sixteenth-century Spain, laws that included limitations on all those who were Jewish in the ethnic sense, even if otherwise they were faithful

7 Cp. Lea 1988, Vol. I, 407ff., Vol II, 143ff.

members of the Roman Catholic Church. They were blocked from all higher state and ecclesial positions.[8] From a historical perspective, modern racist antisemitism is thus a consequence of Christian anti-Judaism.[9]

In Central Europe, for a longer period, Jews could lead relatively unhindered lives. To a large extent, they organized the trade with the Near East and therefore enjoyed a certain protection. The situation took an immense turn for the worse with the beginning of the Crusades. The very first victims of the Crusaders were the Jewish congregations in France and along the Rhine in the course of sometimes extreme Christian riots. It is estimated that several tens of thousands of Jews were murdered in Central Europe during the First Crusade.[10] In the aftermath, we see increasing measures aimed at forcing Jews into a social ghetto. In 1215 the Fourth Lateran Council decided that all Jews should be distinguished by wearing a special Jew's hat and a yellow patch on their coats. They were excluded from the craftsmen's guilds, and from the late Middle Ages on were also not allowed to purchase any property. On the other hand they were allowed to charge interest in financial dealings, which was forbidden to Christians due to religious reasons.[11] Because of this, some Jewish circles were pressed into becoming bearers of the increasingly important financial economy, as a result of which however they were also forced into the role of hated usurers. However, the Jews had to buy their licenses, permissions and protection letters from the Christian authorities with substantial payments, so that in the end a not insignificant proportion of the gain from their financial endeavors flowed back into Christian coffers. But in Central Europe too Jews repeatedly suffered from massive forced expulsions. When the plague broke out in the fourteenth century, many assigned blame for it to the Jews, accusing them of having poisoned public wells. Throughout Europe extensive pogroms occurred with the result that, toward the end of the fourteenth century, Jewish congregations in Europe were largely ruined. From the sixteenth century on their remnants became more and more ghettoized.

Modernity brought some improvements. Of course these came less from the Protestant Reformation but far more from the gradually developing forces of the Enlightenment and Liberalism. Though in his early years Luther had urged people to spare the Jews, he later authored fierce anti-Jewish writings. In these he describes Jews not only as "snakes' spawn and children of the devil"[12] but also actively calls for

8 Cp. Lea 1988, Vol. I, 539-563.

9 Following some Jewish historians, Hans Küng has drawn attention to the fact that Christianity's military fight against Islam led to a general worsening of the Jews' situation, since they were understood to be allies of Islam. (Cp. Küng 1992, 163; 1991, 210). That the fight against Islam also radicalized the anti-Jewish praxis of the Church cannot be disputed. But I would not say there was a "terrible shift in the attitude of the church to Judaism" (ibid.) because the theological motives of Christian anti-Judaism are substantially old and remained unaltered.

10 Cp. Grayzel 1968, 306.

11 Calling upon Lk 6:34 and various Old Testament traditions which did not distinguish between taxes and usury, on the Christian side there had for a long time been an only somewhat restricted law against taxes.

12 Cp. Wengst 2004, 84, n. 28.

the destruction of the synagogues and Jewish houses, the confiscation of valuables, Jewish prayer books, Talmuds, and even Bibles, demanding that rabbis are banned from teaching and preaching and that their safe-conduct is revoked, recommends forced labor, and finally deportation and expulsion. An improvement of the Jewish situation first became apparent in England. There had been a mass expulsion of Jews in 1291. Yet under Cromwell in the seventeenth century, England re-admitted Jews and softened discriminatory laws. The English Enlightenment supported a tolerant attitude, which was carried across to America. In Continental Europe too, the ideas of the Enlightenment led to an improvement in Jewish living conditions and to the liberalization of anti-Jewish laws. By contrast, in Eastern Europe there was continual suppression of Jews, which particularly in the nineteenth century led to large numbers of Jews fleeing Russia for the West. The gradual emancipation of Central European Jews in the nineteenth century was, however, of short duration. The Holocaust, which the National Socialists inflicted on European Judaism in the twentieth century, put a grim end to this. It is reported that Hitler said, on the occasion of a visit by two bishops, that his *Judenpolitik* was only the culmination of what Christianity had taught and practiced for 2000 years.[13] It is true that National Socialism was not a Christian movement but rather an atheism adorned with pseudo-religious features. Yet it is just as true that, as Hans Küng repeatedly wrote, Nazi anti-Semitism: "would not have been possible without the prehistory of the religious anti-Judaism of the Christian church extending over almost two thousand years."[14] This is also the position of *Dabru Emet*, the Jewish declaration published in September 2000 and signed by more than 200 rabbis and Jewish theologians:

> Nazism was not a Christian phenomenon. Without the long history of Christian anti-Judaism and Christian violence against Jews, Nazi ideology could not have taken hold nor could it have been carried out.[15]

Today, many Christian theologians share this understanding. After the Second World War, Christians felt a tremendous burden of complicity regarding the development that ultimately led to the mass murder of six million Jews. As a result, we see the first intensive theological efforts aimed at uncovering and overcoming the theological roots of Christian anti-Judaism.

13 Cp. Ruether 1979, 223f. On this, see also the as shattering as enlightening comparison of National Socialism's anti-Semitic laws and the anti-Jewish decisions in Ecclesial law, in Küng 1992, 234f.

14 Küng 1992, 236 (1991, 292) and 1980, 196, and 1991, 292.

15 *Dabru Emet*, Thesis 5. The original English text of *Dabru Emet* is accessible on various websites, e.g. http://www.icjs.org/resources/dabru-emet. On *Dabru Emet* see also Sandmel 2002 and Kampling, Weinrich 2003.

Theological Roots of Christian Anti-Judaism

In light of the indisputable fact that Christians and Christian motives stand behind the long and sanguinary history of anti-Judaism, there are fundamentally two different possibilities for how one might respond theologically: On the one hand, Christians can heed the Enlightenment's call for religious tolerance and legally guaranteed freedom of religion. In other words, Christians can and should support a governmental and legal framework that precludes from the outset the types of intolerance Judaism has had to suffer. As obvious as this may sound today, we should not forget that as late as 1832 Pope Gregory XVI, in the encyclical *Mirari vos*, literally described the demand for religious freedom as "madness." It was only in 1965 that the Roman Catholic Church took up the call for freedom of religion in the "Declaration on Religious Freedom" (*Dignitatis humanae*) of the Second Vatican Council. Within the dimensions of church history, this is not that long ago. And what is young is often also fragile.

Yet unambiguous support of the Enlightenment demand for freedom of religion does not yet touch on the issue of identifying the specific *theological roots* that were responsible for the rise of Christian enmity towards Jews. So the second theological response must consist of not only a striving for a different legal framework for interreligious co-existence, but also for a different theological foundation for Jewish-Christian relations. The main concern is to expose and overcome the central theological motives of Christian anti-Judaism. Yet how tightly are these linked to the fundamental tenets of the Christian faith? Could it be possible that the Christian faith itself needs to undergo certain changes in order to overcome the roots of Christian anti-Judaism from the inside out?

Looking at the development of anti-Jewish theology in the early church, one can establish that in the anti-Jewish writings of the church fathers—the so-called *Adversus-Iudaeos* literature—the following five interconnected motifs recur:[16]

1) The Jews rejected the Messiah and murdered the Son of God.
2) The church is the true Israel.
3) Only the church understands the Old Testament.
4) Any harm suffered by Jews is divine judgment.
5) The existence of a post-Christian Judaism has no intrinsic theological value.

1) *The Jews rejected the Messiah.* "Jesus Christ" is the shortest conceivable form of the Christian confession of Jesus as the "Christ." "Christ" means "the anointed one" and is the Greek term for "Messiah." In this way the early church proclaimed that the Messiah promised to the people of Israel had indeed appeared. However, as the early church also proclaimed, the people of Israel, at least the vast majority of it, has rejected the Messiah. Given the relatively rapidly developing notion that Jesus was

16 On this cp. especially Ruether 1979, 117-182; Jansen 1990, 137ff.

not only the promised Messiah but also the Son of God become man, the judgment against Israel evolved into the view that the Jews had not only opposed the Messiah but also the Son of God. This was combined with the even harsher accusation that Jews had committed "deicide" by crucifying Jesus, and that all Jews who do not convert to Christianity are guilty of a sort of moral complicity in this. And so it became a standard *topos* of Christian anti-Jewish polemic that already in the old covenant Israel had killed the prophets and finally with Jesus had even murdered the Son of God.

2) *The church is the true Israel.* The allegation that Israel had rejected its Messiah, whereas the church recognized and accepted Jesus as the Messiah, led to the conviction that the Christian church now represents the "true Israel." Already Paul speaks of the church as the "Israel of God" (Gal 6:16). With the notion that the church was the true Israel came the claim that all the promises of the old covenant actually referred to the church and not to the Jewish people. In the church, not in Israel, they find their fulfillment. In conjunction with the idea of the church as the true Israel or the Israel of God, we find the motif of the Jewish people as a false Israel, a people that is no longer the People of God, a people that actually had always obstructed God, beginning with the adoration of the golden calf at Sinai, to their resistance to the prophets, and finally to the crucifixion of Christ. Already in the New Testament a usage develops which applies the expression "the Jews" in this hostile sense. In 1 Thess 2:15, for example, "the Jews" are those "who killed both the Lord Jesus and the prophets, and drove us out; they displease God and oppose everyone." This tendency increases in the Gospel of John, leading to the repeated insistence that "the Jews" do not know God (Jn 7:28; 15:21; 16:3); indeed, as it says in a culminating verse, that they have the devil and not God as their father, and that they fulfill the will of the devil, who "was a murderer from the beginning" (Jn 8:41-44).

3) *Only the church understands the Old Testament.* The tendency also retrospectively to deny that the people of Israel were ever the true people of God correlates with the notion that Jews do not understand the Scriptures given to them. Everything in the Scriptures points in a hidden way to Jesus Christ and the church. But Judaism lacks the key to a true understanding of the Scriptures, which is solely in the hands of the church. Thus, according to Paul,

> … to this very day, when they hear the reading of the old covenant, that same veil is still there, since only in Christ is it set aside. Indeed, to this very day whenever Moses is read, a veil lies over their minds; but when one turns to the Lord, the veil is removed (2 Cor 3:14-16).

Throughout the New Testament we find the idea that only the recognition of Jesus as the Christ (Messiah) produces the correct understanding of the Torah and the Prophets, namely as a promise of the coming of Jesus Christ. On the basis of this idea, the church claimed the Hebrew Bible as her exclusive property, that is, as the "Old Testament," in the sense that the church alone recognizes and understands the Scriptures correctly as finding its fulfillment and its end in the "New Testament."

There was thus no theological justification for a separate and autonomous Jewish way of reading the Torah and the Prophets.

A particular issue in this context, which assumed its own special significance, is the Pauline concept of an opposition between law and gospel. The Torah, at least in its Jewish exposition, is not capable of helping humans attain salvation but rather is an oppressive law, which solely mediates knowledge about sin and the curse of divine judgment. The law "was our disciplinarian until Christ came" (Gal 3:24). Yet as such it becomes superfluous with the coming of Christ and without Christ it has no function as a mediator of salvation. Since this notion refers to the heart of the Jewish religion, it is at one and the same time to be understood as a statement about Judaism as a whole.

4) *Any harm suffered by Jews is divine judgment.* The notion that "the Jews" killed the Messiah, as they had the prophets before him, and that this shows that they have always been a people closed off to God, led to the conviction in the anti-Jewish literature of the church fathers that all the catastrophes suffered by the Jewish people in the time since Jesus' death were expressions of God's wrath and their rejection. So, for example, church fathers like Augustine and Chrysostom interpreted the final destruction of the Temple and the expulsion of the Jews from Israel by the Romans as divine judgment over Israel. This interpretation can also already be found in the New Testament, when Jesus in the twenty-third chapter of the Gospel of Matthew announces the divine punishment for all those who have spilled the innocent blood of the prophets and the righteous ones. Or when in the twenty-seventh chapter of Matthew the Jewish crowd before Pilate loudly demands the crucifixion of Jesus and the Scripture then says:

> Then the people as a whole answered, "His blood be on us and on our children!" (Mt 27:25).

The notion that since the crucifixion of Jesus the Jewish people is no more than the object of divine punishment and that this judgment is inflicted on the Jewish people through all kinds of harm made it possible that the church understood itself and its anti-Jewish measures almost as an aide in the execution of the divine judgment. A characteristic example of this is a comment by Ambrose in his aforementioned writing to the Emperor Theodosius following the destruction of the synagogue in Callinicum. Ambrose, the Bishop of Milan, who in his letters joins in solidarity with the Bishop of Callinicum, writes here that the only reason he himself had not set fire to the synagogue in Milan was because God had already taken this task from him by causing a lightning strike. In this remark the notion that God and the church are working hand in hand in afflicting the Jewish people becomes quite concrete.

5) *The existence of a post-Christian Judaism has no intrinsic theological value.* All the points mentioned up till now—the rejection of the Messiah and the murder of God, the replacement of the people of Israel by the church as the "true Israel," the inability of the Jewish people to understand their own Holy Scriptures properly, and finally their obvious damnation through divine judgment and punishment—cul-

minated in the conviction that there was no theological justification for the continuance of Israel in the sense of a separate Jewish religion. The law, the temple, and circumcision: in the eyes of the church fathers, they have all lost their meaning. Augustine held the view that the remnants of the Jewish people, driven out of the Promised Land and dispersed among the people of the world, only continue to exist in order to safeguard their scriptures. For in this way Christians can show the gentile world that the prophetic announcement and promise of Jesus Christ is indeed found in the Jewish scriptures and has not just been a Christian fabrication.[17] Of course this argument became obsolete to the extent that Europe got Christianized, so that there were no more gentiles to whom one had to prove the credibility of the Christian claims.

So in the end a different argument played the most important role for some toleration of the existence of the Jewish people, namely the hope supported by Romans 11:25f that one day the whole of Israel would convert to Christianity. However, this view did not come across as particularly realistic given the numerous violent, but failed attempts to convert Israel by force. Thus, for example, in the Middle Ages Duns Scotus was of the opinion:

> … that one should not, because of such a few who convert so late, tolerate so many Jews who persist in their law in so many regions of the world and for so many years just because eventually there will be a modest harvest for the church. Hence it would suffice us to allow just a few of them to follow their law and ban them to some island.[18]

Inclusivist Openings

The Unrevoked Covenant

The anti-Jewish stereotypes of the *Adversus-Iudaeos* literature correspond to an exclusivist position in the theology of religions. That is, inclusivist positions were, if at all, only expressed in relation to pre-Christian Judaism. Although there was a strong tendency to ascribe an attitude of denial toward God already to pre-Christian Judaism, the notion that the pre-Christian Israelites were the people of God's covenant and promises was not disputed. The crucial assumption however was, that Judaism had lost this status when it rejected Jesus. The divine covenant and its promises has now been conveyed to the Christian church. There can therefore only be an exclusivist position toward post-Christian Judaism, as Karl Barth explains in §17 of his *Church Dogmatics* in a quite shocking way. According to Barth post-Christian Judaism is just

17 Cp. *De Civitate Dei*, 18,46.
18 In Sententias, 4, d. 4. q. 9, Vives XVI 489b. Cited following Jansen, 1990, 144f.

> a human religion, one that once was the human response to his revelation as demanded and ordered by God, in its practice indicted for unbelief though again and again re-accepted through grace, but one that is now—and even this example had to be made—a rejected, deflated religion, because it is deprived of its basis and object, now the Jewish religion from which God has turned his face, one religion among many others and not more than they! It only has one advantage over them and that is something terrible: that once it has been more than they, yet *definitely* ("endgültig") has been.[19]

The change of thinking that began for numerous Christians after the moral catastrophe of the Holocaust was focused on two particular points. On the one hand, they began to see a connection between Christianity's exclusivist anti-Jewish attitude and the Holocaust. On the other, they wanted to overcome the central assumption of anti-Jewish exclusivism, that is, they wanted to grant theological legitimacy to post-Christian Judaism. Already in 1948, at its constituent assembly in Amsterdam, the World Council of Churches established that the negative image of the Jews promulgated by churches in the past had played a part in the creation of antisemitism, and consequently called upon all member churches to adopt a clear stance opposed to antisemitism.[20] The 1961 general assembly of the World Council of Churches in New Delhi strengthened this position. Nevertheless the question of Jewish-Christian relations remained of rather subordinate significance in the central documents of the World Council of Churches—presumably as a result of political considerations, regarding the extremely critical attitude of the churches of the Near and Middle East towards the State of Israel.

The conflict between the State of Israel and the Palestinians significantly influenced also the prehistory of a declaration against antisemitism that was originally planned by the Second Vatican Council.[21] The draft of the declaration was revised several times and was eventually expanded to become a general declaration of the church about its relationship to non-Christian religions, a declaration that the Council passed in 1965 under the title *Nostra aetate.* On the crucial issue of a theological justification for post-Christian Judaism, *Nostra aetate* (No. 4) explaines:

> As Holy Scripture testifies, Jerusalem did not recognize the time of her visitation, nor did the Jews in large number, accept the Gospel; indeed not a few opposed its spreading. Nevertheless, God holds the Jews most dear for the sake of their Fathers; He does not repent of the gifts He makes or of the calls He issues—such is the witness of the Apostle. (…) Although the Church is the new

19 Barth 1932-70, Vol. I/2, 361. Emphasis by Barth. The English translation is based on the German original. [Here as elsewhere, the standard English translation of Barth's Church Dogmatics by Thomson & Knight is not fully accurate in as much as it significantly softens the harsh statements of the German original (here, for example, by omitting the "endgültig").]

20 Cp. Visser't Hooft 1949, 160-164.

21 For the complicated textual history of this declaration, see Oesterreicher 1967 and Zenger 1997.

people of God, the Jews should not be presented as rejected or accursed by God, ...

In this way, *Nostra aetate* positions itself against the notion that God has terminated his covenant with the Jewish people. But if this Covenant continues to be valid, then the justified existence of a post- and non-Christian Judaism must be theologically recognized. Beyond this, *Nostra aetate* opposes the general burdening of the Jewish people with the guilt for Jesus' crucifixion. It declares that Christian proclamation is no longer to speak of such a collective guilt nor of a divine rejection of the Jews. The church, so the declaration continues, dismisses all forms of persecution and bemoans all manifestations of antisemitism, whenever and by whomever these were or are practiced. In the future, the relationship between Jews and Christians should be marked above all by mutual knowledge and respect, to which end the Council recommends theological studies and fraternal dialogue. It is primarily in this regard that *Nostra aetate* is valued as a milestone in establishing a new relationship between Judaism and Christianity. For as it turned out subsequently the Council was serious about this willingness to dialogue. Not least the pontificate of Pope John Paul II made this unquestionably clear. Especially worth mentioning in this connection is also the cleaning up of the liturgy that began already during preparation for and subsequently to *Nostra aetate*. Pope John XXIII had already deleted the reference to the "faithless (*perfidus* and *perfidia*) Jews" found in the prayer for the Jews in the Good Friday liturgy. Yet it is also true that the schema of promise and fulfillment, according to which Judaism is only a preparation for Christ, remains as before deeply embedded in the structure of the Roman Catholic Church's liturgy; something that can also be said about other churches as well.[22]

In the period after *Nosta aetate*, one also finds its decisive point, the recognition of an enduring covenant between God and Judaism that is not revoked by the rise of Christianity, repeatedly emphasized in the Protestant realm, as for example in the widely known 1980 Declaration of the Protestant Church in the Rhineland. In the meantime, numerous churches have begun to rethink their relationship to Judaism in a self-critical manner,[23] even if much more slowly in some churches, such as the Orthodox Churches, than in others.[24]

However, *Nostra aetate* neither explicitly mentioned the Holocaust nor did it address in any way the issue of a Christian co-responsibility. Even the Vatican's declaration of 1988, "*We Remember: A Reflection on the Shoah*" held back on this score.[25] The confession of sins by Pope John Paul II at the "Day of Pardon" (March 12, 2000) speaks only generally of "the sins...against the people of the Covenant." Yet in the

22 Cp. Pawlikowski 2002, 85.

23 On this, cp. text collections in: Richter 1984; Rendtdorff, Henrix 1989; and Henrix, Kraus 2001.

24 Cp. Kessler 2002, 59f. According to Oeldermann 2003, 198, "the Orthodox-Jewish dialogue is still in its infancy."

25 Cp. Thoma 1998.

last few years, Christian churches, especially Protestant ones, repeatedly admitted a concrete connection between the long history of Christian anti-Judaism and the Holocaust. Thus the 1996 Methodist Declaration "*Building Bridges in Hope*" describes the "Holocaust as the catastrophic culmination of a long history of anti-Jewish attitudes and actions in which Christians, and sometimes the Church itself, have been deeply implicated."[26] But this admission remains linked to a theological problem that has not yet even remotely been tackled. As I said before, Christian anti-Judaism resulted significantly from the theological positions of the early Christian *Adversus-Iudaeos* literature. And these positions found their apogee in the denial of an intrinsic theological value of post-Christian Judaism. How does the affirmation that God's covenant with the Jewish people has not been revoked, in other words, that alongside Christianity, Judaism has its own theological right to exist, relate to the theological presuppositions behind the anti-Jewish literature of the early church? It is not enough to merely declare these as passed or to just remain silent about such questions. For the implications of theologically recognizing Judaism as a non-Christian but nevertheless valid path to salvation are far-reaching.

The church's claim of being the "true" or "real" Israel expresses the notion of Christianity superseding and replacing Judaism. This *supersessionism* (also: "replacement" or "substitution theory") is based primarily on the notion that non- or post-Christian Judaism continues to oppose the idea of Jesus as the "Christ," that is, that it still rejects him as its Messiah, and moreover as the one and only savior of all human beings. Thus, the theological roots of anti-Judaism are intimately connected with Christology and the church's self-understanding. These roots penetrate to the center of Christian faith. The theological wrestling for a solution is thus understandably difficult. In order to theologically recognize the dignity of post-Christian Judaism and its right to exist, Christian supersessionism has to be abandoned. But then—so it seems at least—one would also have to give up the Christological claim that Jesus is the Messiah sent by God to Israel and the absolute savior of all, including the Jewish people. Wilhelm Breuning goes to the heart of the matter when he writes:

> To many, the possibility of interpreting the Christ event in the Christian sense of an absolute savior while at the same time openly encouraging an understanding of Israel as having a presently valid salvific position seems like a squaring of the circle.[27]

This reveals that the central problem in overcoming the theological roots of anti-Judaism is identical with the central problem of inclusivism in the theology of religions. For the Christian supersessionism that contests the theological right of other religions to exist rests on the same interpretation of Jesus as the absolute savior and is a claim that Christianity raises not merely in relation to Judaism but toward

26 Quoted from Kessler 2002, 61 (see also www.jcrelations.net/en/?item=999).
27 Breuning 1991, 29.

all other religions. Let us be reminded here once more of Karl Rahner's clear words, "that Christianity, at least for now, is the only religion founded by God himself through Christ, the absolute religion, intended for all persons, the path of salvation that God's salvific will has created and principally made mandatory for everyone."[28] Therefore, Rahner continues, one "can and must say that these extra-Christian religions are 'in themselves' and in principle abolished and superseded by the advent of Christ (...), so that the historic expansion of Christendom, which even today is not yet simply completed, is identical with a progressive abolition of the legitimacy of these religions"[29] Thus the problem of supersessionism arises not only regarding the relationship between Christianity and Judaism. Rather, it arises with respect to the relationship between Christianity and all non-Christian religions. This connection has been clearly recognized on the Jewish side. Edward Kessler, the director of the Center for Jewish-Christian Relations in Cambridge, correctly establishes that:

> the belief that salvation can only come through Jesus (or through the Church) relegates not only Judaism but all other faiths to a position of inferiority.[30]

The insistence made so often since *Nostra aetate* that God's covenant with Judaism was not, in fact, revoked by the Christ-event is usually based on Paul's explanation in chapters 9-11 of the Letter to the Romans. Paul here speaks of a "mystery" (Rom 11:25) when discussing the meaning of the continued existence of the non- or better post-Christian Israel. On the one hand, in these chapters Paul vehemently supports the perception that all promises of the old covenant are fulfilled in Christ, that he is the end of the Law (10:4), that the non-Christian Jews are smitten with blindness and the hardening of their hearts (10:2; 11:7), and that they are no longer children of the promise (9:8)! On the other hand, Paul emphasizes that God has not rejected his people (11:2), that their election and calling are valid as before, and that the grace given them is irrevocable (11:28f). Israel, says Paul, has not stumbled so as to fall. "But through their stumbling, salvation has come to the Gentiles, so as to make Israel jealous" (11:11). Once all the Gentiles have attained salvation, says Paul, all of Israel will be saved (11:12, 25f.). In the concluding verses of chapter 11, Paul once again emphasizes the unsearchable nature of God's ways with regard to Israel and the Christians.

Some theological conceptions of the Christian-Jewish relationship are intimately connected with such "theology of mystery." The continued existence of the Jewish religious community is, according to these views, something the church should simply accept and tolerate. This means that in the final analysis the theological sense of this continued existence remains mysterious and the knowledge of it confined to God. Yet one sees no reason to make any compromises regarding the Christian claim that the Old Testament promises are fulfilled in and through Jesus.[31] The state-

28 Rahner 1967, 355f.
29 Ibid. 371f.
30 Kessler 2002, 66.
31 Cp. this Pawlikowski, 391.

ments of *Nostra aetate* also point basically in this direction. The tension between the continued existence of post-Christian Judaism and the Christologically supported claim of the church remains more or less unresolved and is, according to this view, to be retained in the spirit of eschatological hope. After all, *Nostra aetate* also maintains that "Jerusalem did not recognize the time of her visitation, nor did the Jews in large number, accept the Gospel; indeed not a few opposed its spreading." (No. 4). Nevertheless "God holds the Jews most dear for the sake of their Fathers; He does not repent of the gifts He makes or of the calls He issues—such is the witness of the Apostle." But it is still the task of the church to proclaim the Cross of Christ "as the fountain from which every grace flows." Together with Paul "the Church awaits that day, known to God alone, on which all peoples will address the Lord in a single voice ..." (No. 4). If the cross of Christ is to be understood in the literal sense as the "fountain" or source of "every grace" and is also to be proclaimed as such, then the Christological basis of the Christian claim to superiority remains untouched. The implication of this is that, as before, Judaism finds itself in the situation of not recognizing its divine "visitation" and of not accepting the Gospel. So why the continuance of a post-Christian Judaism should be theologically connected to something other than the hope that it eventually will still convert to Jesus Christ as its Messiah, does indeed remain a mystery. The actual difficulty of this position is thus that it ascribes the same status to post-Christian Judaism as to pre-Christian Judaism—that of being a precursor of Christianity.

The Issue of Missionizing the Jews

One can see just how theologically problematic and unstable this position is when considering the debate about the question of whether the Christian missionizing of the Jews is still justified. Exclusivist-minded circles have by no means given up the attempt and the practical efforts to convert Jews to Christianity. But anyone who pursues the conversion of Judaism to Christianity is clearly saying that he or she does not consider the continued existence of a non-Christian Judaism as desirable. This cannot be reconciled with the idea of a continuing covenant between God and Judaism. Yet an inclusivist position is also fundamentally geared to the global missionary expansion of Christianity. This causes a dilemma for all those who on the one hand endorse a theological justification of non-Christian Judaism and consequently reject a proselytizing mission to the Jews, but who on the other hand do not want to give up an inclusivist or exclusivist position in the theology of religions because of the associated Christological and soteriological positions.

"Christians and Jews III," a study-document issued by the German Protestant Church (EKD) in 2000, devoted a long section to the "Conflict about Missionizing the Jews." On the one hand, this text uses quite stark words in reaffirming a universal missionary mandate. "Mission" is defined here as "the commission of publicly

witnessing to the faith in Jesus of Nazareth who was raised up by God to be the ruler of the world. (…) Everything that happens in the world is geared toward an encounter with him, so as to find its saving perfection in that encounter."[32] Given his experience that the vast majority of the Jewish people did not accept Jesus as Messiah, Paul, according to this text, became convinced that the church should turn its attention to missionizing the non-Jewish world. God himself would then see to it that, after the completion of the global mission, Israel would finally acknowledge Jesus as its Messiah and be incorporated into his salvation.[33] The great commission in Matthew's Gospel to go out into the world is understood in this document as a mission "to the peoples of the world, that is, to the people outside of the people of God."[34] For this reason, Christians today should still consider themselves obliged to do global missionary work, while excluding Israel from this. Despite "the refusal to believe in Jesus by its majority," Israel "by no means has the status of being far from salvation and without salvation."[35] For since God did not abandon his people, God will "let his people see the consummation of his salvation. He does not need our missionary endeavors for this."[36]

Has the squaring of the circle succeeded here? The document states that Israel in its majority does not believe in Jesus as its Messiah, but neither does it therefore find itself in a state of "being far from salvation" because God has not terminated his covenant and Israel will come to a recognition of Jesus eschatologically, a task God will accomplish without the missionary activity of Christians. At the same time the document retains the necessity for a worldwide mission. This, however, inevitably raises the question of how to think about other peoples and religions that, just like Israel, mostly do not in their majority join the Christian faith in Jesus. Is it also true for them that they do not therefore have the status of being far from salvation and that God will eventually lead them to a recognition of Jesus, for which God does not need our missionary efforts? If so, then why is there a need for the continuation of proselytizing mission? Or are we to assume that somewhat stricter rules apply to non-Jews? Should we assume that the "Noahide Covenant," which according to Jewish belief God made with all human beings, has, according to Christian belief, actually been revoked for those non-Jews who do not accept the Christian faith? That, in other words, God's love and care for our salvation never applied to all people equally? The document clearly states that the "advocate of missionizing Jews in the final analysis puts into question the theological legitimacy of Jewish existence."[37] This is an accurate assessment. Yet the advocate of a global mission likewise questions the theological legitimacy of the existence of all other religions. And

32 Christians and Jews III, 2000, 49.
33 Cp. ibid. 51.
34 Ibid. 53.
35 Ibid. 55.
36 Ibid. 60.
37 Ibid. 62.

the document does not explain why the latter should be theologically (!) justified while the former is not.

The Protestant New Testament scholar Klaus Wengst goes one step further in his deliberations. For him, the "No to missionizing the Jews" is the "litmus test" for a positive relationship of the church to Judaism.[38] Wengst uses sharp and unambiguous words to reject the theological notion that Judaism is "deficient" in comparison to Christianity. He rejects the associated clichés such as "grace and love" in contrast to "righteousness and judgment," of "gospel" *versus* "law," of "fulfillment" here and "promise" there, as implausible rhetoric in light of the fact that before Jesus, and independent of Jesus, Jews testified to the experience of God's faithfulness and "undeserved mercy" with the same authenticity as Christians. According to Wengst, Christians are led through Jesus Christ to the God of Israel; but this does not imply that Jews in comparison to Christians are lacking something.[39] Wengst thus also rejects the designation of Jesus as "Israel's Messiah." According to Wengst, Jesus did not fulfill Israel's specific messianic expectation of national liberation. Instead Jesus became a "Messiah from Israel for the peoples."[40] The Reformation principle of "Christ alone" (*solus Christus*), in the sense of the salvific mediation of Christ, does not hold for Israel, but only—and here "without restriction"—for the peoples of the world.[41] Through Jesus Christ, the "people from among the peoples [can] … turn away from the idols … and turn toward the *one* God, the God of Israel."[42] Yet once again it remains totally unclear why the *one* true God is supposed to be found only on one side (this time the side of Judaism *and* Christianity together), while on the other side there are only idols, and why Christ should be supposed to be the only path to salvation for all non-Jews, while not so for Jews.

Among the reasons for saying "No" to missionizing the Jews, Wengst also names the following:

> I say no to missionizing the Jews in deference to the faithfulness with which the Jewish people builds on God's faithfulness and goes its way in its covenant with God and thus witnesses to him. I cannot wish to convert witnesses. I want to pay heed to God's witnesses.[43]

There is no doubt that Wengst speaks here from his own experience and that this may have contributed decisively to the fact that he no longer views Judaism as a deficient religion when compared to Christianity. But do other peoples not likewise trust in God's faithfulness and in the revelation mediated to them by their prophets, seers, or enlightened ones? Is their testimony any less valuable? Do they deserve less

38 Wengst 2004, 129.
39 Cp. ibid. 134ff.
40 Cp. ibid. 76f.
41 Cp. ibid. 81.
42 Ibid. 136f.
43 Ibid. 140.

respect? Can one thus simply seek to convert them and call upon them to turn away from their "idols" and toward the one God as revealed in Jesus?

Looking at the issue of missionizing the Jews reveals the tendency to retain the Christian claim to superiority, whether in its inclusivist or exclusivist form, and then either to bracket Judaism from it or—as Wengst does—to include it in such a way that religious superiority is now claimed for Christianity in tandem with Judaism. Yet each of these alternatives is even more flawed than the standard version of the Christian superiority claim. For on the one hand neither the exclusion nor the inclusion of Judaism can be made theologically plausible. And on the other hand, in both variants the claim of Christianity's superiority over Judaism is either hollowed out or abandoned, which does not make Christian superiority more probable when it is claimed toward other religions.

According to John Pawlikowski, who for a long time is counted among the leading Catholic thinkers in the Jewish-Christian dialogue, it is true that:

> The extent to which we create theological space for Jewish faith, against which Christianity has defined its identity, to that extent we moderate, albeit implicitly, the absolute claims of Christian faith.[44]

In his opinion, the hesitance and ambivalence found in the various Protestant and Catholic statements on the missionizing the Jews issue are connected to its "profound Christological implications." And yet, according to Pawlikowski, in the long run the "dialogical credibility" of Christianity depends on the clarification of this question.[45] In this regard, both Jews and Christians who engage in the Jewish-Christian dialogue consider it a highly worrying signal that *Dominus Iesus* speaks of the church without any qualification as the "universal sacrament of salvation" (No. 20) and of a "gravely deficient situation" (No. 22) in which non-Christians allegedly find themselves.[46]

Pluralizing Developments or an Inclusivist Alliance?

A number of theologians who in recent years strongly spoke out for a new relationship of the church with Judaism, such as Bertold Klappert[47] or Paul van Buren,[48] have developed positions similar to that of Klaus Wengst. Pawlikowski characterizes this fittingly as "single-covenant theology:"[49] Through Jesus Christ or through the Christian church, never before seen numbers of non-Jews were being familiarized with the God of Israel. However, God's covenant with Israel has not been dis-

44 Pawlikowski 2002, 80.
45 Cp. ibid. 80f.
46 Cp. Kessler 2002, 66; Pawlikowski 2002, 79f.
47 Cp. Klappert 1997.
48 Cp. Van Buren 1983.
49 Cp. Pawlikowski 1988, 393-398.

solved because of this. Rather, the non-Jews were included in this one covenant as Christians. In terms of theological import or substance, Christianity has no advantage over the Jewish people. Rather, as Jacobus Coos Schoneveld expresses it, Jesus is the "Torah in the flesh," the embodiment of the actual message and meaning of the Torah for the gentiles.[50] Since there is only one single covenant, the supersessionist theory according to which the New Covenant replaces the Old Covenant is wrong. The enmity between the church and Israel up to this point should be understood as a sort of schism that can be turned—much as in inner-Christian ecumenism—into a reconciled ecumenical relationship.

Other theologians emphasize more strongly the difference between Israel and the church. According to Didier Pollefeyt, Christianity is not a kind of Judaism for the gentiles. "Judaism and Christianity are not two sides of the same coin. They are two different coins."[51] Pawlikowski designates such positions as "double-covenant theology,"[52] referring to God's covenant with the Jewish people and the covenant that God made through Christ with the world of the gentiles or non-Jews. The decisive point is that the representatives of this approach argue against the notion of the "new" covenant as replacing the "old" one by emphasizing the equal validity of both covenants, and this not merely in any provisional or temporary sense. Otherwise, as Pawlikowski rightly says, "the double-covenant theory would only be a deferral of the Christian ideas about a replacement of Judaism to the eschaton rather than a truly new interpretation of the theology of the Jewish-Christian relation."[53]

Along the lines of such a "new interpretation," the approaches of a "double-covenant theology" represent Judaism and Christianity as manifesting "different but complementary aspects of human religiosity" and at the same time as sharing "a common biblical heritage."[54] The different versions of this model vary in how they assess the complementarity of Judaism and Christianity. James Parkes, one of the early pioneers of Jewish-Christian dialogue, suggested for example that we regard, in light of the revelation at Sinai, the Jewish form of religiosity primarily as oriented toward community, whereas Christian religiosity is supposedly more focused on the relationship of the individual person to God.[55] Others, as also John Pawlikowski himself, hold that the complementary aspects are found in both religions but with different emphases.[56] Either way, these attempts are marked by an effort to emphasize the peculiarities of and differences between Judaism and Christianity in a more pronounced way than is the case in the variants of a "single-covenant theology." In order to do so, they have to determine the revelation of God in Jesus in such a way that leaves room for another, characteristically Jewish revelation which is, in princi-

50 Cp. ibid. 397.
51 Pollefeyt 1997a, 6.
52 Cp. Pawlikowski 1988, 398f.
53 Ibid. 401.
54 Ibid. 400f.
55 Cp. here esp. Parkes 1960. On Parkes see also Everett 1993.
56 Cp. Pawlikowski 1988, 398-401.

ple, of equal value with the Christian one, although it is not mediated by Jesus. This is where genuine concerns of religious pluralism come to the fore. Yet how consistently these concerns can be put into practice depends on whether one indeed gives up the Christian claim to universal and singular mediation of salvation by Jesus or whether it is only modified with regard to Israel. If the latter, the question still stands why such a modification of Jesus' universal mediation of salvation should be justified only with regard to Judaism and not equally so with regard to other religions.

When Christian theology does not sufficiently recognize the connection between the Jewish-Christian relationship and the general issues of a theology of religions, or even plays the former off against the latter, a new version of the Christian claim to superiority may easily arise, albeit now in the sense of a sort of inclusivist alliance which includes Judaism—of course unasked (!)—in the superiority claim separating it from and pitting it against other religions. Sometimes this takes on bizarre forms, as for example in Friedrich-Wilhelm Marquardt's work. According to Marquardt, Israel's election is given absolute priority in relationship between God and humanity. Thus, Marquardt speaks of the "madness" of Muslims, Christians, and other non-Jewish peoples or religions to think that they can have a relationship to God without having a relationship to God's chosen people.[57] According to Marquardt, only the divinely chosen Jews are essentially the "real human beings," so that all others only become "'real humans' through participation in the history of Israel."[58] Thus according to Marquardt, it is neither true that God is equally disposed toward all humans and peoples,[59] nor that all human beings *are* equal—a notion that Marquardt disqualifies as an "ideology of parity."[60] One can easily see how here the same theological patterns that once led to the exclusion of all non-Christian religions, including Judaism, are still at work, but now support the exclusion of all non-Jews and non-Christians—even to the point of implications that almost appear to come close to racism. The irrational and arbitrary nature of such outrageous claims becomes particularly evident when Marquardt declares the election of Israel to be an unquestionable axiom of his theology, but not the existence of God![61]

I will now move on to a theologian who, at a very early stage, recognized the Christological implications of the relationship between Judaism and Christianity, which very clearly led her not only to give up the Christian claim to superiority vis à vis Judaism, but also to turn this into a truly pluralist position in the theology of religions.

57 Marquardt 1994, 183 (similarly also ibid. 133).
58 Marquardt 1990, 139.
59 Marquardt 1994, 183.
60 Marquardt 1996, 269.
61 For a critical appraisal of Marquardt from a theology of religions perspective, see also Winkler 2004.

Rosemary Radford Ruether

The Catholic theologian and historian Rosemary Radford Ruether was born in 1936.[62] Her father was an Episcopelian, her mother a Catholic, and an uncle, who because of the frequent absence of her father during the Second World War often took over the role of father, was a Jew. The strongest religious influence came from her mother, who—as Ruether reports—"cultivated an intellectual catholic tradition of philosophical spirituality, reading classics such as the writings of Meister Eckhart."[63] In 1954 Ruether began her studies in Claremont, California, at first in the fine arts, but soon thereafter in religion, philosophy and history focusing on Greek and Roman classics. Thus from the beginning she studied Christianity in its connection with Judaism, the religions of Mesopotamia, and the ancient Greek-Roman environment. She "became fascinated with the Jewish vision of righteousness enunciated by the Hebrew prophets and Jesus."[64] In contrast to this, she recognized in the religions of Mesopotamia and Greece a spirituality that was cosmological and oriented toward a sanctification of the natural world. Ruether writes that neither of these two forms of spirituality, neither the Jewish-Christian nor the Mesopotamian-Greek, is more true or better than the other. At the time of her studies, the Jewish-Christian emphasis on righteousness was more important to her, while today, in light of a growing ecological concern, she asks whether a symbiosis of both forms of spirituality might be possible.[65] As far back as she can think, she has rejected every form of religious exclusivism. She attributes this on the one hand to the fact that from her childhood she was familiar with three different forms of religiosity—Protestantism, Catholicism, and Judaism—and on the other hand to the fact that she completed her studies at Claremont in an atmosphere marked by an awareness of and high regard for religious plurality.[66]

Radford Ruether wrote her first book about the church as eschatological community; her dissertation had focused on Gregory of Nazianzus. Already since the early 1960s she had engaged in the American civil rights and peace movements, actively participated in the fight against discrimination of the black population, and theologically had increasingly concentrated on the concerns of liberation and feminist theology. In 1966 she accepted a teaching position in Washington D.C. Toward the end of the sixties, two further topics became increasingly important to her: the ecological crisis (the report of the "Club of Rome" appeared in 1966) and antisemitism. According to her own assessment, in all the fields of contemporary problems in which she was engaged, she was always interested in the question of the issues' historical

62 Cp. the following biographical details with Kalsky 2000, 136ff, as well as the autobiographical record in Ruether, 2001, 48-62.
63 Ruether 2001, 49.
64 Ibid. 53.
65 Cp. ibid. 54.
66 Cp. ibid. 147.

roots: "How did it happen this way?"[67] This attitude also determined her response to antisemitism and the Holocaust. Thanks to her competence in ancient history, she saw herself particularly well equipped to research scientifically the roots of antisemitism. The result was her 1974 book, *Faith and Fratricide: The Theological Roots of Anti-Semitism.*[68] This work immediately made her famous in the theological world. In Christian circles, it generated intense discussions. Franz Mussner, for example, calls the book "profound" and "arousing." Although he does not agree with the central thesis, he considers a "rebuttal" "not to be easy."[69] For not only does Ruether use a host of historical evidence to contradict the thesis that Christian anti-Judaism was something essentially alien to Christianity, an aberration that more or less came from elsewhere. Instead, for the first time she asks with unsparing openness to what extent the roots of Christian anti-Judaism reach back to the middle of the New Testament and to the center of Christian beliefs, that is, to early Christology. No one less than the renowned Catholic theologian Gregory Baum wrote the book's Introduction, in which on the one hand he responds to the anticipated indignant reactions, and on the other hand, supports the core of Ruether's findings.

On the Jewish side, the book was greeted enthusiastically and the *B'nai B'rith*, an influential Jewish organization, officially promoted it. From this point on, Jewish institutions often invited Ruether to give lectures and she frequently participated in Jewish-Christian dialogues. In 1976 Garrett-Evangelical Seminary in Evanston, Illinois offered her a chair in historical theology. Yet in the following years, as she herself says, it became increasingly obvious that there was often a "hidden agenda" in Jewish-Christian dialogue. According to Ruether, the Christian admission of a partial responsibility and guilt for antisemitism was instrumentalized to turn Christians into uncritical supporters of the politics of the State of Israel and: "Above all, they were not to ask about justice to the Palestinians."[70] From this point forward, Ruether intensified her efforts to dialogue with the Palestinians and spent 1985 together with her husband, the Islamist Herman Ruether, on an extended research stay in Tantur, a Christian-Palestinian study center in Israel. The results appeared in a 1989 book that took a highly critical stance toward Israeli politics.[71] In her own words she was now a "pariah" in official Jewish-Christian dialogue. So she instead became more involved in Christian-Islamic dialogue. Yet here too she discovered that the demand for self-critique was rather one-sidedly directed to the Christian dialogue partner and was not very pronounced on the Islamic side.

67 Ibid. 56.

68 Translated into German as "Nächstenliebe und Brudermord", see Ruether 1978.

69 Mussner 1979, 356.

70 Ruether 2001, 59.

71 *The Wrath of Jona: The Crisis of Religious Nationalism in the Israel-Palestinian Conflict.* Yet, already in *Faith and Fratricide* Ruether shows a clear understanding of the political issues of the Israeli-Palestinian conflict, though it was only briefly touched upon there. Cp. on this Ruether 1979, 227.

In 1986 Radford Ruether participated in the so-called "Rubicon Conference"[72] at Claremont and was one of the co-authors of the pluralist polemic, *The Myth of Christian Uniqueness.* Since the mid-80s she had participated in the Christian-Buddhist dialogue conferences of the so-called Cobb-Abe group,[73] to which John Cobb, one of her former teachers at Claremont, had invited her. During all these years she continued to work on feminist and ecological theology and her reputation as a leading feminist theologian exceeded the fame she had attained through her contributions to the Jewish-Christian conversation. Through their common work in the Cobb-Abe group, Ruether and the Buddhist feminist Rita Gross eventually developed a more intensive collaboration in which they placed the ecological challenge—alongside the feminist themes—on the agenda of their interreligious dialogues.[74]

The central and, for many Christians then as now, most shocking thesis in *Faith and Fratricide* is that anti-Judaism is the "other side" of Christology[75] or the "left hand" of Christology as Radford Ruether puts it in another place.[76] What is meant by this? As has been shown, the leading theological themes of the *Adversus-Iudaeos* literature are based on the Christian understanding that Judaism in its opposition to Jesus rejected its own Messiah. On the other hand, the confession of Jesus as the Christ and hence as the Messiah of the Jewish prophetic promises is the most fundamental creed of Christianity. Herein lies the root of the problem. According to Ruether, it was impossible for the majority of Judaism to accept the belief in the Messiahship of Jesus because the concrete messianic expectations of final salvation and enduring liberation had not been fulfilled in Jesus. Today—after the painful, evil history that the coming of Jesus actually caused for Judaism—such recognition has become even more impossible from a Jewish perspective.[77] According to Radford Ruether, the Jewish "No" to Jesus as Messiah led in reverse to a process in which the early church reinterpreted central elements of the originally Jewish Messianic or eschatological expectation as applying to the relationship between Judaism and the church. In particular this means:

First, the church insisted that the messianic hope that all peoples of the world would come to Mount Zion where they would recognize and venerate the God of Israel as the one true God had already been fulfilled in the form of the Christian church consisting of many peoples. Whereas Judaism understood itself as one particular people of God and shifted any universal religious claim to God's eschatological future, the church interpreted these claims as referring to itself and based the claim of its own unique and universal validity on this interpretation. In other words, what was and remained eschatological hope to the Jews, the church declared as historically and concretely fulfilled in her own existence.

72 Cp. on this above chapter 1, p. 23.
73 Cp. to this below, chapter 15, p. 414.
74 Cp. Ruether, Gross 2001.
75 Ruether 1979, 246.
76 Ruether 1981, 31.
77 Ruether 1979, 246f.

Second, the pattern of intra-Jewish prophetic self-critique was reinterpreted in the sense of the church's critique of Judaism. This process too involves an eschatological dimension. For Judaism's prophetic self-critique was always understood in light of the divine promise geared toward the future. That is, the prophetic critique that announced the wrath and judgment of God in the face of the failings of the Jewish people was accompanied by the promise of divine forgiveness and God's faithfulness to his promises. The early church severed this connection and applied the former, that is, critique and judgment, to Judaism and the latter, forgiveness and fulfillment, to itself. That is how, based on the claim that the promises had been fulfilled in Jesus, the church transformed the prophetic self-critical dialectic of Judaism into a Christian-Jewish antagonism.

Third, this process came to a head in the development of specific clichés, which present Judaism as the old, but now superseded covenant, distort it as a spiritually deficient religion, and glorify Christianity as the religion of fulfillment: there the superficial and externalized religion, the religion of hypocrisy, of the "letter" of the Law, and here the religion of the truth and the "Spirit;" there the religion of mere legalism, here the religion of grace. None of these clichés can in any way be factually substantiated. Pre-Christian and post-Christian Judaism had always been conscious of the danger of religious superficiality, hypocrisy, and of missing the true spirit. Judaism had always reminded itself of these dangers by means of its prophetic self-critique. Yet the Law could never be presented as the opposite of divine grace because the Law itself was understood as the special gift of God, mediating the Spirit of God.[78] And the idea that love of neighbor is the true core of the Law—as we find it in the teachings of Jesus—is already found independent of, and chronologically before, Jesus in the teachings of the Pharisee Hillel (first century BCE).[79]

Thus, according to Radford Ruether, what can be seen in these standard patterns of the Christian distortion of Judaism is that basic process by which the Christian church converts the eschatologically oriented prophetic self-critique of Judaism into the church's critique of Judaism. This process was set in motion by the church's claim that in Jesus—and therefore also in the church—the eschatological dimension of the prophetic critique had been historically fulfilled. So the central Christological problem of Christian anti-Judaism consists of the "historicizing of the eschatological event."[80] This process transforms the Jewish hope that one day God will make everything new into the Christian-Jewish antagonism by which Christianity defines itself as the "new messianic people" in contrast to and in rejection of the "old one," i.e. the Jews.

> The message of the messianic expectation is imported into history and reified as a historical event in a way that makes it a reality-denying, rather than a reality-discerning, principle. Evil is declared to have been conquered once-for-all

78 Ibid. 241f.
79 Ruether, 1981, 37.
80 Ruether 1979, 246.

> by the Messiah. His victory has been established as the Catholic Church. Let anyone who fails to discern the Kingdom of God in the Christian imperium be anathema. (…) Christ becomes the vengeful instrument to persecute that people who hoped for his coming and who fail to recognize in such a Christ their own redemption.[81]

Given the background of this analysis, is it possible at all to confess one's allegiance to Jesus in a way that is not anti-Jewish? "Is it possible to purge Christianity of anti-Judaism without at the same time pulling up Christian faith?"[82] Ruether answers her question in the affirmative. But to do so it is necessary to understand the Messianic significance of Jesus *first* in a *"proleptic"* sense, that is, as reaching toward the future but not as having been ultimately fulfilled, and *second* in a *"paradigmatic"* sense, that is, in the sense of an example or model that does not pervert the particularity of Jesus and of the church into universality.[83]

The early Christian confession of Jesus as the Messiah arose in the context of the imminent apocalyptic expectation. That is, the first generation of Christians was convinced that Jesus would be returning during their lifetime and that he would *then*, by fulfilling all Messianic promises, finally reveal himself as the Messiah. Yet this did not happen. Christians thus pushed off the expectation of Christ's return into an uncertain future, and instead increasingly glorified the life of Jesus in terms of a completion and fulfillment that had already begun.[84] According to Ruether, we need to undo this wrong development, this "illegitimate historicizing of the eschatological."[85] That is, Christians must confess clearly that Jesus did not bring about the fulfillment of the Messianic promises, but rather that these remain, as before, unfulfilled. "The ultimate eschatological event, the ultimate 'coming' of the Messiah, must still signify that final future when 'every tear will be wiped away.'"[86] We need to discover the truth in the Jewish 'No' to Jesus, which consists of the fact that the final Messianic salvation has actually not yet occurred through Jesus.[87] Therefore Jesus is also not to be understood as the Messiah in this sense. Instead, Jesus is someone who himself lived by the eschatological hope and who exemplified this hope in a clear way through his life and even unto his death. One can view the resurrection of Jesus as divine confirmation of this hope. To this extent Jesus garners *proleptic* significance and it is in this sense that he becomes "the mediator of this hope to us and to our descendants."[88] Since "the final eschatological event of history" has not yet come to pass through Jesus, the event of his life is not:

81 Ibid. 246.
82 Ibid.
83 Ibid. 249. Cp. also Ruether 1981, 42f.
84 Cp. Ruether 1979, 247.
85 Ibid. 248.
86 Ibid.
87 Cp. ibid. 245.
88 Ibid. 249 and 250.

> … placing all history before that time in an obsolescent and morally inferior relation to itself or invalidating the access to God of those who go forward on other grounds. (…)
>
> To reaffirm Jesus' hope in his name, then, is not to be able to claim that in Jesus this hope has already happened, albeit in invisible form. Nor does it mean that it is now only in his name that this hope can be proclaimed.[89]

Jesus and his resurrection therefore depict the *paradigmatic* embodiment of the Christian hope for an ultimate eschatological salvation and a life lived out of this hope. A valid functionally equivalent paradigm for Judaism can be found in the Exodus experience. As the death and resurrection of Jesus, the experience of the Exodus, of the divine liberation from slavery, likewise gives a foretaste of the ultimate salvation. And like the resurrection, this event must continually be recalled in order to remain a source of hope. Yet both events are only "foretastes" and not yet the fulfillment itself.[90] The life, death, and resurrection of Jesus are thus valid parallels to the Exodus experience:

> When Easter is seen, not as superseding and fulfilling the Exodus, but as reduplicating it, then the Christian can affirm his faith through Jesus in a way that no longer threatens to rob the Jew of his past, eliminate his future and surround his present existence with rivalrous animosity.[91]

The insight into the paradigmatic significance of Jesus, however, permits not only the thought that the Exodus experience is an equally valid paradigm of eschatological hope for salvation and its proleptic anticipation, but also that there exist additional paradigmatic experiences of equal value in the religious traditions of other people. Thus while the cross and resurrection are of paradigmatic significance to Christians, Ruether holds that;

> Those who have not chosen to make it their paradigm, because they have paradigms which are more compelling to them from their own histories, are not to be judged as false or unredeemed thereby.[92]

The insight into the proleptic and paradigmatic meaning of Jesus can help Christianity unmasking its own universalistic claims as an illegitimate historicizing of eschatological hopes. Christianity is not the universal religion, but rather as particular as all others. This self-understanding as one particular religion is something that Christianity may freshly learn from Judaism, once it stops misunderstanding itself as Judaism's Messianic fulfillment and substitution.[93]

This pluralist conception already present in *Faith and Fratricide* Ruether later consolidated further, especially in her contribution to *The Myth of Christian Unique-*

89 Ibid. 248 and 249.
90 Cp. ibid. 249f.
91 Ibid. 256f.
92 Ibid. 250.
93 Cp. ibid. 251ff.

ness. Presumably her new experiences with Christian-Islamic dialogue played an important role in this, as well as the experience that some Christians and Jews promoted a Jewish-Christian alliance (even if from different motives) now insisting on the two traditions' joint superiority over all other religions. The idea that Christians should nowadays no longer missionize Jews because Jews have their own valid path to salvation, whereas all non-Jews still need Christianity in order to come into a right relationship with God, in other words, that the two biblical traditions have a monopoly on religious truth, is criticized by Ruether as "an outrageous and absurd religious chauvinism."[94] "Although there is much overlap among religions, they also represent a broad spectrum of possible ways of experiencing the divine. Some may focus on the historical struggle for justice, some on the renewal of natural processes, and some on mystical ecstasy."[95] Only the divine reality itself is truly universal and the fatherly-motherly ground of all beings.[96] God's transcendent reality surpasses all its particular human images and representations. Its purpose is to allow the liberating experience of God to become concrete in our lives, each in their own specific conditions.[97] Religious universality can only be attained under the real conditions of our world if religions stand by the insight into their own particularity and specificity, if they mutually recognize their particularity and as far as possible allow themselves to be enriched through their efforts at reciprocal understanding.[98] What is special and paradigmatic about Jesus for Radford Ruether is his "good news for the poor, his confronting the religious and social systems that embody oppressive privileges, and an affirmation of the despised as those loved and liberated by God"—a message that Jesus exemplified in his life, for which he was prepared to die, and for which he was crucified by those who rejected this message.[99] For Ruether giving up Christian claims to universalism is ultimately fully consonant with this message:

> Nor does it seem to me that the power of Jesus' name will become less if we cease to use that name to deny the validity of other people's experience of God through other names. Indeed only when we cease to use Jesus' name to negate other peoples' experiences of the victory of life over death, can the name of Jesus cease to be a name that creates alienation of Jew from Christian, Christian from Non-Christian. Instead we can begin to find new possibilities of human solidarity in our differing ways of mediating hope in the midst of defeat.[100]

94 Ruether 1987, 141.
95 Ibid. 142.
96 Cp. ibid. 141.
97 Cp. Ruether, Gross 137f. Ruether 1991, 135.
98 Cp. Ruether 1987, 142.
99 Cp. Ruether 1991, 135; similarly Ruether, Gross 2001, 139.
100 Ruether 1981, 43

Pluralist Perspectives

With the two key words "proleptic" and "paradigmatic" that Ruether uses to describe the significance of Jesus, she has given the pluralist perspectives on Jewish-Christian relationship their thematic direction. For a long time it seemed as if the Christian confession of Jesus as Messiah and the Jewish denial of the Messiahship of Jesus were irreconcilably opposed to one another. Yet a *proleptic* understanding of Jesus makes it possible to recognize the truth on both sides and thus to understand the relationship between Judaism and Christianity as one of genuine theological equality.[101] Moreover, a *paradigmatic* understanding of Jesus allows us to protect the relationship between Judaism and Christianity from that theological isolation into which some Christian theologians have tried to maneuver it in recent years, and instead to see it in the horizon of the wider task of developing a theology of religions which is not only a challenge to Christianity but also to Judaism. In what follows, I will explain both these points more fully.

On the Christian "Yes" and the Jewish "No" to Jesus

In the year 1263 a notable disputation took place in the royal palace of Barcelona. King James I of Aragon had invited the Dominican Pablo Christiani, a convert from Judaism, and the distinguished Jewish Kabbalist Nahmanides (Moses ben Nahman) to discuss three questions: "1. Has the Messiah already appeared or not? 2. Is the Messiah promised by the prophets a divine or a human being? 3. Who holds the correct faith, the Jews or the Christians?"[102] To the first question Nahmanides responded that Jesus was not the Messiah since he had not fulfilled the Messianic promises, particularly that of the establishment of a universal peace. Second, according to the Jewish tradition the promised Messiah will be a human being and not God. Third, Christianity could not be true since it contained too many internal contradictions and logical inconsistencies. Nahmanides was considered to be the winner of the disputation. The debate itself was almost prematurely concluded due to concerns for Nachmanides' personal safety. Subsequently the Dominicans pursued his expulsion and even appealed to the Pope to exert pressure on the King. Nachmanides went to Palestine, whether of his own free will or not remains historically disputed.[103] This episode is characteristic in two regards: on the one hand with respect

101 In this respect it is telling that Karl Rahner, in the context of his inclusivist position, could only honor the Jewish No to Jesus in the sense of a good but erroneous conscience. Cp. Lapide, Rahner 1983, 109f.

102 Willi 1980, 14f. Cp. also Cohn-Sherbok 1991, 20f.

103 According to Willi, Nahmanides more or less willingly forestalled a deportation (cp. Willi 1980, 14 and 16f., n. 42); according to Grayzel Nahmanides was expelled (cp. Grayzel 1968, 322).

to the Jewish image of Jesus, because many Jews see Jesus, as Cohn-Sherbok writes, "simply as one preacher among many, a false Messiah, who had failed to fulfil the scriptural predictions of redemption and deliverance."[104] And on the other hand for the Christian response, for once again the Christian affirmation of Jesus as the Messiah was expressed through the use of violence and the attempt to physically get rid of the Jews. As Didier Pollefeyt pointedly explains, if we wish to overcome both the Christian claim of replacing Judaism and the Jewish rejection of Christianity then we need:

> ... theological frameworks within which the Christian "Yes" to Jesus can be spoken without being anti-Jewish, and within which the Jewish "No" to Jesus can be spoken without being anti-Christian.[105]

Can the systematic foundations of a pluralist theology of religions offer such a framework?

For the response to this question it is important to be totally clear that the Jewish 'No' to Jesus does not necessarily imply an overall rejection of the person of Jesus. Rather it is primarily a rejection of the Christian interpretation of Jesus[106] as the Messiah and as the incarnate Son of God.[107] The reasons for this rejection are more than clear: from a Jewish perspective Jesus cannot be accepted as Savior because—as Nahmanides and many other representatives of Judaism have argued time and again—the expectations and promises connected with the coming of the Messiah were not fulfilled through Jesus.[108] Jesus did neither fulfill the expectations of a political Messiah who renews the kingdom of David, restores the Temple, and in so doing satisfies the requirements for the complete observance of the Law. Nor did he fulfill the expectations of an apocalyptic Messiah who brings about the final period of salvation during which lasting peace reigns on earth and—as Isaiah says—even snakes and infants live together in harmony. Additionally, a Jewish perspective cannot accept Jesus as the incarnate Son of God because incarnation transgresses the border between creator and creation, and because the corresponding notion of a triune God seems to contradict the essential Jewish confession of the *one* God, understood in strictly monotheistic terms.[109] The confession of the oneness of God, based on the biblical *Shema Israel* (Deut 6:4-9) "is understood as the most precious and important tradition of faith. [...] Many Jewish martyrs understood themselves as witnesses to the unity and oneness of God."[110] The Jewish side has of course been aware that Christianity also intends to hold fast to monotheism, even if there have always been and still are manifests tendencies toward tritheism. But from a Jewish

104 Cohn-Sherbok 1997, 79.
105 Pollefeyt 1997a, 7.
106 Cp. Swidler 1990, 118f.
107 Cp. also Cohn-Sherbok 1997, 75f. Among the standard Jewish objections that Cohn-Sherbok lists, the interpretation of Jesus as incarnate Son of God and as Messiah top the list.
108 Cp. ibid. 76.
109 Cp. ibid. 75.
110 Thoma 1989, 112f.

perspective, the veneration of Jesus as incarnate Son of God seems inevitably to constitute a watering down of monotheism, in as much as apparently a person is elevated to the divine level and set alongside God. Jewish theology referred to this by the denigrating term *shittuf* (= connection, association),[111] which corresponds to the Islamic allegation raised against Christianity of *shirk*, i.e. placing additional figures at God's side.

For a growing number of Christian theologians it is becoming less and less difficult to show theological understanding for the Jewish 'No' to the Christian confession of Jesus as the Messiah. For after all there is no doubt that the aforementioned expectations were indeed *not* fulfilled in the expected way. Hence today Christians often admit that the confession of Jesus as Messiah implies a highly selective interpretation of the messianic prophecies or a reconceptualization of the concept of "messiah." The messiah expected victoriously to bring about the decisive political change or even the apocalyptic turn of the eon became a messiah who appeared as God's suffering servant.[112] But this implies that Christians too acknowledge that not all promises and expectations are fulfilled in Jesus. This is further confirmed by the Christian belief in Jesus' second coming. For exactly those eschatological expectations that Judaism traditionally connected with the coming of the Messiah are on the Christian side connected with Christ's second coming. This implies a clear admission that these messianic expectations were not—or not yet—realized through Jesus.[113] Jews and Christians thus live with the same eschatological hope for the not yet accomplished final redemption. To the extent that the Jewish 'No' to Jesus as Messiah expresses that the final redemption is yet to come and at the same time implies an enduring hope, it is not in opposition to Christianity. Rather, there lies in this 'No' an important truth which can and must also be acknowledged from the Christian side. It is thanks to Rosemary Radford Ruether that the significance of this insight for Christian-Jewish relations has been pointed out so clearly.

For Christians, of course, Jesus is by no means simply one more among many false Messiahs. This Ruether also makes quite clear in speaking about Jesus' proleptic significance. It is true that the Messianic promises were not fulfilled in Jesus. But one can understand his life, death, and especially his resurrection as a renewed affirmation of these promises, as an anticipatory confirmation of their fulfillment. Yet this means that for Christians, just as for Jews, the basis of their hope in final salvation lies solely in God or—expressed in the context of personal conceptions of transcendence—in the love of God. It is this love that Christians see revealed in Christ. By means of this revelation Jesus mediates the salvation that is based in God alone. As shown above, herein lies the adequate basis for an understanding of incarnation that is also compatible with a pluralist theology of religion.[114]

111 Cp. ibid. 113ff.
112 Cp. for example, Mussner 1982.
113 Thus also Pollefeyt 1997b, 34f, drawing on corresponding opinions of Darrell Fasching and Jürgen Moltmann
114 Cp. above chapter 11.

Yet how does such an understanding of incarnation, one based wholly on the function of Jesus as revealer and mediator of salvation, work in light of the Jewish critique of Christian belief in incarnation? John Hick's interpretation of the doctrine of incarnation as a mythological instead of literal statement has found positive resonance on the Jewish side. According to Dan Cohn-Sherbok, Hick has thus removed the decisive traditional barrier to an authentic Jewish-Christian dialogue.[115] Michael Wyschogrod considers Hick's Christology to be much truer to the biblical witness than Chalcedon's high Christology.[116] Yet it is not clear whether those who agree from a Jewish perspective also recognize that—as I argued earlier—even in Hick's non-mythological interpretation there is nonetheless still a kind of incarnational core, namely the belief that God was at work in and through Jesus in a revelatory and salvific way.[117] Moreover, Michael Wyschogrod articulates his discomfort with the further implications of a pluralist theology of religions. To him, the Christian claim to absoluteness is also a kind of Jewish inheritance. Therefore he does not want the doctrine of incarnation to be criticized from a pluralist perspective but only because it is irreconcilable with the Hebrew Bible which is a canonical scripture also for Christianity.[118]

To the extent that the work of God in and through Jesus is understood along the lines of an inspiration Christology, in other words to the extent that this divine work is understood as the work of the divine Spirit, some Jewish theologians admit that, in principle, there are no reservations about it from a Jewish perspective.[119] After all, such a Christology closely follows the basic prophetic pattern and can moreover claim some affinity with the rabbinic idea of *Shekinah*, God dwelling among humans. "And why," asks Hans Küng, "should not God's presence, Shekinah, for once take its abode in an individual human being instead of a temple, so that in him God's hidden 'glory' can shine out for those who rely on him in trust?"[120] Leonard Swidler emphasizes that "the whole Jewish experience of God" was shaped by "the Word of God"—the world: created through God's Word; the Torah: God's guiding Word to his people; the prophets: mediators of God's Word. Hence it was possible for Jesus' followers to understand him as someone whose life was fully transparent to God's Word and who in this sense is "God's Word become flesh."[121] Yet if—as inspiration Christology suggests—one understands incarnation in the final analysis as following a prophetic pattern and Jesus along those lines as one whose whole life became an expression, i.e. revelation of the divine Word, then one can in turn ask the same question of Jewish theology, that is, whether every genuine prophecy does not in fact presuppose a sort of divine immanence, which can also be understood as

115 Cohn-Sherbok 1991, 21f.
116 Wyschogrod 1988, 181.
117 Cp. on this above chapter 11, pp. 253-258.
118 Cp. Wyschogrod 1988, 183.
119 Cp. Wyschogrod 1988, 1986. Similarly Kogan 1995, 102ff.
120 Küng 1992, 384.
121 Cp. Swidler 1990, 108 and 112.

a kind of incarnation in degrees. This does not threaten the oneness of God. Hence, the doctrine of the Trinity also no longer needs to present an insurmountable contrast between Christianity and Judaism. So long as, in terms of the hermeneutical and epistemological presuppositions of a pluralist theology of religion, one does not interpret it as a description of the divine essence, but rather as an expression of different human forms of experience: the experience of God as the ultimate ground of the world ("Father"), the experience of God as an effective power in people's hearts ("Spirit"), and the experience of God as it is mediated through those persons who let themselves be led by God's Spirit ("Son").

But is there some readiness on the Jewish side to grant Jesus at least something like a prophetic function, that is, to see in him a person who was led by the divine Spirit? The spectrum of Jewish attitudes toward Jesus as a person is extraordinarily broad. Given the long history of horrific suffering that Christian anti-Judaism has caused the Jewish people, it should be no surprise that, for Jewish sensitivity, the figure of Jesus is almost indissolubly linked with this history of suffering. To the question of what he spontaneously associates with "Jesus Christ," the American rabbi and historian Michael Signer responded: "Hatred"—"Hatred and immeasurable suffering that came upon the Jewish people through him."[122] "The Cross," writes Michael Wyschogrod, "has been for Jews not a source of comfort but of fear."[123] Signer and Wyschogrod have no polemical interests in saying this. Both have been engaged in Jewish-Christian dialogue for some time and Signer is one of the co-authors of *Dabru Emet*, the pioneering Jewish statement on Christianity published in 2000. The suffering that Christians have caused Jews in the name of Jesus has not only often strengthened the perception that Jesus was indeed a false messiah, but also that Christianity is "a religion practiced by morally and culturally inferior gentiles, based on unbelievable claims, which had degenerated into idolatry."[124] Therefore, Jewish interest in dialogue with Christianity is quite often rather modest. The only wish many Jews have of Christianity is simply to be left in peace by it.[125] As Leon Klenicki puts it, to invest oneself seriously in understanding Christianity and its central figure demands from the Jewish side a willingness and ability to overcome two thousand years of painful memories and deep-seated negative judgments.[126] Yet *Dabru Emet* has taken a significant step in this direction. It says:

> Jews and Christians worship the same God. (…) While Christian worship is not a viable religious choice for Jews, as Jewish theologians we rejoice that, through Christianity, hundreds of millions of people have entered into relationship with the God of Israel. (…)

122 Reported in Winkler 2004, 30f.
123 Wyschogrod 1988, 179. Similarly also Klenicki 1997, 70.
124 Kessler 2002, 58.
125 Cp. ibid. 57f.
126 Cp. Klenicki 1997, 69f.

> Christians know and serve God through Jesus Christ and the Christian tradition. Jews know and serve God through Torah and the Jewish tradition.[127]

One may read these sentences as a Jewish recognition of Jesus as having a prophetic function at least for non-Jews, since their relationship to the God of Israel is mediated "through Jesus Christ." Yet if so, should such a recognition then not also have consequences for how Jesus is regarded within Judaism? According to Edward Kessler, *Dabru Emet* did not use the opportunity to inquire about the significance of Jesus the Jew for Judaism.[128] Yet of what sort could this significance be?

In the last few decades, a number of Jewish scholars have begun, from a pronounced Jewish perspective, an exploration of who Jesus was: among them pioneers like Joseph Klausner and Martin Buber, Jewish theologians and New Testament scholars like Claude G. Montefiore, Shalom Ben-Chorin, David Flusser, Pinchas Lapide, Israel Abrahams, Samuel Sandmel, Geza Vermes, and many others.[129] Yet this discussion often remains on the tracks laid out by the polemical history of Jewish-Christian relations. Did Jesus understand himself as Messiah or not? That is, was he himself a Messiah-pretender, or is this only a case of a post-Jesus Christian misinterpretation? How are we to evaluate Jesus' position on the Torah? Was he truly so critical of it and claiming a quasi-divine sovereignty with respect to it, as Christian proclamation has often insisted? Or can one interpret Jesus' stance toward the Law in the sense of one among the contemptorary Jewish and proto-rabbinic views or schools? Yet only rarely the question is raised regarding what Jesus' role in Judaism might be. Geza Vermes, however, asked it explicitly:

> Does he [Jesus, PS-L] deserve, as Martin Buber suggested, "a great place in Israel's history of faith?" And if so, what has he to offer to Judaism and what should Jews do about it?[130]

Vermes only hints at his own personal answer to this: The "real Jesus" who "was seen and heard around the countryside of Galilee" has been completely buried up until now by the "rich and majestic figure of the church's Christ."[131] But, speculates Vermes, "is it not possible that Jesus the healer, teacher and helper may yet be invited to emerge from the shadows of his long exile? And not by Christians alone?"[132] According to Vermes, one motif is particularly striking in Jesus' life and teaching: his imitation of God. In this, says Vermes, he is following a proper Jewish motif. Jesus' saying "Be merciful just as your Father is merciful" (Lk 6:36) has almost literal parallels in Jewish writings. Yet Jesus radicalizes this motif in a way that does not exclude anyone from this mercy, neither enemies, nor the despised and outsiders of

127 *Dabru Emet*, Theses 1 and 6.
128 Cp. Kessler 2002, 64.
129 On this cp. also Hagner 1984.
130 Vermes 1991, 39.
131 Vermes 1981, 47.
132 Ibid. 47.

society. It is precisely in this that Jesus imitates what he considers to be God's relationship to human beings.[133]

If we ascribe a prophetic role to Jesus precisely regarding this particular attitude of imitating God, in other words if Jesus truly embodies—or "incarnates"—how God relates to us, then there are two conclusions that may be drawn from this: First, the fact that Christians separate Jesus' message from an exclusive tie to the Jewish people and instead ascribe it universal significance would resonate with his message of God's mercy as one that excludes nobody. Second, this message implies a prophetic critique of the notion of exclusive divine election—be that of the Jewish people, the Christian church, or both—insofar as this notion is connected with the further conclusion that God's mercy applies less to other peoples and religions. If God really has the kind of relationship to us that Jesus prophetically proclaims and embodies, then we can neither ascribe any exclusive significance to Israel's experience of God nor to the church's specific experience of God as it was mediated by Jesus. Rather, as Radford Ruether rightly says, this significance has to be understood paradigmatically. Perhaps this is the prophetic role of Jesus, the Christ, in relation to the self-understanding of the church, and of Jesus, the Jew, in relation to the self-understanding of Israel. In any case, every theological attempt to tie the church and Israel together against the rest of the world would fall directly under such prophetic self-critique.

Election and the Plurality of Religions

Today, for many Christian theologians involved in the Jewish-Christian dialogue, the following is uncontested: A Christian commitment to Jesus must no longer be understood in a sense that explicitly or implicitly contests the theological legitimacy of post- and non-Christian Judaism. It must not lead to the supersessionist theory, according to which the church "replaces" Israel. However, as Didier Pollefeyt appropriately explains, this is not possible if one adopts an understanding of Jesus as constitutive of salvation.[134] Here Pollefeyt draws on the terminology of Schubert Ogden, as described in the previous chapter.[135] If Jesus is constitutive for the salvation of all persons, then there cannot be another equally valid path of salvation and "a constitutive Christology will inevitably end up in substitution."[136] On the other hand, if Jesus' significance for salvation is understood in a representative sense, this leaves space for additional, and different, representations of the sole constitutive source of salvation, the presence of God.[137] And this should not be limited only to the rep-

133 Cp. Vermes 1991, 33f.; Vermes 1981, 43f.
134 Cp. Pollefeyt 1997b, 33.
135 Cp. to this above, chapter 11, pp. 248f.
136 Pollefeyt 1997b, 33.
137 Cp. ibid. 33f.

resentational salvific significance of the Exodus experience or of the revelation of the Torah at Sinai. Marcus Braybrook, Director of the Council of Christians and Jews in Great Britain, writes that it is not enough if we, as Christians, recognize the need to make room for others' theological legitimacy only with reference to Judaism:

> The other is not only the Jewish people, but Hindus, Muslims, Buddhists, Sikhs, indigenous people and many more. It is not enough just to recognize that Jews, like Christians, are people of God. We need to move to a consistent universalism, which recognizes God's presence in every faith community.[138]

For Braybrooke, the future of Jewish-Christian dialogue lies in its conjunction with global interreligious dialogue. This becomes obvious, first of all, by the increasing insight into the significance of the Jewish-Christian-Islamic trialogue.[139] It is only in this way that one can prevent a political, anti-Arabic instrumentalization of the Christian-Jewish dialogue. Beyond this the increasing importance of a Jewish-Buddhist dialogue is also obvious.[140] The astonishingly large number of Jewish conversions to Buddhism shows the strong appeal of Buddhism to Jews today. It is also in light of this that Buddhist-Jewish-Christian trialogues might prove beneficial for all participants.[141] Yet this does not imply the neglect of the special bonds that bind Judaism and Christianity together. Rather, these can and should be recognized, to cite Braybrooke once more, "without suggesting that in some way our two religions are more important to God than other religions."[142] However, a pluralist view of Jewish-Christian relations amounts to more than simply a multi-religious expansion of dialogue. Rather, to use John Pawlikowski's terminology,[143] it is a matter of turning the approaches of "single-covenant" or "double-covenant theology" into a "multiple-covenants theology." This presents a challenge not only for Christian theologians but for Jewish ones as well.[144]

The early biblical conception of the relation between Judaism and non-Jewish people or religions was predominantly exclusivist; "...the world consists first of 'us,' Israel, and then of 'them,' everyone else, the nations (*goyim*). ...In the biblical world, these nations were unanimously idolatrous. ... theologically they are total outsiders, uniform in their failure to recognize Israel's God."[145] In later rabbinic times, this exclusivist conception was replaced by the notion that through Noah and his sons God had made a covenant with all humanity, and then that through Abraham and Mo-

138 Braybrook 2000, 107.
139 See on this Kuschel's important 1994 study, also the ground-breaking Jewish-Christian-Islamic trialogue in Hick, Meltzer 1989 and Cohn-Sherbok 1991b.
140 Cp. to this Lubarsky 1990, 119-128, and Kasimow; Keenan, Klepinger Keenan 2003.
141 In this regard it was a notable step that Eugene Borowitz was included in the Christian-Buddhist dialogues of the Cobb-Abe group. Cp. Cobb, Ives, 1990.
142 Braybrooke 2002, 26.
143 Cp. Pawlikowski 1988, 401f.
144 Cp. Borowitz 1980, 63.
145 Langer 2003, 263f.

ses God had in addition made a special covenant with Israel (Gen 9:1-17).[146] The Noahide covenant compels all people to keep seven laws: the prohibition of idolatry, blasphemy, murder, sexual immorality, theft, eating from a living animal, and living in a lawless state. According to rabbinic understanding, to the extent that non-Jews observe these laws they can participate in eternal bliss. By contrast, God's covenant with Israel stands as a special covenant, one to which God has elected the Jewish people in a particular way. Connected to this covenant are specific promises, but also more obligations, as expressed in the traditional 613 laws that only apply to the Jewish people.

Yet what does this belief in a special election mean? One may recognize here a repercussion of the older exclusivist conceptions, which, though softened by some inclusivist influence, nonetheless give Judaism a clear religious superiority. Not in the sense that the Jewish nation is better than all others. But in the sense of a higher divine vocation and the honor of being given a more comprehensive and pure revelation. This special position of Israel, its special election, enables it to serve and love God in a special way, to be a "light to the nations" and finally to lead these to a full knowledge of God through the Messiah who comes out of Israel.[147] Does a pluralist theology of religions therefore demand of Judaism that it give up its belief in its divine election—as Dan Cohn-Sherbok suggests and actively requests—because this faith is merely an expression of its religious claim to superiority?[148]

According to Radford Ruether, one does not necessarily have to understand this conception of the Noahide covenant with all and the specific covenant with Israel in an inclusivist sense. Rather, this conception leaves room, in principle, for the idea that within the general framework of the Noahide laws other peoples and religions each have their own special status before God and in this sense being "on the same level before God" as Israel.[149] It is precisely this direction that a number of Jewish theologians have taken in recent years as they try to further develop the schema of the Noahide covenant and in so doing transform it into a pluralist conception. Among these are Elliot Dorff,[150] Norman Solomon,[151] Ruth Langer,[152] and most recently also the British Chief Rabbi, Jonathan Sacks.[153]

If one understands the Noahide laws as a type of religious and ethical minimum requirement that applies to all people and if at the same time one leaves room for the notion of a special position for Israel, "why"—asks Norman Solomon—"should

146 Cp. to this Dorff 1982 and 1996; Lubarsky 1990, 17ff; Cohn-Sherbok 1994, 29ff; Langer 2003.
147 Cp. Langer 2003, 263; Dorff 1996, 49f.
148 Cp. Cohn-Sherbok 1994, 169 and 1997, 184.
149 Cp. Ruether 1987, 140.
150 Cp. Dorff 1996.
151 Cp. Solomon 1996.
152 Cp. Langer 2003.
153 Cp. Sacks 2003 esp. 200-205.

other people not understand themselves the same way?"[154] Ruth Langer suggests that the concept of the Noahide covenant allows that

> Jews understand their tradition of "chosenness" not to imply superiority or an exclusive relationship to God, but to be a definition of their particular relationship to God among many others. [...] This, then, allows for Judaism to differentiate between the various religions, to grant them their own theological uniqueness ...[155]

Thus also from a Jewish perspective, the diversity of religions can be understood as the result of a form of revelation or recognition of God that corresponds to the specific particularities of each nation, culture, language, etc.[156] Chief Rabbi Sacks writes that it is a case of recognizing the "value" and the "dignity of difference"—even in the field of religion.[157] In this regard he speaks specifically of God's covenant with humanity as being "inherently pluralistic" and that God's election does not only include the people of Israel (with reference to Isaiah 19:25).[158] According to Solomon, Judaism has always been conscious of the value of diversity: the "diversity in creation," the "diversity of human personality," the "diversity of nations." It saw God glorified in this diversity. Yet what Judaism to this point had rejected was the notion that the "diversity of faith" is likewise a value.[159] According to Solomon, it is precisely this thought that we now need to consider:

> This diversity is to be cherished as testimony to the glory of God, who is too great to be contained in one tradition or reserved for one people.[160]

But, asks the British Reform rabbi, Tony Bayfield, is the recognition of further covenants not deeply painful for Israel? If Christianity is challenged to give up the idea that it is the one religion that replaces all others, must Israel not then, almost as a counter offer, stop thinking of itself "as God's first love"? "I cannot tell you how difficult it has been to write these last sentences," says Bayfield.[161] No! This is not the cost that a pluralist theology of religion demands. For God's love for every people and for every single person is not lessened or made any less personal by embracing all equally. For this love applies to everyone in an equally unique and particular way. Perhaps a word from Shinran Shōnin, one of the great figures of the Amida-Buddhist tradition, may offer some help in this question. Shinran never tired of emphasizing that the promise of Amida-Buddha to save all sentient beings excludes no one, that Amida's boundless love really does encompass everyone. And yet, or per-

154 Solomon 1996, 97.
155 Langer 2003, 276.
156 Cp. Dorff 1996, 63; Solomon 1996, 98; Sacks 2003, 204.
157 Cp. Sacks 2003, 200f.
158 Cp. Sacks 2003, 203f.
159 Cp. Solomon 1996, 85f, 98.
160 Solomon 1996, 98. Similarly also Hartman 1990, 243-266, and 1999, 135-192.
161 Bayfield 2000, 125.

haps precisely because of this, Shinran can write: "When I consider deeply the Vow of Amida, (...) I realize that it was entirely for the sake of myself alone!"[162]

What one sees repeatedly emphasized on the Christian side is that within the framework of the theology of religions the relationship between Judaism and Christianity deserves such special standing that it actually explodes the entire framework.[163] In my mind the Jewish-Christian relationship does indeed have a special role. Not that of being an exception in the theology of religions, but rather that of its vanguard. With reference to Judaism, many theologians have meanwhile recognized where the Christian claim to supersede another religion and the contestation of another religion's theological legitimacy may lead to. They have seriously begun to look for theological ways of overcoming such claims. Today many theologians are prepared to adopt a pluralist position toward Judaism, that is, to recognize Judaism as a different but equally path to salvation, and accept all the Christological implications and consequences of this view. In the past, Christianity's stance toward Judaism often had a paradigmatic function. That is, the attitude of Christians to post-Christian Judaism was for a long time *the* prime example of an exclusivist position. And for many, the Christian position toward pre-Christian Judaism still is that basic model of an inclusivist stance, which they would also like to adopt in relation to other religions: Christianity ought to recognize other religions as its 'precursors' in a similar way as it did with Judaism. Yet Christianity's relation to Judaism could not only be the paradigm of an exclusivist or inclusivist stance to other religions. In an analogical way, the transformed stance toward Judaism that many Christians now take could well become the paradigm of a pluralist position.[164] As Alan Race so aptly states:

> ... once the integrity of Judaism has been liberated from the shackles of fulfilment and supercessionism, the way is opened for other religions not to be placed, as it were, in the equivalent position of being forerunner to Christianity.[165]

162 Tannishō, Postscript. Shinran 1997, 679.
163 See for example Dirscherl 1996, 505ff with an anti-pluralist thrust.
164 Michael Hüttenhoff has criticized my definition of pluralism (as a position in the theology of religions) in that according to this definition a theological position would already count as "pluralist" if it recognizes as equal to Christianity just one further religion, such as Judaism. He sees this definition as being in tension with the "spirit and intention of the pluralist option" (Hüttenhoff 2001, 74f.). Of course, Hüttenhoff is right that the majority of pluralists extend the claim of equal validity to several religions. But he overlooks the fact that the decisive threshold of hope is already crossed when Christianity gives up the claim to superiority with reference to only one other religion. All the rest depends more or less on simply drawing the appropriate consequences with respect to other religions.
165 Race 2001, 61.

13. Christianity and Islam

Historical Burdens

Who is Surpassing Whom? Conquests, Reconquests, and their Religious Background

In the year 610, the then forty-year old merchant Muhammad (570–632), through a series of visions, experiences his call to be the prophet of the One and Only God:

> Say: He is Allah, the One and Only; Allah, the Eternal, Absolute; He begetteth not, nor is He begotten. There is none like unto Him. (Sūrah 112)

At first, Muhammad resists his calling.[1] But then he submits to his calling and proclaims in Mecca the revelations that are bestowed on him at irregular intervals. In his proclamation Muhammad turns against the polytheism of his time and against the worship of idols, which he rejects in the name of the absolute transcendence of God. Since God is highly exalted above everything, none of the numerous deities is equal to him. Nothing and no one is like God, *that is why* God is one and unique (Sūrah 6,100; 16,1ff; 23,91f, 116f; 27,63).[2] It is to God alone that a person is to "submit" him- or herself (this being the literal meaning of "islam.") In the name of God's mercy and righteousness Muhammad also turns against all unrighteousness and hardness of heart. The devotion to the one true God is to be expressed in just and merciful deeds (7,29; 26,181ff.; 30,38; 93).

This message gains Muhammad a following especially among the lower classes of the Meccan society, but it also leads to increasingly strong tensions and conflicts with the established circles, so that finally in 622 Muhammad considers himself forced to emigrate with his followers to Yathrib (later renamed "Medina"). Islamic tradition made this year of the "emigration" (*hijrah*) the beginning of its calendar. In Medina, Muhammad quickly rises to become a political leader. He adamantly opposes the Jewish tribes, who do not support him as expected. By 630, Muhammad is a successful ruler and he conquers Mecca almost without a fight. Here he proves lenient toward his enemies. When he dies two years later, almost the entire Arabic peninsula is united under Islamic rule. After Muhammad's death, his followers gath-

1 Cp. Williams 1973, 72.
2 Cp. here appropriately Askari, 1985, 197: "'One' is not a number but a form of awareness of God's transcendence."

er the preserved revelations and put them together as the "Qur'an." Approximately twenty years later, they are finally edited under Caliph Uthmān and brought into the form we know today. Islamic tradition expresses its belief in the divine origin of the Qur'an by the notion that it is the human image and the earthly manifestation of a heavenly original Qur'an that is located with God.

According to the Qur'an, Muhammad stands in a long line of prophets. To *every* people, says the Qur'an, God has sent his messengers (e.g. 13,7; 35,24).[3] In its essence, the message of these prophets is always the same: "There is no God beside me. Serve me" (21,25). Yet, because people often turn away from the true God and God's commandments on account of their sinfulness, the message has to be continually renewed through the repeated sending of prophets. In light of this understanding, Islam interprets the biblical writings of the Old and New Testaments as containing genuine words of revelation, though partially in distorted and corrupted form. Biblical figures such as Adam, Noah, Abraham, Isaac, Jacob, Moses, Elijah, and others are regarded as prophets and divine messengers. This is also and particularly true of Jesus, whom the Qur'an identifies as a "Word of God" (4,171), as a "Spirit of God" (4,171), and a "mercy of God" (19,22). Muhammad is the "Seal of the Prophets" (33,40), which the Islamic tradition usually interprets as meaning that in him the working of the prophets is complete and in this sense is "sealed" forever. It considers the Qur'an therefore as a pure, trustworthy, and uncorrupted revelatory document. The Qur'an confirms everything that is authentic in the other revelatory documents, at the same time establishing the critical measure by which one can recognize what is wrong and corrupt in the other Holy Scriptures. As the "Seal of the Prophets", Muhammad is of universal importance, a messenger to all men, "giving them glad tidings, and warning them" (34,28; similarly 6,90; 7,158; 68,52). Thus Islam traditionally understands itself as surpassing and fulfilling all other authentic religions.[4]

This self-understanding brought Islam into tough competition with the claims of Christianity, which likewise considered itself to be the surpassing and fulfillment of Judaism and all other religions. The result of this competition was a bitter confrontation that lasted for centuries and continues to the present. The "common past" of Christianity and Islam, Ludwig Hagemann recounts,

> …is predominantly an unholy history of polemic and apologetics, of aggression and despair. Though this history also knows times of cultural enrichment and religious understanding—particularly in the regions of Spain that were once under Muslim rule—what predominates by far are competition and confrontation, conquests and reconquests, wars and campaigns, massacres and

3 The Islamic tradition differentiates between "prophet" (*nabī*) and "envoy" (*rasūl*); of the two only the latter brings a word of revelation. However, such a clearcut distinction is not yet found in the Qur'an itself.

4 Cp. Zirker 1993, 246.

> bloodbaths. Indeed: the history of Christian-Islamic relations is steeped in blood.[5]

After 632, the year of Muhammad's death, Islam experienced unparalleled expansion.[6] From the Arabian Peninsula, it advanced simultaneously to the north, east, and west. By the middle of the seventh century, it had conquered Palestine, Syria, Armenia, Cyprus, and Sicily to the north, Iraq and Persia to the east, and Egypt and Libya to the west. In the next seventy years came the conquest of the rest of North Africa and finally also Spain. With the exception of Persia, all these countries had been predominantly Christian regions, including a series of key Christian countries. In other words, in barely one hundred years almost one third of the Christian world had fallen to Islamic rule. It was only in 732 that Karl Martell stopped the advance of Islam at the Battle of Poitiers. In the East, however, Islam continued its expansion. It took over Central Asia, the area of contemporary Pakistan, including the Indus Delta, and the Punjab. Islam advanced to China's borders, and in the North as far as the Aral Sea. Whereas Muslim rulers often strongly oppressed the adherents of Asian religions,[7] they extended a certain protection to Christians and Jews, the so-called "people of the book".[8] As "protected people" (*dhimmī)* they had to pay a special tax, identify themselves by wearing particular clothing, and were excluded from military service. Yet they were allowed to practice their own religion, provided they refrained from any missionary activities. They could engage in trade and science relatively unhindered and it was not unheard of that individual Jews or Christians rose to positions of high regard—even in governmental services. Nevertheless, the Christian congregations in the formerly Christian regions of Armenia, Syria, and Egypt shrank considerably in size or—as was the case in North Africa—in the course of time disappeared completely.

The shock which the rapid military success of Islam triggered was only intensified by the fact that culturally Islam was in many ways superior to Christian countries as, for example, in mathematics, chemistry, physics, geology, astronomy, and medicine, as well as in various technical areas such as blacksmithing, architecture, shipbuilding, and printing technology. Also in areas such as music and philosophy Islam proved to be more advanced. Due to its cultural superiority, Islam appeared to be even more of a threat, but it also enriched the Christian countries in all these areas, and as a result contributed significantly to the cultural flourishing of the Christian Middle Ages. This was also true of theology: without the Aristotelian philosophy conveyed by Islam, the major theological systems of scholasticism would have been impossible.

5 Hagemann 1999, IX.
6 Cp. on the following the overviews in Goddard 1995, 125-145; Smart 1999, esp. 170–195; Hagemann 1999; Busse 1991, 141–186; Elias 1999, 82-97; Tworuschka 1992, 162–250.
7 For Islam's advance against Buddhism, see Scott 1998.
8 On the status of Christians and Jews under Islamic rule, cp. Busse 1991, 145ff; Goddard 1995, 139ff.

From the eighth century on, the Muslim areas surrounded the rest of Christian Europe like a pair of pliers. It took more than three centuries before Christianity became capable of responding militarily. The retaking of Sicily in the eleventh century came first. In the West, from the eleventh to twelfth centuries, the gradual recapture of Spain began, the so-called Reconquista. This made greater strides from the middle of the thirteenth century on and achieved its goal in the year 1492 with the fall of Granada. Just like in Sicily before, Jews and Muslims were no longer tolerated in re-Christianized Spain. The alternatives were expulsion or baptism. The Spanish Inquisition assured through its own inhumane means that remnants of Jewish and Muslim faith would no longer be secretly practiced by the forced converts.

In the East, the military response to Islam was primarily motivated by the concept of the "Crusade", which arose toward the end of the eleventh century: According to this idea it was the will of God to "free" the sacred sites of Palestine, particularly Jerusalem, from the hands of the Islamic rulers. In 1098, Christian forces succeeded in taking Antioch and in 1099 they conquered Jerusalem. It was here that the crusading knights caused what, even by contemporary standards, was an excessive bloodbath. "All enemies that they could find they felled with the sharpness of their swords, without taking any account of age, status, or gender. There were so many slaughtered lying around that one could find no path or way through other than by going over corpses," the twelfth-century chronicler William of Tyre reported.[9]

After the conquest of Jerusalem, it was indeed possible to establish a Christian kingdom in Palestine. But despite further crusades, this lasted only about one hundred years. The Muslim side gradually succeeded in again bringing all the regions of Palestine under its control. And the Muslim expansion continued. In the fourteenth and fifteenth centuries, Muslims conquered Anatolia and Muslim troops pushed toward the Balkans. Constantinople fell in 1453. Greece and the Balkans came under the rule of the Ottoman Empire. In 1529 and again in 1683, Muslim troops stood before the gates of Vienna. In Africa, Islam now also pushed into countries south of the Sahara. From Central Asia, it expanded in a northerly direction into Russian territory. In India, its rule extended over the northern half of the peninsula up to Bengal. In Southeast Asia, Muslims conquered Indonesia along with parts of the Philippines. In the East, Islam pushed along the Silk Road further and further into Chinese territory.

Islam attained its biggest territorial expansion in the seventeenth century. Yet the Islamic countries were unable to keep pace with the technological advances of the Western nations during modernity. Thus, the colonial age once again changed the power relations quickly and drastically. In the nineteenth century, Holland conquered Indonesia. Britain annexed India, parts of the Arabian Peninsula, Egypt, Sudan, and further regions of Africa (such as Nigeria). Other Western countries divided up the rest of Islamic Africa among themselves: France took Morocco, Egypt,

9 Quoted following Elm, 1992, 408.

Tunisia, Senegal, Mali and Niger, Italy took Libya and South Somalia, and Spain parts of Morocco and the Western Sahara. Of the entire Islamic world, only Turkey, Iran, Afghanistan, and Saudi Arabia were spared Western colonial rule (though not in some cases significant dependence). It has only been since the middle of the twentieth century that many of the aforementioned countries regained their national independence. Western colonial rule had traumatic effects on the Islamic world; more than that, it challenged Islamic faith: Why had God allowed Islam—just at the height of its expansion—to be suddenly forced into the position of a global outsider?[10]

However, Christian hopes of also gaining missionary success among Muslims in the wake of the colonization of Islamic countries soon proved to be completely unrealistic. From a long-term perspective, colonialism seemed rather to have the opposite effect and played its own part in the revitalization of Islam.[11] Only too often, native Christians in Islamic countries were the ones who bore the brunt of anti-colonial resentment.[12] Yet the responses of Islam to the West both during and also after colonial rule proved quite varied in its details. On the one hand, influenced by the values of the Enlightenment, a certain Islamic liberalism arose.[13] On the other, so did various forms of a decidedly anti-Western Islam, which presented itself either in very traditional forms (in the sense of a return to the former Islamic order), or in a modernist way (in the sense of a development of new but not Western Islamic systems). Between these poles exists a broad spectrum of different reform movements and political experiments that extends from the establishment of a secular, laicist state as in Turkey, all the way to the establishment of the Islamic Republic of Iran.[14]

The history of Islamic expansion during early modernity, the subsequent colonization of Muslim countries by the West and the only recently attained independence of numerous Islamic states have left behind on both sides a deep-seated fear of one another. Samuel Huntington's scenario in *Clash of Civilizations*, which Huntington primarily understood as a battle between the Islamic and the Christian influenced civilizations,[15] is just as much an expression of this fear as is the penetrating depiction of Americans and their Western allies as "crusaders" in the pamphlets of militant Islamist groups[16] or the attitude of numerous Muslims to the Israeli-Palestinian conflict. They frequently view the American Christian support of Israel as an attempt to "destroying the Muslim character of Palestine,"[17] which in turn is seen as

10 Cp. Duran 1990, esp. 423ff.
11 Siddiqui (1997, 6-20) offers an overview of Islamic responses to Christian missionary efforts during the colonial era.
12 Cp. Duran 1990, 450f.
13 On this, see the excellent reader by Kurzman 1998.
14 On this, see also the nuanced overview in Rotter 1993.
15 Huntington 1998, 209ff, 246ff, 252ff.
16 On this cp. Kelsay 2003. For the fateful effects of the connection between Western colonialism and Christian mission on the Islamic perception of the West and Christianity, see Zebiri 2001.
17 Maryam Jameelah, cited in Zebiri 2001, 184.

a symbolic expression of a battle of the "West" (understood as an alliance between secularism, Christianity, and Judaism) against Islam. What we can see in numerous current tensions is unmistakably the effect of this long history of religious conflict between Christianity and Islam, which Ludwig Hagemann fittingly characterized as "a history of shattered relationships"[18] and identified its roots as "intolerant exclusivism."[19]

Islam from a Christian Exclusivist Perspective

> ...A rundlet, that hath lost
> Its middle or side stave, gapes not so wide,
> As one I mark'd torn from the chin throughout
> Down to the hinder passage: 'twixt the legs
> Dangling his entrails hung, the midriff lay
> Open to view, and wretched ventrile
> That turns th'englutted ailment to dross
> Whilst eagerly I fix on him my gaze,
> He ey'd me, with his hands laid his breast bare,
> And cried: Now mark how I do ripe me! Lo!
> How is Mohammed mangled![20]

It is with this repulsive vision that Dante Alighieri (1265–1321) in his *Divine Comedy* depicts Muhammad's fate in hell, where, like his son-in-law Ali, the founder of Shi'ite Islam, he is suffering for having sown "scandal and schism." Dante's depiction corresponds to the traditional Christian perception of Islam. For a long time, Christian theologians viewed Islam not as a different religion in its own right, but rather as an extreme Christian heresy. It was assumed that Muhammad had formulated his teachings under the influence of a heretical Christian monk, who was described either as an Arian or as a Nestorian.[21] Thomas Aquinas, only a few years before Dante, had been the first to question the categorization of Islam as a Christian heresy, and he did so with the argument that Islam does not share the same canonical writings with Christianity.[22] This marked the beginning of a clearer realization of the distinctness of Islam as a religion based on its own revelatory document. Even if it is highly uncertain whether Aquinas himself had ever read the Qur'an, it can be no coincidence that Aquinas formulated his view about one hundred years after the completion of the Qur'an's first Latin translation in Toledo in 1143.

18 Thus the subtitle of Hagemann's 1999 book.
19 Ibid. IX.
20 Dante Alighieri, *The Divine Comedy*. Hell. Canto 28, 22-30. Cited following the translation by Henry Francis Cary.
21 Cp. Hagemann 1999, 16ff.
22 *Summa contra gentiles* I, 2.

However, the categorization of Islam as a Christian heresy by no means implied a more moderate judgment. In fact, it was rather the opposite. According to a widespread theological opinion, the prophetic mediation of revelation had come to an end with the death of the last apostle. Thus Christian authors of anti-Islamic treatises generally viewed Muhammad, honored by Islam as the "Seal of the Prophets," as a false prophet. Christian polemicists contested the prophetic mission of Muhammad on the one hand with arguments against the person of Muhammad, and on the other with arguments against the reliability of the Qur'an.[23] There were, Christians argued, neither witnesses to the genuineness of Muhammad's mission nor prophecies that had announced Muhammad beforehand. He himself could point to neither prophecies he fulfilled nor miracles he accomplished as confirmation of his divine calling. In addition, they argued that his life showed no signs of holiness, but rather evidenced an unrestrained sensuality and a brutal striving for power. Regarding the reliability of the Qur'an, they alleged that it was not in agreement with biblical traditions and that it was full of falsehood. In particular, the Christian authors fought against the Qur'anic denial of Jesus' death on the cross (4,157f.). For this denial not only contradicted biblical writings, but apparently also revealed at the same time the uselessness of Muslim religious practice. For in their eyes it is only through the cross of Christ that the path of salvation is opened for people. Furthermore, according to the understanding of the Christian polemicists, the teachings of the Qur'an just reflect the bad character of Muhammad. In particular, they viewed the sexual morality of the Qur'an as permissive, since polygamy and concubinage are permitted. They also criticized the pictorial descriptions of paradise found in the Qur'an as inappropriately sensual.[24] From their perspective the Qur'an does not know true love, but instead preaches only hatred and violence.[25]

The Qur'an repeatedly warns Christians not to endanger the uniqueness of God, and thus criticizes the doctrine of the Trinity as well as the claim that Jesus is the Son of God (e.g. Sūrah 4,171; 5,73 and 116; 112, 1–4). Some Christian theologians were content with dismissing this critique and emphasizing that neither the doctrine of the Trinity nor Christology would contradict monotheism. Others preferred the counter-attack and disputed that the God of the Qur'an was identical with the God of the Bible. According to George Hamartolos (ninth century), Islam was simply a "resumption of Arabic Heathenism."[26] Nicetas of Bizantium (ninth-tenth century) claimed that Muhammad merely used monotheism as a vehicle to lead his adherents astray to idol and devil worship, which Nicetas suspected of being behind the cult of the Ka'ba.[27] However, the real argument is theological in nature: The God of Muhammad could not be identical with the Father of Jesus Christ because God is revealed only through Jesus Christ, and by the same token all genuine knowledge of

23 Cp. this with Khoury 1969 and 1976,
24 For a particularly helpful new treatment of this theme, cp. Hoye 1990.
25 Cp. Khoury 1969, 49.
26 Ibid., 21.
27 Cp. ibid. 23f.

God must also lead to knowledge of God's Son.[28] Christian theologian and Islamic studies scholar Adel Khoury primarily credits the political circumstances when explaining the highly polemical tone found especially in the early anti-Islamic tracts of Byzantine theologians, that is, the excessiveness of the denigration of Muhammad and the Islamic faith, and the almost complete absence of balanced opinions seeking understanding:

> One gets the impression that this unrelenting intransigence and the vehemence of the damning comments...want to take vengeance for the military defeats.[29]

As plausible as it may be to attribute the harsh style of the Christian accusations primarily to time-bound factors, this changes nothing about the fact that we can already see here the development of stereotypical patterns of Christian judgments of Islam. There were of course some exceptions: theologians and thinkers who encountered Islam with more good will and sometimes even sympathy, such as Nicholas of Cusa,[30] Enlightenment scholars such as Hadrian Reland and Gotthold Ephraim Lessing,[31] and also Johann Wolfgang von Goethe, who with his "West-Eastern Divan" likewise aimed at theological bridge-building.[32] The old negative clichés, however, remained dominant in theological circles, where they were repeated again and again. Martin Luther in particular fostered this tendency. Luther saw in Islam, much as he had in Judaism, a purely legalistic religion in which a person tries in vain to earn his salvation through good works. Since the Cross of Christ was for Luther the source of all divine grace, in his judgment of Islam he focused especially on the Qur'anic contestation of Jesus' death on the Cross. According to Luther there is no forgiveness of sins, no grace, and no Holy Spirit in Islam. In reality, concludes Luther, Muhammad and the Qur'an are instruments of the devil.[33] Calvin's opinions are not that different:[34] The Muslim God is false and empty because it is not the God of Jesus Christ. Without recognition of Jesus Christ as the only mediator, the God of the Muslims, like the God of the Jews (!) remains nothing more than an idol. The Muslims, writes Calvin, have been led astray by the "deliria" of the false prophet Muhammad. And according to Calvin, since they in turn lead so many people into falsehood, "they deserve to be killed."[35]

The negative Christian depiction of Islam continues in recent history. In 1996, the eighteenth edition of the three-volume Church History by Bihlmeyer and Tüch-

28 Cp. ibid. 51f.
29 Khoury 1969, 10.
30 Cp. Qirker 1993, 60-7; Hagemann 1999, 68-81.
31 For their conception of Islam, see Hagemann 1999, 98-102.
32 Cp. Mommsen 2001.
33 Cp. Hagemann 1999, 81-95.
34 On this, cp. Slomp 1995.
35 *Calvini Opera Quae Supersunt Omnia,* edited by W. Baum, E. Cunitz, E. Reuss), 27:261. Cited following Slomp 1995, 135.

le says of Muhammad: "Cruelty and lasciviousness distort his character."[36] For Karl Barth, the Islamic God has nothing in common with the Christian God. Rather, Islam is the "potentization of all other heathenism," only "in a yet more primitive fashion." Barth calls the Islamic emphasis on God's uniqueness "fanatical clamor," since Islam allegedly does not proclaim "God as One" but rather "Oneness as God."[37] According to Johannes Witte, a Protestant scholar of mission studies who is very near to the dialectical theology of Karl Barth, the Qur'anic insistence to stand in continuity with biblical revelation is simply absurd. Rather, according to Witte, the revelation claims of Christianity and Islam are mutually exclusive:

> This is a hard either/or. If, as Muhammad says, it really is the same living God who has spoken through Christ and now through Muhammad, then he cannot have revealed through the New Testament, through Christ himself and his disciples, that Christ is the Son of God, and then reveal 600 years later through Muhammad that there is no Son of God! (…) The Gospel talks of the Trinitarian God. And now Christ is denying the Trinity? So where did Christ really speak and where did he speak the truth, in the Gospel or in Muhammad? There can be no doubt about the answer. We are doing Muhammad no injustice if we count these words he put in Christ's mouth among Muhammad's bogus revelations, words that allow whatever suited him to count as "revealed"…[38]

If, as Witte argues, the recognition of God's revelation in Christ excludes the truth of the Qur'anic revelation, then Muhammad's prophetic claim must be viewed as either a case of illusion or of malicious deceit. Witte suggests both these options:

> In Christ an entirely pure prophet really does stand before us, one whose humanity is totally unblemished (the fact that according to his own words and those of his followers he was more than this, we will ignore for now.) Yet in Muhammad we have a man who initially and perhaps honestly believed he had received a divine mission, but who very quickly and in the most crass way became ethically and religiously degenerate, turning into a political tyrant, a depraved promise breaker, a treacherous murderer and a dissolute lecher, as well as a deliberate forger of supposed divine revelations.[39]

According to Witte, it is thus likely that Muhammad made up at least the later prophetic sayings in order to legitimate his personal position of power and his allegedly immoral lifestyle. According to Witte, Muhammad had to reject the notion of Jesus as the Son of God because otherwise he could not have regarded himself as being the greater of the two.[40] At the latest by the time he was in Medina, there can, allegedly, be

36 Vol. I, 248.
37 The "Potenzierung allen sonstigen Heidentums", Barth 1932-70: II/1, 504ff.
38 Witte 1936, 133f.
39 Ibid. 131.
40 Cp. ibid. 134.

> absolutely no doubt that…Muhammad is a massively sinful person, who conceals the offensive desires of his heart, his desire for political power, and his personal desire for revenge through supposed revelations from God…[41]

Witte presents the same argument with regard to the doctrine of salvation. The "entire Old and New Testaments" teach that on account of the holiness of God an "expiatory sacrifice" is needed for sins to be forgiven. According to Witte God reveals in the New Testament that Christ paid this sacrifice through his death on the cross. Muhammad, however, held that Christ did not die on the cross and that God also does not need such a sacrifice, since "God is the Merciful One."[42] That is why, according to Witte, a clear mutual exclusivity also obtains in the realm of soteriology:

> If what Muhammad says about this is a revelation of God, then the entire Old and New Testaments are not a lower form of God's revelation but none at all. (...) We are not talking about higher or lower revelation, but rather about the either/or, about where there is revelation, either in the New Testament or with Muhammad.[43]

For Witte, the answer is "completely clear."[44] The denial of the crucifixion

> … is once again a false revelation, an embarrassed word from Muhammad's own heart, not from God's truth, a lie, not a revelation.[45]

It is revealing how Witte reconstructs the supposed reason for this "lie": If Muhammad had recognized that the way to salvation was opened only by Jesus' death, then he would have had to admit that he himself was in need of this sacrifice, and that he is therefore ranked below Christ:

> If he had recognized Christ's death, then that would be the end of his superior position to Christ. (…) For then Muhammad would have had to become a Christian, and in that case his whole construction of a special revelation, even of a higher revelation, would have come tumbling down.[46]

What Witte presents here betrays much more about his own motivation than about Muhammad's. For if like Witte one makes God's willingness to forgive dependent on Jesus' death on the cross, then one makes God's mercy, which Islam confesses as being autonomous, contingent on the acceptance of Christianity and thereby establishes Christianity's absolute superiority over Islam and all other religions.

After the picture that the exclusivist interpretation has sketched of Islam over more than thirteen centuries, Islam stands as the religious antipode of Christianity. According to this image the Qur'an denies three central Christian teachings: the incarnation of God in Jesus, the divine Trinity, and the salvific meaning (and factual

41 Ibid. 128.
42 Ibid. 149.
43 Ibid. 149f.
44 Ibid. 150.
45 Ibid. 149.
46 Ibid. 149f.

reality) of Jesus' death on the Cross. Thus Islam seems to be irreconcilably opposed to Christianity. From an exclusivist perspective this leads to a decisive rejection of every Islamic claim of revelation. For if Christianity emphasizes the three aforementioned teachings because it believes God revealed them, and if Islam contests these three teachings, because it believes God revealed their falsity, then, as Witte clearly says, it can no longer be a case of "lower or higher revelation" but rather only one of the exclusionary alternative of a true or a "bogus" revelation. This simultaneously passes the verdict on the prophetic claim of Muhammad: based on such argumentation, Christianity has no other choice but to vehemently contest this claim.

We can see that for Witte this argument—and this is more or less true of the entire traditional Christian image of Islam—rests on an instruction-model of revelation.[47] In other words, it understands revelation as the supernatural communication of propositional beliefs that, because of their divine origin, are considered to be infallibly true. On the basis of this concept of revelation, it is not possible that God would reveal something through the Bible that God contests through the Qur'an. Consequently, a Christian perspective demands the rejection of the Qur'an as a document of revelation.

It is not only within Christianity that an instruction-model of revelation has prevailed, even until must recently. It also dominates Islamic theology of revelation: God conveys the revelation to Muhammad through an angel in the form of a mental text.[48] Accordingly Muhammad, during his first revelation experience, is prompted to "read" or "recite" this text (Sūrah 96). The literal meaning of "Qur'an" is correspondingly "(scripture) reading," or "recitation." Thus, the solemn recital of the Qur'an almost represents a ritual reenactment of divine revelation and the human reception of that revelation.[49] Consequently, the exclusivist Christian critique of the Qur'an aims not only at demonstrating the Qur'an's irreconcilability with biblical scriptures. Rather, ever since the first anti-Islamic tracts by Byzantine theologians, this critique has aimed at discovering historical errors or untruths in the Qur'an in order to contest its claim of divine origins. The goal is to show that everything in the Qur'an either comes from Muhammad himself or that it came to him in an entirely "natural" way, especially regarding the Qur'anic material on biblical figures, stories, or doctrines. It is not God from whom Muhammad received this information but hearsay, or more precisely, the particular Christian heretic whom these critiques always suspected of being Muhammad's main informant.

This argument drew, to begin with, upon the fact that in the Qur'an, Mary, the Mother of Jesus, is described as "Aaron's sister" (19,28). Christian theologians regarded this as clear proof of a confusion of the Mother of Jesus with the sister of Aaron and Moses, who likewise is called Maria or Miriam. Another example can

47 On this, cp. above chapter 8, pp. 190-194.
48 In the Qur'an itself, the traditional view of angels as mediators of revelation is not yet that unambiguously present. Cp. Renz 2002, 460f.
49 Cp. Renz, Leimgruber 2004, 110f.

be found in the Qur'an's reports on Jesus and the so-called bird miracle. That is, the story of Jesus as a boy shaping a bird from clay and by blowing on bringing life into it (3,49; 5,110). This miracle story is not found in the New Testament but in the apocryphal writings of the children's stories of the Gospel of Thomas, with which—so it was assumed—Muhammad must somehow have been familiar. From a Christian perspective this served as evidence that it is not God who is the source of the Qur'an, but rather—as in this case—some dubious or at least non-canonical Christian traditions. A third and final example: In the Qur'an it says: "O Jesus the Son of Mary! Didst thou say unto men, 'Worship me and my mother as gods in derogation of Allah'?" (5,116). This was often understood as the Qur'an incorrectly assuming that in Christianity, Mary stands as the third person of the Trinity. This would indicate that Muhammad had highly imprecise ideas of Christianity, which then became the basis of the alleged revelations.

Undoubtedly, Islamic apologetics can without a great deal of effort produce solutions to such objections. That Mary was the sister of some "Aaron" could refer to a tradition that was dominant at that time; the bird miracle does not have to be false just because it is not found in the New Testament; the elevation of Jesus and Mary to a place of divine honor does not refer to the doctrine of the Trinity, but rather to the actual religious praxis.[50] Yet there is something more fundamental than the question of how probable such polemical attacks on the Qur'an or their corresponding apologetic defenses are. For in every case an instruction-model of revelation, whether Christian or Islamic, suffers from the basic weakness explained above in connection with the presuppositions of a pluralist theology of religions. It more or less inevitably leads to a confusion of the revelation's time and culture, of typically human forms of expression as they are already contained in the particular language and terminology of the text, with its supposedly non-human, supernatural and time-less content.[51] Something clearly underlying human conditionality is thereby identified with an unconditionality that only applies to God. After the Enlightenment's radical critique of revelation, Christian theology, though not in its entirety, largely accepted the notion that in connection with revelation the attribute "supernatural" relates to nothing but the supernatural nature of God, and that therefore one should think of revelation strictly as divine self-disclosure. The culturally conditioned form of revelatory testimonies and documents is thus entirely a human affair. It is not the actual revelation itself, but rather part of the way humans receive revelation and witness to it.

On the Christian side, such a change in the understanding of revelation creates an important foundation on which one may overcome the exclusivist "either/or" in Christian-Islamic relations. The affirmation of incarnation, the doctrine of the Trinity, and the salvific meaning of the cross, are not truths revealed by God whose contents are more or less fixed. Rather, they are the results of historically evolving inter-

50 As examples of this, cp. Denffer 1991, 6ff., 27, or Abdullah 1992, 145.
51 Cp. above chapter 8, p. 191-193.

pretations of the role of Jesus as revealer and mediator of salvation. For that reason, these teachings are also fundamentally open to reinterpretation and to a change of meaning if such new interpretations become necessary due to substantive reasons. The question of whether there is an inconsistency between them and Islamic positions is therefore clearly more open than the traditional exclusivist reading suggests.

But is it possible to overcome an instruction-model of revelation also within the framework of Islamic theology? The response to this can of course only proceed from the inner Islamic theological discussion itself. A positive response would in any case imply that the person of Muhammad and the concrete situations in which he lived play a much larger role in how the Qur'an came about than has previously been acknowledged. Muslims too will hardly be inclined to believe that the Qur'an, in exactly the same form, could have been revealed through another prophet at another time and in another culture. This also relativizes the difference that in Christianity it is a person (Jesus Christ), and in Islam it is a book (the Qur'an), that is the central medium of revelation: Without Muhammad and his quite specific historical situation, the Qur'an would simply not be what it is nor how it looks today. And without the writings of the New Testament, the revelation in Jesus would have remained unreceived. Yet what is key is that for both Jesus and the Qur'an we are talking about a truly human medium. Just as Jesus as a child of his time became the mediator of saving knowledge of God, so too does the Qur'an convey its revelation as a "child" or a book of its time.

By differentiating between the earthly or more precisely Arabic Qur'an of the seventh century and a heavenly original Qur'an, Islam obtains over a hermeneutical tool that, at least in principle, enables it to realistically recognize the human nature of the Qur'an and its historical-cultural limitedness. The Qur'an itself confirms that the true word of God infinitely exceeds everything that human beings can write in books (18,109; 31,27). The striking parallels between the Islamic differentiation between the earthly Qur'an and the heavenly original Qur'an on the one hand, and the Christian differentiation between the person of Jesus and the divine Logos on the other have been pointed out repeatedly.[52] Taking up the Chalcedonian formula of "neither confused nor divided," one may state: First and foremost it is necessary to grasp more clearly all the consequences and implications of the unconfused relationship between the earthly and the heavenly Qur'an. One can thus no longer use the fact of the concrete historical shaping of the Qur'an, and hence its human form, as arguments of Christian anti-Islamic polemic against the prophetic function of Muhammad. When Mohammed Arkoun writes from an Islamic perspective that a scientific, historico-philologically oriented perspective on the the Qur'an would in the end strengthen the "theology of revelation,"[53] this holds not only with reference to the intrinsic credibility of Islamic theology of revelation, but also with reference to whether and how this may be conveyed inter-religiously. In any case, the notion of

52 Cp. Watt 1995, 50.
53 Arkoun 1999, 75.

revelation is, as Andreas Renz rightly emphasizes, "the theological focal point in the relationship between Christianity and Islam…in which all other theological themes culminate."[54] The hard "either/or" of the exclusivist position can only be broken up to the extent that the instruction-model of revelation is overcome. This can also be seen in the inclusivist openings in Christian-Islamic relationship.

Inclusivist Openings

The Significance of the Second Vatican Council

Within the Roman Catholic Church, it was above all the proceedings of the Second Vatican Council that introduced[55] a change in Christian-Islamic relations.[56] Both the World Council of Churches and the Orthodox Churches followed Rome in this and likewise started official dialogues with Islam thanks to the influence of the Council.[57] In the "Dogmatic Constitution on the Church" (*Lumen gentium* 16) the Second Vatican Council says:

> …the plan of salvation also includes those who acknowledge the Creator. In the first place amongst these there are the Muslims, who, professing to hold the faith of Abraham, along with us adore the one and merciful God, who on the last day will judge mankind.

The "Declaration on the Relation of the Church to the Non-Christian Religions" examines Islam in a more detailed way *(Nostra aetate* 3). Beyond what is said in *Lumen gentium*, *Nostra aetate* emphasizes that Muslims revere Jesus as a prophet but "do not acknowledge Jesus as God." In addition it notes positively that Islam honors not only Jesus but also "Mary, His virgin Mother." Muslims, continues the text, "value the moral life and worship God especially through prayer, almsgiving and fasting." With respect to the relations between Christians and Muslims, the Catholic Church emphasizes that it regards Muslims "with esteem." Further:

54 Renz, Leimgruber 2004, 120.

55 Cp. Renz 2002, 61.

56 The literature on the relationship between Christianity and Islam has grown enormously within the last few years. Goddard 1995 gives a short, summary presentation of this. A number of contributions to Haddad & Haddad 1995 give multi-faceted insights into the Christian-Islamic relations within various countries and regions. One can also find there a rather extensive bibliography. Siddiqui 1997 offers a more nuanced overview of Islamic attempts at dialogue with Christianity. Renz and Leimgruber 2000 offer an up-to-date introductory portrayal of Christian-Islamic relations.

57 The 1969 consultation in Cartigny, Switzerland, marked the World Council of Churches' entrance into the Christian-Islamic dialogue. But it was only at the 1986 consultation in Geneva that the Orthodox churches first officially entered into this dialogue. On this, cp. the overviews in Renz, 2002, 47–62. The reports about the Christian-Islamic dialogues of the WCC from 1969–1989 can be found in Brown 1989.

> Since in the course of centuries not a few quarrels and hostilities have arisen between Christians and Moslems, this sacred synod urges all to forget (*obliviscentes,* PS-L) the past and to work sincerely for mutual understanding and to preserve as well as to promote together for the benefit of all mankind social justice and moral welfare, as well as peace and freedom.

Particularly new in the Council's statements are the following three aspects: *First* of all, the Council recognizes that, in principle, it is possible for Muslims to be saved and it also positively evaluates their ethical and religious stances. *Second*, the Council proposes concrete steps for future relations, namely efforts for better "mutual understanding" and also cooperation in practical concerns. *Third*—and most fundamentally—*Lumen gentium* acknowledges that Muslims, "professing to hold the faith of Abraham, along *with us* (*nobiscum*) adore the one and merciful God."[58] Apparently the Council used "nobiscum" in order to express that the God who is adored in Islam is the same God to whom Christians turn.[59] With reference to Jews and Christians, the Qur'an emphasizes the same thing: "Our God and your God is One; and it is to Him we bow" (29,46). As we have seen, this is precisely what the Christian exclusivist view of Islam had contested since the early Byzantine theologians all the way to Karl Barth, insinuating that Islam was idol worship or even devil worship.

What circumstances led to the changed position of the Second Vatican Council toward Islam? As far as I can see, this has not yet been sufficiently researched. First, the statements of the Council about non-Christian religions were motivated by the general theological turn from a moderate exclusivism to an inclusivist theology of religions that was proposed by a number of Catholic theologians, most prominently by Karl Rahner. Second, during the Council it was particularly bishops from countries with a non-Christian majority, like India, Japan, Vietnam, Cameroon, and Turkey, who repeatedly urged the Council to expand the originally planned declaration about Judaism to a declaration about the relationship to non-Christian religions in general.[60] The chairman of the working group on Islam was Georges Anawati. He underlined the theological influence of Louis Massignon, which may be seen as the third decisive factor.[61] As a Catholic and Orientalist, Massignon had adopted the Islamic notion of the unity between Judaism, Christianity, and Islam based on the prophetic tradition going back to Abraham. As early as in 1940 he had initiated dialogical meetings between Christians and Muslims in Egypt.[62] Yet what lay beneath all three of these aforementioned factors was the experience of a deep crisis in Christian mission: the recognition of the unholy alliance between mission and West-

58 Emphasis mine.
59 The Catholic theologians Andreas Renz and Stephan Leimgruber put this even more strongly. To their mind, the Council is here "firmly defining for Catholic theology that Christians and Muslims (of course along with the Jews) pray to one and the same God." Renz, Leimgruber 2004, 85.
60 Oesterreicher 1967, 450.
61 Cp. Anawati 1967, 485f.
62 Cp. Busse 1991, 165f.

ern imperialist grasping for power, combined with insight into the pervasive lack of success of Christian mission among the other great world religions. The relationship to Islam quite clearly underscored both of these insights.

The change introduced by the Second Vatican Council was also noticed and appropriately honored on the Muslim side.[63] After the Council, a number of Muslims entered into serious dialogue with Christianity. Yet, some strong reservations remain. Ataullah Siddiqui, who has researched the attitude of Muslims toward dialogue with Christianity, lists among other things the following reasons for these reservations: fears that dialogue is only another strategy for mission; that dialogue with modern Western Christianity opens up for Western secularism a further avenue to influence Islam; that this dialogue is carried out according to Western intellectual rules of the game to which Muslims don't feel equal; that memories of the colonial past act like a psychological barrier; the fear that dialogue could cause a division in, and therefore weakening of, Islam.[64] It is quite conspicuous that the mistrust and repulsion expressed here are the consequence of the, for many Muslims, still fresh and traumatic memory of Western and Christian colonization as well as the result of a long history of conflict. Siddiqui draws attention to the fact that in this context, the Vatican's recommendation "to forget the past" must have a highly ambivalent effect. Without reappraisal and a genuine change of mind, "forgetting" is not a viable option.[65] A concrete "word of regret or a plea for forgiveness for what the Catholic Church and Catholic Christians have done to Muslims, for example during the Crusades or the Reconquista,"[66] is lacking in *Nostra aetate.* However, although it does so in rather general terms, the papal "Confession of Sins and Asking for Forgiveness" on the Day of Pardon in 2000 expresses regret that Christians allowed themselves to be led "by enmity towards members of other religions," that they have "shown contempt for their cultures and religious traditions" and yielded "to a mentality of power."

Unfortunately dialogue is now further burdened by the fact that some communications of the Roman Catholic Magisterium *after* the Council are in part highly ambivalent and do not always match the statements of Council itself. In 1985, Pope John Paul II greeted the Muslim participants of a Christian-Islamic symposium using a phrase that deliberately recalls Sūrah 29,46: "Your God and our God is one and the same, and we are brothers and sisters in the faith of Abraham."[67] Yet the Catechism of the Catholic Church from 1992 lumps all the non-Christian religions together speaking of their "search (…) for the God who is unknown" (the official German edition has: "who is yet unknown to them") (No. 843). *Dominus Iesus*

63 Cp. for example Aydin 2002, 45f; Abu-Rabi 2000, 187.
64 Cp. Siddiqui 1997, 50-55.
65 Cp. ibid. 55f.
66 Renz 2002, 32.
67 Cp. Renz 2002, 38; Ayoub 2000, 175.

(No. 7) contains similar statements.[68] In *Crossing the Threshold of Hope,* John Paul II comments rather negatively on Islam.[69] From a Muslim perspective, Mahmoud Ayoub points out that the constant emphasis on the duty of universal mission undercuts the Roman Catholic Church's commitment to dialogue, making it necessarily appear as an instrument of Christian mission.[70] Why, asks Ayoub, does Pope John Paul II avoid any mention of this missionary duty when addressing Jews, while emphasizing it when speaking to Muslims? According to Ayoub, this ambivalence in the Pope's stance toward Islam does not exactly contribute to constructive dialogue.[71]

By far the most consequential ambivalence concerns the statements of the Second Vatican Council itself. It is true that *Nostra aetate* mentions that Muslims "adore the one God ...who has spoken to men" (No. 3), thereby referring to the belief in the work of the prophets that is constitutive for Muslim faith. Yet the Council passes over the central prophet of Islam, Muhammad, in silence. Hans Küng clearly articulates the ambivalence of this silence: If the Church truly regards Muslims and their faith in the one God "with great respect," "*then*, in my opinion, that Church—and all the Christian Churches—must also 'look with great respect' upon the man" who "alone led the Muslims to the worship of the one God, who spoke through him: Muhammad, the Prophet."[72] So long as Muhammad's prophetic role remains unacknowledged, the recognition of the faith that arose in response to his work also remains up in the air. Already in his remarks on *Nostra aetate*, Georges Anawati noted that the silent omission of Muhammad was "of course the most sensitive point" for Muslims. "Once the dialogue has advanced, one will be forced to be present this central point with more precision."[73] Only a few years after the Council, Mikel de Epalza had to remind the participants of a Christian-Islamic Congress in Cordoba that this task cannot be pushed off into the distant future. In light of the long tradition of weighty Christian polemic against Muhammad, de Epalza bemoaned the fact that up until then,

> ... practically nothing had been done to enhance the status of the prophet of Islam in Christianity. Muslims find this all the more painful when they compare the Christian attitude to Muhammad with the respect with which Muslims approach Christ. The theological controversy about Muhammad is one of the main reasons why the partners in Muslim-Christian dialogue don't understand one another, and this problem must first be resolved positively.[74]

68 Dominus Iesus speaks of "belief in other religions" as "religious experience still in search of the absolute truth and still lacking assent to God who reveals himself." On this, compare the critical comments by Andreas Renz and Hans Zirker in Renz 2002, 37.

69 Cp. Renz 2002, 44 n. 74; Ayoub 2000, 182.

70 Cp. Ayoub 2000, 181.

71 Cp. ibid. 177f.

72 Küng, van Ess, von Stietencron, Bechert 1993, 27 (German original: 1984, 60).

73 Anawati 1967, 487.

74 De Epalza 1974, 396.

Indeed Muslims have repeatedly pointed to the central importance of this question.[75] The Christian hesitation toward acknowledging Muhammad as a genuine prophet seems to cast doubt on how serious Christians really are about valuing Muslim faith. Kenneth Cragg too, one of the great pioneers of Christian-Muslim dialogue, holds that a clear Christian position on Muhammad's prophetic claim is a challenge that in the long run Christians cannot avoid if they wish to take their Islamic dialogue partners seriously.[76]

Muhammad and Jesus in the Writings of Kenneth Cragg

One can hardly overestimate the influence of Kenneth Cragg (1913[-2012]) in changing the Christian perception of Islam, above all within the English-speaking world.[77] His best known work, whose first edition appeared already in 1956, carries the indicative title *The Call of the Minaret.* The title is the program. For, says Cragg, the call that goes out from the minaret not only calls Muslims to prayer. Rather, it also calls upon Christians to take a stand.[78] That is, Christians are called to *understand* Islam from within and to *serve* Muslims in an attitude of Christian solidarity. Moreover, it is a call to look back on and reassess the history of Christian-Muslim relations, a call *to overcome* the *alienation* between both traditions. Therefore, it is simultaneously a call to a *new theological interpretation* of Islam and also of Christianity in its relation to Islam. Ultimately, it is a call *to proclaim* Christ in a way understandable to Muslims and *to wait for an appropriate Islamic response* with patience, faith, and hope.[79] Dialogue is thus for Kenneth Cragg clearly integrated into a missionary purpose. Cragg holds an unambiguously inclusivist position: Jesus Christ is the fulfillment of all religions, including Islam, and it is the Christians' duty to proclaim Jesus Christ to the Muslims.[80] Yet such proclamation has to relate the Gospel to the degree and kind of salvific knowledge of God that is already present in Islam, and which, according to Cragg, is much more substantial than the Christian tradition up till now has been prepared to accept.[81]

According to Cragg, paramount for the relationship between Christianity and Islam is the concept of revelation in both religions or, more precisely, the differences between the respective concepts. In Islam, revelation is essentially understood as text or, better, as "scripture." In revelation God discloses primarily his will. In contrast,

75 On this, cp. Aydin 2002, 169ff.; and Siddiqui 1997, 59.
76 Cp. Cragg 1984, 1-14.
77 On this see the appreciation in Renz, 2002, 185ff, as well as the biographical details in ibid. 127 n. 276. In Renz one can also find a relatively extensive summary of Cragg's analysis of Islam.
78 Cp. Cragg 1956m 176-185.
79 Cp. to this the corresponding division of chapters in Cragg 1956. The closing chapter entitled "The Call to Patience" in later editions was changed to "The Call to Hope and Faith."
80 Cp. Cragg 1956, 355.
81 See also the clear account of Cragg's position in Renz 2002, esp. 127-129 and 185-190.

for Christianity, revelation is personal; that is, God reveals him/her/itself, God's own being, in the life of a particular human being: Jesus.[82] Furthermore, God gives humanity not only a law and direction but rather establishes a relationship: offering community with God by way of repentance, forgiveness, and conversion.[83] The biblical writings are therefore the "Word of God" only in a derivative sense. They are not of themselves revelation, but rather bear witness to the revelation, namely through the mediation of those people who have entered into this relationship with God.

According to Cragg, this basic consideration clarifies three issues: *First,* it can be better determined what kind of continuity we find between the Qur'anic revelation and the revelation of God in Jesus. *Second,* to what extent the revelation in Jesus surpasses and fulfills the Qur'anic revelation. *Third,* how, in the face of the respective Islamic objections, the traditional themes of Christian-Muslim controversies, that is incarnation, Trinity, and the salvific significance of the cross, may be better and more adequately understood if they are viewed strictly as interpretations of the revelation of God in Jesus.

According to Cragg, the Christian side can recognize Muhammad in a genuine sense as a prophet, but as the "prophet of the Qur'an."[84] This would require a more realistic acknowledgement of the socio-historical contingency of the Qur'an, and hence of Muhammad's prophesy, than is usually the case in Islamic tradition. Recognizing that the Qur'anic text is deeply intertwined with the person of Muhammad and the respective temporal circumstances of his prophetic ministry does not mean contesting the revelatory value of the Qur'an. However, it implies that revelation occurs through a concrete person with all his personal, temporal, and spatial particularities and contingencies.[85] This insight has important consequences for the relationship of Muhammad to Jesus. For even if, in contrast to the prophets of the Old Testament, Muhammad comes after Jesus chronologically, and even if Islam invests this with much more than mere chronological meaning—viewing Muhammad as the surpassing fulfillment of all prophets—one can nonetheless judge, from a Christian perspective, that Muhammad's cultural and religious context basically corresponds to a pre-Christian situation.[86] For that reason it is, according to Cragg, possible to count Muhammad among a prophetic tradition that is substantially pre-Jesus, a tradition about which the Letter to the Hebrews (1:1) says, that God "in many and various ways" spoke through the prophets, "but finally through the Son."[87] In a certain sense, explains Cragg, one does not even need to dispute that Muhammad completes and brings to an end the prophetic tradition.[88] For Jesus is actually not the last

82 Cp. Cragg 1956, 271ff; 289f.
83 Cp. ibid. 278.
84 Cragg 1984, 91.
85 Cp. ibid. 87ff.
86 Cp. ibid. 92f.
87 Cp. Cragg 1956, 289.
88 Cp. Cragg 1984, 125.

prophet. Rather, in him we encounter a form of divine revelation that exceeds the prophetic tradition, namely the revelation "through the Son."

According to Qur'anic understanding, prophecy includes divine direction, guidance, leading, teaching, warning, and admonition. The fact that God continually gives people renewed prophetic guidance is evidence of God's relationship to people, of God's mercy. God does not leave a person in the dark concerning the meaning and true direction of life.[89] According to Cragg, the entire prophetic program is in some sense "educational." Prophets act like teachers or tutors, "through whom that divine education of humanity proceeds ... All the world's a school."[90] According to Cragg, the Qur'an trusts deeply that a person can be made more perfect through divine mercy, but through a kind of mercy that reaches human beings in the form of prophetic revelation, instruction, and warning. Yet when prophetic education fails, punishment and judgment follow.[91]

But, asks Cragg, is this kind of divine pedagogy sufficient? Is prophetic instruction and warning really enough in light of the reality of sin?[92] Is God not willing to be involved much more intensively with humans, to let their rectification cost him much more dearly?[93] The Christian response says that precisely this happened in Jesus and it is for this reason that Jesus is "more" than a prophet (Mt. 11:9).[94] That God is deeply interested and involved in the human situation is not a matter of debate between Islam and Christianity. Creation itself is already an expression of God's interest in humanity, and the sending of the prophets all the more so. According to Cragg, what is up for debate between Islam and Christianity is the "degree," or the "extent," to which God shows interest in humans. The Qur'an emphasizes God's sovereignty and enduring transcendence. As a consequence, God acts in the lives of humans by *sending* revelation and *sending* prophets. Yet the Christian understanding is that *God himself came* and revealed himself in Jesus.[95] Jesus is therefore the fulfillment of the inner logic of the prophetic tradition and also its overcoming.[96] In Jesus, God not only teaches out of mercy; in him, God reveals his nature as love and in doing so makes his mercy irrevocably certain.[97]

According to Cragg, the comparison between Muhammad's *hijrah*, his flight or emigration to Medina, and Jesus' death on the cross reveals the central difference between Muhammad, the Prophet, and Jesus, the Son. Both Muhammad and Jesus entered into dangerous conflict with their surroundings on account of their divine calling. Muhammad responded to this conflict by leaving Mecca, ascending to the position of a successful man of power in Medina, and finally returning to Mecca

89 Cp. ibid. 126.
90 Ibid. 125.
91 Cp. ibid. 129f.
92 Cp. ibid. 126.
93 Cp. ibid. 130.
94 Cp. ibid. 126.
95 Cp. ibid. 137; Cragg 1956, 291.
96 Cp. Cragg 1984, 127.
97 Cp. ibid. 159; Cragg 1956, 293.

as a triumphant conqueror. By contrast, Jesus neither took up arms nor forsook his message. Rather, he chose the way of the cross.[98] The path of Jesus that led him to the cross becomes a revelation if one recognizes in it the concrete instantiation of the God-human relationship. That is, the power of human sin in its various forms is made concrete in the powers that crucify Jesus. In the figure of Pilate: the "political and personal sins" of a life shaped by the search for convenience and security. In the figures of the high priests: the "ecclesiastical sins" of pride and prestige. In the form of the mob urging on the death of Jesus: the "social sins" of lazy compromise and dull brutality. In this way, the actors involved in the crucifixion of Jesus represent human sin in its many guises and thus ultimately the sin of all human beings.[99] In contrast, the attitude of Jesus manifests a love that forgives precisely this sin, a love that stays true to itself, even to the point of sacrificing one's own life:

> Here we find a quality of love that makes an end of evil because it freely takes all its consequences upon itself. In revenge and hatred evil is perpetuated. In pardon and long-suffering it finds its term.[100]

If one views Jesus' actions, life, and death as divine revelation, then what is revealed here is divine love toward sinful humanity. Cragg does not question that the Qu'ran too knows about God's mercy and even explicitly states that forgiveness is more demanding and better than retaliation (42,36-43). In particular strands of Islam, such as in Shi'ite Islam and in Sufism, there is also extensive knowledge about the spiritual value of self-sacrifice and suffering on behalf of others.[101] But taken as a whole, says Cragg, Islam knows no true parallel to the cross. Rather, what dominates in Islam is the notion of the triumphant God. Herein lies, according to Cragg, the deepest ground for the Qur'an's denial of Jesus' death on the cross. From a Qur'anic perspective, it could not be accepted that God's enemies emerge as victors. However, God's victory is understood only in the sense of a triumph of his power over the power of the godless. That God's actual triumph over godlessness lies in a forgiving and self-sacrificing love does not become clear in Islam.[102] In this way, the paths of Muhammad and Jesus stand in symbolical opposition: Muhammad becomes the commander who finally conquers his enemies in Mecca with force, while Jesus never conquers nor subdues Jerusalem but rather dies outside the city and makes the cross his throne.[103]

By way of his theology of revelation, Cragg not only clarifies where he sees, on the one hand, the continuity between Muhammad and Jesus, and, on the other hand, the superiority of God's revelation in Jesus. His theology of revelation is also the basis for an interpretation of the doctrine of salvation, the doctrine of the incar-

98 Cp. Cragg 1956, 93 and 298.
99 Ibid. 299.
100 Ibid.
101 Cp. ibid. 302.
102 Cp. ibid. 294ff.
103 Cp. ibid. 302.

nation, and the doctrine of the Trinity, which overcomes the traditional exclusivist oppositions. Thus Cragg rejects as totally mistaken the notion, criticized also by Muslims, that it is the crucifixion that makes God's love possible, or that through the crucifixion God receives satisfaction for sin. Instead, it is through the crucifixion of Jesus that God's love, which is already and everywhere at work on behalf of the sinner, finds its strongest expression:[104]

> Wherever by love an evil situation is redeemed, God is there. In Christ, at the Cross that whole divine concern for human waywardness, bearing its consequences in a great single deed, is seen in cosmic fullness.[105]

According to Cragg, not just the doctrine of salvation but also the Christian doctrine of incarnation must be understood strictly as a statement about Jesus' function as revealer.[106] In other words, incarnation is not about elevating a human teacher to the status of God. Islam rightly criticizes such a notion, but this critique does not reflect what Christianity intends: "When we speak of 'God the Son' we mean God in the act of revelation."[107] Essentially, this nips in the bud every polytheistic and every biological misunderstanding of what is meant by divine Sonship. According to Cragg, when the scriptures say that the Father "begets" the Son, this means nothing more than that God's will to reveal himself has become reality.[108] The unity of God remains unharmed. God reveals here nothing but himself, and God does so via the medium of a human being and his life.

Moving on to the doctrine of the Trinity, Cragg suggests to understand it as an explanation of the unity of God in the act of God's self-revelation. And one should, without limitation, accommodate the Islamic insistence on the strict oneness of God.[109] According to Cragg, this is possible if one assumes that revelation consists of a divine-human relationship and that therefore it is always mediated by the experience of concrete people. When we talk about God, such talking actually reflects our experiences of God's action. Thus we should understand the doctrine of the Trinity as an expression of human experience of God. We speak of God as "Father" because God's nature is revealed to us in Jesus as the "Son." And to the extent that this revelation has concrete consequences in the lives of people, to the extent that people experience a change in their own hearts through the revelation of God's love in Jesus Christ, God is called "Holy Spirit" as the author of this change.[110] Thus, all talk about Father, Son, and Spirit always refers to the one God in relationship to humanity, the God whose will preserves everything, whose love redeems, and whose Spirit transforms. According to Cragg, such an understanding of God is not in contrast to

104 Ibid. 300.
105 Ibid. 301.
106 Cp. ibid. 288ff.
107 Ibid. 290.
108 Cp. ibid. 291.
109 Cp. ibid. 304ff.
110 Cp. ibid. 309-314.

monotheism. Rather, it preserves the oneness and uniqueness of God in the various ways in which humans experience God:

> The Christian faith in the Holy Trinity only carries further the truth implicit in the Muslim faith in revelation and judgement. It is the Christian form of belief in a God who has real and meaningful relation with humanity and the temporal world.[111]

In response to the Islamic critique of the Christian doctrine of the Trinity, Cragg asks rhetorically:

> Was not Muhammad, Prophet, husband, leader, and example? He was no less one Muhammad.[112]

Cragg's position is characteristic both of the opportunities as well as of the limits of an inclusivist interpretation of Islam: On the one hand, Cragg goes further than the Second Vatican Council and acknowledges a genuine prophetic role of Muhammad. Several Christian theologians such as Hans Küng,[113] David Kerr,[114] Reinhard Leuze,[115] and Hendrik Vroom[116] have followed him in this.[117] Others, such as Hans Zirker,[118] appear more cautious, yet do not want to exclude definitively the theological possibility of such an acknowledgment. Yet on the other hand, one can also see in Cragg's argumentation that the price for this recognition is the unambiguous subordination of the prophetic significance of Muhammad to the revelation of God in Jesus Christ. In this respect, for Cragg the "Prophet of the Qur'an" is on the same plane as the Old Testament prophets. To Cragg's mind, both prophetic traditions—Judaism and Islam—are fulfilled and surpassed in Jesus Christ. That is, they are superseded by Christianity.[119]

However, must we not apply also to Islam the insight into the problem of the theory of substitution that a series of Christian theologians have arrived at with reference to Judaism?[120] As shown above, it does not escape attentive Muslims who are engaged in dialogue with Christians that many Christians are inclined to give up missionary efforts toward Judaism, but not toward Islam. Quite justified they ask: For what reason? Is it theologically legitimate to require, with respect to Christol-

111 Ibid. 317.
112 Ibid. 317.
113 Cp. Küng, Ess, Stietencorn, Bechert 1984, 55-61.
114 Cp. Kerr 1991 and 1995.
115 Cp. Leuze 1994, 24-34; Leuze 2001.
116 Cp. Vroom 1996, 114-121.
117 For an overview of the Christian attempts to honor the prophetic role of Muhammad, cp. Kerr 1995.
118 Zirker 1993, 159f; 2001, 14. Cp. on this also Renz 2002, 259ff.
119 For the substitutionary motif in relation to Judaism, cp. Cragg 1956, 244, or also his polemical debate with James Parkes in Cragg 1992, esp. 102-107. For the substitutionary claim in relation to Islam cp. ibid. 333-357.
120 Cp. on this also Renz, Leimbruger 2004, 109. And yet this insight remains surprisingly inconsequential in Renz and Leimgruber. The question is also raised in Renz 2002, 195, but remains unanswered.

ogy, more from Islam than from Judaism? Or put another way: If Christians admit that nothing is missing[121] from the Jewish understanding of God's mercy—despite the rejection of Jesus as Messiah—why should this not also apply to the Islamic understanding of God's mercy?[122] In addition, is it possible, regarding the concept of revelation in Christianity and Islam, to differentiate, as Cragg does, between a revelation of divine will and a revelation of divine being?[123] Is the Islamic understanding of God's mercy really deficient because it is not established on Christology? Is it really appropriate to compare, as Cragg does, Muhammad's *hijrah* with Jesus' crucifixion in relation to their revelatory value, or is this comparison ultimately distorting because it compares two incomparable situations?

Küng and Leuze also combine their recognition of Muhammad's prophetic role with ascribing to Muhammad a proximity to Old Testament prophecy.[124] Like Cragg, Leuze hints at a difference between the prophetic revelation of God's will and the self-disclosure of God's nature in the 'Son.'[125] But in contrast to Cragg, Küng and Leuze attempt to account, theologically, for Muhammad's role as a *post*-Christian prophet by asking what prophetic significance Muhammad has for Christians. According to Küng, Muhammad is for Christians a "prophetic corrective" and a "prophetic warner." His message exhorts Christians to put God alone at the center of their faith, not to associate anyone else with God, and not to separate "faith and life" anywhere, "including politics."[126] According to Leuze, through Muhammad God impresses his enduring transcendence upon Christians as well: "God does not want to dissolve into this world, not even through his revelation in Jesus Christ; he wants to be and to remain entirely the other."[127] Such statements definitely express the intention to not regard Muhammad, and therefore also Islam, merely as precursors of Christianity. Küng and Leuze offer serious attempts to get beyond the impasse of reciprocal superiority claims, and in so doing they clearly point in a pluralist direction.[128]

121 Cp. on this once more Wengst 2004, 134-137. See above chapter 12, p. 288.
122 On this cp. also the corresponding references by Renz 2001, 50ff.
123 Cp. on this Renz' questions, 2002, 199.
124 Cp. Küng 1984, 57f.; Leuze 1994, 28, and Leuze 2001, 39.
125 Cp. Leuze 1994, 206f., n. 36; 2001, 39ff.
126 Cp. Küng, Ess, Stietencron, Bechert 1993, 129 (German original: 1984, 200).
127 Leuze 1994, 54.
128 Renz then rightly point out pluralist tendencies in Küng and Leuze (cp. Renz 2002, 234 and 337f). With reference to Küng, Kerr (1995, 441) makes similar judgments.

Wilfred Cantwell Smith

Wilfred Cantwell Smith (1916-2000),[129] who is one of the "fathers" of a pluralist theology of religions,[130] early on proposed a pluralist conception of the Christian-Islamic relationship. Smith was born in Toronto, Canada, and it was there that he first read Oriental Studies. In 1938, he transferred to Cambridge, England where he added Theology to Oriental Studies. In 1941 he went to Pakistan as a missionary, and in 1943 he was ordained as a minister of the United Church of North India. In Lahore, Pakistan, he taught Indian and Islamic history. On the basis of his experience of lived Islam, Hinduism, and Sikhism, and especially on the basis of close personal friendships with adherents of these religions, Smith revised his formerly conservative, even "fundamentalist," theological position.[131] In 1948 he graduated from Princeton with a degree in Oriental Studies and in 1949 he became Professor of Comparative Religion at McGill University in Montreal. From 1964-1973 he taught as Professor of World Religions at Harvard, from 1973-1978 once again in Canada at Dalhousie University of Halifax, and from 1978-1984, before he became an emeritus professor, once again at Harvard.

In his early publications, Smith concerned himself almost exclusively with the history of Modern Islam. His 1957 work, *Islam in Modern History*, is considered a modern classic. It was translated into numerous languages, including German, making it the only one of Smith's books available in German.[132] Beginning in the sixties, his publications focused on basic methodological questions of religious studies as well as on research into how faith is understood from the perspective of comparative religion. Since the seventies, questions surrounding a theology of religions increasingly preoccupied his publications. These, however, had also been present in his early works. This is particularly true of his renowned 1967 treatise, in which Smith tackles the question: "Is the Qur'an the Word of God?"[133]

Smith begins his exploration with the simple observation that for centuries a large section of humanity, namely Muslims, has answered this question with a decisive "Yes," whereas it has been decisively rejected for an equally long time by another large section of humanity, namely Christians. According to Smith, there can be no doubt that there were and are highly educated representatives of both answers on both sides. So why is it that this question has for such a long time been answered in such contrary ways? According to Smith the actual reason for this is that *both* responses work and thus each has its own justification, but that at the same time both sides have till now largely been blind to the insights of the other. Smith explains his thesis as follows:

129 Extensive bibliographic details can be found in Grünschloss 1994, 27-66.
130 On Smith, cp. also above chapter 6, p. 151, and chapter 10, pp. 228-232.
131 Cp. Grünschloss 1994, 32f., esp. n. 16.
132 W.C. Smith, *Der Islam in der Gegenwart*, Frankfurt 1963.
133 Smith 1967, 39-62, 84-95.

The "Yes" response, says Smith, is not the result of a critical examination but rather a response of faith. "Muslims do not read the Qur'an and then conclude that it is divine; rather, they believe that it is divine, and then they read it."[134] In this way, the "Yes" response has received a pragmatic confirmation:

> Those who have held the Qur'an to be the word of God have, by holding this, found that God does in fact speak to them through it. They have ordered their lives in accord with it, and have found that that pattern rewards them by bringing them into the divine presence. The Book promises to those who submit to its letter and spirit, guidance and boldness and inner peace and endurance in this world, and felicity in the next. We have no evidence on affairs in the next world, but so far as this world is concerned the promise, to those who believe, has in fact been redeemed.[135]

In this regard, Smith gives an enlightening clue. If one of his students reads the Qur'an and asks what in all the world might cause Muslims to consider this book to be the Word of God, he, Smith, recommends the opposite approach: the student should first imagine the Qur'an to be the Word of God, and then read it. Perhaps in this way the student may sense something of the deep impression that this book can make.

According to Smith, the No-response, however, has also found its confirmation. The notion, considered to be obvious by Christianity for centuries, that the Qur'an is not the Word of God, has come down in Oriental Studies, a child of modernity, as an unquestioned presupposition. In their research, Western scholars have taken for granted that the Qur'an is of purely worldly origin. They have searched for and found its worldly source: in Muhammad's psychology, in the circumstances of his life, in the tradition of which he was a part, and in his socio-economic context. According to Smith, this research has brought to light a whole series of uncontestable or at least extremely well-testified facts that have led to a historical interpretation of the Qur'an which is hard to dismiss.

According to Smith, the actual error of both sides lies in the fact that they have negated whatever truth is present in the other's response. Smith thus suggests the following solution: The question of whether the Qur'an is the Word of God cannot be posed in an abstract or ahistorical manner. God does not speak into a vacuum. When God speaks, God always speaks to concrete persons in concrete situations. So, properly stated, the question should be: Has God spoken through the Qur'an at particular places and times to concrete persons? When asked in this way, says Smith, the answer can be clearly affirmative: God has indeed spoken through the Qur'an to many, though not to all, people. In other words, as part of the Islamic religious tradition the Qur'an could indeed become the medium of divine revelation, but only as mediated through the faith of the persons participating in this tradition. As a re-

134 Ibid. 49.
135 Ibid. 51.

sponse that takes into account both the historical and the religious facts and thus integrates the truth of both sides, Smith therefore suggests:

> ...that the Qur'an was the word of Muhammad, historically conditioned, and that it was at the same time (...) the closest approximation to the eternal word of God to which Muhammad was capable of rising; and that since that time, thanks to the place that it has been given in the Islamic religious tradition, it has become and continues to be the word of God to many Muslims, varying in authenticity and largeness and intimacy from person to person and from hour to hour...[136]

Smith holds that the revelation of God through Jesus Christ should be understood in a strictly analogous way. Here too he suggests:

> Rather than saying that Jesus Christ is the full revelation of God, I would say rather that He is a revelation of God to me, and has been to many other people, though I know others to whom He has not been.[137]

Would such an integrative response that corresponds to a basically pluralist view of the relationship between Christianity and Islam prove to be acceptable to both sides? According to Smith, on the Christian side this depends above all on the further developments in the theology of religions. On the Muslim side, everything depends on the extent to which Islamic theology opens or closes itself to the insights of a historically oriented research of the Qur'an. According to Smith it is very clear that:

> The historical facts that give sense to the proposition that the Qur'an is a mundane product, can no more be gainsaid by Muslims than can, by outside observers, the religious facts that give sense to the proposition that it is a divine word, a power of God unto salvation for those that believe.[138]

Three aspects of Smith's theological interpretation of the Qur'an must be underlined here: *First,* Smith emphasizes that it would be inadequate to place the Qur'an on the same level as the Bible theologically. Whereas in Christianity the central medium of revelation is Jesus Christ and the Bible is only the testimony to this revelation, in Islam the central medium of revelation is the Qur'an.[139] In this respect Smith agrees in principle with Cragg. Yet for Smith the parallelism of Jesus and the Qur'an leads, *second,* to the need of understanding both Jesus and the Qur'an in their historical reality. Jesus and the Qur'an are both media of true revelation, but they are so as concrete, finite manifestations of human history. They mediate revelation to the extent that they elicit faith. And they fulfill this function to the extent that they belong to a living religious tradition that continues to the present. In this way, Smith

136 Ibid. 93.
137 Ibid. 91.
138 Ibid. 59.
139 Smith suggests that the position of the Bible corresponds better to that of the Hadith-literature, that is, the collection of Muhammad's sayings. Cp. Smith 1981, 239.

shows that neither the historical consideration of the Qur'an nor the historical consideration of Jesus necessarily entails disputing their functions as media of revelation. According to Smith both Jesus and the Qur'an work in a virtually sacramental[140] manner: as tangible realities they make present the intangible reality of God for the believer.[141] Smith thereby arrives, *third,* at a position in the theology of revelation that clearly goes far beyond Cragg. Whereas for Cragg the parallelism between Jesus and the Qur'an leads to the notion that in Christianity revelation is understood as the self-revelation of God and in Islam by contrast it is understood as the revelation of the divine will, Smith rejects this distinction. Although in this respect Smith's own position was initially similar to Cragg's,[142] he later concluded that every revelation is a divine self-communication: "what God reveals is always Himself."[143] Since, according to Smith, in Islam God's will is not distinct from God him/her/itself, Islam is no exception to this.[144] Smith's understanding of the parallel between Jesus and the Qur'an as central media of revelation thus matches his basic understanding of religious traditions as channels of divine self-disclosure: Jesus and the Qur'an are media of divine self-communication to the extent that they are central elements of their respective religious traditions.[145]

Smith's response to the question, "Is the Qur'an the Word of God?" consists, as we have seen, of a historicizing reformulation: "Has the Qur'an served God as his Word?" This can be answered in the affirmative because, among many Muslims, the Qur'an has elicited what can be assessed as an attitude of genuine saving faith.[146] In his later writings, Smith left a kind instructive postscript on this position: What is the religious significance of holy scriptures today? The fundamentalist movements, as they are now found in various religions, seem to indicate that today holy scriptures are a much less suitable instrument for God to rescue humanity from their evils and stupidities.[147] Yet this situation could take a turn for the better if religious communities learn to better understand that, and how, God is at work in the traditions and scriptures of other religions.[148]

A criticism often made of Smith is that he does not take seriously enough the doctrinal differences between religions in his understanding of faith and religious tradition. By postulating faith as a general attitude in which people of different religions respond to the divine self-communication, he would not sufficiently account for the influence that the sometimes grave differences between the beliefs of the var-

140 Cp. Smith 1993, 240. See also Renz 2002, 82ff.
141 Cp. Smith 1987, 61-66; Smith 1989, 174f.
142 Cp. Smith 1981, 36f (this contribution originally stems from 1961). But even here it already says: "In the Qur'ān, God makes Himself and His purpose known to man in the form of words." Ibid. 31.
143 Cp. Smith 1989, 173. See also Smith 1991, 21.
144 Cp. Smith 1989, 173f. Similarly Smith 1993, 47.
145 On this see also the discussion in chapter 10, p. 230.
146 Cp. Smith 1967, 84-95.
147 Cp. Smith 1992, 61.
148 Cp. ibid. 61f and Smith 1993, 216ff.

ious religions have on the respective faith of their adherents. Does Smith indeed level the differences between the religions, including those in the existential attitude of faith, too much? Kenneth Cragg has also made this criticism of Smith.[149] Yet Smith poses the decisive counter question: Is it not the reverse that is true? That we overestimate the significance of the theological or doctrinal differences when talking about saving faith?[150] Do we not all too easily assume that a Christian is not a Muslim and a Muslim is not a Christian? If, as Islamic tradition holds, the one who lives in true submission to God is a "Muslim," then—as Islam itself acknowledges—Abraham was just as much a Muslim as Jesus. But then, continues Smith, Christians are also "Muslims" in the true sense of the word.[151] And if a "Christian" is someone who follows and honors Jesus, then Muslims have also always been Christians.[152] For by their own understanding they honor Jesus and follow him in his adoration of God.[153]

Pluralist Perspectives

Incarnation and Trinity

Both Cragg's and Smith's work confirms how significant the concept of revelation is for the theological understanding of Christian-Islamic relations. Cragg has already shown that the Christian understanding of incarnation and the Christian doctrine of the Trinity are not affected by Islamic criticism if we interpret both strictly as claims about the role of Jesus as revealer: One can only speak of an incarnation of the eternal "Word of God" in the person of Jesus to the extent that Jesus is the mediator of a genuine divine revelation. And Islam does not contest that Jesus is a genuine mediator of revelation. To the contrary: the basis of Islamic Christology is the Qur'anic teaching that Jesus is a "sign" of God for the world.[154] That is, the Islamic interpretation of Jesus is also based primarily on Jesus' function as a revealer. Moreover, an inspiration Christology, as it is held by John Hick, has been met with great sympathy in the Islamic world.[155] Martin Bauschke—a scholar who, in the German speaking world, intensively examined the Islamic understanding of Jesus—emphasizes in his significant theses on Qur'anic Christology: In light of both Christian-Islamic and

149 Cp. Cragg 1992, esp. 260f.
150 "Our beliefs differ, and that is important. Yet it is not ultimately important; it is not what God Himself is finally interested in." Smith 1981, 281.
151 Cp. Smith 1981, 262.
152 Cp. ibid. 263.
153 Cp. ibid. 261.
154 Cp. Bauschke 2001, 123-129; Zirker 1993, 142ff.
155 Cp. Siddiqi 1989, 213; Cohn-Sherbok 1991, 18f. Hick's book, *The Myth of God Incarnate* was translated into Arabic soon after publication. Hick was the first Christian theologian to be invited to give a lecture at the Islamic University of Saudi Arabia, an invitation which however he did not accept. Cp. Goddard 1995, 7.

also Christian-Jewish dialogue, we must take fully into account the insights of New Testament exegesis into the theocentric attitude of Jesus. That is, Christology has to accommodate the fact that Jesus distinguished himself strongly from the one God to whom he had completely oriented his life. And in this way, Jesus also becomes understandable as someone whose life was utterly saturated by the Spirit of God.[156]

If, in the context of an inspiration Christology, it is possible to find more sense in the Chalcedon formula than Hick himself does, this does not necessarily have to mean a step backward for a Christian-Islamic understanding concerning Christology. For if—as suggested above[157]—one can interpret the Chalcedonian affirmation of the two natures of Jesus Christ as implying that every human or created reality that becomes a medium of divine revelation has a divine nature in the sense that what is revealed is truly divine (while the medium itself is not), then this is also true of the Qur'an. According to Frithjof Schuon, from an Islamic perspective one can speak of God becoming human wherever genuine revelation takes place since such revelation always assumes that the Divine expresses itself in human language. Consequently, according to Schuon, the phrase "true God and true man" applies in analogous fashion also to God's revelation through books.[158]

Moreover, Schuon emphasizes that the notion of Trinity "does not oppose anything within Islam's doctrine of unity," so long as Trinity is understood as "unfolding" or "appearance" (*tajallī*).[159] In so doing, Schuon picks up on a term that can stand both for cosmic and for quite personal forms of divine manifestations within Islam. This corresponds to the basic understanding of the doctrine of the Trinity as an expression of diverse human ways of experiencing the one God—a view that is already found in Cragg, but likewise also in Hick.[160] With reference to the Christian-Islamic dialogue, Hans Küng and Reinhard Leuze have emphasized that the Christian doctrine of the Trinity should not be understood as a statement "about God in himself and his innermost nature," but rather as a statement "about the manner in which God reveals himself."[161] This notion of a God who reveals himself requires, according to Leuze, that we "understand God's unity as a unity in difference." In this way, monotheism can be consistently preserved: "If we could succeed in making this understanding intelligible to Islam, then we would in one fell swoop be able to get rid of the problems which arise for Christian-Islamic dialogue in relation to this issue."[162]

Up to this point, such considerations have not yet been widely acknowledged on the Muslim side. The Christian-Islamic dialogue is still far too young for that. But it becomes unmistakably clear: An interpretation of the Trinity as referring not

156 Cp. Bauschke 2001a, 136-152 esp. 137f., 141ff., 146f.
157 Cp. above chapter 11, pp. 257-262.
158 Cp. Schuon 1985, 169 and ibid. n. 19. Similarly also Nasr 2000, 33ff.
159 Schuon 1993, 68.
160 On this, cp. again Hick 2001a, 154. Cp. above chapter 11, p. 266.
161 Cp. Küng, Ess, Stietencron, Bechert 1993, 120 (German original: 1984, 188).
162 Leuze 1994, 133.

to God's inner nature but rather to the diverse forms in which the one God reveals himself to people, cannot be affected by the Islamic critique since such understanding does not threaten monotheism. And an interpretation of incarnation according to which incarnation refers strictly to the issue of revelation neither places a human being on a level with God, nor does it pull God down to the level of the creature.

Joachim Gnilka has denounced such reflections, as they have been suggested within the context of pluralist theology of religions, as attempts at "finding unity by means of quasi diplomatic negotiation." According to Gnilka, such efforts would "do a disservice to both religions" and cause "serious harm" to both traditions.[163] This criticism is completely misplaced. For it ignores in a surprisingly ahistorical way that the doctrines of incarnation and Trinity evolved in the course of history and are, to a large extent, liable to interpretation and change. They are interpretaments of the revelation in Jesus, and not the revealed, immutable content of the revelation itself. Gnilka also overlooks the fact that the critique which Islam directed at these doctrines in the past does not necessarily hit that understanding of Trinity and incarnation as it, for various reasons, suggest itself today. To establish old oppositions as insurmountable would amount to denying to both Islamic and Christian theology any possibility of further development and advancement in knowledge. In contrast, we need to emphasize, in the words of Hans Zirker, that:

> If the dialogue partner is to be taken seriously, one cannot have dialogue without *relativizing* one's own position toward *the possibility of some kind of better insight*—perhaps even in relation to some element that had been regarded as "essential." (…) Either we expose ourselves to the experiment of reaching a common understanding (…) or we remove ourselves from the risk of such openness by excluding part of our convictions as being absolutely definite.[164]

Muhammad and Jesus

Has the revelation of God as Christians believe they recognize it in Jesus also been heard by Islam? According to Kenneth Cragg, the "Jesus of the Gospels" is "unrecognizable" in the Jesus of the Qur'an.[165] Since the Qur'an denies Jesus' crucifixion it also denies, says Cragg, not only the true nature of Jesus but also the true nature of God as it is disclosed in Jesus' fate. In the final analysis, Muhammad—according to Cragg—knows only the God of power, of triumph, and of glory. He does not know the love that is revealed on the cross, the love that is offered to the sinner to the utmost. According to Cragg, this becomes evident in a paradigmatic way in the biographies of Jesus and Muhammad, since two diametrically opposed decisions are

163 Gnilka 2004, 184.
164 Zirker 1993, 139f.
165 Cp. Cragg 1956, 296.

contrasted here: The decision of Jesus not to defend himself against the hostility of his opponents, not to counter evil with evil, brought him to the cross.[166] The decision of Muhammad, in light of the resistance he encountered, to go to Medina and rise to political leadership brought him back to Mecca as a victorious conqueror. According to Cragg, both these decisions are equally comprehensive—and as Cragg writes—equally "formative" for Christianity and Islam.[167]

Muslim authors also sometimes share the opinion that the Qur'anic Jesus "has little in common with the Jesus of the Gospels,"[168] or that "the Jesus of the Gospels, who consorts with sinners, is not often encountered in the Muslim gospel..."[169] So is Cragg right in saying that the mercy of God finds a far more radical expression in Jesus than in Muhammad? Does this mean the revelation witnessed to in Christianity is superior to what we find in the Islamic testimony of revelation? And does this imply that with regard to Islam a pluralist interpretation of the relationship must ultimately fail?

In a short essay John Hick offers some noteworthy reflections regarding the comparison of Muhammad and Jesus and their respective paradigmatic significance.[170] To begin with, says Hick, we need to think of the totally different life contexts of Jesus and Muhammad: Jesus was a craftsman and a member of a people oppressed by Rome. He had neither political power nor responsibility. But above all it was his apocalyptic expectation of an imminent end of the world that kept him away from any kind of political activity. Thus his message was totally oriented to the individual and focused on individual repentance, but not on political or social change. He never faced those problems, says Hick, which fell upon Christianity after the year 310 with the uniting of ecclesial and state power: From that point on Christianity also had to offer a political framework for the life of society. "When this happened...the original gospel of love, with its pacifist implications, quickly gave way to the harsh law of the Church-State."[171]

In contrast, Muhammad grew up as a member of one of the leading tribes of Arabia. He lived in a society in which the founding of a new religious movement necessarily implied the founding of a new community. And founding a new community necessarily meant founding a new political power. In order to survive, the new religious community was forced to follow the rules of politics. A development that only happened gradually in Christianity over the course of more than three centuries, happened in Islam within the short time span of the life of its founder.[172]

166 Cp. ibid. 298.
167 Cp. ibid. 93.
168 Khalidi 2003, 16.
169 Ibid., 57.
170 Cp. Hick 1991e.
171 Ibid. 115.
172 With this reflection, says Renz (2002, 193f), Hick brings things "to the heart of the matter."

Like Cragg, Hick too holds that the differences between Jesus and Muhammad are of paradigmatic significance. But in contrast to Cragg, Hick sees embodied in them two equally important aspects of religious truth:

> One is the transforming claim of God upon the individual, thereby creating a redeemed community of saints, the church, as a select minority in an unredeemed world. The other is the claim of God upon society as a whole, sinners and saints alike, but with laws inevitably written with sinners in mind.[173]

According to Hick, both aspects are complementary. Christianity and Islam have actually developed both of these complementary aspects. Christianity began with the high ideals of the Sermon on the Mount that were totally geared to the individual, and by which no state could ever be governed. But when Christianity was challenged to assume responsibility, it quickly developed doctrines of the state that incorporated all kinds of force and violence: police force, punitive force, the teaching about just war and the sanctioning of violence to defend and disseminate faith. By contrast, the Qur'an contains an ethic which, compared to the Sermon on the Mount, is much less demanding and idealistic, but is thus easier to practice and hence from the beginning could serve as the basis of general laws. Yet at the level of individual piety, Islam also developed very high and ideal notions of perfect love. According to Hick both aspects need one another. That is, at the individual level the challenge set out by divine reality can and should always be greater than the challenge at the level of society, which must find generally practicable, but thus also *sub-ideal* regulations, whose implementation in a number of cases demands the use of force.

One can find similar judgments regarding the paradigmatic positions of Jesus and Muhammad on the Islamic side. In response to the pervasive Christian accusation that Islam is a religion of the sword whereas Christianity by contrast is a religion of love, the Muslim scholar Seyyed Hossein Nasr writes:

> It is true that Islam has legislation for even war whereas Christianity orders man to turn the other cheek, and is mild and gentle in its teachings. But what is forgotten is that either a religion is made for saints as Christ said: "My Life is not of this world," in which case it leaves aside political, social and economic questions and envisages all of its followers as potential saints and, in fact, can only function in a society of saints. Or a religion tries to encompass the whole of man's life, in which case it must take into account the whole of man's nature with all the weaknesses and shortcomings it has, and legislate for the political and economic life of man as well as for the purely religious aspects of his existence.[174]

In this sense Nasr, like Hick, sees Jesus as the representative of high ideals centered on individual saintliness. By contrast, Muhammad is a saint "who sanctifies the very life of the world by living in it and accepting it with the aim of integrating it into a

173 Ibid. 118.
174 Nasr 2000, 18.

higher order reality."[175] As distinct from Jesus, Muhammad's revelation thus also includes legal regulations that form the basis for implementing the divine will within societal life.[176]

Therefore neither Hick nor Nasr dispute that in the case of Jesus the ethical and spiritual demands are more radical than in the case of Muhammad. But this is not the same as saying that there is a difference in the perception of the determination of God's mercy and thus a difference in the quality of revelation—as has been suggested by Cragg. Rather, it is about a difference in the moral demands at the different levels of individual and societal life. The high demands of personal saintliness cannot be transferred wholesale to society. And the neglect of societal realities at the level of a very high individual ethos can only too easily—as Nasr notes—lead to this ethos losing all its relevance at the societal level.[177]

Yet how is Islam doing in relation to its claim of implementing God's will at the societal level? One cannot claim that the legal requirements of the Qur'an are simply an expression of Muhammad's high-handed, autocratic power consciousness. Compared to the conditions of the time, they actually reveal clearly humanizing tendencies:[178] punishments were reduced and blood vengeance was curbed. Some completely new forms of punishment were introduced, such as feeding the poor. The killing of newborn girls was sharply condemned and forbidden. Slaves were to be treated humanely and if possible were to be ransomed. The state had the duty to support the poor and the needy by means of the newly introduced obligatory social tax. In all business dealings, fairness was the guiding principle. Even the Qur'anic rules on warfare offer evidence of a humanizing spirit:

> The Muslim warriors are not allowed to be "unrestrained in their killing."[179] People in the enemy zone who are not participating in the warfare (like women, children, monks, hermits, the old, the blind, and mentally ill persons) are not to be bothered. During battle, Muslim soldiers may not perpetrate any atrocities, for example by additionally disfiguring dead enemies, or spearing severed heads on their lances. Unnecessary devastation and destruction of the enemy's and the stranger's property and possessions is to be avoided.[180]

In the opinion of C. Weeramantry, former Vice-President of the International Criminal Court in The Hague, the regulations regarding prisoners of war found in Islamic law in many ways anticipate the Geneva Convention and in part even exceed it.[181] In light of a long tradition of martial law, which clearly aims at justice and the limitation of violence, many Muslim scholars today emphasize that the murderous acts of

175 Ibid. 61.
176 Cp. ibid., 17ff; 94ff.
177 Cp. ibid. 19.
178 Cp. Khoury 1995, 20.
179 Sūrah 17,33.
180 Khoury 1995, 35. On this, cp. the extended treatment of Islamic rules of war in Weeramantry 2002, 134-138. For the basic ideas of Islamic law, see ibid., 59-93.
181 Cp. Weeramantry 2002, 135.

"Islamic terrorists" who show no regard for the life of non-combatants, or who take the lives of women and children, are in stark contrast to the spirit and letter of Islamic law.[182]

The fundamental Qur'anic idea of the equality of all human beings before God and the resulting call for just treatment led, among other things, to the fact that slaves within traditional Islamic societies had a much better legal status than they did in the societies of Ancient Greece and Rome, or even in the Christian-shaped societies of the Americas in the early modern period.[183] For this reason it is not surprising that the particularly strong acceptance of Muhammad's message among slaves and members of the lower social classes is not limited to the beginnings of Islam in Mecca. Rather, this has remained a characteristic of Islam until the recent past. The nineteenth century slave revolt of Bahia in Brazil led to the establishment of the first Islamic republic of modern times, although it did not last long, suffering military defeat soon after its formation.[184] It is widely known that in the second half of the twentieth century many African Americans considered an Islamic state to be their only hope for equality in the U.S., the establishment of which was for some time the goal of the "Black Muslims."[185]

Hans Küng and Hendrik Vroom emphasize that the acknowledgement of the prophetic mission of Muhammad is imperative also because "Muhammad linked his monotheism to a humanism" and "to the demand for social justice,"[186] and because he "moved people to a righteous and compassionate life."[187] At the same time, the strong focus on society and law found in Islamic ethics does not preclude an Islamic appreciation of the ideals embodied by Jesus and their significance for the individual person. Already in the Qur'an (57,27) we find the following about Jesus as the Word of Allah:

> We sent after them [i.e. the preceding messengers] Jesus, the Son of Mary, and bestowed on him the Gospel; and We ordained in the hearts of those who followed him compassion, mercy and monasticism.

"Monasticism" here likely also stands for the high individual ethic of a freely chosen, ascetic life. The following hadith clearly shows how much Islam views what Jesus embodied as valid at the level of individual piety:[188]

182 On this, see the contributions in Çapan 2004. See also Hofmann 2002, 50; "There was and is no Islamic justification for the killing of thousands in New York and Washington." Abou El Fadl, 2001, presents a nuanced discussion of terror and rebellion within the Islamic legal tradition.
183 Cp. Weeramantry 2002, 139.
184 Cp. Duran 1990, 440.
185 Cp. ibid. 445-449.
186 Küng, Ess, Stietencron, Bechert 1993, 26 (1984, 58).
187 Vroom 1996, 121.
188 A *hadith* is typically a saying of Muhammad that has been passed down. A word of Muhammad that contains not the opinion of the prophet but a word of God is known as a "holy hadith" (*hadith qudsi*) and thus constitutes something like an extra-Qur'anic revelation.

> Allah (mighty and sublime be He) will say on the Day of Resurrection: 'O Son of Adam, I fell ill and you visited Me not. He will say: O Lord, and how should I visit You when You are the Lord of the worlds? He will say: Did you not know that My servant So-and-so had fallen ill and you visited him not? Did you not know that had you visited him you would have found Me with him? O son of Adam, I asked you for food and you fed Me not. He will say: O Lord, and how should I feed You when You are the Lord of the worlds? He will say: Did you not know that my servant So-and-so asked you for food and you fed him not? Did you not know that had you fed him you surely would have found that with Me? O son of Adam, I asked you to give Me to drink and you gave Me not to drink. He will say: O Lord, how should I give You to drink when You are the Lord of the worlds? He will say: My servant So-and-so asked you to give him to drink and you gave him not to drink. Had you given him to drink you would have surely found that with Me.'[189]

It is evident that this hadith constitutes a positive Islamic reaction to Mathew 25:31ff. Yet this is by no means an isolated occurrence. There are several clear parallels between the Islamic Jesus-tradition and the New Testament tradition. But precisely because Islam has its own distinct way of perceiving Jesus,[190] there is the danger in Islam of ignoring the Christian view of Jesus, or of only perceiving it through the filter of the Islamic depiction of Jesus. It is one of the great opportunities of Christian-Muslim dialogue to change this situation so that the biblical testimony may, in the future, enrich the Islamic understanding of Jesus to a much greater degree than has thus far been the case.[191] From a pluralist perspective it is by no means advisable to level the difference between the Qur'anic and biblical image of Jesus. Equally unsatisfactory is the traditional solution that acknowledges the differences but simply discards the differences in the depiction of Jesus on the other side as misunderstandings and falsifications. Instead we need to fully recognize the differences and simultaneously consider the possible complementarity of the insights found in those different views.

In principle, such a complementarity is conceivable because for the Qur'an too it is beyond question that "my Lord is indeed full of mercy and loving-kindness" (11,90). Or as it says even more pointedly in one of the holy hadiths:

> When Allah decreed the Creation He pledged Himself by writing in His book which is laid down with Him: My mercy prevails over My wrath.[192]

This hadith speaks of the heavenly original Qur'an, of God's eternal word whose earthly manifestation is held to be the Arabic Qur'an. If we turn again to the parallel of Jesus and the Qur'an as the central mediators of revelation, then the following holds true for both religious communities: The God who reveals him/her/itself

189 Ibrahim; Johnson-Davies 1997, 88ff.
190 Cp. Risse 1989; Bauschke 2001a; Khalidi 2003.
191 Cp. on this Bauschke 2001a, 133f; Zirker 1993, 18-22.
192 Ibrahim; Johnson-Davies 1997, 40.

to humans in the Qur'an and in Jesus is that God whose mercy is stronger than his righteous anger at sin.

Kenneth Cragg's paradigmatic contrast between the cross of Jesus and the *hijrah* of Muhammad is therefore wrong in its central point. That is, one cannot derive from the Qur'anic denial of the crucifixion of Jesus that Islam lacks a deeper understanding of God's mercy. It is also true in Islam that when it comes to the relation of God to humans the *lex talionis* in which God repays measure for measure does not have the last word. The power of God over the sin of humans does not consist of the triumph of divine anger but rather of the triumph of divine mercy. And the response of humans to the goodness of God correspondingly consists of being good to others, even one's enemy:

> Allah said: "Give, O Son of Adam, I give for you.[193]

and

> Nor can Goodness and Evil
> Be equal. Repel (Evil)
> With what is better:
> Then will he between whom
> And thee was hatred
> Become as it were
> Thy friend and intimate!
> (Sūrah 41,34).

But then what does the Qur'anic denial of Jesus' crucifixion mean? It is rather difficult to discern the exact sense of the Qur'anic verses (4,157f). The translation possibilities vary significantly, and no less so the interpretations within Islamic tradition.[194] A large portion of Islamic tradition understands the text as saying that God made another person (many think Judas) look similar to Jesus and crucified him in Jesus' place. Others, especially those in the Ahmadiyya tradition, assume that Jesus survived the crucifixion and subsequently escaped to India. Still others say that God, unnoticed by the executioners, elevated Jesus to himself and in so doing protected him from death. The assumption into heaven happened, so to say, directly from the cross. A related view speculates that only the external bodily husk of Jesus was crucified, while his true being was preserved from death.

Despite all these various theories, one central concern of the Qur'anic message remains fairly clear: In the final analysis, the powers that were opposed to God and wanted to annihilate Jesus were not successful. Mahmoud Ayoub thus interprets the Qur'anic denial of the killing of Jesus as "a denial of the power of men to vanquish and destroy the divine Word, which is forever victorious."[195] Hans Zirker agrees that

193 Translation follows Denffer 1987, 50.
194 Cp. the overview in Zirker 1993, 135-142 and especially in Bauschke 2001, 83-114.
195 Ayoub 1980, 117. On Ayoub's place in the Islamic-Christian dialogue see also Siddiqui 1997, 97-109.

this interpretation is also "acceptable from a Christian perspective." Seen in this way, the relevant Qur'anic passage even contains a "bit of the Easter message." According to Zirker, this is a "fundamentally" possible interpretation for Muslims, even if the majority of Muslims would presumably (for now?) not accept it.[196] Yet however one interprets the Qur'anic denial of the crucifixion of Jesus, it is in any case not the intention of the Qur'an hereby to dispute God's absolute mercy and willingness to forgive.

Kenneth Cragg imputes that the Qur'an understands God's victory over the forces opposed to God one-sidedly as merely a triumph of power. For Cragg Islam thus propagates an image of God that is concretely realized in Muhammad's power politics and that has allegedly exercised a "formative" influence on the entire Islamic tradition. In so doing, Cragg in the end succumbs to a polemical, apologetically motivated depiction of Islam that does not correspond to the historical facts. The politics of Christian states have not relied any less on military might than is the case with Islamic states. And Islam need not shy away from a historic comparison of the humane aspects between the Christian and Islamic exercise of power. What Cragg addresses here is actually a danger that affects both Islam and Christianity, since this danger is unavoidably connected to the challenge of shaping political life on the basis of a religious spirit. No religion that has taken on this challenge has been left unscathed by the danger of an overly close entanglement between power and religion or even of a perversion of religion into political power.

Christians share with Muslims the concern that the goodness and justice of God must also become visible in how people regulate their civil cohabitation. Apart from the relic of the Vatican State, today Christians have largely abandoned the notion of a state dominated and shaped only by Christianity or by a particular Christian denomination. The separation of religion and state might be comparatively harder to endorse by Muslims since Islam has not developed an ecclesial institution, but rather became woven into the fabric of civil politics from the beginning. Yet Islam has also a long experience of existing within non-Islamic states, so that both theoretically and practically Islam is familiar with the separation of religion and state. Therefore, the actual challenge to Islam will presumably be the question of to what extent it can endorse, on the basis of its own theological presuppositions, the concept of an open, ideologically pluralistic society. This is strongly debated within contemporary Islam,[197] and the answer will largely depend on whether, and to what extent, one regards the concrete legal regulations of the Qur'an and of Islamic law as historically contingent and therefore as potentially changeable. A further problem in this regard lies in the question of how Islam relates to religious diversity. Referring to the Qur'anic designation of Muhammad as the "Seal of the Prophets," Reinhard Lenze writes:

196 Zirker 1993, 141f.

197 Cp. on this also the overview in Ridgeon 2004, as well as the contributions in Kurzmann 1998.

> Don't we find here the same consciousness of finality that Christians have cultivated for nearly two thousand years, only in order to recognize now that in their enthusiasm for their faith they were defending claims that are too grandiose? And don't we have to ascertain in relation to Muslims as well as to Christians, that they irresponsibly restrict the sovereignty of God in the interests of their particular faith by furnishing their own faith perspective with the claim of finality?[198]

Can Islam relativize this kind of self-understanding? Can it give up its traditionally inclusivist stance toward Judaism and Christianity as well as its exclusivist tendencies toward almost all other religions, and instead accept a pluralist position? Or will it have to remain the goal of Islam to strive for the Islamization of the world and the overcoming of all other religions, so that at best—according to the traditional model—only a subordinated, tolerated status can be granted to these other religions within the framework of an Islamic society?

Pluralist Islam

Under traditional presuppositions, says Hans Zirker, "there are no starting points in Islam for a 'pluralist theology of religions'" except for in Islamic mysticism, which "occasionally (crosses) theologically defined boundaries."[199] There is no doubt that Islam, in accordance with its traditional presuppositions, is just as non-pluralist as any of the other major religious traditions. Hence there is no question that the few Muslim voices that are beginning to edge toward a pluralist position are not representative, as Zirker rhetorically notes.[200] And Zirker's observation that these voices often allude to Islam's mystical tradition is equally correct. But why should these observations establish anything other than that Islam does actually offer certain roots that allow Muslim thinkers to embark on a pluralist path and in so doing modify or even change the traditional presuppositions? This is exactly what is happening in a whole series of Muslim scholars such as Mohammed Arkoun, Hasan Askari, Adnan Aslan, Mahmut Aydin, Mahmoud Ayoub, Ashgar Ali Engineer, Farid Esack, Seyyed Hossein Nasr,[201] Abdulaziz Sachedina, Abdulkarim Soroush, and others who, though with different consistency, are moving in a pluralist direction.[202]

198 Leuze 2001,41.
199 Zirker 1996, 198.
200 Cp. ibid. 200.
201 Like all representatives of the "traditional school" Nasr is of course just as opposed to the idea of changing or modifying the tradition as he is to the notion that there could be something of spiritual value in modernity. Yet this changes nothing about the fact that Nasr actually in many respects does deviate from conventional Islamic positions and represents viewpoints that were developed in the engagement with the challenges of modernity. As Aslan ironically but appropriately comments, the "traditional point of view is not traditional in the sense that traditional people understood it." Aslan 1998, 129.
202 On this, cp. the bibliographical information in chapter 6, p. 155.

The theological foundation of an Islamic pluralism rests above all on the following three Qur'anic pillars: *First*, the emphasis on a universal chance of salvation for all those who live in righteousness and true fear of God, even if they are nominally not Muslims (2,62. 112. 213; 5,72; 20,112). *Second,* the conviction that God has left no people without the necessary revelation or prophetic direction (5,19. 48; 10,47; 14,4; 35,24). *Third,* the confession of the absolute transcendence of God that surpasses all human forms of expression (17,43; 37,180; 112,4).

But not unfrequently Muslim authors vacillate between a broadly conceived inclusivism and a pluralist position. The decisive and for Muslims thorny question concerns the place of Muhammad, or more exactly, the finality of the Qur'an. This corresponds to the centrality of Christology in the Christian discussion of a pluralist theology of religions. So we see here once again the functional parallelism between Christ and the Qur'an. One of the Muslim pluralists, Mahmut Aydin, who teaches in Turkey, has consciously addressed this parallelism. Aydin suggests to define the place of the Qur'an in a similar way as Paul Knitter does regarding the place of Jesus Christ, so

> … that Muslims not consider God's revelation to the prophet Muhammad as "full, definitive, and unsurpassable" but, rather, as the "universal, decisive, and indispensable" message of God.[203]

Aydin explains this position in the following way: *First,* the Qur'anic revelation is not *full,* because it does not exhaust all the truth of divine revelation, that is, "since, theologically speaking, no created medium can exhaust the fullness of the Infinite."[204] *Second*, the Qur'an is *not the definitive* Word of God in as much as normative expressions of the Word of God are also found outside of the Qur'an. *Third,* the revelation of God in the Qur'an is not *unsurpassable* because Muslims cannot hold "that God could not reveal Godself in other ways apart from the Qur'an at other times."[205]

On the other hand the revelation of God in the Qur'an is *universal,* because the Qur'anic message of the grace of God and a life that is pleasing to God has significance for all people at all times. Yet this does not exclude the possibility that other religious figures and other divine revelations may be of similar universal significance. *Second*, the Qur'anic revelation is of *decisive* importance insofar as it gives life a salvific orientation. It offers a decisive norm, one which excludes some other norms as incompatible, but which does not deny the validity of all other norms. *Third*, the Qur'anic revelation is indispensable in the sense that it has enriched and transformed the lives of Muslims and can have the same effect in the lives of others.[206]

203 Aydin 2001, 349, with reference to Knitter 1997b, 7f.
204 Aydin 2001, 349.
205 Ibid.
206 Cp. ibid. 349f.

In this way, says Aydin, the significance of the Qur'an and of the Prophet Muhammad can be affirmed without absolutizing them. Muhammad and the Qur'an are and will remain central for Muslims. But this does not preclude the possibility of Muslims recognizing a similarly central role of other figures and media of revelation for people of other faiths. It is for this reason, says Aydin, that interreligious dialogue must become a formative factor in future Islamic theology.[207] That is, in and through dialogue Muslims can and should try to understand their non-Muslim partners from the perspective of their respective self-understanding. Muslims and non-Muslims alike should be open to being challenged by the other's perspective and to learning from one another so that new theological developments become possible. One can better recognize the limitations of one's own position in light of the message of the other, so that jointly both sides can arrive at a deeper understanding of transcendent reality or better, of their experiences with this reality. Absoluteness and finality should not be claimed for religious systems and not be posed against one another. Absoluteness and finality rather refer to the existential claim that each particular message makes with regard to its practical realization in our life. Therefore the aim is not to convert the other to one's own religion, but rather a deeper conversion of all dialogue partners to divine reality.[208]

Are Islamic pluralists prepared also to expand such ideas beyond the circle of Abrahamic religions, the "people of the book," to include the great religious traditions of Asia? As far as I know, Aydin does not explicitly address this question. Yet the Qur'anic notion to which Aydin frequently refers, that God has sent his messengers to every people, seems to imply this possibility. Based on these Qur'anic statements, Adnan Aslan holds that among God's messengers are also those "who are not mentioned in the Qur'an, including Gautama the Buddha and the avatars of the Hindus."[209] Mahmoud Ayoub makes a similar judgment. As the criterion for discerning genuine prophets, Ayoub suggests that they are in substantial conformity with the two basic tenets of the Qur'an: the affirmation/preservation of divine transcendence and of its ethical-spiritual significance in human life.[210] Seyyed Hossein Nasr points out that various Qur'an commentators supported the view that the prophet *Dhu'l-kifl* (mentioned in the Qur'an 21,85f.; 38,48) was actually the Buddha.[211] And Nasr adds that some Muslim jurists seriously considered to count Buddhists and Hindus among the "people of the book."[212] Nasr himself explicitly includes the major Asian religions such as Hinduism, Buddhism, and Daoism in the circle of valid religions. For according to Nasr, these neither lack the basic elements of a path to salva-

207 Cp. ibid. 350f.
208 Cp. Aydin 2001a, 245f.
209 Aslan 1996, 174. Similarly also Engineer 2003.
210 Cp. Ayoub 1997, 110ff.
211 Cp. Nasr 1997, 523.
212 Cp. ibid. 528. Also Scott 1998, 208. Yet Nasr is silent about the fact that for the greater part, Islamic tradition has considered Buddhism to be idol worship (cp. Scott 1998, 196ff) and Hinduism to be polytheism.

tion (knowledge, love, righteous works), nor the testimony to an ultimate transcendent reality: According to Nasr, behind the ostensible polytheism of Hinduism one finds the deeply profound metaphysics of the non-duality of ultimate reality. And in Buddhism, much like in Daoism, one understands divine reality in an impersonal way. According to Nasr, such differences merely reflect a diversity of viewpoints.[213] For in the end, divine reality in its absolute transcendence stands above all finite designations, whether these are of a personal or an impersonal nature.[214] The one transcendent reality is infinitely elevated above the multiplicity of all forms. Yet at the same time it creatively produces this multiplicity as the medium of its revelation.[215]

Islam is linked with Hinduism and Buddhism through a long history of encounters: in Central Asia, China, India, and South East Asia. All too often these encounters were marked by tensions and violent conflicts. But there are also examples of Islamic, Hindu, and Buddhist spirituality having a fruitful impact on one another: such as Indian Sufism, which draws extensively on Hindu and Buddhist roots; or the great figures of the North Indian *nirguna bhakti* movements, such as Kabir or Guru Nanak, who were deeply shaped by the Islamic emphasis on the absolute transcendence and oneness of God, and who had just as many Hindus as Muslims among their followers. In more recent times, however, there have been two events which demonstrate with much symbolic force the potential for conflict between these religions: the destruction of the almost five hundred years old Babri mosque in Ayodhya by an incited Hindu mob in 1992 with the subsequent rioting that claimed the lives of several hundred people, and the destruction of the fifteen hundred year-old Buddha statues and frescoes in Bamiyan by the Taliban in 2001. Dialogue between Hinduism and Islam and between Buddhism and Islam is more important and urgent today than ever before. Despite a long history of encounter, the dialogue between these religions is in its infancy at best.[216] Muslim pluralists have begun to carry out a good deal of important theological preparation necessary for this dialogue.[217] It is only desirable, also from a Christian perspective, that this development grows much stronger in the coming years. For a Christian and pluralist theology of religions does not only appreciate those interreligious relationships in which Christianity is involved.

213 Cp. Nasr 1993, 38, 56ff., 67 n. 11, 72f.; Nasr 1999.
214 Cp. ibid. 7ff.
215 Cp. on this esp. Nasr 1989, 280-308. For a comparison between Hick's and Nasr's positions, see Aslan 1998.
216 On Muslim-Buddhist dialogue see Ikeda, Tehranian 2004. On the multifaceted tensions between Hindus and Muslims in India, see Weiss et al., 1996. For a theological interpretation of Hindu-Muslim relations, see Smith 1981, 217-230.
217 Cp. for example Hasa Askari's sensitive appreciation of the Bhagavadgita in Askari 1991b, 71-79.

14. Christianity and Hinduism

Colonialism and Neo-Hinduism

The Beginnings of Indian Christianity

Possibly Christianity reached India already in the first Christian century.[1] There is a tradition according to which the Apostle Thomas brought the message of Jesus to the South Indian coast and proclaimed it both to the Jewish congregations there and also to adherents of other non-Christian religions. He allegedly died a violent death in India, on which there are however different accounts: some say he suffered a martyr's death at the command of an enraged king; some say he was accidentally struck by a stray arrow; others that he died at the hand of a Brahmin—although this last version was only written down toward the end of the sixteenth century.[2] In any case, native accounts agree that pre-colonial Indian Christians trace their origins back to the ministry of the Apostle Thomas, and for this reason call themselves "Thomas-Christians."

We are able to corroborate very little about the beginnings of Christianity in India historically. However, India had trade relations with the Mediterranean world early on. Thanks to the conquests of Alexander the Great, the land route to North India was opened up, as well as the sea route to Alexandria via the ports on the southwest coast of India. For this reason one cannot exclude the possibility of a rather early Christian presence in India. However, clearer evidence of Christian churches in India only exists since the beginning of the sixth century.[3] These were churches composed mainly of Syrian- and Nestorian-influenced Christians. The location of early Christian centers along the area of the most important ports of the southwest coast of India indicates that the Christian communities presumably profited greatly from the presence of Christian traders and seafarers, and probably recruited heavily from among them originally. The burgeoning of Islam, however, led to a massive reduction in Christian-dominated trade relationships and caused an almost complete isolation of the Indian Christians from Western Christianity.

1 The contributions in Coward 1989 offer an overview on the encounter of Hinduism and Christianity from the beginnings to the present. Sharpe 1977 mainly covers the religions' encounters of the nineteenth and twentieth centuries. Kuttianimattathil 1995 gives an excellent overview of theology in India. Both the 1997 and 1998 volumes by Bsteh offer, in loose thematic order, some more and some less relevant aspects.

2 Cp. Neill 1984, 27, 33f.; Thomas, P. 1954, 17.

3 Cp. Neill 1984, 49.

Early Christianity was apparently able to establish itself in South India without choosing the path of radical confrontation with the indigenous religions. Christians in the coastal region of Kerala were in general well-to-do and well regarded. To a certain extent, they adapted themselves to their Hindu context and in many cases conducted friendly exchange with the Hindus. They were integrated into the caste system as somewhat like a caste on their own.[4] There are no plausible indications of intensive missionary efforts,[5] but, as already mentioned in chapter 6, there are signs that the Thomas Christians even cultivated something akin to proto-pluralist attitudes.[6]

Christian Mission under Portuguese and British Rule

The face of Christianity in India changed drastically with the arrival of Portuguese Catholics at the beginning of the modern era. The successful circumnavigation of Africa at the end of the fifteenth century opened up a new sea route to India and hence a way to circumvent the barrier of Islamic countries. Portugal now established itself as the dominant seafaring power and made Goa in southern India its main colonial outpost. In 1498, Vasco de Gama landed in India and twelve years later (1510) the Portuguese conquered the then Muslim-ruled town of Goa. They burned down the mosques and killed thousands of Muslims. The King of Portugal's immediate claim of being the "Lord of India" was, of course, utterly exaggerated. Till 1961, Goa remained a Portuguese enclave in India. But a particularly profitable one, for this granted Portugal control of the sea trade for a century to come.

In 1418, Pope Martin V called Christianity to conquer the unbelievers and root out their false beliefs. In 1452, Pope Nicholas V gave the King of Portugal and his successors the authority to attack the lands of unbelievers, conquer them, and make the inhabitants subject to the Portuguese Crown and the Catholic faith, a dictate reaffirmed by Pope Sixtus IV in 1481.[7] The theological understanding of legal authority from which one derived the dispensation of such "commission" is clearly expressed by Pope Innocent IV, an important canonist of the thirteenth century:

> We believe that the pope, who is the vicar of Christ, has power not only over Christians but also over all unbelievers, since Christ has power over all.[8]

4 Cp. Amaladass 1990, 18f.
5 Cp. Neill 1984, 49.
6 Cp. above chapter 6, pp. 148f.. Besides the literature mentioned there in n. 4, see also Amaladass 1990.
7 Cp. Neill 1984, 111f.
8 Quoted following Neil 1984, 400.

The Christian presence in conquered Goa manifested itself in all its ambivalence. On the one hand, it resulted in the establishment of Christian charity such as hospitals, orphanages, and the support of the needy. On the other hand, it also resulted in the persecution of people of other faiths, and in the establishment of the Inquisition. Initially, the Portuguese religious politics in Goa, at least toward the Hindus, was still marked by relative tolerance: It "merely" prohibited the open practice of Hindu rituals and the public erection of Hindu images. But this was followed very quickly by the destruction of all Hindu temples, which was completed in 1545. In 1559, the Portuguese forbade the possession of Hindu ritual objects on pain of life-long galley slavery. In 1560, they began expelling Brahmins who were unwilling to convert.[9] In 1567, the Church in Goa forbade the practice of all "heathen rites" as well as paying "honour ... to the name of Muhammad." Conversion was allowed only to Christianity, not in any other direction.[10] The Church now also undertook missionary activities beyond Goa, but primarily focused on those southwest and southeast regions of India in which there were already Thomas Christians.

According to Francis Xavier, who first set foot in Goa in 1542, "the invocations of the pagans are hateful to God, since all their gods are devils."[11] In a letter to the King of Portugal, Saint Francis recommended bringing the Inquisition to India in order—following the Spanish model—to consolidate the faith of the newly converted Christians.[12] Formally, the Inquisition was launched in India in 1560 and already within the first seven years of its existence it organized eleven official auto-da-fés, which caused fear and horror to spread throughout Goa.[13] According to the careful reckoning of the historian Stephen Neill, there were a total of 16,172 Inquisition trials during this time. However, as Neill explains, "it is ... impossible to calculate the number of those who died miserably in the dungeons without ever having been brought to trial ..."[14] Even the Thomas Christians, to the extent that they tried to maintain their theological and liturgical traditions, were for many years massively oppressed and partially expelled by the Portuguese Catholics.

A very different picture emerged at the same time in the empire of the Mogul Emperor Akbar (1556-1605). Born as a Muslim, Akbar's personal religiosity was apparently strongly influenced by Sufism as well as Hindu mysticism. Contrary to the will of the Muslim religious leaders, Akbar largely pursued a politics of far-reaching religious tolerance. He allowed the building and renovation of Hindu temples as well as the public worship of Hindu deities. His liberal religious politics, however, included not only Hindus, but extended also to Jains, Zoroastrians, and Christians. He even abolished the poll tax for non-Muslims. The religious discussions that Akbar organized at his court became highly renowned. To these debates Akbar also in-

9 Cp. Neill 1984, 130f., 226f.
10 Cp. ibid. 233.
11 Cited following ibid. 143.
12 Cp. ibid. 160.
13 Cp. ibid. 230.
14 Ibid. 231.

vited Portuguese missionaries; yet they were unable to achieve any missionary success on those occasions.[15]

Another example of a moderate but at times overestimated openness has become widely known: The Jesuit Roberto de Nobili (1577-1656), who ministered in Madurai in South India, learned Sanskrit and Tamil, studied Hindu scriptures, and adapted his way of life, his diet, and clothing to that of the Brahmins. Yet in his writings he presented Christianity as being the only truth, and denied Hinduism any salvific meaning.[16] It is therefore beyond question that de Nobili understood his accommodation solely as a missionary strategy and pursued it only with respect to Indian culture, and not the Hindu religion, although—as one might imagine—he too was likely quite conscious of the close connection between the two. After initial resistance, de Nobili achieved numerous conversions of Brahmins to Christianity and to some extent gained a certain respect even among Hindu Brahmins.[17] De Nobili allowed the converted Brahmins to continue living according to the respective rules of the caste system, including the restriction not to interact with members of the lower castes.[18] There were some concerns about this within the wider church. And yet de Nobili found broad support for his successful missionary methods, eventually also from Pope Gregory XV (in 1623). However, as a result of the so-called "Malabar Rites controversy" about a hundred years later (1744), Rome rescinded the permission for Catholic Christians to participate in certain Brahmin rituals. Yet Rome remained more liberal when it came to concessions about the caste system, as this system was interpreted as being primarily a social rather than a religious institution. Catholic missionaries continued to make efforts to spread Christianity in other regions of India—all the way to Tibet—but only with rather modest results.

At the beginning of the seventeenth century, a British, a Dutch, and a French East India Company entered the lucrative trade with Asia and followed the Portuguese example in setting up military settlements on Indian soil. After lengthy and particularly bitter battles between the British and the French, the British finally attained supremacy in the second half of the eighteenth century. In 1774, British parliament handed over ruling power to the East India Company. In the nineteenth century British power was further expanded, and finally, in 1858, India was formally made subject to the British crown. In 1877 Queen Victoria declared herself "Empress of India." Only eight years later the "Indian National Congress," was founded, which was to develop into the central instrument of anti-colonial resistance and which took over power in 1947 when India achieved independence.

Initially, the interests of Holland, France, and Britain in India were of a purely economic and political nature. In particular, the increasingly powerful British East India Company did not, at first, want to see any missionaries in the country, be-

15 Cp. Embree, Wilhelm 1990, 237-240; Neill 1984, 166-190.
16 Cp. Neill 1984, 299f.
17 Cp. ibid. 287.
18 Cp. ibid. 283f., as well as Forrester 1980, 15f.

cause they feared unrest and hence a disruption of their goals. Toward the end of the eighteenth century, the call for missionizing India became increasingly loud in the British homeland. Since 1813, various Protestant missionary societies (Anglicans, Presbyterians, Lutherans, Baptists, Methodists, Congregationalists etc.[19]) could act unhindered and with state support in India. Generally, their theological perspective was shaped by exclusivism. Many of the missionaries held views similar to that of the Scottish missionary John Wilson, who depicted Hinduism as "the grandest living system of heathen error" and according to whom "in India ... Satan has triumphed more fearfully than in any other region of the Globe."[20] Exclusivist-minded missionaries found support for their positions in the injustices and in part degrading character of the caste system, in practices such as sati, widow burning, or the killing of newborn girls, as well as in the widespread social and religious discrimination against women in traditional Indian society. But above all they repeatedly attacked Hindu ritual practices, which they condemned as superstition and idolatry. If at all, Hindu scriptures were only used with apologetic and polemical intent. The ideas found in them were presented as being contradictory and as the basis for the rejected Hindu practices.[21] However, apart from a few exceptions, Christian missionaries' knowledge of Hindu ideas and scriptures remained rather paltry. Nevertheless, despite the undeniable anti-Hindu motivation, the missionaries' persistent demand for more social and legal equality, as well as their initiatives to promote a broadly applied, western-oriented educational system undoubtedly made a positive contribution to the development of modern Indian society.[22] This will also become clear when we look at the Neo-Hindu response.[23]

The Neo-Hindu Response

"Neo-Hinduism" refers to a series of Hindu reform movements that arose in India in the nineteenth and twentieth century. These movements responded to the three challenges of first the Christian mission, second the principles of the European Enlightenment including the scientific venture, and third the presence of the British colonial power. In light of these challenges, the Neo-Hindus strove first for a response to Christianity from within the spirit of their own religious tradition, second for a renewal of the Indian religious traditions out of a spirit of critique and reform and in partial absorption of Western impulses, so that, third, they could, for the first time, define "Hinduism" and elevate it to be the ethical-religious basis of a new Indian national consciousness.

19 Overview in Neill 1985, 460-468.
20 Wilson 1849, 113. Cp. also Sharpe 1977, 12 and 15.
21 Cp. Neufeldt 1989a, 31.
22 Thomas, P. 1954, 185-203.
23 On what follows, see also: Thomas 1969; Klostermaier 1989, 385-414; 2000, 266-284; 2002, 139-170; Neufeldt 1989a, 1989b; Dupuis 1993, 15-45; Halbfass 1988, 197-262.

In 1829, Rāmmohan Roy (1772-1833), often termed the "Father of Modern India," founded the association *Brāhmo Samāj*, which became an influential bearer of Neo-Hindu ideas. The Brāhmo Samāj pursued an enlightened theism, turned against numerous "superstitious" practices (Roy became renowned primarily for his successful opposition against widow burning), and declared the Upanishads to be the true and real basis of Hinduism. In his writing, *The Precepts of Jesus: The Road to Peace and Happiness* (1820), Roy proclaimed Jesus as the perfect religious ideal. From the Christian side, this spurred accusations that he was reducing and distorting the gospel, since, allegedly, Roy had not understood the true nature of Jesus as the incarnate savior. Other important figures of Reform Hinduism are connected to the Brāhmo Samāj, such as Devendranāth Tagore (1817-1905), the father of the famous poet Rabindranath Tagore, and Keshab Chandra Sen (1838-1884). Like Roy, Devendranāth Tagore also dismissed the belief in Jesus as God incarnate, while Keshab Chandra Sen in contrast embraced a sort of inspiration-Christology: Jesus is filled with the Holy Spirit and is therefore "God-in-man," but not "God-become-man."[24] In this sense, according to Sen, Jesus is by no means the only incarnation. Rather, Jesus had realized in a perfect way what is fundamentally possible for every person, since all persons share in the presence or immanence of God.

A parallel organization, called *Ārya Samāj*, was founded by Swami Dayananda Saraswati (Dayānanda Sarasvatī) (1824-1883). In some respects, the Ārya Samāj was similar to the Brāhmo Samāj: it embraced an enlightened theism, recognized only the Vedas or certain basic ideas of the Vedas as authoritative, and was radically opposed to "superstition," idol worship, and societal injustices. The Ārya Samāj assumed an extremely polemical attitude toward non-Hindu religions, and particularly toward Christianity. Saraswati also inverted the common critique from the missionaries and directed it toward Christianity, accusing Christianity of being a religion full of inconsistencies and absurdities. The Ārya Samāj developed a special ritual for the re-conversion of former Hindus and in turn carried out its own missionary activities.

The *Ramakrishna Mission*, founded by Vivekananda (1863-1902), is the third influential organization of Neo-Hinduism. Its name refers to Vivekananda's teacher, the Hindu mystic Ramakrishna (1836-1886) and simultaneously also to Rāma and Krishna, as two revered divine incarnations or *avatāras* central to Hinduism. The Ramakrishna Mission is, however, less theistically oriented, following instead primarily the tradition of the non-theistic Advaita-Vedānta. The Ramakrishna Mission too is motivated by a strong sense of mission. It teaches the unity and equality of all religions, an equality, however, which can only be explained from a Hindu or more precisely Advaita-Vedānta perspective. Much like Sen, Vivekananda showed a high regard for Jesus and considered him to be a divine incarnation in terms of the Hindu Avatāra-doctrine (*avatāra* = "descent"). According to the *Bhagavadgītā* (4, 7-8),

24 Cp. Neufeldt 1989b, 165.

from time to time God (Vishnu) takes on human[25] form, in order to re-establish the true Dharma and to overcome injustice.[26] Like Sen, Vivekananda also rejected any claim to the uniqueness of the incarnation of God in Jesus:

> Let us … find God not only in Jesus of Nazareth, but in all the great Ones that have preceded him, in all that came after him, and all that are yet to come. (…) They are all manifestations of the same Infinite God. They are all pure and unselfish; they struggled and gave up their lives for us …[27]

Vivekananda's journeys through the USA and Europe as well as his rhetorical talent made him both a renowned and impressive representative of Hinduism. The way in which he was able to present the spiritual riches of the Hindu tradition spurred serious questions regarding the justification of Christian mission in the very countries that organized the mission.[28] Auborbindo Ghose (1872-1950) embraced a position similar to Vivekānada's, as did Sarvepalli Radhakrishnan (1888-1975), the Oxford philosopher of religion and later President of India, who had been influenced by Vivekananda. The extent to which Mahātma Gandhi venerated Jesus and tried to follow him in his own life as a Hindu (!) became known far beyond India's borders.

With respect to the understanding of the crucifixion of Jesus, the Neo-Hindus unanimously reject any interpretation of it as an atonement for our salvation. For Sen, Vivekananda, and Radhakrishnan, the cross signifies Jesus' complete self-surrender for the sake of the truth, in that he offers his own sacrifice as a sign and example for others, thereby serving their salvation.[29] Neo-Hindus thus very early on, and with remarkable clarity, recognized the need to understand the death of Jesus as representative rather than constitutive of salvation.[30] As Ronald Neufeldt summarizes, Jesus counts for nearly all Neo-Hindus as an "ideal for living," in a Hindu sense. Thus they all emphasize consistently that Jesus was not only Asian geographically speaking, but also and particularly in his teaching and lifestyle.[31] Jesus has been unjustly monopolized by the Christians—suggests the tenor of various Neo-Hindus. Moreover, the exclusivist Christian interpretation of Jesus stands in tension with the teaching and life of Jesus himself.[32] According to many Neo-Hindus, Jesus and his religious significance can be understood much better and more adequately from the perspective of Hindu insights than from the perspective of Christian missionaries and their exclusivist views.

25 This appears to be assumed in the Gītā. The Purāṇas also assume incarnations of God in non-human forms.
26 On the *avatāra* concept in Hinduism and its diverse interpretations, cp. Parrinder 1997, 13-127.
27 Vivekananda 1994, Vol. 4, 152.
28 On this cp. the anecdote related on pp. 20f above on Vivekananda's presentation at the first World Parliament of Religions in Chicago in 1893.
29 Cp. Neufeldt 1989b, 167 and 170f.
30 On this difference, see above, pp. 248f.
31 Cp. Neufeldt 1989b, 170 and 173.
32 Vivekananda's lecture, "Christ the Messenger" offers a particularly clear example of this, in Vivekananda 1994, vol. 4., 138-153.

To exclusivist-minded Christianity, Neo-Hinduism posed a tremendous challenge. Not simply due to the critique of Christian exclusivism that Neo-Hindus expressed, but even more so because of the veneration which many Hindus were showing for Jesus in such an authentic way. For how could Hinduism be a satanic aberration if Hindus, from the roots of their own spiritual tradition, arrived at such an appreciation of Jesus—an appreciation shown not only by their words but also by their deeds? In order to defend itself, Christian exclusivism had to reach for one of its last, and least credible, weapons: that new version of the old theory of *imitatio diabolica*, the "demonic imitation" of the sacred, as we find in Hendrik Kraemer's note, that "the whole problem of, for instance, Gandhi" reminds one that the "most sincere representative of the most impressive forms of piety or of quality of life may happen to be the farthest from the Kingdom of God."[33] Yet for other Christians it seemed necessary to relinquish their exclusivist approach to Hinduism and change over to an inclusivist position.

Inclusivist Openings

Among missionaries, there had been some early occasional examples of an attitude cautiously leaning in an inclusivist direction. Particularly noteworthy in this regard is the Lutheran Bartholomäus Ziegenbalg (1682-1719), who was the first German Protestant missionary sent to India to work for the Danish-Halle Mission ("Tranquebar Mission"). He learned Tamil and studied the traditions of South Indian Hinduism. While he held fast to the belief that there was no salvation in Hinduism,[34] he nonetheless conceded that not everything in this religion was wrong, but that here and there one could find "a small light of the Gospel" as well as passages that are "according to God's Word."[35]

Yet a true rethinking was first set in motion by the enormous impression that the Hindu reformers made on Christianity. The blossoming of Indology, which had in turn inspired many of the Neo-Hindu movements themselves, served as an additional, reinforcing factor.[36] Through the translations, historical analyses, and comparative religious studies by Indologists such as Max Müller, H.T. Colebrooke, H.H. Wilson, M. Monier-Williams and others, it became much easier to gain a better knowledge and more profound understanding of Hinduism.[37] Hence it is not surprising that the actual beacon for a new theological perception of Hinduism appeared in the form of a voluminous work of comparative religion. It was published in 1913, came from the

33 Kraemer 1956, 365. Cp. above p. 112.
34 Cp. Neill 1985, 32.
35 Cited following Kuttianimattathil 1995, 18.
36 Neufeldt 1989a, 36.
37 The significance of early Indology for the change of theological thought in India has often been highlighted. Cp. for example, Boyd 1974, Sharpe 1977, 10-16; Kuttianimattathil 1995, 25-27.

pen of the Scottish missionary John Nicol Farquhar (1861-1929) and bore the significant title *The Crown of Hinduism*, by which was meant no other than Jesus Christ and Christianity.[38]

"The Crown of Hinduism"

Farquhar's central message is that Jesus came "not to destroy, but to fulfil" (Mt 5:17).[39] With reference to Hinduism, this means that not everything in Hinduism is dark and evil, but rather that much can also be found that is valuable from a Christian perspective:

> ...the noble art of India, the power and spirituality of its best literature, the beauty and simplicity of Hindu village life, the love and tenderness of the Hindu home, the devotion and endurance of the ascetic schools.[40]

According to Farquhar, all this is not destroyed by Christ and Christianity but rather "purged," "restored," "explained," and "consummated." And yet this "consummation" or "fulfillment" requires that Hinduism as a "system" dies. It is only in this way that the truths found in its philosophy and theology can be set free and attain new life: "Hinduism must die in order to live. It must die into Christianity."[41]

As a historical example of this process, Farquhar points to Judaism and the religious philosophy of Ancient Greece and Rome: Judaism was from God, says Farquhar. Yet it was not intended to be permanent, but rather to find its fulfillment through its transformation into Christianity.[42] Similarly the religion and philosophy of the Romans and Greeks: It was a preparation for Christ. Although it died out, everything valuable about it was preserved by Christianity, and it thus found a new life.[43]

Farquhar understands the relation between Christianity and non-Christian religions in the sense of an evolutionary continuity.[44] Much in the non-Christian religions may have been right and even necessary "for the childhood of the world." Today, however, it has mostly been superseded and is merely a hindrance. Rather than being universally valuable, the religious notions and legal rules of non-Christian religions have, for the most part, only temporally and culturally limited value. Yet everything in them that is of universal validity is recognized, liberated, pre-

38 According to Sharpe (1977, 23-25), Farquhar relates this attribute more to Christ than to Christianity. Yet Farquhar himself also speaks repeatedly of Christianity as the "crown" and "fulfillment" of Hinduism (cp. for example, Farquhar 1913, 55, 58, 64.) Of course, to Farquhar Christianity is the "crown" not apart from Jesus but because of him (ibid. 58).

39 Farquhar 1913, 53f.

40 Ibid. 54.

41 Ibid. 51.

42 Cp. ibid. 51.

43 Cp. ibid. 53.

44 Cp. ibid. 51; see also Sharpe 1977, 27.

served, and surpassed by its fulfilment in Christ and Christianity.[45] The Christian ideas and doctrines of faith are the "true spiritual successors" of those notions that appear in the early days of human religious history.[46] Thus, only Christ "supplies the religious basis necessary for modern society."[47] According to Farquhar, this has brought about the civilizational superiority of the West, which in turn proves the superiority of Christ:

> Despite our [the West's, PS-L] pitiable failure, there is abundance in our life to show the supremacy of Christ. The West surpasses all the world in practical philanthropy, in eager endeavours to serve man, in the uprightness and purity of its government, and in general efficiency.[48]

In most of his book, Farquhar tries to concretize and substantiate his claim of surpassing fulfillment. In this regard he focuses *first,* on the cosmic, social, and moral order (or *Dharma*, in Hindu terms); *second,* on the underlying concept of God; *third,* on the religious ideal; and *fourth,* on the interpretation of Jesus.

The Indian reformers, says Farquhar, strive for liberty, equality, fraternity, and social justice.[49] Yet these principles can neither be justified nor realized on the basis of the caste system. The caste system depends on the untenable and outdated cosmological ideas of reincarnation and karma, and it is deeply embedded in Hinduism. Therefore, the caste system cannot be reformed from within the Hindu system. It can only die out along with the Hindu system.[50] Nevertheless Christianity shares with Hinduism the concern for the sanctity of the social order and the wish for it to have a moral foundation. For without the moral principles of brotherly love and justice, the principles of freedom and equality would lead to chaos.[51] Christianity thus preserves the fundamental concern of Hinduism; indeed, in Christianity it will be much more securely anchored. For one can easily derive the principles of freedom, equality, brotherhood, and social justice from Jesus' image of God as the common father of all people.[52] By contrast, the Hindu God is beyond morality and moral principles. The Hindu tendency toward an impersonal concept of God undermines the concept of a God who created the world, acts in the world, is interested in the world and its people, and is in personal relationship with them.[53] The Christian concept of God is superior to the Hindu one because it assumes a genuine, ethically informed relationship between God and persons.[54] Hence it is only in the Christian concept of God that those theistic tendencies of Hinduism that speak of God's

45 Cp. Farquhar 1913, 55-65.
46 Cp. ibid. 77.
47 At least this is how Farquhar titles section IV, 9 (cp. ibid. 6).
48 Ibid. 62f.
49 Cp. on this ibid., 134-210.
50 Cp. ibid, 198, 455.
51 Cp. ibid. 200ff.
52 Cp. ibid. 198ff.
53 Cp. ibid. 219-246.
54 Cp. ibid. 408ff.

love and grace find their actual justification.[55] And so Christianity transforms and surpassingly fulfills the Hindu ideal of religious life: not a renunciation of the world, but liberation from the world for selfless service to the world.[56]

According to Farquhar, Christianity also adopts and purifies the Hindu inclination to worship religious images because here it becomes focused on Christ as the one true image of God.[57] The Hindu belief in *avatāras* is to Farquhar a mythic anticipation of the incarnation of God in Jesus Christ. It is "mythical" because the people regarded as *avatāras* in the Purāṇas such as Rāma, Krishna, or Gautama Buddha, although they were historical figures, did not regard themselves as incarnations, and neither did their immediate followers. Rāma and Krishna were not even religious teachers, but rather warriors, and the Buddha would have found it revolting to be seen as an incarnate God.[58] By contrast, Jesus identified himself as the Son of God and claimed divine authority in his teaching and ministry.[59] Hinduism is thus correct to cultivate belief in God becoming human. But it confuses myth with historical reality by believing that God became man in Rāma and Krishna.[60] In Jesus, however, the Hindu expectation was really fulfilled.[61] And Jesus is "Savior" in a comprehensive sense, including also the social order. He brings the longed for redemption of biological, social, and spiritual life: the improvement of the medical situation; social relations that are based on freedom, equality, brotherhood, and justice; ultimate fellowship with God, made possible through the forgiveness of sins brought by his death on the cross.[62]

So it is only when Hinduism dies into Christianity that its deepest hopes can be fulfilled and its universal values can be liberated from the shell of the outdated Hindu system. The true reform of Hinduism must be its baptism, its transformation into Christianity. According to Farquhar, only in this way will the construction of a Modern India as it is desired by the Neo-Hindu reformers become possible. Farquhar ends his book with the pathetic summons:

> The time has come when the Indian patriot must choose between tradition and the health of his country.[63]

55 Cp. ibid. 421.
56 Cp. ibid. 247-296.
57 Cp. ibid. 343ff.
58 Cp. ibid. 423.
59 Cp. ibid. 426ff.
60 Cp. ibid. 425.
61 Cp. ibid. 437.
62 Cp. 443f.
63 Ibid. 457.

Catholic Inclusivism after the Second Vatican Council

Farquhar's book had its effect less on the "Indian patriot" whom he invoked, than on those Protestant missionaries for whom it became *the* standard work of the Indian Mission for years to come.[64] In 1938, however, Hendrik Kraemer published his book *The Christian Message in a Non-Christian World* which, in the name of an exclusivism influenced by Karl Barth, spoke out against everything for which Farquhar stood.[65] By doing so, Kraemer could indeed diminish Farquhar's influence. Yet he did not manage to root it out completely. For, five decades later, Farquhar's work once again found a marked resonance in the transformation that the theology of religions began to undergo in the Roman Catholic Church at the time of the Second Vatican Council. Thus, on the eve of the Council, Josef Neuner wrote (with obvious echoes of Farquhar):

> It is the mission of the Church to fill the entire Indian society with divine life. It may therefore not destroy, but must rather elevate, complete, purify, and deify. Christianity's task is not to kill Hinduism, but to save it by Christianizing all the positive and genuine values in Hinduism. A Hinduism that has become Christian will never look as it did before its baptism. But baptism means sacrifice and supernatural elevation…[66]

The move toward inclusivist positions brought about by the Second Vatican Council not only meant that Roman Catholic theologians now held views similar to those of Farquhar, but also that they went beyond Farquhar in one important way. Farquhar had remained unclear about the central question of a theology of religions: the salvific significance of Hinduism. According to Farquhar, salvation became possible only through the crucifixion of Jesus.[67] But Farquhar says nothing about whether this salvation reaches only those persons who explicitly confess Christ. He confirms that it is the light of Christ that can be recognized in Hinduism,[68] and affirms that individual Hindu theologians had even foreseen that the God-become-man must suffer for us out of love.[69] He explicitly states that the "institutions" of the non-Christian religions, their "pictures, symbols, prophecies" had their validity and even necessity in the past,[70] although Christianity has now superseded them. But he is silent about whether this also implies that the light of Christ that is mediated by non-Christian religions may be understood as a *saving* knowledge of God. Roman Catholic theologians such as Jacques Dupuis and his Indian student Jose Kuttianimattathil have therefore accused Farquhar that he and similar versions of "fulfillment theology," do

64 Cp. Sharpe 1977, 123.
65 As rightly stated by Sharpe 1977, 93.
66 Neuner 1962, 245.
67 Cp. Farquhar 1913, 444.
68 Cp. ibid. 54f, 458.
69 Cp. ibid. 444.
70 Cp. ibid. 52.

not acknowledge a salvific role of non-Christian religions.[71] Roman Catholic theologians insist on more clarity at this point, and those who follow Karl Rahner's inclusivism argue clearly for such acknowledgement.[72]

According to Dupuis, non-Christian religions contain true though incomplete signs of Christ's salvation, meaning that they can indeed mediate this salvation to their adherents through their respective religious practices.[73] These signs are incomplete because the true "human face of God," in other words Jesus, remains unknown outside of Christianity.[74] To support this claim with regard to Hinduism, Dupuis repeats what is in substance Farquhar's position. In its classic formulations, the Hindu *avatāra* teaching remains mythical and does not refer to a concrete entering of God into history.[75] The *avatāra* teaching thus finds its real historical basis only in Jesus. The same is true for the Upanishads and the Advaita-Vedāntic teaching of the non-dual unity of Ātman (the true self) and Brahman (the divine or cosmic self). In a literally true sense, this unity can only be ascribed to Jesus and his non-dualist unity with the Father.[76] Yet through their relationship with Jesus, every Christian is called upon to participate in the consciousness of Christ and therefore in Jesus' non-dualist relationship to God, so that this constitutes something like a Christian Advaita.[77] Thus—says Dupuis in an obvious reminiscence of Farquhar—Jesus is "the crown and fulfillment of the intuition of the seers of the *Upanishads*."[78] Yet according to Dupuis, this does not mean that the intuitions and anticipations of Hinduism remain unfulfilled as long as they are not transformed into Christianity. In a symbolic and quasi "sacramental" way they mediate the same reality, but do so in an incomplete and "secret" manner.[79]

How far theologically does this path really take us beyond Farquhar? Does it not ultimately remain the goal even here to transform that which is "incomplete" and "secret" into its complete and revealed form, in other words into Christianity? As I pointed out above in connection with my discussion of inclusivism, Dupuis is seriously engaged in creating space, within an inclusivist framework, for the notion that the non-Christian religions are divinely willed and of a lasting legitimacy. Yet under the inclusivist premise of Christianity's superiority, this unintentionally but unavoidably results in the absurd position that according to God's will the non-Christian majority of humanity would have to be permanently satisfied with an imperfect and concealed form of revelation.[80] If this consequence is to be avoided, then inclu-

71 Cp. Dupuis 1993, 127f; Kuttianimattathil 1995, 237.
72 Nevertheless, this question has recently once again been debated in the Roman Catholic Church, cp. above pp. 98f.
73 Cp. Dupuis 1993, 145-151.
74 Cp. ibid. 150.
75 Cp. Dupuis 1993, 202; 1997, 302.
76 Cp. Dupuis 1993, 62.
77 Cp. ibid. 65f.
78 Ibid. 63.
79 Cp. Dupuis 1997, 303.
80 Cp. above pp. 135ff.

sivism permits only the path indicated by Farquhar: Hinduism dying into Christianity, or—to use Josef Neuner's words—the Christian "baptism" of Hinduism. This is nothing other than the program of inculturation that has been pursued so intensively in the last few decades. That is, the indigenous Christianity emerging in India adapts some elements of Hinduism, yet in so doing presents itself as being the fulfillment of Hinduism. That this notion does not exactly meets with applause on the Hindu side is understandable. The Hindu side views all such Christian efforts to enter into dialogue with Hinduism, in as much as they are part of this program, with skepticism and suspicion. In this vein, a 1982 study on the status of Hindu-Christian dialogue complains that:

> The Hindus fear that the Christians enter into dialogue with a hidden agenda, even if they do not aim at immediate conversion, they nonetheless want to establish the idea of Christ's primacy above all religious striving and effort.[81]

But aren't such fears well-founded?[82]

As we can see from Farquhar to Dupuis, the key question is on what evidence the Christian claim of superiority over Hinduism is finally based. The argument presented by Farquhar, even on the eve of the First World War, that Christianity's superiority was among others apparent in the high morality of Western governments, will presumably no longer be an option for anyone after the horrendous experiences of the twentieth century. And his attempt to ascribe to Christianity the principles of the Enlightenment along with the successes of science and technology and from this to gain capital in the theology of religions, not only ignores the long and considerable tensions between Enlightenment and science on the one hand and the Christian churches on the other. It furthermore neglects that the intellectual force behind Enlightenment and science was by no means only Christianity, but also the renewal of the spirit of antiquity during the Renaissance.[83] In the end the only remaining argument is the revelation and incarnation of God in Jesus.

Now Christian inclusivists do not dispute that Hinduism acknowledges the notion of a loving and forgiving God who has become incarnate in human life—a God who in the words of the Bhagavadgītā (11,44) turns to us "like the father to the son, like the friend to the friend, like the lover to the beloved," a God who is likeminded to all people (9,29-33) and to whom all are equally welcome, regardless of caste, gender, and religion (7,21f.). A God of whom Tulsī Dās can say:

> From the love that he bore to his followers, Rāma took the form of a man, and by himself enduring misery secured their happiness.[84]

81 Nayak, Abrard 1982, 28.

82 As examples of Hindu reactions to Christian inclusivism of a post-Conciliar bent, cp. the contributions of Mukerji and Yadav in Griffiths 1990, 228-246.

83 On the critique of such strategies to establish the superiority of Christianity, see also John Hick's contribution in Hick, Knitter 1987 esp. 24-29.

84 Quoted in Farquhar 1913, 442.

And about whom Tiru Mular writes:

> The ignorant think that love (…) and God (…) are two [different things]; they do not know that love is God. After knowing that love is God they remain possessed of love which is God.[85]

What Christian inclusivists contest is that these notions have a justified historical basis in Hinduism. *Through Jesus alone* has that about which Hindu myth speaks become reality. And, so goes a common argument, does not the concrete praxis of the *caste system* show that in Hinduism the mythological message of God's love is belied by Hinduism's own reality? The critical examination of the Christian claim to superiority over Hinduism must therefore refer primarily to these two core questions.[86] Regarding the first question, that of the historicity and uniqueness of the incarnation, an important step in a pluralist direction was already made at a relatively early stage by Raimon Panikkar.

Raimon Panikkar

Panikkar counts among the pioneers of Christian-Hindu dialogue and already his biography disposed him to this. He was born in Barcelona in 1918, the son of a Hindu father and a Catholic mother. In 1946 he was ordained as a Roman Catholic priest. In 1953 he moved to India where he stayed until 1960 and to which he was to return repeatedly thereafter. He received a doctorate in philosophy, chemistry, and theology. He held the chair in religious studies at the University of Santa Barbara, California, and was also a member of the faculty at various universities in India, Europe, and America.

In his early works, Panikkar embraced an inclusivist position that at that time and in the context of Roman Catholic theology was both progressive and pioneering. God has entered into a salvific relationship with all human beings, and Christ is present to all in a hidden way—so goes the tenor of his 1963 book *Die vielen Götter und der eine Herr* ("The Many Gods and the One Lord"). Panikkar expounds this position with respect to Hinduism in his work *The Unknown Christ of Hinduism,* which first appeared in English in 1964 and one year later in German. Apart from the fact that Panikkar affirms the saving presence of Christ in Hinduism much more clearly than does Farquhar, Panikkar's approach is nevertheless quite similar.[87] This is true even to the extent that he partly uses the same metaphors and historical examples. Thus Panikkar writes:

85 Shaiva Siddhānta, Tirumubai 257. Quoted from Dhavamony 1971, 128.

86 By contrast, Francis Clooney, in accordance with the basics of his understanding of "comparative theology" (cp. this to above pp. 80-87), holds that the question of whether God incarnated himself only in Jesus and not also in Rāma or Krishna is urgent but cannot (or cannot yet) be answered. Cp. Clooney 2001, 179f.

87 For the same assessment see Boyd 1974, 121f and Sharpe 1977, 125f.

> That Christ which is already in Hinduism, which, therefore, Christianity recognises and worships, that Christ has not unveiled his whole face, has not yet completed his mission there. He still has to grow up and to be recognised. Moreover, he still has to be crucified there, dying with Hinduism as he died with Judaism and with the Hellenistic religions in order to rise again, as the same Christ (who is already in Hinduism), but then as a risen Hinduism, as Christianity. (...)
>
> Christ is there in Hinduism, but Hinduism is not yet his spouse. (...)
>
> The presence of Christ in Hinduism makes it, in the eyes of Christian theology, (...) a vestibule of Christianity, a first and valuable stage of the *sanātana dharma* which has to find its fullness in the truly *sanātana* but *dharma-siddhi* of Christianity (the *dharma-sādhana* of Hinduism being Christianity).[88]

According to Panikkar, Christianity is "the fulfilment of religion."[89] The Christ who is at work in every religion found his perfect manifestation in the incarnation in Jesus Christ. For this reason, all other religions are geared toward this fulfillment. For Christians it is important to discern in dialogue with Hinduism the so far unknown working of Christ and to proclaim to Hindus the fulfillment of this work through the incarnation of Christ in Jesus:

> Hinduism is the starting point of a religion that culminates in Christianity. (...) Hinduism ... is a kind of Christianity in potency, because it has already a Christian seed, because it is the desire of fullness, and that fullness is Christ ...[90]

Fifteen years later Panikkar produced a substantially revised second edition of this book[91] (which appeared in German translation in 1986 under the title *Der unbekannte Christus im Hinduismus*[92]). In this revised edition Panikkar sharply critiques and radically changes the "fulfillment theology" which he had himself previously embraced.[93] He now maintains that the model of potency and fulfillment cannot be applied to the relationship between Hinduism and Christianity. Rather, potency and fulfillment are found equally within each of the two religions, though in different ways. Christianity is not the unilateral fulfillment of Hinduism, but rather, according to Panikkar, "a mutual fecundation" could take place between Hindu-

88 Panikkar 1964, 17-18. [*sanātana dharma* = eternal teaching; *dharma-siddhi* = teaching perfection; *dharma-sādhana* = realization of the teaching].

89 Ibid. 22.

90 Ibid. 59f.

91 *The Unknown Christ of Hinduism,* 1981 (the preface dates from 1979). There are, however, essentially twenty years separating the two versions since the first draft of the first edition goes back to 1957.

92 A second printing of the German translation was published in 1990. On p. 50 of the German edition of Paul Knitter's *No Other Name,* (*Ein Gott—viele Religionen,* 1988) it incorrectly says that the important revised edition of Panikkar's *The Unknown Christ of Hinduism* had not been translated into German, although the German translation had actually appeared two years earlier.

93 Cp. Panikkar 1981, 89ff.

ism and Christianity.[94] "Christ," Panikkar now clarifies, is simply the Christian name for the mystical unity of World, God, and Man.[95] Christians discovered this reality in and through Jesus and continue to express it in the compound of "Jesus" and "Christ." Yet in other religions too the same mystical unity can be found where it is then named accordingly, for example in Hinduism as Rāma or Krishna or Īśvara or Purusha.[96] Each of these names, says Panikkar, "is a new aspect, a new manifestation and revelation of it. Yet each name teaches or expresses, as it were, the undivided Mystery."[97] None of the two religions can therefore claim to be superior to the other.[98]

What led Panikkar to this revised understanding? Comparing the texts of the two versions of *The Unknown Christ* provides some revealing clues.

The idea of a mutual "fecundation" or "fulfillment" already appears in the 1964 version, though not as a Christian proposal but in connection with Panikkar's account of of the Neo-Hindu standpoint. Here Panikkar states that according to "modern Hinduism," Christianity can be received "as a younger sister religion," and that both siblings "meet as *two* religions, two ways, which eventually may even need mutual correction and mutual enlightenment...."[99] Tellingly, in the 1981 edition, this passage is no longer found at this place,[100] yet—as cited above—it now reemerges as Panikkar's own proposal of how to understand Christian-Hindu relations. So the change in Panikkar's position consists of Panikkar having made the insights of Neo-Hinduism his own. But why?

In the 1964 version, Panikkar writes about the Christian discernment of Christ's presence in Hinduism:

> Christ is already at work in any Hindu prayer as far as it is really prayer; Christ is behind any form of worship, in as much as it is adoration made to God.[101]

This formulation is preserved in the 1981 edition with some smaller changes:

> The Spirit of Christ is already at work in Hindu prayer. Christ is already present in every form of worship, to the extent that it is adoration directed to God.[102]

Yet what is new is that Panikkar now adds a very similar observation from a Hindu perspective, an observation not yet present in the 1964 edition:[103]

94 Cp. ibid. 93.
95 Cp. ibid. 19f.
96 Cp. ibid. 27.
97 Ibid. 29.
98 Cp. ibid. 75-89.
99 Panikkar 1964, 14.
100 Cp. Panikkar 1981, 46.
101 Panikkar 1964, 17.
102 Panikkar 1990b, 56.
103 Yet at another place Panikkar writes that Hinduism could acknowledge the work of God in both religions and refer to this by using a term like "Īśvara" (Lord). Cp. Panikkar 1964, 24.

> The Bhagavad Gītā says that all worship is ultimately directed to Krishna, that it is he who brings all religious acts to fulfilment, even those devoted to other Gods. Thus, if we were to follow these and similar teachings of other schools, we could arrive at a Hindu meeting-point called Krishna....[104]

One can see from these examples that Panikkar has become much more aware than before of the possibility that inclusivist positions can be and are actually taken reciprocally. However, he has also reached the conviction that both sides do so with a certain theological legitimacy. That is why he now speaks of reciprocal "fulfillment" or "fecundation." Yet what lies behind his assessment of such legitimacy? On the one hand, the recognition that a one-sided Christian claim of superiority over Hinduism has become totally unbelievable. Whereas in the 1964 edition of *The Unknown Christ* Panikkar had only rejected exclusivist black/white depictions—which see in Hinduism nothing but lies, darkness, sin, damnation, and so forth, while in Christianity truth, light, holiness, and salvation—in the 1981 edition, he uses the same arguments against inclusivist claims of fulfillment and superiority.[105] Whereas Panikkar, for example, had initially only concluded that the concrete history of Hinduism and Christianity offered no basis for the exclusivist contrasts, he now concludes that a Christian attitude of superiority can likewise not prevail in light of the historical facts.[106] On the other hand, quite concrete personal experiences[107] could well be behind Panikkar's shift to a pluralist position, as Panikkar indicates in an "objectified autobiographical" essay of 1970.[108]

The decisive theological point for the implementation of his new pluralist perspective on the relationship between Christianity and Hinduism lies in Christology. To be more precise, it lies in the relationship between that "meeting-place" of World, God and Man—for which Panikkar coined the word "cosmotheandric," and to which he refers in Christian terminology as "Christ"—and the concrete person of Jesus of Nazareth. In the 1964 version of *The Unknown Christ*, Panikkar still identified in a sort of one-to-one relationship the God-human meeting-place, which he called "Christ", with the concrete person of Jesus:

> The stumbling-block (for Hinduism, PS-L) appears when Christianity ... identifies Christ with Jesus the Son of Mary. A full Christian faith is required to accept this identity.[109]

104 Panikkar 1981, 46. Compare this with the corresponding section in Panikkar 1964, 14-16.
105 Cp. Panikkar 1964, 35-57, with Panikkar 1981, 70-89.
106 Cp. Panikkar 1964, 46ff, with Panikkar 1981, 78ff.
107 And beyond this perhaps also the experiences of other, contemplative pioneers of the Christian-Hindu dialogue such as Bede Griffiths and Henri Le Saux.
108 This essay originally (1970) appeared in Spanish as "Fe y creenca," then in abbreviated form under the title "A Multireligious Experience. An Objectified Autobiographical Fragment" in the Anglican Theological Review (1971, 53), and finally it was included in Panikkar's *The Intrareligious Dialogue* (Panikkar 1978). Since the translation of his book under the title *Der neue religiöse Weg*, this important essay is also available in German (cp. Panikkar 1990, 50-81).
109 Cp. Panikkar 1964, 24; cp. also ibid. 138.

In the 1981 edition, Panikkar softens this statement by saying that such an identity "characterizes the Christian belief."[110] However, a new introduction has been added to the 1981 version in which Panikkar makes a crucial modification:

> ...though a Christian believes that "Jesus is the Christ" ... this sentence is not identical to "the Christ is Jesus." (...) The Christian ... cannot say that "Christ is *only* Jesus"....[111]

Does this mean that Panikkar assumes that the "cosmotheandric" meeting-point identified as "Christ" is also manifest or incarnate in other concrete persons of history? Even if Panikkar's deliberations remain rather cautious at this point, he seemingly must be understood in this way.[112] In his function as savior, Jesus Christ, according to Panikkar, cannot be understood as unique because this would lead to the untenable exclusivism. In his message and in his lived praxis, Jesus is likewise not unique, since one can find parallels to those in many non-Christian saints, prophets, and traditions. Jesus is certainly unique as an individual, yet "everyone is unique" in this sense.[113] According to Panikkar the religious meaning of confessing the "uniqueness" of Jesus Christ lies in the relationship between this confession and the personal language of love: "Christ is unique, as any loved child is unique for its parents..."[114] On the other hand, Panikkar writes, "The Christian pluralist will not affirm that there are many saviors."[115] Yet he explains this statement by saying that the saving power called "Christ" is beyond quantification ("is neither one nor many.")[116] It is incarnate in every reality and can neither be limited to history as such nor to a particular part of history.[117] This view has considerable consequences for the contradistinction between Hindu myth and Christian history that has been so popular and common since Farquhar. According to Panikkar, we find myth and history in both religions. Panikkar speculates that as the Christian-Hindu dialogue continues the historical dimension of Krishna could become more important to Hindus than it has been before, and the Christian could become more inclined to admit "the trans-historical nature of Christ."[118]

At this point it is worth emphasizing once more that for Panikkar, "Christ" and "Krishna" are not simply different names for one and the same thing. Though in both cases we are dealing with revelations or disclosures of the cosmotheandric unity, that is, the unity of the World, God and Man, these are nonetheless revelations

110 Cp. Panikkar 1981, 57.
111 Panikkar 1981, 14. Emphasis is Panikkar's! Cp. also ibid. 82f.
112 Cp. Kuttianimattathil 1995, 280, n. 315: "...for him Jesus of Nazareth is only one of the manifestations of Christ, and he is unique only for Christians."
113 Panikkar 1997, 112.
114 Panikkar 1987, 108; similarly also Panikkar 1996, 271.
115 Panikkar 1987,111.
116 Ibid.
117 Ibid. 114.
118 Panikkar 1978, 17.

in the sense of different manifestations and different representations of this unity.[119] They are thereby each embedded in the specific systematic connections within their own religions, namely in Christianity in the doctrine of the Trinity, and in Hinduism in the theistic systems of Viśiṣṭādvaita- or Dvaita-Vedānta or of Nyāya and in the various traditions of Vishnuism and Shivaism.[120] Each of these systems expresses the cosmotheandric unity in both specific and comprehensive ways, and that is why they cannot be integrated into an even bigger meta-system. This would eliminate pluralism, which for Panikkar amounts to a destruction of these systems.[121] Nevertheless it is possible to learn to understand the different systems as different revelations, and this means to conceive them as "functional," or as Panikkar prefers to call them, "homeomorphic equivalents."[122] Thus when Panikkar judges that Christ is not "only" Jesus, then "Christ" becomes the Christian symbol for the fundamental theological possibility of reckoning with the existence of such equivalents in a genuine theological sense. But in order to understand these equivalents from within, one has to move beyond the Christian idiom and enter into the other religious system with its own specific network of meanings.

Pluralist Perspectives

Mutual Enrichment

Panikkar's reflections have proven to be extraordinarily fruitful, and by no means only with regard to the Christian-Hindu dialogue. Some theologians have made efforts to more closely elucidate the "homeomorphic equivalence", or, as Hans Küng aptly put it many years ago, "equivalence"[123] but "not sameness" of Hindu and Christian beliefs. Under the unmistakable influence of Panikkar, Michael von Brück relates the Christian doctrine of the Trinity to the non-dualist conception of unity in Shankara, the chief representative of Advaita-Vedānta.[124] Franics D'Sa correlates the Trinity with the cosmological view of unity in "Bhagavadgītā-Theism," which he interprets in the sense of Viśiṣṭādvaita-Vedānta founded by Rāmanuja.[125] Von Brück and D'Sa both show how a pluralist understanding of the differences and functional

119 Cp. once more Panikkar 1981, 27-30.

120 In this connection, Panikkar had already relatively early on proposed the doctrine of the Trinity as the Christian equivalent of the philosophy of unity found in both Advaita-Vedānta and in theistic belief systems. Cp. Panikkar 1967, 101-138; Panikkar 1973.

121 Panikkar increasingly emphasizes this point in his later writings. Cp. Panikkar 1987, 109ff, as well as in many republished contributions that appear in Panikkar 1995.

122 Cp. Panikkar 1978, XXI-XXIII.

123 "Gleichwertigkeit." Cp. Küng, Ess, Stietencron, Bechert 1984, 269f (1993, 180).

124 Cp. von Brück 1987.

125 Cp. D'Sa 1987. In line with the teaching of Rāmanuja, D'Sa identifies the cosmos as the body of God. Cp. ibid. 48, 69.

equivalents between Hinduism and Christianity can lead to what Panikkar described as mutual fecundation. Christians, says von Brück, will particularly appreciate how Advaita-Vedānta begins and ends in its philosophical reflections with mystical experience.[126] Christians can adopt Hindu meditation and contemplative practices as a way of attaining a more effective spiritual internalization of that which is also emphasized by the Christian doctrine of justification: that we are already redeemed and need to live by this awareness.[127] For D'Sa as well, it is primarily the contemplative and meditative ways of Hinduism that can enrich and deepen Christian spirituality and may lead it to the "basic experience of being borne by the wholeness-and-totality."[128] Behind these opinions stand the concrete experiences of those who, like the Christian monks Henri Le Saux (Swami Abhishiktānanda) and Bede Griffith, have deeply immersed themselves in the practice of Hindu spiritual ways.[129] Regarding the reverse possibility of a Christian fecundation of Hinduism, D'Sa and von Brück both emphasize that Christianity's "historical realism in salvation-theology" (von Brück) may continuously goad Hinduism toward translating the awareness of ultimate unity and wholeness into "cosmic solidarity" and a "true and just community."[130] Thus, Hinduism and Christianity need not be in competition with one another; rather, they can complement each other precisely because of their differences.[131]

Another major pioneer of Christian-Hindu dialogue, M.M. Thomas, on the one hand clearly expressed his sympathy for the pluralist cause[132] but on the other hand warned, in his contribution to the anti-pluralist volume edited by D'Costa, against a pluralistically minded diminishing of the centrality of Jesus Christ. For in doing so one runs the risk of depriving modern India of one of its most important spiritual ferments, a ferment that had demonstrated its enormous efficacy especially through its influence on the Neo-Hindu reform movements.[133] Thomas' warning needs to be taken seriously. But a pluralist view of the relation between Hinduism and Christianity does not have to lead to a leveling of the two religions and to a de-emphasizing of Jesus' significance as "God's identification with suffering humanity and as the pattern of true humanity..."[134] The notion of mutual enrichment and fulfillment can take this fully into account without simultaneously having to insist on the uniqueness or superiority of God's revelation in Jesus.

126 Cp. von Brück 1987, 215.
127 Cp. von Brück 1993, 94ff, and 102ff.
128 D'Sa 1987, 124l cp. also ibid. 89-95.
129 Von Brück explicitly refers to this (cp. von Brück 1987, 25).
130 Cp. von Brück 1993, 95l D'Sa 1987, 113-122; D'Sa 1998, 171.
131 Cp. D'Sa 1987, 123f.
132 Cp. Thomas, M.M. 1990, 60.
133 Cp. Thomas, M.M. 1990, 52-55. In this regard it is telling that Thomas gave his important study of Neo-Hinduism (published in 1969) the title *The Acknowledged Christ of the Indian Renaissance*. In this title, Thomas clearly alludes to Panikkar's *The Unknown Christ of Hinduism*, thereby expressing his own contrary approach.
134 Thomas, M.M. 1990, 53.

Much like M.M. Thomas, Stanley Samartha initially responded to the Neo-Hindu challenge by insisting on the uniqueness of Jesus and rejecting the interpretation of Jesus as one *avatāra* among others.[135] However, in the course of his work as the first director of the dialogue unit of the World Council of Churches, Samartha grew ever closer to a pluralist position.[136] He eventually concluded that the theory of many *avatāras* was theologically the most appropriate position because it accounts for both the mystery of God and the fact that people have responded to this mystery in multiple ways.[137] Christian and Hindu notions each refer to this mystery in the language of their own cultural context. None of these notions is absolute, none exhausts the mystery, nor does the sum of them all. Yet they possess their own characteristic differences.[138] Therefore, the thesis of a plurality of *avatāras* has its theological benefit especially in that it encourages a truly mutual exchange of religious messages. Christians take it as most natural that they are to tell the world the story of Jesus, and Samartha does not want to contest this. But what about people of other faiths? Do Christians seriously expect that these likewise have something to share? Perhaps stories which are also of great significance, such as the story of the Buddha, of Rāma, or of Krishna? Samartha recounts that whenever he presented Christian theologians with this question, their response has been silence, indifference, or "a refusal to even consider" it. According to Samartha, the reason for this is that Christians do not take seriously the mediators of salvation in other religions as such mediators in a Christian-theological sense.[139] Each of these three figures has his own real historical background and his specific message of salvation mediated through doctrine and myth: the proclamation of liberation and enlightenment in the case of the Buddha, the promise of liberating divine grace in the case of Rāma and Krishna.[140] According to Samartha, Christians are right in seeing Jesus as the normative promise and mediation of God's presence. But in this respect he should be considered neither unique nor absolute.[141] Indian mediators of salvation can therefore also shed new light on Jesus. The ideals of letting go, non-attachment, and selflessness that are characteristic of Hinduism as well as Buddhism can also be discerned in the life of Jesus. His inner non-attachment to the things of the world set him free for his liberating service to others.[142]

> When Mahatma Gandhi was assassinated (1948) there were only four things in his possession: a pair of wire-rimmed spectacles, a fountain pen, a watch attached to a chain tucked in his *dothi* (waist cloth), and a pair of chappals

135 Samartha 1970, 175.
136 Cp. Samartha, 1981 and 1991.
137 Cp. Samartha 1991, 131.
138 Cp. ibid. 82ff.
139 Cp. ibid. 130f and X.
140 Cp. ibid. 124-131.
141 Cp. ibid. 84.
142 Cp. ibid. 136f.

(leather sandals). When Jesus died on the cross all that he had was a loincloth.[143]

If Jesus is seen in one line with the other Asian mediators of salvation, then, says Samartha, the common thread is this link between inner letting go and liberation and the selfless engagement for the liberation of others. This understanding of Jesus has a place and a meaning in and for Asia. The Christ who is supposed to "conquer" Asia, does not.[144]

Farquhar criticized the Neo-Hindu expansion of the *avatāra* concept to include Jesus and other religious founding figures primarily because, from a historical perspective and in contrast to Jesus, neither the Buddha, nor Rāma, nor Krishna understood themselves as the incarnation of God nor did their immediate disciples view them in this way. Farquhar viewed the difference between myth and history therefore as coinciding with the difference between true and false. In other words, in Hinduism belief in the incarnation remains a myth, not because Rāma, Krishna, or the Buddha were not historical figures (Farquhar does not contest their historicity) but rather because these figures, historically, did not understand themselves to be divine incarnations. By contrast, in Christianity the belief in incarnation corresponds to a historical reality. Yet this contradistinction in untenable. For Jesus too, in all historical probability, did not understand himself to be the "Son of God" in the sense of a divine incarnation. And the genesis of the Christian concept of incarnation went through lengthy theological developments that are still not over and perhaps never will be over, because their point is to express the significance of Jesus, a significance that Christians necessarily understand in new and different ways as the circumstances change. In this sense we are talking here too about a "myth,"[145] a myth, however, that in expressing the significance of Jesus simultaneously emphasizes the significance of historically concrete existence. Von Brück, D'Sa, and Samartha all show, each in his own way, that this aspect of the Christian message can be related to Hinduism as a necessary and fruitful ferment. But they likewise show that in doing so, Christianity can also receive from Hinduism a deeper understanding of other aspects of the message and life of Jesus. Such reciprocal fecundation becomes possible precisely when Christianity no longer sets Jesus up against or elevates him above the other mediators of salvation as the only mediator, the only revealer, and the only divine incarnation, and instead interprets him as standing in a relation of complementarity to the others.

Regarding the question, raised by Neo-Hinduism, of whether the *avatāra* concept may be applicable to Jesus, the point is therefore not whether Neo-Hindus ac-

143 Ibid. 136.
144 Cp. ibid.
145 Hans-Peter Müller noted in connection with the Christian-Hindu dialogue that "the Old Testament Lord of history" would also become a victim of a radical critique of myth. Cp. Müller, H.-P. 1998, 71.

tually use the concept of *avatāra* in the traditional Hindu sense,[146] or whether this traditional sense is identical to the traditional Christian understanding of incarnation,[147] and so forth (besides, such questions may also be hard to answer because there is no such thing as *the* traditional understanding of either *avatāra* or "incarnation"). The crucial point is rather that Hindus, in freely drawing on their tradition, feel encouraged by this tradition to take a twofold step: first, to recognize the presence of God in Jesus ("God in man" not "God as man"), and second, to contest the uniqueness of this presence. This raises the challenge for Christians of whether they can share this view and then find a way to express, in the context of Hindu spirituality, the particular but not unique role of Jesus as a mediator of salvation. Or, whether in contrast they continue insisting on Jesus as the only mediator and the unique divine incarnation, so that ultimately Hinduism would have to disappear into Christianity as the fulfillment of its allegedly purely mythological hopes and the only legitimate form of Hinduism's afterlife would be that of a Christianity inculturated into India, that is, into an India that, at least religiously, has been "conquered."

The fact that the real challenge lies here has become obvious once again in a debate between Michael Amaladoss and Hans Staffner, both Jesuits, and both important advocates of an inculturated Indian theology.[148] In response to a remark by Amaladoss, according to whom the particularities of Christianity do not make it "a better, superior, surer, or easier way to God," Staffner sharply asked Amaladoss whether he wanted to declare the major religions as being equally valid. Because, as held by the Christian faith, Jesus is the only Son of God, the "assumption that the religion founded by the Son of God is not better than any other religion is simply absurd."[149] If one does not regard Jesus as one *avatāra* among others, then conversion to Christianity will remain the goal of the Christian proclamation in India. Amaladoss' response reveals the entire problem: On the one hand, Amaladoss continues to reject the language of Christianity's superiority.[150] On the other hand, however, he emphasizes that he has not applied the title of "Christ" to other mediators, and also that he does not share the view that Jesus is only one *avatāra* among others.[151] Yet Staffner's question was precisely about how it should be possible to derive from the insistence on Jesus as the only Son of God anything else but the superiority of Christianity. To this question Amaldoss gave no answer, presumably because there is no answer to it.

From the perspective of exclusivist Christians in India, the pluralist position undermines the Christian witness.[152] In the words of Martin Alphonse, the plural-

146 Cp. Kuttianimattathil 1995, 291-296.
147 Cp. Schoonenberg 1982, D'Sa 1993.
148 Cp. Staffner 1988 and Amaladoss 1992.
149 Staffner 1991, 38.
150 Amaladoss 1991 43; likewise also Amaladoss, 1997, 27.
151 Ibid. 43f.
152 Cp. on this a number of the contributions in Bage et al. 1992.

ist theology of religions is "alarming, even blasphemous!"[153] To Alphonse, a pluralist theology of religion is simply a Christian adaptation of the Hindu "syncretism," which proclaims the universality and equality of all religions.[154] There is no doubt that the influence of Neo-Hinduism has indeed been a significant factor for those Christian and pluralist positions which developed in the context of the Christian-Hindu dialogue. But what is wrong with that? This would only be wrong if it were clear from the outset, in an exclusivist manner, that nothing good or true can come from Hinduism. Is there any other reason, one that does not arise from such theological bias? Yes, there is one indeed, and it is particularly the exclusivists—including Alphonse[155]—who keep quoting it: It is the insistence that the dehumanizing characteristics of the Indian caste system are inextricably enmeshed in Hinduism, and that this reveals a spirit that is in flat opposition to the gospel.

A Pluralist Theology of Religions and the Question of Caste

In the first place, the Indian caste system[156] presents an enormous challenge to the Christian churches in India themselves. Since the time of the Thomas Christians and since the strategic missionary accommodation of de Nobili, Indian churches have made compromises with the caste system and therefore must continually ask the self-critical question at which point they might be compromising the message of Jesus itself.[157] M.M. Thomas is clearly right when he states that in India—and in view of the message of *koinonia* or fellowship in Christ—the Christian churches' "approach to caste and race distinction …is of paramount importance."[158] In light of the traditional prohibition of inter-dining between members of different castes (to avoid religious and ritual contamination), this challenge repeatedly shows up in the real-symbolic question of whether the ecclesial practice of Eucharist or Communion need take heed of differences in caste, or whether it should instead consciously and deliberately disregard them. In both its significance and symbolic message, this question may very well equal the conflict between Peter and Paul about table fellowship between Jewish and Gentile Christians (see Gal 2:11-13).

In as much as the caste system results in contesting the equal worth and dignity of all human beings, it is incompatible with the message of Jesus. For this reason, the caste question is by no means only a challenge to the Indian churches' own inner-ecclesial practice. It also affects the relationship of Christianity to Hinduism. A high proportion of Indians who have converted to Christianity (Ariarajah speaks of

153 Alphonse 1992, 46.
154 Ibid. 45.
155 Cp. ibid. 52.
156 For a brief overview see Meisig 1988 and Böck, Rao 1995.
157 On this cp. Forrester's excellent 1980 study.
158 Thomas, M.M. 1969, 253.

75-80% with reference to the Protestant churches[159]) come from the "casteless," the "untouchables" or "Dalits" (meaning "broken ones"). The "casteless" are ranked below even the lowest castes and look to Christianity for recognition of their human dignity. Roughly 20% of the Indian population is considered to be part of the "casteless" or "untouchables." That means roughly 200 million individual persons who day in and day out suffer from being systematically despised and from living in the atrocious conditions which have been assigned to them. Every dialogue with Hinduism—so say the critical voices—undermines the credibility of Christianity because the Hindu dialogue partners are the "oppressors," those who are responsible for and support the caste system, and who benefit from it.[160] In this issue, the question of whether a Christian and at the same time pluralist theology of religions ascribes to Jesus a normative function becomes quite concrete. Can Hinduism seriously be included in the circle of those religions that are equal to Christianity in the mediation of salvific knowledge of transcendence? To this I wish to respond in four points.

First, Christian pluralists must be unambiguously clear in their rejection of the debasing, dehumanizing characteristics of the caste system. Pluralists like John Hick,[161] Paul Knitter,[162] Wesley Ariarajah,[163] and others have taken an unequivocal position on this matter. Hick, for example, writes that the "influence of Christianity, Marxism, and Islam upon Hinduism must be toward the final purging of the blight of caste from the life of India."[164]

Second, one cannot deny that the caste system is rooted in the religious concepts and scriptures of Hinduism. However, pluralists hold that Hinduism also comprehends an *opposite potential,* so that, in principle, it seem possible to reform the caste system *within the context of Hinduism* and in the long term to overcome it completely. The caste system emerged from the Vedic belief in a divinely ordained system of estates. Influenced by the belief in reincarnation and karma as it came up in the Upanishads, the caste system came to be viewed as an external expression of stages on the path of spiritual progress. Each person is re-born into that particular caste which corresponds to his or her ethical-spiritual development. Thus, each person himself is responsible for his own caste status. It is for this reason that a Hindu perspective views the system not as unjust but rather as an expression of karmic retributive justice: The person reaps what he or she sows! The later Hindu legal treatises, the *dharmaśāstras*, and particularly the *Manu-Smṛti*, make the caste system even more rigid (meaning that the barriers between the castes are raised and made less permeable), and the understanding of religious and social rights and duties increasingly assumes a caste-specific form. That is, there are different rights depending on one's caste and thus the religious and legal status of the lowest castes and the

159 Cp. Ariarajah 1999, 78.
160 Cp. ibid. 79ff.
161 Cp. Hick 1982, 132f.
162 Cp. Knitter 1995, 197ff.
163 Cp. Ariarajah 1999. 79-84.
164 Hick 1982, 133.

casteless is accordingly menial. *However*, these developments did not imply a negation of the fundamental equality of all people before God or of their divine dignity: Every person, regardless of caste and gender, has the Ātman, which, depending on the respective philosophical-theological school, is understood either in the sense of a metaphysical unity with God or of a substantial likeness to God (as for example in Madhva's Dvaita-Vedānta). And no one—according to Krishna's message in the Bhagavadgītā—is excluded from God's redeeming love. In the context of lived Hindu spirituality, the various Bhakti-movements in particular have emphasized the irrelevance of one's caste status for one's relationship to God. And Bhakti-spirituality, the loving devotion to God, is by no means limited to the theistic forms of Hinduism. In the form of the Nirgun-Bhakti[165] it could even integrate the non-theistic conception of God of Advaita-Vedānta (as for example in the particularly renowned and popular hymns and poems of Kabīr). In my opinion, without these opposite tendencies it would indeed be impossible to acknowledge that in Hinduism too we find a mediation of salvific knowledge of transcendence that is equivalent to what is found in Christianity.

The existence of such tendencies makes it feasible that Hinduism can overcome the caste system without thereby losing its own identity. The historical development that led to the solidifying of the caste system with all its evil manifestations seems to be fundamentally reversible. The first important step, namely the abandonment of a caste-dependent legal system, has already been taken with the establishment of the Indian Constitution. The next step would be to overcome the belief that the stage of an individual's karmic-spiritual developmental can be told by his social status at birth. Early Buddhism had already reacted to the beginnings of this idea by arguing that it is solely one's character and behavior that reveals the state of one's spiritual maturity or immaturity, and not one's birth. This Buddhist objection also shows that getting rid of the caste system does not require giving up belief in karma and reincarnation. Finally, it is both possible and necessary to reinterpret these Vedic teachings that formed the basis of the caste system in light of a modern society that, after all, has long since ceased to correspond to the Vedic system of estates. This can be done in a variety of ways, for example, along the lines of the spiritual reinterpretation that Swami Agnivesh suggests (with the four main castes as symbolical expressions of diverse spiritual callings).[166]

Third, from a pluralist perspective, *Hindus* themselves must therefore drive the reform and incremental overcoming of the caste system. However, Christians may consider it their task to cooperate with Hindus on this whenever the opportunity presents itself and, as far as possible, also to involve followers of other religions, primarily Buddhists and Muslims. In other words, from a pluralist perspective the Christian contribution to the improvement of living conditions in Indian society and the efforts to overcome the religious motives that stand in the way of such an

165 Cp. Lorenzen 1996.
166 Cp. Amaladoss 1997b, 65f, 100f.

improvement must assume the form of *interreligious cooperation*.[167] There is a strong caste-critical potential in the major Neo-Hindu reform movements that is far from exhausted.[168] The abolition of the caste-specific legal system by the Indian Constitution of 1949 has to be defended against restorative tendencies, something that can only be done effectively through the Hindu majority. Islam, as well as Ambedkar's[169] Neo-Buddhism, have become havens for the casteless, just like Christianity. It is therefore particularly important that Muslims and Buddhists participate in the joint efforts to overcome the caste system. But these efforts also have to be interreligious for a further reason: Only interreligious cooperation can counter the strong tendency within the non-Hindu religious communities of gaining apologetic capital from the issue of caste. Instrumentalizing the critique of the caste system to buttress one's own religion's superiority claims will ultimately help those powers on the Hindu side that in the name of preserving Hindu identity ("Hindutva") also aim at the retention and legal restitution of the caste system. Interreligious efforts to overcome the caste system are also to be combined with feminist efforts, since the social and religious subordination of women in traditional Hindu society[170] draws on the same sources and notions as the caste system, and indeed cannot be separated from it. However, the caste system is deeply entrenched in the consciousness of many Indian people, often even in those who do not identify as Hindus. Thus, one cannot reasonably count on quick success in overcoming the caste system.

Fourth, we must finally point out that from a Christian and pluralist perspective evils similar to the caste system are not unknown in Christianity. Although, for example, at several places in the New Testament it is very clearly stated that neither the difference between man and woman, nor between slave and free, nor between Jew and non-Jew (Gal 3:26-29) is of any relevance to God, it has taken many centuries for this to filter down to societal implementation. Right up until late modernity (and partially till the present) Christians have defended slavery, racial segregation, and legal gender inequality as divinely ordained arrangements. It is by no means only within Brahminical Hinduism that full religious equality for women—including the practice of priestly functions—is still pending. Just as conservative Hindu defenders of the caste system consider this system not as an injustice but rather as an expression of a just and divinely willed world order, so too have Christians caused untold suffering in believing that their actions corresponded with divine law. *One* example of this also concerns the Christian mission in India. As shown at the beginning of this chapter, Christians perceived the conquering and violent conquest

167 On this demand, often raised in India itself, and its practical implementation see the examples in Knitter 1995, 157-180 as well as in Kuttianimattathil 1995, 521-534.

168 Cp. the overview in Forrester 1980, 155-172, as well as, somewhat more generally, Halbfass 1988, 310-333.

169 On Ambedkar, see Jürgens 1994. The abolition of a caste-specific legal system by the Indian Constitution was primarily Abedkar's accomplishment, who as the Chairman of the Constitution Drafting Committee "practically singlehandedly" drafted the constitution. Cp. Jürgens 1994, 31.

170 Rothermund, C. and D. 1995 give a short overview.

of non-Christian countries and the extermination of their religions not as an injustice but rather as divine right, even as a God-given duty. The Hindu caste system therefore gives Christians no occasion to boast. Rather, the positive experiences that Christians have made by transforming their own religious tradition should give them occasion to wish for and, as far as possible, to support similar processes in Hinduism.

Repressive Tolerance?

Unlike many Neo-Hindus, and in contrast especially to Mahatma Gandhi, Bhimrao Ambedkar (1891-1956), who was himself a casteless and became their uncontested leader, argued that it would be impossible to achieve, within Hinduism, an adequate reform of the caste system. Therefore, Ambedkar endorsed the conversion of the casteless to Christianity or to Islam, and finally, shortly before his death in 1956, turned to Buddhism in a public ceremony together with five hundred thousand followers. Millions more took the same step in the subsequent years. His intention to abandon Hinduism in favor of another religion was something that Ambedkar had already made publicly known in 1935.[171] Gandhi by contrast was no friend of conversions and from the beginning of the 1930s took a particularly dismissive attitude towards Christian missionary efforts. In part, Gandhi justified his dismissal of mission work with the pluralist argument "that all religions are fundamentally equal" and that people of each religion owe other religions "the same innate respect ... as we have for our own."[172] Ambedkar therefore attacked Gandhi with the most fervor. He argued that it was impossible for all religions to be equally true or of equal value. Hence one could not demand equal respect for all of them. Rather, it was the duty of members of different religions, according to Ambedkar, to openly criticize what they perceived as being untrue and ethically wrong in another religion. The call to conversion would thus be fully in line with this obligation. Ambedkar regarded Gandhi's rejection of mission and his pluralist justification of this rejection only a strategy for immunizing Hinduism from the critique of other religions. And he anticipated the danger that one day such argumentation might be used to oppress Christianity in India.[173]

This fear was by no means simply plucked out of thin air. The call to legal regulation and restriction of missionary activities is virtually omnipresent in India.[174] Such tendencies as predicted by Ambedkar are certainly present in the context of parties and organizations that are part of the so-called *Hindutva*-movement, such as BJP,

171 Cp. Jürgens 1994, 35.
172 Thus Gandhi in the magazine "Harijan" of 1936, p. 330. Cited from Ambedkar 1989, 446.
173 Cp. Ambedkar 1989, 445-450. This is a passage taken from one of Ambedkar's posthumously published writings.
174 Cp. Thomas M.M. 1990, 59; Samartha 1991, 142-154.

RSS and VHP. M. S. Golwalkar, leader of the RSS from 1940-1973, openly advocated a Hindu national state, in which there would be no room for Muslims and Christians. Oddly enough, his justification for this position is that only Hinduism offers the spiritual bases for a universal brotherhood of humankind and the unity of religions. Hinduism alone, he argues, is in a position to appreciate all religions and see them as equally valid. This is Hinduism's gift to the world, the treasure entrusted to it by God. It is for this reason, that is, for the good of the whole world, that one must protect this treasure in India from the harmful influence of those religions that do not share this same spirit. Thus in the name of a pluralist conception of religion an intolerant religious politics is demanded.[175]

The Indian controversies about mission and the intolerant ideas on religious politics in the *Hindutva*-movement direct our attention to two basic dangers of which a pluralist theology of religion must remain aware: *First,* the notion of pluralist equality must not lead to an inability to be critical. By the way, the same is true of intra-Christian ecumenism, in which the efforts at mutual recognition and unity in diversity only too easily lead to the danger of no longer being at all critical of one's ecumenical partner. If in former times one polemically overshot the goal, now one is too often silent. The same problems present themselves at the level of pluralistically conceived interreligious relations. Good relations, whether ecumenical or interreligious in nature, must also allow for mutual criticism. The question of the appropriate criteria for such criticism therefore proves foundational once again.[176] As much as it is of crucial importance to first understand each religion on the basis of its own principles and assesses it according to its own norms, as little would it be sufficient to stop at this point. The normative foundations of each religion themselves need to be checked for their interreligious compatibility or, better, acceptability. Only to the extent that such fundamental compatibility has been established can one, as part of interreligious critique, scrutinize another religion by drawing on that religion's own norms. Otherwise, that is, if one would support an unqualified pluralism and hold that the validity of all norms is entirely context-dependent, it would be impossible to avoid the danger of a relativism that lacks any criteria and is incapable of any criticism.[177]

Second, a pluralist theology of religions too must remain bound to the principle of tolerance. Precisely when it is understood that a pluralist position is not about tolerance, that it does not suggest the toleration but the appreciation of other religions,[178] then it becomes all the more important to practice genuine tolerance toward those who do not share this appreciation. Otherwise there is the real danger

175 Cp. Frei 1996; Klostermaier 2002, 155f.
176 On this, cp. again above pp. 41-50.
177 In his discussion on human rights—against the backdrop of the Indian caste system—Raimon Panikkar comes dangerously close to such relativism and only avoids succumbing to it because of his principle of "mutual fecundation". Cp. Panikkar 1995, 109-133.
178 Cp. on this above pp. 162-164.

that a pluralist notion will degenerate into what Herbert Marcuse, in another context, once identified as "repressive tolerance."[179]

Yet these critical and self-critical words should not obscure the fact that the long and multi-layered Hindu tradition contains an immense philosophical, theological, and spiritual treasure, from which not only Christianity but all religions may benefit. Undoubtedly part of this treasure is also the particular contribution that Hinduism can make—and has made through the great Neo-Hindus—to a pluralist understanding of religious diversity: Its insight into the manifoldness of God's presence that Hinduism has so often testified to throughout its history, as for example in the following verse by Abhinavagupta (10./11. Ct.), Kashmir's great Shaivite master:

> In you alone, the benevolent one,
> The highest
> Who transcends the thicket [of the world],
> Who is without beginning,
> Who is one only,
> Who rests in people's hearts in many different ways,
> Who is the foundation of everything,
> Who inhabits all things, the quick and the dead,
> I take refuge.[180]

179 Of course this danger is not exclusively connected with a pluralist position. Rather, it is a basic problem linked to self-affirmation and has been appropriately analyzed by Gerd Neuhaus who describes it as the "Sarastro-Syndrome." Cp. Neuhaus 2003.

180 Paramārthasāra vs. 1. Quoted after Mayer-König 1995, 153. On Abhinavagupta, see also Bäumer 1992 and 2003.

15. Christianity and Buddhism

On the History of Christian-Buddhist Encounter

An Explosive Pre-History?

In comparing the canonical writings of Christianity and Buddhism one finds a surprisingly large number of similar stories, nearly identical miracle reports, related or even identical metaphors, and surprisingly synonymous proverbial wisdom sayings. The increasing awareness of this in the West around the end of the nineteenth century spurred intense research into possible mutual borrowings.[1] Could it be that the New Testament is substantially influenced by Buddhism? And did Christianity in turn inspire those striking developments within Buddhism that led to the emergence of Mahāyāna Buddism? The bulk of the research interest lay in the first question. But all the extensive research that was done did not lead to an even remotely probable result. The fact that there were already intensive trade relations between India and the Mediterranean region makes it conceivable, in principle, that there was also an exchange of religious ideas.[2] Yet there is no solid evidence of a substantial Christian-Buddhist influence in either of the two possible directions. Nearly everything on this topic remains a matter of speculation. Particularly lacking is some kind of link, that is, some source of Christian ideas that at the same time would undeniably display Buddhist influence. Richard Garbe's 1914 work *India and Christianity* ("Indien und das Christentum") concluded that a few Christian miracle reports[3] as well as the expression "the wheel of births" in James 3:6 were likely inspired by Buddhist sources, but presumably no more than that.

Since then, interest in this area of research has diminished considerably, even though it continues to flicker up from time to time, even to the present. For example, toward the end of the 1970s the Canadian religious studies scholar Roy C. Amore suggested a far-reaching Buddhist influence on the New Testament.[4] In particular, Amore believed that he had found the missing link. He proposed this to be

1 Benz, Nambara 1960, 53ff contains a bibliographical overview of this. On the question of mutual borrowings, see my extensive treatment in Schmidt-Leukel 1992, 22-35.

2 Halbfass 1988, 2-23 offers a good overview of the early exchange of ideas between India and Greek-Roman antiquity.

3 Garbe's thesis was later supported by the work of Norbert Klatt 1982, who considers the New Testament stories of walking on water very likely to have been influenced by Buddhism.

4 Cp. Amore 1978.

the text called "Q" (short for "Quelle" = source) that has been postulated by New Testament exegetes but never actually been discovered. A widespread thesis assumes that the Gospels of Matthew and Luke used two common sources: the Gospel of Mark and a lost source referred to as "Q." If Q really existed its content would thus include the material that Matthew and Luke have in common but is not found in the Gospel of Mark. The thus reconstructed Q source displays, according to Amore, a vast number of stunning parallels to the *Dhammapada,* an ancient Buddhist collection of sayings, which in its *Gāndhāri* version was used by the Dharmaguptaka School in its westward-directed mission. Apart from that, Amore even allows for the possibility of an immediate Buddhist influence on Jesus himself through the possible presence of Buddhist missionaries in Palestine. Moreover, he suggests a Hindu and/or Buddhist influence on the development of the Christian incarnation doctrine which he regards as clearly following the schema of the *avatāra* motif. However, as we may add *en passant*, the legend that Jesus himself had been in India, which is widespread in esoteric circles, has been unmasked as being largely an invention of the nineteenth-century.[5]

Currently, Duncan M. Derrett[6] and Christian Lindtner[7] are still defending the thesis of far-reaching Buddhist influence on the New Testament. Yet one problem of their works is that often the possibility of a Buddhist influence is not sufficiently balanced against the alternative explanation of the respective passages through Hellenistic influence and intra-Jewish developments. The same is also true in the reverse situation. Much in Mahāyāna Buddhism can be more easily and more plausibly explained by intra-Buddhist tendencies and by Hindu influence than by making use of the hypothesis of a Christian inspiration. Moreover, those theses that assume a massive mutual borrowing between religions too often traffic in adventurous speculation and thus have—as far as the New Testament is concerned—to date found as good as no support among broader exegetical circles. Perhaps even more important than this observation is the following admission by Amore: Even if there was, as Amore himself assumes, indeed a Buddhist influence on Q and possibly on Jesus himself, the Buddhist ideas were in the process of adoption creatively transformed by the dominant factor of Jewish theism.[8] Thus even if there was such an influence, it was unable to relativize the theistic setting.

This differentiates it from another starting point in the research for possible historical dependencies. It is undisputed that the strong mystical strands in Judaism, Christianity, and Islam were all to a great extent influenced by the Neoplatonist phi-

5 On this cp. Grönbold 1985.

6 Cp. Derrett 2000, 2004.

7 Cp. Lindtner 2001. Lindtner even assumes that the evangelists themselves used Buddhist Sanskrit texts (ibid. 240). Lindtner's theses are unfortunately not free from more than dubious, and even racist, background assumptions. He postulates that Christianity emerged under two opposing influences: The influence of Semitic cultures on the one hand and the influence of the allegedly superior Aryan cultures on the other, represented by Greece and the Sanskrit culture of India.

8 Cp. Amore 1978, 184.

losophy going back to Plotinus (third century C.E.). Of particular relevance here is, on the one hand, the Neoplatonic notion of unity or oneness and, on the other, the strong pull to "negative theology": the conviction that ultimate reality (the "one"= *hen*) is necessarily above and beyond the level of the mind/reason (*nous*), that is, above and beyond the level of conceptual comprehension and representation. Now there are some grounds to speak of the possibility of, if not a specifically Buddhist, at least a general Indian influence on Plotinus, perhaps mediated by Plotinus' mysterious teacher Ammonios Sakkas. These reasons have to do not only with a striking similarity between the content of the Neoplatonic system and certain Indian ideas but also with a series of further circumstances: First, Plotinus quite obviously used meditative contemplative practices. Second, there is good evidence that at the time of Plotinus some information about India and also about the Buddha was available in Alexandria, the place where Ammonios taught.[9] Third, Plotinus' student Porphyry reports in his biography of Plotinus that Plotinus, after the death of his teacher Ammonios, decided to leave Alexandria and go to Asia to study the philosophy of the "Persians and Indians" there (Porphyrius, *Vita Plotinii*, 3, 15-17). To this end Plotinus joined Gordian III's campaign, which however failed, with the result that Plotinus did not reach India and had to turn back. Thus Plotinus himself never was in India. But one will have to assume that he nonetheless knew so much about India and Indian philosophy that it was worthwhile to him to embark on the risky adventure of getting there in order to learn more from it.

Now even if there was some sort of Indian influence on Plotinus, this still does not yet imply that the Neoplatonically-influenced mysticism is therefore a kind of alien element in Judaism, Christianity, and Islam.[10] For far more important than the possibility of an Indian influence on Neoplatonism—at least from a theological perspective—is the question of how the Neoplatonic philosophical inheritance was able to become so enormously influential in the three Abrahamaic religions. Both the persuasiveness of the Neoplatonic ideas and an apparently strong readiness to accept these ideas must have played an important role here. And this openness to Neoplatonic influence must have its own foundation in the Abrahamic traditions themselves, independent and in advance of any possible Indian influence.

More solid traces of a Buddhist influence can be found among individual ancient Gnostics, particularly in Manichaeism. These influences are as a whole rather peripheral and had no significant effects on Christianity. The emergence and rapid spread of Islam from late Antiquity on formed an almost insurmountable barrier blocking further opportunities for encounter between Western Christianity and Buddhism. It is true that individual Buddhist narrative motifs found entry into Christianity by way of Islam, among them incidentally the Buddha legend itself, so that the Buddha was honored as a saint in the West in the form of the legend-

9 For example, the Buddha is mentioned by Clement of Alexandria (*Stromata* I, XV, 71,6) and later by Saint Jerome/Hieronymus (*Libri ad Jovianum* I, 42).

10 As is the tendency in Nambara 1960.

ary persons Barlaam and Josaphat. Yet apart from a very few exceptions, there were no actual encounters. Marco Polo, who met Buddhism on his journeys in the thirteenth century, held the opinion that as a Christian the Buddha would have become a great saint.[11] Marco Polo, like the few Western missionaries who reached Buddhist regions (such as the Franciscans who reached Tibet and China in the thirteenth and fourteenth centuries), categorized the Buddhists as "idolaters" ("idololatrae").[12] Since there is no image worship in Judaism and Islam, and given that the Christian veneration of images was of course not counted as "idolatry" (who in the world of religions would have ever understood his or her own cult as "idolatry"?), Buddhism was the only religion known at that time to which this biblical label seemed to fit. At a later stage it was then also applied to Hinduism.

The situation was quite different among the Nestorian Christians in Asia. Not only did they live in India ("Thomas Christians"[13]), they also advanced to Central Asia and China, where they partly practiced a close exchange with Buddhists. Unfortunately we do not know much more than that this exchange existed and that it was not without consequences for the theology of the Asian Nestorians.[14] At the beginning of the ninth century there appeared to have been more than 200,000 Nestorian Christians in China. Together with Buddhism, Nestorian Christianity was hit hard by the persecution of "foreign religions" under Emperor Wu-tsung (841-846). Western Christianity at that time did not receive any closer knowledge about the Nestorian experiences of Buddhism. In the fourteenth century there was a Franciscan mission in China, but it perished rather quickly. More intensive encounters between European Christianity and Buddhism only became possible at the beginning of the modern era with the successful circumnavigation of the Islamic countries. Now the European seagoing nations pushed through not only to India (where by this time Buddhism had already died out) but also to vital Buddhist centers such as Sri Lanka, China, and Japan. However, what followed was to a great extent tragic and brought with it ongoing burdens for Christian-Buddhist relations.

Historical Burdens

Jesuit missionaries came to Sri Lanka, together with the Portuguese, at the beginning of the sixteenth century. By the mid-sixteenth century, led by Francis Xavier, they reached Japan and by the end of the sixteenth century, China.[15] In Sri Lanka, the Portuguese quickly succeeded in conquering and colonizing the coastal regions that were to them of particular commercial interest. In these regions the Portuguese

11 Cp. Lubac 1952, 39f.
12 Cp. Welbon 1968, 13ff.
13 Cp. above chapter 14, pp. 352f.
14 Cp. Klimkeit 1981.
15 See also von Brück, Lai 1997, 79ff; 109ff, 149ff.

persecuted Buddhism in a harsh and sanguinary manner. And after an attack on the Buddhist kingdom of Kandy in the Central Highlands, the Portuguese bragged about having robbed and destroyed a tooth relic of the Buddha that had been protected there for nearly two thousand years and was considered the most precious religious possession of Sri Lanka. The Buddhist guardians of the relic, however, explained that they only allowed a copy of the relic to fall into Portuguese hands.

Toward the end of the sixteenth century, in Japan the well-founded suspicion arose that Christian missionary activities represented the precursors of colonial intentions.[16] Among other things, it was the news of similar processes in the Philippines and in South America that fed this suspicion. The Buddhists became increasingly hostile toward Christianity because Catholic missionaries incited those Japanese Lords whom they had successfully proselytized to destroy Buddhist temples and drive out Buddhist monks from their regions. When Japan's fears of a Portuguese military threat strengthened, Christianity became outlawed, which resulted in several strong waves of persecution. After the overthrow of the Christian-led Shimabara uprising (1638), the Japanese authorities completely closed off their country. Throughout the country, they sought out Christians and made frequent use of horrific tortures to force them into apostasy. By the end of the seventeenth century, Christianity in Japan had been almost entirely destroyed. Only a few small groups managed, in complete hiding, to keep their faith.

In China, Christians and Buddhists also got involved in serious polemical conflicts with harsh attacks from both sides at a rather early stage of their encounter.[17] Soon, influential Buddhists demanded the expulsion of the Christian missionaries. Yet at this time, Buddhism in China was much less powerful than in Japan, with the result that Christianity managed to survive there until the middle of the eighteenth century. It was only after Rome forbade any adaptation to Chinese religious rituals and symbolic forms of expression that Christians became persecuted—primarily on the demand of Confucians and the Christian mission in China found its temporary end.

Over the long haul the Asian countries could not effectively thwart the military might of the Western colonial powers. In the mid-seventeenth century, the Dutch conquered large parts of southern Sri Lanka. At the end of the eighteenth century, the British arrived and finally managed to bring all of Sri Lanka under their control, including the Buddhist kingdom of Kandy that had successfully protected itself for a comparatively long time. In the second half of the nineteenth century, Great Britain also conquered Buddhist Burma and expanded its influence to parts of Thailand. During this same period, the French conquered the Buddhist countries of Vietnam, Laos, and Cambodia, then known as Indo-China. Several Western colonial powers, first of all Great Britain, also pushed into China, which though never totally con-

16 For an overview of the history of Japan in the sixteenth and seventeenth centuries, see Boxer 1967. Gössman 1965 gives a portrayal of the entire history up to the present.

17 On this cp. especially Kern 1992.

quered was brought to the state of a semi-colonial dependency. In the opium wars, Britain forced the Chinese to permit the import and trade of opium. Not only Britain but also Portugal, France, Germany, and Russia took over regions of China. Even Japan once again began to feel pressure from the West. Here it was the Americans who in the mid-nineteenth century used military power to force the opening of the country. Yet while the USA did not colonize the country, Japan itself operated as a colonial power expanding its reign over Korea and parts of weakened China.

The effects of the massive establishment of Western rule in the Buddhist countries of Asia reverberated back to Europe. During the nineteenth century, Buddhist texts became known here for the first time. Toward the end of the nineteenth century, scholarly editions and translations of Buddhist writings in European languages increased greatly in number, resulting in the establishment of European Buddhism. That is, under the influence of Buddhist writings, individual European intellectuals adopted Buddhist thought and propagated Buddhism in the West as an alternative to Christianity. This sparked heated disputes between Christian apologists and European Buddhists. And this situation had in turn its repercussions on Asia. The resistance of the Asian nations against Western colonialism, especially against the British colonial rule, now combined with efforts to demonstrate Buddhism as the religion superior to Christianity. In Sri Lanka, for example, after centuries of being humbled by Christian colonial powers, an equally nationalistic as well as decidedly anti-Christian Buddhism developed that is often known as Buddhist "modernism." But also in countries like Japan, where after the forced opening of the country there was gradual allowance for Christian mission, Buddhist opposition arose which tied in with both the anti-Christian literature of the seventeenth century persecutions of Christianity and with the contemporary parallel developments in other Buddhist countries.[18] In Korea, Japan used its colonial might to revitalize the significantly weakened Korean Buddhism and privilege it, also in order to combat the growing influence of Catholic and Protestant missions.[19] For Korea, this meant that the anti-colonial resistance was directed not against a Christian but against a Buddhist colonial power which allowed the Christians to present Christianity as an ally of the Korean people. This unique circumstance is presumably a major reason for the startling missionary success of Christianity in Korea that has no parallel in Asia.[20]

As a whole the modern encounter between Christianity and Buddhism—first in Asia and then, from the middle of the nineteenth century on, also in the West—was characterized by strong mutual polemic and partly also by deep hostility. In six-

18 On this see the excellent work of von Thelle 1987.

19 Cp. Grayson 2002, 184.

20 Unique with respect to those Asian countries that are under the influence of the Asian major religions of Hinduism, Buddhism, Confucianism, and Daoism. From the outset the situation was different in the Philippines. None of the major Asian religions dominated there. Hence it was easy for the Portuguese to conquer and almost completely Christianize the land within a few decades (with the exception of those parts of the south in which there had been a strong Muslim presence since the fourteenth century).

teenth-century Sri Lanka, Christians spilled the blood of Buddhists; in seventeenth century Japan it was the Buddhists who tortured and murdered Christians. Yet particularly the Buddhist side learned over the course of the centuries that Christian mission went hand in hand with colonial intentions and that in those places where Christian rule was established, Buddhists had to reckon with various forms of discrimination including open oppression and persecution. In this respect, the example of Sri Lanka is especially effective: After roughly 150 years of Portuguese rule, a further 150 years of Dutch rule, and then finally another 150 years of British colonial rule, Sri Lanka not only became sufficiently acquainted with different European nations but also with a relatively broad palette of different Christian denominations: initially Roman Catholics, then Reformed Christians, and finally Anglicans and Methodists. In each of those versions Christianity always pursued one and the same goal: exploiting colonial rule to disrupt Buddhism and usurp its position. These experiences became deeply carved into the collective memory and consciousness of the Buddhist in Sri Lanka (and not only there!). One of the impressive frescoes of the large Buddhist temple in Kelaniya near Colombo shows the Buddhist faithful how in the past Portuguese soldiers destroyed this temple and how Buddhist monks watched non-violently but also aghast.

It is true that the era of direct colonial rule is now over, but not the era of serious tensions. Sri Lanka, shattered by the long civil war between the Buddhist Singhalese and Hindu Tamils is currently besieged by massive well-funded missionary campaigns that originate predominantly in the USA. For political reasons Sri Lanka can hardly defend itself against this. In South Korea, Christianity has meanwhile become numerically as strong as Buddhism and here too the political situation plays more to the Christians. In recent years there have been frequent attacks on Buddhist temples and Buddha statues by Christians, as well as "defamation, spraying with feces, assaults, destruction and arson and other violent attacks of all types."[21]

Just as in the relationship of Christianity to Judaism, Islam, and Hinduism, it is also true that in Christianity's relationship to Buddhism primarily exclusivist positions shaped the broadly aggressive history of this relationship. Although neither Christian nor a Buddhist exclusivism necessarily has to lead to religious polemic, intolerance, and violent humiliation, or even violent attempts at annihilation, neither can we deny that exclusivist conceptions were almost always involved. Christians—and in response also Buddhists—have often seen in the other's religion no more than a dangerous and false path. It is, however, worth looking more closely at these exclusivisms since they contain relatively stable stereotypes and distortions that continue to have their effect on both sides to the present day.

21 Younghae Yoon, in Rötting 2001, 124.

Mutual Exclusivism

In the eyes of the Jesuit missionaries of the early modern era, Buddhism was precisely that as which the Christian Middle Ages had already categorized it, that is, "idolatry"[22] or even devil worship:

> Above all else, we hate and abhor the devil; the bonzes revere and worship him, build temples for him, and offer him great sacrifices.[23]

This was the judgement of the missionary to Japan, Louis Frois S.J., in 1585. When the missionaries encountered parallels to Christianity, they assessed them either as not genuine, or as diabolical imitations, or even as elaborate demonic enticement. An example of the latter can be found in the now famous words of the Visitor of Missions Valignano who in the sixteenth century reported that the teachings of Japanese Amida Buddhism are the same as the heresy of Luther and that both had been inspired by the devil.[24]

Although the sixteenth and seventeenth century missionaries certainly made an effort to understand the to them quite foreign teachings of the different Buddhist schools, their knowledge for the most part remained rather sketchy and imprecise, thus leaving little chance of correcting their theological assessments and prejudices. And yet, rather early on the question of how to correctly understand transcendent reality emerged as the fulcrum of Christian interpretation of Buddhism. Whereas the Christian missionaries initially realized that Buddhism also knew of an ultimate transcendent reality without, however, conceiving this as a personal god,[25] their judgment later hardened into the opinion that Buddhism is *idolatry* pure and simple. As Matteo Ricco (1552-1610) wrote:

> We differ from Buddhism by the following: (1) It is based on emptiness, we on reality; (2) it is focused on what is selfish, we on the common good; (3) it is ambivalent and contradicts itself, whereas we have a sole basis. Those are the *small* differences. It revolts (against the Lord of Heaven) and denies (him); we obey and serve (the Lord of Heaven). That is the *big* difference. That's it, and nothing else.[26]

Another contemporary text explained the underlying argument in the following way: If the Buddha really had not known about the existence of God, that would

22 Cp. Schurhammer 1939, 83.
23 Frois (1585) 1955, 157.
24 Cp. Valignano 1944, 161. I am grateful to the excellent unpublished work of Bucsek 1990 for identifying the exact source of this quotation.
25 Thus Juan Fernandez in 1551 for example reports regarding one of the early Christian-Buddhist disputations: "We asked them many things, in order to make it clear to them that there is a principle (principio) which gives all other things their beginning (principio). They admitted such was the case by saying, 'This is a principle from which all things come: Men, animals, plants. (…) This principle, they say, is neither good nor bad, has neither pleasure nor pain, neither lives nor dies, which means it is a Nothing.'" Schurhammer 1929, 67.
26 Kern 1984/85, 79f.

have been a sign of "greatest ignorance." But if the Buddha recognized but did not profess the existence of God, then that would have been the "greatest rebellion"[27]—an argument that has been repeated endlessly all the way into modern apologetics. According to this line of apologetics, the existence of God is recognizable to every thinking person by the natural light of reason. So anyone who denies God is either unspeakably stupid or—and more likely—deeply evil. What Ricci called the "big difference" continues to have its effects up to the present.

With the beginning of academic research on Buddhism and particularly with Bartélemy Saint-Hilaire's book, *Le Bouddha et sa religion* (*The Buddha and his Religion*) of 1860, a strand of interpretation established itself in the West that described Buddhism with four terms: *atheism, materialism, nihilism*, and *pessimism*. All four labels were at that time already being used in the ideological conflicts of the West. They served to identify the various non- or anti-Christian philosophies that in the wake of the Enlightenment had differentiated themselves from Christianity. And now the West began to apply these labels to Buddhism.[28]

The characterization of Buddhism as atheism had the most central and lasting significance. This view interpreted the lack of a personal concept of God in the Buddha's teaching as a clear and deliberate denial of God. It can often be observed that such labels, once applied, quickly become immune to possible objections. For example, in response to the objection that the Buddha did not deny the existence of God but was simply silent on the matter, the Protestant scholar of religion Hilko Schomerus countered that Buddha was so much an atheist that he did not even find it necessary to contest the existence of God explicitly.[29]

From the Buddha's supposed atheism significant consequences were derived for the interpretation of the Buddhist teachings on the "not-self" (*anātman*) and of Nirvāṇa. It was argued that Buddha not only denied God but all mental reality, and therefore also the existence of an immortal soul. That Buddhism had actually not denied the reality of the human mind or mental capacities, but rather only contested the notion of an *immutable* soul, was of no consequence to the Western interpretation of Buddhism. And so they interpreted the Buddhist not-self teaching as "a denial of the soul" and thus as evidence of a materialist view of the world and of human beings. From the alleged atheism and materialism it followed that there could be no life after death. Thus one understood Nirvāṇa as the ultimate annihilation and extinguishing of the person, which then lead to the characterization of Buddhism as "nihilism."

However, neither the Buddhist claims about rebirth nor about Nirvāṇa as a positive and worthwhile goal of salvation fit into this view. Representatives of this strand of interpretation noticed such discrepancies, but explained them this way: The fact that despite his materialist denial of the soul the Buddha nonetheless taught reincar-

27 Ibid. 96.
28 Cp. on this Schmidt-Leukel 1992, 36-116.
29 Schomerus 1931, 25.

nation simply revealed the confused and underdeveloped character of his philosophy. In his teaching on Nirvāṇa as the final termination of all reincarnation the Buddha's fundamentally nihilistic orientation would find its clearest expression. The only reason why the Buddha declared Nirvāṇa as a desirable and worthwhile goal was that he hated life. Given the belief in perpetual reincarnations, Nirvāṇa appears positive only because it finally brings about the longed for total annihilation. This argument cemented the characterization of Buddhism as a pessimist worldview. It is the Buddha's stance toward life that was regarded as pessimistic since he allegedly despised life and considered it altogether as suffering. Again and again the Buddhist teaching was summarized with the words: "All life is suffering."[30]

From these cornerstones of a Western interpretation of Buddhism a series of further characterizations were derived that, from a theological perspective, appeared as particularly important, that is, as important regarding Buddhism's comparison with Christianity.

Given the Buddhist teachings on reincarnation and Nirvāṇa, one realized that Buddhism understood itself as a message of salvation. Western apologists, however, interpreted the Buddhist goal of salvation nihilistically as a salvation *from* existence. Regarding the concrete path to salvation, Buddhism was depicted as the dark counterpart to Christianity. Since Buddhism was supposedly atheistic, it allegedly taught self-salvation whereas Christianity proclaimed salvation through divine grace. The fact that the notion of self-salvation stands in tension with the Buddhist "not-self" teaching was—if one was even aware of this tension—regarded as yet another inconsistency of Buddhism. Because Buddhism was seen as a form of materialism supposedly denying the human soul but at the same time teaching a path of self-salvation, one concluded that in the context of Buddhism the idea of a genuine altruistic love of neighbor was impossible. If good works were done at all, then they were done not for the good of the other but only for one's own ego-centered progress along the path of salvation. The actual goal of this path was viewed as the extinction of all the dictates of the heart, no longer doing any good works, but having blunted all affects meeting the desired ultimate annihilation. In this way, Buddhism was assessed as thoroughly escapist, weary, and culturally subversive. Buddhism's meditative practices were regarded as dangerous relics from the dark beginnings of humanity and as forms of shamanistic self-hypnosis whose goal was a narcoticization and blunting of one's heart. The Buddha himself appeared as a philosopher disgusted by life whose ideas were confused and contradictory and who led people astray to depressive and passive aversion to the world. Jesus Christ and Christianity are therefore not only incomparably higher than the Buddha and Buddhism ("as man is superior to the animal," as Archibald Scott put it[31]), Christianity is its complete opposite, the

30 This is often cited rather freely as being the content of the first noble truth, though such a phrase is not to be found there. From a Buddhist perspective the life of the unenlightened beings is unsatisfying and full of suffering. By contrast, the life of the enlightened one is pervaded with the peace and happiness of Nirvāṇa.

31 Scott 1971, 41.

bright way of salvation compared to the way of deep darkness and confusion (they differ, according to W. Englert, by then a theologian of the University of Bonn, like "the true dew of paradise from the poison spread by the snakes"[32]). Ernst Haack, a Protestant High Consistory member, ended his widely distributed lecture published in 1898 with the following words, characteristic of this strand of the Western interpretation of Buddhism:

> There is absolutely no way in which Jesus Christ, the Holy One of God, could be placed alongside Siddharta Gautama of Kapilavastu. The latter, with his teaching about suffering, is also no positive preparation for salvation through Christ, let alone that he himself could save man. We rather have to stick with the alternative: Christ or Buddha, and with the apostle's exclusion (Acts 4:12): "There is salvation in no one else, for there is no other name under heaven given among mortals by which we must be saved."[33]

As I said before, some elements of this exclusivist perspective on Buddhism continue to have theological effect. I will mention at least a few examples: In his contribution to the 1997 Christmas edition of the *Süddeutsche Zeitung* (No. 296), the renowned theologian Johann Baptist Metz in a disastrous manner deployed the overused clichés of the allegedly escapist Buddhism on the one hand and of Christianity facing the world with love on the other.[34] Christianity, according to Metz, teaches "not a mysticism of closed eyes, but a mysticism of eyes wide open"—"a mysticism of compassion." Its opposite is "the mysticism of closed eyes, the in the end only self-centered mysticism of suffering, as found in the Far Eastern and especially Buddhist traditions." Buddhism has a normative figure who upon encountering the suffering of others "finally escapes to the royal palace within his own mind in order to find in the mysticism of closed eyes the land that is immune to all suffering. Jesus on the other hand … opens … the way of compassion." What effect must such statements have on Buddhists, given their concrete historical experiences with Christianity? Why does Metz not demonstrate a similar sensitivity toward other religions as he does to Judaism? How shall one explain his claims about Buddhism given that the entire Buddhist tradition in all its various branches honors the Buddha as the embodiment of compassion (*karuṇā*), and that the Buddha legend actually only begins where Metz has it end, namely *with* enlightenment, and that the Buddha, *after* his enlightenment, "out of compassion" (as it says in the canonical report) for forty-five years led a life of active commitment to the world? Presumably the most obvious answer is that Metz simply—and carelessly—followed a widespread cliché that fits only too well with his own theological agenda. But the days in which one could allow oneself such recklessness in the wider public sphere should really be a thing of the past. For by now undoubtedly there are also Buddhists among the readers of the *Süddeutsche Zeitung*.

32 Englert 1898, Foreword (no page numbers).
33 Haack 1898, 23f.
34 Metz 1997, 57.

The remarks of Pope John Paul II about Buddhism in his book, *Crossing the Theshold of Hope,* offer another inglorious example that caused great irritation in the Buddhist world. In this book, the Pope criticizes Buddhism as a "negative soteriology," an "'atheistic' system," and as an escapist, pessimistic teaching of self-salvation. On this the Theravāda monk Bhikkhu Bodhi living in Sri Lanka rightly commented:

> In criticizing Buddhism for its so-called "negative soteriology," Pope John Paul is echoing an evaluation of the Buddhist teaching that was widely disseminated by Christian missionaries in the 19th century. This view depicted Buddhism as a bleak doctrine of world-negating escapism aimed at personal annihilation in a nameless nothingness. Serious scholars of Asian religions, including open-minded Christians, have long recognized this characterization of Buddhism to be erroneous. The negative view of Buddhism was rooted partly in simple misunderstanding, partly in deliberate distortion aimed at justifying the evangelical ambitions of the Christian missions.[35]

As is well known, the Pope's comments drew considerable protests from Theravāda Buddhists preceding and during his visit to Sri Lanka in 1995. Many Christians, especially those engaged in dialogue with Buddhism, had hoped that the Pope would use this occasion to find suitable words to correct his judgment. Yet the threshold of this hope was unfortunately not crossed.[36]

In recent times, exclusivist clichés have also been spread by the former Buddhist Paul Williams after his re-conversion to Christianity. Buddhism, says Williams, does believe in the existence of gods. Yet these "gods" are still inner-worldly beings, subject to the reincarnation cycle (*saṃsāra*). What, according to Williams, Buddhism does not know is a God who is the basis and guarantor of salvation. From a Christian perspective Buddhism would thus have to count as a form of atheism.[37] Given that Buddhism explicitly rejects the belief in a divine creation, it cannot in the end elicit genuine love and real virtue, Williams claims. For both, love and virtue, presuppose humility, and true humility would come only from insight into one's own creatureliness. And it is precisely this insight that Buddhism allegedly lacks.[38]

As I indicated before, exclusivist interpretations of Christianity by Buddhists arose mainly in reaction to the exclusivist attitude of Christians. This does not mean that the Buddhist judgments were less demeaning than those of the Christians. Zhixu (1599-1655), who is counted among the "four great monks from the end of the Ming-dynasty" and who stands in the tradition of Zen and Amida Buddhism, makes the following judgment about Christian missionaries:

> At first [they learned] the words and writing of our country. Next, in secret they studied many books on the three teachings (…) pulled things from Buddhism and connected them with Confucianism, turned everything around and

35 Bodhi 1995, 20.

36 Cp. the 1995 issue of *Dialogue N.S.* which was totally devoted to this problem, as well as the Buddhist contributions in Sherwin, Kasimow 2000, 85-122.

37 Cp. Williams 2002, 25ff.

38 Cp. Williams 2004, 110f.

> created these false teachings in order through them to deceive the world, defraud the people, and destroy the country's foundation of well-being.[39]

The consequences derived from the disapproving stance toward Christianity were no less grim. In the seventeenth century, the Chinese Buddhist Huang composed a summons—pathetically titled "Remaining silent is unbearable to me"—in which he demanded that one prohibit Christianity and burn its writings.[40]

On the Buddhist side we can discern one central point of criticism. This criticism clearly has something to do with what Ricci had earlier called the "big difference." Zen master Yuanwu (1566-1642) formulated it in this way:

> If the Lord of Heaven has no insight, he too is (like) a man thrown back and forth in the three worlds and cannot give men a spiritual soul. Yet if in the three worlds a man has insight, then nothing will prevent him from being the lord in his place and the chief in his circumstances. In heaven he guides gods; (…) among men he guides men. He is neither a god nor a man, but he commands gods and men. (…) If this is so, then what is called the Lord of Heaven is an empty name. Yet that which calls upon the Lord of Heaven is not empty, but rather the reality of original nature. If it is the reality of original nature then it is common to all beings and the suchness of all beings. (…) The one who peers cannot discern its limits, neither can the one who searches explore its origins. It comprehends heaven and earth and penetrates past and present. It brings the sun and the moon to their clarity and the souls to their spiritedness. (…) It rules over gods and men, but gods and men cannot rule over it. It pervades birth and death, but birth and death cannot pervade it. The reality of original nature is the greatest miracle!"[41]

Ricci and Yuanwu thus each defend different notions of ultimate transcendent reality, and accuse each other of totally misapprehending this reality, or indeed of reversing its meaning into the opposite. For Ricci, transcendent reality is a personal other, whom a human being must approach with humility and grateful reverence. By contrast, for Yuanwu transcendent reality is beyond all differentiation. It includes all beings and is their original nature. The correct attitude toward it is insight into its absolute transcendence and the existential translation of its unmediated presence. It is only in this way that humans will be raised up above gods and men and above birth and death, that is, only so will they be liberated from Saṃsāra. In Yuanwu's eyes fixing ultimate reality on a concrete personal vis-à-vis—such as the Lord of Heaven—is completely misguided. He can understand the "Lord of Heaven" only as a deity that is itself part of the Saṃsāra. In this, Yuanwu is following that old Buddhist pattern according to which Indian Buddhism declared the Hindu deities to be beings still caught in the cycle of reincarnation and thus lacking any transcendent status.

39 Kern 1992, 262.
40 Ibid. 30.
41 Ibid. 129f.

These deities cannot save. Only the knowledge of absolute reality, which transcends all limitation, can be salvific.

During British colonial rule in Sri Lanka, several debates between Christians and Buddhists were held that garnered a great deal of public participation. The most well-known took place in Panadura in 1873. It is hard to imagine a debate more defined by mutual polemics, reciprocal misunderstanding, and the obvious attitude of not wishing to understand the other. The learned Buddhist monk Mohattiwatte Gunānanda (1823-1890) contended that Christianity is a thoroughly false religion, that the God of Christianity is a bloodthirsty demon who is afraid of iron, and that no one who adopts the Christian faith can possibly hope for a happy future life.[42]

Anagārika Dharmapāla (1864-1933), the renowned leader of the modern Buddhist revival in Sri Lanka, wrote about the founder of Christianity:

> Jesus as a human personality was an utter failure. He made no impression on the public during the three years of his ministry. No thinker or philosopher took the least notice of his philosophy which helped to create imbeciles. The few illiterate fishermen of Galilee followed him as he had promised to make them judges to rule over Israel.[43]

According to Dharmapāla, the spiritual level of devotees is reflected in their deities, for, "Each man according to his intelligence makes his own god."[44] Dharmapāla reckons Christianity to be among the lowest class of religions, i.e. the destructive cults,[45] as opposed to the Buddha who "taught that man can get his salvation without the help of angry, blood thirsty deities."[46] His way is a path of "scientific wisdom," on which one "can attain the highest peace, bliss and freedom by individual effort and personal purity of heart."[47] The only thing Dharmapāla exempted from his critique was the ethics of the Sermon on the Mount. Yet this, he conjectured, could have been borrowed from Buddhism.[48]

At the present time, an exclusivist Buddhist view of Christianity is primarily found in the work of the Sri Lankan philosopher Gunapala Dharamsiri.[49] Dharmasiri, who did his Ph.D. with Ninian Smart in Great Britain, presented an exhaustive critique of the Christian concept of God for which he substantially drew on arguments from the Western critique of religion. Most notably, however, he focuses his attacks on the connection between the idea of God and ethical practice. Belief in a personal God who as an expression of ultimate reality stands above all—and hence also above all validity of ethical norms—implies, according to Dharmasiri, a latent unethical and deeply dangerous potential that, in the history of all theistic religions

42 Cp. Copper 1873, esp. 18ff.
43 Dharmapāla, 1991, 475.
44 Dharmapāla 1989, 13.
45 Cp. ibid. 6f.
46 Ibid. 12.
47 Ibid. 12f.
48 Dharmapāla 1991, 26f.
49 Cp. Dharmasiri 1974 and the enlarged edition of 1988.

including Christianity, has time and again become manifest with fateful results. In this, Dharmasiri is primarily following an argument of Ludwig Feuerbach. Yet similar reflections can already be discerned in the critique that classical Buddhist philosophers in India leveled at Hindu concepts of God.[50] According to Dharmasiri, Christianity ties salvation to submission to God's authority and is thus, in the end, unable to support human beings in developing a truly autonomous posture and hence also incapable of helping them to achieve a mature religiosity. In Buddhism, by contrast, salvation is connected only to morality and insight and not to some kind of submission to the Buddha. Instead, every person is called to attain by his or her own insight the same enlightened and liberated status as the Buddha himself. For Dharmasiri, in the hierarchy of religions Christianity stands at the very bottom end.[51]

To be sure, neither Christianity nor Buddhism are bound to exclusivist positions in their reciprocal attitudes. But what makes it possible for Christians and Buddhists to move beyond the exclusivist ways of defining their relationship in favor of an inclusivist position? And how far will the adoption of inclusivism lead them in their mutual relationships?

Inclusivist Openings

Contrary to the interpretation of Buddhism as a form of atheism, a few scholars in the nineteenth century suggested Buddhism was neither atheistic nor nihilistic, but that rather it belongs to the branch of mystical religiosity.[52] Nirvāṇa, they held, was essentially identical to the goal of all mysticism, supposed to be the union of the soul with God. While the interpretation of Buddhism as a form of atheism became dominant, particularly in theological circles, the interpretation of Buddhism as a form of mysticism initially remained restricted to some circles within the science of religion, although individual academics who represented this direction—such as Friedrich Heiler and Gustav Mensching—clearly pursued Christian theological interests.

Characteristic of this strand of interpretation is the ascription of a mystical notion of God to Buddhism, in contrast to the personal notion of God found in Christianity. According to Gustav Mensching, for example, Buddhism is not lacking the notion of God as such; rather, what is missing are the personal traits of it. Mensching interprets the experience of Nirvāṇa as an experience of union with the impersonal numinous. If God is conceived as an impersonal reality, then, says Mensching, it is understandable that Buddhism teaches the de-personalization of human beings as a way to the unification with this impersonal divine reality. As a result, this line of interpreting Buddhism led to more or less the same view of Buddhism's

50 Cp. on this the texts in Lindtner 1999, esp. 69ff.
51 Cp. esp. the new "Postscript" in Dharmasiri 1988, 259-271.
52 See the extensive presentation in Schmidt-Leukel 1992, 13ff., 73f.

concrete path of salvation as it is found in its interpretation as atheism: Buddhism is allegedly concerned with overcoming earthly existence, and the doing away with all individuality and all emotional stimuli directed to concrete life. Thus also in its interpretation as mysticism, Buddhism is in the end characterized as escapist, as incapable of honoring the human person or of doing actual deeds of charitable love.

The extent to which such judgments became hardened and were retained even in the face of an increasingly better knowledge can be seen in a comment by Albert Schweitzer. Schweitzer never tires of emphasizing that in contrast to Jesus, the Buddha does not demand any charitable acts of love, and indeed on the basis of his teachings cannot even aspire to do so. At this point in time, that is, in 1936, scholars were already quite familiar with those canonical texts in which not only lay followers but also Buddhist monks are reminded to do "acts of love," and in which the Buddha himself sets the model for doing so; as for example in that passage of the monastic rule which recounts how the Buddha once himself looked after one of his neglected confrères who was sick with dysentery. He washed and cared for this monk and later admonished the other monks by stating: "Whosoever ... would wait upon me, he should wait upon the sick."[53] Schweitzer too knew and mentions this passage. Yet he concludes from it that the Buddha, in contrast to his own teaching, "allowed himself to be carried away, and acted from the motive of love." In the personality of the Buddha, says Schweitzer, ethics was "so strong and so living" that it actually could not be accommodated by his teaching.[54] Thus Western scholars were at times more prepared to exclude the Buddha from Buddhism than to correct their own gridlocked image of Buddhism.

Similar examples can still be found in contemporary Western religious studies. In a 2002 comparison between the Buddha and Jesus, the indologist Axel Michaels first quotes from one of the most significant texts[55] of ancient Buddhism on the Buddhist understanding of love (*mettā, maitrī*) the verse:

> As a mother watches over and protects her only child, even to the endangerment of her own life, so one should lovingly embrace the whole world with beneficent, unlimited kindness.[56]

Michaels then comments on this verse with the following words:

> This feeling of friendship is marked by gentleness and indifference, however, not by empathy. *Maitrī* is in a sense nothing more than an indifferent goodwill or liking without affection.[57]

53 Vinaya-Piṭaka: Mahāvagga VIII, 26:1-4.

54 Cp. Schweitzer 1936, 114.

55 The so-called *Mettā-Sutta*= *Sutta Nipāta*, 143-152.

56 Cited following the translation in Luz, Michaels 2006, 84 (see also Luz, Michaels 2002, 98).

57 Quoted after the German original (Luz, Michaels 2002, 98). What the English translation (Luz, Michaels 2006, 84) just renders as "an indifferent goodwill or liking" reads in the original version "indifferentes Wohlwollen ohne Zuneigung". The phrase "ohne Zuneigung" ("without affection") has been supressed in the English version and is restituted here.

If it was the intention of the Buddhist text to propagate "indifference" and "indifferent goodwill without affection," why then does the text use as the normative analogy of this love the image of a mother who protects her only child with her own life? Does Michaels seriously believe that this example illustrates particularly well the notions of "indifference" and "goodwill without affection"? Hardly. Once again, here Michaels is simply holding on to deeply engrained patterns of interpretation, even if they do not fit the factual evidence.[58] In any case, the actual assertion of the text is clear: just as the mother feels for her only child and is prepared to sacrifice her own life on behalf of the child, so too shall the one who follows the Buddha embrace the whole world and share his goodness not only with some but with all beings without discrimination,[59] for it is only the love that does not differentiate that proves itself to be free of egocentric interest.

Within religious studies the difference between the Christian-personalist image of God and the supposed Buddhist mystical understanding of God was meant to remain unjudged as the task of religious studies was often regarded as providing a purely neutral description. Yet when theologians adopted the interpretation of Buddhism as mysticism, they explicitly gave it an evaluative character. Given that, according to this line of interpretation, Buddhism was supposed to accept, in principle, the existence of a divine reality, it could now be assessed more positively than within the context of its interpretation as atheism. However, its allegedly mystical concept of God and the corresponding path of salvation still appeared deficient when compared to Christianity. Christianity, one argued, contains certain decisive elements in its knowledge of God that Buddhism lacks and which give Christianity an advanced understanding: that God is a person, that God is the creator of an essentially good world, that all humans are likewise persons because they are created in the image of God, and that salvation consists of a personal loving relationship between God and human, the reflection and actualization of which is found in the love of neighbor among humans. From this perspective, the Buddha appears as the seeker who remains only dimly aware of the divine secret, while Jesus by contrast is the revealer who comes straight from God and discloses God's true nature to humanity.

This line of interpretation became significant for the beginnings of the Christian-Buddhist dialogue.[60] The important pioneering works of the 1960s by Hugo

58 It is also odd when Michaels, in order to substantiate his view, contrats Albert Schweitzer and Mother Teresa, as Christian role models, with the fourteenth Dalai Lama as a Buddhist example (cp. 2006, 76f). He thereby simply ignores the ground rules of scholarly interreligious comparison. An adequate comparison to the Dalai Lama might include Christian Church leaders such as Pope John Paul II, the Archbishop of Canterbury, etc, and as comparisons to Albert Schweitzer and Mother Teresa, one might think of Buddhist activists such as Ariyaratne or Mahaghosananda.

59 Including also non-human life forms (cp. Sutta Nipāta 146-147).

60 On this cp. the extensive overviews in: Spae 1980, Ingram 1988, Schmidt-Leukel 1992; von Brück, Lai 1997; 2001.

Enomiya-Lassalle,[61] Heinrich Dumoulin,[62] and Winston King,[63] all clearly stand in this tradition. Yet there were also some noticeable changes.

(1) Personal contacts with living Buddhism quickly showed that Buddhism by no means despises charitable love or encourages unethical behavior. Thus soon the voices of praise for the high ethical ideals and often impressive moral praxis of Buddhism increased. Yet there continued to be those who insisted that such praxis and ideals would actually contradict the content of Buddhist teaching.

(2) Personal experiences with the meditative practices of Buddhism resulted in an interpretation of Buddhism that not only paid more attention to such practices but also evaluated them in a much more positive light. Pioneers of Christian-Buddhist dialogue such as Enomiya-Lassalle or Thomas Merton triggered a relatively broad reception of Buddhist forms of meditation among Christians.

(3) A more intimate familiarity with Buddhist teachings created doubt about the notion that Buddhism embraces a mystical notion of God. Rather, one finally could not avoid the realization that Buddhism actually has no concept of God. The central religious terms in Buddhism, such as Buddha, Dharma, Nirvāṇa, and in Mahāyāna Buddhism terms like Śūnyatā, Dharmakāya or Dharmatā could not be properly understood in the sense of a curtailed concept of God. Rather, they required their own specific interpretation from within their genuine Buddhist context. Yet given the high regard with which the Christian side had in the meantime come to view Buddhist praxis, they were also not in a position to simply return to the atheist-nihilist view of Buddhism.

In the course of Christian-Buddhist dialogue, the following solution emerged: Christians were inclined to acknowledge that Buddhists can and had have genuine experiences of God. Yet at the same time Christians argued that Buddhism did not recognize and address such experiences *as* experiences of God. It was, so to say, only the human side of God experience that was more or less adequately reflected in Buddhism.

For example, Enomiya-Lassalle was of the opinion that the enlightenment experience of Zen Buddhism represents a genuine experience of God that has many experiential similarities with the accounts of the Christian mystics. But Buddhism falsely interpreted it as a monistic experience of unity with the cosmos. It is only through the revelation in Jesus Christ that it becomes possible to interpret the Zen experience of enlightenment correctly, that is, as that which it, according to Enomiya-Lassalle really is, namely an experience of unity with God. At the level of doctrine, Buddhism is therefore atheistic or at best pantheistic, but at the level of living experience it is in contact with the salvific presence of God. Heinrich Dumoulin argues in manner similar to Enomiya-Lassalle. Nothing in Buddhist praxis can be faulted, and this is also true from an ethical perspective. Moreover, Buddhist teach-

61 Cp. Enomiya-Lassalle 1966.
62 Cp. Dumoulin 1966.
63 Cp. King 1963.

ings reflect genuine mystical experiences with the divine reality. What is missing is the knowledge of God as a personal reality and also the correct knowledge of human's personhood. Buddhist praxis is thus actually ahead of Buddhist doctrine and therefore Buddhist doctrine cannot properly substantiate Buddhist praxis. Whereas Dumoulin held on to this position even in his old age,[64] Enomiya-Lassalle became ever more reticent over the years. One can even assume that he eventually moved toward a pluralist perspective on the relationship between Christianity and Buddhism.[65]

Christian interpretations of Buddhism that follow an inclusivist approach have, broadly speaking, only two options: Either they say that Buddhist doctrine and Buddhist praxis are in harmony with one another. Then they have to postulate that Buddhist doctrine and hence also Buddhist praxis is deficient compared to Christianity: that Buddhism has a deficient image of God since it lacks insight both regarding the personal nature of God and the fact that God is a reality different from the world and humanity. Correspondingly, Buddhist praxis would lack the full realization of personal values and of an appropriate relationship to the world.[66] Yet if Christian inclusivists opt for a more positive assessment of Buddhist praxis saying that at the level of praxis Buddhism does not lag behind Christianity, then they are forced to maintain either a contrast or at least a considerable tension between Buddhist praxis and Buddhist doctrine. From an inclusivist position it is impossible to maintain that in Buddhism, teaching and praxis are in harmony with one another and to assert simultaneously that both, praxis and teaching, despite their differences from Christianity, are not deficient. This view would demand the shift to a pluralist approach.

Something similar can be observed on the Buddhist side. Buddhists who suggest an inclusivist interpretation of Christianity either see a close connection between what is to them a deficient Christian teaching and Christian praxis, or they claim that the lived spirituality of Christians surpasses its inadequate teaching. Some representatives of the so-called Kyoto school—for example Shin'ichi Hisamatsu[67] and the early Masao Abe[68] who was influenced by Hisamatsu—have made the accusation that Christianity, as a result of its personal concept of God, privileges belief over insight, remains chained to a heteronomous spirituality, fails to advance to full human self-realization, and, finally absolutizes words and concepts in a dogmatist way, instead of understanding their true purpose as instruments in service of experience.

The Theravāda Buddhist Nyanaponika Mahāthera held the widespread Buddhist view that a "theist," to the extent that his faith motivates him to lead a morally good life, may thereby attain a better rebirth, "possibly one in a heavenly world that re-

64 Cp. Dumoulin's extremely critical remarks about Enomiya-Lassalle in Dumoulin 1990, 160ff.
65 Cp. the sensitive analysis in von Brück, Lai 1997, 502-516.
66 Mark Heim's work discussed above in chapter 5 is very much in this vein. See above pp. 126-131.
67 Cp. for example Hisamatsu 1978
68 Cp. for example Abe 1981 and Abe 1989, 186-202.

sembles his own conceptions of it..."[69] This is of course not the ultimate salvation of Nirvāṇa—although from a Buddhist perspective an improvement of Karma can also result in coming closer to salvation. Quite similar considerations are found in the writings of the fourteenth Dalai Lama: "*nirvana* is only explained in the Buddhist scriptures, and is achieved only through Buddhist praxis."[70] But in order to reach a heavenly paradise, a perfect understanding of reality is not necessary; to this purpose one only needs to accumulate a sufficient amount of karmic merit.[71] According to the Dalai Lama, it is also possible for a Christian to follow the path of a Bodhisattva. In so doing he could, even as a Christian—similar to followers of other Mahāyāna schools—attain a limited degree of enlightenment or spiritual realization, though not perfect enlightenment.[72] In the case of a Christian, the chief obstacle on the way to perfect enlightenment is, according to the Dalai Lama, the belief in a creator God.[73] Buddhists like Nyanaponika and the Dalai Lama thus represent a standpoint that is also often found, in reverse, in Christian inclusivism: Although the teachings of non-Christian religions are in the final analysis wrong, they may nonetheless inspire their adherents to lead a morally good live und to that extent they contribute positively to their salvation. Inclusivist positions only admit a limited appreciation of the other.

Lynn A. de Silva

One of the major pioneers of Christian-Buddhist dialogue is the Sri Lankan Methodist, Lynn A. de Silva (1919-1982).[74] De Silva studied theology in Bangalore, New York, and Birmingham, and Buddhism at the Viyalankara University in Sri Lanka. From 1964-1982 he worked as one of the main translators of the Singhalese edition of the Bible. From 1962 until his death he was director of the Ecumenical Institute for Study and Dialogue in Colombo. He also founded the journal *Dialogue*, the first ever academic theological journal for Christian-Buddhist dialogue. At the same time, de Silva was active in various capacities for the World Council of Churches in Geneva, where he decisively supported the interreligious commitment of the WCC.

De Silva initially also entered dialogue with Buddhism from an inclusivist position. However, the evolution of this dialogue allowed him to develop conceptions that moved beyond the typical impasses of inclusivism toward a pluralist position. De Silva's original concern was a missionary one. According to de Silva, who worked

69 Nyanaponika 1981, 2.
70 Thus the fourteenth Dalai Lama in the famous Bodhgaya Interviews of 1981, reprinted in Griffiths 1990, 169.
71 Ibid.
72 Cp. Dalai Lama 1996, 153-158.
73 Ibid. 146.
74 On de Silva cp. Schmidt-Leukel 1992, 185-202; von Brück, Lai 1997, 92ff., 104ff., 388ff. as well as the Introduction by Petrus Höhensteiger to de Silva 1998, 7-33.

for almost twenty years on translating the Bible into Singhalese, merely translating the Christian message into another language is not enough. The gospel must also be conveyed into the conceptual horizon of this Buddhist-influenced culture. "Translation" is therefore primarily a theological task. For this, says de Silva, it is necessary to clarify the existential implications of Christianity and Buddhism and to relate them to each other in the sense of Paul Tillich's method of correlation.

Already by 1957 de Silva had turned against the notion of Buddhism as a form of atheism. Buddhism, he said, assumes the existence of an ultimate reality, because without such a reality salvation would not be feasible.[75] As evidence de Silva quotes the following famous passage which is found twice, in identical words, in the Pāli Canon:

> There is, bhikkhus, a not-born [*ajātaṁ*], a not-brought-to-being [*abhutaṁ*], a not-made [*akataṁ*], a not-conditioned [*asaṅkhataṁ*]. If, bhikkhus, there were no not-born, not-brought-to-being, not-made, not-conditioned, no escape would be discerned from what is born, brought-to-being, made, conditioned. But since there is a not-born, not-brought-to-being, not-made, not-conditioned, therefore an escape is discerned from what is born, brought-to-being, made, conditioned.[76]

According to de Silva, Buddhism has only a vague idea of this ultimate reality. Buddhism concentrates far more on analyzing the human need for salvation, which it aptly describes in its teaching on the three marks of existence (transience, suffering, and not-self). Here it is in fundamental agreement with Christianity. For Christianity also teaches of creation's impermanence, suffering or need for salvation, and, at least in its original biblical form, it disputes the existence of an eternal, unchangeable soul.

According to de Silva, the Christian doctrine of the Trinity correlates to the Buddhist teaching on the three marks of existence (see the diagram below).[77] That is, the Buddhist teaching on the transience of all things corresponds to the Christian message of the Father as the only Eternal One, compared to whom all else is naught. The Buddhist teaching on the unsatisfactory and sorrowful character of unredeemed life corresponds to the Christian message of the Son as the redeemer, who in his "kenotic" disposition, that is, in his self-emptying, has shown us the way to salvation. This way to salvation is finally expressed in the third correlation, the correspondence of the Buddhist *not-self (anattā) teaching* and the Christian concept of the *pneuma,* of the *Holy Spirit.* No component of the human being is immortal, as the Buddhist not-self teaching correctly recognizes. And yet humans are related to the Immortal as their true salvific goal. The Christian teaching about the Spirit expresses, according to de Silva, this human relatedness to transcendence.

75 Cp. de Silva 1957, 1 and 6.

76 Udāna 8,3 and Itivuttaka 43. Translation from Ireland 1997, 103. In his earlier writing of 1957 de Silva however misplaces this passage as being in the Dīgha-Nikāya.

77 Thus in his programmatic essay "Buddhist-Christian Dialogue" (de Silva 1967).

Three Marks of Existence (*tilakkhaṇa*)	Trinity
Transience (*anicca*)	God, the Eternal One (Father)
Suffering (*dukkha*)	God, the Redeemer (Son)
Not-Self (*anattā*)	God, the Sanctifier (Spirit)

Moreover, the Buddhist not-self teaching also has a spiritual and practical aspect, namely the concrete turning away from any kind of self-attachment or self-centeredness. From a Christian perspective, says de Silva, this is a feature inherent in any genuine kind of love. For love has both, a centrifugal side of self-denial and a centripetal side of becoming a person through turning to the other and turning away from the self. If Christianity uses the term "Kingdom of God" to describe salvation as a perfect fellowship of love, the Buddhist Nirvāṇa describes so to say the centrifugal side of this love and hence presents one aspect of the Kingdom of God. Hence de Silva interprets Nirvāṇa not as an expression of a mystical, curtailed concept of God, but as one particular aspect of the human relation to God. Accordingly, in an early piece of his writings de Silva calls God the "source" of Nirvāṇa.[78]

It seems that de Silva originally intended to develop theologically more fully each of the three correlations between the Christian Trinity and the Buddhist marks of existence. Yet he managed to compose an extensive study only on the third correlation, that of not-self and Spirit (*anattā-pneuma*), a text which in the meantime has become one of the classics of Christian-Buddhist dialogue.[79] On the first two correlations De Silva left only two shorter tracts.[80]

De Silva's conception expressed a clear appreciation of Buddhist teaching and understood it as being in total harmony with Buddhist praxis. However, in this conception too Buddhism came across as deficient and in need of fulfillment: Although Buddhism fully understands the human need for salvation and knows of a path of salvation, the presupposed relation to transcendence remains, according to de Silva, too unspecific and finds a far more precise expression in the Christian teaching on Trinity. But de Silva did not stop at this inclusivist understanding. The Tillich-inspired correlation he developed between Christianity and Buddhism eventually pushed him to understand the need for fulfillment increasingly in a reciprocal sense, that is, in the sense of a mutual complementarity.

The central theological motif that led to this change can already be discovered in a text from 1970.[81] Here de Silva accuses traditional theology of having spoken too often about God in a reified way, for example about the nature of God as it is in itself, independent of human beings. But according to de Silva, we can only speak of God with reference to human beings and in respect to the human experience of

78 Cp. de Silva 1967, 202f.
79 De Silva 1975 and 1979.
80 De Silva 1966 and 1970.
81 De Silva 1970.

God. And in our experience, God is present as the one who surpasses all understanding.[82] This insight into God's absolute transcendence on the one hand and the relatedness of all language about God to human God-experience on the other has decisive consequences for how one understands the attributes ascribed to God. In this sense de Silva writes about the crucial point of God's personality: "To say that God is personal does not mean that He is *a* person. It means that he is the ground and source of everything personal."[83]

By taking the path of relating all talk about God not to the being of God as it is in itself, but rather to the human experience of God, de Silva fulfills one of the essential presuppositions of a pluralist theology of religions.[84] This enabled him to interpret Buddhist teachings as an expression of different but nevertheless equally valid aspects of the experience of transcendence. De Silva thus eventually came to the conclusion that Buddhism does not constitute a deficient path of salvation but rather one that, although different from Christianity, is in principle equally valid.

De Silva sketched his new conception of Buddhist-Christian relationship in his last, only posthumously published, essay that he gave the telling title: "Buddhism and Christianity Relativised."[85] Here de Silva asserts that Buddhism affirms the existence of a salvific transcendent reality primarily by using impersonal terms, such as in the passage from the Udāna cited above, which speaks of the transcendent as the unborn, the unoriginated, the uncreated, and the unconditioned. Christianity by contrast speaks of transcendent reality primarily in personal terms, that is, of a personal Creator God, of an eternal "Thou." Yet there is no need to interpret these impersonal and personal terms of speech as being mutually exclusive if we understand them as expressing different aspects of the experience of transcendence. De Silva identifies these aspects as "ultimacy" and "intimacy." If ultimacy is emphasized, then religious language tends to use impersonal terms. If the emphasis is instead on intimacy, then religious language tends to use personal expressions.

Transcendent Reality

The experience of ultimacy	The experience of intimacy
Impersonal language: "That"	Personal language: "Thou"

The personal "Thou" of the Christian God and the impersonal "That" of the Buddhist Nirvāṇa express two different aspects of the experience of transcendence and thereby also evoke different experiences. While these experiences or aspects of expe-

82 Ibid. 59-62.
83 Ibid. 57.
84 Cp. on this above chapters 7-9.
85 De Silva 1982.

rience are indeed different, they are complementary rather than contradictory: For the experience of ultimacy coalesce with to the experience of a deep closeness and intimacy, and by the same token there is always an element of ultimacy in that experience of transcendent which is marked by loving intimacy. According to de Silva, this complementarity explains why both aspects can be found in both religions. That is, despite the dominance of impersonal language in Buddhism, one also finds in it numerous examples of a verbalization or depiction of transcendence in personal terms and images, as for example in the diverse forms of Buddha worship and the representation of transcendent reality via supra-natural Buddhas, as it is particularly characteristic of Mahāyāna Buddhism. Similarly, despite its dominant use of personal forms of expression, Christianity also knows of some forms of expression that are more impersonal in nature, like for example the Old Testament traditions of neither making any images of God nor uttering God's name, or the apophatic tradition in Christianity. Both aspects complete one another, correct one another, and balance one another: "In fact ultimacy gives depth to intimacy and intimacy gives vitality to ultimacy."[86]

This new conception has repercussions for de Silva's understanding of the Trinity. It no longer appears as a clearer understanding of the transcendent reality that Buddhism would only vaguely realize. Rather, de Silva now sees the doctrine of the Trinity as a theological formula that, within the context of Christianity, liaises the aspects of ultimacy and intimacy. The Father stands for the ultimacy of transcendence, the Son for its manifestation in personal concreteness, and the Spirit holds both together. In this regard, the doctrine of the Trinity finds its functional equivalent in the Buddhist Trikāya teaching, the teaching on the "Three Bodies" (or levels of reality) of the Buddha. Here too the transcendent, ultimate Dharmakāya (the highest, absolute, and ineffable reality) is intermediated with its manifest concreteness in the Nirmāṇakāya (that is, the level of the earthly Buddha). Thus Gautama Buddha and Jesus Christ represent for both religions the presence of ultimate transcendent reality in familiar human form: "the Ultimate … became intimate by becoming man."[87]

De Silva emphasizes that what underlies the Christian faith in God's becoming man is the New Testament notion of "*kenōsis*" or "self-emptying" (Phil 2:6-11). The unconditioned empties itself of its self and enters the conditioned nature of human existence. Yet, according to de Silva, Paul in this text is particularly interested in the spiritual meaning of this *kenōsis*, as the immediately preceding verse (Phil 2:5) makes clear: "Let the same mind be in you that was in Christ Jesus." To empty oneself and in so doing becoming transparent to the presence of ultimate reality has an unmistakable parallel in Buddhism in the two closely connected teachings on *śūnyatā* (emptiness) and the *Bodhisattva*. The Bodhisattva unselfishly puts his life in service of the liberation of all other beings, and in so doing realizes the true reality of emptiness. In this connection, de Silva speaks of "mythical or typological anal-

86 De Silva 1982, 51.
87 Ibid. 55.

egies to what Christians mean by Christ."[88] Yet "Christians would say that Jesus is the guarantee of liberation that lived into history."[89] De Silva does not pursue further whether he considers Jesus to be the *only* historically concrete guarantee of liberation, or whether—as he hints in his explanations on the Buddhist Trikāya teaching—he recognizes Gautama Buddha as having a similar role.

Unfortunately de Silva died before he could further develop his new conception and clarify the resulting questions regarding the relationship between Christianity and Buddhism. But the basic elements of a pluralist understanding emerge clearly with him and point the way forward: first, the reference of Christian and Buddhist language to different forms of human experience of transcendence; second, the corresponding possibility of understanding personal and impersonal forms of speech as complementary and not contradictory; and third, the resulting necessity of finding a new way to reflect on Buddha and Christ as incarnations of transcendence. In this way, de Silva became able to describe the relationship between Christianity and Buddhism both in the sense of reciprocal complementarity and in the sense of reciprocal relativization.

Pluralist Perspectives

Christian-Buddhist Complementarity

One can argue whether de Silva's categories of ultimacy and intimacy are particular suitable to characterize the specific differences between the Christian and Buddhist relationship to transcendence. The Sri Lankan Jesuit and close colleague of de Silva, Aloysius Pieris—who edited the journal *Dialogue* after de Silva's death and is one of the most eminent liberation theologians of Asia—proposed the categories of wisdom and love as a way to characterize the typical differences in Christian and Buddhist parlance.[90] According to Pieris, Buddhism primarily expresses the liberating experience of transcendence within a "gnostic" idiom, that is, an idiom of wisdom, while Christianity uses an "agapeic" idiom, in other words, one formed by the experience of love. The two idioms are complementary. Each idiom is both aware of the importance of the central insight of the other idiom and is in a position to integrate it into its own. In both idioms we find the view that the process of salvation remains inadequately expressed if the complementary aspect is lacking. Put concretely, Christianity knows the necessity of wisdom as a central element of genuine love of God and

88 Ibid. 58.
89 Ibid. 60.
90 Cp. esp. Pieris 1975, 1986, 122-130; 1988, 110-135 (= 1989, 157-194). Cp. also to Pieris, Schmidt-Leukel 1992, 222-231; von Brück, Lai 1997 esp. 545-557; Flemming 2002, esp. 201-265.

love of neighbor, and Buddhism knows love as the condition, correlation, and consequence of liberating wisdom.

I consider neither de Silva's nor Pieris' characterizations (ultimacy and intimacy, wisdom and love) to be wrong. Undoubtedly, in using these terms both theologians have correctly identified crucial features of Christianity and Buddhism. But I believe it is possible to describe the particularities of Buddhism and Christianity, especially with respect to the formative phases of both religions, in a still more precise and differentiated manner. I agree with de Silva and Pieris that explaining the differences between Buddhism and Christianity should be done in relation to differences in experience. Yet I suggest we begin with differences in the interpretation and emphasis of basic existential experiences, that is, with experiences that are constitutive of human life. The Christian idiom seems to be characterized by an understanding of human existence that is primarily shaped by the basic experience of interpersonal relatedness, whereas in the Buddhist idiom it seems to be the basic experience of transience or mortality that primarily shapes the respective understanding of human life. From these differences in their understanding of human existence many further differences between the teachings of both religions can be made intelligible.

Thus in Buddhism, the human predicament is primarily understood as one of suffering from transience. This may be demonstrated by countless details of early Buddhist teaching. I will mention only a few examples:[91] It is not for nothing that the teaching on the three marks of existence begins with the mark of transience and continues by saying that what is transient is also unsatisfactory, full of suffering, and should therefore not be considered to be the true self. Another central teaching of early Buddhism, the schema of the Four Noble Truths, offers in the First Noble Truth a description of misery or suffering (*dukkha*) and likewise begins with the experience of transience: "Birth is suffering, old age is suffering, illness is suffering, death is suffering." Old age, illness, and death form a standard triad that in Buddhist texts points to the existential experience of transience. "Birth" is mentioned because in Buddhist understanding it marks the beginning of the end, the entrance into transient existence starting from birth on. The background to this is the teaching on the cycle of rebirth, in which being born is not primarily understood as new life but as the prolongation—and potentially infinite prolongation—of transient existence. For that reason one often finds the term "re-death" instead of "re-birth." Also in the well-known legend of the life of the Buddha it is the encounter with an old man, a sick person, and a dead person on the first three of his four excursions that make the young prince aware of his own mortality. When on the fourth excursion he sees a religious ascetic, he decides to choose the life of an ascetic himself in order to attain the liberation from old age, illness, and death.

By contrast, for the Christian understanding of human existence it is not the experience of transience that is decisive, but rather the experience of interpersonal relatedness. Here, the human predicament is understood as sin (and death as the

91 For an extensive treatment, see Schmidt-Leukel 1992, esp. 457-521.

"wages of sin," Rom 6:23). But the meaning of "sin" is broken relationship, the inability to love God and one's neighbor truly, and the being curved inward on oneself.

The categories that Buddhism and Christianity use to express their understanding of the human predicament shape their notions of salvific transcendence. When the Buddha in his enlightenment reached the goal of his long search, he proclaimed: "The deathless has been found!" (*Majjhima-Nikāya* 26). The "deathless" (*amata, amṛta*) is a synonym for Nirvāṇa, frequently used in Buddhism right up to the various branches of later Mahāyāna. For this reason, the widespread translation of the first mark of existence as "all is transient" or of the First Noble Truth as "all is suffering" is incorrect. It is only true of saṃsāric existence that everything about it is transient and unsatisfactory or full of suffering. By contrast, Nirvāṇa is free of all transience and suffering. And this is the reason—as is argued in various classic Buddhist tracts (such as in the *Milindapañha* or the *Visuddhimagga*)—why Nirvāṇa must be thought of as a not-conditioned or un-conditioned reality. For everything that is conditioned is transient and therefore unsatisfying. Because Nirvāṇa is an unconditioned reality it cannot, so the argument continues, be conceived as being only a state. As the mere state of the enlightened human being, it would be a conditioned reality, conditioned by those factors that caused this state to arise. Rather the reverse is true: The unconditioned existence of transcendent reality is itself the very condition that makes enlightenment and liberation possible.

In Judaism, and therefore also Christianity, transcendent reality is understood as a personal God, that is, as a reality whom a human being can approach and trust like a person, that is, like a merciful father. Here too the existence of transcendent reality is seen as the condition of salvation, but this is expressed in the categories of interpersonal relations. That is, trust in the love of the divine Father saves a person from his or her sinful self-centeredness. The love of God sets human beings free to love God and his or her neighbor in return. Because God loves us although we are sinners and therefore as Paul says, "enemies of God" (Rom 5:8), the love of one's enemy becomes a sign of divine love. As Jesus proclaims in the Sermon on the Mount, God sends the life-giving light of the sun and the life-giving water of rain indiscriminately to both the righteous and the unrighteous. And hence we too should not only love our friends but also our enemies (Mt 5:43-48).

Christianity and Buddhism are also aware of the significance of that basic human experience that is of formative importance in the idiom of the other. The liberating love that comes from God and evokes its reflection in peoples' hearts overcomes, according to Paul, not only sin but also "its wages," which is death. For "love covers all sins" (Prov 10:12) and nothing in the world, not even death, proclaims Paul, can separate us from the love of God that appeared in Christ (Rom 8:38f). But if nothing in the world can separate us from the love of God, then in a certain sense the love of God separates us from the world. It frees us from enslavement to this world and its powers. Receiving the love of God and responding to it therefore involves a release from the entanglements of the world of death. Paul advises that we should not hold on to the things of the world as if we owned them, for "the present form of this world is passing away" (1 Cor 7:29ff). Or as it is expressed in the Gospel of John, we are in the world but not of it (Jn 17:9-19).

According to the Buddhist analysis, our transient existence causes suffering because we actually strive for the intransient, for what is free of birth, old age, illness, and death (cp. *Majjhima-Nikāya* 26). We cling to what is transient because we are driven by the persistent illusion that the fleeting things of the world and the impermanent constituents of our own existence could fulfill our deepest striving. This deluded orientation of our existential striving, falsely directed to the transient things of the world, is what Buddhism describes as "thirst" (*taṇhā, tṛṣṇā*). A telling metaphor in the hot climate of India! The pleasures that we derive from worldly possessions can only temporarily quench the "thirst;" they cannot satisfy it forever. This "thirst" that manifests itself in attachment chains us to the Saṃsāra, the cycle of birth and death, and forces us again and again into repeated transient existence. Death and the suffering under our mortality can therefore only be overcome by the liberation from all attachment. But because the thought "This is me" is the strongest form of attachment, liberation from attachment means, above all, liberation from any kind of self-centeredness. This liberation, however, only becomes possible through the experience of the transcendent, "deathless" reality itself. This experience forms the core of the final liberating enlightenment and it is mediated through the life and teaching that flows from the Buddha's enlightenment. Thus the teaching of the Buddha is capable of guiding a person on the right path and leading him or her to the liberation from their fetters. The Buddha, his teaching, and his community are therefore liberating mediators of salvific experience of transcendence. The ultimate liberation from "thirst" and "attachment," however, cannot be our "work." It is rather the result of one's own final enlightenment experience, that is, of one's own perfect encounter with the "deathless."

Whereas in Christianity the correlate of divine unselfish love is likewise a form of detachment, that is, a liberating separation from the world, in Buddhism it is exactly the inverse. Here the correlate of detachment is selfless love. For greed and hatred arise from attachment. They are the morally unwholesome forms of clinging self-centeredness. Yet every genuine form of love, that is, of love that primarily seeks the wellbeing of the other rather than one's own, contains an element of selflessness or detachment, and so contributes to the liberation of the mind, as it says in *Itivuttaka* 27. Perfect love in the Buddhist ideal would be a completely detached and fully selfless love. The sign of complete detachment and selflessness is that this love is extended to all without distinction, whether powerful or weak, whether friend or foe. Thus the notion of love of enemy is already found in Buddhism in a distinct form long before Christianity: Even if one is being cut into pieces by an enemy, one is meant not to cease embracing this person with undiminished loving kindness (*Majjhima-Nikāya* 21). In Buddhism, the great example of perfect selfless love is the Buddha himself (about whom it is in fact reported that in one of his previous lives he was indeed cut into pieces, while feeling boundless compassion for the evildoer).[92] With his enlightenment the Buddha had achieved everything he could achieve for himself. So all his actions after his enlightenment are therefore an expression of perfect altruism. The forty-five years of service to the world after his enlightenment are a manifestation of his compassion for the unredeemed beings. Out of loving kindness and compassion he proclaims the teaching, and out of loving kindness and compassion he establishes the Buddhist community. Mahāyāna Buddhism even goes one step further and concludes that the Buddha's motive was altruistic already *before* his enlightenment: He was not seeking his own salvation. He sought enlightenment in order that as an enlightened Buddha he could serve all other beings in the best possible way. This is the attitude of a Bodhisattva, which we are called to follow.

Buddhism and Christianity experience life by means of different categories, whose difference, I suggest, is best understood by the different priorities that they assign to the respective basic experiences of human existence. In the case of Buddhism, the priority lies in the experience of transience, and in the case of Christianity in the experience of interpersonal relatedness. In both contexts transcendent reality appears as that which makes salvation possible. Christianity presents this reality in terms of a personal vis-à-vis, whereas Buddhism presents it as the impersonal reality of the deathless. Both religions, however, integrate also those experiences which are central in the context of the other. Therefore Buddhism and Christianity coincide in the ideal of detached love or loving detachment. The concrete manifestation of this ideal for Christians is Jesus Christ and for Buddhists Gautama Buddha. They both mediate the liberating experience of transcendence to the lives of those who follow them.

At the *existential* level, the complementarity of Buddhism and Christianity thus rests on the complementarity of detachment and loving involvement. In this regard both traditions may spiritually enrich, challenge, and correct one another. The idiomatic dominance of the experience interpersonal relatedness in Christianity is in danger of neglecting the element of detachment in love, whereas the idiomatic dominance of the experience of transience in Buddhism carries the danger of insufficiently considering the element of love in the midst of detachment. Yet both traditions have also developed their own sub-traditions that place a greater emphasis than usual on the complementary aspect: the mystical and monastic spirituality of Christianity has always emphasized the value of detachment, and in Buddhism it is particularly the ideal of the Bodhisattva that represents the sublime value of loving involvement. For that reason it is by no means surprising that on the Christian side the Christian-Buddhist encounter is leading to a revitalization of contemplative spirituality, and on the Buddhist side it is renewing the sense of social responsibility.

At the *doctrinal* level, the complementarity of both idioms entails first of all that characterizing Buddhism as atheism is largely erroneous. Of course, Buddhism is not a theistic religion. But in its traditional form it does not deny the existence of a transcendent reality, but rather posits it—as we need to insist against Paul Wil-

92 Cp. *Jātaka 313* and *Jātakamāla 28.*

liams[93]—as the condition of salvation. However, Buddhism approaches this reality primarily by way of impersonal notions and does not conceptualize it as a personal God as in Christianity. If both Christianity and Buddhism remain conscious of the fact that their respective notions of transcendence are each connected to different forms of experience of transcendence, then this does indeed imply—as de Silva suggested—a relativization of the supposed antagonism between personal and impersonal notions of transcendence.

Christian-Buddhist Relativization

Are there also Buddhists who agree with such a relativization? Lynn de Silva himself refers to two Western Buddhist authors in whose writings he found similar thoughts: Maurice O'C. Walshe[94] and Marco Pallis.[95] It is worth noting that Marco Pallis belongs to the traditional school established by René Guenon and Frithjof Schuon that holds its own particular version of religious pluralism.[96] However, even Buddhist thinkers who tend toward a pluralist position within a Buddhist 'theology' of religions often only support a one-sided relativization, that is, personal notions of transcendence are relativized by impersonal ones and not the other way around. An example of this is the Thai reformer, Bhikkhu Buddhadāsa (1906-1993). According to Buddhadāsa, talking about God as a person is unavoidably linked to an anthropomorphic notion of God. But then ultimate reality would be misunderstood as a finite, limited being, as a being that is still subject to attachment, because it manifests behaviors like greed and anger.[97] If, however, one divests the conception of God of its anthropomorphic—and for Buddhadāsa that means its personal—traits, then in some respects it is functionally similar to the impersonal Buddhist concept of Dharma.[98] But one would need to go beyond even this, since God actually has no attributes and no form at all.[99] It is only by being completely detached that one becomes aware of God.[100]

Buddhadāsa's approach is pluralist in as, from his perspective, a personal concept of God can be overcome not only in Buddhism but also in Christianity. In addition, Buddhadāsa affirms that the Sermon on the Mount, if put into practice, contains more than enough for attaining complete liberation.[101] He describes the particularities of Buddhism, Christianity, and Islam as three different, but equally salvif-

93 Cp. again Williams 2002, 26.
94 Cp. Walshe 1982.
95 De Silva refers to Marco Pallis, *A Buddhist Spectrum*, London 1980.
96 Cp. above chapter 6, p. 152.
97 Cp. Buddhadāsa 1967, 62ff.
98 Cp. ibid. 66ff.
99 Cp. ibid. 74.
100 Cp. Buddhadāsa 1989, 152.
101 Buddhadāsa 1967, 29 and 26.

ic paths: the path of wisdom, the path of trust or faith, and the path of will-power. They are different and complementary. They converge in their essential concern "… not to cherish self-love (egoism-selfishness) but Dhamma-love devoted to the truth, or you may say God-love."[102] Nevertheless, Buddhadāsa himself finds only little value in personal language about transcendent reality (although he resorts to it surprisingly often), because for him it is inevitably connected to the notion of a finite being caught up in the passions. In this respect, Buddhadāsa is a typical example of the phenomenon (so often met in Asian religions) of identifying "personality" or "person" with "limitation" and "egocentrism."[103]

Things are different with Keiji Nishitani, one of the main representatives of the Kyoto school. It is startling to read Nishitani write, in his work *Religion and Nothingness*:

> The idea of man as person is without doubt the highest conception of man yet to appear. The same may be said of the idea of God as person.[104]

Yet for Nishitani, the idea of person is ambivalent both with respect to the question of the personhood of God as well as the personhood of humans. For Nishitani, much like for Buddhadāsa, the term 'person' is often connected to the notion of an *ego* that separates oneself from and asserts oneself against others: "Hating one's enemies and loving one's friends are sentiments typical of human love. They belong to the field of the ego."[105] When applied to God, the concept of a "person" suggests the notion of a God who arbitrarily elects one particular people and repudiates others, or who loves the righteous and punishes sinners.[106] But Nishitani contrasts with this the word of Jesus from the Sermon on the Mount, according to which God lets the sun shine on the evil and the good, and sends rain to both the righteous and the unrighteous. This love, says Nishitani, is a "non-differentiating love beyond enmity and friendship."[107] Such a non-differentiating love corresponds to the Buddhist ideal. It presupposes the overcoming of the discriminatory perspective of egocentric love. Non-differentiating love is therefore selfless love. According to Nishitani, Buddhism expresses this by its teaching of the "not-self" (*anātman*), and Christianity through the teaching of *kenōsis* or self-emptying.[108] When by emptying himself Jesus imitates the Father, this implies that this kenōtic self-emptying or selflessness is essential to God.

From this Nishitani draws three far-reaching conclusions: *First*, the non-differentiating, selfless love of God corresponds to the Buddhist ideal of great compassion *(mahā karuṇā)*. *Second*, since non-differentiating love is selfless love, and since only

102 Buddhadāsa, 1967, 24.
103 Waldenfels 1982, 45.
104 Nishitani 1982, 69.
105 Ibid. 59.
106 Cp. ibid. 60.
107 Ibid. 58.
108 Cp. ibid. 58f.

this non-differentiating love reflects the perfect, divine love, personhood can only be ascribed to God by including this impersonal or "transpersonal" element. Thus, God's impersonality manifests itself in selflessness and non-discrimination. But because it is selfless and non-differentiating *love*, God's personality is also manifest, so that it would be more accurate to speak of the personal impersonality or impersonal personality of God. According to the Christian teaching on *kenōsis* and the Buddhist Bodhisattva ideal, it is humanity's calling to strive for the realization of perfect love. Hence also with regard to human beings, personhood must not be understood in the sense of the self-centered ego, but rather in the sense of a call to the realization of selfless, non-differentiating love. *Third*, to the extent that the Buddhist teaching on "emptiness" (*śūnyatā*) entails not only a negation of all concepts but aims at an "existential conversion away from the mode of being person-centered person,"[109] *śūnyatā* or emptiness can be set in close relation to the actual being of God and to the vocation of humanity, that is, to their true nature.

These reflections, which, as I showed earlier, are already hinted at in Lynn de Silva (incidentally without any influence by Nishitani), form the basis for the so far longest and most intense debate in the history of Christian-Buddhist dialogue. This debate was not led by Nishitani himself, but (and this probably primarily for reasons of language) by another representative of the Kyoto School: Masao Abe. Abe had already ignited this debate in the 1960s. At that time it took place mainly through a series of publications in the journal *Japanese Religions*. In the mid-1970s there was a second round of this debate, again in *Japanese Religions*. The zenith was reached in the 1980s with the symposia of the so-called "Cobb-Abe Group," a Buddhist-Christian circle of scholars co-chaired by Abe and John Cobb. The development of this debate, in which numerous Christian theologians and Buddhist thinkers participated, is in part highly intricate, much ramified in subject matter, and at times extremely abstract. Since it has been repeatedly and extensively recounted, I can refrain from doing this again.[110] Yet I wish to clarify the point at which this debate touched on a question that is significant for a pluralist conception of the relationship between Christianity and Buddhism: whether, and if so, in what sense, we can speak of a mutual relativizing of personal and impersonal notions of transcendence as it had become apparent in Nishitani's thought.

Masao Abe criticizes a mythological understanding of *kenōsis*. The "Son of God" *was* not originally God and then *became* man. Rather, Jesus is at one and the same time true man and true God, because, and insofar as, he lived his life as an act of complete self-emptying.[111] This presupposes that God's nature itself is understood as *kenōsis*, as self-negating or self-emptying, as Abe suggests with reference to the Buddhist term *śūnyatā* or "emptiness." Can Christianity imagine such self-emptying as

109 Ibid. 70.
110 Cp. on this Brück, Lai 1997 esp. 269-288 and 412-478; Münch 1998, 155-249. For parts of the debate itself see Cobb, Ives 1990 and Corless, Knitter 1990.
111 Cp. Abe in Corless, Knitter 1990, 13.

God's nature and thus take the idea of *kenōsis* to its radical end? Or does God in the final analysis remain unaffected by self-emptying, in that God remains, as before, the unchangeable counterpart to the world, who is conceived of as the one reality completely different from the world? According to Abe, the consistent and comprehensive self-emptying of God implies that God is no longer thought of as being different from the world, but rather that "God *is* each and every thing"[112] without, as Abe emphasizes, understanding such a non-differentiation between God and the world as simply a monistic, pantheistic identity.[113] Rather, God is truly God (and different from the world) by not being—unlike the entities of the world—just a further, objective, separate entity alongside the world.[114]

Standing behind Abe's suggestion is the long tradition of Mahāyāna Buddhist philosophy going back to Nāgārjuna (2-3 century CE) and his writings on "emptiness." For Nāgārjuna, as for the Buddhist tradition before him, the ultimate reality of Nirvāṇa is an unconditioned and therefore unoriginated and imperishable, and in the end inconceivable reality. That which is inconceivable, what cannot be expressed in the form of any concept, Buddhism calls "formless." This leads to the unavoidable paradox of this "formlessness" becoming a new kind of form, and inconceivability a new conception. Hence there is the danger of undercutting the inconceivability of transcendent reality, so that it can be grasped and conceived by the concepts of formlessness or inconceivability. From a Buddhist perspective, this is no purely intellectual problem. For conceptual grasping may well be a form of attachment and thus of delusion. The inconceivability and formlessness of transcendent reality therefore also entails that experiencing it must be combined with detachment. This explains why the approach that quietly makes the formlessness of the transcendent into a concept is seen not only as an intellectual problem but as a spiritual danger.

Nāgārjuna, and to a great extent the Mahāyāna philosophy that follows him, draw two consequences from this. If we are to preserve the inconceivability of the unconditioned reality of Nirvāṇa, then we must *first* counteract the tendency to conceptualize Nirvāṇa as the counterpart of Saṃsāra. Hence Nāgārjuna famously stated that Nirvāṇa is not different from Saṃsāra.[115] This, however, can easily produce the misunderstanding of conceptualizing Nirvāṇa in a monistic sense as being identical to Saṃsāra. Nāgārjuna guards against this by *secondly* declaring the world to be just as inconceivable as Nirvāṇa.[116] According to Nāgārjuna, the conceptually mediated picture of the world as constituted by different entities and the various kind of relations between them, proves to be full of unsolvable logical contradictions and thus as unsustainable. It is a mental construct. Such a construct, however, is indispensable. It is useful and essential for our orientation in the world. Yet if we mistake this construct to be reality itself, we are ensnared by attachment. The truth rather is

112 Ibid. 18.
113 Cp. ibid.
114 Cp. ibid. 17-19.
115 Mūlamadhyamakakārikā 25, 19f.
116 Mūlamadhyamakakārikā 25, 22-24.

that everything in the world is just as unconditioned, without origination and cessation, as Nirvāṇa itself and is therefore equally inconceivable.[117] As an aside, it is worth noting that Nāgārjuna is thus far from reducing the unconditioned reality of Nirvāṇa to the conditioned reality of the world—an understanding one can sometimes find among contemporary Buddhists influenced by Western secularism. Instead, Nāgārjuna in a sense elevates the world to the level of the absolute, thus understands transcendent reality as the ultimate reality of everything.

The link between "emptiness" and "detachment" remains crucial. For Nāgārjuna, "emptiness" means that our concepts are "empty." Or more precisely that the supposed "things" are empty of those substances and relations ascribed to them by the respective concepts. The substances and relations expressed in our concepts cannot be discerned in reality, that is, beyond those concepts. Hence "emptiness" or *śūnyatā* signifies inconceivability. Reality is ungraspable and for this reason "emptiness" itself must also be emptied—that is, one must not misunderstand it as a new but now correct concept of reality.[118] Rather, the function of the teaching of "emptiness" is to foster the attitude of not-grasping or unattachment, which simultaneously manifests itself as great compassion. The teaching of "emptiness" thus becomes the epitome of the Buddhist doctrine as such. The conceptually formulated doctrines of Buddhism fulfill a primarily spiritual and practical purpose. They are intended to point beyond themselves to a realization of absolute truth beyond all concepts. They are means, instruments, or as Nāgārjuna says, "relative" or "veiled" truth. Yet one can point toward absolute truth *only* by means of relative truth.[119] And therefore the Buddhist teaching is indispensable.

This conception lies behind Masao Abe's question about whether Christianity is capable of consistently following the idea of God's self-emptying or becoming empty up to its radical end, or whether in the final analysis it continues to view God as the counterpart of the world. In the latter case, God would remain reified and graspable serving as the starting point for Christian dogmatism. In other words, Abe treats the Christian concept of God in a similar fashion as Nāgārjuna treats the Buddhist concept of Nirvāṇa. Nāgārjuna empties Nirvāṇa by means of the teaching on "emptiness," that is, he presents the relationship between Nirvāṇa and Saṃsāra as being neither different nor identical. Similarly, Abe suggests thinking of God as neither different nor identical to the world, but rather as kenotically "empty." Yet what are the implications of this position for a theology of religions? Does it relativize the absolute claims of Buddhism and Christianity and their particular concepts of transcendence to the same extent? The answer turns out to be ambivalent.

Drawing on the Buddhist schema of the "three bodies" of the Buddha (*trikāya*), Abe suggests to interpret ultimate transcendent reality not only in the sense of the self-emptying *śūnyatā* but rather as a reality that manifests itself in the various de-

117 Mūlamadhyamakakārikā 18, 7-10 and 25, 9.
118 Mūlamadhyamakakārikā 13, 8.
119 Mūlamadhyamakakārikā 24, 7-12.

pictions of God in the different religions, and which gains historically concrete form in their key figures and founders.[120] That is, "emptiness"—or "boundless openness" as Abe also says with reference to the Zen-Buddhist tradition[121]—assumes the place of the "Dharmakāya" (the highest of Buddha's three "bodies" or levels of reality). The level of "Sambhogakāya" (traditionally this is the level of supra-worldly Buddhas) then corresponds to "Yahweh," "Allah," "Shiva," "Vishnu," "Amida Buddha," and even to an impersonal concept such as the Hindu "Brahman". At the level of "Nirmānakāya" (which traditionally refers to the historical Buddha), we find Jesus, Muhammad, and Krishna alongside Gautama Buddha.[122]

LORD: (Nirmānakāya)	Jesus	Muhammad	Krishna	Gautama
GOD: (Sambhogakāya)	Yahweh	Allah	Ishvara (Shiva, Vishnu, Brahman[123])	Amida

BOUNDLESS OPENNESS: Formless and boundless Reality of Emptiness (Openness) (Dharmakāya)

This schema can be viewed as a pluralist conception. Yet it is striking that the highest[124] position of Dharmakāya is occupied exclusively by the Buddhist *śūnyatā* or in Zen Buddhist terms, "boundless openness." Though Abe defends himself against an understanding of his position as an affirmation of a Buddhist superiority claim,[125] it does come dangerously close to this. The decisive question is how one understands *śūnyatā*. If one uses the Buddhist teaching on *śūnyatā* to claim a standpoint above all others, without the limitation of a particular perspective,[126] thus a Buddhist version

120 Cp. Ave 1985, reprinted with minor revision in Abe 1995, 17-39.

121 The legendary Bodhidharma, who is said to have brought Zen from India to China, famously responded to the question "What is the first principle of the sacred truth?" with the answer, "Wide openness, nothing sacred." Cp. Dumoulin 1985, 90.

122 Cp. Abe 1985, 186.

123 Thus in the original edition of 1985. When this essay was reprinted in Abe 1995, 35, "Brahman" was turned into "Brahmā." Yet Abe says quite unequivocally in the text that he refers to the impersonal "Brahman," not the personal deity, "Brahmā."

124 There is no change in this status even if in his graphic representation Abe inverts the hierarchy.

125 Ibid. 189.

126 Against my attempt to demonstrate that the Buddhist experience and understanding of transcendence are also bound to a particular perspective, Armin Münch has objected that this attempt is "not correct," since the "whole point of Buddhism" consists precisely in "abandoning the ego-bound perspective!" (Münch 1998, 132). Yet Münch seems to overlook that the claim to a perspective-free understanding of reality constitutes a Buddhist parallel to Christian claims of absoluteness, which in my opinion are both implausible with regard to the claimed absoluteness. The demonstration that Buddhism too in its experience of transcendence is bound to a particular perspective and remains dependent on it (at least as soon as Buddhism expresses itself doctrinally) is among other things directed against such Buddhist

of a "God's eye view," then this clearly constitutes a Buddhist superiority claim.[127] In this case we cannot even speak of an equal ranking of personal and impersonal conceptions of transcendence but Buddhism's impersonal notion of transcendence as *śūnyatā* would stand above the personal and impersonal conceptions of transcendence of all other religions. Such an interpretation no doubt fits with broad swaths of Buddhist self-understanding within the Buddhist tradition, in which one often encounters inclusivist hierarchies: One's own teaching represents the highest truth, the teachings of other Buddhist schools represent deficient forms of one's own highest insight, and in comparison to this, non-Buddhist teachings are either still less perfect or even totally wrong.

In my opinion, however, we do not necessarily have to understand Abe's proposal in this way. We can also interpret the fact that Abe describes ultimate reality only with the Buddhist term *śūnyatā* or the Zen-specific term of "boundless openness" in the sense of a hermeneutic inclusivism.[128] Alfred Bloom, an adherent of Pure-Land Buddhism, has suggested a very similar view of the religions as Abe, except that he presents the Dharmakāya as qualified by Amida Buddha, so that other religions appear as means by which Amida reveals and extends his boundless compassion to the people of those religious traditions.[129] Bloom too emphasizes that this is not to claim any kind of superiority for Buddhism and he thus accepts the possibility that other religions express the same facts through their own religious terminology, so that, for example, Hindus might speak of the manifestations of Brahman or Christians about the work of the Logos.[130]

A pluralist interpretation of Abe's proposal would require that *śūnyatā* too is ranked at the level of form realities, in other words at the level of different particular concepts (personal and impersonal) of transcendence,[131] but at the same time acknowledging its function of pointing beyond itself to the actual inconceivable nature of transcendence.[132] Then the decisive question to Buddhists (and also to Christians) is whether they can allow the Christian notion of God a similar dual function; that is, whether in their eyes the Christian concept of God is similarly a concept which on the one hand articulates transcendent reality but on the other hand points beyond itself to the inconceivability of ultimate reality. In light of the strong presence of negative and apophatic theology in the Christian tradition, it should not be that

claims to absolutism. For a critical analysis of this version of a Buddhist claim to absoluteness, see also Hick 1989, 292-295.

127 This is roughly how Sundermeier (1991, 179ff) interprets Abe.

128 Cp. on this above chapter 3, p. 68.

129 Cp. Bloom 1992, 26.

130 Cp. ibid. 26f.

131 It is understandable that for traditional Buddhists this thought must seem like an imposition, since *śūnyatā* is clearly defined as being "without form." And yet the Buddhist tradition is also aware of the paradox that "emptiness" is a concept and as such not formless but "form." However, it is directed against all conceptual grasping and thus also against its own form as a concept (and this is why Buddhist tradition talks about the "the emptiness of emptiness").

132 Cp. on this Hick 1989, 287-292, who points out the dual character of *śūnyatā* very clearly.

hard to answer this question in the affirmative. On the other hand, we cannot deny that Mahāyāna philosophy emphasizes the necessity to go beyond every conception more radically than almost any other tradition. Mahāyāna Buddhists can therefore rightfully consider this to be their particular contribution to the dialogue of religions.[133] The insight into the spiritual complementarity of detachment and loving involvement entails, however, that detachment in connection with a personal concept of transcendence, as in Christianity, can assume different but by no means less radical forms. In the Christian context, the emphasis is not on detachment but on love. And this difference in emphasis is also reflected in the criteriology of interreligious assessment. Hence it is understandable that in their assessment of Christianity, Buddhists apply criteria that focus above all on the spiritual value of detachment in Christianity, whereas conversely Christians consider how serious Buddhism is about loving involvement. It should therefore be equally important for both sides to become, through dialogue, more aware of the complementarity of detachment and love, and, as a result, to broaden their criteriological standards. The pluralist maxim of combining difference with equality therefore holds a challenge for both sides.

This challenge becomes concrete in the question of the reciprocal assessment of the Gautama Buddha by Christians and of Jesus Christ by Buddhists.[134] The different perceptions of this challenge prove characteristic of the peculiarities of each tradition. Mahāyāna Buddhists have repeatedly affirmed that they have no problem with the basic notion of "incarnation", since the Mahāyānist three-body teaching itself is a form of incarnation teaching, according to which Gautama Buddha is the incarnation not only of a supra-mundane Buddha, but also of the highest truth of the Dharmakāya.[135] As José Cabezón has made clear, the problems are more about the Christian claim of the uniqueness of incarnation, and further about the kind of God that is supposedly incarnate in Jesus.[136] For in his biblical, Old Testament form this God possesses, according to Cabezón, highly dubious characteristics from an ethical point of view. And in the Christian metaphysical form of a personal, eternal creator, this God would be irreconcilable with the Buddhist understanding of reality. For this reason, says Cabezón, it is difficult for Buddhism to see Jesus as an incarnation of the Dharmakāya, and thus as an enlightened Buddha. The problem is almost exactly the opposite in Christianity. For Christianity one difficulty is to accept the possibility of multiple incarnations, while the other difficulty consists in the absence of an infinite loving God in Buddha's message, even if no less than Romano Guardini thought that precisely the freedom and loving kindness displayed in the Buddha's life could suggest the idea "to move him close to Jesus."[137]

To the extent that each side grows in their understanding of the particularities and of the complementarity of their respective experiences of transcendence

133 Cp. on this Bloom 1992, 29 and similarly Makransky 2003, 359.
134 On this cp. the collections of Gross, Muck 2000, and Schmidt-Leukel 2001a.
135 Cp. Schmidt-Leukel 2001a, 29.
136 Cp. Cabezón 2000, 24ff.
137 Literally: "ihn in die Nähe Jesu zu rücken." Guardini 1997, 376.

and their corresponding verbalizations and to the extent that each recognizes the spiritual opportunities and dangers on both sides, Gautama Buddha could gain in importance for Christians and Jesus Christ for Buddhists. That is, Christians may increasingly better understand why Buddhists see in the Buddha an incarnation of the highest reality and will no longer feel the need to contest the truth found therein.[138] In this way, the Buddha may become a mediator of salvific experience of transcendence for Christians as well and will be able to teach them the importance of detachment. In this light, the Christian understanding of Jesus will broaden and deepen, because they will then understand Jesus not only as the embodiment of God's unconditional love, but also as the embodiment of the radical detachment associated with it. For their part, Buddhists may increasingly better understand the sense in which Christians regard Jesus as the human face of the invisible God without feeling that they need to contest the truth found therein. In this way, Jesus may become also for them a mediator of salvific knowledge of transcendence and show them anew the spiritual importance of unconditional love. And in this light they will more clearly recognize that Gautama Buddha is not only the fully enlightened one, but is also fully a *person*, permeable to the all-encompassing goodness flowing from ultimate reality. Doing so does not require the introduction of foreign elements into Buddhism. The Pāli Canon already has one of Buddha's followers state that he knew of God Brahmā's steady kindness only from hearsay, but that in Gautama he had seen this with his own eyes.[139] And Shinran Shōnin (1173-1262) qualifies the famous Zen saying "mind is Buddha"[140] with the words:

> The aspiration to save all beings is the mind that grasps sentient beings and brings them to birth in the Pure Land of happiness. This mind is the mind of ultimate equality. It is great compassion. This mind attains Buddhahood. This mind is Buddha.[141]

The pluralist perspectives presented here on the relationship between Christianity and Buddhism by no means explain all the questions of Christian-Buddhist dialogue. Numerous problems remain unsolved and call for further dialogical work, such as the question of cosmology, that is, the understanding of the world as creation and the understanding of God as creator,[142] or the question of reincarnation,[143] which is more deeply entangled with the issue of creation than one might initial-

138 Cp. on this Schmidt-Leukel 2003a. Other works on this are soon to be published.

139 Majjhima-Nikāya 55.

140 However the word originally comes not from Zen Buddhism but from the Amida Buddhist tradition and can be found for the first time, at least as far as I know, in the so-called *Amitāyur-dhyāna-Sūtra* 17 (it is not clear if there was a Sanskrit original).

141 *Passages on the Pure Land Way.* A Translation of Shinran's *Jōdo monrui jushō*, Kyoto 1982, 53.

142 The European Network of Buddhist Christian Studies organized a symposium on this question in 2003. See Schmidt-Leukel (ed.), *Buddhism, Christianity, and the Question of Creation*, Aldershot 2005.

143 On this cp. for example de Silva 1968 and 1998, 200-211; Hick 1990c, Kochanek 1992, Bischofberger 1996, Schmidt-Leukel 1996b.

ly think because from a Buddhist perspective the world is continually being created through the karma of beings. We can approach such questions in a more relaxed manner if we do not fundamentally deny the other tradition a salvific knowledge of transcendence or allow it only in a deficient sense. But above all, such questions point beyond the limited horizon of Christian-Buddhist dialogue. They can only be properly discussed when we include the context in which Buddhism developed its original positions on these questions, that is, when we expand the Christian-Buddhist dialogue to a Hindu-Buddhist-Christian trialogue.[144] This is a step we should take soon.

144 For an attempt at a Hindu-Buddhist dialogue see Singh, Ikeda 1988.

16. Steps to the Future

A Plausible Theological Hypothesis

Is the pluralist interpretation of religious diversity true? Do humanity's major religious traditions really embody different but essentially equally valid forms of the salvific knowledge of a transcendent reality? The truth of the pluralist position cannot be proved in any strict sense of proof—we cannot even prove that there is a transcendent reality![1] Yet also the opposite, that is, the atheist or naturalist denial of a transcendent reality is unproved. Belief in God, in whatever form, remains a belief rather than indubitable knowledge. Faith ought to know that it believes, rather than believe that it knows. However, as long as faith does not suffer from irresolvable contradictions and as long as it does not stand in irresolvable contradiction to other well-confirmed knowledge, trusting in the presence of a transcendent reality and allowing one's life to be determined by such confidence has to count as a rationally justified option.

The basis of faith is religious experience. As far back as we can trace human existence, there are signs that human beings were convinced of the presence of some kind of transcendent reality, and as far back as we have written records of religion, these records witness to the living experience of transcendent powers and beings. However, if one wanted to view the religious experience of all other religions as deceitful, why would this not also hold true of one's own religion? Already at the end of the nineteenth century, Ernst Troeltsch commented on this:

> To apply Feuerbach's theory [according to which religion is based on projection; PS-L] to non-Christian religions while applying the theory of supernatural revelation to the Christian religion is clearly a dangerous experiment at which the truth of Christianity in whatever form will seem to be able to prevail to just a few.[2]

It is particularly for this reason that in every religion exclusivist theories are hardly plausible. And for the same reason inclusivism, which is in principle prepared to acknowledge that religious experience is also genuine if it occurs in other religions, is much more probable than exclusivism.

Inclusivist claims to superiority are just as little a Christian peculiarity as exclusivist theses are. Francis Clooney paraphrases the inclusivist attitude that is nowa-

1 Cp. on this Schmidt-Leukel 1999a, 93-110.
2 Troeltsch 1895, 375.

days found among many religions and which has not infrequently replaced exclusivist positions as follows:

> … "By an honest appreciation of universal spiritual values recognizable in all great traditions, one can see that while your tradition is adequate in many respects, ours contains the complete and integral representation of all these values. So, for the sake of the very values you hold dear, should you not leave behind your tradition and join ours?"[3]

Yet how great is the overall plausibility of such inclusivist superiority claims? If the superiority claims of several religions are strictly related to the same issue, then it is logically excluded that mutual superiority claims are equally true. Among several religions, each one cannot be superior to every other one in exactly the same respect, just as in a group of people it is impossible that everyone is older than everyone else. Of course, one person might be more clever, another more helpful, a third more patient, and a fourth more dependable, etc. Similarly, particular aspects of the human relationship to transcendence can be expressed more markedly in some religions than in others, so that in some respects certain religions can indeed be superior to others. Yet with respect to the fundamental issue of the mediation of salvific knowledge of transcendence, there can be no reciprocal superiority, though there can be a genuine equality in diversity. As the preceding overview of the relations of Christianity to some other religions has shown, inclusivist positions succeeded in all cases to break the exclusivist deadlocks, but they lead to the impasse of mutual superiority claims. By contrast, pluralist approaches lead beyond such impasses. However, whether or not one considers pluralism as a whole to be more plausible than inclusivism depends on the extent to which one is theologically prepared to appreciate the value of diversity not only in the realm of aesthetic beauty, but also in the realms of truth, goodness, and holiness. Let me repeat: The intention is not mixing a true religion with a false one, a good with a bad, and a holy with a demonic one. The question is rather whether we can accept that at the level of concrete human existence in all its cultural and individual diversity there can be true knowledge, good life, and the veneration of the holy in a genuine variety of equally valid forms. There are plenty of signs of this in the numerous religious traditions. But are the religions or better their adherents prepared to take these signs seriously? If they do so and if they want to cherish diversity also in the field of religion, then the transition from an inclusivist to a pluralist position becomes unavoidable.

To the extent that the pluralist position is a *theological* hypothesis, it is in principle not more probable than an atheist or naturalist explanation of religious diversity, which interprets religious diversity just as a diversity of lies and deception. Yet *within the spectrum of possible theological interpretations*, there is much to be said for the pluralist position as the most plausible hypothesis. What then, will be the results of religious pluralism in a practical sense?

3 Clooney 2003, 332.

Practical Consequences

It is said that Kenneth Cragg's presentation of Christian superiority on the basis of Islamic values and beliefs was so convincing to some Muslims that they converted to Christianity under his influence.[4] On the other hand, we know that Wilfred Cantwell Smith not only cultivated intensive friendships with Muslims,[5] but also in at least one case had a decisive role in someone's reconversion.[6] I am referring to Mahmoud Ayoub, who was born in 1935 in Lebanon to a religious Muslim family. Under the influence of the Christian school that Ayoub attended, he converted to Christianity and later became a member of the Southern Baptists. While he was a student at Harvard in the 1960s, he left the Southern Baptists, gave up their conservative evangelical theology, and turned to the Quakers as part of his religious quest. Smith, who was then Ayoub's teacher at Harvard, encouraged him to return to his Islamic roots. This eventually led to Ayoub finding his way back to Islam. Yet he did so not with the oft-encountered mentality of a polemical, zealous convert, but rather with that ecumenical attitude that Ayoub became known for in the Christian-Islamic dialogue.

The differences between Smith and Cragg in their relations to Muslims have an almost paradigmatic value. In Clooney's paraphrase of an inclusivist attitude cited above, the practical heart of inclusivism once more becomes clear: "should you not leave behind your tradition and join ours?" Of course this holds even more true for an exclusivist position. Because exclusivism and inclusivism assume that salvific truth is either exclusively or in its highest form only found in one's own religion, it necessarily seems ideal to these positions that other religions disappear in favor of one's own. In their missionary efforts exclusivists and inclusivists try to work towards the realization of this ideal. In contrast, it follows from a pluralist position that, when it comes to the religions perceived as equal, all proselytizing missionary efforts are to be ceased. In this context, "conversion" can only mean repeatedly turning anew to God. This neither excludes that in so doing, significant spiritual impulses will be received from other religions. Nor does it exclude the possibility that individual persons arrive at the conclusion that it is better for themselves to pursue their own spiritual path in the context of a different religion, or even just find their path there for the first time, and thus convert to this religion. But what is incompatible with the pluralist position is the deliberate attempt to supersede other religions on behalf of one's own through active missionary efforts.

According to their own self-understanding, religions have to accomplish a task in the world. "Mission," writes Stanley Samartha, "is God's continuing activity through

4 Cp. Renz 2002, 188, n. 627.
5 Cp. Grünschloss 1994, 32f. Among his closest friends Smith also numbered Hasan Askari, who—by his own admission—agreed "through and through" with Smith's ideas. Cp. Siddiqui 1997, 110f.
6 Cp. on this Siddiqui 1997, 97f.

the Spirit to mend the brokenness of creation, to overcome the fragmentation of humanity, and to heal the rift between humanity, nature, and God."[7] If one understands mission in this sense as a grounding of the religious task in transcendent reality itself, as the divine "calling" to work for the wellbeing and healing of the world, or—using the words of the Second Vatican Council—as the task of being the "sign and instrument" of God's Kingdom,[8] then from a pluralist perspective each religion has its own divine "mission." The future of Christian mission, according to Wilfred Cantwell Smith, will depend on learning a new understanding of mission in this enlarged sense:

> The mission of the Church is world-wide; but it is not God's only mission. It is not even His only world-wide mission. (…)
>
> Few of us Christians know much about God's mission in the Islamic venture; God's mission to India, and nowadays … to the world, through the Hindu complex; God's mission to East Asia, and nowadays to the world, in the Buddhist movement. Few Christians have any apprehension of God's mighty mission to the world in the post-biblical Jewish community. But we can learn. We are learning. (…) Only as we learn to see God's activity in other movements and other communities shall we serve Him well in and through our own.[9]

When we recognize that in this sense other religions also have a divine "mission" in the world, then the missionary task has to be carried out in dialogue and cooperation. But if religions close themselves off to dialogue and cooperation and instead continue to work against one another, then not only are they not living up to their duty, they are in fact themselves standing in the way. That "mission" today has to mean dialogue and cooperation for the salvation and wellbeing of the world has also been emphasized by Kenneth Cracknell and Paul Knitter, both of whom have tried to reconceptualize mission in a more pluralist fashion.[10] It is however a fair question of whether the term "mission" is still useful, from a pluralist perspective, for describing the task of religions in the world. Is not the concept of "mission" too strongly connected, perhaps irretrievably, to the notion of proselytization? It might be possible to convey a transformed understanding of mission to a relatively small circle of theologically educated Christians. But I fear that beyond this circle the word "mission" itself cannot be redeemed. Especially among members of non-Christian religions, any Christian talk of "mission" *as* or *through* dialogue and cooperation will have the opposite effect. That is, it will inevitably encourage the fear that the Christian invitation to dialogue and cooperation is no more than the old proselytizing efforts in a new disguise. Simply the word "mission" can thus make representatives of other religions reluctant or even adverse to dialogue and cooperation. The word is

7 Samarth 1991, 149.

8 See on such a sacramental approach to the concept of mission, which comes close to a pluralist position, the position of the sadly far too early deceased Swiss scholar of mission studies, Anton Peter, in Peter 1996, 383-401.

9 Smith 1988, 366f.

10 Cp. Cracknell 1986, and Knitter 1996.

so charged that today it can hardly serve the task that religions have in this world and that they should accomplish jointly. It would therefore presumably make sense to give up not only the goal of proselytization but also the term "mission" itself, as it is so closely tied to this idea.

Regarding Judaism, many theologians are now prepared to do both: that is, many not only reject the actual "mission to the Jews," they also find the word "mission" itself to be obsolete. So, with reference to the matter of the "mission to the Jews," one typically does not find any theological attempts to reconceptualize the word "mission" so as to retain its use. It would be desirable to transfer this consistent attitude to the relation of Christianity to the other religions as well.

There is another way in which the developments in the relationship of Christianity to Judaism have an important pioneering role. As reported above, already in 1961 Pope John XXIII deleted the words about the "faithless Jews" from the Good Friday liturgy.[11] But John Pawlikowski is indeed correct to point out that the notion of Christianity as the fulfillment and supersession of all other religions remains deeply embedded in the structure of the liturgy and worship of the Christian churches. This requires a deep-seated change not only with respect to Judaism.

And it is not enough only to change those liturgical formulas that either explicitly or implicitly denigrate other religions. Although Christian liturgy remains shaped primarily by the experience of God in Jesus Christ, liturgical praise should also go beyond this and speak of the works of God among all peoples. Christian praise would then join the many voices of praise, and also the silent reverence, in the face of ultimate reality. This will involve searching for new liturgical forms of expression that emphasize a genuine appreciation for the true, the good, and the holy in other religions.[12] Of course, this will not be accomplished by such changes in our liturgy that would assign these religions a similar precursor status as we have with Judaism. This was and remains the problem of those much discussed Indian liturgical experiments in which readings from the sacred scriptures of Indian religions stand in for readings from the "Old Testament," that is, from the Hebrew Bible. It is no surprise that such experiments led to unenthusiastic responses from the members of those religions. For such changes only reinforce, this time via liturgy, the claim that Christianity fulfills and surpasses these religions, presenting it as the *one* new covenant that makes obsolete the many "old" covenants.

Caution is also needed when developing new liturgical or ritual forms within the context of such interreligious events that have the character of a worship service. One must pay attention to the distinctiveness and integrity of the groups participating in interreligious worship. At the same time, interreligious events have high symbolic value, particularly if they are of a decidedly religious nature. Today they can be an excellent sign of mutual appreciation between religions, and become so ever more clearly in the future. The development of liturgical forms that are useful and

11 Cp. above chapter 12, p. 283.
12 On this, cp. also the relevant comments in Hick 1993a, 163f.

appropriate is therefore an important desideratum. And this offers a special opportunity: for it is only through joint conversation that we can develop liturgical and ritual forms of interreligious prayer, meditation, etc.

A pluralist theology of religions must have further important consequences in the sphere of religious education and development. First of all, it is crucial that all levels of Christian catechesis convey solid and reliable information about other religions and avoid distorted pictures and the unfair comparisons of the ideals of one's own religion with less than ideal realities in other religions. In addition, concrete encounters with people of other religions—and with their living religiosity—need to become an integral part of Christian formation[13] and theological education. The purpose of such encounters should not only be to impart respect for the faith of the other but, as far as possible, also a sensitivity for the rich variety of human experience of transcendence preserved within it.

Presumably, the main challenge of religious education is to contribute to the formation of a religious identity that is shaped by a positive openness toward the religious other. For a closer characterization of this attitude, I find the categories originally developed in 1997 by the British Commission on "Islamophobia" and then taken over in the rightly much praised Parekh Report (of the "Commission on the Future of a Multi-Ethnic Britain") to be particularly helpful. This report differentiates between a closed and an open attitude to people of other religions/cultures in eight different areas:[14]

1. *Monolithic/diverse*: Is the religious Other seen as a monolithic, static, unchangeable block, *or* as a differentiated group in which there are debates and the possibility of further development?
2. *Separate/interacting*: Is the religious Other seen as being completely separate from me, with whom I share no common values, by whom I am not affected, and on whom I exercise no influence, *or* do I see my relationship to the Other as interdependent, that is, as a relationship of shared values and aims with the possibility of mutual influence and enrichment?
3. *Inferior/different:* Is the religious Other seen as inferior, for example as "barbaric," "irrational," "fundamentalist," *or* as different but of equal worth?
4. *Enemy/partner:* Is the religious Other seen as violent, aggressive, and threatening, as to be defeated or dominated, *or* is the Other seen as an actual or potential partner in joint co-operative enterprises and in the solution of shared problems?
5. *Manipulative/sincere:* Is the religious Other seen as manipulative and deceitful, as concerned only with material or strategic advantage, *or* as sincere and not hypocritical in their belief?

13 For a presentation and discussion of more recent pedagogical efforts and experiments that take into account particularly strongly the reality of religious diversity, see the contributions in Heumann 2003.

14 See the Parekh Report 2000, 245-247. I follow closely though not always literally the wording of the report.

6. *Criticism of the self rejected/considered:* Is criticism toward oneself by the religious Other discarded from the outset *or* is such criticism considered and debated?
7. *Discrimination defended/criticized:* Is hostility toward the religious Other used to justify discriminatory practices and exclusion of the Other from the mainstream society, *or* is it accepted that debates and disagreements with the religious Other do not diminish efforts in combatting discrimination and exclusion?
8. *Hostility towards the Other seen as natural/problematic:* Are fear and hostility towards the religious Other accepted as natural and "normal" *or* are critical views of the religious Other themselves subjected to critique, lest they be inaccurate and unfair?

Of course, it is not only on the basis of a pluralist theology of religions that an open attitude toward the religious Other, described in this way, can be cultivated. But such an attitude is more or less congenial to a pluralist position. However, the pluralist position has its own specific dangers: It will have to be particularly sensitive regarding the practical attitude it creates towards those who cannot and will not share a pluralist position. Precisely because a pluralist theology of religions is shaped primarily by the notion of appreciation and not of toleration, pluralists are no less susceptible to intolerance than exclusivists or inclusivists when dealing with manifestations of religions which they do not appreciate. The law of tolerance, that is, the broadest possible toleration of that which is not appreciated, is therefore equally important for all three positions in the theology of religions.[15]

Above all, the pluralist stance in interreligious dialogue is characterized by the expectation of encountering signs of God's presence everywhere in other religions. And what particularly distinguishes the pluralist position is the justified confidence that this divine presence is no less salvific and no less clearly reflected in other religions than in one's own religions. As Mahmoud Ayoub says:

> Therefore, the ultimate goal of all interfaith dialogue ought to be the ability of all women and men of faith to listen to and obey the voice of God as it speaks to all communities through their own faith-traditions…[16]

In order to draw the theological consequences from this understanding of dialogue, it is necessary to strive purposefully toward the goal of a world theology.[17]

15 Cp. on this once more above chapter 6, pp. 162-164.
16 Ayoub 2004, 318.
17 Cp. the foundational discussion in Swidler 1987b.

Toward a World Theology

In the preceding chapters on Christian dialogue with Judaism, Islam, Hinduism, and Buddhism, I have tried at numerous points to show that in relation to the theological content a broadening of these dialogues is both desirable and necessary. It makes sense, for example, to extend dialogue with Judaism and dialogue with Islam into a Jewish-Christian-Islamic trialogue. The same holds true of dialogue with Hinduism and Buddhism where there is much to be said for pursuing a Hindu-Buddhist-Christian trialogue. This in no way means that the time for bilateral dialogue is coming to an end. All in all, these are still quite young and each has to be pursued in its own right—with and also without Christian participation! From a pluralist perspective, dialogue between Judaism and Islam, between Hinduism and Buddhism, between Judaism and Buddhism, Judaism and Hinduism, Hinduism and Islam, or Islam and Buddhism are clearly desirable and they are theologically significant. Nevertheless, various interreligious relationships are so tightly interconnected, partly as a result of their historical preconditions and in every case because of contemporary constellations, that it is urgently advisable to supplement bilateral dialogue with trialogues and multilateral colloquies. Also to be included both at the level of bilateral and multilateral conversation are the traditional Chinese religions as well as smaller religious communities such as tribal religions or religions like the Jains, the Parses, the Sikhs, the Baha'i, and so forth. They too have important aspects to contribute to the global colloquy of religions. Since these religions are often closely related or interconnected with some of the major religious traditions, like for example the Chinese religions with Buddhism, the Jains with Buddhism and Hinduism, the Sikhs with Islam and Hinduism, the Baha'i with Islam, and the tribal religions with the world religions found in their region, including them seems obvious even on historical grounds. In this way, interreligious dialogue results in a global colloquy of religions. Already more than 40 years ago, Wilfred Cantwell Smith described this process and his preferred way of conducting it with the following words:

> The traditional form of Western scholarship in the study of other men's religion was that of an impersonal presentation of an "it." The first great innovation in recent times has been the personalization of the faiths observed, so that one finds a discussion of a "they." Presently the observer becomes personally involved, so that the situation is one of a "we" talking about a "they." The next step is a dialogue, where "we" talk to "you." If there is listening and mutuality, this may become that "we" talk *with* "you." The culmination of this progress is when "we all" are talking *with* each other about "us."[18]

From a theological perspective this means—according to Smith—that we are jointly proceeding toward an understanding of the world in which we no longer think in the old contrasts of "we" and "they" or "we" and "you," but are rather aware that

18 Smith 1959, 34.

"*some of us* are Muslims, some are Hindus, some are Jews, some are Christians" and "some of us are skeptics."[19] If theology is to be an expression of faith controlled by scholarly rules, then, according to Smith, in this day and age it has to express "the faith of all of us" and "our modern perception of the world."[20] If theology is meant to express the truth about God on the basis of God's self-manifestation or revelation, then today's theology must take the complete human history of religion as its material basis.[21] In such a "theology of religions," the religions are no longer just the object but become the subject of this theology. It is a world theology to which the theologies of the different religious traditions—in other words Christian, Jewish, Islamic, Hindu and their analogous counterparts in the non-theistic traditions—each make their own contribution. This intended world theology has to be pursued by means of a global colloquy of all religions.[22] One cannot realistically expect that this global theology will ever assume anything like a generally accepted form. Even inside the religious traditions there is no such thing as a single generally accepted form of theology. So it is all the more unlikely for this to be possible with an interreligious world theology. Yet it is clear that global theology can and should be practiced through a global dialogical process. It materializes in that theological effort that no longer tries to formulate its own understanding of the truth without open and serious regard for the relevant insights of other religious traditions, and which contributes the result of these efforts to the global dialogue.[23]

For every participating religious tradition, the project of a world theology entails two important and closely connected tasks: the effort for comprehensive integration and for thorough consistency. For example, what will the insights that from a Christian perspective have been won in the dialogue with Judaism mean for the dialogue with Hinduism or vice versa? What do insights from the dialogue with Buddhism mean for the dialogue with Islam and so forth? It takes a special kind of theological effort to interconnect the theological developments within different dialogues as closely as possible with each another. And it requires particular work to strive for the inner consistency of the Christian position whilst paying attention to the various dialogues. This is all the more important if one does not regard the Christian position in an unhistorical manner as set-in-stone, but rather as a position that can undergo transformations in response to new insights and in fact actually does so.

By now there are already some important pioneering works on the Christian side for this global theological project. Smith himself has contributed two significant studies: his comparative work on the concept of faith[24] and his work on the role of sacred scriptures in interreligious perspective.[25] John Hick explicitly related

19 Cp. ibid. 58 and Smith 1989, 101.
20 Cp. Smith 1989, 125.
21 Cp. Smith 1987b, 52-61.
22 Cp. Smith 1989, 124-129, 193.
23 Cp. ibid. 130-179.
24 Cp. Smith 1979.
25 Cp. Smith 1993.

his major study on eschatology to the project of a global theology.[26] Geoffrey Parrinder's comparative study on the notion of incarnation,[27] though written primarily from a religious studies perspective, nonetheless displays a clear theological interest. Ninian Smart and Steven Konstantine[28] offer a Christian doctrinal outline in a multi-religious horizon. In Germany, Hans-Martin Barth has published a similar attempt.[29] In this context we must above all draw attention to the pioneering work of the former Oxford systematic theologian, Keith Ward. His comparative study on the concept of God or transcendence[30] was followed by four volumes of comparative theology that discuss in turn the notion of revelation,[31] the understanding of creation,[32] issues of soteriology and eschatology,[33] as well as ecclesiology,[34] all from an interreligious perspective.

Not all the authors named here represent a pluralist position. Ninian Smart and Steven Konstantine as well as Hans-Martin Barth are inclusivists in terms of a theology of religions. This shows that even from a non-pluralist position the need for, as Barth puts it, "a Christian dogmatics oriented to interreligious dialogue"[35] is noticed and taken seriously. To be sure, the primary interest is then to give the assumed superior truth of Christian faith a clearer profile in light of other religions. This does not necessarily imply that the theological interest amounts to nothing more than that. Even from an inclusivist perspective it is theologically possible and desirable not only to talk *about* religions, but also to speak "*with* their representatives" and in so doing not only to view them "as objects, but rather as subjects of theology" as Barth says in following Hans Waldenfels.[36] However, the readiness to learn theologically from other religions remains limited if it is based on inclusivist presuppositions. The primal expectation here is to arrive at a "deepened insight into the basic statements of Christian faith."[37] Yet how far can such a deepening go? Does the openness to "deepened insight" also include an essential willingness to make changes in one's religious self-understanding as well as in specific matters of doctrinal content, as Keith Ward calls for as a prerequisite of comparative theology?[38] A pluralist theology of religions depends on the conviction that what we have so far recognized as true about and in the other religions already requires a change in one's own religious self-understanding. And this is expressed not only theologically but also at the level of lived spirituality.

26 Cp. Hick 1990c, 29-34.
27 Cp. Parrinder 1997.
28 Cp. Smart, Konstantine 1991.
29 Cp. Barth 2001.
30 Cp. Ward 1987.
31 Cp. Ward 1994.
32 Cp. Ward 1996.
33 Cp. Ward 1988.
34 Cp. Ward 2000.
35 Barth 2001, 39.
36 Cp. ibid. 49f.
37 Cp. ibid. 50f.
38 Cp. Ward 1994, 48. On this see above chapter 3, p. 83.

Interreligious Spirituality

> Each religion, being placed in a multi-religious world, should have long before developed an interreligious consciousness. But for centuries, this interreligious consciousness was suppressed …

… says Hasan Askari in his small but remarkably dense and rich compendium of interreligious spirituality.[39] The reasons for his demand are many, though one reason stands out above all the rest: Every one of the major religions is imprinted with a universalistic spirit. They are all focused on a truth that concerns *all* people, about a transcendental reality that is for *all* people the highest good or the basis of their salvation. This universalistic characteristic manifests itself either in an attitude that is opposed to all other religions, especially in the attempt to overcome these through missionary efforts, or, according to Askari, it manifests itself as an "interactive universality":

> By an interactive universality, a real universal spirit is experienced. Then only do we start unravelling the secret: God spoke to every nation in its own language. Religion, in its universal statement, is an inter-universality of different cultures.[40]

As summary and conclusion, I would like to characterize in more detail this attitude of an interactive religious universality, or, put another way, of an interreligious spirituality as it corresponds to a pluralist theology of religions in terms of seven virtues.

Confidence. Like all genuine religiosity, interreligious spirituality is shaped above all by trust in the existence of an ultimate reality as the basis for our salvation. Or to put it another way, it is shaped by the confidence that all surface reality, which suffers from so many obvious limitations and in part from horrendous evils, is infinitely transcended by, while also deeply infused with, this ultimate reality; the hope that this reality, if it really exists, justifies that which John Hick has termed "cosmic optimism."[41] It is in and through confidence that such trust combines with this hope. "The kind of spirituality," writes Hick, "that is appropriate to the contemporary pluralistic vision is one that is basically trusting and hopeful and stirred by a sense of joy in celebration of the goodness, from our human point of view, of the ultimately Real."[42]

Confidence, as it is rooted in the transcendent, is of crucial significance for our understanding of reality as a whole, for our self-understanding, and also for our understanding of our fellow humans:

39 Askari 1991b, 12.
40 Ibid. 16.
41 Cp. Hick 1989, 56-69, and 1999, 47-73. See also above chapter 7, pp. 188f.
42 Hick 1996, 409.

> … he is not far from each one of us. For "In him we live and move and have our being …" (Acts 17:27b-28a)

In this speech given on the Aeropagus in Athens, Paul freely admits that non-Christians have also recognized the universal presence of God. The fact that the ultimate reality is close to everyone in a very personal way is the basis of what in Christianity is called God's "universal salvific will." And indeed, we can find analogous testimonies in all the major religions: For example, the word of the prophet Amos that God is not only the liberator of Israel but likewise the liberator of other peoples (Amos 9:7); the Qur'anic emphasis that God has set his messengers to all people so as not to leave anyone without the necessary "guidance" (Qur'an 16:36); Krishna's promise in the Bhagavadgītā that he receives the prayer of all even if these are directed to other gods (Gītā 9:23); the revelation of the supernatural Buddha in the Lotus-Sūtra, that he directs his wisdom to all beings, good or bad, without distinction, just as the sun gives light to all and the rain brings the same water for all, in order to lead them to salvation (Lotus-Sūtra 5). Interreligious spirituality lives by the confidence that such affirmations are not empty words, but rather that they come from the presence of the transcendent itself.

Humility. If transcendent reality exceeds everything, then it also exceeds our abilities to grasp it. To cite Anselm of Canterbury once again: If God is that than which nothing greater can be conceived, then God must be greater than anything that can be conceived (Proslogion 15). As shown before, this view also has numerous parallels within all the major religious traditions.[43] It commands us with almost brazen sternness not to make for ourselves an image of the divine reality, not even a theological one! Or, to say it more accurately, this divine reality reveals that all our human images are provisional, since the divine reality always remains greater than what these images can grasp or express. None of our images of God and none of our concepts of transcendence must be allowed to take the place of this reality itself. Humility in the face of absolute transcendence forbids any absolutizing of its symbolic, dogmatic, or cultic representation. No finite pointer to the infinite can exhaust its infinity, let alone replace it. On the one hand, this insight can guard us against absolutizing our own religious tradition. And on the other hand, it can lead us to the insight that there is no idolatry where we find an equally radical emphasis on the all-surpassing eminence of this ultimate reality.

Divine reality, however, would not be truly and absolutely unlimited it if were somehow limited by its own transcendence. As a truly transcendent reality it is therefore at the same time also deeply immanent. This is the only reason why transcendent reality is accessible to us without losing its transcendent nature: "Transcendence can only be known through immanence; yet it is known as transcending that immanence"[44]—as Wilfred Cantwell Smith formulated it so precisely. That

43 Cp. above chapter 7, pp. 181-184.
44 Smith 1993, 246 n. 16. Cp. also Smith 1990.

is, transcendent reality is accessible to people in and despite its inconceivability. Its presence can indeed and genuinely be experienced, but in those limited and diverse ways which reflect both our own limitations as finite beings and also the diversity of humanity. What moves us to explore this more deeply is something akin to religious curiosity.

Curiosity. In the Christian tradition, curiosity is hardly reckoned to be one of the virtues. Augustine in particular considered it to be rather a vice. Yet I am not referring to that meddlesome, insensitive, and undue curiosity which has no respect for the integrity of the other. Rather, I am speaking about something like the curiosity or inquisitiveness of a researcher or scientist. In the interreligious context, it signals a genuine interest in what God means to other people in their lives. In this sense, curiosity represents the wish to discern the "treasures a generous God has distributed among the nations of the earth" (*Ad gentes* 11). "How many ways to God are there?" Peter Seewald asked Cardinal Ratzinger, and Ratzinger's response was: "As many as there are human beings."[45] This is precisely what curiosity—as a virtue of interreligious spirituality—takes seriously. It wants to find out more about the many ways of humanity to God, and to learn from them. It is the sincere wish to expand our own spiritual horizon by better understanding our neighbors in other faith communities, through a better understanding of their experience, their wisdom, and their truth. This kind of curiosity automatically leads to a fundamental dialogical stance, and this brings us to our next virtue, that of friendship.

Friendship. The curiosity about which I just spoke includes reading and studying the writings of other religions, becoming familiar with their cultural and cultic forms of expression and under certain circumstances also participating in other forms of religious praxis. Yet everything that we can observe, study, or explore is only the expression of something much more profound, and at the same time much less objectifiable, namely the faith of concrete persons. We must not forget that the so-called religions are in the final analysis not abstract entities. If a religion is not the religion of concrete, living people, then it has either died out or it never really existed. All too often we carry around with us an image of other people's religion that is completely fictional, because the religion that we imagine does not coincide with the religion that these people actually live and experience. We can know and study many facts about other religious traditions. But what these traditions actually mean to those people who live in and through them, can ultimately only be understood when we become their friends—their close friends.

No one has emphasized this basic principle of modern religious studies and the theology of religions as much as Wilfred Cantwell Smith, including through his own praxis as an academic teacher. We can see this in numerous examples. Let me mention at least one: When Smith became the director of the "Center for the Study of World Religions" at Harvard University, the newly erected building contained not only the rooms of students and guest lecturers but also a large room that was in-

45 Ratzinger 1996b, 35.

tended to serve as an "inter-faith chapel." The library, on the other hand, was in a smaller room on the ground floor. One of the first things that Smith did was to move the library into the big chapel room. However, he did not convert the erstwhile library into the intended chapel, but rather turned it into a common room that offered opportunities for casual interaction. As he himself reports, it seemed to Smith that a place in which friendships could develop between students of different religions and cultural origins was far more important than a place to experiment with interreligious prayers.[46]

Friendship includes many good things, such as the effort and opportunity to understand our friends as they understand themselves. This also opens up understanding for their "religion." In order to understand Buddhism, says Smith, we should not primarily look at what can be described as "Buddhism," but rather, as far as possible, look at the world through Buddhist eyes![47] Only when we share our friends' joy and sorrow will we have the opportunity to truly understand how their faith helps them to overcome their pain, to nourish their hope and to keep their love from growing cold. This kind of understanding is central to an interreligious spirituality that makes friendship its key virtue.

Honesty. Friends *can* be honest with one another. And they *must* be honest if they want to remain true friends. Interreligious friendship therefore includes the virtue of honesty—an honesty toward both the friend's religion as well as one's own. In such honesty there is no reason to boast and no place for contempt. It excludes double standards. Jesus' parable about the speck in the neighbor's eye and the log in one's own is almost nowhere as relevant as in an interreligious context. If there is a reason to be critical, criticism ought to be expressed carefully, sensitively, and without triumphally patting oneself on the back. Christianity is familiar with the tradition of *correctio fraterna* or "brotherly correction." I suggest that when and where interreligious critique is necessary, that it be practiced in this spirit.

When interreligious friendship is coupled with honesty, then we will not only learn to see the world through the eyes of our friends but also to see ourselves and our own religion in that way. It is a clear sign of maturing interreligious relationships when we as Christians begin to see ourselves through the eyes of our non-Christian friends. There are signs that interest in such a change of perspective has been increasing in the last few years.[48] Undoubtedly, this constitutes a huge challenge. Yet this challenge implies in a special way the potential of transforming our self-perception. And this requires the virtue of courage.

Courage. It takes courage to let oneself and one's own religion be confronted by insights coming from another religious tradition. Undoubtedly, such openness allows us to discern and overcome misunderstandings and misinterpretations. Yet to

46 Cp. Smith 1992, 55f.
47 Cp. Smith 1989, 82.
48 See for example Griffiths 1990, Grünschloss 1999, Gross, Muck 2000, Schmidt-Leukel 2001a, Ridgeon 2001.

realize how people of other faiths see us will often imply an extremely irritating experience, especially when this realization stands in tension with our usual self-perception. Here let us be reminded once more of the aforementioned examples from Jewish-Christian dialogue: What Christian would not be horrified and shocked to hear Michael Signer say that what above all he associates with the name "Jesus Christ" is hatred and suffering, or to hear Michael Wyschogrod say that it is the feeling of fear that he mostly associates with the symbol of the cross?[49] On the other hand who would deny that it is deeply important and healing to become aware of such external perceptions of Christianity? With their help we can arrive at a more realistic, truer self-understanding, especially also in as much as it concerns our theological claims about other religions. Christians have begun to learn this lesson with regard to Judaism. But this lesson is no less important with respect to other religions. And this learning process is often still pending.

As a result, interreligious dialogue, if it is genuine and serious, leads to an "intra-religious dialogue," as Raimon Panikkar aptly put it three decades ago.[50] Intra-religious or inner-religious dialogue begins when we truly allow ourselves to be touched by the insights of our friends and their religious traditions: Do they challenge us to alter our thinking, feeling, and believing? Courage here means being prepared to accept any spiritual consequence that results when we honestly open ourselves to a religious tradition other than our own. It is the willingness to change. Quite a number of people who have seriously immersed themselves into interreligious encounter, interreligious dialogue, and interreligious friendship for many years, exhibit signs of such change: Some of them go as far as to say that they now experience a sort of double or even multiple religious belonging.[51] That is, they simply note quite honestly that dialogue has so much changed their own spiritual life, that it is no longer nourished by only one religious tradition. Undoubtedly this is a serious change and can include intense moments of crisis, since it does have a direct impact on one's own religious identity. Yet among those who have gone through this experience, it leaves them in the end with a sense of a transformation that is profoundly enriching spiritually and existentially decisive, accompanied by a sense of deeply felt gratitude.

Gratitude completes my list of the seven virtues of interreligious spirituality: gratitude for the religious other, gratitude both for what we have in common *and*

49 Cp. above chapter 12, p. 303.

50 Cp. Panikkar 1978.

51 To name just a few prominent examples: Raimon Panikkar (Christian-Hindu-Buddhist), Henri Le Saux (Christian-Hindu), Bede Griffith (Christian-Hindu), Roger Corless (Christian-Buddhist), Sallie King (Christian-Buddhist), Julia Ching (Christian-Buddhist-Taoist-Confucian), Frithjof Schuon (Christian-Muslim). For other examples and a beginning theological reflection on this see Ching 1999; Cornille 2002; Kasimow, Keenan, Klepinger Keenan 2003; Pannikar 1999; Phan 2003. Although double or multiple religious belonging is still a relatively new phenomenon in the West, there is a long tradition of this in the Chinese cultural sphere, and thus this plays an important role in the dialogue with Chinese religions (cp. Berthrong 1994, 165-187). For the most part, theological reflection on multiple religious belonging and the related question of religious identity is still pending, but it ought to become an important task of future theology.

for what differentiates us from one another. I once read in a review how the reviewer criticized the author under review by saying that this author was "not clear on whether what is good about the world religions is that we are all the same, or that we are all different." What a false and superficial alternative! Both are reasons for joy and gratitude: our unity *and* our diversity. And both belong together. Without diversity, unity would be unbearable conformity or dreary uniformity. Yet without unity, diversity would be either irrelevant or mean only confusion, division, and war.

If gratitude is profound, then it includes what in German mysticism is known as "Gelassenheit" (composure): stillness, serenity, non-attachment—without lethargy or passivity. In grateful composure, detachment may unite with loving engagement, thus joining two of the most prominent essentials of the spirituality of both Eastern and Western religions. With this attitude we can stride into the future with realism and confidence, a future in which we—all of us—handle our religious diversity in a wiser, friendlier, and more fruitful way than has been the case in the past.

Bibliography

Abdullah, Muhammad Salim 1992: *Islam für das Gespräch mit Christen*. Gütersloh: Gütersloher Verlagshaus.

Abe, Masao 1981: Toward a Creative Encounter between Zen and Christianity. In: *A Zen-Christian Pilgrimage. The Fruits of Ten Annual Colloquia in Japan. 1967-1976*. (No place) The Zen-Christian Colloquium, 36-44.

– 1985: A Dynamic Unity in Religious Pluralism: A Proposal from the Buddhist Point of View. In: J. Hick, H. Askari (eds.): *The Experience of Religious Diversity*. Aldershot: Gower Publishing, 163-190.

– 1989: *Zen and Western Thought*, ed. by W.R. LaFleur. Reprint of 1985 edition. Honolulu: University of Hawai'i Press.

– 1995: *Buddhism and Interfaith Dialogue*. Ed. by St. Heine. Basingstoke: Macmillan.

Abou El Fadl, Khaled 2001: *Rebellion and Violence in Islamic Law*. Cambridge: Cambridge University Press.

Abu-Rabi, Ibrahim M. 2000: John Paul II and Islam. In: B. Sherwin, H. Kasimow (eds.): *John Paul II and Interreligious Dialogue*. Maryknoll: Orbis, 185-204.

Al- Ghazālī, Abū-Hāmid Muhammad 1987: *Die Nische der Lichter* (Miskāt al-anwār). Hamburg: Felix Meiner.

Aleaz, Kalarikkal Poulose 1995: *Dimensions of Indian Religion. Study, Experience and Interaction*. Calcutta: Punthi Pustak.

Allen, John 1999: Doubts About Dialogue. In: *National Catholic Reporter* (27.8.1999).

– 2000: Perils of Pluralism. In: *National Catholic Reporter* (15.9.2000).

Alphonse, Martin 1992: Witnessing to Christ in a World of Religious Pluralism. In: Bage, M. et. al.,: *Many Other Ways?* Delhi: ISPCK, 44-58.

Alston, William 1988: Religious Diversity and Perceptual Knowledge of God. In: *Faith and Philosophy* 5,433-448.

– 1991: *Perceiving God. The Epistemology of Religious Experience*. Ithaca – London: Cornell University Press.

Amaladass, Anand 1989: Dialogue between Hindus and the St. Thomas Christians. In: H. Coward (ed.): *Hindu-Christian Dialogue. Perspectives and Encounters*. Maryknoll: Orbis, 13-27.

Amaladoss, Michael 1990: *Making All Things New. Dialogue, Pluralism and Evangelism in Asia*. Maryknoll: Orbis.

– 1991: New Wine and Old Bottles. In: *Vidyajyoti* 55, 41-45.

– 1992: *Becoming Indian. The Process of Inculturation*. Published by Centre for Indian and Inter-relgious Studies (CIIS), Rom, and Dharmaram Publications (DP), Bangalore.

– 1997: A Simple Solution. In: L. Swidler, P. Mojzes (eds.): *The Uniqueness of Jesus. A Dialogue with Paul Knitter*. Maryknoll: Orbis, 25-28.

– 1997b: Life in Freedom. Liberation Theologies From Asia. Maryknoll: Orbis.

Ambedkar, B.R. 1989: *Writings and Speeches*. Vol. 5. Compiled by Vasant Moon. Bombay: Government of Maharashtra.

Amore, Roy C. 1978: *Two Masters, One Message*. Nashville: Abingdon.

Anawati, Georges C. 1967: Exkurs zum Konzilstext über die Muslim. In: *Lexikon für Theologie und Kirche*. Das Zweite Vatikanische Konzil. Teil II. Freiburg – Basel – Wien: Herder, 485-487.

Ariarajah, Wesley 1985: *The Bible and People of Other Faiths*. Geneva: WCC.

– 1989: A World Council of Churches' Perspective on the Future of Hindu-Christian Dialogue. In: H. Coward (ed.): *Hindu-Christian Dialogue. Perspectives and Encounters*. Maryknoll: Orbis, 251-261.

– 1994: *Die Bibel und die Andersgläubigen*. Frankfurt a.M.: Lembeck.

– 1997: The Need for a New Debate. In: L. Swidler, P. Mojzes (eds.): *The Uniqueness of Jesus. A Dialogue with Paul Knitter*. Maryknoll: Orbis, 29-34.

– 1999: *Not Without My Neighbour. Issues in Inter-Faith Relations*. Geneva: WCC.

Arkoun, Mohammed 1993: Islam and the Hegemony of the West. In: A. Sharma (ed.): *God, Truth and Reality*. Basingstoke: Macmillan, 72-86.

– 1998: Rethinking Islam Today. In: Ch. Kurzman (ed.): *Liberal Islam. A Sourcebook*. Oxford: OUP, 205-221.

– 1999: *Der Islam. Annäherung an eine Religion*. Heidelberg: Palmyra.

Arnal, William E. 2000: Definition. In: W. Braun, R.T. McCutcheon (eds.): *Guide to the Study of Religion*. London – New York: Cassell, 21-34.

Askari, Hasan 1985: Within and Beyond the Experience of Religious Diversity. In: J. Hick, H. Askari (eds.): *The Experience of Religious Diversity*. Aldershot: Gower, 191-218.

– 1991: Inmitten und jenseits der Erfahrung religiöser Vielfalt. In: R. Kirste, P. Schwarzenau, U. Tworuschka (Hg.): *Gemeinsam vor Gott* (RIG 1). Rissen: EBV, 106-127.

– 1991b: *Spiritual Quest. An Inter-Religious Dimension*. Pudsey: Seven Mirrors.

– 1992: Vom Teilen zur Begegnung. In: R. Kirste, P. Schwarzenau, U. Tworuschka (Hg.): *Engel, Elemente, Energien* (RIG 2). Balve: Zimmermann, 66-73.

– 2002: Die theologischen und anthropologischen Herausforderungen an den interreligösen Dialog. In: R. Kirste, P. Schwarzenau, U. Tworuschka (Hg.): *Neue Herausforderungen für den interreligiösen Dialog* (RIG 7). Balve: Zimmermann, 11-30.

Aslan, Adnan 1996a: Islam and Religious Pluralism. In: *The Islamic Quarterly: A Review of Islamic Culture* 40, 172-187.

– 1996b: Religions and the Concept of the Ultimate. An Interview with John Hick and Seyyed Hossein Nasr. In: *The Islamic Quarterly: A Review of Islamic Culture* 40, 266-283.

– 1998: *Religious Pluralism in Christian and Islamic Philosophy: The Thought of John Hick and Seyyed Hossein Nasr*. Richmond: Curzon.

Augustinus, Aurelius 1976: *Die Retractationen in zwei Büchern. Retractationes Libri Duo* (Aurelius Augustinus Werke, hg. von Carl Johann Perl). Paderborn: Schöningh.

Aydin, Mahmut 2000: Is There Only One Way To God? A Muslim View. In: *Studies in Interreligious Dialogue* 10, 148-159.

– 2001: Religious Pluralism: A Challenge for Muslims – A Theological Imagination. In: *Journal of Ecumenical Studies* 38, 330-352.

– 2002a: *Modern Western Christian Theological Understanding of Muslims Since the Second Vatican Council* (Cultural heritage and Contemporary Change. Series IIA. Islam, Vol. 13). Washington: The Council for Research in Values and Philosophy.

– 2002b: Globalization and the Gospel: A Muslim View. In: Th. Foust et. al. (eds.): *A Scandalous Prophet. The Way of Mission after Newbigin*. Grand Rapids, Cambridge: Eerdmanns, 174-181.

Ayoub, Mahmoud 1980: Towards an Islamic Christology, II: The Death of Jesus, Reality or Delusion. In: *The Muslim World* 70, 91-121.

– 1997: Islam and Pluralism. In: *Encounters. Journal of Inter-Cultural Perspectives* 3, 103-118.
– 2000: Pope John Paul II on Islam. In: B. Sherwin, H. Kasimow (eds.): *John Paul II and Interreligious Dialogue*. Maryknoll: Orbis, 171-184.
– 2004: Christian-Muslim Dialogue Goals and Obstacles. In: *The Muslim World* 94, 313-319.
Bage, M. et al. 1992: *Many Other Ways?* Questions of Religious Pluralism. Papers from a Symposium on Religious Pluralism conducted by the Church Growth Research Center McGavran Institute at the Gurukul Lutheran Theological College Chapel, Madras on 23 June, 1990. Delhi: ISPCK.
Baillie, Donald M. 1997: *God was in Christ. An Essay on Incarnation and Atonement* (1st ed. 1948). London: Faber and Faber.
– 1959: *Gott war in Christus*. Göttingen: Vandenhoeck & Ruprecht.
Balasuriya, Tissa 1988a (ed.): Emergence of Third World Theology. From Dar es Salaam to Mexico (*Voices from the Third World*. Vol XK, No. 1). Colombo.
– 1988b (ed.): Christologies in Encounter (*Voices from the Third World*. Vol XI, No. 2). Colombo.
– 1988c: Humanity's Fall and Jesus the Saviour. In: T. Balasuriya (ed.): Christologies in Encounter (*Voices from the Third World*. Vol XI, No. 2). Colombo, 41-75.
Barnes, L. Philip 1990: Relativism, Ineffability, and the Appeal to Experience: A Reply to Myth Makers. In: *Modern Theology* 7, 102-144.
Barth, Hans-Martin 2001: *Dogmatik. Evangelischer Glaube im Kontext der Weltreligionen*. Ein Lehrbuch. Gütersloh: Gütersloher Verlagshaus.
Barth, Karl 1932-1970: *Church Dogmatics*. English translation as in "The Digital Karl Barth Library". See: http://solomon.dkbl.alexanderstreet.com/cgi-bin/asp/philo/dkbl/volumes_toc.pl?&church=ON
Barth, Karl 1987 (1923): Von der Paradoxie des »positive Pardoxes«. Antworten und Fragen an Paul Tillich. In: *Theologische Blätter* 2 (1923), Sp. 287-296, reprinted in: J. Clayton (ed.): Paul Tillich. Writings in the Philosophy of Religion – Religionsphilosophische Schriften (= Paul Tillich: Main Works – Vol. 4). Berlin – New York: De Gruyter, 98-109.
Basinger, David 2002: *Religious Diversity. A Philosophical Assessment*. Aldershot: Ashgate.
Bäumer, Bettina 1992: *Abhinavagupta. Wege ins Licht*. Texte des tantrischen Shivaismus aus Kaschmir. Zürich: Benziger.
– 2003: *Trika: Grundthemen des kaschmirischen Shivaismus*. Hg. Von E. Fürlinger. Innsbruck – Vienna: Tyrolia.
Bauschke, Martin 2001a: *Jesus im Koran*. Cologne: Böhlau.
– 2001b: Der koranische Jesus und die christliche Theologie. In: *Münchener Theologische Zeitschrift* 52, 26-33.
Bayfield, Rabbi Tony 2000: Response. In: M. Braybrooke. *Christian-Jewish Dialogue. The Next Steps*. London: SCM Press, 113-126.
Becker, Gerhold 1987: *Die Ursymbole in den Religionen*. Graz: Styria.
Beeh, Volker 1994: Bilderverbot, Zeichenlosigkeit und Unbeschreiblichkeit. In: *Hōrin. Vergleichende Studien zur japanischen Kultur* 1, 105-119.
– 1995: Nāgārjunas Zehntes Tor. In: *Hōrin. Vergleichende Studien zur japanischen Kultur* 2, 113-123.
Benz, Ernst; Nambara, Minoru (Hg.) 1960: *Das Christentum und die nichtchristlichen Hochreligionen*. Leiden, Cologne: E.J. Brill.
Bernhardt, Reinhold 1990: *Der Absolutheitsanspruch des Christentums. Von der Aufklärung bis zur Pluralistischen Religionstheologie*, Gütersloh: Gütersloher Verlagshaus.

– 1991 (Hg.): *Horizontüberschreitung. Die Pluralistische Theologie der Religionen.* Gütersloh: Gütersloher Verlagshaus.
– 1993: Deabsolutierung der Christologie? In: M. v. Brück, J. Werbick (Hg.): *Der einzige Weg zum Heil?* Freiburg i. Br.: Herder, 144-200.
– 1996: Philosophische Pluralismuskonzepte und ihre religionstheologische Rezeption. In: G. Risse, H. Sonnemans, B. Theß (Hg.): *Wege der Theologie* (FS Waldenfels). Paderborn: Bonifatius, 461-480.
– 1997: Prinzipieller Pluralismus oder mutualer Inklusivismus als hermeneutisches Paradigma einer Theologie der Religionen? In: P. Koslowski (Hg.): *Die spekulative Philosophie der Weltreligionen.* Vienna: Passagen Verlag, 17-31.
– 1998: Die Herausforderung. Motive für die Ausbildung der »pluralistischen Religionstheologie«. In: H.-G. Schwandt (Hg.): *Pluralistische Theologie der Religionen. Eine kritische Sichtung.* Frankfurt a.M.: Lembeck, 19-38.
– 1999: Auf dem Weg zur »größeren« Ökumene: Paradigmenwechsel in der ökumenischen Theologie. In: R. Kirste, M. Klöcker, P. Schwarzenau, U. Tworuschka (Hg.): *Vision 2001. Die größere Ökumene.* Köln, Weimar, Wien: Böhlau, 23-50.
– 2000: Trinitätstheologie als Matrix einer Theologie der Religionen. In: Ökumenische Rundschau 49, 287-301.

Berthrong, John H. 1994: *All under Heaven.* Transforming Paradigms in Confucian-Christian Dialogue. Albany: SUNY.

Bischofberger, Norbert 1996: *Werden wir wiederkommen? Der Reinkarnationsgedanke im Westen und die Sicht der christlichen Eschatologie.* Mainz – Kampen: Matthias Grünewald Verlag.

Bloom, Alfred 1992: Shin Buddhism in Encounter with a Religiously Plural World. In: *The Pure Land. New Series,* Nos. 8-9, 17-31.

Böck, Monika; Rao, Aparna 1995: Aspekte der Gesellschaftsstruktur Indiens: Kasten und Stämme. In: D. Rothermund (Hg.): *Indien. Kultur, Geschichte, Politik, Wirtschaft, Umwelt.* Ein Handbuch. München: C.H. Beck, 111-131.

Bodhi, Bhikkhu 1995: Replies to Questions from »Source«. In: »Pope and Buddhism«. *Dialogue* N.S. 22, 20-28.

Böhle, Josef 2001: *Inter-Religious Co-operation in a Global Age.* Thesis submitted to the University of Birmingham. Department of Theology. Birmingham.

Bongardt, Michael 2000a: Aufs Ganze sehen. Der Inlusivismus eines glaubenden Blicks auf die Welt. In: *Salzburger Theologische Zeitschrift* 4, 142-154.
– 2000b: Haltungsfragen. In: *Salzburger Theologische Zeitschrift* 4, 163-166.
– 2000c: Veraltete Grenzen? In: *Salzburger Theologische Zeitschrift* 4, 186-188.

Bornkamm, Günther 1988: *Jesus von Nazareth.* Stuttgart: Kohlhammer, 14th edition.

Borowitz, Eugene 1980: *Contemporary Christologies: A Jewish Response,* New York: Paulist Press

Boxer, C.R. 1967: *The Christian Century in Japan. 1549-1650.* Berkeley: University of California Press.

Boyd, R.H.S. 1997: *India and the Latin Captivity of the Church. The Cultural Context of the Gospel.* Cambridge: Cambridge University Press.

Braybrooke, Marcus 2000: *Christian-Jewish Dialogue.* The Next Steps. London: SCM Press.
– 2002: Christian-Jewish and Wider interfaith Dialogue. In: E. Kessler, J. Pawlikowski, J. Banki (eds.): *Jews and Christians in Conversation. Crossing Cultures and Generations.* Cambridge: Orchard Academic, 25-31.

Breid, Franz 1999 (Hg.): *Beten alle zum selben Gott?* Steyr: Ennsthaler Gesellschaft m.b.H. & Co. KG.

Breuning, Wilhelm 1991: Mit dem Stamm Abrahams geistlich verbunden. In: *Israel und Kirche heute. Beiträge zum christlich-jüdischen Dialog* (FS E.L. Ehrlich), hg. von M. Marcus, E. W. Stegemann, E. Zenger. Freiburg i.Br.: Herder, 22-34.

Brown, Stuart E. 1989 (ed.): *Meeting in Faith. Twenty Years of Christian-Muslim Conversations Sponsored by the World Council of Churches*. Geneva: WCC.

Brück, Michael von 1987: *Einheit der Wirklichkeit. Gott, Gotteserfahrung und Meditation im hinduistisch-christlichen Dialog*. 2nd edition, Munich: Kaiser.

– 1991: Mystische Erfahrung, religiöse Tradition und die Wahrheitsfrage. In: R. Bernhardt (Hg.): *Horizontüberschreitung. Die Pluralistische Theologie der Religionen*. Gütersloh: Gütersloher Verlagshaus, 81-103.

– 1992: *Weisheit der Leere*. Munich: Koesel Verlag.

– 1993: Heil und Heilswege im Hinuismus und Buddhismus – eine Herausforderung für christliches Erlösungsverständnis. In: M. von Brück, J. Werbick (Hg.): *Der einzige Weg Zum Heil? Die Herausforderung des christlichen Absolutheitsanspruchs durch pluralistische Religionstheologien* (QD 143). Freiburg i.Br.: Herder, 62-106.

Brück, Michael von; Lai, Whalen 1997: *Buddhismus und Christentum. Geschichte, Konfrontation, Dialog*. Munich: Beck.

– 2001: *Christianity and Buddhism. A Multi-Cultural History of Their Dialogue*. Maryknoll: Orbis.

Brück, Michael von, Werbick, Jürgen 1993 (Hg.): *Der einzige Weg zum Heil? Die Herausforderung des christlichen Absolutheitsanspruchs durch pluralistische Religionstheologien* (QD 143). Freiburg i. Br.: Herder.

Besteh, Andreas 1997 (Hg.): *Der Hinduismus als Anfrage an christliche Theologie und Philosophie* (Studien zur Religionstheologie 3). Mödling: St. Gabriel.

– 1998 (Hg.): *Christlicher Glaube in der Begegnung mit dem Hinduismus* (Studien zur Religionstheologie 4). Mödling: St. Gabriel.

Buber, Martin 1949: *Die Erzählungen der Chassidim*. Zurich: Manesse Verlag.

Bucsek, Claudia 1990: *Die Begegnung des Christentums mit dem Buddhismus in der japanischen Mission des 16. und 17. Jahrhunderts*. Staatsexamensarbeit im Fach Systematische Theologie. Ludwig-Maximilians-Universität. Munich.

Buddhadāsa, Indapañño 1967: *Christianity and Buddhism* (Sinclair Thompson Memorial Lecture). Bangkok.

– 1989: *Me and Mine. Selected Essays of Buddhadāsa*. Ed. by D. Swearer. Albany: SUNY.

Bultmann, Rudolf 1958: Welchen Sinn hat es, von Gott zu reden? In: *Glauben und Verstehen*, Bd. I. Tübingen: Mohr, 26-37.

Burrell, David 1986: *Knowing the Unknowable God: Ibn-Sina, Maimonides, Aquinas*. Notre Dame: University of Notre Dame Press.

Busse, Heribert 1991: *Die theologischen Beziehungen des Islams zu Judentum und Christentum. Grundlagen des Dialogs im Koran und die gegenwärtige Situation*. 2nd edition. Darmstadt: Wissenschaftliche Buchgesellschaft.

Byrne, Peter 1989: *Natural Religion and the Nature of Religion. The Legacy of Deism*. London – New York: Roudledge.

– 1995: *Prolegomena to Religious Pluralism. Reference and Realism in Religion*. Basingstoke: Macmillan.

– 2003a: It Is Not Reasonable to Believe that Only One Religion is True. In: M.L. Peterson, R.J. VanArragon (eds.): *Contemporary Debates in Philosophy of Religion*. Oxford: Blackwell, 201-210.

– 2003b: Reply to Yandell. In: M.L. Peterson, R.J. VanArragon (eds.): *Contemporary Debates in Philosophy of Religion*. Oxford: Blackwell, 215-217.

Cabezón, José 2000: A God, but not a Savior. In: R. Gross, T. Muck (eds.): *Buddhists Talk about Jesus. Christians Talk about the Buddha.* New York: Continuum, 17-31.

Cahill, Joseph 1982: *Mended Speech. The Crisis of Religious Studies and Theology.* New York: Crossroad.

Çapan, Ergün 2004 (ed.): *Terror and Suicide Attacks. An Islamic Perspective.* New Jersey: Light.

Copper, John 1873: *A Full Account of the Buddhist Controversy Held at Pantura.* Colombo: Ceylon Times.

Chia, Edmund 2003: *Towards a Theology of Dialogue. Schillebeeckx's Method as Bridge between Vatican's Dominus Iesus and Asia's FABC Theology.* Bangkok: Edmund Chia.

Ching, Julia 1999: Living in Two Worlds: A Personal Appraisal. In: A. Sharma, K.M. Dugan (eds.): *A Dome of Many Colours.* Harrisburg: Trinity Press, 7-22.

Christen und Juden III 2000: *Schritte der Erneuerung im Verh*ältnis zum Judentum. Eine Studie der Evangelischen Kirche in Deutschland. Gütersloh: Gütersloher Verlagshaus.

Christian, William A. 1964: *Meaning and Truth in Religion.* Princeton: Princeton University Press.

– 1987: *Doctrines of Religious Communities. A Philosophical Study.* New Haven, London: Yale University Press.

Christlicher Glaube und nichtchristliche Religionen 2003. Theologische Leitlinien. Ein Beitrag der Kammer für Theologie der Evangelischen Kirche in Deutschland (EKD Texte 77). Hannover.

Clooney, Francis X. 1990: Reading the World in Christ. From Comparison to Inclusivism. In: G. D'Costa (ed.): *Christian Uniqueness Reconsidered. The Myth of a Pluralistic Theology of Religions.* Maryknoll: Orbis, 63-80.

– 1993: *Theology after Vedanata. An Experiment in Comparative Theology.* Albany: SUNY.

– 1995: Comparative Theology: A Review of Recent Books (1989-1995). In: *Theological Studies* 56, 521-550.

– 1996: *Seeing Through Texts. Doing Theology among the Srivaisnavas of South India.* Albany: SUNY.

– 2001: *Hindu God, Christian God. How Reason Helps Break Down the Boundaries between Religions.* Oxford: Oxford University Press.

– 2003: Hindu Views of Religious Others: Implications for Christian Theology. In: *Theological Studies* 64, 306-333.

Cobb, John 1999: *Transforming Christianity and the World. A Way beyond Absolutism and Relativism.* Edited and Introduced by P. Knitter. Maryknoll: Orbis.

Cobb, John; Ives, Christopher 1990 (eds.): *The Emptying God. A Buddhist-Jewish-Christian Conversation.* Maryknoll: Orbis.

Cohn-Sherbok, Dan 1991: Incarnation and Trialogue. In: D. Cohn-Sherbok (ed.): *Islam in a World of Diverse Faiths.* Basingstoke: Macmillan, 18-32.

– 1991b (ed.): *Islam in a World of Diverse Faiths.* Basingstoke: Macmillan.

– 1992: *The Crucified Jew: Twenty Centuries of Anti-Semitism.* London: HarperCollins.

– 1994: *Judaism and Other Faiths.* Basingstoke – New York: Macmillan.

– 1997: *The Jewish Messiah.* Edinburgh: T&T Clark.

Congregation for the Doctrine of the Faith 2000, *Dominus Iesus*, http://www.vatican.va/roman_curia/congregations/cfaith/documents/rc_con_cfaith_doc_20000806_dominus-iesus_en.html

Congregation for the Doctrine of the Faith 2001a, Notification on the book *Toward a Christian Theology of Religious Pluralism* (Orbis Books: Maryknoll, New York 1997) by Father

Jacques Dupuis, S.J., http://www.vatican.va/roman_curia/congregations/cfaith/documents/rc_con_cfaith_doc_20010124_dupuis_en.html

Congregation for the Doctrine of the Faith 2001b, Commentary on the Notification of the Congregation for the Doctrine of the Faith Regarding the Book Towards a Christian Theology of Religious Pluralism by Father Jacques Dupuis, S.J., http://www.vatican.va/roman_curia/congregations/cfaith/documents/rc_con_cfaith_doc_20010312_dupuis-2_en.html

Conway, Martin 1996: "Together in Birmingham – Strength Through Racial Diversity". In: *Studies in Interreligious Dialogue* 5, 117-140.

Coomaraswamy, Ananda 1977: *Metaphysics* (ed. by R. Lipsey). Princeton: Princeton University Press.

Corless, Roger; Knitter Paul 1990 (eds.): *Buddhist Emptiness and Christian Trinity. Essays and Explorations*. New York: Paulist.

Cornille, Catherine 2002 (ed.): *Many Mansions Multiple Belonging and Christian Identity*. Maryknoll: Orbis.

Council for a Parliament of the World's Religions 1999: *A Call to our Guiding Institutions*. Presented on the 1999 Parliament of the World's Religions. December 1 through 8, 1999. Cape Town, South Africa.

Coward, Harold 1989 (ed.): *Hindu-Christian Dialogue. Perspectives and Encounters*. Maryknoll: Orbis.

Cracknell, Kenneth 1986: *Towars a New Relationship. Christians and People of Other Faith*. London: Epworth Press.

Cragg, Kenneth 1956: *The Call of the Minaret*. New York: Oxford University Press

– 1984: *Muhammad and the Christian. A Question of Response*. Maryknoll: Orbis.

– 1985: *The Call of the Minaret*. Second Edition, Revised and Enlarged. Maryknoll: Orbis.

– 1992: *Troubled by Truth. Life-Studies in Inter-Faith Concern*. Durham: Pentland Press.

Craig, William Lane 1989: "No Other Name": A Middle Knowledge Perspective on the Exclusivity of Salvation Through Christ. In: *Faith and Philosophy* 6, 172-188.

– 1993: Talbott's Universalism Once More. In: *Religious Studies* 29, 497-518.

– 1994: *Reasonable Faith: Christian Truth and Apologetics*. Wheaton: Crossway Books.

– 1995: Middle Knowledge and Christian Exclusivism. In: Sophia 34, 120-139.

– 2003: Response to David Myers. In: Religious Studies 39, 421-426.

D'Costa, Gavin 1986: *Theology and Religious Pluralism. The Challenge of Other Religions*. Oxford: Blackwell.

– 1987: *John Hick's Theology of Religions. A Critical Evaluation*. Lanham – New York – London: University Press of America.

– 1990 (ed.): *Christian Uniqueness Reconsidered. The Myth of a Pluralistic Theology of Religions*. Maryknoll: Orbis.

– 1990b: ›Extra ecclesiam nulla salus‹ revisited. In: I. Hamnett (ed.): *Religious Pluralism and Unbelief. Studies Critical and Comparative*. London – New York: Routledge, 130-147.

– 1991: John Hick and Religious Pluralism: Yet Another Revolution. In: H. Hewitt (ed.): *Problems in the Philosophy of Religion. Critical Studies of the Work of John Hick*. Basingstoke: Macmillan, 3-18.

– 1993: Whose Objectivity? Which Neutrality? The doomed quest for a neutral vantage point from which to judge religions. In: *Religious Studies* 29, 79-95.

– 1993b: Creating Confusion: A Response to Markham. In: *New Blackfriars* 74 No. 867, 41-47.

– 1996: The Impossibility of a Pluralist View of Religions. In: *Religious Studies* 32, 223-232.

– 2000: *The Meeting of Religions and the Trinity.* Maryknoll: Orbis.

D'Holbach, Paul Thiry 1978: *System der Natur* (First edition 1770). Frankfurt a.M.: Suhrkamp

– 2005: *The System of Nature,* vol II, chapter 3. Translated from French by Samuel Wilkinson. Online reprint as Project Gutenberg ebook: http://www.gutenberg.org/files/8910/8910-h/8910-h.htm#link2H_4_0005

D'Sa, Francis X. 1987: *Gott, der Dreieine und der All-Ganze. Vorwort zur Begegnung zwischen Christentum und Hinduismus.* Düsseldorf: Patmos.

– 1993: Die christliche Inkarnation und das hinduistische Avatara. In: *Concilium* 29, 146-152.

– 1998: "Christus – Buddha – Krishna ..." -- Zum Gespräch zwischen Christus und Krishna, zwischen dem Apostel Paul (Knitter) und dem Missionar Franz-Xaver (D'Sa), dem universal-christlichen D'Costa und dem christlich-hinduistischen D'Sa. In: H.-G. Schwandt (Hg.): *Pluralistische Religionstheologie.* Frankfurt a.M.: Lembeck, 153-174.

Dalai Lama 1996: *Beyond Dogma. Dialogues & Discourses.* Ed. by M. Dresser. Berkeley: North Atlantic Books.

Davis, Caroline Franks 1989: *The Evidential Force of Religious Experience.* Oxford: Clarandon Press.

Davis, Stephen 1988 (ed.): *Encountering Jesus. A Debate on Christology.* Atlanta: John Knox Press.

– 1990: Universalism, Hell and the Fate of the Ignorant. In: *Modern Theology* 6 173-186.

Denffer, Ahmad von 1987 (Hg.): *Vierzig Heilige Hadite* (Schriftenreihe des Islamischen Zentrums München Nr. 14). Munich.

– 1995: Der Islam und Jesus (Schriftenreihe des Islamischen Zentrums München Nr. 18). Munich.

Derret, Duncan M. 2000: *The Bible and the Buddhists.* Bornato/Italy: Casa Editrice Sardini.

– 2004: The Buddhist Dimension of John. In: *Numen* 51, 182-210.

Descartes, René 1994: *Meditationen über die Grundlagen der Philosophie mit den sämtlichen Einwänden und Erwiderungen.* Übers. Und hg. von A. Buchenau. Hamburg: Felix Meiner.

Dharmapāla, Anagārika 1989: *The Arya Dharma of Sakya Muni, Gautama Buddha or The Ethics of Self Discipline (1917).* Reprint. Calcutta: Maha Bodhi Book Agency.

– 1991: *Return to Righteousness. A Collection of Speeches, Essays and Letters of the Anagarika Dharmapāla.* Ed. by A. Guruge. Colombo: The Government Press.

Dharmasiri, Gunapala 1974: *A Buddhist Critique of the Christian Concept of God.* Colombo: Lake House.

– 1988: A Buddhist Critique of the Christian Concept of God. (Enlarged edition with new Postscript). Antioch: Golden Leaves.

Dhavamony, Mariasusai 1971: *Love of God According to Saiva Siddhānta. A Study in the Mysticism and Theology of Saivism.* Oxford: Clarendon Press.

Dialogue and Proclamation 1991: In: *Catholic International.* Vol 2, No. 17 (1.-14.10.1991), 805-823.

Die Theologie der Religionen in der Diskussion 2000: Themenheft *Salzburger Theologische Zeitschrift* 4, Heft 2.

DiNoia, Joseph A. 1990: Varieties of Religious Aims: Beyond Exclusivism, Inclusivism, and Pluralism. In: B.D. Marshall (ed.), *Theology and Dialogue. Essays in Conversation with George Lindbeck.* Notre Dame: University of Notre Dame Press, 249-274.

– 1992: *The Diversity of Religions. A Christian Perspective.* Washington: Catholic University of Amaerica Press.

Dionysius Areopagita 1981: *Von den Namen zum Unnennbaren*. Auswahl und Einleitung von Endre von Ivánka. 2nd edition. Einsiedeln: Johannes Verlag.

Dirscherl, Erwin 1996: Die besondere Nähe zwischen Judentum und Christentum als Anfrage an die pluralistische Religionstheologie. In: G. Risse, H. Sonnemans, B. Theß (Hg.): *Wege der Theologie: and der Schwelle zum dritten Jahrtausend* (FS Hans Waldenfels). Paderborn: Bonifatius Verlag, 495-511.

Donovan, Peter 1993: The Intolerance of Religious Pluralism. In: *Religious Studies* 29, 217-229.

Dorf, Elliot N. 1982: The Covenant: How Jews Understand Themselves and Others. In: *Anglican Theological Review* 64, 481-501.

– 1996: A Jewish Theology of Jewish Relations to Other Peoples. In: H. Ucko (ed.): *People of God, Peoples of God. A Jewish-Christian Conversation in Asia*. Geneva: WCC, 46-66.

Dörman, Johannes 1988: *Die eine Warheit und die vielen Religionen* (Respondeo 8). Abensberg: Verlag Josef Kral.

Driver, Tom 1987: The Case for Pluralism. In: J. Hick, P. Knitter (eds.): *The Myth of Christian Uniqueness*. Maryknoll: Orbis, 203-218.

Dulles, Avery 1983: *Models of Revelation*. Dublin: Doubleday.

Dumoulin, Heinrich 1966: Östliche Meditation und christliche Mystik. Freiburg – Munich: Alber.

– 1985: *Geschichte des Zen-Buddhismus*. Band 1: Indien und China. Bern: Francke.

– 1990: *Zen im 20. Jahrhundert*. Munich: Koesel.

Dunn, James D.G. 2003: *Christology in the Making. A New Testament Inquiry into the Origins of the Doctrine of the Incarnation*. 2nd ed. London: SCM Press.

Dupuis, Jacques 1993: *Jesus Christ at the Encounter of World Religions*. 2nd printing. Maryknoll: Orbis.

– 1997: *Toward a Christian Theology of Religious Pluralism*. Maryknoll: Orbis.

– 1999: 'The Truth Will Make You Free': The Theology of Religions Revisited. In: *Louvain Studies* 24, 211-263.

– 2002: *Christianity and the Religions: From Confrontation to Dialogue*. Maryknoll: Orbis.

– 2002b: Christianity and the Religions. Complementarity and Convergence. In: Catherine Cornell (ed.): *Many Mansions? Multiple Religious Belonging and Christian Identity*. Maryknoll: Orbis, 61-75.

Duran, Khalid 1990: Der Islam in der Mehrheit und in der Minderheit. In: *Der Islam III: Islamische Kultur – Zeitgenössische Strömungen – Volksfrömmigkeit* (Die Religionen der Menschheit. Bd. 25, 3). Stuttgart: Kohlhammer, 423-451.

Eck, Diana L. 1993: *Encountering God. A Spiritual Journey from Bozeman to Banaras*. Boston: Beacon Press.

Eckel, Malcom David 1987: *Jñānagarbha's Commentary on the Distinction Between the Two Truths*. Albany: SUNY.

Eddy, Paul Rhodes 2002: *John Hick's Pluralist Philosophy of World Religions*. Aldershot: Ashgate.

Eicher, Peter 1977: *Offenbarung. Prinzip neuzeitlicher Theologie*. Munich: Koesel.

Elias, Jamal J. 1999: *Islam* (Religions of the World, ed. by N. Smart). London: Routledge.

Elm, Kaspar 1992: »Guck Dir doch bloß die Kreuzzügge im Mittelalter an ...«. Di Kreuzzüge – Kriege im Namen Gottes? In: M. Müller (Hg.): *Plädoyer für die Kirche. Urteile über Voruteile*. 3rd edition. Aachen: MM-Verlag, 407-422.

Embree, Ainslie T; Wilhelm, Friedrich 1990: *Indien. Geschichte des Subkontinents von der Induskultur bis zum Beginn der englischen Herrschaft* (Fischer Weltgeschichte, Bd. 17). Frankfurt a.M.: Fischer.

Epalza, MIkel de 1976: Der islamisch-christliche Kongreß von Córdodba (September 1974). In: *Concillium* 12, 395-397.

Engineer, Ashgar Ali 2001: *Rational Approach to Islam.* New Dehli: Gyan Publishing House

– 2003: Islam and Pluralism (unpublished manuscript; forthcoming) [published in: P. Knitter (ed.). *The Myth of Religious Superiority.* Maryknoll: Orbis 2005, 211-219].

Englert, W. Ph. 1898: *Christus und Buddha in ihrem himmlischen Vorleben.* Vienna: Verlag von Mayer & Co.

Enomiya-Lassalle 1966: *Zen-Buddhismus.* Cologne: J.P. Bachem.

Esack, Farid 1997: *The Qu'ran, Liberation and Pluralism. An Islamic Perspective of Interreligious Solidarity against Oppression.* Oxford: Oneworld.

Everett, Robert A. 1993: *Christianity Without Anti-Semitism.* James Parkes and the Jewish-Christian Encounter. Oxford: Butterworth-Heinemann.

Evers, Georg 1997: Kontextuelle Theologie in Asien. Zur Exkommunikation Tissa Blasuriyas. In: *Stimmen der Zeit* 122, 374-386.

Farquhar, John N. 1913: *The Crown of Hinduism.* London: Oxford University Press.

Feldkeller, Andreas 1998: Verlangt der gesellschaftliche Pluralismus nach einer »pluralistischen« Religionstheologie? In: *Evangelische Theologie* 58, 445-460.

– 2000: Interreligiöser Dialog und Pluralistiche Religionstheologie – ein Traumpaar? In: Ökumenische Rundschau 49, 273-285.

Fine, Lawrence 1984: Kabbalistic Texts. In: B.W. Holtz (ed.): *Back to the Sources. Reading the Classic Jewish Texts.* New York: Summit, 305-359.

Firth, Raymond 1996: *Religion. A Humanist Interpretation.* London – New York: Routledge.

Flannery, Edward H. 1985: *The Anguish of Jews. Twenty-three Centuries of Antisemitism.* Revised and updated. New York: Paulist.

Flasch, Kurt 1990 (Hg.): *Logik des Schreckens.* Augustinus von Hippo. De diversis quaestionibus ad Simplicianum I 2. Mainz: Dieterich'se Verlagsbuchhandlung.

Flemming, Kenneth 2002: *Asian Christian Theologians in Dialogue with Buddhism.* Oxford: Peter Lang.

Fletcher, Jeannine Hill 1993: Shifting Identity. The Contribution of Feminist Thought to Theologies of Religious Pluralism. In: *Journal of Feminist Studies in Religion* 19, 5-24.

Flew, Antony 1966: *God and Philosophy.* London: Hutchinson.

Forrester, Duncan B. 1980: *Caste and Christianity. Attitudes and Politics on Caste of Anglo-Saxon Protestant Missions in India.* London, Dublin: Curzon.

Foust, Thomas F; Hunsberger, Georg R.; Kirk, J. Andrew; Ustorf, Werner 2002 (eds.): *A Scandalous Prophet. The Way of Mission after Newbigin.* Grand Rapids – Cambridge: Eerdmans.

Fredericks, James L. 1995: A Universal Religious Experience? Comparative theology as an alternative to a theology of religions. In: *Horizons* 22, 67-87.

– 1999: *Faith among Faiths. Christian Theology and Non-Christian Religions.* New York: Paulist.

Frei, Fritz 1996: Religiöse Tradition als Rettung der Nation und der Welt. Universaler Wahrheitsanspruch der hinduistischen Bewegung RSS. In: A. Peter (Hg.): *Christlicher Glaube in multireligiöser Gesellschaft.* Immensee: Neue Zeitschrift für Missionswissenschaft, 170-186.

Fritsch-Oppermann, Sybille 2000: *Christliche Existenz im buddhistischen Kontext. Katzumi Takizawas und Seiichi Yagis Dialog mit dem Buddhismus in Japan.* Münster: LIT Verlag.

Frois, Luis 1955: *Kulturgegensätze Europa – Japan (1585).* Kritische Ausgabe von Josef Franz Schütte S.J. (Monumenta Nipponica 15). Tokyo: Sophia Universität.

Gäde, Gerhard 1998: *Viele Religionen – ein Wort Gottes. Einspruch gegen John Hicks pluralistische Religionstheologie,* Gütersloh: Gütersloher Verlagshaus.
– 2002: Der Zumutungscharakter der christlichen Botschaft. In: *Freiburger Zeitschrift für Philosophie und Theologie* 49, 166-188.
Gandhi, Mohandas K. 1957: *An Autobiography. The Story of My Experiment With Truth.* Boston: Beacon Press.
Geivett, R. Douglas; Phillips, W. Gary 1995: A Particularist View: An Evidentialist Approach. In: D. Okholm, T. Phillips (eds.): *More Than One Way? Four Views on Salvation in a Pluralistic World.* Grand Rapids: Eerdmans, 213-245.
– 1995b: Conclusion. In: D. Okholm, T. Phillips (eds.): *More Than One Way? Four Views on Salvation in a Pluralistic World.* Grand Rapids: Eerdmans, 259-270.
Gerth, André 1997: *Theologie im Angesicht der Religionen. Gavin D'Costas Kritik an der pluralistischen Religionstheologie John Hicks.* Paderborn: Schoeningh.
Gilkey, Langdon 1987: Plurality and Its Theological Implications. In: J. Hick, P. Knitter (eds.): *The Myth of Christian Uniqueness.* Maryknoll: Orbis, 37-50.
– 1993: The Pluralism of Religions. In: A. Sharma (ed.): *God, Truth and Reality.* Basingstoke: Macmillan, 111-123.
Gillis, Chester 1993: *Pluralism. A New Paradigm for Theology.* Louvain: Peeters.
Glasenapp, Helmuth von 1972: *Die fünf Weltreligionen.* Düsseldorf-Köln: Eugen Diederichs. 3rd edition.
Gnilka, Joachim 1990: *Jesus von Nazert. Botschaft und Geschichte.* Freiburg i.Br.: Herder.
– 1997: *Jesus of Nazareth: Message and History.* Peabody: Hendrickson Publishers.
– 2004: *Bibel und Koran. Was sie verbindet, was sie trennt.* 3rd edition. Freiburg i.Br.: Herder.
Goddard, Hugh 1995: *Christians and Muslims. From Double Standards to Mutual Understanding.* Richmond: Curzon.
Goodall, Dominic 1996 (ed.): *Hindu Scriptures.* London: Phoenix.
Gössmann, Elisabeth 1965: *Religiöse Herkunft, profane Zukunft? Das Christentum in Japan.* Munich: Max Hueber.
– 1996: Feministische Kritik an universalen Wahrheitsansprüchen. In: A. Peter (Hg.): *Christlicher Glaube in multireligiöser Gesellschaft. Erfahrungen. Theologische Reflexionen. Missionarische Perspektiven.* Immensee: Neue Zeitschrift für Missionswissenschaft, 312-350.
Grayson, James Huntley 2002: *Korea – A Religious History.* Revised edition. London – New York: Psychology Press.
Grayzel, Solomon 1968: *A History of the Jews.* New Revised Edition. New York: New American Library.
Greschat, Hans-Jürgen 1988: *Was ist Religionswissenschaft?* Stuttgart: Kohlhammer.
Griffith, Bede 1983: *Die Hochzeit von Ost und West. Hoffnung für die Menschheit.* Salzburg: Otto Müller.
– 1990: *Eine neue Wirklichkeit. Westliche Wissenschaft, östliche Mystik und christlicher Glaube.* Grafing: Aquamarin Verlag.
Griffiths, Paul 1990 (ed.): *Christianity Through Non-Christian Eyes.* Maryknoll: Orbis.
Grönbold, Günter 1985: *Jesus in Indien. Das Ende einer Legende.* Munich: Koesel.
Gross, J. 1965: Die Ur- und Erbsündenlehre der Schule von Laon. In: *Zeitschrift für Kirchengeschichte* 76, 12-40.
Gross, Rita M.; Muck, Terry C. 2000 (eds.): *Buddhists Talk about Jesus – Christians Talk about the Buddha.* New York – London: Continuum.

Grünschloss, Andreas 1994: *Religionswissenschaft als Welt-Theologie. Wilfred Cantwell Smiths interreligiöse Hermeneutik*. Göttingen: Vandenhoeck & Ruprecht.
– 1999: *Der eigene und der fremde Glaube. Studien zur interreligiösen Fremdwahrnehmung in Islam, Hinduismus, Buddhismus und Christentum*. Tübingen: Mohr Siebeck.
Guardini, Romano 1997: *Der Herr.* 16th edition. Mainz. Paderborn: Schöningh.
Haack, Ernst 1898: *Christus oder Buddha?* Schwerin i.W.
Haag, Herbert 1992: Die Rede vom Heil. In: *Theologische Quartalschrift* 172, 81-97.
Hackbarth-Johnson, Christian 2003: *Interreligiöse Existenz. Spirituelle erfahrung und Identität bei Henri Le Saux (O.S.B.) / Swami Abhishiktanada (1910-1973)*. Frankfurt a.M.: Peter Lang.
Haddad, Y.Z.; Haddad, W.Z. 1995 (eds.): *Christian-Muslim Encounters*. Gainesville: University Press of Florida.
Hagemann, Ludwig 1999: *Christentum contra Islam. Eine Geschichte gescheiterter Beziehungen*. Darmstadt: Wissenschaftliche Buchgesellschaft.
Hagner, Donald A. 1984: *An Analysis and Critique of Modern Jewish Study of Jesus*. Grand Rapids: Zondervan Academic Books.
Hahn, Ferdinand 1995: *Christologische Hoheitstitel*. 5th enlarged edition. Göttingen: Vandenhoeck & Ruprecht.
Haight, Roger 1992: The Case for Spirit Christology. In: *Theological Studies* 53, 257-287.
– 1999: Jesus. Symbol of God. Maryknoll: Orbis.
Halbfass, Wilhelm 1988: *India and Europe. An Essay in Understanding*. Albany: SUNY.
Hall, Elton: Gandhi's Religious Universalism. In: J. Hick, L.C. Hempel (eds.): *Gandhi's Significance for Today*. New York: Saint Martin's Press, 166-181.
Härle, Wilfred 1992: Der Toleranzgedanke im Verhältnis der Religionen. In: W.E. Müller, H.H.R. Schulz (Hg.): *Theologie und Aufklärung* (FS for G. Hornig). Würzburg: Königshausen u. Neumann, 323-338.
Hartman, David 1990: *Conflicting Visions*. New York: Schocken Books.
– 1999: *A Heart of Many Rooms. Celebrating the Many Voices within Judaism*. Woodstock: Jewish Lights Publishing.
Heelas, P. 1978: Some Problems With Religious Studies. In: *Religion* 8, 1-14.
Heijden, B. van der 1973: *Karl Rahner. Darstellung und Kritik seiner Grundpositionen*. Einsiedeln: Johannes Verlag.
Heiler, Friedrich 1963: Die Religionsgeschichte als Wegbereiterin für die Zusammenarbeit der Religionen. In: M. Eliade, J. Kitagawa (Hg.): *Grundfragen der Religionswissenschaft*. Salzburg: Otto Müller Verlag, 40-70.
– 1967: Vivekānada, der Künder der Harmonie der Religionen. In: R. Thomas (Hg.): *Religion und Religionen* (FS f. Gustav Mensching). Bonn: Röhrscheid, 35-49.
Heim, Mark 1985: *Is Christ the Only Way? Christian Faith in a Pluralistic World*. Valley Forge: Judson Press.
– 1992: The Pluralistic Hypothesis, Realism and Post-Eschatology. In: *Religious Studies* 28, 207-219.
– 1994: Salvations: A More Pluralistic Hypothesis. In: *Modern Theology* 10, 341-360.
– 1995: Eine Weite in Gottes Barmherzigkeit. Evangelikale Theologie überdenkt religiösen Pluralismus. In: *Dialog der Religionen* 5, 67-76.
– 1995b: *Salvations. Truth and Difference in Religion*. Maryknoll: Orbis.
– 2001: *The Depth of the Riches. A Trinitarian Theology of Religious Ends*. Grand Rapids – Cambridge: Eerdmans.
– 2001b: The Depth of the Riches: Trinity and Religious Ends. In: *Modern Theology* 17, 21-55.

Heller, Christian 2001: *John Hicks Projekt einer religiösen Interpretation der Religionen. Darstellung und Analyse – Diskussion – Rezeption*. Münster: LIT Verlag.

– 2003: Auf dem Weg zu einer christlichen Theologie des religiösen Pluralismus. In: *Zeitschrift für Katholische Theologie* 125, 167-185.

Helfenstein, Pius F. 1998: *Grundlagen des interreligiösen Dialogs. Theologische Rechtfertigungsversuche in der ökumenischen Begwegung und die Verbindung des trinitarischen Denkens mit dem pluralistischen Ansatz*. Frankfurt a.M.: Lembeck.

Hemming, Laurence Paul 2000 (ed.): *Radical Orthodoxy? – A Catholic Enquiry*. Aldershot: Ashgate.

Hempelmann, Heinzpeter 2000: Christus allein. Skizze der Voraussetzungen und biblisch-theologischen Begründunszusammenhänge einer exklusivistischen Religionstheorie. In: *Salzburger Theologische Zeitschrift* 4, 112-126.

Henrix, Hans Hermann; Kraus, Wolfgang 2001 (Hg.): *Die Kirchen und das Judentum. Dokumente von 1986-2000*. Paderborn: Bonifatius.

Herrmann, Peter 1996 (Hg.): *Glaubenskriege in Vergangenheit und Gegenwart*. Göttingen: Vandenhoeck&Ruprecht.

Hessen, Johannes 1963: *Der Absolutheitsanspruch des Christentums*. München: Ernst Reinhardt Verlag.

Heumann, Jürgen 2003 (Hg.): *Religion im Bildungsangebot der Schule. Vom Religionsunterricht zur Praxis religiöser Bildung in Projekten und Unterrichtsfächern*. Oldenburg: Universität Oldenburg.

Hewitt, Harold 1991 (ed.): *Problems in the Philosophy of Religion. Critical Studies of the Work of John Hick*. Basingstoke: Macmillan.

Hick, John 1970: *Arguments for the Existence of God*. Basingstoke: Macmillan.

– 1973: *God and the Universe of Faiths*. Basingstoke: Macmillan.

– 1974 (ed.): *Truth and Dialogue. The Relationship between World Religions*. London: Sheldon Press.

– 1977a (ed.): *The Myth of God Incarnate*. London: SCM Press.

– 1977b: *The New Nazism of the National Front and National Party. A Warning to Christians*. Birmingham: AFFOR.

– 1977c: Jesus and the World Religions. In: Hick (ed.), *The Myth of God Incarnate*. London: SCM Press, 167-185.

– 1979 (Hg.): *Wurde Gott Mensch?* Gütersloh: Gütersloher Verlagshaus.

– 1979b: Jesus und die Weltreligionen. In: idem. (Hg.): *Wurde Gott Mensch?* Gütersloh: Gütersloher Verlagshaus, 175-194.

– 1980a: *God Has Many Names. Britain's New Religious Pluralism*. Basingstoke: Macmillan.

– 1980b: *Apartheid Observed*. Birmingham: AFFOR.

– 1982: *God Has Many Names* (US-edition). Philadelphia: Westminster Press.

– 1983a: *The Second Christianity*. London: SCM Press.

– 1983b: On Conflicting Religious Truth Claims. In: *Religious Studies* 19, 485-491.

– 1987: The Non-Absoluteness of Christianity. In: J. Hick, P. Knitter (eds.): *The Myth of Christian Uniqueness. Toward a Pluralistic Theology of Religions*. Maryknoll: Orbis, 16-36.

– 1988: *Problems of Religious Pluralism*. Repr. Basingstoke: Macmillan.

– 1988b: Religious Pluralism and Salvation. In: *Faith and Philosophy* 5, 365-377.

– 1988c: *Faith and Knowledge*. Second Edition reissued with a new preface. Basingstoke: Manmillan.

– 1989: *An Interpretation of Religion: Human Responses to the Transcendent*. Basingstoke: Macmillan.

- 1989b: Trinity and Incarnation in the Light of Religious Pluralism. In: J. Hick, E. Meltzer (eds.): *Three Faiths – One God. A Jewish, Christian, Muslim Encounter*, Basingstoke: Macmillan, 197-210.
- 1990: *Philosophy of Religion*, 4th ed. Englewood Cliffs: Prentice Hall.
- 1990b: Straightening the Record. Some Responses to Critics. In: *Modern Theology* 6, 187-195.
- 1990c: *Death and Eternal Life* (1st edition, 1976). Basingstoke: Macmillan.
- 1991: Reply (to Mesle). In: H. Hewitt (ed.): *Problems in the Philosophy of Religion. Critical Studies of the Work of John Hick*. Basingstoke: Macmillan, 82-85.
- 1991b: Reply (to D'Costa and Kellenberger). In: H. Hewitt (ed.): *Problems in the Philosophy of Religion. Critical Studies of the Work of John Hick*. Basingstoke: Macmillan, 24-27.
- 1991c: Response to Mesle. In: C.R. Mesle, *John Hick's Theodicy. A Process Humanist Critique*. Basingstoke: Macmillan, 115-134.
- 1991d: Islam and Christian Monotheism. In: D. Cohn-Sherbok (ed.): *Islam in a World of Diverse Faiths*. Basingstoke: Macmillan, 1-17.
- 1991e: Jesus and Mohammad. In: D. Cohn-Sherbok (ed.): *Islam in a World of Diverse Faiths*. Basingstoke: Macmillan, 114-118.
- 1993a: *The Metaphor of God Incarnate*. London: SCM Press.
- 1993b: *Disputed Questions in Theology and the Philosophy of Religion*. Basingstoke: Macmillan.
- 1994: Eine Philosophie des religiösen Pluralismus. In: *Münchener Theologische Zeitschrift* 54, 304-318.
- 1995: *The Rainbow of Faiths. Critical Dialogue on Religious Pluralism*. London: SCM Press.
- 1995b: Religiöse Erfahrung: Ihr Wesen und ihre Zuverlässigkeit. In: P. Schmidt-Leukel (Hg.): *Berechtigte Hoffnung. Über die Möglichkeit, vernünftig und zugleich Christ zu sein*. Paderborn: Bonifatius, 85-98.
- 1996: *Religion. Die menschlichen Antworten auf die Frage nach Leben und Tod*. Munich: Diederichs.
- 1998: Eine Artwort auf Kardinal Ratzingers Ausführungen zum religiösen Pluralismus. In: *Dialog der Religionen* 8, 91-94.
- 1999: *The Fifth Dimension. An Exploration of the Spiritual Realm*. Oxford: Oneworld.
- 2001a: *Gott und seine vielen Namen*. 2nd completely revised edition. Frankfurt a.M.: Lembeck.
- 2001b: *Dialogues in the Philosophy of Religion*. Basingstoke: Macmillan.
- 2001c: Review of 'S.M. Heim, The Depth of the Riches'. In: *Reviews in Religion and Theology* 8, 411-414.
- 2002: *An Autobiography*. Oxford: Oneworld.

Hick, John; Hebblethwaite, Brian 2001 (eds.), *Christianity and Other Religions. Selected Readings*. Revised edition, Oxford: Oneworld.

Hick, John; Knitter, Paul 1987 (eds.): *The Myth of Christian Uniqueness. Toward a Pluralistic Theology of Religions*. Maryknoll: Orbis.

Hick, John; Meltzer, Edmund S. 1989 (eds.): *Three Faiths – One God. A Jewish, Christian, Muslim Encounter*. Basingstoke: Macmillan.

Hillman, Eugene 1989: *Many Paths. A Catholic Approach to Religious Pluralism*. Maryknoll: Orbis.

Hintersteiner, Norbert 2001: *Traditionen überschreiten. Angloamerikanische Beiträge zur interkulturellen Traditionshermeneutik*. Vienna: WUV-Universitätsverlag..

Hismatsu, Shin'ichi 1978: Atheismus. In: *Zeitschrift für Missions- und Religionswissenschaft* 62, 268-296.

Hofmann, Murad Wilfried 2002: Müssen die Religionen zum Konflixt führen? In: *Islam im Dialog* 1, 45-47.

Holenstein, Elmar 1985: *Menschliches Selbstverständnis. Ichbewußtstein – Intersubjektive Verantwortung – Interkulturelle Verständigung*. Frankfurt a.M.: Suhrkamp.

Hopkins, Jasper 1985: *On Learned Ignorance* (De Docta Ignorantia) by Nicholas of Cusa. Minneapolis: The Arthur J. Banning Press.

Hopkins, Jasper 1994: *A Miscellany on Nicholas of Cusa*. Minneapolis: The Arthur J. Banning Press.

Hoye, William J. 1990: Die Paradiesjungfrauen des Korans und die Eschatologie des Thomas von Aquin. In: L. Hagemann, E. Pulsfort (Hg.): *"Ihr alle aber seid Brüder"*(FS A. Th. Khoury). Würzburg – Altenberge: Echter, 521-537.

Hughes, Edward J 1986: *Wilfred Cantwell Smith: A Theology for the World*. London: SCM Press.

Hübner, Reinhard M. 1996: Εις Θεος Ιησους Χριστος. Zum christlichen Gottesglauben im 2. Jahrhundert – ein Versuch. In: Münchener Theologische Zeitschrift 47, 325-344.

Hume, David 2000: *Enquiries Concerning Human Understanding and Concerning The Principles of Morals*. Third edition with text revised and notes by P.H. Nidditch, Oxford: Clarendon Press.

Huntington, Samuel P. 1998: *The Clash of Civilizations and the Remaking of World Order*. London – New York: Touchstone Books.

Hüttenhoff, Michael 2001: *Der Religiöse Pluralismus als Orientierungsproblem. Religionstheologische Studien*. Leipzig: Evangelische Verlagsanstalt.

Ibrahim, Ezzedin; Johnson-Davies, Denys 1997: *Forty Hadith Qudsi*. Cambridge: Islamic Text Society.

Ikeda, Daisaku; Tehranian, Majid 2004: *Global Civilization. A Buddhist-Islamic Dialogue*. London – New York: British Academic Press.

Ipgrave, Michael 2003: *Trinity and Inter-Faith Dialogue: Plenitude and Plurality*. Frankfurt a.M.: Peter Lang.

Ingram, Paul. O. 1988: *The Modern Buddhist-Christian Dialogue. Two Universalistic Religions in Transformation*. Lewiston/Queenston: Edwin Mellen Press.

– 1997: *Wrestling with the Ox. A Theology of Religious Experience*. New York: Wipf & Stock.

Insole, Christopher J. 2000: Why John Hick cannot, and should not, stay out of the jam pot. In: *Religious Studies* 36, 25-33.

International Theological Commission 1997: *Christianity and the World Religions*, see: http://www.vatican.va/roman_curia/congregations/cfaith/cti_documents/rc_cti_1997_cristianesimo-religioni_en.html

Inwagen, Peter van 1995: Non est Hick. In: Th. D. Senor (ed.): *The Rationality of Belief and the Plurality of Faith* (FS W. Alston). Ithaka: Cornell University Press, 216-241.

Ireland, John D. 1997 (transl.): *The Udāna & The Itivuttaka*. Kandy: Buddhist Publication Society.

Irenäus von Lyon 1993: *Gegen die Häresien II*. Transl. and introduced by Norbert Brox (Fontes Christiani 8/2). Freiburg i.Br.: Herder.

Jackson, Roger; Makransky, John 2000 (eds.): *Buddhist Theology. Critical Reflections by Contemporary Buddhist Scholars*. Richmond: Curzon.

Jansen, Reiner 1990: Christliche Kirche und Judentum von den Kirchenvätern bis zu den Reformatoren. In: *Judaica* 46, 134-163.

Jenkins, Philip 2002: *The Next Christendom. The Coming of Global Christianity.* Oxford: Oxford University Press.

Johannes Paul II. 1979: *Redemptor Hominis* (Verlautbarungen des Apostolischen Stuhls 6). Bonn.

– 1990: *Redemptoris Missio* (Verlautbarungen des Apostolischen Stuhls 100). Bonn.

Joswowitz-Schwellenbach, Kirsten 2000: *Zwischen Chalcedon und Birmingham. Zur Christologie John Hicks.* Neuried: Ars Una Verlag.

Jürgens, Bernd Sebastian 1994: *B.R. Ambedkar – Religionsphilosophie eines Unberührbaren.* Frankfurt a.M.: Peter Lang.

Justin 1913: *Die beiden Apologien Justins des Märtyrers.* Bibliothek der Kirchenväter, Bd. 12. Kempten – München: Kösel, 55-155.

Kalsky, Manuela 2000: *Christaphanien. Die Re-Vision der Christologie aus der Sicht von Frauen in unterschiedlichen Kulturen.* Gütersloh: Gütersloher Verlagshaus.

Kampling, R.; Weinrich, M. (eds.) 2003, *Dabru emet—redet Wahrheit: Eine jüdische Herausfordering zum Dialog mit den Christen.* Gütersloh: Gütersloher Verlagshaus.

Kaplan, Stephen 2002: *Different Paths, Different Summits. A Model for Religious Pluralism.* Lanham: Rowman & Littlefield.

Kärkkäinen, Veli-Matti 2004: *Trinity and Religious Pluralism. The Doctrine of the Trinity in Christian Theology of Religions.* Aldershot: Ashgate.

Kasimow, Harold; Kennan, John Pl Klepinger Keenan, Linda 2003 (eds.): *Beside Still Waters. Jews, Christians, and the Way of the Buddha.* Boston: Wisdom Publications.

Kaufman, Gordon 1987: Religious Diversity, Historical Consciousness, and Christian Theology. In: J. Hick, P. Knitter (eds.): *The Myth of Christian Uniqueness.* Maryknoll: Orbis, 3-15.

– 1991: Geschichtlichkeit der Religionen als Herausforderung an die Theologie. In: R. Bernhardt (Hg.): *Horizontüberschreitung.* Gütersloh: Gütersloher Verlagshaus, 47-59.

– 1993: Religious Diversity and Religious Truth. In: A. Sharma (ed.): *God, Truth and Reality.* Basingstoke: Macmillan, 143-164.

Kellenberger, J. 1993 (ed.): *Inter-Religious Models and Criteria.* Basingstoke: Macmillan.

Kelly, J.N.D. 1977: *Early Christian Doctrines.* Fifth, revised edition. London: Adam & Charles Black.

Kelsay, John 2003: War, Peace and the Imperatives of Justice in Islamic Perspectives: What Do the 11 September 2001 Attacks Tell Us about Islam and the Just War Tradition? In: P. Robinson (ed.): *Just War in Comparative Perspective.* Aldershot: Ashgate, 76-89.

Kenny, Anthony 2004: *The Unknown God. Agnostic Essays.* London – New York: Continuum

Kerber, Walter 1993 (Hg.): *Der Begriff der Religion. Ein Symposion.* München: Kindt.

Kern, Iso 1984/85: Matteo Riccis Verhältnis zum Buddhismus. In: *Monumenta Serica* 36, 65-126.

– 1992: *Buddhistische Kritik am Christentum im China des 17. Jahrhunderts.* Berne: Peter Lang.

Kern, Walter 1980: »Außerhalb der Kirche kein Heil«. In: idem.: *Disput um Jesus und um Kirche,* Innsbruck: Tyrolia, 88-112.

Kerr, David 1991: The Prophet Mohammad in Christian Theological Perspective. In: D. Cohn-Sherbok (ed.): *Islam in a World of Diverse Faiths.* Basingstoke: Macmillan, 119-133.

– 1995: »He Walked in the Path of the Prophets«. Toward Christian Theological Recognition of the Prophethood of Muhammad. In: Y.Y. Haddad, W.Z. Haddad (eds.): *Christian-Muslim Encounters.* Gainesville: University Press of Florida, 426-446.

Kessler, Edward 2002: Working Towards an Appreciation of Common Purpose. In: E. Kessler, J. Pawlikowski, J. Banki (eds.): *Jews and Christians in Conversation. Crossing Cultures and Generations*. Cambridge: Orchard Academic, 53-73.

Kessler, Hans 2001: Der universale Jesus Christus und die Religionen. In: *Theologische Quartalschrift* 181, 212-237.

Khalidi, Tarif 2002: *Der muslimische Jesus. Aussprüche Jesu in der arabischen Literatur*. Düsseldorf: Patmos Verlag.

– 2003: *The Muslim Jesus. Sayings and Stories in Islamic Literature*. 4th repr. Cambridge – London: Harvard University Press.

Khoury, Adel Theodor 1969: *Der theologische Streit der Byzantiner mit dem Islam*. Paderborn: Schoeningh.

– 1976: Der Islam im ostchristlichen Denken während des Mittelalters. In: *Concilium* 12, 334-337.

– 1995: Religiöse Ideale als Motive prosozialen Verhaltens gezeigt am Beispiel des Islams. In: W. Kerber (Hg.): *Religion und prosoziales Verhalten*. Munich: Kindt, 15-46.

King, Ursula 1998: Feminism: The Missing Dimension in the Dialogue of Religions. In: J. D'Arcy May (ed.): *Pluralism and the Religions: The Theological and Political Dimensions*. London: Cassell, 40-55.

King, Winston 1963: *Buddhism and Christianity. Some Bridges of Understanding*. London: Allen and Unwin.

Kirste, Reinhard 1991: Der eine und drei-eine Gott im Christentum. In: *Gemeinsam vor Gott. Religionen im Gespräch*, Bd. 1. Hg. von R. Kirste, P. Schwarzenau, U. Tworuschka. Rissen: EBV, 165-195.

– 1999: Interreligiöser Dialog und religiöser Pluralismus in Deutschland: Geschichte und Entwicklungen. In: R. Kirste et al., (Hg.): *Vision 2001. Die größere Ökumene*. Cologne: Böhlau, 122-181.

– 2002: Die religiös plurale Situation in Deutschland und Forderungen für interreligiöses Lernen in der Schule. In: *Neue Herausforderungen für den interreligiösen Dialog*. Religionen im Gespräch. Bd. 7. Balve: Zimmermann, 298-313.

Kitagawa, Joseph 1963: Gibt es ein Verstehen fremder Religionen? In E. Benz (Hg.): *Joachim Wach-Vorlesungen I*. Leiden: E.J. Brill, 37-66.

Klappert, Bertold 1997: Fellow Heirs and Partakers of the Promise: An Alternative for Christian Subsitution-Theology and –Christology. In: D. Pollefeyt (ed.): *Jews and Christians: Rivals or Partners for the Kingdom of God? In Search of an Alternative for the Theology of Substitution*. Leuven: Peeters, 38-61.

Klatt, Norbert 1989: *Literarkritische Beiträge zum Problem christlich-buddhistischer Parallelen*. Cologne: Brill.

Klenicki, Leon 1997: On Christianity: Towards a Process of Historical and Spiritual Healing – Understanding the Other as a Person of God. In: D. Pollefeyt (ed.): *Jews and Christians: Rivals or Partners for the Kingdom of God? In Search of an Alternative for the Theology of Substitution*. Leuven: E.J. Brill, 62-94.

Klimkeit, Hans Joachim 1981: Christentum und Buddhismus in der innerasiatischen Religionsbegegnung. In: *Zeitschrift für Religions- und Geistegeschichte* 33, 208-220.

Klostermaier, Klaus 1989: *A Survey of Hinduism*. Albany: SUNY

– 1989b: The Future of Hindu-Christian Dialogue. In: H. Coward (ed.): *Hindu-Christian Dialogue. Perspectives and Encounters*. Maryknoll: Orbis, 262-274.

– 2000: *Hinduism. A Short History*. Oxford: Oneworld.

– 2002: *Hinduism. A Short Introduction*. Repr. Oxford: Oneworld.

Knitter, Paul 1985: *No Other Name? A Critical Survey of Christian Attitudes Toward the World Religions.* Maryknoll: Orbis.
- 1986: Katholische Religionstheologie am Scheideweg. In: *Concilium* 22, 63-69.
- 1987: Toward a Liberation Theology of Religions. In: J. Hick, P. Knitter (eds.): *The Myth of Christian Uniqueness.* Maryknoll: Orbis, 178-200.
- 1988: *Ein Gott – viele Religionen. Gegen den Absolutheitsanspruch des Christentums.* München: Kösel.
- 1988b: Dialogue and Liberation. Foundations of a Pluralist Theology of Religions. The 1987 Frances Youngker Vosburgh Lectures, in: *The Drew Gateway* 58:1, 1-53.
- 1989: Nochmals die Absolutheitsfrage. Gründe für eine pluralistische Theologie der Religionen. In: Evangelische Theologie 49, 505-516.
- 1991: Religion und Breifreiung. Soteriozentrismus als Antwort an die Kritiker. In: R. Bernhardt (Hg.): *Horizontüberschreitung.* Gütersloh: Gütersloher Verlagshaus, 203-219.
- 1995: *One Earth Many Religions. Multifaith Dialogue and Global Responsibility.* Maryknoll: Orbis.
- 1996: *Jesus and the Other Names. Christian Mission and Global Responsibility.* Maryknoll: Orbis.
- 1997a: *Horizonte der Befreiung. Auf dem Weg zu einer pluralistischen Theologie der Religionen.* Herausgegeben von B. Jaspert. Frankfurt a.M.: Lembeck.
- 1997b: Five Theses on the Uniqueness of Jesus. In: L. Swidler; P. Mojzes (eds.): *The Uniqueness of Jesus. A Dialogue with Paul F. Knitter.* Maryknoll: Orbis, 3-16.
- 1999: Catholics and Other Religions. Bridging the Gap between Dialogue and Theology. In: *Louvain Studies* 24, 319-354.
- 2002: *Introducing Theologies of Religions.* Maryknoll: Orbis.

Kochanek, Hermann 1992 (Hg.): *Reinkarnation oder Auferstehung? Konsequenzen für das Leben.* Freiburg i. Br.: Herder.

Kogan, Michael S. 1995: Toward a Jewish Theology of Christianity. In: *Journal of Ecumenical Studies* 32, 89-106 u. 152.

Koziel, Bernd Elmar 2001: *Kritische Rekonstruktion der Pluralistischen Religionshteologie John Hicks vor dem Hintergrund seines Gesamtwerks.* Frankfurt a.M.: Peter Lang.

Kraemer, Hendrik 1956: *Religion and the Christian Faith.* London: Lutterworth Press
- 1962: *Why Christianity of All Religions?* London: Westminster Press.

Kraft, Charles 1979: *Christianity in Culture.* Maryknoll: Orbis.

Kreiner, Armin 1992: *Ende der Wahrheit? Zum Wahrheitsverständnis in Philosophie und Theologie.* Freiburg i. Br.: Herder.
- 1992b: Versöhung ohne Kapitulation. Überlegungen zu George A. Lindbecks »The Nature of Doctrine«. In: *Catholica* 46, 307-321.
- 1993: Demonstratio religiosa. In: H. Döring, A. Kreiner, P. Schmidt-Leukel: *Den Lauben denken. Neue Wege der Fundamentaltheologie* (QD 147). Freiburg i. Br.: Herder, 9-48.
- 1996a: Kritische Erwägungen zum pluralistischen Wahrheitsverständnis. In: A. Peter (Hg.): Christlicher Glaube in multireligiöser Gesellschaft. Immensee: *Neue Zeitschrift für Missionswissenschaft,* 249-267.
- 1996b: Philosophische Probleme der pluralisischen Religionstheologie. In: R. Schwager (ed.): *Christus allein? Der Streit um die pluralistische Religionstheologie.* Freiburg i.Br.: Herder, 118-131.

Küng, Hans 1978, *On Being a Christian,* Glasgow: Collins.
- 1980: *Christ sein* (DTV paperback edition). 4th edn. Munich: DTV.
- 1986: Zu einer ökumenischen Theologie der Religionen. In: *Concilium* 22, 76-80.
- 1991: *Das Judentum. Die religöse Situation der Zeit.* Munich: Piper.

– 1992: *Judaism. The Religious Situation of Our Time*. London: SCM Press.
– 1995 (Hg.): *Ja zum Weltethos*. Munich: Piper.
Küng, Hans; Ess, Josef van; Stietencron, Heinrich von; Bechert, Heinz 1984: *Christentum und Weltreligionen*. Munich – Zurich: Piper.
Küng, Hans; Ess, Josef van; Stietencron, Heinrich von; Bechert, Heinz 1993: *Christianity and the World Religions*. London: SCM Press.
Kunin, Seth D. 2003: *Religion: The Modern Theories*. Edinburgh: Edinburgh University Press.
Kurzman, Charles 1998: *Liberal Islam. A Sourcebook*. New York—Oxford: OUP.
Kuschel, Karl-Josef 1994: *Streit um Abraham. Was Juden, Christen und Muslim trennt—und was sie eint*. Munich: Piper.
Kuttianimattathil, Jose 1995: *Practice and Theology of Interreligious Dialogue. A Critical Study of the Indian Christian Attempts since Vatican II*. Bangalore: Kristu Jyoti Publications.
Lampe, Geoffrey W.H. 1977: *God as Spirit. The Bampton Lectures 1976*. Oxford: Clarendon Press.
Langer, Ruth 2003: Jewish Understandings of the Religious Other. In: *Theological Studies* 64, 255-277.
Lanz, Eddy 1996: Ist der Gedanke, dass Heiden ohne Jesus ewig verlorengehen, mit dem Glauben an einen liebenden Gott vereinbar? In: A Holzhausen (Hg.): *Mission under Beschuss. Missionspraktiker antworten auf kritische Fragen*. Neuhausen—Stuttgart: Hänssler, 56-65.
Lapide, Pinchas; Rahner, Karl 1983: *Heil von den Juden? Ein Gespräch*. Mainz: Grünewald.
Laun, Andreas 1992: "Kirche und Religionsfreiheit—ein schwarzer Schimmel?" Die Gewissens- and Religionsfreiheit nach dem II. Vatikanischen Konzil. In M. Müller (Hg.): *Plädoyer für die Kirche. Urteile und Vorurteile*. 3rd edition. Aachen: MM Verlag, 263-273.
Lea, Henry Charles 1988: *Geschichte der Spanischen Inquisition*. 3 vols. (Reprint of 1911 edition). Nördlingen: Greno Verlagsanstalt.
Leuze, Reinhard 1994: *Christentum und Islam*. Tübingen: J.C.B. Mohr.
– 2001: Der Prophet Muhammad in christlicher Perspektive. In: *Münchener Theologische Zeitschrift* 52, 26-33.
Lienemann-Perrin, Christine 1991: *Mission und interreligöser Dialog* (Ökumenische Studienhefte 11). Göttingen: Vandenhoeck&Ruprecht.
Lindbeck, George 1984: *The Nature of Doctrine. Religion and Theology in a Postliberal Age*. Philadelphia: Westminster Press.
– 1997: The Gospel's Uniqueness: Election and Untranslatability. In: *Modern Theology* 13, 423-450.
Lindtner, Christian 1982: *Nagarjuniana. Studies in the Writings and Philosophy of Nāgārjuna*. Copenhagen: Akademisk Forlag.
– 1999: Madhyamaka Causality. In: *Hōrin. Vergleichende Studien zur japanischen Kultur* 6, 37-77.
– 2001: Review Article: The Bible and the Buddhists. In: *Buddhist Studies Review* 18, 229-242.
Lipner, Julius 1999: *Hindus. Their Religious Beliefs and Practices*. Reprint, London—New York: Routledge.
Loichinger, Alexander 1999: *Ist der Glaube vernünftig? Zur Frage nach der Rationalität in Philosophie und Theologie*. 2 vols. Neuried: Ars Una.
Lorenzen, David 1996: *Praises to a Formless God. Nirgunī Texts from North India*. Albany: SUNY.
Loughlin, Gerald 1987: Noumenon and Phenomenon. In: *Religious Studies* 23,493-508.

- 1990: Prefacing Pluralism: John Hick and the Mastery of Religion. In: *Modern Theology* 7, 29-55.

Lubac, Henry de 1952: *La Rencontre du Bouddhisme et de L'Occident.* Paris: Aubier.

Lubarsky, Sandra B. 1990: *Tolerance and Transformation. Jewish Approaches to Religious Pluralism.* Cincinnati: Hebrew Union College Press.

Luz, Ulrich; Michaels, Axel 2002: *Jesus oder Buddha. Leben und Lehre im Vergleich.* München: C.H. Beck.

- 2006: *Encountering Jesus & Buddha. Their Lives and Teachings.* Minneapolis: Fortress Press.

MacIntyre, Alasdair C. 1985: *After Virtue.* 2nd ed. London: Duckworth.

- 1988: *Whose Justice? Which Rationality?* London: Duckworth.

Mackie, John Lesley 1982: *The Miracle of Theism. Arguments for and against the existence of God*, Oxford: OUP.

Macquarrie, John 1993: *Jesus Christ in Modern Thought.* 3rd ed. London—Philadelphia: SCM Press, Trinity Press.

- 1995: *The Mediators: Nine Stars in the Human Sky.* London: SCM Press.

- 1997: Revisiting the Christological Dimension of Uniqueness. In: L. Swideler, P. Mojzes (eds.): *The Uniqueness of Jesus. A Dialogue with Paul F. Knitter.* Maryknoll: Orbis, 94-99.

Makransky, John 2003: Buddhist Perspectives on Truth and Other Religions: Past and Present. In: *Theological Studies* 64, 334-361.

Mall, Ram Adhar 2003: Zur Hermeneutik des Einen mit vielen Namen: Eine interkulturelle Perspektive. In: F. Uhl, A.R. Boelderl (Hg.): *Die Sprachen der Religion.* Berlin: Parerga, 39-375.

Markham, Ian 1993: Creating Options: Shattering the Exclusivist, Inclusivist, and Pluralist Paradigm. In: *New Blackfriars* 74, No. 867, 33-41.

Marquardt, Friedrich-Wilhelm 1990: *Das christliche Bekenntnis zu Jesus, dem Juden. Eine Christologie.* Vol. 1. Munich: Kaiser.

- 1994: *Was dürfen wir hoffen, wenn wir hoffen dürfen? Eine Eschatologie.* Vol. 2. Gütersloh: Gütersloher Verlagshaus.

- 1996: *Was dürfen wir hoffen, wenn wir hoffen dürfen? Eine Eschatologie.* Vol. 3. Gütersloh: Gütersloher Verlagshaus.

Marshall, Molly Truman 1993: *No Salvation Outside the Church? A Critical Inquiry.* Lewiston: Edwin Mellen Press.

Margull, H.-J. 1963 (Hg.): *Zur Sendung der Kirche. Material aus der ökumenischen Bewegung.* Munich: Kaiser.

May, John D'Arcy, 2003: *Transcendence and Violence: The Encounter of Buddhist, Christian and Primal Traditions.* New York - London: Continuum.

Mayer-König, Birgit 1995: Transzendenz im Licht von Karman und Gnade. Eine Untersuchung zum nicht-dualistischen Shivaismus und zur buddhistischen Lehre von der Verdienstübertragung. In: *Hōrin. Vergleichende Studien zur japanischen Kultur* 2, 149-168.

McGrath, Alister E. 1992: The Christian Church's Response to Pluralism. In: *Journal of the Evangelical Theological Society* 35/4, 487-501

- 1995: A Particularist View: A Post-Enlightenment Approach. In: D. Okholm T. Phillips (eds.), *More Than One Way? Four Views on Salvation in a Pluralistic World.* Grand Rapids: Zondervan, 151-180.

Meisig, Konrad 1988: Das Kastensystem des Hinduismus. In: A Th. Khoury, P. Hühermann (Ed,): *Wer ist mein Nächster? Die Antwort der Weltreligionen.* Freiburg i. Br.: Herder, 11-58.

Menke, Karl-Heinz 1995: *Die Einzigkeit Jesu Christi im Horizont der Sinnfrage*. Einsiedeln. Freiburg: Johannes Verlag.

Mensching, Gustav 1955: *Toleranz und Wahrheit in der Religion*. Heidelberg: Quelle & Meyer.

– 1964: Das Christentum in der Ausinandersetzung der Religionen heute. In: E.v. Dungern (Hg.): *Das Grosse Gespräch der Religionen*. München – Basel: Reinhardt, 11-27.

Metz, Johann Baptist 1997: Mit der Autorität der Leidenden. In: *Süddeutsche Zeitung*, 24./25./26. Dezember 1997, Nr. 296, 57.

Milbank, John 1990: *Theology and Social Theory*. Oxford: Blackwell.

– *The World Made Strange: Theology, Language, Culture*. Oxford: Blackwell.

Milbank, John; Pickstock, Catherine; Ward, Graham 1999 (eds.): *Radical Orthodoxy. A New Theology*. London – New York: Routledge.

Mommsen, K. 2001: *Goethe und der Islam*. Frankfurt a.M.- Leipzig: Insel Verlag.

Müller, Gerhard Ludwig 1998: Ist die Einzigkeit Jesu Christi im Kontext einer pluralistischen Weltzivilisation vermittelbar? In: R. Schwager (Hg.): *Relativierung der Wahrheit? Kontextuelle Christologie auf dem Prüfstand* (QD 170). Freiburg i.Br.: Herder, 156-185.

– (Hg.): *Erinnern und Versöhen. Die Kirche und die Verfehlungen in ihrer Vergangenheit*. Einsiedeln, Freiburg: Johannes Verlag.

– 2003 (Hg.): *Die Heilsuniversalität Christi und der Kirche*. Würzburg: Echter.

Müller, Gerhard Ludwig; Serretti, Massiimo 2001 (Hg.): *Einzigkeit und Universalität Jesu Christi. Im Dialog mit den Religionen*. Freiburg: Johannes.

Müller, Hans-Peter 1998: Rechtfertigung des Mythos in bibeltheologischer und hermeneutischer Hinsicht. In: A. Bsteh (Hg.): *Christlicher Glaube in der Begegnung mit dem Hinduismus*. Mödling: St. Gabriel, 63-77.

Münch, Armin 1998: *Dimensionen der Leere. Gott als Nichts und Nichts als Gott im christlich-buddhistischen Dialog*. Münster: LIT.

Mussner, Franz 1979: *Traktat über die Juden*. Göttingen: Vandenhoeck&Ruprecht.

– 1982: Der Messias Jesus. In: H-J. Greschat, F. Mussner, S. Talmong, R. J. Zwi Werblowsky: *Jesus –Messias? Heilserwartung bei Juden und Christen*. Regensburg: Pustet, 89-107.

Myers, David B. 2003a: Exclusivism, eternal damnation, and the problem of evil: a critique of Craig's Molinist soteriological theodicy. In: *Religious Studies* 39, 407-419.

– 2003b: Rejoinder to William Lane Craig. In: *Religious Studies* 39, 427-430.

Nagel, Thomas 1987: *What Does It All Mean? A Very Short Introduction to Philosophy*. New York – Oxford: Oxford University Press.

Nambara, Minoru 1960: Die Idee des absoluten Nichts in der deutschen Mystik und seine Entsprechungen im Buddhismus. In: *Archiv für Begriffsgeschichte*. Vol. IV. Bonn: Meiner, 143-277.

Nasr, Seyyed Hossein 1989: *Knowledge and the Sacred*. Albany: SUNY.

– 1990: *Die Erkenntnis und das Heilige*. München: Diederichs.

– 1993: *The Need for a Sacred Science*. Albany: SUNY.

– 1993b: *Ideal und Wirklichkeit des Islam*. Munich: Diederichs.

– 1995: Comments on a Few Theological Issues in the Islamic-Christian Dialogue. In: Y.Y. Haddad; W.Z. Haddad (eds.): *Christian-Muslim Encounters*. Gainesville: University of Florida Press, 457-467,

– 1997: Der Islam. In: A. Sharma (Hg.): *Innenansichten der grossen Religionen*. Frankfurt a.M.: Fischer, 387-538.

– 1999: Religion, Globality, and Universality. In: A. Sharma, K.M. Dugan (eds.): *A Dome of Many Colours. Studies in Religious Pluralism, Identity, and Unity*. Harrisburg: Trinity Press, 152-178.

– 2000: *Ideal and Realities of Islam*. New Revised Edition. Chicago: ABC International Group.

Nayak, Anand; Abrard, Anne-Marie 1982: Hindu-Christlicher Dialog in India. In: *Pro Muni Vita Bulletin* 88 (Brüssel).

Neil, Stephen 1984: *A History of Christianity in India. The Beginnings to AD 1707*. Cambridge: Cambridge University Press.

– 1985: *A History of Christianity in India. 1707-1858*. Cambridge: Cambridge University Press.

Netland, Harrold 1991: *Dissonant Voices. Religious Pluralism and the Question of Truth*. Grand Rapids: Eerdmans.

– 2001: *Encountering Religious Pluralism. The Challenge to Christian Faith and Mission*. Downers Grove—Leicester: InterVarsity Press, Apolllos.

Neufeldt, Ronald 1989a: The Response of the Hindu Renaissance to Christianity. In: H. Coward (ed): *Hindu-Christian Dialogue. Perspectives and Encounters*. Maryknoll: Orbis, 28-46.

– 1989b: Hindu Views of Christ. In: H. Coward (ed.): *Hindu-Christian Dialogue. Perspectives and Encounters*. Maryknoll: Orbis, 162-175.

Neuhaus, Gerd 1999: *Kein Weltfrieden ohne christlichen Absolutheitsanspruch* (QD 175). Freiburg i. Br.: Herder.

– 2003: Der Absolutheitsanspruch des Christentums. In: H. Schmidinger (Hg.): *Identität und Toleranz. Christliche Spiritualität im interreligösen Kontext*. Innsbruck: Tyrolia, 115-150.

Neuner, Josef 1962: *Hinduismus und Christentum. Eine Einführung*. Freiberg i.Br.: Herder.

Neuner, Josef; Roos, Henrich 1979: *Der Glaube der Kirche in den Urkunden der Lehrverkündigung*. Neubearbeitet von Karl Rahner und Karl-Heinz Weger. 10th edition. Regensburg: Friedrich Pustet.

Neuner, Peter 2003: Toleranz und Wahrheit in pluralistischer Zeit. In: H. Wadenfels (Hg.): *Religion. Entstehung – Funktion – Wesen*. Freiburg – Munich: Alber, 175-214.

Newbigin, Lesslie 1989: *The Gospel in a Pluralist Society*. Grand Rapids – Geneva: Eerdmans, WCC.

– 1990: Religion for the Marketplace. In: G.D'Costa (ed.): *Christian Uniqueness Reconsidered*. Maryknoll: Orbis, 135-148.

– 1995: *The Open Secret. An Introduction to the Theology of Mission*. Revised Edition. London: SPCK.

Nicholas of Cusa, 1952: *Der verborgene Gott. Ein Gespräch zwischen einem Heiden und einem Christen*. Lateinisch und Deutsch. Übertragung und Nachwort von Fritz Stippel. 3. Verbesserte Auflage. Freiburg i. Br.: Erich Wewel Verlag.

– 1964: *Die belehrte Unwissenheit*. Buch I. Übersetzt und mit einem Vorwort und Anmerkungen herausgegeben von Paul Wilpert. Berlin: Akademie Verlag.

Niles, D.T. 1969: Karl Barth—A Personal Memory. In: *The South East Asia Journal of Theology* 11, 10f.

Nishitani, Keiji 1982: *Religion and Nothingness*. Berkeley: University of California Press.

Nyanaponika 1981: *Buddhism and the God-Idea* (The Wheel Publication No. 47). Kandy: Buddhist Publication Society.

O'Collins, Gerald 2003: Jacques Dupuis's Contribution to Interreligious Dialogue. In: *Theological Studies* 64, 388-397.

O'Grady, Paul 2002: *Relativism*. Chesham Bucks: Acumen Publishing.

Oeldermann, Johannes 2003: Orthodoxe Theologen im interreligiösen Dialog mit dem Judentum und dem Islam. In: *Catholica* 57, 193-206.

Oesterreicher, Johannes 1967: Erklärung über das Verhältnis der Kirche zu den nichtchristlichen Religionen. Kommentierende Einleitung. In: *Lexikon für Theologie und Kirche*. 2. Auflage. Anhangbände: Das Zweite Vatkanische Konzil. Teil II Freiburg: Herder, 406-478.

Ogden, Schubert 1991: Gibt es nur eine wahre Religion oder mehrere? In: *Zeitschrift für Theologie und Kirche* 88, 81-100.

– 1992: *Is There Only One True Religion or Are There Many*? Dallas: Southern Methodist University Press.

Ohlig, Karl-Heinz 1999: *Ein Gott in drei Personen? Vom Vater Jesu zu "Mysterium" der Trinität*. Mainz-Luzern: Matthias Grünewald Verlag.

Okholm, Dennis; Phillips, Timothy 1995 (eds.): *More Than One Way? Four Views on Salvation in a Pluralistic World*. Grand Rapids: Zondervan.

Osborn, Eric 1987: *Anfänge christlichen Denkens: Justin, Irenäus, Tertullian, Klemens*. Übersetzt, bearbeitet und herausgegeben von Johannes Bernard. Düsseldorf: Patmos.

Osterman, Heinrich 1963: *Die Weltreligionen und das Christentum*. Augsburg: Verlag Winfried Werk.

Otto, Rudolf 1923: *The Idea of the Holy*: an inquiry into the non-rational factor in the idea of the divine and its relation to the rational. London: Oxford University Press.

Oxtoby, Willard 1986: *Offenes Christentum*. München: Piper.

Paden, William E. 1990: *Am Anfang war Religion. Die Einheit in der Vielfalt*. Gütersloh: Gütersloher Verlagshaus.

Pallis, Marco 1989: *Spektrum buddhistischer Leitgedanken*. Dietikon: Garuda Verlag.

Panikkar, Raimon (Raimundo) 1963: *Die vielen Götter und der eine Herr. Beiträge zum ökumenischen Gespräch der Weltreligionen*. Weilheim: O.W. Barth.

– 1964: *The Unknown Christ of Hinduism*. London: Darton, Longman & Todd.

– 1965: *Christus der Unbekannte im Hinduismus*. Luzern, Stuttgart: Räber.

– 1967: *Keryga und Indien. Zur heilsgeschichtlichen Problematik der christlichen Begegnung mit Indien* (Kerygma und Mythos V—Supplementary volume III). Hamburg—Bergstedt: Herbert Reich – Evangelischer Verlag.

– 1973: *The Trinity and the Religious Experience of Man: Icon-Person-Mystery*. London-Maryknoll: Orbis.

– 1975: Verstehen als Überzeugtsein. In: H.G. Gadamer, P.Vogler (Hg.): *Neue Anthropologie*, Bd. 7. Stuttgart: DTV, 132-167.

– 1978: *The Intrareligious Dialogue*. New York: Paulist.

– 1981: *The Unknown Christ of Hinduism. Completely Revised and Enlarged Edition*, Maryknoll: Orbis.

– 1987: The Jordan, the Tiber, and the Ganges. Three Kairlogical Moments of Christic Self-Consciousness. In: J. Hick; P. Knitter (eds.): *The Myth of Christian Uniqueness. Toward a Pluralistic Theology of Religions*. Maryknoll: Orbis, 89-116.

– 1989: The Ongoing Dialogue. In: H. Coward (ed.): *Hindu-Christian Dialogue. Perspectives and Encounters*. Maryknoll: Orbis, IX-XVIII.

– 1990: *Der neue囲 religöse Weg. In Dialog der Religionen leben*. Munich: Kösel.

– 1990b: *Der unbekannte Christus im Hinduismus* (1st edition, 1986), 2nd edition, Mainz: Grünewald.

– 1991: *Der Weisheit eine Wohnung bereiten*. Hg. von C. Bochinger. Munich: Kösel.

– 1995: *Invisible Harmony. Essays on Contemplation and Responsibility*. Edited by Harry James Cargas. Minneapolis: Fortress Press.

– 1996: A Self-Critical Dialogue. In: J. Prabhu (ed.): *The Intercultural Challenge of Raimon Panikkar*. Maryknoll: Orbis, 111-115.

– 1999: Religious Identity and Pluralism. In: A. Sharma, K.M. Dugan (eds.): *A Dome of Many Colours. Studies in Religious Pluralism, Identity, and Unity.* Harrisburg: Trinity Press, 23-47.

Pannenberg, Wolfhart 1979: *Erwägungen zu einer Theologie der Religionsgeschichte.* In: idem., *Grundfragen Systematischer Theologie.* 3rd edition. Göttingen: Vandenhoeck&Ruprecht, 252-295.

– 1987a: *Wissenschaftstheorie und Theologie.* Frankfurt a.M.: Suhrkamp.

– 1987b: Religion und Religionen. In A. Bsteh (Hg.): *Dialog aus der Mitte christlicher Theologie.* Mödling: St. Gabriel, 179-196.

– 1988: *Sytematische Theologie,* Bd. I. Göttingen: Vandenhoeck&Ruprecht.

– 1989: Die Religionen als Thema der Theologie. In: *Theologische Quartalschrift* 169, 99-110.

– 1991: *Systematische Theologie,* Bd. II. Göttingen: Vandenhoeck&Ruprecht.

– 1994: *Systematic Theology,* Vol. 2. Transl. by G.W. Bromiley. Grand Rapids: Eerdmans Publishing.

Papendreou, Damaskinos 1998: Möglichkeit und Notwendigkeit interreligöser Dialoge. In: *Una Sancta* 53, 115-125.

Paret, Rudi 1989: *Der Koran.* Stuttgart: Kohlhammer. 5th edition.

Parkes, James 1960: *The Foundations of Judaism and Christianity.* London: Vallentine, Mitchell and Co.

Parrinder, Geoffrey 1997: *Avatar and Incarnation. The Divine in Human Form in the World Religions* (repr.). Oxford: Oneworld.

Paul, Gregor 1994: Argumente für die Universalität der Logik. In: *Hōrin. Vergleichende Studien zur japanischen Kultur* 1, 57-86.

– 2000: Die Vielfalt der Religionen aus atheistischer Sicht. In: *Salzburger Theologische Zeitschrift* 4, 84-93.

Pawlikowski, John T. 1988: Judentum und Christentum. In: *Theologische Realenzyklopaedie,* Bd. 17, Berlin-New York: De Gruyter, 386-403.

– 2002: Maintaining Momentum in a Global Village, In: E. Kessler, J. Pawlikowski, J. Banki (eds.): *Jews and Christians in Conversation. Crossing Cultures and Generations.* Cambridge: Orchard Academic, 75-91.

Peter, Anton 1996 (Hg.): *Christlicher Glaube in multireligöser Gesellschaft. Erfahrungen, theologische Reflexionen, missionarische Perspektiven.* Immensee: Neue Zeitschrift für Missionswissenschaft.

Phan, Peter 2003: Multiple Religious Belonging: Opportunities and Challenges for Theology and Church. In: *Theological Studies* 64, 495-519.

Phidas, Vlassios 1997: Le dialogue interreligieux dans une perspective orthodoxe. In: Joseph Doré (ed.): *Le christianisme vis-à-vis des religions.* Namur: Artel, 81-98.

Phillips, D.Z. 1988: *Faith after Foundationalism.* London: Routledge.

Pieris, Aloysius 1975: God-Talk and God Experience. In a Christian Perspective. In: *Dialogue* N.S. 2, 116-128.

– 1986: *Theologie der Befreiung in Asien. Christentum im Kontext der Armut und der Religionen.* Freiburg i.Br.: Herder.

– 1988: *Love Meets Wisdom.* Maryknoll: Orbis.

– 1989: *Liebe und Weisheit. Begegnung von Christentum und Buddhismus.* Mainz: Grünewald 1989.

– 1994: *Feuer und Wasser. Frau, Gesellschaft, Spiritualität in Buddhismus und Christentum.* Freiburg i.Br.: Herder.

Pinnock, Clark H. 1995: An Inclusivist View. In: D.Okholm, T. Phillips (eds.): *More Than One Way? Four Views on Salvation in a Pluralistic World.* Grand Rapids: Zondervan, 95-123.

– 1997: *A Wideness in God's Mercy. The Finality of Jesus Christ in a World of Religions.* Reprint of 1992 edition. Eugene: Wipf and Stock.

Plantinga, Alvin 1997: Ad Hick. In: *Faith and Philosophy* 14, 295-298.

– 2000: Pluralism: A Defense of Religious Exclusivism (1995), reprinted in: P. Quinn, K. Meeker (eds.): *The Philosophical Challenge of Religious Diversity.* New York – Oxford: OUP, 172-192.

Plantinga, Richard 1999 (ed.): *Christianity and Plurality. Classic and Contemporary Readings.* Oxford: Blackwell.

Pollefeyt, Didier 1997a: In Search of an Alternative for the Theology of Substitution. In: D. Pollefeyt (ed.): *Jews and Christians: Rivals or Partners for the Kingdom of God? In Search of an Alternative for the Theology of Substitution.* Leuven: Peeters, 1-9.

– 1997b: Jews and Christians after Aufschwitz: From Substitution to Interreligious Dialogue.In: D. Pollefeyt (ed.): *Jews and Christians: Rivals or Partners for the Kingdom of God? In Search of an Alternative for the Theology of Substitution.* Leuven: Peeters, 10-37.

Pröpper, Thomas 1991: *Erlösungsglaube und Freiheitsgeschichte. Eine Skizze zur Soteriologie.* 3. Aufl., Munich: Kösel.

Pye, Michael 1978: *Skilful Means: A Concept in Mahayana Buddhism.* London: Duckworth.

Quinn, Philip 1995: Towards Thinner Theologies: Hick and Alston on Religious Diversity. In: *International Journal for Philosophy and Religions* 38, 145-165.

Quinn, Philip; Meeker, Kevin 2000 (eds.): *The Philosophical Challenge of Religious Diversity.* New York – Oxford: OUP.

Race, Alan 1983: *Christians and Religious Pluralism. Patterns in the Christian Theology of Religions*, London: SCM Press.

– 1986: Christianity and Other Religions: Is Inclusivism Enough? In: *Theology* 89, 178-186.

– 1991: Christus und das Skandalon der Partikularitäten. In: R. Bernhardt (Hg.): *Horizontüberschrietung.* Gütersloh: Gütersloher Verlagshaus, 137-150.

– 2001: *Interfaith Encounter. The Twin Tracks of Theology and Dialogue.* London: SCM Press.

Radhakrishnan, Sarvepalli 1961a: *Meine Suche nach Wahrheit.* Gütersloh: Bertelsmann.

– -1961b: *Weltanschauung der Hindu.* Baden-Baden: Holle.

Rahner, Karl 1964: Das Christentum und die nichtchristlichen Religionen. In: idem.: *Schriften zur Theologie* V. Einsiedeln-Zürich-Köln: Benziger, 136-158.

– 1964b: Einige Bermerkungen über die Frage der Konversionen. In: idem.: *Schriften zur Theologie* V. Einsiedeln-Zürich-Köln: Benziger, 356-378.

– 1964c: Was ist eine dogmatische Aussage? In: idem.: *Schriften zur Theologie* V. Einsiedeln-Zürich-Köln: Benziger, 54-81.

– 1967: Kirche, Kirchen und Religionen. In: idem.: *Schriften zur Theologie* VIII. Zürich-Einsiedeln-Köln: Benziger, 355-373.

– 1968: *Ich glaube an Jesus Christus* (Theologische Meditationen 21). Einsiedeln: Benziger.

– 1970: Anonymes Christentum und Missionsauftrag der Kirche. In.: idem., *Schriften zur Theologie* IX. Einsiedeln – Zürich – Köln: Benziger, 251-282.

– 1976: *Grundkurs des Glaubens. Einführung in den Begriff des Christentums.* 9. Aufl. Freiburg i.Br.: Herder.

– 1978: *Foundations of Christian Faith. An Introduction to the Idea of Christianity.* Translated by William v. Dych. New York: The Seabury Press.

Rahner, Karl; Weger, Karl-Heinz 1979: *Was sollen wir noch glauben? Theologen stellen sich den Glaubensfragen einer neuen Generation.* Freiburg i. Br.: Herder.

– 1981: *Our Christian Faith: Answers for the Future.* New York: Crossroad [transl. of "Was sollen wir noch glauben?"].

Rainer, Michael J. 2001 (Hg.): *"Dominus Iesus": Anstössige Wahrheit oder anstössige Kirche? Dokumente, Hintergründe, Standpunkte und Folgerungen.* Münster: LIT.

Ratzinger, Josef 1969: *Das neue Volk Gottes. Entwürfe zur Ekklesiologie,* Düsseldorf: Patmos.

– 1996: Zur Lage von Glaube und Theologie heute. In: *Internationale Katholische Zeitschrift 'Communio'* 25, 359-372. For the English version ("The Current Situation of Faith and Theology", also published as "Relativism: The Central Problem of Faith Today") see: http://www.vatican.va/roman_curia/congregations/cfaith/incontri/rc_con_cfaith_19960507_guadalajara-ratzinger_en.html

– 1996b: *Salz der Erde. Christentum und katholische Kirche an der Jahrtausendwende. Ein Gespräch mit Peter Seewald.* Stuttgart: DVA.

– 2003: *Glaube-Wahrheit-Toleranz. Das Christentum und die Weltreligionen.* Freiburg i.Br.: Herder.

Religionen, Religiosität und christlicher Glaube: eine Studie (1991). Herausgegeben im Auftrag der Vereinigten Evangelisch-Lutherischen Kirche Deutschlands (VELKD) und der Arnoldshainer Konferenz, Gütersloh: Gütersloher Verlagshaus.

Religious Plurality. Theological Perspectives and Affirmations (Baar 1990) In: *Current Dailogue* 19 (1991) 47-51.

Rendtorff, Rolf; Henrix, Hans Hermann 1989 (Hg.): *Die Kirchen und das Judentum. Dokumente von 1945 bis 1985.* 2. Aufl., Paderborn-Munich: Bonifatius, Kaiser.

Renz, Andreas 2001: Der Islam: Keine 'Gesetzreligion', sondern Religion des Glaubens und der Barmherzigkeit Gottes. In: *Münchener Theologische Zeitschrift* 52, 43-55.

– 2002: *Der Mensch unter dem An-Spruch Gottes. Offenbarungsverständnis und Menschenbild des Islam in Urteil gegenwärtiger christlicher Theologie.* Würzburg: Ergon.

Renz, Andreas; Leimgruber, Stephan 2004: *Christen und Muslime. Was sie verbindet – was sie unterscheidet.* Munich: Kösel.

Richards, Glyn 1989: *Towards a Theology of Religions.* London – New York: Routledge.

Richter, Klemens 1984 (Hg.): *Die katholische Kirche und das Judentum. Dokumente von 1945-1982.* Freiburg i.Br.: Herder.

Ridgeon, Lloyd 1999: *Crescents on the Cross. Islamic Visions of Christianity.* Glasgow: Glasgow University Press.

– 2001 (ed.): *Islamic Interpretations of Christianity.* Richmond: Curzon.

– 2004: War and Peace in Islam. In: P. Schmidt-Leukel (ed.): *War and Peace in World Religions.* London: SCM Press, 148-180.

Risse, Günter 1989: *"Gott is Christus, der Sohn der Maria." Eine Studie zum Christusbild im Koran.* Bonn: Borengässer.

Rolston, Holmes III 1985: *Religious Inquiry—Participation and Detachment.* New York: Philosophical Library.

Rolt, C.E. (no year): Dionysius The Areopagite, *On the Divine Names and the Mystical Theology.* Montana: Kessinger Publishing. Online: http://www.ccel.org/ccel/rolt/dionysius.i.html

Rössler, Andreas 1990: *Steht Gottes Himmel allen offen? Zum Symbol des kosmischen Christus.* Stuttgart: Quell.

Rötting, Martin 2001: *Berge sind Berge, Flüsse sind Flüsse. Begegnung mit dem koreanischen Zen Buddhismus. Ein Beitrag zum christlich-buddhistischen Dialog.* St. Ottilien: EOS Verlag.

Rosenstein, Gustav 1991: *Die Stunde des Dialogs. Begegnung der Religionen heute*. Hamburg: EBV Rissen.

Roth, John K. 1989: Can John Hick Say What He Said? In: L. Tessier (ed.): *Concepts of the Ultimate*. Basingstoke: Macmillan, 159-62.

Rothermund, Chitra und Dietmar 1995: Die Stellung der Frau in der Gesellschaft. In: D. Rothermund (Hg.): *Indien. Kultur, Geschichte, Politik, Wirtschaft, Umwelt. Ein Handbuch*. Munich: Beck, 132-139.

Rotter, Gernot 1993 (Hg.): *Die Welten des Islam. Neunundzwanzig Vorschläge, das Unvertraute zu verstehen*. Frankfurt a.M.: Fischer.

Rowe, William 1999: Religious Pluralism. In: *Religious Studies* 35: 139-150.

Ruether, Rosemary (Radford) 1978: *Nächstenliebe und Brudermord. Die theologischen Wurzeln des Antisemitismus*. Munich: Kaiser.

- 1979: *Faith and Fratricide. The Theological Roots of Anti-Semitism*. New York: Seabury Press (first edn. 1974).
- 1981: *To Change the World. Christology and Cultural Criticism*. London: Crossroad.
- 1987: Feminism and Jewish-Christian Dialogue. In: J. Hick, P. Knitter, (eds.): *The Myth of Christian Uniqueness*. Maryknoll: Orbis, 137-148
- 1991: Kann Christologie befreit werden vom Patriarchalismus? In: R. Bernhardt (Hg.): *Horizontüberschreitung*. Gütersloh: Gütersloher Verlagshaus, 120-136.

Ruether, Rosemary (Radford); Gross, Rita M. 2001: *Religious Feminism and the Future of the Planet. A Buddhist-Christian Conversation*. London-New York: Continuum.

Ruster, Thomas 2000: *Der verwechselbare Gott. Theologie nach der Entflechtung von Christentum und Religion*. Freiburg i.Br.: Herder.

Sachedina, Abdulaziz 2001: *The Islamic Roots of Democratic Pluralism*. Oxford: OUP.

Sacks, Jonathan 2003: *The Dignity of Difference. How to Avoid the Clash of Civilizations*. Rev. edn. London-New York: Continuum.

Sainsbury, R.M. 1993: *Paradoxien*. Stuttgart: Reclam.

Samartha, Stanley J. 1970: *Hindus vor dem universalen Christus*. Stuttgart: Evangelisches Verlagswerk.

- 1974: *The Hindu Response to the Unbound Christ*. Bangalore: CISRS.
- 1981: *Courage for Dialogue. Ecumenical issues in inter-religious relationships*. Geneva: WCC.
- 1991: *One Christ – Many Religions. Toward a Revised Christology*. Maryknoll: Orbis.

Sanders, E.P. 1996: *Sohn Gottes. Eine historische Biographie Jesu*. Stuttgart: Klett-Cotta.

Sandmel, David Fox 2002: Dabru Emet and the Future Direction of Jewish-Christian Relations. In: E. Kessler, J. Pawlikowski, J. Banki (eds.): *Jews and Christians in Conversation. Crossing Cultures and Generations*. Cambridge: Orchard Academic, 93-102.

Sanneh, Lamin 1996: *Piety and Power. Muslims and Christians in West Africa*. Maryknoll: Orbis.

Scheffczyk, Leo 1999: Der eine Heilsweg und die vielen Religionen. In: Franz Breid (Hg.): *Beten alle zum selben Gott?* Steyr: Ennsthaler Gesellschaft m.b.H. & Co. KG, 50-78.

Schenk, Richard 1999: In universum mundum. Das Zeugnis des Evangeliums im Zeitalter pluralistischer Religionstheologien. In: W. Schreer, G. Steins (ed): *Auf neue Art Kirche sein* (FS Josef Homeyer). München: Don Bosco, 514-530.

Schimmel, Annemarie 1995: *Al Halladsch—"O Leute, rettet mich vor Gott". Texte islamischer Mystik*. Freiburg i.Br.: Herder.

- 1996: *Wie universal ist die Mystik? Die Seelenreise in den grossen Religionen der Welt*. Freiburg i.Br.: Herder.

Schlette, Heinz Robert 1998 (Hg.): *Religionskritik in interkultureller und interreligiöser Sicht.* Bonn: Borengässer.

Schleiermacher, Friedrich 1958: *On Religion. Speeches to its Cultured Despisers.* New York: Harper and Row.

– 1985: Über die Relig*ion. Reden an die Gebildeten unter ihren Verächtern* (1. Aufl. 1799). Stuttgart: Reclam.

– 1960: *Der christliche Glaube*. Hg. von Martin Redeker. 2 Bde. Berlin: De Gruyter.

Schmidt-Leukel, Perry 1984: *Die Bedeutung des Todes für das menschliche Selbstverständnis im Pāli-Buddhismus.* St. Ottilien: EOS Verlag.

– 1992: *"Den Löwen brüllen hören"—Zur Hermeneutik eines christlichen Verständnisses der buddhistischen Heilsbotschaft*, Paderborn: Schöningh.

– 1992b: Der schwierige Weg vom Gegeneinander zum Miteinander der Religionen. Neue Dokumente zur theologischen Grundlegung des interreligösen Dialogs. In: *Una Sancta* 47, 54-77.

– 1993a: Zur Klassifikation religionstheologischer Modelle. In: *Catholica* 47, 163-183.

– 1993b: Christliche Buddhismus-Interpretation und die Gottesfrage. In: *Münchener Theologische Zeitschrift* 44, 349-358.

– 1993c: Das Pluralistische Modell in der Theologie der Religionen. Ein Literaturbericht. In: *Theologische Revue* 89, Sp. 353-364.

– 1995: Buddhismus und Christentum. Ausdruckgestalten und Kontexte underschiedliche Erfahrungen mit derselben transzendenten Wirklichkeit. In: *Hōrin. Vergleichende Studien zur japanischen Kultur* 2, 169-192.

– 1996: Die religionstheologischen Grundmodelle: Exklusivismus, Inklusivismus, Pluralismus. In: A. Peter (Hg.): *Christlicher Glaube in multireligöser Gesellschaft. Erfahrungen, theologische Reflexionen, missionarische Perspektiven.* Immensee: Neue Zeitschrift für Missionswissenschaft, 227-248.

– 1996b: Der Reinkarnationsgedanke—Eine Herausforderung an die christliche Theologie. In: P. Schmidt-Leukel (Hg.): *Die Idee der Reinkarnation in Ost und West.* Munich: Diederichs, 177-204.

– 1997: *Theologie der Religionen. Probleme, Optionen, Argumente.* Neuried: Ars Una.

– 1998a: "Niemand hat Gott je gesehen'? Zu den anthropologischen Rahmenbedingungen der Gotteserfahrung bei Thomas von Aquin und John Hick. In: M. Thurner (Hg.): *Die Einheit der Person. Beiträge zur Anthropologie des Mittelalters. Festschrift für Richard Heinzmann.* Stuttgart: Kohlhammer, 263-280.

– 1998b: Review: *Gerhard* Gäde, Viele Religionen—ein Wort Gosttes. Einspruch gegen John Hicks pluralistische Religionstheologie. In: *Religionen im Gespräch* 5, 592-603.

– 1998c: Wie ist das Wirken Gottes in den Religionen zu denken? In: *Una Sancta* 53, 98-108.

– 1991: *Grundkurs Fudmanetaltheologie. Eine Einführung in die Grundfragen des christlichen Glaubens.* Munich: Don Bosco.

– 1998b: Die Wahrheit des Buddhismus aus christlicher Sicht—ein dialogisches Zwischenresümee. In: *Salzburger Theologische Zeitschrift* 3, 52-69.

– 2000: Ist das Christentum notwendig intolerant? In: R. Forst (Hg.): *Toleranz. Philosophische Grundlagen und gesellschaftliche Praxis.* Frankfurt a.M.: Campus Verlag, 177-213.

– 2001a (ed.): *Buddhist Perceptions of Jesus.* St. Ottilien: EOS.

– 2001b: Zum Gesamtwerk von John Hick. In: *Hick, John: Gott und seine vielen Namen.* 2. Völlig neu bearbeitete Auflage. Frankfurt a.M.: Lembeck, 179-209.

– 2002: Beyond tolerance: towards a new step in interreligious relationships. In: *Scottish Journal of Theology* 55, 379-391.

– 2003a: Buddha and Christ as Mediators of Salvific Transcendent Reality. In: H. Eisenhofer-Halim (Hg.): *Wandel zwischen den Welten. Festschrift für Johannes Laube*. Frankfurt a.M.: Peter Lang, 647-667.
– 2003b: Sag und Unsagbarkeit von Transzendenz. Zur Hermeneutik menschlicher Gottesrede. In: Florian Uhl, Artur Boelderl (Hg.): *Die Sprachen der Religion*. Berlin: Parerga, 31-47.
– 2004 (ed.): *War and Peace in World Religions*. London: SCM Press.

Schmitz, Rudolf Michael 1999: Eine Theologie der Religionen? In: Franz Breid (Hg.): *Beten all zum selben Gott?* Steyr: Ennsthaler Gesellschaft m.b.H. & Co. KG, 9-49.

Schoen, Ulrich 1996: Islam und Christentum. In: *Theologische Rundschau* 61, 1-47; 177-227.

Schomerus, Hilko W. 1931: *Buddha und Christus*, Halle-Saale: Buchhandlung des Waisenhauses.

Schoonenberg, Piet 1974: Versuch einer christlich-theologischen Sicht des Hinduismus. In: G. Oberhammer (Hg.): *Offenbarung, Geistige Realität des Menschen*. Vienna: De Nobili Research Library, 171-187.
– 1982: Christologie angesichts der Avatara-Lehre. In: G. Oberhammer (Hg.): *Epiphanie des Heils. Zur Heilsgegenwart in indischer und christlicher Religion*. Vienna: De Nobili Research Library, 179-192.

Schulz, Michael 2001: Die Gretchenfrage der pluralistischen Religionstheologie: Einer is Gott, nur einer auch Mittler? In: G.L. Müller, M. Serretti (Hg.): *Einzigkeit und Universalität Jesu Christi. Im Dialog mit den Religionen*. Einsiedeln, Freiburg: Johannes, 113-153.

Schuon, Frithjof 1981: *Von der inneren Einheit der Religionen*. Interlaken: Ansata.
– 1984: *Das Ewige im Vergänglichen*. Bern: O.W. Barth.
– 1985: *Christianity/Islam. Bloomington*: World Wisdom Books.
– 1986: *The Essential Writings of Frithjof Schuon* (ed. by S. H. Nasr). Shaftsbury: Element Books.
– 1993: *Den Islam verstehen*. Freiburg i. Br.: Herder.

Schurhammer, Georg 1929: *Die Disputationen des P. Cosme de Torres S.J. mit den Buddhisten in Yamaguchi im Jahre 1551*. Tokyo: Deutsche Gesellschaft fürNatur- und Völkerkunde Ostasiens.

Schwager, Raymund 1996 (Hg.): *Christus allein? Der Streit un die pluralistische Religionstheologie* (QD 160). Freiburg i.Br.: Herder.

Schwandt, Hans-Gerd 1988 (Hg.): *Pluralistische Theologie der Religionen. Eine kritische Sichtung*, Frankfurt a.M.: Lembeck.

Schwarzenau, Paul 1993: *Das nachchristliche Zeitalter. Elemente einer planetarischen Religion*. Stuttgart: Kreuz Verlag.
– 1999. *Ein Gott in allem. Aufsätze zum Gottesbild der Religionen*. Cologne: Böhlau.

Schwarzenau, Paul; Gerlitz, Peter 1999: Religionstheologisches Streitgespräch. In: R. Kirste et al. (Hg.): *Vision 2001. Die grössere Ökumene*. Cologne: Böhlau, 72-85.

Schweitzer, Albert 1931. *Indian Thought and Its Development*, London: Hodder & Stoughton.

Scott, Archibal 1971: *Buddhism and Christianity: A Parallel and a Contrast* (1890). Reprint. Port Washington: Kennikat Press

Scott, David 1998: Buddhismus und Islam: Von der Vergangenheit bis zur Gegenwart—Begegnungen und interreligiöse Lektionen. In: P. Schmidt-Leukel (Hg.): *Wer is Buddha? Eine Gestalt und ihre Bedeutung für die Menschheit*. Munich: Diederichs, 195-210.

Seager, Richard Hughes 1993 (ed.): *The Dawn of Religious Pluralism. Voices from the World's Parliament of Religions, 1893*. LaSalle: Open Court.

Seckler, Max 1981: Aufklärung und Offenbarung. In: *Christlicher Glaube in moderner Gesellschaft*. Volume 21. Freiburg i.Br.: Herder, 5-78.

- 1985: Der theologische Begriff der Religion. In: *Handbuch der Fundamentaltheologie. Bd. 1. Traktat Religion*, hg. von W. Kern, H.J. Pottmeyer, M. Seckler. Freiburg i.Br.: Herder, 173-194.
- 1985b: Der Begriff der Offenbarung. In: *Handbuch der Fundamentaltheologie. Bd. 2. Traktat Offenbarung*, hg. von W. Kern, H.J. Pottmeyer, M. Seckler, Freiburg i.Br.: Herder, 60-83.
- 1986: Theologie der Religionen mit Fragezeichen. In: *Theologische Quartalschrift* 166, 164-184.

Seckler, Max; Kessler, Michael 1985: *Handbuch der Fundamentaltheologie. Bd. 2. Traktat Offenbarung* hg. von W. Kern, H.J. Pottmeyer, M. Seckler. Freiburg i.Br., 29-59.

Shankara 1990: *Die Erkenntnis der Wahrheit*. Düsseldorf: ECON.

Sharma, Arvind 1990: *A Hindu Perspective on the Philosophy of Religion*. Basingstoke: Macmillan.

Sharpe, Eric J. 1977: *Faith Meets Faith. Some Christian Attitudes to Hinduism in the Nineteenth and Twentieth Centuries*. London: SCM Press.

Sherwin, Byron L; Kasimow, Harold 2000 (eds.): *John Paul II and Interreligious Dialogue*. Maryknoll Orbis.

Shinran 1997: *The Collected Works of Shinran. Vol. I: The Writings*. Kyoto: Jōdo Shinshū Hongwanji-Ha.

Siddiqi, Muzammil H, 1989: A Muslim Response. In: J. Hick. E. Meltzer (eds.): *Three Faiths—One God. A Jewish, Christian, Muslim Encounter*. Basingstoke: Macmillan, 211-213.

Siddiqui, Ataullah, 1997: *Christian-Muslim Dialogue in the Twentieth Century*. Basingstoke - New York: Macmillan.

Siedler, Dirk Chr. 1999; *Paul Tillichs Beiträge zu einer Theologie der Religionen. Eine Untersuchung seines religionsphilosophischen, religionswissenschaftlichen und theologischen Beitrags*. Münster: LIT.

Silva, Lynn A. de 1957: *Belief in God* (C.P.C.L. Pamphlets, No. 2). Colombo: C.P.C.L.

- 1966: *Why Can't I Save Myself? The Christian Answer in Relation to Buddhist Though* (Dialogue Publications No. 1). Colombo: Ecumenical Institute for Study and Dialogue.
- 1967: Buddhist-Christian Dialogue. In: H. Jai Singh (ed.), *Inter-Religious Dialogue*. Bangalore, The Christian Institute for the Study of Religion and Society, 170-203.
- 1968: *Reincarnation in Buddhist and Christian Thought*. Colombo: Ecumenical Institute for Study and Dialogue.
- 1970: *Why Believe in God? The Christian Answer in Relation to Buddhism* (Dialogue Publications, No. 2). Colombo: Ecumenical Institute for Study and Dialogue.
- 1975: *The Problem of the Self in Buddhism and Christianity*. Colombo: Ecumenical Institute for Study and Dialogue.
- 1979: *The Problem of the Self in Buddhism and Christian*. Second edition with a Foreword by John Hick. Basingstoke: Macmillan.
- 1982: Buddhism and Christianit Relativised. In: *Dialogue* N.S. 9, 41-72.
- 1998: *Mit Buddha und Christus auf dem Weg*. Einleitung von Petrus Höhensteiger OSB. Nachwort von Aloysisus Pieris SJ. Freiburg i.Br.: Herder.

Singh, Karan; Ikeda, Daisaku 1988: *Humanity at the Crossroads. An Inter-cultural Dialogue*. Delhi: Oxford University Press.

Sinha, Harendra Prasad 1993: *Religious Philosophy of Tagore and Radhakrishnan. A Comparative and Analystical Study*. Delhi: Motilal Banarsidas.

Slater, R.L.; Lewis, H.D. 1966: *World Religions, Meeting Points and Major Isues*. London: Watts.

Slomp, Jan 1995: Calvin and the Turks. In Y. Y. Haddad; W.Z. Haddad (eds.): *Christian-Muslim Encounters*. Gainesville: University of Florida Press, 126-142.

Smart, Ninian 1984: Scientific Phenomenology and Wilfred Cantwell Smith's Misgivings. In: F. Whaling (ed.): *The World's Religious Traditions. Current Perspectives in Religious Studies* (FS Wilfred Cantwell Smith). Edinburgh: T&T Clark, 257-269.

– 1999 (ed.): *Atlas of the World's Religions*. Oxford: OUP.

Smart, Ninian; Konstantine, Steven 1991: *Christian Systematic Theology in a World Context*. London: Harper Collins.

Smith, Huston, 1991: Two Traditions—and Philosophy. In: S.H. Nasr, W. Stoddart (eds.): *Religion of the Heart*. (FS F.Schuon). Washington: Foundation for Traditional Studies, 278-296.

Smith, Huston; Griffin, David R. 1989: *Primordial Truth and Postmodern Theology*. Albany: SUNY.

Smith, Wilfred Cantwell 1957: *Islam in Modern History*. Princeton: Princeton University Press.

– 1959: "Comparative Religion: Whither—and Why?" In: Mircea Eliade, Joseph Kitagawa (eds.), *The History of Religions. Essays in Methodology*, Chicago: The University of Chicago Press, 31-58.

– 1967: *Questions of Religious Truth*. London: Victor Gollancz.

– 1976: *Religious Diversity*. Edited by W.G Oxtoby. New York: Harper & Row.

– 1977: *Belief and History*. Charlottesville: University Press of Virginia.

– 1978: *The Meaning and End of Religion: A Revolutionary Approach to the Great Religious Traditions* (First edition 1962). New York: Harper & Row.

– 1979: *Faith and Belief*. Princeton: Princeton University Press.

– 1981: *On Understanding Islam*. Selected Essays. The Hague – Paris – New York: Mouton Publishers.

– 1984: The World Church and the World History of Religion: The Theological Issue. In: *The Catholic Theological Society of America. Proceedings* 39, 52-68.

– 1987: Idolatry. In Comparative Perspective. In: J. Hick, P. Knitter (eds.): *The Myth of Christian Uniqueness*. Maryknoll: Orbis, 53-68.

– 1987b: Theology and the World's Religious History. In: L. Swidler (ed.): *Toward a Universal Theology of Religion*. Maryknoll: Orbis, 51-72.

– 1988: Mission, Dialogue and God's Will for Us. In: *International Review of Mission* 77, 360-374.

– 1989: *Towards a World Theology. Faith and the Comparative History of Religions*. 2nd edition. Maryknoll: Orbis.

– 1990: Thoughts on Transcendence. In: *Zeitschrfit für Religions- und Geistesgeschichte* 42, 32-49.

– 1991: Christian-Muslim Relations: The Theological Dimension. In: *Studies in Interreligious Dialogue* 1, 8-24.

– 1992: Can Believers Share the Qu'ran and the Bible as Word of God? In: J.D. Bort, H.M. Vroom, R. Fernhout, A. Wessels (eds.): *On Sharing Religious Experience. Possibilities of Interfaith Mutuality*. Amsterdam—Grand Rapids, 55-63.

– 1993: *What is Scripture? A Comparative Approach*. London: SCM Press.

– 1997: *Modern Culture from a Comparative Perspective*. Edited by J.W. Burbidge. Albany: SUNY.

Solomon, Norman 1991: Stereotyping Other Theologies. In: Cohn-Sherbok, Dan (ed.): *Islam in a World of Diverse Faiths*. Basingstoke: Macmillan, 104-113.
- 1996: Faith in the Midst of Faiths: Traditional Jewish Attitudes. In: H.Ucko (ed.): *People of God, Peoples of God. A Jewish-Christian Conversation in Asia*. Geneva: WCC, 84-99.

Soroush, Abdulkarim 2000: *Reason, Freedom, and Democracy in Islam*. Transl. and ed. by M. Sadri and A. Sadri. Oxford: OUP.

Spae, Joseph 19980: *Buddhist-Christian Empathy*. Chicago: Chicago Institute of Theology and Culture; Tokyo: Oriens Institute for Religious Research.

Sprung, Mervin 1973 (ed.): *The Problem of Two Truths in Buddhism and Vedanta*. Dordrecht: Springer.

Stace, Walter 1952: *Time and Eternity*. Princeton: Princeton University Press.

Staffner, Hans 1988: *Jesus Christ and the Hindu Community.* Is a synthesis of Hinduism and Christianity possible? Anand/India: Gujarat Sahitya Prakash.
- 1991: Are All Religions Really Equal? Some Reflections on a book by Fr Michael Amaladoss. In: *Vidyajyoti* 55: 37-41.

Stetson, Brad 1994: *Pluralism and Particularity in Religious Belief.* London: Praeger.

Stosch, Klaus von 2001: *Glaubensverantwortung in doppelter Kontingenz. Untersuchungen zur Verortung fundamentaler Theologie nach Wittgenstein*. Regensburg: Pustet.
- 2002: Komparative Theologie—ein Ausweg aus dem Grunddilemma jeder Theologie der Religionen? In: *Zeitschrift für Katholische Theologie* 124, 294-311.

Strange, Daniel 2002: *The Possibility of Salvation Among the Unevangelised. An Analysis of Inclusivism in Recent Evangelical Theology*. Carlisle—Waynesboro: Paternoster.

Streng, Frederick 1985: *Understanding Religious Life*. 3rd ed. Belmont: Wadworth.

Striet, Magnus 2003: *Offenbares Geheimnis. Zur Kritik der negativen Theologie*. Regensburg: Pustet.

Sturm, Hans P. 1996: *Weder Sein noch Nichtsein*. Würzburg: Ergon.

Suchocki, Marjorie Hewitt 1987: In Search of Justice. Religious Pluralism from a Feminist Perspective. In: J. Hick, P. Knitter (eds.): *The Myth of Christian Uniqueness*. Maryknoll: Orbis, 149-161.

Sullivan, Francis 1992: *Salvation outside the Church? Tracing the History of the Catholic Response*. New York: Paulist.

Sundermeier 1991: Evangelisation und die "Wahrheit der Religionen." In: R. Bernhardt (Hg.): *Horizontüberschreitung*. Gütersloh: Gütersloher Verlagshaus, 175-190.
- 2000: Grundlagen und Voraussetzungen für das interreligöse Gespräch. In: *Ökumenische Rundschau* 49, 318-331.

Swidler, Leonard 1987: Interreligious and Interideological Dialogue: The Matrix For All Systematic Reflection Today. In: L. Swidler (ed.): *Toward a Universal Theology of Religion*. Maryknoll: Orbis, 5-50.
- 1987b (ed.): *Toward a Universal Theology of Religion*. Maryknoll: Orbis.
- 1990: *After the Absolute. The Dialogical Future of Religious Reflection*. Minneapolis: Fortress.
- 1990b: A Dialogue on Dialogue. In: L. Swidler, J. Cobb, P. Knitter, M. Hellwig: *Death or Dialogue?* London: SCM Press - Philadelphia: Trinity Press, 56-78.
- 1991: Eine Christologie für unsere kritisch-denkende, pluralistische Zeit. In: R. Bernhardt (Hg.): *Horizontüberschreitung*. Gütersloh: Gütersloher Verlagshaus, 104-119.
- 1992: *Die Zukunft der Theologie. Im Dialog der Religionen und Weltanschauungen*. Regensburg: Pustet.
- 1994: Heutige Implikationen des jüdisch-christlichen Dialogs über Jesus Christus. In: *Zeitschrift für Religions- und Geistesgeschichte* 46, 333-351.

Swidler, Leonard; Mojzes, Paul 1997 (eds.): *The Uniqueness of Jesus. A Dialogue with Paul F. Knitter*. Maryknoll: Orbis.

Swinburne, Richard 1989: *Responsibility and Atonement*. Oxford: OUP.

Szczesny, Gerhard 1971: *Die Antwort der Religionen*. Reinbek bei Hamburg: Rowohlt.

Takeuchi, Yoshinori 1983: *The Heart of Buddhism. In Search of the Timeless Spirit of Primitive Buddhism*. New York: Crossroad.

The Christian Life and Message in Relation to Non-Christian Systems. Report of the Jerusalem Meeting of the International Missionary Council. March 24th – April 8th, 1928. Volume 1, 1928, London: Oxford University Press.

The Parekh Report 2000: *The Future of Multi-Ethnic Britain*. The Runnymede Trust. London: Profile Books.

Thelle, Notto R. 1987: *Buddhism and Christianity in Japan. From Conflict to Dialogue, 1854-1899*. Honolulu: University of Hawai'i Press.

Thich Nhat Hanh 1995: *Living Buddha, Living Christ*. London: Rider.

Thoma, Clemens 1989: *Theologische Beziehungen zwischen Christentum und Judentum*. Darmstadt: Wissenschaftliche Buchgesellschaft.

– 1998: Vatkanische Reue mit Einschränkungen. "Wir erinnern uns: Nachdenken über die Schoa". Mit einem einführenden Kommentar von Clemens Thoma. In: *Freiburger Rundbrief* 5, 161-177.

Thomas, M.M. 1969: *The Acknowledged Christ of the Indian Renaissance*. London: SCM Press.

– 1990: A Christ-Centered Humanist Approach to Other Religions in the Indian Pluralistic Context. In: G. D'Costa (ed.): *Christian Uniqueness Reconsidered*. Maryknoll: Orbis, 49-62.

Thomas, O.C. 1969 (ed.): *Attitudes Toward Other Religions*. London: SCM Press.

Thomas, P. 1954: *Christians and Christianity in India and Pakistan. A General Survey of the Progress of Christianity in India from Apostolic Times to the Present Day*. London: Allen & Unwin.

Thomas von Aquin 1986: *Der Prolog des Johannes-Evangeliums*. Übersetzung, Einführung und Erläuterungen von Wolf-Ulrich Klünker. Stuttgart: Verlag Freies Geistesleben.

Thurman, Robert 1976 (transl.). *The Holy Teaching of Vimalakīrti. A Mahāyāna Scripture*. Pennsylvania University Park: Pennsylvania University Press.

Tilley, Terrence W. 1999: "Christianity and the World Religions" – a Recent Vatican Document. In: *Theological Studies* 60, 318-337.

Tillich, Paul 1994: Die Bedeutung der Religionsgeschichte für den systematischen Theologen. In: K.-J. Kuschel (ed): *Christentum und Nichtchristliche Religionen*. Darmstadt: Wissenschaftliche Buchgesellschaft, 51-64.

– 1980: Das Wesen der religiösen Sprache. In: *Tillich-Auswahl*, Bd. 2, hg. von M. Baumotte, Gütersloh: Gütersloher Verlagshaus, 29-38.

Troeltsch, Ernst 1895: Die Selbständigkeit der Religion (Part 1 and II). In: *Zeitschrift für Theologie und Kirche* 5, 361-436.

– 1994: Die Stellung des Christentums unter den Weltreligionen. In: K.-J. Kuschel (Hg.): *Christentum und Nichtchristliche Religionen*. Darmstadt: Wissenschaftliche Buchgesellschaft, 23-38.

Tworuschka, Monika and Udo 1992: *Religionen der Welt. Grundlagen, Entwicklung und Bedeutung in der Gegenwart*. Munich: Bertelsmann.

Ueda, Shizuteru 2001: Jesus in Contemporary Japanese Zen. With Special Regard to Keiji Nishitani. In: P Schmidt-Leukel (ed.): *Buddhist Perceptions of Jesus*. St. Ottilien: EOS, 42-58.

Unser Glaube (1991). Die Bekenntnisschriften der evangelisch-lutherischen Kirche, herausgegeben vom Lutherischen Kirchenamt. Bearbeitet von Horst Pöhlmann. Dritte erweiterte Auflage. Gütersloh: Gütersloher Verlagshaus.

Ustorf, Werner 1995: Von der Unheiligkeit heiliger Plätze. Theologische Arbeit in der multireligiösen Industriestadt Birmingham. In: J. Mehlhausen (Hg.): *Pluralismus und Identität*. Gütersloh: Gütersloher Verlagshaus, 592-606.

Valignano, Alexandro 1944: *Historia del principio y progresso de la Compana de Jesus en las Indias Orientale (1542-64)*, herausgegeben und erläutert von Josef Wicki. Roma: Institutum historicum S.I.

Van Buren, Paul 1983: *A Christian Theology of the People of Israel*. New York: Harper & Row.

Vardy, Peter 1990: *The Puzzle of God*. London: HarperCollins.

Vermes, Geza 1981: *The Gospel of Jesus the Jew*. University of Newcastle Upon Tyne.

– 1991: Jesus the Jew: Christian and Jewish Reactions. In: E.-W. Böckenförde, E. Shils (eds.): *Jews and Christians in a Pluralistic World*. London: Weidenfeld & Nicolson, 25-42.

– 1993: *Jesus der Jude. Ein Historiker liest die Evangelien*. Neukirchen-Vluyn: Neukirchner Verlag.

– 2000: *The Changing Faces of Jesus*. London – New York: Penguin.

– 2001: *Jesus the Jew* (1st edn. 1973). London: SCM Press.

Vetter, Tilmann 1964: *Erkenntnisproblem bei Dharmakīrti* (Österreichische Akademie der Wissenschaften. Philosophisch-Historische Klasse. Sitzungsberichte, 245. Vol. 2. Abhandlung). Vienna.

Visser't Hooft, W.A. 1949 (ed.): *The First Assembly of the World Council of Churches*. London: Student Christian Movement Press.

Vivekananda 1994: *The Complete Works of Swami Vivekananda*. Vols. I-VIII. 6th reprint of the 1989 edition. Calcutta: Advaita Ashrama. Publication Department.

Vroom, Hendrik 1990: Do All Religious Traditions Worship the Same God? In: *Religious Studies* 26, 73-90.

– 1993: Right Conduct as a Criterion for True Religion. In: J. Kellenberger (ed.): *Inter-Religious Models and Criteria*. Basingstoke: Macmillan, 106-131.

– 1996: *No Other Gods. Christian Belief in Dialogue with Buddhism, Hinduism and Islam*. Grand Rapids—Cambridge: Eerdmans.

Waldenfels, Hans 1976: *Absolutes Nichts. Zur Grundlegung des Dialogs swischen Buddhismus und Christentum*. Freiburg i.Br.: Herder.

– 1982: *Faszination des Buddhismus. Zum christlich-buddhistischen Dialog*. Mainz: Grünewald.

– 1987 (Hg.): *Die Friedensgebete von Assisi*. Eingeleitet von F. König, Kommentar von H. Waldenfels. Freiburg i.Br.: Herder.

– 1989: Assisi 1986. In: *Theologische Quartalschrift* 169, 24-33.

– 1996: *Einführung in die Theologie der Offenbarung*. Darmstadt: Wissenschaftliche Buchgesellschaft.

– 1999: 'Unterwegs zu einer christlicher Theologie des religiösen Pluralismus', Anmerkungen zum 'Fall Dupuis'. In: *Stimmen der Zeit*, 219, 217f.

Walshe, M. O'C. 1982: Buddhism and Christianity. A Positive Approach. In: *Dialogue* N.S. 9, 3-39.

Ward, Keith 1987: *Images of Eternity. Concepts of God in Five Religious Traditions*. London: Darton, Longman and Todd.

– 1990: Truth and the Diversity of Religions. In: *Religious Studies* 26, 1-18.

– 1991: *A Vision to Pursue. Beyond the Crisis in Christianity*. London: SCM Press.

- 1993: Divine Ineffability. In: A Sharma (ed.): *God, Truth and Reality. Essays in Honour of John Hick*. Basingstoke: Macmillan, 210-220.
- 1994: *Religion and Revelation. A Theology of Revelation in the World's Religions*. Oxford: Clarendon.
- 1996: *Religion and Creation*. Oxford: Clarendon.
- 1998: *Religion and Human Nature*. Oxford: Clarendon.
- 2000: *Religion and Community*. Oxford: Clarendon.

Watt. W. Montgomery 1995: *Islamic Philosophy and Theology. An Extended Survey*. Edinburgh: Edinburgh University Press.

Weeramantry, C.G. 2002: *Islamic Jurisprudence. An International Perspective* (London: Macmillan – New York: St. Martin's Press 1988). Repr. Ratmalan/Sri Lanka: Sarvodaya Vishva Lekha.

Weiss, Christian; Weichert, Tom; Hust, Evelin; Fischer-Tiné, Harald 1996: *Religion – Macht – Gewalt. Religiöser 'Fundamentalismus' und Hindu-Moslem-Konflikte in Südasien*. Frankfurt a. M., Berlin: Iko Verlag.

Welbon, Guy Richard 1968: *The Buddhist Nirvana and Its Western Interpreters*. Chicago, London: University of Chicago Press.

Wengst, Klaus 2004: *Jesus zwischen Juden und Christen. Re-Visionen im Verhältnis der Kirche zu Israel*. Zweite, durchgesehene und erweiterte Auflage. Stuttgart: Kohlhammer.

Whittaker, J.H. 1981: *Matters of Faith and Matters of Principle*. San Antonio: Trinity University Press.

Wiertz, Oliver 2000: Eine Kritik an John Hicks pluralistischer Religionstheologie aus der Perspektive der philosophischen Theologie. In: *Theologie und Philosophie* 75, 388-416.
- 2003. Der eine Gott und die vielen Religionen. Kritische Anmerkungen zu einigen Argumenten für die pluralistische Theologie der Religionen. In: *Theologie und Philosophie* 78, 321-338.

Wietzke, Joachim 1993 (Hg.): *Mission erklärt. Ökumenische Dokumente von 1972 bis 1992*. Leipzig: Evangelische Verlagsanstalt.

Wiles, Maurice 1992: *Christian Theology and Inter-religious Dialogue*. London: SCM Press.
- 1993: The Meaning of Christ. In: A. Sharma (ed.): *God, Truth, and Reality. Essays in Honour of John Hick*. Basingstoke: Macmillan, 221-235.

Wilfred, Felix 1988: *Verlass den Tempel: Antyodaya – indischer Weg zur Befreiung*. Freiburg i.Br.: Herder.
- 1993a: *Beyond Settled Foundations. The Journey of Indian Theology*. Madras: University of Madras.
- 1993b: Some Tentative Reflections on the Language of Christian Uniqueness: An Indian Perspective. In: *Vidyajyoti* 57, 654-672.

Willi, Thomas 1980: Judentum, Christentum und Islam in der geistesgeschichtlichen Situation Spaniens im 13. Jahrhundert. In: Ina Willi-Plein und Thomas Willi (Hg.): *Glaubensdolch und Messiasbeweis. Die Begegnung von Judentum, Christentum und Islam im 13. Jahrhundert in Spanien*. Neukirchen-Vluyn: Neukirchner Verlag, 9-20.

Williams, John A. 1973: *Der Islam* (Die grossen Religionen der Welt). Geneva: Edito-Service.

Williams, Paul 2002: *The Unexpected Way. On Converting from Buddhism to Catholicism*. Edinburgh – New York: Continuum.
- Aquinas Meets the Buddhists: Prolegomenon to an Authentically Thomas-ist Basis for Dialogue. In: *Modern Theology* 20, 91-121.

Wilson, John 1849: *The Evangelization of India*: Considered with Respectful to the Duties of the Christian Church at Home and of Its Missionary Agents Abroad. Edinburgh: William Whyte & Co.

Winkler, Ulrich 2004: Christologie im Kreuzverhör. Wider die Diastase von Israeltheologie und Religionstheologie. In: *Salzburger Theologische Zeitschrift* 8: 30-61.

Witte, Johannes 1936: *Die Christus-Botschaft und die Religionen*. Göttingen: Vandenhoeck&Ruprecht.

World Missionary Conference 1910: *Report of Commission IV, The Missionary Message in Relation to Non-Christian Religions*. Edinburgh – London: Oliphant, Anderson and Ferrier.

Wyschogrod, Michael 1988: A Jewish Postscript. In: S. Davis (ed.): *Encountering Jesus. A Debate on Christology*. Atlanta: Estminster John Knox, 179-187.

Yagi, Seiichi 1987: "I" in the Words of Jesus. In: J. Hick, P. Knitter (eds.): *The Myth of Christian Uniqueness*. Maryknoll: Orbis, 117-134.

– 1988: *Die Front-Struktur als Brücke vom buddhistischen zum christlichen Denken*. München: Kaiser.

Yandell, Keith 1993: Some Varieties of Religious Pluralism. In: J. Kellenberger (ed.): *Inter-Religious Models and Criteria*. Basingstoke: Macmillan, 187-211.

– 1994: *The Epistemology of Religious Experience*. Cambridge: Cambridge University Press.

– 1999: *Philosophy of Religion. A contemporary introduction*. London – New York: Routledge.

– 2004a: How to Sink in Cognitive Quicksand: Nuancing Religious Pluralism. In: M.L. Peterson, R. J. VanArragon (eds.): *Contemporary Debates in Philosophy of Religion*. Oxford: Blackwell, 191-201.

– 2004b: Reply to Bryne. In: M.L. Peterson, R.J. VanArragon (eds): *Contemporary Debates in Philosophy of Religion*. Oxford: Blackwell, 211-214.

Yong, Amos 2000: *Discerning the Spirit(s): A Pentecostal-Charismatic Contribution to Christian Theology of Religions* (Journal of Pentecostal Theology Supplement Series 20). Sheffield: A&C Black.

– 2003: *Beyond the Impasse. Toward a Pneumatological Theology of Religions*. Carlisle – Grand Rapids: Baker Academic.

Zebiri, Kate 2001: Muslim Perceptions of Christianity and the West. In: L. Ridgeon (ed.): *Islamic Interpretations of Christianity*. Richmond: Curzon, 179-203.

Zehner, Joachim 1992: *Der notwendige Dialog. Die Weltreligionen in katholischer und evangelischer Sicht*. Gütersloh: Gütersloher Verlagshaus.

Zenger, Erich 1997: Nostra aetate. Der notwendige Streit um die Anerkennung des Judentums in der katholischen Kirche. In G.B. Ginzel, G. Fessler (Hg.): *Die Kirche und die Juden. Versuch einer Bilanz*. Gerlingen: Lambert Schneider, 49-81.

Zirker, Hans 1993: *Islam. Theologische und gesellschaftliche Herausforderungen*. Düsseldorf: Patmos.

– 1993b: Wegleitung Gottes oder Erlösung durch Christus? Zum Heilsverständnis und Geltungsanspruch von Christentum und Islam. In: M. von Brück, J. Werbick (Hg.): *Der einzige Weg zum Heil? Die Herausforderung des christlichen Absolutheitsanspruchs durch pluralistische Religionstheologien*. Freiburg i. Br.: Herder, 107-143.

– 1996: Zur "Pluralistischen Religionstheologie" im Blick auf den Islam. In. R. Schwager (Hg.): *Christus allein: Der Streit um die pluralistische Religionstheologie*. Freiburg i.Br.: Herder, 189-202.

– 2001: Der Koran in christlicher Sicht. In: *Münchener Theologische Zeitschrift* 52, 3-15.

Index of Names